UNDERSTANDING SCIENCE & NATURE

Resource Guide

AND MASTER INDEX

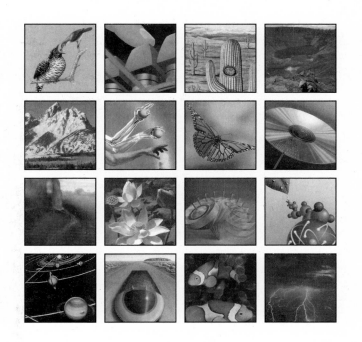

CONTENTS

Introduction   3

Earth and Space Science   4
Resource Guide _____ 5
Activities _____ 9
Index _____ 12

Life Science   28
Resource Guide _____ 29
Activities _____ 36
Index _____ 38

Physical Science   65
Resource Guide _____ 66
Activities _____ 72
Index _____ 74

Master Index   93

Introduction

The 16 volumes in the Understanding Science & Nature series pick up where most textbooks leave off. Thanks to their striking visuals—detailed cutaway drawings, expansive diagrams, electron micrographs, maps, charts, and graphs—these lavishly illustrated science books make concrete the abstract ideas that are taught in textbooks. The artwork captivates students as they browse through the books, giving them an appreciation for the drama of science.

Each volume in the series focuses on intriguingly familiar aspects of basic science. A discussion of physical force, for example, centers on how a pitcher makes a baseball curve in midair. An examination of phase change explores not just the phenomenon of water turning into ice but also the formation of crystals in ice cream. These topics are discussed in an accessible question-and-answer format: The questions are ones that students would naturally ask, and the answers are concise and direct. The books explain such everyday mysteries as how microwaves warm food, why fireflies light up the night sky, and how weather forecasts are made—subjects of immediate interest in students' lives.

Students will also benefit from the scope of this series. Individual topics are often explored in more than one book, each time from a fresh perspective. Phase change, for example, is discussed in five volumes. *Physical Forces* describes water, ice, and steam; *Structure of Matter* presents dry ice, the effect of salt on freezing water, and the process of making ice cream; *Weather & Climate* explores rain clouds, fog, and cloud seeding; *Underwater World* shows how certain antarctic fish use a natural antifreeze to keep their body fluids from freezing; and *Machines & Inventions* explains how pressure cookers raise the temperature at which water converts to steam. This multiple perspective helps students understand the relationships among different branches of science.

This *Resource Guide and Master Index* shows teachers how they can use the books in Understanding Science & Nature to explore these relationships. The Master Index at the back of this volume lists every topic covered in the series. The books in the series are grouped into three separate sections, each representing a different discipline: earth and space science, life science, and physical science. Each of these three sections offers an index and a resource guide with activities, labs, and experiments that teachers can use in the classroom to reinforce what students have learned.

After looking through the series, you will undoubtedly come up with classroom applications of your own. For example, the books can provide introductory material for teachers beginning a unit. Students can browse through the volumes to find possible subjects for their research projects, or they can use the books for enrichment reading in independent study. The books also make excellent sources of information for classroom displays.

In short, the books in the Understanding Science & Nature series are valuable classroom supplements not just because of the information they provide but also because of the way they provide it. Their dynamic design and clear-cut text can help teachers energize even the most reluctant student. To spark a student with a fascination for science is a worthy goal indeed. This series—and this book—can help you reach that goal.

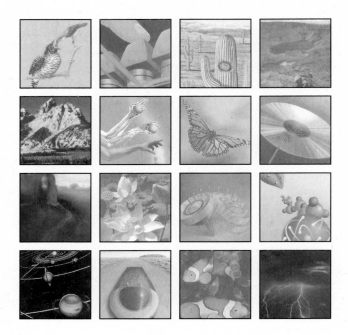

Earth and Space Science

The Earth and Space Science group consists of four volumes that ideally complement any Earth Science curriculum. Photographs, illustrations, diagrams, charts, and maps help students visualize objects that are too large—or too far away—to be observed directly. This pictorial approach also reveals the dynamic forces at work inside the Earth.

The four books chart a course from the faraway to the here and now. *Space & Planets,* for example, provides an overview of the universe but focuses on the planets of our Solar System and the Sun that anchors their orbits. *Planet Earth* peels away the hidden inner layers of the world we live on. It explains how the Earth formed and how earthquakes, volcanoes, and the oceans continue to sculpt the planet today. *Geography* takes a closer look at surface features, detailing everything from the art and science of mapping to the fantastic diversity of landforms to the impact of human enterprise on a fragile planet. *Weather & Climate* recounts the history of Earth's atmosphere and explains the powerful forces that interact to create both harmless and havoc-laden phenomena. This volume also shows how forecasters use advanced technology to predict and report the weather.

The concept of geologic time can be difficult for students to grasp. Most planetary changes take place far too slowly to be completed in a millennium, much less a single lifetime. To overcome this hurdle to understanding, the four titles in the Earth and Space Science group employ a battery of graphic devices—time lines, historical maps, cutaway views, sequenced illustrations, and step-by-step drawings and diagrams—that constitute a sort of "time-lapse photography" of the geologic time scale. In addition to helping students understand the surface features they can directly observe, this method of presenting information enables them to see that the entire pageant of human history occupies but the merest fraction of Earth's five-billion-year life span.

Space & Planets

Space & Planets highlights a range of topics related to astronomy. The book examines every aspect of the universe, from the endless waltz of the Earth and Moon to the prospects for interplanetary space travel. Commissioned artwork and photographs enable students to visualize the universe as it would appear from a viewpoint beyond its boundaries.

Chapter 1: The Solar System. After explaining the origin of the Solar System, this section paints portraits of the planets, asteroids, comets, and meteoroids that populate it. Cutaway drawings show the inside of moons and planets and explain the mechanics of the atmospheric storm known as Jupiter's Great Red Spot. Using data collected during the missions of the Voyager spacecraft, the chapter probes volcanoes on Io (one of Jupiter's 16 known moons), the atmosphere of Titan (the largest of Saturn's 18 moons), and the makeup of the rings that are now known to encircle four planets: Saturn, Jupiter, Uranus, and Neptune. The discussion of comets includes findings gleaned during the recent Earth visit of Halley's comet.

Chapter 2: The Sun. This chapter clarifies the process of nuclear fusion that fuels the Sun, our nearest star. Drawings of the Sun's atomic and molecular structure help to explain its chemical constituents. Illustrations depicting the "life history" of the Sun introduce the concept of geologic time and give students an idea of how long the Sun will continue to shine. Drawings re-create the changes the Sun has undergone in the last 5 billion years—and project the changes that are likely in the future as the Sun reaches the ripe old age of 12 billion years or so.

Chapter 3: The Motion of the Earth. Brought to light here are the fundamental forces that cause the Earth to spin on its axis and orbit the Sun. Diagrams show the actual motion of the Earth and explain how that differs from the apparent motion of stars and planets seen in the sky. The chapter devotes special attention to the scientific observations and discoveries that enabled early scientists to deduce that the Earth is a rotating body moving through space.

Chapter 4: The Moon. This chapter conveys the excitement of planetary research by presenting four competing views of the origin of the Moon: the collision theory, the sister theory, the fission theory, and the capture theory. Cutaway drawings reveal similarities in the internal composition of the Earth and Moon. A chart tracks the Moon's orbital path over the last 4.6 billion years and explains why the Earth's satellite is moving away from us at the rate of 1.2 inches per year.

Chapter 5: The Stars. A simplified discussion of mass, temperature, and basic elements helps students understand why the visible stars differ in brightness and color. This leads into a series of drawings that elucidate the life cycle of a typical star, including the buildup and explosion of Type I and Type II supernovas. The chapter explores the frontiers of stellar research by showcasing black holes, neutron stars, and the changing shape of the constellations.

Chapter 6: Galaxies and the Universe. This chapter presents a number of unusual views, starting with a map of our home galaxy, the Milky Way, and showing the Solar System's position within it. Diagrams drawn from imaginary viewpoints in space help students visualize the spiral arms of the Milky Way galaxy and likely scenarios for the formation and structure of the universe.

Chapter 7: Watching the Skies. The work of astronomers is explained in this close-up look at today's observational tools: optical telescopes, radio telescopes, and satellites. The chapter also takes students on a virtual tour of a planetarium.

Chapter 8: Life in Space. The book's final section focuses on the lessons people have learned from 40 years of life in space: the functioning of the space shuttle, eating and sleeping in zero gravity, the rigors of astronaut training, space probes, space colonies, and how and where humans might travel next in space.

Planet Earth

Planet Earth investigates the relationship between the world's internal structure and its external features. The text and illustrations work in tandem to take students on a voyage to the center of the Earth.

Chapter 1: This Majestic Planet. This chapter goes back some 4.6 billion years to explain how planetesimals—infinitesimal planets—smashed into one another and stuck together to form the third planet from the Sun. A grasp of this process helps students understand current models of the Earth's inner makeup, which is shown in cutaways, cross sections, pullouts, and core samples. Readers will be intrigued to learn about the instruments used to measure the Earth's size, density, gravity, and magnetism—and to plumb its depths.

Chapter 2: When Continents Collide. Many geologic phenomena fit into the theory of plate tectonics, or continental drift, which holds that Earth's outer layer is composed of huge, rocky plates creeping across the face of the globe at speeds of up to four inches per year. Photographs of the Earth's surface and cutaway drawings of its inner layers show how crustal plates collide, pull apart, or grind past one another. These plate-boundary interactions are in turn responsible for seafloor spreading, volcanic islands, and earthquakes.

Chapter 3: Earthquakes: Movers and Shakers. Elaborating on the concepts introduced in chapter 2, this section reveals how and why earthquakes stem from slight shifts of the Earth's crust. Drawings detail the three major types of earthquake—reverse fault, normal fault, and strike-slip fault. Three-dimensional representations of the Earth's crust explain how scientists are working to minimize future disasters by improving the tools of earthquake prediction.

Chapter 4: Volcanoes: Earth's Power Unleashed. This chapter conducts an in-depth examination of a topic that mesmerizes students—volcanoes. The chapter diagrams the mechanics of catastrophe: how lava forms, accumulates, and is vented; how one type of explosion differs from another; and the aftermath of an outburst. Illustrations then re-create a trio of notorious but instructive explosions: Pompeii's Mount Vesuvius in AD 79, Indonesia's Krakatoa in 1883, and Mount St. Helens in 1980. The chapter concludes with case studies showing what happens when volcanoes come in contact with seawater and ground water.

Chapter 5: Rock of Ages. A short section on the formation and classification of rocks explains how igneous, sedimentary, and metamorphic rock came to be, and how each type evolves and weathers over the unimaginably vast stretches of geologic time. The chapter points out that rocks reveal not just their origins and ages but also the story of life's evolution on the planet.

Chapter 6: Harvesting Earth's Mineral Bounty. Building on the foundation set forth in chapter 5, these pages describe the lengthy and hidden processes that have made the Earth a treasure trove of fossil fuels (coal, oil, natural gas) and mineral riches (salt, sulfur, gold). The chapter presents the cutting-edge technologies that geologists use to predict, locate, and extract underground resources. It also explains the urgency and feasibility of finding alternative sources of energy.

Chapter 7: The Oceans: Sculptors of the Planet. Roughly one fourth of *Planet Earth* is devoted to the past, present, and future condition of the world's oceans. Maps and diagrams show "rivers in the sea"—that is, currents on the surface of the ocean as well as in its depths. The chapter also analyzes waves, whirlpools, and tides: What causes them? What effects do they have on the Earth? Finally, the book scrutinizes the oceans as future providers of food and minerals, and discusses what we can do today to steward this precious resource.

Geography

Geography focuses on the Earth's surface features and the transformations that stem from wind erosion, water erosion, and climatic change. The volume pays special attention to the impact that human activity has had on the planet and its atmosphere. All of the material in the book is closely linked to observations that students can actually make. It encourages them to question why the Earth looks the way it does, and to examine the changes that are taking place as the result of both natural processes and human intervention.

Chapter 1: Mapping the Surface of the Earth. This chapter explores how maps and the demanding discipline of making them have evolved from ancient times to the present. Diagrams show how cartographers solved the problem of depicting a spherical Earth on flat maps. The chapter also delves into more advanced techniques, including aerial photography, electronic surveying, and computerized relief maps.

Chapter 2: Earth's Colossal Stonecutters. Examined here are the roles that water and ice have played in shaping the Earth's surface. Rivers, for example, give rise to all sorts of landforms—V-shaped valleys, oxbow lakes, flood plains, terraces, estuaries, and alluvial fans and deltas. In Europe, they have been tamed to create a network of interconnected canals. The sculpting action of glaciers is even more dramatic; their migration across the landscape produced kettle lakes, moraines, eskers, bowl-shaped depressions known as cirques, and the Great Lakes.

Chapter 3: Ground Water and Lakes. The ebb and flow of ground water and its impact on topography are perfect subjects for the cutaway drawings and diagrams that fill chapter 3. Any student who has ever wondered what causes a cave, an oasis, a sinkhole, or a spring (hot or cold) will find the answer here. The chapter also discusses the need to preserve this underground network, which functions as both a water supply and a drainage system for planet Earth.

Chapter 4: Oceans in Action. This chapter spotlights some true fringe elements—the worldwide boundary lines where the oceans meet the shore. The section addresses the current and future give-and-take between water and land by discussing marine erosion, the formation of sea cliffs, the growth of coral reefs, and the potential for polar melting brought on by the greenhouse effect.

Chapter 5: Molding the Face of a Planet. Many forces—plate tectonics, erosion, winds, and heat from the Sun and from the Earth's molten core—are responsible for creating and destroying the planet's most monumental landforms. This chapter roams the globe to explain the causes and effects of that molding process. Case studies include French farmland, a Norwegian fjord, the Appalachian Mountains, the Grand Canyon, and the Himalayas (which grow two inches taller each year).

Chapter 6: Climate as a Force of Change. Chapter 6 covers the ways in which climate dictates topography—and, interestingly, vice versa. The chapter features the landscaping action of steady winds, which create not only deserts but the dunes and monoliths that populate them. The chapter concludes with an intriguing turnabout—a discussion of how seaside mountain ranges can cause microclimates, and how warm ocean currents can temper the cold of northern climes.

Chapter 7: The Pace and Price of Progress. The final section in the volume focuses on the relationship between humans and the Earth—and on the radical changes that people have made to the face of the planet. Charts and maps examine the population explosion, water management, and the production of food and lumber. The challenges of urban planning, irrigation, and reclaiming land from the sea are topped off by a look at innovative solutions to the shortage of land.

Weather & Climate

Weather & Climate is designed to help teach students how an everyday phenomenon—weather—translates into the long-term patterns of global climate. In addition to presenting contemporary topics of inquiry such as acid rain, ozone holes, and the greenhouse effect, *Weather & Climate* puts these and other climatic changes in the context of the five-billion-year history of the Earth.

Chapter 1: The Air Above. The book's first chapter explores the makeup of Earth's atmosphere in order to explain why the planet's thin covering is a precious resource with a complex structure. The book examines each atmospheric layer in turn, from the troposphere (where weather occurs) to the ozone layer (which protects Earth by absorbing ultraviolet rays) to the ionosphere (without which teenagers could not tune in radio stations). Clear text and diagrams reveal the forces responsible for such atmospheric pyrotechnics as a beautiful sunset or the northern lights.

Chapter 2: The Air in Motion. Only when the air is in motion can its presence be felt. This chapter explains why it moves (because the Sun warms the planet unevenly). The global circulation of the atmosphere is made clear by pages showing what happens when the vertical convection caused by solar heating interacts with the Coriolis effect caused by the spinning Earth. The chapter also reveals how surface features such as mountains and oceans modify these basic motions.

Chapter 3: Storm Machines. Chapter 3 delves into the dynamics of cloud formation and the diverse results: rain, fog, sleet, hail, snow, lightning, and thunderstorms. In addition to teaching students how to tell a cumulus cloud from its cirrus and stratus counterparts, these pages explain the forces at work inside those clouds: air currents rise or fall, water changes state from gas to liquid to solid, and electric currents accumulate until they are released as lightning. The chapter also visits jet vapor trails, ice storms, cloud seeding, and tropical squalls.

Chapter 4: Atmospheric Pressure. This chapter investigates the movement of air on a grand scale: the formation, migration, and collision of high- and low-pressure systems. It devotes special attention to the growth of tropical depressions into destructive hurricanes and typhoons.

Chapter 5: Aerial Wonders. Chapter 5 traces the discovery of the secrets beyond some mysterious displays: rainbows, mirages, ball lightning, and halos (bright rings that sometimes encircle the Sun, the Moon, or mountains). The chapter places these phenomena in a broader context by mentioning what they have taught scientists about the Earth's atmosphere and the laws of physics.

Chapter 6: Watching the Weather. An astonishing variety of mechanical eyes and ears track weather around the globe. Among them are ships, buoys, island observatories, mountaintop radar stations, weather rockets, atmospheric drift balloons, aircraft, and satellites. This chapter explains how computers transform the data thus collected into maps meteorologists use to forecast the weather.

Chapter 7: The Climate of System Earth. The book's final chapter establishes links and relationships between weather (local, short term) and climate (regional or global, long term). It explains why deserts are dry, why certain Asian countries have a rainy season, and how the world's ocean currents affect its climate. Besides examining short- and long-range cycles of climatic change (El Niño, the ice ages), chapter 7 points out the impact that human activities have had on the planet's weather and climate.

Classroom Applications

Each volume in the Earth and Space Science group was written to be evocative and easy to read. Because the material in the books can be understood without being formally presented by the teacher, the books make ideal classroom resources. They also motivate students to find out more about a topic on their own.

The following topic list suggests portions of the four books that can be tied to the major subject areas in an Earth- or space-science curriculum:

Astronomy	*Space & Planets* (entire volume)
Atmosphere	*Weather & Climate* (entire volume) *Geography* (pages 100-117)
Oceanography	*Planet Earth* (pages 108-144) *Geography* (pages 68-82)
Fresh Water	*Geography* (pages 24-66) *Weather & Climate* (pages 56-81, 122-124)
Structure of the Earth	*Planet Earth* (pages 4-83) *Geography* (pages 84-99)
The Earth's Surface	*Geography* (entire volume) *Planet Earth* (pages 84-95)
Mineral Resources	*Planet Earth* (pages 96-107)
Technology	*Space & Planets* (pages 116-144) *Planet Earth* (pages 52-57, 98-99, and 136-144) *Geography* (pages 4-23, 118-144) *Weather & Climate* (pages 108-122)

Activity: Sky Watch

Background. For most students today, naked-eye observations of the sky are a thing of the past. Many of them are unaware of seasonal changes in the apparent position of the Sun and the planets, or they cannot identify common constellations in the night sky. Yet it was precisely this type of celestial observation that allowed early scientists to deduce the structure of the Solar System.

In the activity that follows, students have a chance to observe objects visible in the sky and report their findings to the class. The four books from the Earth and Space Science group can serve as reference material to help the students explain the phenomena they observe.

Group Size. Three or four students per group.

Skills needed. You may want to team up students in such a way that each small group has *art skills* (for drawings or models included in the class report), *writing skills* (for the written class report), *math skills* (for taking measurements and organizing the data), and *communication skills* (for presenting the report in class).

Duration. The teacher will need about one day to introduce and present the activity. Allow six weeks of nonclass time for students to complete their observations. At the end of the observing period, allow the students two days to complete the reports and prepare a presentation (recommended length: 5 to 10 minutes). Finally, set aside an additional two or three days of class time for the presentations.

Scope. Assign each small group to observe one of the following: Sun; Moon; stars; planets; sky (colors, unusual phenomena such as lightning or rainbows); clouds. Give each group about six weeks to complete its observations and prepare a class report. This report should contain both a summary and an ex-

planation of the group's observations. In addition, ask each student (or each small group) to write a report that includes their on-site observations, a copy of the oral report, and a list of references used in preparing the report.

Procedure.

Sun: Students record the time and location of sunrise and sunset each day. They measure the angle of the Sun above the horizon at the same time each day. (This teaches that the Sun does not travel the same path across the sky throughout the year.) The recording can be done safely by measuring the length and direction of the shadow of a meter stick at the identical time each day.

You can also direct your students to observe changes in the brightness and color of the Sun at different times of day or under different weather conditions. *Caution them strongly never to view the Sun directly!* Instead, demonstrate the proper observing technique by projecting the Sun's image through a pinhole in a file card onto a sheet of paper. This method allows them to safely observe the brightness and color changes that the Sun exhibits at sunrise and sunset; like the other measurements, these should be recorded.

Moon: Students record the time and location of moonrise and moonset each day. They sketch the shape of the Moon each day or night it is visible, as well as any surface features they can see. Students observe the path the Moon follows across the sky; does it change from night to night? They also record the Moon's color–especially any changes that occur just after moonrise or just before moonset.

Stars: Students learn to recognize the constellations. To help orient them to night-sky observation, teach them the profile and position of a few basic constellations, such as Orion, the Big Dipper, Cassiopeia, Ursa Major (the Great Bear), and Ursa Minor (the Little Bear). Students must observe *the same group of stars* several times in the course of a night if they are to successfully determine the stars' daily motion. In addition, they must observe each constellation *at the same time* each night so that they begin to see the pattern of annual movement.

Planets: Most students——and adults, for that matter—will need help locating planets in the sky. Star charts, available from local libraries or bookstores, can help orient the observer; the planets are often easiest to find when one or more of them appears near the Moon in the sky. The daily weather map of many newspapers includes a list of visible planets, along with the approximate time and location of their appearance in the sky. If this information is unavailable in the students' local newspaper, have them look for it in the *New York Times.* Each planet should be observed several different times in a single night to discern its 24-hour movement. To ascertain long-term patterns of planetary motion, each planet should also be observed at the same time each night.

Sky: Students observe the sky during daylight and nighttime hours. They record the colors that appear in different parts of the sky (near the horizon as opposed to directly overhead, near the Sun or Moon as opposed to far away from it, etc.) and at different times of the day and night. The most dramatic color changes will occur shortly before and after the Sun or Moon sets or rises. Alert students to be on the lookout for unusual phenomena such as rainbows, Sun or Moon halos, and the "green flash" sometimes witnessed at the precise moment of sundown.

Clouds: Students observe and describe the three main types of clouds (cumulus, cirrus, and stratus) and record the weather (including any precipitation, fog, or frost) that accompanies them within 12, 24, and 48 hours. If it is possible, this group's data collection also includes readings for temperature, barometric pressure, and humidity.

Tides (optional): Teachers who live near coastal areas can assign a small group of students to observe the tides. This group should record the times of the two high tides and the two low tides in each 24-hour period, as well as the difference in water level between each tidal extreme.

Reference Guide. Students may find these sections helpful in understanding their observations:

Sun: *Space & Planets,* pages 50-59
Moon: *Space & Planets,* pages 64-71
Stars: *Space & Planets,* pages 50-61, 76-81, and 90-91; *Geography,* pages 10-11
Planets: *Space & Planets,* pages 4-27, 50-61
Sky: *Weather & Climate,* pages 22-23, 96-107
Clouds: *Weather & Climate,* pages 56-89
Tides: *Planet Earth,* pages 128-129; *Space & Planets,* pages 72-73

Activity: Moon Base

Background. Students are assigned to work as astronomers, geologists, or life-support specialists in creating a drawing or a model of a human colony on the Moon. Working in small, specialized groups, the students research a number of questions related to the development and survival of a lunar colony. The answers to these questions are then incorporated into the colony's design.

Group Size. Three teams of two to four students each.

Skill Set. You may want to team up students in such a way that each small group includes someone with *art skills* (for producing the drawing or model of the moon base), someone with *writing skills* (for the written report), and someone with *communication skills* (for presenting the report to the class).

Duration. The teacher will need about one day to introduce and present the activity. Allow students two to three days to research and design the lunar colony. You will also need two or three days' class time for the students to present their reports (recommended length: 5 to 10 minutes per report).

Scope. Assign each small group to research and design a practicable human settlement on the moon. Ask each team to present its ideas and findings in an oral report to the class. This report should contain both a description and a drawing (or model) of the lunar colony, along with an explanation of how the group arrived at that particular design. In addition, have each student (or each small group) write a report that includes their answers to the questions below, a copy of their oral report, and a list of the references they used to design the colony.

Questions.

For the ASTRONOMER Team:

1. Where are observatories located on Earth?
2. How will you decide where to locate your observatory on the Moon?
3. What kinds of telescopes would be best for a lunar observatory?
4. What are some of the advantages that an astronomer on the Moon would have over an astronomer on the Earth? The disadvantages? List three of each.
5. What site would you select as the best place for the Moon base?

For the GEOLOGIST Team:

1. What resources might be obtained from Moon rocks?
2. How could the colonists use those resources?
3. Will moon-quakes be a danger to the colony?
4. How did the Moon's surface features form? Are they still changing?
5. What site would you select as the best place for the Moon base?

For the LIFE-SUPPORT Team:

1. Does the Moon have a "light" side and a "dark" side?
2. Which side of the Moon would be best for the base–or does it not matter?
3. How will you supply the colony with energy?
4. What will you do to protect the base against meteorite collisions?
5. Will it be necessary to shield the colony from radiation?
6. How will you provide air? Food? Water?
7. What will you do with waste?

Reference Guide. Students may find it helpful to consult these sections of *Space & Planets* as a first step in answering the questions above:

Overview and introduction: pages 74-75
Astronomer Team: pages 64-65, 116-125
Geologist Team: pages 64-65, 68-69, 74-75
Life-Support Team: pages 34-35, 48-49, 68-71, 74-75

Animal Behavior
AN

Computer Age
CO

Ecology
EC

Evolution of Life
EV

Geography
GE

Human Body
HU

Insects & Spiders
IN

Machines &
Inventions **MA**

Earth and Space Science Index

Numerals in italics indicate an illustration of the subject mentioned.

A

Aberration of starlight: SP 55

Absolute vs. apparent magnitude: SP 80-81

Absorption lines: SP 29, 78; redshift of, SP 115

Abyssal currents: PE 116-117

Abyssal plains: PE *map* 112-113, 115

Accretion disks around black holes: SP 94, 95

Acid rain: WE 28-29

Adiabatic cooling: WE *24*

Adriatic Sea and bora winds: WE 48-49

Advection fog: WE 71

Aerial surveys: GE 6-7, 19; of ore deposits, PE 99; of volcanoes, PE 79

Aerosol plasma theory of ball lightning: WE *107*

Africa: cattle, GE *131*; climate zones, GE *112-113*; diamond formation, PE *91*; Great Rift Valley, PE *22-23, 40-41*; Nile River, GE *4-5, 33*; Sahara dunes, GE *100-101, 105, 109*; savanna, GE *113*

Aftershocks following earthquakes: PE *54*

Agriculture: climate and, GE *130-131, 136-137*; dryland farming, GE 138; grain production, GE *122-123*; irrigation, GE *35, 63, 138-139*; Mediterranean, GE *131, 136-137*; slash-and-burn, GE *107*; South America, GE *141*; transhumance, GE *142-143*; Whittlesey's zones, GE *map* 130-131

Air: *See* Atmosphere of Earth; Wind

Air circulation: in Earth's atmosphere, SP *48*

Aircraft: air turbulence and, WE *52-53*; cloud seeding from, WE *78-79*; contrails, WE *64-65*; hurricane hunters, WE *94-95*; in weather observation, WE *94-95, 111, 116, 123*

Air eddies: and contrails, WE *64*; mountains and, WE *69*

Airplanes: *See* Aircraft

Air pollution: WE *26-27*; and acid rain, WE *28-29*; and ozone holes, WE *30-31*

Air pressure: *See* Atmospheric pressure

Air turbulence: WE *52-53*

Akiyoshi Cave, Japan: GE *54-55*

Alaska, U.S.: aurora, WE *16*; rainbow, WE *99*

Albedo: WE *map* 123

Alcaid (star): movement, SP *90-91*

Algae: and formation of atmosphere, WE *7*; fossil (stromatolites), WE *6*

Algol (binary star system): SP *82-83*

Alioth (star): movement, SP *90-91*

Alluvial fans: GE *27, 30-31*

Alluvium: terraces from, GE *88-89*

Alpine glaciers: GE 42; landforms created by, GE *44-45*

Alpine zone of Alps: GE *142, chart* 142

Alps (mountains), Europe: GE *45, 142-143*; Dinaric, Yugoslavia, bora winds over, WE *48-49*

Altiplano (plateau): Bolivian, GE *140-141*

Altitude: and gravity, PE *18*

Altocumulus clouds: WE *61, 63*

Altostratus clouds: WE *61, chart* 74

Amazon River, Brazil-Peru: GE *36-37*

Amino acids: formation, SP *23*

Ammonia: Jupiter's, absorption pattern, SP *29*

Anak Krakatoa (volcanic island), Indonesia: PE *72*

Andesite: PE *89*

Andes (mountains), South America: PE *map* 39; Altiplano, GE *140-141*; and fog, WE *72-73, 135*; formation of, PE *38-39*; source of Amazon, GE 36

Andromeda (galaxy): SP *103*

Annular eclipse of Sun: SP *63*

Antarctica: GE *52-53*; albedo, WE *map* 123; atmospheric pressure over, WE *122*; icecap, possible melting of, effects of, GE *72-73*; ice fog and solar displays, WE *103*; moraines, GE *46*; ozone hole over, WE *30-31*; weather observation of, WE *122-123*

Antarctic Transverse Range: GE *53*

Anthracite and bituminous coal: deposits, PE *map* 104; formation of, PE *105*

Anvil clouds: WE *62, 63*; stratocumulus, WE *60*

Apollo asteroids: SP *34-35*

Apollo 11 mission: view of Moon from, SP *69*

Apollo 17 astronauts: Moon buggy used by, SP *74*

Appalachian Mountains, U.S.: formation of, GE 87, *96-97*

Apparent vs. absolute magnitude: SP *80-81*

Aquifers: GE 56; and artesian water, GE *56*; formation of, GE *57*; and oases, GE *62, 63*; and subsidence, GE *64-65*

Arable zone of Alps: GE *142, chart* 142

Arches: sea cliffs and, GE *68-69, 76-77*

Arctic Circle: summer, SP *58-59*

Arizona, U.S.: Grand Canyon, GE *84-85, 94-95*; Monument Valley, GE *110-111*; Sun City, planned community in, GE *118-119*

Artesian springs: GE *56*; and oases, GE 62, 63

Artesian wells: GE *56*; at oases, GE *62*

Asteroids: SP *30-31*; Apollo, SP *34-35*; belt, SP *4-5*, 30, *31, 35*; orbits, SP *31, 35*

Asthenosphere: PE *9, 28, 29*

Astronauts: *See* Space travel

Atlantic Ocean: continental margin, PE *114-115*; fishing grounds, GE *126*; Sargasso Sea, PE *132-133*; seacoast, formation of, GE *28-29*; temperatures, PE *117*

Atmosphere of Earth: WE 4-31; acid rain, WE *28-29*; aurora, WE *8, 11, 16-17*; composition of, WE 6, *8*, 10, *14-15*; Earth's protection by, WE *20-21*; end of, WE *10-11*; formation of, WE 4, *6-7*; greenhouse effect, WE *136-137, 139*; history of, PE 6, 110, *111*; inversion layer, WE *60, 138-139*; ionosphere, WE 4, 8, *9*, 10, *14-15*, 16; layers of, WE 4, *8-9, 10-11, 112-113*; optical phenomena, WE *96-105*; ozone layer, WE 4, *7, 8-9, 12-13*, 25, *30-31*; pollution, WE *26-27*; pollution effects, WE *28-29, 30-31*; sky color, WE *22-23*; from space, WE *10*; spacecraft above, SP *124, 130-131*; Sun's radiation and, SP *48-49*; Sun through, WE *4-5*; temperature of, altitude and, WE 24, 25, *113*; Van Allen belts, WE *10-11, 18-19*. *See also* Atmospheric pressure; Wind

Atmospheres: Jupiter, SP *14-15, 16, 17, 28*; Sun's chromosphere, SP *40, 41, 42-43*; Sun's corona, SP *40, 41, 50-51, 63, 123*; Titan (moon of Saturn), SP 22, *23*; Venus, SP 10, *11*

Atmospheric circulation: WE *34-35, 36-37, 112-113*, 124, *134*; and jet streams, WE *38, 53*

Atmospheric pressure: WE 82; altitude and, WE *24*; at center of hurricane, WE *charts* 92-93; isobars, WE *40, 41, 44, 84, 85, 93, 118-119, 122*. *See also* High pressure; Low pressure

Atolls: GE *81*; coral, PE *114-115*

Atoms: birth of, SP *108*

Aurora: WE *16-17*; in atmospheric layers, WE *8, 11*; australis, WE 16; borealis, WE 16; in Norway, SP *49*

Auroral oval: WE *17*

Planet Earth
PE

Plant Life
PL

Physical Forces
PH

Structure of Matter
ST

Space & Planets
SP

Transportation
TR

Underwater World
UN

Weather & Climate
WE

Australia: capital (Canberra), GE *128-129*; Great Barrier Reef, GE *80-81*; in map projections, GE *17*; sheep, GE *131*

Austria: Alps in, GE *45*

Autumnal equinox: SP *56, 57*

B

Babylonian world map: GE *14*

Background radiation: cosmic, SP *113*

Baker, Mount, Wash., U.S.: study of, PE *79*

Bali (island), Indonesia: tropical squall on, WE *76*

Ball lightning: WE *106-107*

Balloons: atmospheric, WE *116*; radiosondes, WE 11, *112, 116, 118, 123*

Baltic Sea: predecessors of, GE *maps* 66-67

Barchan dunes: GE *108*; movement of, GE *109*

Barchanoid dunes: GE *108*

Barges: on Rhine River, GE *40*

Barometric (pressure) gradient force: WE *40, 41*

Barred spiral galaxies: SP *103*

Barrier reefs: GE *80-81*

Barringer Crater, Ariz., U.S.: SP *35*

Basalt: PE *89*; columnar, PE *84-85*; in layers of Earth's crust, PE *10*; lunar maria, SP *69*

Bathymetric map: GE *19*

Bays: Carmel Bay, Calif., U.S., GE *19*; estuaries, GE *38-39*; Osaka Bay, Japan, GE *144*; and sand bar formation, GE *74, 75*; in sea cliffs, GE *76-77*; Suruga Bay, Japan, GE *23*

Beach drift: GE 74

Beaches: sand ridge with, GE *75*; sea cliffs and, GE *68-69, 76-77*

Behaim, Martin: globe by, GE *14*

Benches: coastal, wave-cut, GE *77*

Bench marks: GE *6*

Beryl: PE *100*

Bessel, Friedrich: SP *54*

Beta Lyrae (binary star system): SP *83*

Betelgeuse (star): magnitude, SP *80*; spectrographic analysis of, SP *78-79*

Big Bang: aftermath of, SP *108-109, 112-113*

Big Crunch in closed universe: SP *115*

Big Dipper (Ursa Major constellation): SP *60, 90*; changes in, SP *90-91*

Binary star systems: with black hole, possible, SP *94-95*; eclipsing variables, SP *82-83*; with neutron star, SP *96-97*; and Type I supernova, SP *85*

Bingham mine, Utah, U.S.: PE *96-97*

Bird's-foot deltas: GE *33*

Bituminous coal and anthracite: deposits, PE

map 104; formation of, PE *105*

Black dwarf (star): SP *93*

Black holes, possible: SP *94-95*; at galactic centers, SP 98, 105; in quasars, SP 112, 113; as supernova remnants, SP 84, *85, 93*

Black ore: PE *100*

Black smokers: PE *106, 107*

Blowholes in sea cliffs: GE *77*

Blueshift: SP *91*

Blue-white supergiant (star): SP *94-95*

Bode, Johann: SP 31

Bolivia: Altiplano of, GE *140-141*

Booster rockets: space shuttle, SP *130, 131*

Bora winds: WE *48-49*

Borneo (island), Malay Archipelago: logging on, GE *125*

Bottom currents: ocean, PE *116-117*

Bottomset beds of deltas: GE *33*

Bow shock: WE *16, 19*

Bradley, James: SP 55

Brazil: Amazon River in, GE *36-37*

Breakers (ocean waves): PE *108-109, 126, 127*

Breezes: regular, WE *42-43, 76*

Brightness of stars: SP *chart* 79; magnitude, SP *80-81*; variable, SP *82-83*

British Isles: climate of, GE *116*

Buildings: wind around, WE *52, 54-55*

Buoys: remote, weather, WE *110, 117*

Burley Griffin, Lake, Canberra, Australia: GE *128, map* 129

Buttes in Monument Valley, Ariz., U.S.: GE *110*

C

Calcite in formation of cave features: GE 61

Calderas: PE *67, 68*; formation of, PE *68-69*; hot-spot volcanic island, PE *77*; Krakatoa, PE *72*; Yellowstone, PE *80*

California, U.S.: Carmel Bay, GE *19*; Death Valley, GE *115*; Loma Prieta earthquake (1989), effects of, PE *55, 61*; San Andreas fault, PE *42-43*, 49

California Current: WE 126

Calms: morning and evening, WE *42, 43*

Cambrian period: species, WE *142*; temperatures, WE *chart* 142

Canada: forests, GE *125*; Laurentian Plateau, GE *29*; Rockies, GE *24-25*

Canals: European, GE *map* 41; locks, GE *40*

Canberra, Australia: GE *128-129*

Cap clouds: WE *68-69*

Capes, sea cliffs': GE *76-77*

Capture theory of Moon's origin: SP *67*

Carbon: content of coal, PE *104*; diamonds, PE *90-91*

Carbon dioxide: in cities, and greenhouse effect, WE *139*; and global warming, GE *72, 73*, WE *136, 137*; and greenhouse effect, GE *73*, WE *136-137, 139*; rain and, rock dissolved by, GE 58, *110*

Carbon-14 dating: PE *95*

Carboniferous period: coal formation beginning in, PE *104*; species, WE *142*; temperatures, WE *chart* 142

Cargo transport, Europe's: GE *40, map* 40-41

Carmel Bay, Calif., U.S.: GE *19*

Cartography: *See* Maps and mapping

Cassiopeia (constellation): SP *60*

Cassiopeia A (supernova remnant): SP *85*

Cattle raising: GE *130, 131*; in Alps, GE *143*; overgrazing and desertification, GE *107*

Caves: GE *54-55*; formation of, GE *59, 60-61*; in sea cliffs, GE *76, 77*

Cavity geyser: PE *81*

Celestial sphere: GE *10, 11, 21*, SP *50, 60-61, 100*; ecliptic on, SP *54-55, 60-61, 70*

Cenozoic era: configuration of continents during, PE *102*; species during, WE *143*

Centrifugal force: in Earth-Moon system, SP *73*; and Earth's rotation, PE *18*; and hurricanes, WE *91*; and tides, PE *128*; and wind, WE *41*

Cepheid variables (stars): SP *83*

Cepheus (constellation): SP *60, 61*

Chemical surveys of mineral deposits: PE *99*

Chert (rock): PE *87*

Chesapeake Bay, Md.-Va., U.S.: GE *38*

Chiba Peninsula, Japan: earthquake effects on, PE *54, 55*

China: oasis, GE *63*; tower karst, GE *59*; Yellow River, course changes in, GE *34-35*

Chinooks: WE *44-45*

Chlorofluorocarbons (CFCs): destruction of ozone layer by, WE *30-31*

Chromosphere: SP *40, 41, 42-43*

Cinder cones: PE *67*

Circulation, atmospheric: WE *34-35, 36-37, 112-113, 124, 134*; and jet streams, WE *38, 53*

Circumpolar Currents: Antarctic, PE *map* 120-121; bottom, PE *116-117*

Cirques: GE *45*; horns formed from, GE *44*

Cirrostratus clouds: WE *61, chart* 74

Cirrus clouds: WE 60, *61*; in atmospheric layers, WE *8, 11*; from cumulonimbus top, WE *63*; and subtropical jet stream, WE *38*

Clear-cutting of rain forest: GE *125*

Clear-weather turbulence: WE *53*

Cliffs: sea, GE *68-69, 76-77, 88-89*

| Animal Behavior **AN** | Computer Age **CO** | Ecology **EC** | Evolution of Life **EV** | Geography **GE** | Human Body **HU** | Insects & Spiders **IN** | Machines & Inventions **MA** |

Climate: GE 100-117, WE 124-144; and agriculture, GE *130-131, 136-137*; of Alps, GE *142-143*; of Andes, GE *140*, GE *charts* 140; changes over time, WE *142-143*; cities vs. suburbs, WE *138-139*; deserts, GE *51, 100-101, 104-109*, WE *72, 124-125, 134-135*; El Niño phenomenon, WE *140-141*; factors determining, WE *128-129*; geography's effect on, GE 100, *114-115, 116-117*; greenhouse effect, WE *136-137, 139*; ice ages, WE 142, *chart* 143, *144*; land elevation and, GE *maps* 114, *142-143*; and landslides, GE *102-103*; monsoon seasons, WE *130-131, 132*; and Monument Valley's formation, GE *110-111*; ocean currents and, GE 70, *71, 116-117*, WE *72-73, 126-127, 140-141*; Pleistocene glaciations, GE *charts* 50, *maps* 51; rainy season, WE *88-89, 132-133*; and soil types, GE 112, *map* 113; and vegetation zones, GE *maps* 51, 112, *map* 113, 142, *chart* 142; in water cycle, global, GE 82, *83*; western U.S. zones, GE *map* 114; world zones, GE *charts* 112, WE *128-129, map* 128-129. *See also* Wind

Clinch River, Tenn.-Va., U.S.: dam on, GE *134*

Closed vs. open universe: SP *115*

Clouds: WE 56; and adiabatic cooling, WE *24*; over Antarctica, WE *122*; around low pressure, WE *86, 87, 111, 122*; atmospheric layers and, WE *8-9, 10, 11*; bora winds and, WE *49*; cap, WE *68-69*; cirrus, WE *8, 11, 38*, 60, *61, 63*; contrails, WE *64-65*; cumulonimbus, WE *9, 10, 50, 51*, 60, *62-63*, 66, 67, *74-75*, 76, 78, *89, 90-91*; electricity in, WE 66, *67*; equatorial waves, WE *132*; and foehns, WE *45*; fog, WE *70-71, 72-73*; formation and growth of, WE *58-59, 60-61, 62-63, 89*; on Jupiter, SP *14-15*; and mountain halos, formation of, WE *104-105*; in primitive atmosphere, WE *6*; and radar, WE *115*; satellite images, WE *111, 121*; seeding of, WE *78-79*; shapes, WE *60-61*; sirocco and, WE *46, 47*; solar energy reflected and absorbed by, WE *20-21*; squalls, tropical, and, WE 76, *77*; test-tube, WE *58*; thermal air turbulence and, WE *52*; on Venus, SP *10-11*

Cloud seeding: WE *78-79*

Clusters and superclusters of galaxies: SP *110-111*; Local Group, SP 102, *110-111*; recession of, SP *graph* 115

Coal: formation of, PE *104-105*; locations of, PE *100, 101*; reserves of, PE *map* 104; strip mining of, PE *105*

Coastal areas: aerial surveying of, GE *19*; deltas, GE *4-5*, 26, *32-33*, 39; estuaries, GE *38-39*; inundation of, GE *90-91*; plains, formation of, GE *28-29*; rain, sea winds and, GE *114-115*; saltwater intrusion in, GE 64; sand bars, formation of, GE *74-75*; sea's shaping of, GE *68-69, 76-77, 88-89*

Coastal plain estuaries: GE *38*

Coastal terraces: GE *88-89*

Collision theory of Moon's origin: SP *66-67*

Colonization of space, possible: SP 128, *140-141*; and Moon base, SP *74-75*; and transport, SP *143*

Colorado Plateau, U.S.: and Grand Canyon, GE *94-95*; and Monument Valley, GE *110-111*

Colorado River, Mexico-U.S.: Grand Canyon formed by, GE *84-85, 94-95*

Columbia Icefield, Canada: GE *24-25*

Coma (head) of comet: SP *32-33*

Comets: SP *32-33, 35*; orbits, SP *4-5, 32-33*

Compasses: working of, PE *20-21*

Compressional (P) waves, seismic: and shear (S) waves, PE 15, 50, *51*; S-P time, PE 51, 52, 53, *chart* 53

Computer maps: GE *19, 22-23*

Computer models and simulations: weather conditions, WE 108

Condensation of liquids: of water vapor, WE *70*

Condensation trails (contrails): WE *64-65*

Conglomerates (rocks): PE *87*

Conic map projections: GE *13*

Conrad, Pete: SP *133*

Constant-pressure maps: WE *119, 122*

Constant-pressure surfaces: WE *40*

Constellations: changes in, SP *90-91*; precession and, SP *60-61*; zodiac, SP *54-55*. *See also individual names*

Contact vs. regional metamorphic rock: PE *87*

Continental crust: collisions, PE *11, 34, 36-37, 48-49, 64-65*; splitting of, PE *29, 33, 40, 41*; vs. oceanic crust, PE 8, *9*, 10

Continental drift: WE *142-143*; and mountain building, GE 86, *87, 96-99*; and seafloor spreading, GE *78-79*. *See also* Plate tectonics

Continental margin (continental shelf and continental slope): PE *114-115*

Contrails: *See* Condensation trails

Convection: atmosphere, PE *120*; in plate tectonics, PE *28, 29*

Convection currents: WE *59*; and atmospheric circulation, WE 34; formation of, WE *40-41*

Convection zone of ocean: PE 134, *135*

Convection zone of Sun: SP *17, 40, 41, 42*

Convergence of trade winds: WE *90, 132-133*

Convergent boundaries: and mountain building, PE *11, 34, 36-37, 38-39, 49*. *See also* Subduction

Cooling, kinds of: adiabatic, WE *24*; insulation, WE *58, 64*; radiation, WE *76, 85*

Copernicus, Nicolaus: SP 52

Copper mine: PE *96-97*

Coral: atolls, PE *114-115*; reefs, formation of, GE *80-81*

Core of Earth: PE *8*; formation of, PE 7; magnetic field, PE 20, *21*; and seismic waves, PE *15*

Cores: Mars, SP *12*; Milky Way, SP *104-105*; Moon, SP *68*; Neptune, SP *29*; Saturn, SP *29*; Sun, SP *17, 40, 41*; Uranus, SP *29*; Venus, SP *11*

Coriolis force and effect: SP *53*; on climate, WE 124; and ocean currents, GE 70, *71*, PE 118, *119*; on prevailing winds, WE 36

Corn: production of, GE 122, *123*

Corona: atmospheric, WE *105*; of comet, SP *32-33*; lunar, WE *105*; solar, SP *40, 41, 123*, WE *105*; solar, telescopes for studying, SP *122, 123*; solar, during total eclipse, SP *41, 50-51, 63*

Coronagraph: SP *123*; photograph by, SP *123*

Cosmic background radiation: SP *113*

Cosmic rays: WE *9*; and electricity in clouds, WE 67; and Van Allen belts, WE *18*

Cotton: growing, GE *map* 130, *131*

Crab nebula: SP *85, 96*

Crater Lake, Oreg., U.S.: PE *68*

Craters: asteroids, SP *30*; Earth, SP *35*; Mercury, SP *8-9*; Moon, SP *64-65, 68-69*; Triton (moon of Neptune), SP *27*. *See also* Calderas; Meteor craters

Creep meter: PE *57*

Cretaceous period: species, WE *143*; temperature, WE *chart* 143

Critical density of universe: SP 115

Crop plants: and climate, GE *130-131*

Cross winds in tornado formation: WE 50

Crusts: Earth, PE 8, *9, 10-11*; Earth, formation of, PE *7, 111*; Earth, igneous rocks in, PE *88, 89*; Io (moon of Jupiter), SP *18-19*; Mars, SP *12*; Moon, Earth's, SP *68*; Venus, SP *11*. *See also* Plate tectonics

Crystals: ice, images formed by, WE *102-103*

Cuesta ridges: GE *92-93*

Cumulonimbus clouds: atmospheric layers and, WE *9, 10*; and cloud seeding, WE 78; formation of, WE *60, 62-63, 89*; and

Planet Earth
PE

Plant Life
PL

Physical Forces
PH

Structure of Matter
ST

Space & Planets
SP

Transportation
TR

Underwater World
UN

Weather & Climate
WE

hurricanes, WE *90-91*; and lightning, WE *66, 67*; and precipitation, WE *63, 74-75*, 76; and tornadoes, WE *50, 51*

Cumulus clouds: WE *60*; cumulonimbus clouds from, WE *50, 62*

Currents, auroral: WE *16-17*

Currents, ocean: GE 68, *70-71*, WE *126-127*; bottom, PE *116-117*; cause of, SP *49*; effect of, on climate, GE 100, *116-117*; and fishing areas, GE *126-127*; and garúa, WE *72-73*; and sand bars, GE *74-75*; and Sargasso Sea, PE *132-133*; southern oscillation and, WE *140-141*; surface, PE *118-119*, *map* 120-121; warm and cool, PE *120-121*; and whirlpool formation, PE *122-123*

Cyclones: Coriolis force affecting, SP *53*; formation of, WE 86

Cygnus (constellation): and precession, SP *60*; x-ray sources in, SP *94, 97*

Cygnus X-1 (x-ray source): SP *94*

Cylindrical map projections: GE *13*

D

Dams: for irrigation, GE *138*; in the Netherlands, GE *133*; Ogouchi Dam, Tokyo, Japan, WE *79*; Tennessee Valley Authority (TVA) projects, GE *134, map* 134-135; tidal, PE *139*

Dark nebulas: SP *87*

Darwin, Charles: GE 81

Dating: geological, PE *94, 95*

Death Valley, Calif., U.S.: GE *115*

Deep-sea drilling: PE *31*

Deltas: GE 26, *32-33*; estuaries from, GE *39*; Nile River, GE *4-5, 33*

Deneb (star): distance and magnitude, SP *81*

Density: of planets, SP *28-29*

Deposition: terraces formed by, GE *88-89*

Depositional plains: GE 28, *29*; alluvial fans, GE *27, 30-31*; deltas, GE *4-5, 26, 32-33, 39*; flood plains, GE *27, 29*

Depressions: tropical, WE 82, *90-91*

Depth charts: GE *18*; soundings for, GE *18*

Desalinization plants: PE *139*

Desertification: and overgrazing, GE *107*

Deserts: GE 100, WE *124-125, 134-135*; creation of, by wind, GE *104-105*; distribution of, WE *map* 135; dunes, GE *100-101, 105, 108-109*; expansion and contraction of, GE *106-107*; human activities causing, GE 106, *107*; ice ages' effect on, GE *51*; mirages, WE *100, 101*; Monument Valley's floor, GE *110-111*; oases in, GE *62-63*; rain-shadow, formation of, WE *134-135*; sirocco from, WE

46-47; South American coastal, WE *72, 135*

Deuteron formation: SP *44*

Dew point: WE 58, 62

Diamonds: PE *90*; formation of, PE *90-91*

Diffraction: WE *104*; effects, WE *104-105*

Dikes: in the Netherlands, GE *132*; Yellow River's, GE 34, *35*

Dinaric Alps (mountains), Yugoslavia: bora winds over, WE *48-49*

Dinosaurs: WE *143*

Discontinuities between layers of Earth: PE *14*

Divergent boundaries: PE *34*; and normal faults, PE *48*. *See also* Mid-ocean ridges; Rift valleys

D layer of ionosphere: WE 9, *14-15*

Doppler effect (Doppler shift): SP *91*; redshift, SP *91, 115*

Downdrafts: and air turbulence, WE *52-53*; mountain and valley breezes, WE *43*; in tornado formation, WE *50, 51*; in wind formation, WE *41*

Draco (constellation): SP *60, 61*

Drift motion in Van Allen belts: WE *18-19*

Dropsondes: use of, WE *95*

Drowned valleys: GE *90-91*

Drumlins: glaciers' formation of, GE *44-45*

Dryland farming: GE *138*

Dubhe (star): movement, SP *90-91*

Dunes: formation of, GE *108-109*; Sahara's, GE *100-101, 105, 109*

Dust tail of comet: SP *33*

Dwarf stars: SP *93*; Sun as, SP *47*; and supernova, SP *85*

Dynamo theory of Earth: PE *20*

E

Earth: PE entire volume; PE *4-5*; density, SP *29*; eclipses seen from, SP *41, 50-51, 62-63*; formation of, PE *6-7, 110-111*; gravitational variation, PE 17, *18-19*; heat, internal, PE *12-13*, 28, *29*; magnetic field, PE *20-21*; Mercury's view of, SP *8*; meteorite crater, SP *35*; midnight Sun, land of, SP *58-59*; and Milky Way, SP *100-101*; Moon's distance from, increasing, SP *72-73*; Moon's eclipses caused by, SP *62-63*; and Moon's formation, theories of, SP *66-67*; Moon's orbit around, SP *70-71*; Moon's view of, SP *67*; motion of, SP 50, *52-61*; nebulas seen from, SP *86-87*; nuclear fusion, experimental, SP *45*; orbit, SP *54-55*; precession, SP *60-61*; rotation, effects of, SP *52-53*; rotation, slowing of, SP *73*; satellites above, SP *124*; satellite views of, PE *4-5, 133*; seasons,

cause of, SP *56-57*; seismic study of, PE *14-15*, 98, *99*; shape, PE *4-5*, 16, *17*; size, PE *16-17*; solar radiation on, SP *45, 48-49*; star motions relative to, SP *90-91*; stars' distances from, and magnitude, SP *80-81*; tides, cause of, SP *73*; universe's evolution seen from, SP *112-113*. *See also* Earthquakes; Layers of Earth; Minerals; Oceans; Plate tectonics; Rocks; Volcanoes

Earth-approaching asteroids: orbits, SP *31, 35*

Earthquakes: PE *46-61*; around volcanoes, detecting, PE *79*; cause of, PE 42, 46, *48-49*; effects of, PE *46-47*, 48, *54-55, 58-59, 60-61*; focus, locating, PE *52-53*; and liquefaction of ground, PE *55, 60-61*; predicting, PE *56-57*; S-P time of seismic waves from, PE 51, 52, 53, *chart* 53; studying seismic waves from, PE *14-15*; traveling of seismic waves from, PE *50-51*; and tsunamis, PE *54, 58-59*

Earth's Moon: *See* Moon, Earth's

Easterlies (winds): WE *34-35*, 36, 37; convergence of trade winds, WE *90, 132-133*; southern oscillation, WE *140-141*

East Pacific Rise: PE *35*

Eating in space: SP *132, 133*

Echo sounder: survey ship using, GE *18*

Eclipses: of Moon, SP *62-63*; of Sun, SP *41, 50-51, 62-63*

Eclipsing variables (stars): SP *82-83*

Ecliptic: SP *54-55, 60-61, 70*

Eddies, air: and contrails, WE *64*; mountains and, WE *69*

Egypt: Nile, GE *4-5*, 33; Sahara, GE *100-101*

Einstein, Albert: SP 44, 95

Ekman spiral (current): PE *119*

E layer of ionosphere: WE 9, *14-15*

Electrical and gravitational studies: of ore deposits, PE *98*; of volcanoes, PE *79*

Electricity: in clouds, WE *66, 67*

Electricity theory of ball lightning: WE *107*

Electromagnetic wave theory of ball lightning: WE *107*

Electrons: and auroras, WE 16, *17*; in ionosphere, WE *14*; in Van Allen belts, WE *18-19*

Elliptical galaxies: SP *103*

El Niño phenomenon: PE *124-125*, WE *140-141*

Eltanin Fracture Zone: PE *map* 112-113

Emission lines in spectra of stars: SP *78*

Emission nebulas: SP *86*

Emperor seamounts: PE *44*

Encke comet, orbit: SP *32*

England: Greenwich meridian, GE *21*; London, GE *116*, 128; Thames River, GE *38*

Animal Behavior
AN

Computer Age
CO

Ecology
EC

Evolution of Life
EV

Geography
GE

Human Body
HU

Insects & Spiders
IN

Machines &
Inventions **MA**

Epicenter of earthquake: PE 50; locating, PE 52-53

Equal-area map projections: GE 17

Equator, Earth's: Foucault pendulum at, SP 52-53; stars' apparent motion at, SP 53; Sun's angle to, and seasons, SP 56-57

Equatorial convergence zone: WE 90, 132-133

Equatorial waves (clouds): WE 132

Equinox: autumnal, SP 56, 57; vernal, SP 56

Eratosthenes (Greek scientist): PE 16, 17

Erosion: in Appalachian Mountains' formation, GE 96-97; aquifers exposed by, GE 62, 63; cuestas formed by, GE 92-93; by Himalayan rivers, GE 98-99; of limestone, GE 58-59; marine, effects of, GE 68-69, 76-77, 88-89; Monument Valley's formation by, GE 110-111; plains formed by, GE 28, 29; and terraces, GE 88-89

Erosional plains: GE 28, 29

Eskers: GE 66; formation of, GE 44, 67

Estuaries: GE 38-39

European Space Agency: satellites launched by U.S. and, SP 124, 125

Evaporation: in global water cycle, GE 68, 82; vs. precipitation, GE 83

Exercising in space: SP 132, 133

Exosphere: WE 8-9

Expanding universe: SP 98, 114-115

Explorer 1 (satellite): WE 18

Extensometer: PE 57

Extrusive vs. intrusive igneous rocks: PE 87, 89

Eye of hurricane or typhoon: WE 91, 92, chart 93, 95, 115

F

Fabricus, David: SP 82

Faculae: SP 41

Fall equinox: SP 56, 57

Farallon plate: subduction of, PE 42, 43

Farming: *See* Agriculture

Fault-block mountains: GE 86

Faults: PE 48, 49; measuring movement of, PE 56, 57; from shallow-focus earthquakes, PE 54; transform, PE 34, 35, 42-43, 49

Felsic rocks: PE 88, 89

Ferrel cells: WE 34-35, 38, 53, 112

Field-aligned current, auroral: WE 16-17

Fiji Islands: GE 21

Finland: landscape formation in, GE 66-67

Fireballs: WE 106-107

Firn zone of Alps: GE 142, chart 142

Fish farming: PE 142-143

Fishing areas: GE 126-127

Fission theory of Moon's origin: SP 67

Fjords: GE 91

Flares, solar: SP 36-37, 40, 41

F layer of ionosphere: WE 9, 14-15

Flooding of rivers: and alluvial fans, GE 30-31; and estuaries, GE 39; Yellow River, GE 34

Flood plains: GE 27; of Mississippi, GE 29

Flood tides: and estuaries, GE 38; South American, GE 36, 37

Flow (landslide): GE 103

Flux tubes: Sun, SP 42

Focal point: in telescopes, SP 118, 119

Focus of earthquake: locating, PE 52-53; seismic waves traveling from, PE 50-51

Foehns: WE 44-45; in Sicily, WE 47

Fog: WE 70-71; advection, WE 71; garúa, WE 72-73; ice, WE 103; and mountain halos, formation of, WE 104-105; radiant, WE 70; sliding, WE 71; South America, WE 72-73, 135; steam, WE 71

Fog forests: WE 72

Fontana Dam, N.C., U.S.: power station, GE 134

Forecasts, weather: WE 108, 120-121

Forests: lumber exports from, GE 124, maps 124-125, 125

Fossil algae (stromatolites): WE 6

Fossil fuels: coal, PE 104-105; and greenhouse effect, WE 136; locating deposits of, PE 98, 99; locations of, PE 100, 101; oil and natural gas, formation of, PE 102-103; pollution by, WE 26, 27, 28-29

Fossils: and continental drift, PE 26; and Earth's history, PE 94; index fossils, PE chart 95; trilobites, PE 95

Foucault, Jean-Bernard-Léon: rotation of the earth proven by, SP 52

Foucault's pendulum: SP 52-53

France: beach, Normandy, GE 68-69; cuestas, GE 93; temperature, Paris's, GE chart 116

Fringing reefs: GE 81

Fronts: WE 84, 86, 87; Antarctica, WE 122; and cloud formation, WE 59, 60, 61; and downpours, WE 88, 89, 133; occluded, WE 87; stationary, WE 120-121; on weather maps, WE 118-119, 120-121

Fuji, Mount, Japan: GE 22-23, WE 24, 25; cap cloud, WE 68; radar antenna, WE 115

Funnel cloud in tornado: WE 50, 51

Fusion, nuclear: on Earth, SP 45; stars, SP 76, 92; Sun, SP 40, 44-45

G

Gabbro as layer of crust: PE 32, 89

Galaxies: SP 98; evolution of, SP 108-109, 112-113; groups of, SP 102, 110-111, graph 115; infant, quasars as, SP 112, 113; recession of, SP 98, 114-115; shapes of, SP 103; spiral, SP 89, 98-99, 103, 106-107. See also Milky Way

Galaxy clusters: SP 110-111; Local Group, SP 102, 110-111; recession of, SP graph 115

Galileo Galilei: SP 116

Gamma rays: Sun's production of, SP 40, 44

Garúa (fog): WE 72-73

Gas, natural, and oil: formation of, PE 102-103; in reservoir rocks, PE 103

Gas jets: at galactic center, SP 104; from quasar, SP 113

Gas-type planets vs. rock-type planets: SP 7, 28-29

Geiger counters: use of, PE 57

General circulation of atmosphere: WE 34-35, 36-37, 112-113, 124, 134; and jet streams, WE 38, 53

Geochemical surveys: PE 99

Geography: GE entire volume

Geoid: Earth as, PE 17

Geologic surveys: PE 98; improved, PE 98-99

Geology: PE entire volume

Geomagnetism: See Magnetism

Geostationary satellites: WE 11, 94, 110-111, 117

Geothermal (hot) springs: PE 12, 82-83; distribution, PE map 83

Geysers: PE 80-81

Ghawar oil field, Saudi Arabia: PE 102

Giant stars, red: See Red giants

Glaciation: WE map 144

Glaciers: GE 24, 52-53; Columbia Icefield, GE 24-25; continental drift and, PE 26; Finland, effect on, GE 66-67; and fjord formation, GE 91; formation of, GE 42-43; Great Lakes formed by, GE 48-49; landforms created by, GE 44-45, 46-47; melting, possible, effects of, GE 72-73; Pleistocene glaciations, GE charts 50, maps 51

Global warming: GE 72, 73, WE 136, 137, 138

Globes: Martin Behaim's, GE 14

Gneiss (rock): PE 7, 87

Gobi Desert, China-Mongolia: effect of ice ages on, GE 51; oasis in, GE 63

Gold: PE 101

Grain production: GE 122-123

Grand Canyon, Ariz., U.S.: GE 84-85, 94-95, PE 94

Granite in Earth's crust: PE 10, 88; erosion of, PE 92

Granodiorite (rock): PE 88

Planet Earth	Plant Life	Physical Forces	Structure of Matter	Space & Planets	Transportation	Underwater World	Weather & Climate
PE	**PL**	**PH**	**ST**	**SP**	**TR**	**UN**	**WE**

Granules: photosphere, SP *41*

Grapes: growing, GE *136-137*; roots, GE *137*

Graphite vs. diamonds: PE *chart* 90

Grasslands: savanna (African), GE *113*

Gravitational interactions with Earth: and precession, SP *60-61*; and tides, PE *128*, SP *73*

Gravitational lens: SP *95*

Gravity: detecting ore deposits with, PE *98*; Earth's, variations in, PE *17*, *18-19*; lunar, and tides, PE *128*; volcano's, measuring, PE *79*

Gravity waves: SP *95*

Great Barrier Reef, Australia: GE *80-81*

Great circles: GE *17*, *21*

Great Dark Spot, Neptune: SP *27*

Great Lakes, Canada-U.S.: formation of, GE *48-49*

Great Mazarin (galaxy): SP *103*

Great Plains, Canada-U.S.: GE *29*; wheat crop, GE *123*

Great Red Spot, Jupiter: SP *14-15, 16*

Great Rift Valley, Africa: PE *22-23*; formation of, PE *40-41*

Greenhouse effect: GE *73*, WE *136-137*; in cities, WE *139*; Venus, SP *11*

Greenhouse gases: buildup of, GE *73*; in primitive atmosphere, WE *6*

Greenland: gneiss formations in, PE *7*

Greenstone: PE *87*

Greenwich, England: prime meridian at, GE *21*

Ground moraine: GE *46*

Ground subsidence: GE *64-65*

Ground water: GE *54*; and caverns, GE *54-55, 59, 60-61*; landscape shaped by, GE *58-59*; movement of, gravity and, GE *56-57*; and oases, GE *62-63*; overpumping of, and subsidence, GE *64-65*

Guilin, China: tower karst of, GE *59*

Gulf Stream: WE *126, 127*; whirlpool formation in, PE *122-123*

Guyots: PE *115*

Gyoki Bosatsu: map by, GE *15*

Gyres (circular currents): GE *70, 71*, PE *118, 119, map* 120-121, *132*

H

Hadley cells: WE *34-35, 36-37, 38, 112*

Hail: cause of, WE *74, 75*; electricity produced in clouds by, WE *66, 67*

Haleakala (extinct volcano), Hawaii, U.S.: PE *45*

Hale telescope, Mount Palomar, Calif., U.S.: SP *118-119*

Halley, Edmond: SP *90*

Halley's comet: SP *32-33*

Halos: mountain, WE *104-105*; solar and lunar, WE *102-103*

Hawaii, U.S.: formation of, PE *44-45*; ocean wave, PE *108-109*; tsunami damage to, PE *59*; volcanically extinct islands, PE *77*; volcanic lava, makeup of, PE *chart* 65; volcanoes, PE *45, 62, 64, 68, 78, 79*

Hawaiian type of volcanic eruptions: PE *66*

HDE226868 (star): SP *94-95*

Head (coma) of comet: SP *32-33*

Heat, internal, of Earth: PE *12-13*; and plate tectonics, PE *28, 29*

Heat balance map: WE *34*

Heat island: WE *138-139*

Heat transfer: WE *20, 21*; in atmospheric circulation, WE *34-35*, 124; by ocean currents, WE 126, 127

Helium: in history of universe, SP *108, 109, 113*; hydrogen conversion to, in Sun, SP 40, *44-45, 46-47*

Herculaneum and Pompeii (ancient cities), Italy: destruction of, PE *74-75*

Hercules (constellation): SP *61*

Hertzsprung-Russell diagram: SP *chart* 79

High pressure: WE *40, 41*, 82, *84-85*; belts, WE *34-35, 37, 134*; cold systems, WE *85*; and deserts, WE *134*; forecast map, WE *120, 121*; jet streams and, WE *39, 88*; migratory vs. stationary systems, WE *85*; Pacific, WE *85, 88, 93, 133*; Sea of Okhotsk, WE *133*; warm systems, WE *85*; Yugoslavia, WE 48

Hilo harbor, Hawaii, U.S.: tsunami damage to, PE *59*

Himalayas (mountains), Asia: PE *36*; formation of, PE *11, 36, 49*, 101; and gravity, PE *19*; and limestone deposit, PE *101*; rivers crossing, GE *98-99*

Hokkaido (island), Japan: sand spit on, GE *75*

Honshu (island), Japan: mountain on, GE *22-23*; tsunami hitting, PE *map* 59

Hornfels: PE *87, 92*

Horns: glacial, GE *44*

Horsehead nebula: SP *87*

Hot spots: mantle, volcanoes formed by, PE *44-45, 76, 77*

Hot springs: PE *12, 82-83*; distribution of, PE *map* 83; geysers, PE *80-81*

Hubble, Edwin P.: SP *114*

Hubble's law: SP *114*, *graph* 115

Hubble Space Telescope: SP *124*

Humboldt (Peru) Current: WE *127*; and garúa, WE *72-73*

Hundred Dishes (terraced pools), Akiyoshi Cave, Japan: GE *54-55*

Hurricanes and typhoons: WE *82-83*, *90*; cause of, WE *90-91*; development of, WE *92-93*; eye of, WE *91, 92, chart* 93, *95, 115*; observing, WE *94-95, 115*; storm tides and waves caused by, PE *130-131*; zones, WE *map* 91

Hydrogen: in history of universe, SP *108, 109, 113*; Jupiter's, SP *15, 17, 28*; Jupiter's absorption pattern, SP *29*; Sun's conversion to helium, SP 40, *44-45, 46-47*

Hydrothermal deposits: PE *100, 101, 106-107*

I

Ice: crystals, WE 102, *103*; and optical phenomena, WE *102-103*

Ice ages: GE 50, *charts* 50, *maps* 51, WE 142, *chart* 143; cause of, WE *144*; vs. interglacial periods, effect of, on deserts, GE *51, 106-107*; melting after, and estuaries, GE 38

Icecaps, polar: GE *52-53*; changes in, effect of, on deserts, GE *106-107*; Mars, SP *12*; melting, possibility of, GE *72-73*

Ice fog: WE *103*

Ice sheets: *See* Glaciers

Icing: WE *80-81*

Igneous rocks: classification of, PE *88-89*; columnar basalt, PE *84-85*; cycle of, PE 93; extrusive vs. intrusive, PE *87, 89*; formation of, PE 86

Ijssel, Lake, the Netherlands: GE *133*

Impact craters: *See* Craters

Index fossils: PE *chart* 95

India: collision of, with Asia, GE *98-99*; equatorial convergence zone and, WE *132-133*; monsoon, WE *130*; satellite, WE *111*

Infinium planetarium: Tsukuba Expo Center, Japan, SP *126*

Influent streams: formation of, GE *30-31*

Infrared Astronomical Satellite: SP *124*

Infrared detector: satellite with, WE *110-111*

Infrared images: satellite, WE *121*

Infrared light and observatory: SP *124*

Infrared radiation: WE *9, 11, 24*; and greenhouse effect, WE *136, 137*

Infrared sensors: PE *79, 136*

Infrared spectroscopy: SP *29*; telescope, SP 28

Inlets: drowned valleys with, GE *90*; and sand bar formation, GE *74-75*

Insolation: varying, and ice ages, WE *144*

Insulation cooling (insulation expansion): and contrails, WE *64*; demonstration of, WE *58*

Interferometry: radio, SP *121*; very long

Animal Behavior
AN

Computer Age
CO

Ecology
EC

Evolution of Life
EV

Geography
GE

Human Body
HU

Insects & Spiders
IN

Machines &
Inventions **MA**

baseline (VLBI), uses of, PE *31, 56-57*
International Date Line: GE *20, 21*
International Ultraviolet Explorer (IUE satellite): SP *125*
Intrusive igneous rocks: PE *88*; vs. extrusive, PE *87, 89*
Inversion layer: WE *60*; heat island, WE *138-139*
Io (moon of Jupiter): orbit, SP *19*; volcanoes, SP *18-19*
Ion engine: SP *143*; craft using, SP *142-143*
Ionosphere: WE *4, 8, 9, 10, 14-15*; and aurora, WE *16*
Ion tail of comet: SP *33*
Irkutsk, Russia: climate of, GE *117*
Iron meteorite: SP *34*
Irregular galaxies: SP *103*
Irrigation: GE *138-139*; kanats for, GE *63, 139*; with Yellow River water, GE *35*
Island-arc volcanoes: formation of, PE *76*; Pacific Rim, PE *115*
Islands: Antarctic, GE *52-53*; coastal terraces around, GE *89*; coral reefs around, GE *80-81*; drowned valleys with, GE *90*; hot-spot, formation of, PE *44-45, 76, 77*
Isobars: WE *40, 41, 84, 85, 118-119*; Antarctica, WE *122*; chinook, WE *44*; typhoon, WE *93*
Isochrones: seismic waves', PE *53*
Isostasy: theory of, PE *10*
Isotherms: WE *126, 139*
Italy: agriculture, GE *131, map 137*; climate, GE *chart 137*; Tiber River delta, GE *33*
Iwaki, Japan: GE *77*
Izu Peninsula, Japan: earthquake's effect on, PE *55*

J

Japan: air pollutants, WE *chart* 27; airport construction, GE *144*; Akiyoshi Cave, GE *54-55*; alluvial fan, GE *31*; ball lightning, WE *106*; coal formation, PE *105*; computer mapping, GE *22-23*; delta, GE *26*; earthquake effects, PE *54, 55*, 60; Fuji, Mount, GE *22-23*, WE *24, 25*, 68, *115*; Gyoki map of, GE *15*; heat island, Tokyo's, WE *map* 139; Iwaki, GE *77*; landslide, GE *103*; Notsukezaki, Cape, GE *75*; Ogouchi Dam, Tokyo, WE *79*; planetarium, SP *126*; radio astronomy, SP *105, 120-121*; satellite, WE *111*; subsidence, GE *65*; terraces, GE *89*; tsunami, PE *map* 59; volcanoes, PE *62-63, 67, 78*; V-shaped canyon, GE *26*; whirlpools, PE *122, 123*; x-ray observatory, SP *125*; Zao, Mount, ice formations on, WE *80*
Japan Current: PE *123*
Jasper National Park, Canada: GE *24-25*

Jet aircraft: air turbulence and, WE *52-53*; contrails, WE *64-65*
Jets, gas: galactic center, SP *104*; from quasar, SP *113*
Jet streams: WE *37, 38-39, 112*; and clear-weather turbulence, WE *53*; and downpours, WE *88-89*; and monsoons, WE *130-131*
Jizuki, Mount, Japan: landslide on, GE *103*
Jupiter (planet): SP *14-17, 28*; Great Red Spot, SP *14-15, 16*; moon of (Io), SP *18-19*; rings, SP *16, 20*; spectrum, SP *29*; Sun compared to, SP *17*; Voyager missions to, SP *139*
Jurassic period: species, WE *143*; temperatures, WE *chart* 143

K

Kahoolawe (island), Hawaii, U.S.: PE *77*
Kaibab Plateau, Ariz., U.S.: GE *95*
Kanats: GE *63, 139*
Karrens: formation of, GE *58-59*
Karst topography: GE *58*; development, GE *58-59*
Katashina River, Japan: terraces, GE *89*
Kauai (island), Hawaii, U.S.: rainfall on, GE *115*
Kekaha, Hawaii, U.S.: rainfall on, GE *115*
Kelp: giant, beds of, PE *142*
Kilauea, Mount, Hawaii, U.S.: PE *45, 62, 64*, 68, 78, *79*; lava, makeup of, PE *chart* 65
Kimberlite pipes: formation of, PE *90-91*
Köppen, Wladimir: WE *128-129*
Köppen system: WE *128-129, map 128-129*
Krakatoa (volcanic island), Indonesia: eruption of, PE *62, 72-73*
Kurobe Canyon, Japan: GE *26*
Kwanto earthquake, Japan (1923): effects of, PE *54, 55*

L

Lagoons, formation of: by coral reefs, GE *80-81*; by sand ridges, GE *74*
Lakes: artificial, for irrigation, GE *138*; Burley Griffin, Canberra, Australia, GE *128, map* 129; Finland's, formation of, GE *66-67*; Great Lakes, formation of, GE *48-49*; Ijssel, the Netherlands, GE *133*; oxbow, formation of, GE *26-27*; Titicaca, Bolivia-Peru, GE *140, 141*
Laminar air currents: WE *69*
Land and sea breezes: WE *42, 43, 76*
Landfill: airport constructed on, GE *144*
Land of midnight Sun: SP *58-59*
Land reclamation: GE *132-133*
Landsat satellites: PE *136*; volcanoes studied

with, PE *79*
Landslides: GE *102-103*
La Niña phenomenon: WE *141*
La Paz, Bolivia: GE *141*; climate, GE *chart* 140
Laser beams: Moon's distance measured with, SP *72*
Laser range finder: fault movement measured with, PE *56*
Laser telemeters: GE *8-9*
Lateral moraines: GE *44, 46-47*
Latitude: GE *10, 11*; and gravity, PE *18*; on Mercator projections, GE *16*
Laurentian Plateau, Canada: GE *29*
Lava: PE *62-63*; formation of, PE *64-65*; makeup of, PE *chart* 65, 66; pillow, PE *32, 77, 106-107*; and type of eruptions, PE *66*; and type of volcanoes, PE *67*
Lava domes: PE *45*, 67
Lava plateau: PE *67*
Layers of Earth: PE *4, 8-9*; discontinuities between, PE *14*; formation of, PE *7, 111*; and gravity, PE *19*; heat from, PE *12-13, 28, 29*; magnetic field, core and, PE *20, 21*; makeup of crust, PE *10-11*; seismic study of, PE *14-15, 98, 99. See also* Plate tectonics; Rocks
Lenses, mechanical: telescope, SP *118, 123*
Lenticular clouds: WE *69*
Leveling: surveyors' use of, GE *8, 9*
Libration: Moon, SP *71*
Life expectancy and population: GE 120
Life on Titan (moon of Saturn): question of, SP *22, 23*
Light: absorption, by seawater, PE *chart* 135
Lightning: WE *56-57, 67*; artificial, WE *66*; ball, WE *106-107*; cause of, WE *66-67*; fireballs related to, WE *107*; from ground up, WE *67*; and thunder, WE *67*
Lignite: PE *map* 104; formation, PE *105*
Limestone: PE *101*; caverns, GE *54-55, 59, 60-61*; karst topography, formation of, GE *58-59*; shoreline, GE *68-69*
Liquefaction of ground: earthquakes and, PE *55, 60-61*
Lithosphere: PE *9, 28, 29*; regeneration, PE *32*
Little Dipper (Ursa Minor constellation): SP *60, 61*
Little Tennessee River, U.S.: power station on, GE *134*
Livestock raising: GE *130, 131*; llamas, GE *140, 141*; overgrazing and desertification, GE *107*; transhumance, GE *142-143*
Local Group of galaxies: SP *102, 110-111*
Local Supercluster of galaxies: SP *110*
Locks, canal: Rhine River's, GE *40*
Loess Plateau, China: GE *34, map* 34

Planet Earth
PE

Plant Life
PL

Physical Forces
PH

Structure of Matter
ST

Space & Planets
SP

Transportation
TR

Underwater World
UN

Weather & Climate
WE

Loma Prieta earthquake, Calif., U.S. (1989): effects of, PE *55, 61*

Longitude: GE 10, *11*; on Mercator projections, GE *16*; and time zones, GE *20-21*

Longitudinal dunes: GE *109*

Love waves: PE *51*

Low pressure: WE *41*, 82, *86-87*; above cold high-pressure systems, WE *85*; over Antarctica, WE *122*; belts, WE *34-35, 37*; and bora winds, WE *48-49*; and chinooks, WE *44-45*; forecast map, WE *120, 121*; jet streams and, WE *38-39*, 88, 89; and monsoon, WE *130*; monsoon lows, formation of, WE *132-133*; in satellite image, WE *111*; and seasonal downpours, WE 88, 89, *133*; and sirocco, WE *46-47*; tropical depressions, WE 82, *90-91*; troughs, WE *84*, 86, 87; warm system, WE *87*

Low-velocity zone (asthenosphere): PE *9*, 28, *29*

Lunar coronas: WE *105*

Lunar eclipses: SP *62-63*

Lunar halos: WE *102-103*

Lyot, Bernard-Ferdinand: invention, SP *123*

Lyra (constellation): and precession, SP *60, 61*; Ring nebula in, SP *87*

M

Maar volcano: PE *67*

McMath solar telescope, Ariz., U.S.: SP *122-123*

Mafic and ultramafic rocks: PE *88, 89*

Magma: in formation of Andes, PE *38*; in formation of hot springs, PE *82, 83*; in formation of igneous rocks, PE 86, 88, 89, 93; in formation of minerals, PE 100, *106*; in formation of ocean floor, PE *32*; in formation of rift valley, PE *41*; in formation of volcanoes, PE *44-45*, 64, 65, *66, 67, 69, 76, 77*, 79, 83; Moon, SP *68, 69*

Magma reservoirs: PE *64, 65*; and caldera formation, PE *68, 69*; and Mount St. Helens eruption, PE *70*; Yellowstone, PE *80*

Magnesium gas: spectrum of, SP *78*

Magnetic field lines: of Earth, PE *21*

Magnetic fields: of Earth, PE *20-21*, WE *10-11*, 16, 17, 19; of Galaxy, and gas jet, SP *104*; of neutron star, SP *97*; of Sun, SP *42-43*, 46, WE 16

Magnetism: as dating method, PE *94*; in detection of ore deposits, PE *99*; as proof of continental drift, PE *27*; as proof of seafloor spreading, PE *30, 94*

Magnetogram of Sun: SP *43*

Magnetopause: WE *16, 19*

Magnetosheath: WE *16*

Magnetosphere: WE *10-11*, 16

Magnetotail: WE *16, 19*

Magnitude of stars: SP *80-81, 82-83*

Main sequence of stars: SP *chart* 79

Malaysia: rain forests of, GE 124

Manganese deposits: PE *100*; nodules on ocean floor, PE *140-141*

Manned Maneuvering Unit (MMU): SP *135*

Mantle, Earth's: PE *8, 9*; convection in, PE *28, 29*; diamond formation in, PE *90-91*; formation of, PE *7*; heat from, PE *12-13, 28, 29*; hot spots, volcanoes formed by, PE *44-45, 76, 77*; in magma formation, PE *64*; peridotite rock in, PE *88, 89*

Mantles: Io (moon of Jupiter), SP *18-19*; Mars, SP *12*; Moon, Earth's, SP *68, 69*; Venus, SP *11*

Maps and mapping: GE 4-23; computer, GE *19, 22-23*; first, GE *14-15*; forecast map, WE *120-121*; latitude and longitude, GE *10-11, 16*; nautical charts, making of, GE *18-19*; printing of, GE *7*; projection types, GE *13, 16-17*; scale, GE *12*; surveying for, GE *6-7, 8-9, 18, 19*; time zones on, GE *20-21*; topographic vs. thematic, GE *12*; weather, WE *118-119*

Maria: Moon, SP *69*

Marine erosion: effects of, GE *68-69, 76-77, 88-89*

Mariner spacecraft: SP *125*; *Mariner 9*, Martian features studied by, SP *12-13*; *Mariner 10*, Mercury photographed by, SP *8*

Mars (planet): SP *12-13, 29, 31*; moon of (Phobos), SP *30*; travel to, possible, SP *144*; Viking missions to, SP *125*

Mass: of planets, SP *28-29*; of stars, and lifetimes, SP 46, 76, 92, *93*; of Sun and Jupiter, SP *17*; Sun's conversion of, into energy, SP 44

Matterhorn (mountain), Switzerland: GE *142*

Maui (island), Hawaii, U.S.: PE *77*; Haleakala, PE *45*

Mauna Kea (volcano), Hawaii, U.S.: observatory, SP *28*

Meanders: development of, GE *26-27*

Mechanical weathering: desert sand created by, GE *104-105*

Medial and lateral moraines: GE *46-47*

Mediterranean Sea: agriculture around, GE *131, 136-137*; Nile meeting, GE *4-5, 33*; and the sirocco, WE *46-47*

Megrez (star): movement, SP *90-91*

Merak (star): movement, SP *90-91*

Mercator projections: GE *16-17*

Mercury (planet): SP *8-9, 29*

Meridians: GE 10, *11*; on Mercator map, GE *16*; and time zones, GE *20-21*

Mesosphere: WE *8-9, 10-11*

Mesozoic era: life in, WE *143*

Metallic hydrogen in planets: SP *17, 28-29*

Metamorphic rocks: PE 86, *87, 92*

Meteor craters: Barringer Crater, Ariz., U.S., SP *35*; Mercury, SP *8-9*

Meteorites: SP *34*

Meteoroids and meteors: SP *34*

Meteor showers: SP *34*, 35

Methane: on Titan (moon of Saturn), SP *22-23*

Mexico City, Mexico: earthquake destruction in, PE *46-47*

M51 (galaxy): SP *106*

Microwaves: radar, WE 115

Mid-Atlantic Ridge: exposed portion of, PE *34*; and seafloor spreading, PE *30*

Mid-ocean ridges: GE 78, *79*, PE *10, 34, 35*, 112, *map* 113; formation of, PE *29*; hydrothermal deposits at, PE *106*; as location of normal faults, PE *49*; and ocean-ridge volcanoes, PE *77*; and San Andreas fault, PE *42, 43*; and seafloor building, PE *32*; and seafloor spreading, PE *30, 94*

Migratory high pressure: WE *85*

Mihara, Mount, Japan: PE *62-63, 78*

Milankovitch, Milutin: WE *144*

Milky Way (galaxy): SP 98, *100-107*; and celestial sphere, SP *100*; center, SP *100, 102, 104-105*; Earth's view of, SP *100-101*; shape, maintenance of, SP *106-107*; stars in, locations of, SP *101*; structure of, SP *102-103*

Minerals: PE 96-107; coal, formation of, PE *104-105*; copper mine, PE *96-97*; diamonds, PE *90-91*; locating, PE *98-99*; locations of, PE *100-101*; in oceans, PE *100, 101, 106-107, 138-139, 140-141*; oil and natural gas, formation of, PE *102-103*. See also Rocks

Mines: copper, PE *96-97*; strip, PE *105*

Minolta optical projector: SP *127*

Mir (space station): SP *144*

Mira (star): SP *82*

Mirages: WE *100-101*

Mirrors: telescope, SP *118, 119, 122, 123*; radio telescope, SP *121*

Mission specialists: space shuttle, SP 136, 137

Mississippi River, U.S.: delta, GE *33*; flood plains, GE *29*

Missouri, U.S.: cotton growing, GE *131*; St. Louis, topographic maps of, GE *12*

Miura Peninsula, Japan: earthquake's effects on, PE *maps* 55

Animal Behavior
AN

Computer Age
CO

Ecology
EC

Evolution of Life
EV

Geography
GE

Human Body
HU

Insects & Spiders
IN

Machines &
Inventions **MA**

Mizar (star): movement, SP *90-91*

Mock suns: WE *102, 103*

Mohorovičić discontinuity (Moho): PE 14

Monsoon lows: formation of, WE *132-133*

Monsoons: PE *118*, WE *130-131*; flooding, WE *132*

Monument Valley, Ariz., U.S.: GE *110-111*

Moon, Earth's: SP *64-75*; coronas around, WE *105*; crater formation, SP *64-65, 68*; Earth rising over, SP *67*; eclipses of, SP *62-63*; far side, visible portion of, SP *71*; halos around, WE *102-103*; human bases on, possible, SP *74-75*; inside, SP *68-69*; motion of, SP *63, 70-73*; origin, SP *64, 66-67*; and precession of Earth, SP *60-61*; recession from Earth, SP *72-73*; role of, in tides, PE *128-129*; and solar eclipses, SP *41, 50-51, 62-63*; surface features, SP *64, 69*

Moons: formation of, SP *7*; of Jupiter (Io), SP *18-19*; of Mars (Phobos), SP *30*; of Neptune (Triton), SP *26-27*; of Saturn (Titan), SP *22-23*; of Uranus, SP *25*

Moraines: formation of, GE *44-45, 46-47*

Moscow, Russia, climate of: GE *116-117*

Mother-of-pearl clouds: WE *8, 11*

Mountain and valley breezes: WE *42, 43*

Mountain halos: WE *104-105*

Mountains: GE *86-87*; air currents over, WE *59, 68-69*; Alps, GE *45, 142-143*; Andes, GE *36, 140-141*, PE *38-39, map* 39, WE *72-73, 135*; Antarctica, GE *52, 53*; Appalachians, formation of, GE *87, 96-97*; cap clouds over, WE *68-69*; climate, effect on, GE *114-115*; and deserts, rain-shadow, WE *134-135*; Dinaric Alps, Yugoslavia, bora winds over, WE *48-49*; fault-block, GE *86*; and foehns, WE *44-45*; and fog, WE *71, 72, 135*; formation of, GE *86, 87, 96-99*, PE *11, 34, 36-37, 38-39, 49*; glaciers in, GE *24-25, 42-47*; and gravity, PE *19*; Himalayas, rivers crossing, GE *98-99*, PE *11, 19, 36, 49, 101*; icing on, WE *80-81*; in isostasy theory, PE *10*; landslides on, GE *102-103*; mineral deposits in, PE *100*; pressure and temperature on, WE *24, 25*; Rocky Mountains, Canada-U.S., GE *24-25, 115*, WE *44-45, 53*; subduction and, GE *87*; Teton Range, Wyo., U.S., GE *86*; turbulence over, WE *52, 53*; weather observation on, WE *108-109, 115*; young Earth's volcanoes, WE *7. See also* Mid-ocean ridges; Volcanoes; *and individual names*

Mountain-wave turbulence: WE *53*

M33 (galaxy): location, SP *110*

Mudflows from Mount St. Helens: PE *70, 71*

Mudstone: PE *87*; and fossil fuels, PE *102,*

103; hornfels from, PE *87, 92*; layers of, PE *86*

N

National Weather Service forecasts: WE 121

Natural gas and oil: formation of, PE *102-103*; in reservoir rocks, PE *103*

Natural resources: *See* Minerals

Nautical charts: making of, GE *18-19*

Navigation: maps used for, GE *18-19*; Mercator projections used for, GE *16-17*; portolans used for, GE *15*; satellites used in, PE *16, 137*

Nazca plate: boundary of, PE *35*; and formation of Andes mountains, PE *38-39*

Neap tides: cause of, PE *129*

Nebulas: SP *86-87*; Crab, SP *85, 96*; in Orion, SP *6, 86, 87, 121*; Pleiades, SP *86, 88*; and star formation, SP *76-77, 87, 88-89*; Sun's formation from, SP *6, 38*; x-ray sources, location of, SP *97*

Neptune (planet): SP *5, 26, 27, 29*; moon of (Triton), SP *26-27*; rings, SP *20, 26-27*; Voyager mission to, SP *138*

Netherlands, the: land reclamation in, GE *132-133*

Neutrinos: Sun's production of, SP *40, 44*

Neutron core of supernova: SP *84*

Neutrons: in nuclear fusion, SP *44-45*

Neutron stars: SP *93, 96, 97*; Crab nebula and, SP *85, 96*

NGC1073 (galaxy): SP *103*

NGC1300 (galaxy): SP *103*

NGC3031 (galaxy): SP *103*

NGC5128 (galaxy): SP *103*

Niagara Falls, N.Y., U.S.: rainbow over, WE *96-97*

Nile River, Africa: GE *4-5*; delta, GE *4-5, 33*

Nimbostratus clouds: WE *61, chart* 74

Ninetyeast Ridge: PE *map* 112-113

Nitrogen in atmosphere: WE *8*; and aurora, WE *17*; ionosphere, WE *14*

Nitrogen oxides: in ionosphere, WE *14, 15*; and sulfur oxides, pollution by, WE *26, 27, 28-29*

Nitrogen volcanoes: Triton (moon of Neptune), SP *27*

Nobeyama Radio Observatory, Japan: radio map from, SP *105*; telescope, SP *120-121*

Normal vs. reverse faults: PE *48*

Normandy (region), France: cuestas, GE *93*; shoreline of, GE *68-69*

Norris Dam, Tenn., U.S.: GE *134*

North: true vs. magnetic, PE *21*

North America nebula: SP *86*

North American plate and San Andreas fault: PE *42, 43*

North Atlantic Drift (ocean current): effect of, GE 116

North Carolina, U.S.: Appalachian Mountains, GE *96*; dam's power station, GE *134*

North Pole: Foucault pendulum at, SP *52, 53*; precession, SP *60-61*; seasons at, SP *59*; solar wind, effects of, SP *49*; stars' apparent motion at, SP *53*

North Sea, rivers emptying into: Rhine, GE *map* 41; Thames, GE *38*

North Star: changing of, SP *60-61. See also* Polaris

Norway: fjords in, GE *91*

Notsukezaki, Cape, Japan: GE *75*

Nuclear fusion: Earth, SP *45*; stars, SP *76, 92*; Sun, SP *40, 44-45*

Nucleus of comet: SP *32, 33*

O

Oases: GE *62-63*

Observatories: *See* Telescopes

Occluded front: WE *87*

Ocean currents: *See* Currents, ocean

Oceanic crust: vs. continental crust, PE *8, 9, 10*; formation of, PE *32, 41*; and seamounts, PE *44, 76-77, 114-115. See also* Subduction

Oceanic plate interactions: GE 86, *87*

Oceanic ridges: *See* Mid-ocean ridges

Oceanographic satellites: PE *136-137*

Oceanographic vessels: PE *31, 137*

Ocean-ridge volcanoes: formation of, PE *77*

Oceans: GE *68-83*, PE *108-144*; advection fog, WE *71*; bottom currents, PE *116-117*; breakers, PE *108-109, 126, 127*; changes in, with depth, PE *117, 134-135*; continental margins, PE *114-115*; coral reefs, formation of, GE *80-81*; desalinization of, PE *139*; and deserts, WE *134, 135*; El Niño phenomenon, PE *124-125*; as energy source, PE *139*; farming of, PE *142-143*; fishing areas, GE *126-127*; floor, GE *78-79*; formation of, PE *7, 33, 110-111*, WE *6-7*; fossil fuels formed in, PE *102*; future uses of, possible, PE *144*; in global water cycle, GE 68, *82-83*; heat flow, PE *map* 13; hurricanes, WE *82-83, 90-95, 115*; importance of, PE *108*; invasion of land by, GE *90-91*; vs. land, PE *chart* 113; manganese nodules in, PE *140-141*; maps for navigating, GE *15, 16-17, 18-19*; melted icecaps' effect on, possible, GE *72-73*; as mineral location, PE *98, 100, 101, 106-107, 138-139, 140-141*; mirages over, WE *100*; and monsoons, WE *130*; saltwater intrusion from, GE *64;*

| Planet Earth **PE** | Plant Life **PL** | Physical Forces **PH** | Structure of Matter **ST** | Space & Planets **SP** | Transportation **TR** | Underwater World **UN** | Weather & Climate **WE** |

Sargasso Sea in, PE *132-133*; satellite scanning of, PE *136-137, 143*; sea and land breezes, WE *42, 43, 76*; seafloor building, PE *32-33, 41*; seafloor spreading, PE *30-31, 32, 94*; seamounts, PE *44, 76-77, 114-115*; storm waves, PE *130-131*; terrain under, PE *112-113*; tsunamis, PE *54, 58-59*; wave motions, PE *126-127*; weather ships and buoys, WE *110-111, 117*; whirlpools, PE *122-123. See also* Coastal areas; Currents, ocean; Tides, ocean; Trenches, ocean; *and individual names*

Ocean tides: *See* Tides, ocean

Ocean trenches: *See* Trenches, ocean

Ogouchi Dam, Tokyo, Japan: WE *79*

Oil: distribution of, in rock layers, PE *103*; formation of, PE *102-103*; locating deposits of, PE *98, 99*

Oil fields: Saudi Arabian, PE *102*

Okhotsk, Sea of: high (weather system), WE *133*

Old Faithful (geyser), Yellowstone National Park, U.S.: PE *80*

Olive (tree): growing, GE *131, 136-137*

Olympus, Mount, Mars: SP *12-13*

Omori formula for earthquake focus: PE *53*

O'Neill, Gerard: space colony designed by, SP *140-141*

Open vs. closed universe: SP *115*

Optical telescopes: SP *118-119*; Galileo's, SP *116*; Hubble Space Telescope, SP *124*; for solar astronomy, SP *122-123*

Orange trees: GE *131*

Orbits: asteroids, SP *31, 35*; comets, SP *4-5, 32-33*; Earth, SP *54-55*; Earth, and ice ages, WE *144*; Io (moon of Jupiter), SP *19*; Moon, Earth's, SP *63, 70-73*; planets, SP *4-5, 25, 31, 35*

Ordovician period: species, WE *142*; temperatures, WE *chart* 142

Orion (constellation): movement, apparent, SP *54*; nebulas in, SP *6, 86, 87*, 121; stars in, SP *78, 80*

Orion nebula: SP *6, 86*; gas analysis, SP *121*

Orogeny (mountain building): PE *11, 34, 36-37, 38-39, 49*; belts of, PE *map* 11

Osaka Bay, Japan: as airport site, GE *144*

Oshima Island, Japan: volcanoes on, PE *62-63, 78*

Ota River delta, Japan: GE *26*

Overgrazing and desertification: GE *107*

Oxbow lakes, formation of: GE *26-27*

Oxygen in atmosphere: WE *8*; and acid rain, WE *29*; and aurora, WE *17*; formation of, WE *7*; ionosphere, WE *14*; ozone from, WE *13*; and ozone holes, WE *30, 31*

Oyashio Current: PE *123*

Ozone layer: WE 4, *8-9, 12-13*, 25; formation of, WE *7*; holes in, WE *30-31*

P

Pacific Ocean: Andes along, GE *36, 140-141*; coral reefs, GE *81*; currents, WE *72-73, 127*; El Niño phenomenon, PE *124-125*, WE *140-141*; fishing areas, GE *126-127*; and garúa, WE *72-73*; high pressure, WE *85, 88, 93, 133*; International Date Line, GE *21*; low pressure, WE *86, 111*; saltiness, variation in, PE *chart* 134; satellite information on, WE *84, 111*; tides, PE *map* 129; typhoon birthplace, WE *maps* 90, 91, 93; vertical layers of, PE *135*; winds, rain from, GE *114-115*

Pacific plate: boundary of, PE *35*; and San Andreas fault, PE *42, 43*

Pacific Rim: PE *114-115*

Pahoehoe lava: PE *65*

Pakistan: kanat access holes in, GE *139*

Paleozoic era: life in, WE *142*

Palomar, Mount, Calif., U.S.: Hale telescope, SP *118-119*

Pangaea (hypothetical supercontinent): breakup of, PE *24-25, 38-39*

Parallax: stellar, SP *55*

Parhelia (mock suns): WE *102, 103*

Paris Basin, France: cuesta ridges in, GE *93*

Parry arcs: WE *102*

Payload specialists on space shuttle: SP *133*, 136, *137*

Peat: formation of, PE *104*

Pendulums: Foucault's, SP *52-53*

Peneplains vs. structural plains: GE *28*

Peninsulas: drowned valleys with, GE *90*; sand spits, GE *75*; Sinai, GE *5*

Penumbra and umbra: SP *62, 63*

Perched ground water: GE *56*

Peridotite (rock): PE *88, 89*

Permian period: species, WE *143*; temperatures, WE *chart* 143

Peru: coast of, garúa along, WE *72-73*; Lima, weather conditions in, WE *chart* 73

Peru-Chile Trench: PE *map* 112-113

Peru (Humboldt) Current: WE *127*; and garúa, WE *72-73*

Phecda (star): movement, SP *90-91*

Phobos (moon of Mars): SP *30*

Photosphere: SP *40, 41, 42-43*

Photosynthetic organisms: SP *48, 49*

Pillow lava: PE *32*; around hydrothermal deposit, PE *106-107*; and hot-spot volcanic islands, PE *77*

Pioneer Venus-Orbiter spacecraft: Venus photographed by, SP *10, 11*

Plages: SP *41*

Plains and plateaus: GE *28-29*; Altiplano and puna region, GE *140-141*; Antarctic, GE *53*; coastal plain estuaries, GE *38*; Colorado Plateau, history of, GE *94-95, 110-111*; Gobi Desert as, GE *51*; karst, GE *58-59*; Loess Plateau, China, GE *34*; undersea, GE *78. See also* Depositional plains

Planetariums: SP *126-127*

Planetary nebulas: SP *87*

Planetesimals: PE *110*; collisions, SP *7, 66*; formation of, PE *6*, SP *6*; in history of Earth, WE *6*

Planets: density, SP *28-29*; formation of, SP *7, 17, 20*; gas- vs. rock-type, SP *7, 28-29*; Jupiter, SP *14-17*, 18, *19, 20, 28, 29, 139*; Mars, SP *12-13, 29*, 30, *31*, 125, *144*; Mercury, SP *8-9, 29*; Neptune, SP *5, 20, 26-27, 29, 138*; orbits, SP *4-5, 25, 31, 35*; Pluto, SP *29*; Saturn, SP *20-21*, 22, *28-29*, 138, *139*; travel between, SP *142-143, 144*; Uranus, SP *20, 24-25, 29, 138*; Venus, SP *8, 10-11, 29. See also* Earth

Plankton theory of manganese nodules: PE *141*

Planned cities: GE *118-119, 128-129*

Plants: and climate zones, GE *112*, *map* 113

Plasma, atmospheric: WE *10-11*, 14; in solar wind, WE *19*

Plateaus: *See* Plains and plateaus

Plate tectonics: PE *11*, 22-45; Andes mountains, formation of, PE *38-39*; boundaries of plates, kinds of, PE *34-35, 42, 48-49*; collision of continents, PE *11, 34, 36-37, 49*; and continental margins, PE *115*; and earthquakes, PE *46, 48-49*; force behind, PE *28-29*; and Great Rift Valley, PE *22-23, 40-41*; Hawaii, formation of, PE *44-45*; history of continental drift, PE *24-25, 38-39*; and hot springs, PE *map* 83; igneous rocks, formation of, PE *86*; and lava formation, PE *64-65*; major plates, PE *map* 35; and mineral deposits, PE *100, 101, 106*; and mountain building, GE *86-87, 96-97, 98-99*; ocean formation, PE *33*; and ocean terrain, PE *112*; proof of continental drift, PE *26-27*; San Andreas fault, PE *42-43*, 49; seafloor building, PE *32-33, 41*; seafloor spreading, GE *78-79*, PE *30-31, 32, 94*; and seamounts, PE *44, 76-77, 114-115*

Pleiades star cluster: SP *86*, 88

Pleistocene glaciations: GE *charts* 50, *maps* 51

Pluto (planet): SP *29*

Pointed deltas: GE *33*

Polar circulation cells: WE *34, 35, 37, 38, 53, 112*

Animal Behavior
AN

Computer Age
CO

Ecology
EC

Evolution of Life
EV

Geography
GE

Human Body
HU

Insects & Spiders
IN

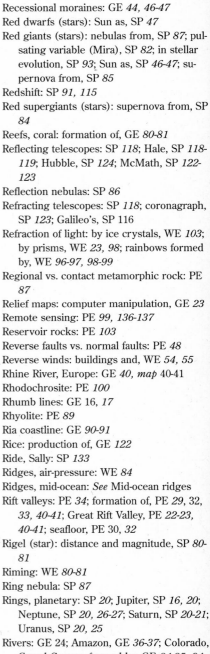
Machines &
Inventions **MA**

Polar easterlies: WE *35, 36, 37*

Polaris (star): SP 90; distance and magnitude, SP *81*; and precession, SP *60, 61*; stars circling, SP *52*

Polar jet stream: WE *37, 38-39, 112*; and clear-weather turbulence, WE *53*

Polar orbit satellites: WE *10, 94*, 110, *111, 117*

Polders: in the Netherlands, GE *133*

Pollution: acid rain, WE *28-29*; of atmosphere, WE *26-27*; and ozone holes, WE *30-31*

Pompeii (ancient city), Italy: destruction of, PE *74-75*

Pools, terraced: in limestone caves, GE *54-55, 60-61*

Population explosion: GE *120-121*

Pororoca (flood tide): GE *36, 37*

Portable Life-Support Subsystem (PLSS): SP *134*

Portolan chart: GE *15*

Potassium-argon dating: PE 95

Power plants (power stations): oceans' energy used by, PE *139*

Precambrian shields: PE 10, 11

Precession: SP *60-61*

Precipitation: Andes region, GE *charts* 140; climate zones, GE *charts* 112; vs. evaporation, GE *83;* glaciation and, GE *chart* 50; in Mediterranean countries, GE *charts* 136-137. *See also* Rain

Pressure, atmospheric: *See* Atmospheric pressure

Pressure gradient force: WE *40, 41*

Prevailing winds: WE *34-35, 36-37*; convergence of trade winds, WE *90, 132-133*; and El Niño phenomenon, PE *124-125*; and ocean currents, PE *118, 119, 120, 132, 133*; southern oscillation and, WE *140-141*

Primary (P; compressional) waves, seismic: and secondary (S; shear) waves, PE *15, 50, 51*; S-P time, PE 51, 52, 53, *chart* 53

Prime focus of Hale telescope: SP *119*

Prisms: SP *78*; Hale telescope, SP *118*; light split by, WE *23, 98*

Probes: *See* Space probes

Procyon (star): spectrographic analysis of, SP *78*

Projection types: maps', GE *13, 16-17*

Prominences: solar, SP *41, 43, 46*

Protogalaxies: evolution of, SP *108-109, 112-113*

Protons: in nuclear fusion, SP *44-45*; and solar wind, SP 16-17; in Van Allen belts, WE *18-19*

Protostar: SP *92*

Ptolemy, Claudius: GE 14, *map* 15

Pulsars: SP 96, *97*

Pulsating variables (stars): SP 82, *83*

Puna region, South America: GE 140

P (compressional) waves, seismic: S-P time, PE 51, 52, 53, *chart* 53; and S (shear) waves, PE *15*, 50, *51*

Q

Quasars: SP *112-113*; spectra of, redshift in, SP *115*; very long baseline interferometry using, PE *31, 56-57*

Quaternary period: species, WE *143*; temperatures, WE *chart* 143

R

Radar: Antarctica mapped with, GE *52*; cloud development, observation of, WE *63*; weather, WE *94, 108, 114-115, 118, 123*

Radar map of Venus: SP *11*

Radiant fog: WE *70*

Radiation belts: Van Allen, WE *10-11, 18-19*

Radiation cooling: WE *76, 85*

Radiation zone of Sun: SP *17, 40, 41*

Radioactive decay: and dating, PE *94, 95*; and Earth's internal heat, PE *12*; ore deposits detected with, PE *99*

Radio astronomy: galactic center, map of, SP *105*; telescopes, SP *120-121, 122, 124*

Radio interference from solar wind: SP *48*

Radiosondes: WE 11, *112, 116, 118, 123*

Radio waves: WE *9*; ionosphere and, WE *15*; use of, in weather radar, WE *114*, 115

Radon: Geiger counter for measuring, PE *57*

Rain: GE 100; acid, WE *28-29*; artificial, WE *78-79*; with carbon dioxide, rock dissolved by, GE 58, *110*; cause of, WE 74, *75*; clouds producing, WE *58-59, 63*; coastal, sea winds and, GE *114-115*; days of, annual, WE *chart* 77; and deserts, rain-shadow, WE *134-135*; downpours, seasonal, WE *88-89, 132-133*; equatorial convergence zone and, WE *132-133*; ground water from, GE *57*; and icing, WE *80-81*; landslides caused by, GE *102-103*; monsoon and, WE 130, 131, *map* 131; radar and, WE *115*; South America, WE *map* 73; southern oscillation and, WE 140, 141; squalls, tropical, WE *76-77*; and stratus clouds, WE *61*; and tornado formation, WE *50*; western U.S., variations in, GE *map* 114; on young Earth, WE *6*

Rainbows: WE *96-97, 98-99*

Rain forests: logging of, GE 124, *125*

Rain shadow: Death Valley in, GE *115*; deserts, formation of, WE *134-135*

Rainy season: WE *88-89, 132-133*

Rayleigh scattering: WE *23*

Rayleigh waves: PE *51*

Reber, Grote: SP 120

Recessional moraines: GE *44, 46-47*

Red dwarfs (stars): Sun as, SP *47*

Red giants (stars): nebulas from, SP *87*; pulsating variable (Mira), SP *82*; in stellar evolution, SP *93*; Sun as, SP *46-47*; supernova from, SP *85*

Redshift: SP *91, 115*

Red supergiants (stars): supernova from, SP *84*

Reefs, coral: formation of, GE *80-81*

Reflecting telescopes: SP *118*; Hale, SP *118-119*; Hubble, SP *124*; McMath, SP *122-123*

Reflection nebulas: SP *86*

Refracting telescopes: SP *118*; coronagraph, SP *123*; Galileo's, SP 116

Refraction of light: by ice crystals, WE *103*; by prisms, WE *23, 98*; rainbows formed by, WE *96-97, 98-99*

Regional vs. contact metamorphic rock: PE *87*

Relief maps: computer manipulation, GE *23*

Remote sensing: PE *99, 136-137*

Reservoir rocks: PE *103*

Reverse faults vs. normal faults: PE *48*

Reverse winds: buildings and, WE *54, 55*

Rhine River, Europe: GE *40, map* 40-41

Rhodochrosite: PE *100*

Rhumb lines: GE 16, *17*

Rhyolite: PE *89*

Ria coastline: GE *90-91*

Rice: production of, GE *122*

Ride, Sally: SP *133*

Ridges, air-pressure: WE *84*

Ridges, mid-ocean: *See* Mid-ocean ridges

Rift valleys: PE *34*; formation of, PE *29, 32, 33, 40-41*; Great Rift Valley, PE *22-23, 40-41*; seafloor, PE 30, *32*

Rigel (star): distance and magnitude, SP *80-81*

Riming: WE *80-81*

Ring nebula: SP *87*

Rings, planetary: SP *20*; Jupiter, SP *16, 20*; Neptune, SP *20, 26-27*; Saturn, SP *20-21*; Uranus, SP *20, 25*

Rivers: GE 24; Amazon, GE *36-37*; Colorado, Grand Canyon formed by, GE *84-85, 94-95*; deltas, GE *4-5, 26, 32-33, 39*; development projects, GE *134-135*; estuaries, GE *38-39*; and ground water, GE *57*; Himalayas crossed by, GE *98-99*; land-

Planet Earth
PE

Plant Life
PL

Physical Forces
PH

Structure of Matter
ST

Space & Planets
SP

Transportation
TR

Underwater World
UN

Weather & Climate
WE

forms created by, GE *26-33*; oasis water provided by, GE *62*; Rhine, GE *40, map* 40-41; terraces, GE *27, 88-89*; Yellow, GE *34-35*

Rockets: weather, WE *11, 112, 116, 123*

Rocks: PE 84-95; ages of, PE *84, 94, 95*; classifications of, PE *86, 87, 88-89*; coastal, sea's shaping of, GE *68-69, 76-77*; cuestas from, GE *92-93*; cycle of, PE *92-93*; desert sand from, GE *104-105*; diamonds in, PE *90-91*; dissolved by rain with carbon dioxide, GE *58, 110*; erosional plains, formation of, GE *28, 29*; formation of, PE *7, 84, 86-87, 92, 93*; glacial deposits, GE *44-45, 46-47*; Grand Canyon's, GE *94-95*; ground water's shaping of, GE *58-59*; history of Earth in, PE *94-95*; igneous, PE *84-85, 86, 87, 88-89, 93*; landslides, GE *102-103*; magnetic orientation of, PE *27, 30, 94, 99*; metamorphic, PE *86, 87, 92*; in Monument Valley's formation, GE *110-111*; in mountain formation, GE *86, 87, 96-97*; reservoir, fossil fuels in, PE *103*; sedimentary, PE *84, 86, 87, 92, 94, 95, 101, 103*. See also Aquifers; Minerals

Rock salt: deposit of, PE *101*

Rock-type planets vs. gas-type planets: SP *7, 28-29*

Rocky Mountains, Canada-U.S.: GE *24-25, 115*; chinooks, WE *44-45*; turbulence over, type of, WE *53*

Rotation: Earth's, effects of, SP *52-53*; Earth's, slowing of, SP *73*; Moon's, SP *70-71*

Royal Observatory, Greenwich, England: GE *21*

Russia: climate of, GE *116-117*

S

Sado Island, Japan: coastline of, GE *89*

Sagami trough, Japan: PE *55*

Sahara (desert), Africa: GE *100-101, 105, 109*, SP *45*, WE *124-125, 135*; sirocco from, WE *46-47*

St. Helens, Mount, Wash., U.S.: PE *70-71*, 78

St. Louis, Mo., U.S.: topographic maps of, GE *12*

Salinity levels: and bottom currents, PE *116*; of ocean waters, GE *70-71*, PE *chart 134*

Salt: rock, deposit of, PE *101*

Salt content of bodies of water: *See* Salinity levels

Saltwater intrusion: GE *64*

San Andreas fault, Calif., U.S.: PE *42-43, 49*

Sand: desert, creation of, GE *104-105*; wind-

blown, rock cut by, GE *111*

Sand bars: formation of, GE *74-75*

Sand dunes: GE *108-109*; Sahara's, GE *100-101, 105, 109*

Sand ridges: GE *74, 75*

Sand seas: formation of, GE *108*

Sand spits: GE *75*

Sandstone: PE *87*; formations, Monument Valley's, GE *110-111*; and fossil fuels, PE *102*, 103; layers of, PE *86, 92*

Sargasso Sea: PE *132-133*

Satellite photos: Chesapeake Bay, GE *38*; Earth, PE *4-5, 133*; Grand Canyon area, GE *95*; Middle East, GE *4-5*; Osaka Bay, GE *144*

Satellites: SP *123, 124-125*; over Antarctica, WE *123*; *Explorer 1*, WE *18*; geostationary vs. polar orbit, WE *10-11, 94*, 110, *111, 117*; global network, WE *111*; ground station monitors, WE *110*; hurricanes observed by, WE *82-83, 84, 111, 121*; navigation using, PE *16, 137*; repair of, in space, SP *136*; surveyors' use of, GE *9*; use of, PE *16, 99, 136-137, 143*; volcanoes studied by, PE *79*; weather, PE *4-5, 136*, WE *10-11, 110-111, 113, 117, 118*

Saturation: and cloud formation, WE *58, 62*; and fog, WE *70*

Saturn (planet): SP *20-21, 28-29*; moon of (Titan), SP *22-23*; ring formation, SP *20-21*; Voyager missions to, SP *138, 139*

Savanna, African: GE *113*

Scale of maps: GE *12*

Scarps: creation of, by slumps, GE *103*

Sea breezes: and land breezes, WE *42, 43*, 76

Sea cliffs: GE *68-69, 76-77, 88-89*

Seafloor building: PE *32-33, 41*

Seafloor spreading: GE *78-79*, PE *30-31, 32, 94*

Seafloor terrain: PE *112-113*

Sea level: Antarctica above, GE *52-53*; changes in, and formation of plains, GE *28-29*; drop in, and terraces, GE *88-89*; increase in, effects of, GE *23, 38, 39, 72-73, 90-91*

Seamounts: PE *76-77*; Emperor, PE *44*; Pacific Rim, PE *114-115*

Sea of Okhotsk high: WE *133*

Seas: ancient, Finland's, GE *maps 66-67*; land reclaimed from, GE *132-133*; lunar, SP *69*. *See also* Oceans; *and individual names*

Seasons, cause of: SP *56-57*; in land of midnight Sun, SP *58-59*

Sea stacks: GE *76, 77*

Sea waves (tsunamis): PE *54, 58-59, map 73*

Secondary (S; shear) waves, seismic: and primary (P; compressional) waves, PE *15*, 50, *51*; S-P time, PE 51, 52, 53, *chart* 53

Sediment: seafloor, PE *10, 102*

Sedimentary rock: Appalachian Mountains, formation of, GE *96-97*; composition of, PE *87*; cuestas from, GE *92-93*; formation of, PE *86, 87, 92*; fossil fuels in, PE *103*; in Grand Canyon, GE *94-95*; history of Earth in, PE *94, 95*; layers of, PE *84, 86, 92, 94, 95*; limestone, PE *101*; in Monument Valley's formation, GE *110-111*; in Teton Range, GE *86*

Sedimentation: *See* Depositional plains

Seismic tomography: PE *15*

Seismic waves: PE *14-15*; isochrones, PE *53*; ore deposits detected with, PE *98, 99*; S-P time, PE 51, 52, 53, *chart* 53; traveling of, PE *50-51*

Seismograms: PE *51*

Seismographs: PE *56*; waves reaching, PE *50-51*; working of, PE *51*

Seismometers: volcanoes studied with, PE *79*

Senegal: cattle in, GE *131*

Shadow zone: seismic, PE *15*

Shallow-focus earthquakes: PE *53*; fissuring by, PE *54*

Shear (cross wind): WE *50*

Shear (transform) boundaries: PE *34, 35, 42-43, 49*

Shear (S) waves, seismic: and compressional (P) waves, PE *15, 50, 51*; S-P time, PE 51, 52, 53, *chart* 53

Sheep: raising of, GE *map 130, 131*

Shield volcanoes: formation of, PE *67, 77*

Shipping: European, GE *40, map* 40-41

Ships: navigation, satellite use in, PE *16, 137*; oceanographic, PE *31, 137*; survey, GE *18*; in weather observation, WE *111, 117*

Shoals: sand bars formed from, GE *74-75*

Shooting stars: SP *34-35*

Shortwaves: radio, WE *15*

Showa New Mountain, Japan: PE *67*

Shuttle: *See* Space shuttle

Sicily (island), Italy: foehn in, WE *47*; olive trees on, GE *131*

Silica (silicon dioxide): lava, silica content of, PE *chart* 65

Silurian period: species, WE *142*; temperatures, WE *chart* 142

Silver iodide: cloud seeding with, WE *78-79*

Simulations and models, computer: weather conditions, WE *108*

Sinai Peninsula, Egypt: GE *5*

Sinkholes: formation of, GE *58-59*

Animal Behavior
AN

Computer Age
CO

Ecology
EC

Evolution of Life
EV

Geography
GE

Human Body
HU

Insects & Spiders
IN

Machines &
Inventions **MA**

Sirius (star): magnitude, SP *81*; spectrographic analysis of, SP *78*

Sirocco: WE *46-47*

Sister theory of Moon's origin: SP *67*

Skarn: PE *100*

Sky color: cause of, WE *22-23*

Skylab (space station): coronagraph, photograph by, SP *123*

Sky Water Project: WE 79

Slash-and-burn agriculture: GE *107*

Slayton, Deke: SP *133*

Sleep: in space, SP *132, 133*

Sliding fog: WE *71*

Slip surfaces: creation of, GE *103*

Slumps (landslides): GE *102-103*

Smoke: pollution by, WE *26, 27*

Smoke machines: cloud seeding with, WE *79*

Snow: cause of, WE 74, *75*; melted by chinooks, WE 44

Sodium gas: spectrum of, SP *78*

Soil: types, climate and, GE 112, GE *map* 113

Solar coronas: WE *105*

Solar eclipses: SP *41, 50-51, 62-63*

Solar energy: Earth, effects on, SP *48-49*; for Moon, possible, SP *75*

Solar flares: SP *36-37, 40, 41*

Solar halos: WE *102-103*

Solar Max satellite: repair of, SP *136*

Solar panels: spacecraft with, SP *142-143*

Solar pillars: WE *102, 103*

Solar prominences: SP *41, 43, 46*

Solar System: SP 4-35; asteroids, comets, and meteors, SP *4-5, 30-35*; in Milky Way, SP *100-101, 102, 103, 111*; origins, SP *6-7, 17*; Voyager routes in, SP *138-139*. *See also* Planets; Sun

Solar telescopes: SP *122-123*

Solar wind: WE *19*; and aurora, WE *16, 17*; effects of, SP *48, 49*

Solstices: summer, SP *56, 58-59*; winter, SP *57, 58*

Sound waves: speed of, in ocean, PE 134, PE *chart* 135

South Africa: diamond formation in, PE *91*

South America: Altiplano, GE *140-141*; Amazon River, GE *36-37*; Andes mountains, formation of, PE *38-39*; deserts, WE *72, 135*; El Niño phenomenon, PE *124-125*; garúa, WE *72-73*; rainfall, WE *map* 73; southern oscillation, effect of, WE *140-141*

Southern oscillation and trade winds: WE *140-141*

South Pole: and atmospheric circulation, WE 34. *See also* Antarctica

Space: SP entire volume

Space colonization, possible: SP 128, *140-141*; Moon base, SP *74-75*; transport, SP *143*

Spacelab: SP *132*, 136; simulator, SP *137*

Space probes: SP 124, *125*; ion-powered, SP *143*; Mars studied by, SP *12-13*; Mercury studied by, SP *8*; Venus studied by, SP *10, 11*. *See also* Voyager space probes

Space shuttle: SP *128-129*; living in, SP *132-133*; propulsion of, SP *130-131*; replicas, SP *137*; specialists, SP *136-137*

Space stations: possible, SP 128, *142, 144*

Spacesuits: SP *134-135*

Space travel: SP *128-144*; colony designs, SP *140-141*; interplanetary, craft for, SP *142-143, 144*; ion-powered craft, SP *142-143*; shuttle, SP *128-133, 136-137*; space stations, SP 128, *142, 144*; suits for, SP *134-135*; training for, SP *136-137*

Spain, agriculture in: GE *131, map* 136; climate for, GE *chart* 136

Spectra: Doppler shifts in, SP *91, 115*; infrared, SP *29*; prisms and, SP *78, 118*

Spectral types of stars: SP *78, chart* 79

Spectrometers: Voyager, SP *139*

Spectroscopy: SP *29*; radio, SP *121*; telescope for, SP *28*

Spectrum: solar, WE *23*

Spicules: Sun's atmosphere, SP *41*

Spiral galaxies: SP *98-99, 103*; shape, maintenance of, SP *106-107*; and star formation, SP *89*. *See also* Milky Way

Spits: sand, GE *75*

Spring (vernal) equinox: SP *56*

Springs: alluvial fans and formation of, GE *30-31*; artesian, GE *56, 62, 63*

Spring tides: cause of, PE *128-129*

S-P time: PE 51, 52, 53, *chart* 53

Squall line: WE *51*

Squalls: tropical, WE *76-77*

Stalactites: GE *60-61*

Stalagmites: GE *60-61*

Star dunes: GE *109*

Starlight: aberration of, SP *55*

Stars: SP *76-97*; birth of, SP *6, 7, 38-39, 76-77, 87, 88-89, 92*; black hole in binary system, SP *94-95*; brightness, SP *chart* 79, *80-81*; colors, SP *78-79*; evolution, SP *46-47, 92, 93*; Hertzsprung-Russell diagram, SP *chart* 79; in Milky Way, SP *101*; motion, apparent, SP *52, 53, 54, 55*; motion, proper, SP *90-91*; and nebula types, SP *86-87*; North Star, changing of, SP *60-61*; nuclear reactions in, SP 40, *44-45, 76, 92*; planetariums projecting, SP *126-127*; Pleiades, cluster of, SP *86, 88*; pulsars, SP *96, 97*; sizes, comparative, SP *78-79*; spectral types, SP *78, chart* 79;

supernova explosions and remnants, SP *76, 84-85, 89, 93-97*; variable, SP *82-83*. *See also* Galaxies; Sun

Stationary front: WE *120-121*

Stationary vs. migratory high pressure: WE *85*

Station models: WE *118-119*

Steam fog: WE *71*

Storms: Great Red Spot, Jupiter, SP *14-15, 16*; Neptune, SP *27*; thunderstorms, WE 51, *56-57, 66-67, 89*. *See also* Hurricanes and typhoons

Storm tides and storm waves: PE *130-131*

Stratavolcanoes: PE *67*; caldera formation in, PE *68*

Stratified zone of oceans: PE 134, *135*

Stratocumulus cloud: WE *60*

Stratosphere: WE 4, *8-9, 10-11, charts* 25; ozone layer, WE 4, *8-9, 12-13, 25, 30-31*; weather observation in, WE *112-113*; winds in, WE *36, 112-113*

Stratus clouds: WE 60, *61, chart* 74

Street winds: WE *55*

Strike-slip faults: PE *42-43, 48, 49*

Strip mine: PE *105*

Stromatolites: WE *6*

Strombolian type of volcanic eruption: PE *66*

Structural plains vs. peneplains: GE 28

Subalpine zone of Alps: GE 142, *chart* 142

Subduction: PE *11*, 28, *33, 34, 48-49*; active theory of, PE *29*; of Farallon plate, PE *42, 43*; island arcs as result of, PE *76, 115*; and magma formation, PE *64-65*; mountains formed by, GE *87*; and rock formation, PE 86

Subreflector of radio telescope: SP *120*

Subsidence: ground, GE *64-65*

Subtropical deserts: WE *134*

Subtropical jet stream: WE 37, *38-39, 112*

Sulfur: on Io (moon of Jupiter), SP *18-19*

Sulfur deposits: PE *100*

Sulfuric acid: Venus, SP *10, 11*

Sulfur oxides: and nitrogen oxides, WE 26, *27, 28-29*

Summer: Arctic Circle, SP *58-59*

Summer monsoon: WE *130*; flooding, WE *132*

Summer solstice: SP *56*; in Arctic, SP *58-59*

Sun: SP *4-5, 17, 36-49*; and aurora, WE 16; chromosphere and photosphere, SP *40, 41, 42-43*; corona, SP *40, 41, 50-51, 63, 123*; corona, atmospheric, WE *105*; Earth, radiation received by, SP *45, 48-49*; Earth's angle to, and seasons, SP *56-57*; Earth's protection from, WE *20-21*; eclipse of, SP *41, 50-51, 62-63*; in eclipse of Moon, SP *62-63*; flares, SP *36-37, 40, 41*; formation of, SP *6, 7, 38-39*; future

Planet Earth
PE

Plant Life
PL

Physical Forces
PH

Structure of Matter
ST

Space & Planets
SP

Transportation
TR

Underwater World
UN

Weather & Climate
WE

of, SP 36, *46-47*; and greenhouse effect, WE *136, 137*; halos around, WE *102-103*; on Hertzsprung-Russell diagram, SP *chart* 79; inside, SP *17, 40, 41*, 44; insolation from, and ice ages, WE *144*; Jupiter compared to, SP *17*; life history of, SP *39, 46-47*; magnetic field, WE *16*; magnetic field lines, SP *42-43, 46*; midnight, land of, SP *58-59*; mock, WE *102, 103*; and mountain halos, WE *104-105*; nuclear fusion in, SP 40, *44-45*; path on celestial sphere (ecliptic), SP *54-55, 60-61, 70*; and precession of Earth, SP *60-61*; and rainbows, WE *96-97, 98-99*; reflection of (albedo), WE *map* 123; size, comparative, SP *79*; and sky color, WE *22-23*; spectrum, WE *23*; stars around, SP *101*; sunspots on, SP *41, 42-43*; telescopes for studying, SP *122-123*; temperatures, SP *17, 39, 41, 47*; through atmosphere, WE *4-5*; and tides, PE 128, *129*; and tropical squalls, WE *76*; ultraviolet light from, WE *7, 9, 11, 12-13, 14, 15, 30*; uneven heating by, and air movement, WE 32, 34, 40, 42, 124; and wind and ocean currents, PE *118, 119, 120*

Sun City, Ariz., U.S.: GE *118-119*

Sunlight: *See* Light

Sunrise and sunset: sky color at, WE *22*

Sunspots: SP *41, 42, 43*; cycle of, SP *graph* 43; formation of, SP *42-43*

Superclusters of galaxies: SP *110*

Supercomputers: weather conditions modeled by, WE 108

Supergiants (stars): and black holes, SP *94-95*; and supernovas, SP *84, 93*

Supergranules and granules: SP *41*

Supernova explosions: SP 76, *84-85, 89, 93*

Supernova remnants: black holes and neutron stars as, SP 76, *85, 93-97*

Superposition of strata: law of, PE 94, *95*

Surface currents: PE *118-119, map* 120-121

Surface waves, seismic: PE 50; Love vs. Rayleigh, PE *51*

Suruga Bay, Japan: GE *23*

Surveying: GE 6, *8-9*; aerial, GE *6-7, 19*; for nautical charts, GE *18, 19*

S (shear) waves, seismic: and P (compressional) waves, PE *15*, 50, *51*; S-P time, PE 51, 52, 53, *chart* 53

Switzerland: Alps in, GE *142-143*

Syenite (rock): PE *88*

Synchronous rotation of Moon: SP *70-71*

T

Tails of comets: SP *33*

Tectonic plate interactions: and mountain building, GE *86-87, 96-97, 98-99*; and seafloor spreading, GE *78-79*

Tectonic plates: *See* Plate tectonics

Telemeters: laser, GE *8-9*

Telescopes: SP *116-125*; earliest, SP 116; Mauna Kea, SP *28*; optical, SP 116, *118-119, 122-123, 124*; radio, SP *120-121, 122, 124*; satellites and probes, SP *123, 124-125*; solar, SP *122-123*

Temperature: altitude and, WE 24, 25, *113*; Andes region, GE *charts* 140; chinooks, WE 44, *chart* 45; climate zones, GE *charts* 112, WE *128-129*; of earth, changes over time, WE 142, *chart* 142-143; and electricity in clouds, WE *67*; glaciation and, GE *chart* 50; global warming, WE 136, *137*; isotherms, WE *126, 139*; land and sea, WE *chart* 43; in Mediterranean countries, GE *charts* 136-137; and mirages, WE *100, 101*; ocean currents and, GE *charts* 116-117; of oceans, depth and, GE *70-71*, PE *117*, 134, *chart* 135; and saturation, WE 58, 70; and wind, WE *40-41*; worldwide, GE *map* 117

Temperature inversion layer: WE *60*; heat island, WE *138-139*

Tenma (x-ray observatory): SP *125*

Tennessee River, U.S.: Tennessee Valley Authority (TVA) projects on, GE *134-135*

Terminal moraine: GE *44-45, 46-47*

Terpen in the Netherlands: GE *132*

Terraced farms: GE *141*

Terraced pools in caves: GE *54-55, 60-61*

Terraces: GE *27, 88-89*; slump's creation of, GE *103*

Tertiary period: WE *143*; coal formation beginning in, PE *105*

Teton Range, Wyo., U.S.: GE *86*

Thailand: rice harvest in, GE *122*; summer monsoon in, WE *132*

Thames River, England: estuary of, GE *38*

Thematic maps: GE 12

Thermal air turbulence: WE *52-53*

Thermal power stations: PE *139*

Thermocline: oceans', PE 134, *135*

Thermosphere: WE *8-9, 10-11*; and winds, WE *36, 38*

3C273 (quasar): SP *113*

Thuban (star): SP *60*

Thunder: production of, WE *67*

Thunderclouds: *See* Cumulonimbus clouds

Thunderstorms: development of, WE 66, *89*; lightning, WE *56-57, 66-67*; squall line, WE *51*

Tiber River, Italy: delta of, GE *33*

Tidal dams: PE *139*

Tidal forces in Earth-Moon system: SP *73*

Tidal pools: PE *128*

Tidal range: PE 128, *map* 129

Tide gauge as indicator of earthquakes: PE *56*

Tides, ocean: GE *36, 37*, PE *128-129*; cause of, SP *73*; and estuaries, GE *38*; storm tides, PE *130-131*

Tilting: vs. centrifugal force in hurricane, WE *91*

Tiltmeters: water-tube, PE 56, *79*

Timber exports: GE 124, *maps* 124-125, *125*

Time: and gravity, PE 18

Time zones: GE *20-21*

Titan (moon of Saturn): SP *22-23*

Titicaca, Lake, Bolivia-Peru: GE *140, 141*

Tokyo, Japan: heat island, WE *map* 139; Ogouchi Dam, WE *79*; subsidence in, GE 65

Topographic maps: GE 12; of seabed, GE 19

Tornadoes: WE *32-33, 50*; formation of, WE *50-51*

Tower karst: Guilin, China, GE *59*

Trade winds: PE 118, *119, 132, 133*, WE *34-35, 36, 37*; convergence of, WE 90, *132-133*; deserts created by, GE *104-105*; and deserts' expansion and contraction, GE *106-107*; and El Niño phenomenon, PE *124-125*; and ocean surface currents, GE 70, *71*; and rainfall, GE *115*; southern oscillation and, WE *140-141*

Transform boundaries and transform faults: PE *34, 35, 49*; San Andreas fault, PE *42-43*, 49

Transhumance: GE *142-143*

Transverse dunes: GE *108*

Tree icing: WE *80-81*

Trees: in Appalachian Mountains, GE *96*; crop-bearing, GE *131*; Gobi Desert formerly covered by, GE *51*; lumber exports, GE 124, *maps* 124-125, *125*

Trenches, ocean: GE 78, 79, PE *33, 34, map* 35, *42, 43, 48-49, 65, 76*, 112, *map* 112, *map* 115; Pacific Rim, PE *115*

Trilobites: PE *95*

Triton (moon of Neptune): SP *26-27*

Tropical convergence belt: WE 90, *132-133*

Tropical depressions: WE 82, *90-91*

Tropical oceans: *See* Hurricanes and typhoons

Tropic of Cancer: SP *56-57*

Tropic of Capricorn: SP *56-57*

Tsunamis: earthquakes and, PE 54, *58-59*; volcanoes and, PE 58, *map* 73

Tube geyser: PE *81*

Type I supernova: SP *85*

Type II supernova: SP *84*

Typhoons: *See* Hurricanes and typhoons

Animal Behavior
AN

Computer Age
CO

Ecology
EC

Evolution of Life
EV

Geography
GE

Human Body
HU

Insects & Spiders
IN

Machines &
Inventions **MA**

U

Ulm ice period: glaciation during, WE *map* 144

Ultramafic and mafic rocks: PE *88, 89*

Ultraviolet astronomy: satellite, SP *125*

Ultraviolet photograph of Sun: SP *41*

Ultraviolet radiation: and ozone layer, WE *30*; and primitive atmosphere, WE *7*; solar, WE *9, 11, 12-13, 14, 15*

Umbra and penumbra: SP *62, 63*

Universe: SP *98*; birth, SP *108*; evolution, SP *108-109, 112-113*; expansion, SP *98, 114-115*; fate, SP *115*; structure, SP *110-111*

Updrafts: and air turbulence, WE *52-53*; in tornado formation, WE *50, 51*; valley and mountain breezes, WE *43*; in wind formation, WE *41*

Upwelling of cold water: PE *121*

Uranium dating: PE *95*

Uranium recovery from seawater: PE *138*

Uranus (planet): SP *24-25, 29*; rings, SP *20, 25*; Voyager mission to, SP *138*

Ursa Major (Big Dipper constellation): SP *90*; changes in, SP *90-91*; and precession, SP *60*

Ursa Minor (Little Dipper constellation): SP *60, 61*

Utah: irrigation in, GE *138*

V

Valles Marineris (canyon), Mars: SP *13*

Valley and mountain breezes: WE *42, 43*

Valleys: drowned, GE *90-91*; flooding of, and estuaries, GE *39*; glaciers in, GE *24-25, 42-47*; limestone, formation of, GE *58-59*; rivers' creation of, GE *26, 27, 99*. See *also* Rift valleys

Valley winds: buildings and, WE *55*

Van Allen, James: WE *18*

Van Allen belts: WE *10-11, 18-19*

Vapor trails (contrails): WE *64-65*

Variable stars: SP *82-83*

Vega (star): SP *61*; distance and magnitude, SP *81*

Vegetation zones: climate and, GE *maps 51, 112, map 113, 142, chart 142*

Venus (planet): SP *10-11, 29*; as seen from Mercury, SP *8*

Vernal equinox: SP *56*

Very long baseline interferometry (VLBI): in earthquake prediction, PE *56-57*; seafloor spreading measured with, PE *31*

Vesuvius, Mount, Italy: eruption of, PE *74-75*

Viking 1 (spacecraft): SP *125*; Mars photographed by, SP *13*

Virgo (galaxy cluster): location, SP *110*

VLBI (very long baseline interferometry): in earthquake prediction, PE *56-57*; seafloor spreading measured with, PE *31*

Volcanic hot springs: PE *82*

Volcanic (extrusive) igneous rocks: PE *87, 89*

Volcanic pipes: kimberlite, PE *90-91*

Volcanism and seafloor building: PE *32*

Volcanoes: PE *62-79*; along rift valleys, PE *41*; Andes formed by, PE *38, 39*; calderas, PE *67, 68-69, 72, 77, 80*; differences among, PE *66-67*; Fuji, Mount, Japan, WE *24, 25, 68, 115*; from hot spots, PE *44-45, 76, 77*; and hot springs, distribution of, PE *map 83*; Io (moon of Jupiter), SP *18-19*; Krakatoa, Indonesia, PE *62, 72-73*; lava formation, PE *64-65*; Mars, SP *12-13*; Pompeii's destruction by, PE *74-75*; predicting eruption of, PE *78-79*; seamounts, PE *44, 76-77, 114-115*; St. Helens, Mount, Wash., PE *70-71, 78*; thermal air turbulence over, WE *52*; Triton (moon of Neptune), SP *27*; and tsunamis, PE *58, map 73*; wind around, WE *68*; on young Earth, PE *111*, WE *7*

Volumetric strain gauge: PE *56*

Voyager space probes: Jupiter, mission to, SP *14, 16, 18*; missions, SP *138-139*; Neptune, mission to, SP *26*; Saturn, mission to, SP *20, 22*; Uranus, mission to, SP *24, 25*; *Voyager 1*, SP *138-139*; *Voyager 1* studies, SP *16, 22*; *Voyager 2*, SP *26, 125, 138-139*; *Voyager 2* studies, SP *16, 20, 24, 25, 26*

Vulcanian type of volcanic eruption: PE *66*

W

Waialeale, Mount, Hawaii, U.S.: rainfall on, GE *115*

Water: irrigation with, GE *35, 63, 138-139*; land reclamation from, GE *132-133*; vapor, WE *70*. See *also* Glaciers; Ground water; Lakes; Oceans; Rain; Rivers

Water circulation: Earth, SP *49*

Water cycle: global, GE *24, 68, 82-83*

Waterfalls: migration of, GE *27*

Water-layer geyser: PE *81*

Water table: GE *56, 57*; sinking of, subsidence from, GE *64-65*

Water vapor: condensation of, WE *70*

Wave-form clouds: WE *61*

Wave-form currents over mountains: WE *69*

Waves, ocean: PE *108-109*; marine erosion from, GE *68-69, 76-77, 88-89*; motion of, PE *126-127*; as power source, PE *139*; and sand bar formation, GE *74*; storm waves, PE *130-131*

Waves, seismic: PE *14-15*; isochrones, PE *53*; ore deposits detected with, PE *98, 99*; S-P time, PE *51, 52, 53, chart 53*; traveling of, PE *50-51*

Weather: WE entire volume. See *also* Atmosphere of Earth; Climate; Clouds; Rain

Weather forecasts: WE *108, 120-121*

Weathering: in desert sand's formation, GE *104-105*; in Monument Valley's formation, GE *110-111*

Weather maps, making: WE *118-119*; forecast map, WE *120-121*

Weather observation: WE *108-109*; of Antarctica, WE *122-123*; forecasts from, WE *108, 120-121*; history of, WE *108*; of hurricanes and typhoons, WE *94-95, 115*; maps, making, WE *118-119, 120-121*; models from, supercomputer, WE *108*; sources, kinds of, WE *10-11, 116-117, 123*; of upper atmosphere, WE *112-113, 119*

Weather radar: WE *94, 114-115*; Antarctica, observation of, WE *123*; antennas on, WE *108, 114, 115, 118*; cloud development, observation of, WE *63*; range of, WE *114, 115*

Weather satellites: PE *136*; WE *10-11, 18, 82-83, 84, 94, 110-111, 113, 117, 118, 121, 123*; image of Earth from, PE *4-5*

Weather stations: WE *116, 117*; maps, making, role in, WE *118*; on mountains, WE *108-109, 115*; network, international, WE *map 117*; satellites and, WE *110*

Wegener, Alfred: PE *24*

Weightlessness in space: SP *132*; simulating, SP *136-137*

Wells, water: GE *139*; artesian, GE *56, 62, 139*; earthquake effects on, PE *55*; overpumping of, and subsidence, GE *64-65*

Well-to-well surveys: PE *99*

Westerly winds: PE *119, 132, 133*, WE *35, 36, 37*; and El Niño phenomenon, PE *124-125*; and low-pressure troughs, WE *84, 86*; and ocean currents, GE *71*

Wet tongue: WE *88-89*

Wheat: production, GE *122, 123*

Whirlpools, formation of: PE *122-123*

White dwarfs (stars): SP *93*; Sun as, SP *47*; and supernova, SP *85*

Whittlesey, Derwent: agricultural zones classified by, GE *map 130-131*

Wind: GE *100*, WE *32-55*; air turbulence, WE *52-53*; around buildings, WE *52, 54-55*; atmospheric circulation, WE *34-35, 36-37, 38, 53, 112-113, 124, 134*; bora winds, WE *48-49*; breezes, regular, WE

Planet Earth
PE

Plant Life
PL

Physical Forces
PH

Structure of Matter
ST

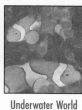
Space & Planets
SP

Transportation
TR

Underwater World
UN

Weather & Climate
WE

42-43, 76; cause of, WE *40-41*; and clouds over mountains, WE *68-69*; and coastal rain, GE *114-115*; convergence of trade winds, WE *90, 132-133*; deserts created by, GE *104-105*; deserts' dunes shaped by, GE *100-101, 105, 108-109*; and deserts' expansion and contraction, GE *106-107*; foehns, WE *44-45, 47*; of hurricanes, WE *82-83, 90-95*; and icing, WE *80-81*; jet streams, WE *37, 38-39, 53, 88-89, 112, 130-131*; monsoon, WE *130-131*; Monument Valley monoliths formed by, GE *110-111*; and ocean surface currents, GE *70, 71*; and ocean waves, PE *126, 127*; pressure and, WE *82, 84*; prevailing, and El Niño phenomenon, PE *124-125*; prevailing, and ocean currents, PE *118, 119, 120, 132, 133*; prevailing, kinds of, WE *35, 36-37*; siroc-

co, WE *46-47*; southern oscillation and, WE *140-141*; storm tides and storm waves caused by, PE *130-131*; in stratosphere, WE *36, 112-113*; tornadoes, WE *32-33, 50-51*
Wind patterns: Jupiter, SP *14*
Wind shadows and dune formation: GE 108
Winter monsoon: WE 130, *131*
Winter solstice: SP *57, 58*
Winter winds: warm, WE *44-45*
Wisconsinan glaciation: Gobi Desert during, GE *51*
Wood: exports, GE 124, *maps* 124-125, *125*
Wyoming, U.S.: Teton Range in, GE *86*

X

X-ray observatory: SP *125*
X-ray photograph of Sun: SP *41*

X-rays: sources of, SP *97*; black hole as possible source of, SP *94, 95*

Y

Yardangs: formation of, GE *111*
Yellow River, China: changes in, GE *34-35*
Yellowstone National Park, Wyo., U.S.: columnar basalts, PE *84-85*; geysers, PE *80-81*
Yoldia Sea, ancient Finland: GE *map* 67
Yugoslavia: bora winds, WE *48-49*; Dubrovnik, WE *49*

Z

Zao, Mount, Japan: ice formations, WE *80*
Zeiss, Carl: planetariums, SP 126
Zodiac: constellations of, SP *54-55*

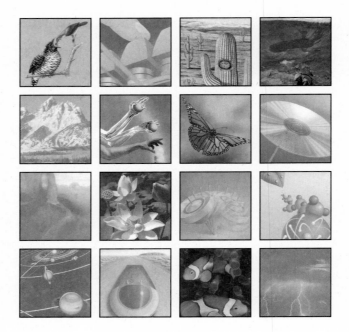

Life Science

The life science group, consisting of seven volumes of the Understanding Science and Nature series, explores the range of life on Earth, from the relationships that affect life on the cellular level to those that shape the planet's ecosystem. Because the books detail life at all levels and in all its variety, they are a valuable resource for the study of life science at any grade level.

Of the volumes in the life science group, two—*Human Body* and *Plant Life*—begin with a basic description of cells, followed by detailed explanations of how those cells are organized to form complex animals and plants. A third volume, *Evolution of Life,* traces the development of life on Earth by showing how the world's first few primitive cells evolved through natural selection to become the plants and animals that live today. The remaining volumes—*Insects & Spiders, Underwater World, Animal Behavior,* and *Ecology*—celebrate the diversity of living things and demonstrate the complex interrelationships among plants, animals, humans, and the environment.

The books in this section, like all the books in this series, have a strong visual orientation that makes difficult concepts easy to understand and motivates students to learn more. This approach is particularly useful in life science, where so many features are too small to be seen or are hidden inside the body. Large, colorful drawings, photographs, and electron micrographs help students visualize even the smallest organisms. By making abstract theories more concrete, these books will help students understand how the biological and ecological concepts they learn apply to their world.

Human Body

An excellent introduction to life science, *Human Body* examines the body's structures and systems through large cutaway drawings, photographs, step-by-step illustrations of the body's processes, and carefully written explanations. Beginning with an overview of the different cells that make up the body, this volume goes on to explore each system in order to give students a clear understanding of their own internal structure.

Chapter 1: The Mysteries of Human Life. The first chapter of *Human Body* explores the body's basic building blocks. A detailed cutaway illustration shows the structure of a typical cell, identifies the major organelles, and briefly describes the function of each one. A series of sketches shows the stages of mitotic cell division. Another section explores DNA, using drawings to unravel a chromosome down to its DNA and to demonstrate how DNA replicates. This chapter also contains a discussion of human reproduction. Illustrations of the reproductive organs help students understand how human life begins. Later sections trace the production of sperm and egg cells and describe the stages of fetal development.

Chapter 2: Your Super Structure. Skin, muscles, and bones are the subject of this chapter. Together, they form the body's framework, a flexible construct that supports and protects the body's delicate internal organs. *Human Body* avoids standard diagrams that show the entire skeletal and muscular systems. Instead, the book zeroes in on specific parts of those systems to answer questions that are often posed by students but seldom explained by textbooks. How bones grow, why people sweat, how cuts heal, and what causes goose bumps are among the topics covered in this chapter.

Chapter 3: Respiration and Circulation. The cells of the human body need two things to make the body run: fuel, supplied by proteins, fats, and carbohydrates, and oxygen to burn the fuel. These needs are answered by the respiratory and circulatory systems, which work together to keep the body going. In addition to explaining how the heart and lungs function, this chapter describes the way these organs get their oxygen and fuel. Drawings show the components of blood at a cellular level and explain the role of each. Cutaways highlight the structural differences among various kinds of veins and arteries. Blood pressure—what it is and how it is measured—is explained with the help of a graph that identifies the high, normal, and low ranges.

Chapter 4: Digestion. From the mouth, through the stomach, to the intestines, this chapter explores the structure and function of the organs that contribute to the digestive process. Macroscopic and cellular-level drawings illustrate the workings of each organ. Additional diagrams show the formation and function of digestive enzymes. The section concludes with a diagram of the digestive system as a whole, pointing out the absorption site of each major food component.

Chapter 5: The Amazing Nervous System. The complex communications network that forms the body's nervous system is the subject of this chapter. Focusing on the senses, the chapter uses cutaways to show the inner structure of each sensory organ, while the text explains how each organ works. Maps of the body's neural pathways demonstrate how nerve impulses are sent to and from the spinal column and the brain.

Chapter 6: Disease and Immunity. The final section of *Human Body* investigates the immune system. Schematic illustrations reveal how the body creates its network of defenses. Drawings also demonstrate how the immune system fights disease and infection, protecting the body on both a cellular and a molecular level. Segments on measles, the common cold, cancer, AIDS, and respiratory allergies dramatically illustrate how and why our immune systems are so essential.

Plant Life

Plant Life follows the same format as *Human Body*, beginning with a description of the basic building blocks of plants—their cells—and working through a plant's anatomy. Cutaway drawings and diagrams of life cycles and other processes are paired with photographs of a broad range of plant species to help teach students the basics of botany.

Chapter 1: Plant Cells and Growth. This chapter explores the specialized cells that make up plants. First, a comparison between a typical plant cell and a typical animal cell shows students the similarities between the two life forms. A chart identifies the major cell organelles and their functions. Other sections explain plant reproduction and growth on a cellular level, helping students to identify and differentiate types of plant tissue.

Chapter 2: Roots and Stems. A plant's roots and stem serve two purposes: They support the plant as it grows, and they supply it with water and nutrients absorbed from the soil. This chapter takes a close look at how roots and stems function. It also answers questions about plant features, explaining what causes tree rings, why some plants have thorns, and how vines support themselves.

Chapter 3: Structure and Function of Leaves. A plant's leaves are its food factories. Thanks to photosynthesis, leaves convert water from the soil and carbon dioxide from the air into the sugars that sustain the plant's life. In addition to explaining the form and function of leaves, this chapter investigates insect-eating plants such as the Venus's-flytrap and the pitcher plant, as well as the sensitive mimosa, whose leaves curl when touched.

Chapter 4: Beauty with a Purpose. Humans see flowers as symbols of fragile beauty; this chapter explores their botanical role as the hard-working reproductive tools of angiosperms. Discussions of bloom time, color, and gender help to outline the basics of pollination.

Chapter 5: Fruits and Seeds. This chapter investigates the later stages of plant reproduction, from the development of seeds and fruits to their dispersal. Photos of plants and plant parts, extensive illustrations of specialized cells and tissues, and diagrams detailing seed growth and dispersal routes inform students about the varied reproductive methods plants use to ensure the survival of their species.

Chapter 6: Plants without Flowers. Though not as complex as flowering plants, nonflowering plants are an interesting subject of study. These organisms—including fungi, mushrooms, diatoms, algae, seaweed, lichens, mosses, and ferns—were among the earliest forms of life on Earth. Today, they serve a vital role in the food chain as decomposers. In this chapter, students can examine the physiology and life cycles of these unusual plants.

Chapter 7: Astonishing Adapters. Environment is a key factor in the evolution of plants, forcing many of them to adapt to new conditions. This chapter explores the ways in which plants have evolved through the ages, as well as the ways in which they maintain the Earth's equilibrium. Sections on unusual plants—such as cacti, living stones, and giant redwoods—are followed by a look at plants in the food chain and how they contribute to the changing face of our planet.

Chapter 8: The Human Connection. The final section of *Plant Life* investigates botany's research frontiers. A segment on medical breakthroughs discusses Sir Alexander Fleming and his discovery of penicillin. This section also examines in genetic engineering, grafting, cross-breeding, and other techniques for improving the yield and quality of food crops. The chapter ends by stressing the importance of maintaining the plant world's genetic resources.

Evolution of Life

Most students remember the names of at least a few of the dinosaurs they learned about in elementary school; others have a fairly extensive knowledge of prehistoric creatures. *Evolution of Life* provides a context for that knowledge. It also presents the latest paleontological research.

Chapter 1: The Evolution of Species. The first section of *Evolution of Life* reviews different theories of evolution, including Charles Darwin's explanation of the evolution of species, natural selection, and adaptation. Comparisons of Darwin's ideas and those of other scientists such as Gregor Mendel and Jean-Baptiste Lamarck reveal that theories, not just organisms, can evolve through time. Illustrated charts and graphs show how evolution and genetics have worked in tandem to create the amazing diversity of life on Earth.

Chapter 2: Where Life Began. This chapter tells the story of the first life on Earth, starting with an investigation of the planet's formation from a cloud of dust and gases. Drawings show how organic molecules—the progenitors of the first living things—developed in the Earth's primitive oceans. A discussion of the formation of simple cells and their evolution into oxygen producers suggests how life on Earth probably began. The introduction of oxygen drastically changed the Earth's atmosphere, preparing the planet for the evolutionary changes to come.

Chapter 3: The Paleozoic: Dawn of Modern Life. During the 325 million years of the Paleozoic era, the mold was cast for every form of modern life. This chapter traces the progress of those life forms, from trilobites through fishes and amphibians to reptiles. Students will be familiar with this sequence of change and will recognize many of the animals mentioned. Drawings track the progress of the external physical changes, while cutaway illustrations explore internal changes. Charts and time lines show students which organisms coexisted and when they lived. Many students will be surprised to discover that mammals evolved along with the dinosaurs, not after them.

Chapter 4: When Dinosaurs Ruled. Many groundbreaking theories—among them the now-accepted theory that birds developed from dinosaur ancestors, the idea that at least some dinosaurs were warm blooded, and new concepts about coloration, external appearance, and various aspects of dinosaur "social" behavior—have come to light in recent years. This section, on dinosaurs and the other animals and plants of the Mesozoic era, explores these new ideas. Traditional ways of thinking are juxtaposed against modern theories so students can see for themselves how the new ideas were developed and, eventually, accepted.

Chapter 5: The Humans Arrive. The catastrophic events that ended the Mesozoic era 66 million years ago created new opportunities for the plants and animals that survived. The Cenozoic era, often called the Age of Mammals, was an era when many life forms flourished—including birds, flowering plants, and of course mammals. This chapter investigates the ascendance of mammals in particular. After examining evolutionary changes in horses, elephants, whales, bats, and primates, it explains how humans evolved from the tiny nocturnal mammals that populated the planet at the dawn of the era.

Chapter 6: Scientific Proofs of Evolution. Modern evolutionary theory rests on a wide base of scientific evidence gathered before and after Charles Darwin performed his pioneering research. This chapter presents that evidence, which supports the concepts of evolution and natural selection. Touching on extinction and the environmental impact of human beings, it also explains why evolution is an unfinished business.

Insects & Spiders

More than one million insect species and more than 30,000 spider species belong to the two classes of animals profiled in this book. Photographs and magnified drawings introduce readers to the beauty and diversity of the planet's most populous group of animals. They reveal features too small to be seen without a microscope—such as the hairy feet of a water strider—and events too fast to be observed directly—such as the beating of a honeybee's wings.

Chapter 1: Body Form and Function. Basic anatomy is the starting point for this chapter on insect physiology. Graphic techniques such as cutaway diagrams and ghosted drawings reveal several internal layers of an insect in a single illustration. The chapter also compares sense organs, forms of locomotion, and coloration. Of particular appeal are discussions of how some insects—such as water striders and insects living in glacier ice—have adapted to unusual environments.

Chapter 2: Eating Habits. This chapter explores the methods insects and spiders use to find their food. Cutaway drawings show the unique way each insect species tracks, catches, and digests its meals. From the glowworm's lure to the spider's web, the chapter investigates who eats what (and when, and where, and how) in the insect kingdom.

Chapter 3: Life Cycles of Insects. This chapter explains the surprisingly complex life cycle of many insects. Included are 17-year cicadas, honeybees, aphids, butterflies and moths, and dragonflies. The processes of metamorphosis and hypermetamorphosis—described in diagrams and charts—will intrigue students learning about the amazing changes insects go through as they mature. Students will also encounter the unusual mating rituals of insects such as the praying mantis, the scorpionfly, and the mosquito.

Chapter 4: Insect and Spider Nests. The nesting habits of insects and spiders are the subject of this chapter. Topics range from the individual homes built by solitary species to the small "cities" built by social insects such as wasps and bees. The text also examines the way in which insect and spider bodies are adapted to build their specialized nests.

Chapter 5: A Diversity of Defenses. The chapter explains the principles of adaptation, camouflage, and mimicry, as well as the more specific defenses that are used by bees, ants, and bombardier beetles. Colorful drawings illustrate each technique in action.

Chapter 6: The Complex Lives of Social Insects. The final section of *Insects & Spiders* probes the fascinating behavioral patterns—as well as anatomy—of so-called "social" insects. Honeybees, ants, termites, and aphids are examples.

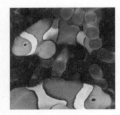

Underwater World

Underwater World describes the wide range of animals and other organisms that live under the water, as well as crustaceans, amphibians, and mammals that live near the water. These animals coexist in an ecosystem that covers more than three-quarters of the Earth's surface.

Chapter 1: All Creatures Wet and Wild. Through pictures and comparison charts, this chapter surveys the diversity of life underwater. Cutaway drawings reveal the anatomy of fish and explore how different fish breathe, drink, and control buoyancy and body temperature. The chapter highlights the adaptations underwater creatures have made to their unusual environment—such as the development of glowing organs in deep-sea fish and the ability of some fish to breathe out of

water. The chapter also examines land crabs, deep-diving sperm whales, and the creatures that live around anaerobic hot-water vents.

Chapter 2: Sensible Swimmers. Like land animals, fish use a wide array of senses to find food and avoid predators. This chapter focuses on underwater species' sensory adaptations. One section, for example, explores the sonar system that allows river dolphins to navigate in muddy water. Another investigates the ability of sharks to detect electrical impulses from their prey.

Chapter 3: Mating, Reproduction, and Growth. This section is devoted to the reproductive rituals that have evolved among aquatic animals. Angelfish, for instance, can change gender when it is time to mate. Other fish, such as tetras, lay their eggs out of water. Young frogs undergo an insectlike metamorphosis from tadpole to adult. Drawings and clear life-cycle diagrams help explain the complicated processes of mating, birth, and development in an underwater environment.

Chapter 4: Desperately Seeking Sustenance. This chapter offers a comparison of aquatic animals' diverse hunting and feeding techniques, from simple filter feeding on krill by a giant blue whale to the expert marksmanship of an archerfish. Illustrations show how feeding methods are reflected in anatomy.

Chapter 5: The Art of Self-Defense. Self-defense is the focus of the last chapter of *Underwater World*. The text examines species with poisonous skin, fish that fly out of the water to escape danger, and animals whose camouflage protects them from predators.

Animal Behavior

Animal Behavior explores the usual—and unusual—behavior of animals, ranging from the feeding habits of the single-celled paramecium to the use of language by chimpanzees. With all animal life as its subject, this book emphasizes the similarities among the animal species, as well as their differences. Photographs, drawings, charts, and diagrams help students better compare and understand complex animal behavior patterns.

Chapter 1: Finding Food. The entries in this section focus on the most basic need of all animals—food. From a barn owl's keen hearing to a snake's unusual ability to smell its prey through its tongue, animals have developed remarkable senses and abilities to help them in their quest for food. This chapter addresses such diverse habits as how ants "milk" honeydew from aphids, how bats hunt at night, and how chimpanzees use tools to gather bugs.

Chapter 2: Animal Defenses. Many animals spend their lives in danger from predators. In response, those animals have developed the effective defense mechanisms that are the focus of the second chapter. Several species use mimicry or protective coloration. Some insect species have misleading eye spots. Other animals may change color with the seasons. But appearance does not provide the only defense. A few species, such as the hermit crab and the anemone, have learned to form partnerships that benefit both. And other animals, such as fish, gather in groups whose sheer numbers protect them.

Chapter 3: Mating and Parenting. This chapter, on reproduction and parenting, shows how different animals pursue this fundamental drive. In doing so, it also answers some basic questions about animal behavior—such as why crickets chirp, what the summertime flash of fireflies means, and why grunions lay their eggs during the full moon. The chapter also discusses how different species, such as alligators and penguins, care for their young.

Chapter 4: Animal Social Behavior. Many animals have developed elaborate social structures that enable them to work well together. In order to live as a group, animals such as ants and chimpanzees have had to learn a special set of skills. This chapter explores how social species divide their work, communicate with each other, and protect one another. The division of labor in a beehive and the migrating behavior of birds show how social behavior has developed at all levels of the animal kingdom. A comparison of matriarchal macaques and patriarchal chimpanzees helps explain dominance hierarchy in primates. The chapter also explores language use by chimpanzees and the evidence for learned behavior in groups of monkeys.

Ecology

While the other books provide windows into specific areas of life on Earth, *Ecology* brings all those elements together. This volume helps students understand the interdependence among plants, animals, and the environment. Using population studies and maps, *Ecology* shows how the planet itself has affected evolution. Students will learn that plants, animals, climate, and the land are all linked together, and that any change in one of them is likely to cause changes in the others.

Chapter 1: Patterns of Life. Through the last three billion years, the interplay between animals, plants, and the Earth itself has shaped and re-shaped our planet. The first section of *Ecology* examines how this interaction has created the world we know today. A study of isolated species, such as those from the Galápagos Islands and Australia, shows students how diversity and adaptation work within a closed environment. A comparison of wildlife from different regions demonstrates the impact that changes in the Earth's surface can have on evolution. This chapter also examines climate's role in natural phenomena, such as the extinction of North American monkeys.

Chapter 2: Adapting to Life on Earth. This chapter surveys the nine major biomes, or zones of shared plant and animal life, that cover the Earth's surface. Desert, grassland, rain forest, polar, alpine, and coastal biomes are among those explored. Each biome study includes a survey of the plants and animals that occupy it. The studies also describe the evolutionary adaptations and relationships living organisms have developed to survive in each zone.

Chapter 3: Continuing the Species. As each species of plant or animal strives to create a healthy new generation, it must find ways to ensure that generation's safety within the context of its environment. Chapter 3 outlines the unusual ways in which some plant and animal species have adapted for survival. The chapter also examines life cycles, showing how each organism must die in order to maintain the health of its environment. Rapidly reproducing lemmings illustrate cycles in population as an example of unusual population-control mechanisms.

Chapter 4: The Food Chain. As a final example of how all living things depend on each other for survival, the last section of *Ecology* explains the nature of the food chain, as well as the roles played by key organisms. Problems associated with human activity—the dangers of pesticide accumulation in the environment, the disasters created by oil spills—conclude the volume.

Classroom Applications

The information found in the life science group relates naturally to the topics covered in most life science and biology courses. One of the most valuable aspects of this set of books—and of the life science group in particular—is that each volume allows students to approach those topics from any of several different angles. The topic list below shows just a few of the possible connections.

Biochemistry	*Human Body* pages 8-11 *Plant Life* (p. 10-11)
Biomes	*Ecology* (p. 30-95)
Cell Structure	*Human Body* (p. 8-9) *Plant Life* (p. 6-7)
Cold-Blooded Vertebrates	*Underwater World* (p. 6-31, 46-59, 64-91, 104-113, 122-135) *Evolution Of Life* (p. 56-97)

Complex Invertebrates
  Mollusks, Arthropods, Insects,
  and Spiders
	Insects & Spiders (entire volume)
	Animal Behavior (p. 8-13, 26-31, 54-55, 64-65,
	  76-79, 90-97, 126-131)
	Ecology (p. 110-111)
	Underwater World (p. 36-39, 96-99, 136-137)

Diseases	*Human Body* (p. 128-144)
Ecosystems	*Ecology* (p. 6-27, 126-144)
Human Body	Support and Movement: *Human Body* (p. 32-51) Digestion: *Human Body* (p. 78-95) Circulation: *Human Body* (p. 60-73) Respiration: *Human Body* (p. 54-59) Nervous System: *Human Body* (p. 98-125) Development and Heredity:*Human Body* (p. 6-29)
Human Interaction with **the Biosphere**	*Plant Life* (p. 132-144) *Ecology* (p. 142-144)
Natural Selection	*Ecology* (p. 98-123) *Evolution of Life* (entire volume)
Plants	*Plant Life* (entire volume) *Evolution of Life* (p. 34-35, 52-53, 102-103) *Ecology* (p. 44-45, 54-57, 64-69, 72-79)
Protists and Fungi	*Plant Life* (p. 94-101) *Animal Behavior* (p. 6-7) *Ecology* (p. 134-135)
Simple Invertebrates	*Evolution of Life* (p. 36-45, 98-99) *Underwater World* (p. 40-43, 60-61, 100-101, 138-143)
Warm-Blooded Vertebrates	*Underwater World* (p. 32-33, 92-95, 114-117) *Evolution Of Life* (p. 100-101, 106-129)

Activity: Digesting a Meal

Background. Most students know little about digestion. Many believe that all food is digested in the stomach and then absorbed in the intestines. They are often aware of the other organs of digestion—the liver, the kidneys, the gallbladder—but few understand how those organs fit into the whole process. In this activity, students will learn that digestion and absorption are complex processes that begin as soon as they put food into their mouths. After choosing a meal, your students will trace each kind of food through the digestive system, learning where different items are broken down and absorbed. When they complete this activity, they should have a more complete knowledge of the system that keeps bodies running.

Group Size. Four or five students in each group.

Duration. The teacher will need one class day to introduce the activity and divide the class into groups. Students will take three to five days to learn about the digestive process and to trace their chosen foods through the digestive system. You will want to leave about two days for summary and evaluation.

Procedure. To begin, each group of students should select foods to fill an imaginary lunchbox. There should be at least one item for each student: a group of five students, for example, might choose a peanut butter and jelly sandwich, carrot and celery sticks, chocolate chip cookies, an apple, and a thermos of milk.

Each student will then choose one item to follow through the digestive process. To do that, the students will first need to know which of the following elements are in their food: starches and sugars, fats, and proteins.

Although your students won't need to know vitamin and mineral content for this activity, collecting that information would be an interesting extension. Most nutritional information can be found on food product labels. *Bowes and Church's Food Values of Portions Commonly Used,* published by Lippincott and available in most libraries, is another valuable resource.

Once your students have found out which nutrients their food contains, they can use the *Human Body* volume to track the food as it progresses through the digestive system. They should pay attention to how and where each component is digested and absorbed and to the enzymes and organs that are responsible for each step in the process. The students will then explain what they've learned to the others in their group. This exchange will show them that not all foods are digested the same way and will help them understand the role and importance of each part of the digestive system.

To evaluate the students' progress, you can ask each group to prepare a written report of its findings. You can also have the group make an oral presentation to the whole class.

Extension. Instead of asking every group to create a lunch menu, try assigning each group a different meal. Using vitamin and mineral information, they can determine whether their menu would give them a balanced diet. By showing them the possible effects of bad eating habits, you can help your students understand the importance of a nutritious diet. Students can also use *Human Body* to learn about the nutritional problems of diseases such as diabetes or ulcers.

Reference Guide. Students may find these sections in *Human Body* helpful as they work on this activity:

The digestive process: pages 92-93	Pancreas: pages 84-85, 142-143
Mouth: pages 78-79	Liver: pages 86-87
Esophagus: pages 80-81	Small intestine: pages 88-89
Stomach: pages 82-83	Large intestine: pages 90-91

Activity: Evolution Time Line

Background. Most students have trouble imagining how the ancient events of prehistory fit together. How long ago did life begin? When did the first mammals arrive? Did humans and dinosaurs live at the same time? A large, classroom-size time line, researched and created by your students, will help them understand how evolution progressed from Precambrian times to the present.

Group size. Five or six students per group. Each group will represent a different era in the Earth's evolutionary history:

Cenozoic Era: 65 million years ago (mya) to the present
Mesozoic Era: 240 mya to 65 mya
Paleozoic Era: 570 mya to 240 mya
Precambrian Era: 4.6 billion years ago to 570 mya

Duration. Your students will need three to five days of class time to create the time line and to deliver their reports.

Materials.

10 m strip of chart paper or butcher paper
Art materials such as markers, crayons, paints, colored paper, and glue

Procedure. Using the 10 m strip of paper, the class will create a time line to show the events of the last 600 million years of Earth's history. Each group will be responsible for a different era. The group's first step will be to decide how much of the 10 m strip it is responsible for. The students will then research the evolutionary changes of their era. Although the Precambrian group will only have 30 million years worth of paper and will illustrate only that period on the time line, the students should investigate the changes that occurred during the entire era and include those changes in their reports. They should also calculate how long their part of the time line would be if the paper were long enough to include the whole era.

Each group will then need to perform these tasks:

First, the students should illustrate their section of the time line to show the life forms that lived during their era.

Next, each group should present an oral report to the class, outlining the important evolutionary developments of their time period.

Last, the group should also prepare a written report that summarizes the findings of the oral report. It should include a list of the references consulted in the research.

Reference Guide. Students will want to use the entire volume of *Evolution of Life* to complete this project. The following sections will help students focus on specific eras in evolutionary history:

Cenozoic Era: pages 104-129
Mesozoic Era: pages 60-103
Paleozoic Era: pages 40-59
Precambrian Era: pages 26-39

|  | | | | | | |  |

| Animal Behavior **AN** | Computer Age **CO** | Ecology **EC** | Evolution of Life **EV** | Geography **GE** | Human Body **HU** | Insects & Spiders **IN** | Machines & Inventions **MA** |

Life Science Index

Numerals in italics indicate an illustration of the subject mentioned.

A

Abalone, single-shelled red: reproduction by, UN *98*

Abscission layer, leaf stalk's: PL *41, 43*

Acacia plants: bull-horn, IN *99*

Acanthodians: EV 48

Acarina (extinct arachnid): EV *50*

Acellular organisms: EV 39

Acid rain: effects of, EC *74-75*

Acinar cells: HU *85*

Acquired immune deficiency syndrome (AIDS): HU *136-137*

Actin and myosin: HU *36, 37*

Active submission: wolves, AN *45*

Adam's apple: HU *58*; development of, HU *59*

Adapis (extinct primate): EV *122*

Adaptation: EV 5, *20-21*, PL 110; alpine plants, PL *120-121*; baobab tree, PL *116-117*; cacti, PL *111, 112-113*; stone plant, PL *110, 114-115*

Adaptive radiation: EV *24-25*, 138

Addax: EC *91*

Adélie penguins: AN *88-89, 112-113*, EC 9, 46, *47*

Adenosine triphosphate (ATP): HU 36, *37, 57*

Adrenal glands: HU *75*

Aedes albopictus mosquito: AN *11*

Aerial roots: PL *22*

Africa: beetles, IN *60, 61, 107*; catfish, UN 57, *84-85, 86-87*; cichlids, UN *79, 84-85*; desert animals, EC 89, *91*; driver ants, IN 138, *141*; electric fish, UN *56-57*; elephants, EC *10, 82-83, 84-85,* 113; hunting dogs, EC *13,* 82; and India, animals of, EC *10-11*; killifish, UN *64*; locust swarming, IN *map* 87; lungfish, UN *30-31*; savannas, EC 29, 76, *80-85*; vs. South America, animals of, EC *20-21*

Africanized honeybees: IN *136-137*

Agave: EC *95*

Agglutinins: HU *70-71*

Agglutinogens: HU *70-71*

Aggregate fruits: PL *67*

Aggressive mimicry: AN *30-31*

Agnathans: EV *46-47,* 48

Agouti: EC *20*

AIDS (acquired immune deficiency syndrome): HU *136-137*

Air (swim) bladder: UN *12-13*; for hearing, UN *52, 53*; and pressure, UN 23

Air-breathing fish: UN *28-29, 30-31*

Air plants: *See* Epiphytes

Air roots: plants with, EC *68-69*

Air sacs in lungs: HU *56-57*

Akagi stink bugs: IN *120*

Akebia flowers: PL *59*

Albatrosses: Galápagos, courtship of, AN *102*; short-tailed, EC *33*

Albino long fin guppy: UN *65*

Alevins: UN *82*

Alexander's horned aphid: IN *144*

Alfonsino: UN *23*

Algae: PL *95, 102-103, 104-105*; chlorophyll in, EV *37*; diatoms, PL *100-101*; evolution of, EV *6-7,* 53; fossil (stromatolites), EV *26-27, 34-35*; in lichens, PL *106, 107*

Allergies: HU 135; hay fever, HU *134-135*

Alligators: and alligator holes, EC *138-139*; planthopper resembling, IN *112, 119*; and young, AN *110-111*

Alligator snapping turtle: UN *110-111*

Allosaurus (dinosaur): EV *74-75*

Alpha waves, brain's: HU *120, 124, 125*

Alpine butterflies: EC *52-53,* 57

Alpine meadows: EC *56-57*

Alpine plants: PL *120-121*

Alpine tundra: EC 54, *55,* 57

Alternation of generations: *See* Spore-bearing plants

Alveoli and alveolar sacs: HU *56-57*; carbon monoxide in, HU *72-73*

Amaranth: PL *75*

Amazon River dolphins: UN *59*

Ammonites: EV *98-99*; mosasaurs eating, EV *94-95*

Amniotic sac: HU *19*; of twins, HU *22, 23*

Amoebas: evolution of, EV *6*

Amphibians: evolution of, EV *56-57*; frogs, AN 15, *56-57, 66-67,* 73, EC 93, *127, 138, 139*; newts, AN *52,* 67; newts, development of, EV *133*; reproduction in, UN *62-63, 88-89, 90-91*; and reptile evolution, EV *58-59*; salamanders, EC 28, *42*; toads, AN *51, 52, 54-55,* EC *92-93, 125*

Ampullae and ampullar crests: HU *114, 115*

Ampullae of Lorenzini: shark's, UN *55*

Anaerobic bacteria: EV *32, 33,* 37

Anal fin: mouthbrooder's, spots on, UN *81*

Analogous parts: PL *28, 29, 30*

Anal pore: paramecium, AN *7*

Anal sphincter: HU *91*

Anancus (elephant ancestor): EV *110*

Anapsids: EV *chart* 63; *Hylonomus*, EV *58, 62*

Anchiceratops (dinosaur): EV *75*

Andrews, Roy Chapman: EV 78

Andrewsarchus (extinct mammal): EV *112*

Anemones, sea: AN *22-23, 48-49*, UN *34*; and clown fish, AN *70-71*, UN 144; crabs living in, UN *39*; and hermit crabs, AN *78-79*

Angelfish: blackspot, sex changes in, UN *66-67*; coloration, UN *132-133*

Angiosperms: *See* Flowers and flowering plants

Anglerfish: UN 110, *111, 112*; devil angler, UN *23*; goosefish, UN *102-103, 110-111*; reproduction, UN *70-71*

Animal behavior: AN entire volume

Animals: Antarctic and Arctic, EC *8-9,* 28, *46-49*; cell, PL *6-7*; as consumers, PL 124, *125*; crowding of, EC *100-101*; endangered, EC *96-97, 112-113*; extinct, EC *18-19,* 20, 112, EV 8, 20, *24, 60-61, 144*; after forest fire, EC *136-137*; of Galápagos, EC *6-7, 113, 119*; plant reproduction aided by, EC *96-97, 114-115, 122-123*; plants' defenses against, EC *118-119*; by region, EC *4-5*; seeds spread by, PL 65, *74-75,* 77, *78-79,* 82; soil, PL *110-111, 127. See also* Africa; Amphibians; Biomes; Birds; Food chain; Habitats; Insects; Mammals; Reptiles; *and individual names*

Ankle joint: HU 38

Annularia (Paleozoic plant): EV *52*

Anomalops: UN *26*; photophore, UN *27*

Antarctica: animals, EC 9, *46-47,* 48, *49*; plants, EC *44-45,* 46

Antarctic cod: body fluids of, UN *chart* 16

Antarctic Ocean: fish in, UN *16-17*

Antarctic toothfish: UN *17*

Anteater: banded, EC *17*

Antelope: AN *60-61*; African, EC 10, 21, *82-85,* 91; pronghorn, AN *61*

Antennae, insect: IN *26-27*; ants', AN *12*; butterflies' vs. moths', IN *32*; flies', AN 8, 9; mosquitoes', AN *10*; moths', AN *94*

Anther culture: PL *140*

Anthers: mistletoe, PL *83*; pine cone, PL *89*

Anthracosaur: EV 58

Antibiotics: PL *132-133*

Antibodies: HU *133*; B cells producing, HU *126, 128, 129, 132, 135*; immune globulin E, HU 134, *135*

|  | | |  | | | | |

Planet Earth **PE** | Plant Life **PL** | Physical Forces **PH** | Structure of Matter **ST** | Space & Planets **SP** | Transportation **TR** | Underwater World **UN** | Weather & Climate **WE**

Ant plants: IN *98*

Ants: aphids' use of, AN *12-13*; army, AN *124-127*; defenses, IN *123, 126-127*; food gathering, IN *42-43, 99, 138*; societies, IN *138-139*; symbiosis, IN *78-79, 98-99*; termites attacked by, IN *140, 141*; as wingless insects, IN *85*

Anus: HU *91*

Apanteles wasps: IN *114*

Apes: arboreal, EC *70, 71*; chimpanzees, AN *46-47, 124-125, 141, 142-143*; evolutionary ancestry, EV *123, 124*; gorillas, EC *112*; social groups, AN *140-141*

Aphids: ants' use of, AN *12-13*; and butterfly-ant coevolution, IN *79*; hover flies and, AN *118-119*; reproduction, IN *72-73*; soldier, IN *144*; as wingless insects, IN *72-73, 85*

Aphytis (parasitic wasp): IN *91*

Apocrine sweat glands: HU *43*

Appendix: HU *90*; lining of, HU *77*

Apples: PL *67*

Aquatic insects: *See* Water dwelling insects

Aquatic mammals: UN *63*; dolphins, EV *136*, UN *18-19, 58-59, 114-115*; otters, EC *130, 131, 142*; sea lions, EC *7*; seals, EC *46-47, 49*, UN *92-93*; Stellar's sea cows, EV *144*; whales, EC *112*, EV *112-113*, UN *4-5, 32-33, 94-95, 107, 114-115, 116-117*

Aquatic plants: EC *26-27*; moose feeding on, EC *58-59*

Arachnids: first, EV *50-51*. *See also* Spiders

Araucaria (gymnosperm): EV *102*

Arborescent lichens: PL *107*

Archaeopteryx (early bird): EV *68, 69, 70-71*

Archerfish: UN *108-109*

Arctic animals: EC *8, 28, 48-49*; gray whales, UN *94*; seals' birthplace, UN *92*; seasonal color changes in, AN *50-51, 58-59*; terns, AN *135*

Arctic temperature vs. Antarctica's: EC *chart 45*

Ardis tyrannus amurensis (moth): IN *32*

Areole: cactus's, PL *113*

Argiope amoena (spider): IN *54-55*

Argiope bruennichi (spider): insect trapping by, IN *38-39*

Argyros (water spider): IN *96-97*

Arm, human: movements, HU *30-31, 39*; nerves, HU *103*; wings, relationship to, EV *131, 135*

Army ants: AN *124-127*

Arrow-poison frogs: UN *90*

Arsinoitherium (extinct mammal): EV *117*

Arteries: HU *62-63*; blood pressure in, HU *68-69*; clogged, HU *144*; of fetus and mother, HU *20-21*; renal, HU *94, 95*

Arthropods: EV *42*; flying, first, EV *54-55*; earliest, EV *50-51*; larvae, similarity of, EV *132*; trilobites, EV *40-41, 42, 44-45*

Artiodactyls: EC *20*

Ascending colon: HU *90*

Ascocarps: lichen's, PL *106*; perithecia, PL *97*

Ascomycetes fungi: PL *98*

Asian horned toad: AN *51, 52*

Asian warbler: AN *98*

Assassin bug: IN *114*; mantis resembling, AN *31*

Astrapotherium (extinct mammal): EV *120*

Atherosclerosis: HU *144*

Atlantic salmon: reproduction by, UN *82-83*

Atlantic snipe eel: UN *112*

Atlas moth: IN *112-113*

ATP (adenosine triphosphate): HU *36, 37, 57*

Auditory system of fish: UN *52-53*; carp, UN *44*; sharks, UN *55*

Auditory system of humans: receptors and cortex, HU *113*

Auks: EC *8*; great, EC *8*, EV *144*

Aurelia jellyfish: UN *43*

Australia: animals, EV *138-139, 144*; bulldog ants, IN *139*; cockroaches, IN *131*; desert, EC *87*; gastric-brooding frogs, UN *90-91*; ladybug from, IN *91*; lungfish, UN *31*; marsupials, EC *16-17, 114*; pollinators, EC *114*; stromatolites, EV *35*

Australian brown newt: AN *52*

Australian honeycomb spider: AN *27*

Australian Region: animals of, EC *4-5*

Australopithecus (extinct hominid): EV *124-126*; skeleton, EV *105*

Axis cylinder: HU *100-101*

Axons: HU *100*; terminal, HU *100-101*

Azaleas: PL *50, 52*; Japanese, EC *118*

Aztec ants and trumpet trees: IN *98-99*

Azure-winged magpies: AN *115*; eggs, AN *114, 115*

B

Baboons: AN *140*

Baby (milk) teeth: HU *26, 27, 35*

Bacilli: coliform, HU *91*

Back: strained, HU *40-41*

Backboned animals: early development of, EV *132-133*; evolution of, EV *46-47*. *See also* Amphibians; Birds; Fish; Mammals; Reptiles

Bacteria: EV *32, 33, 37*, HU *141*; and antibiotics, PL *132, 133*; in conch's gills, UN *35*; as decomposers, PL *126*; decomposition by, EC *128, 129*; evolution of, EV *6*; in food chain, UN *126*; intestinal, HU *89*,

91; luminous, sea creatures with, UN *24, 25, 26, 27, 111, 140, 144*; in ocean trenches, UN *35*; plasmodium and, PL *97*; white blood cell engulfing, HU *65*

Bagworm moths: IN *85*; nests, IN *102-103*

Bait: green heron's use of, AN *36-37*

Balance: organs of, UN *52*

Bald cypress: PL *22*

Bald notothen: UN *17*

Baleen plate, blue whale's: UN *116, 117*

Baleen whales: AN *40*; blue, UN *116-117*; gray, AN *41*; humpback, AN *40*

Ball-and-socket joint: HU *38*

Balsam seeds: PL *67*; germination of, PL *13*

Bamboo: PL *32-33, 91*

Bandicoots: long-nosed, EC *16*

Banks' pine cone: PL *89*

Baobab tree: PL *116-117*

Barbel eel: UN *123*

Barbels: of catfish and loaches, AN *20-21*

Barberry: PL *29*

Barbets: crimson-breasted, EC *61*

Bark beetles: IN *49, 131*

Bark of tree: PL *25, 26-27*

Barley: PL *144*

Barnacles: EC *100-101*, UN *40-41*; early stages of, EV *132*

Barn owls: AN *4-5, 38-39*

Barracudas as predators: UN *103, 104-105*

Barrel cacti: EC *94*, PL *113*

Baryonyx (dinosaur): EV *77*

Basidia: EC *135*

Basidiomycetes vs. Ascomycetes: PL *98*

Basilosaurus (whale ancestor): EV *113*

Basophils: HU *128*

Bass: cherry, UN *62, 66*; largemouth, EC *138, 141*; sea, EC *141*; sea, swim bladder type in, UN *13*

Batesian mimicry vs. Müllerian: AN *69*; of poisonous butterflies, AN *68*; of stinging insects, AN *54-55*

Bats: AN *42-43*; cave dwellers, EC *28, 38-39*; droppings (guano), EC *40*; evolution of, EV *114-115*; as insect predators, IN *24-25*; as pollinators, EC *114*; wing of, EV *130, 134*

B cells: HU *126, 128, 129, 131*; and allergies, HU *135*; and measles, HU *132, 133*

Beans: PL *142*; germination, PL *12-13*; soybeans, PL *13, 54, 67*; starch granules, PL *11*

Bears: EC *142*; anthill attacked by, IN *127*; black, EC *137*; polar, EC *49*; stinging of, IN *124, 125*

Beautyberries: PL *78*

Beavertail cacti: EC *86, 87*

Beech trees: EC *25, 75*; Japanese, fruit of, PL *77*

| Animal Behavior **AN** | Computer Age **CO** | Ecology **EC** | Evolution of Life **EV** | Geography **GE** | Human Body **HU** | Insects & Spiders **IN** | Machines & Inventions **MA** |

Bees: AN 125, *130*; Africanized, IN *136-137*; antennae, use of, IN *26-27*; dancing, IN *26, 128-129, 134-135*; drones' roles, AN *130-131*; evolutionary path, IN *7*; flying method, IN *15*; foot structure, IN *21*; ground, nests of, IN *108-109*; head, IN *5, 22*; and mimics, AN *54-55*; ocelli, effect of, IN *23*; as pollinators, EC *115*; reproduction, IN *70-71, 131, 132-133*; respiration, IN *10-11*; spider's capture of, AN *26*; stinging, IN 124, *125, 137*; workers' roles, AN *128-129, 131*

Beetles: bark, IN *49, 131*; bombardier, IN *122-123*; in caves, EC *43*; *Damaster blaptoides*, IN *85*; dung, IN *92-93, 106-107, 130, 131*; egg laying, EC *108-109*; evolutionary path, IN *7*; family life, range of, IN *130-131*; feeding order, EC *110-111*; fireflies, AN *88-89, 92-93*; foot structures, IN *21*; ground, IN *12*; horns, use of, IN *60-61*; hypermetamorphosis, IN *81*; ladybugs, AN *13*, EC *108-109*, IN *4-5, 20, 91, 113, 120, 144*; leaf-rolling weevils, IN *104-105*; long-horned, AN *55, 69*, IN *15, 21, 29, 49*; net-winged, AN *69*; as pollinators, EC *115*; snout beetle, bluffing by, AN *85*; in soil, EC *36, 37*; spiracles, IN *10*; tiger, larva of, as wasp's prey, IN *110*; water, IN *11*

Beggar-ticks (bur marigold seeds): EC *123*, PL *75*

Belemnites as food for ichthyosaurs: EV *95*

Bellflowers: PL *59*

Bent grass and Bermuda grass: PL *63*

Berries: PL *66, 67*; eaten by birds, PL *78-79*; mistletoe, PL *82*

Bess beetles: IN *130*

Bighead smoothhead: UN *22-23*

Bighorn sheep: AN *106-107*

Bile canaliculi and bile ducts: HU *86, 87*

Bioelectric sensing system of shark: UN *55*

Biological accumulation: EC *144*

Biological pest control: IN *90-91*

Bioluminescence, sea creatures with: UN *24-25, 26-27*; anglerfish, UN *23, 70-71, 111, 112*; cardinalfish, UN *144*; lanternfish, UN *22*; squid, UN *140*

Biomes: EC *4-5, 24-25, 28-29*; desert, EC *28, 86-95*; tundra, Arctic, EC *28, 48*. *See also* Grasslands; Rain forests

Birch, white: bark of, PL *27*

Bird-hipped vs. lizard-hipped dinosaurs: EV *chart 66-67, 74-75*

Birds: aquatic (penguins), swimming style of, UN *18-19*; bluffing, AN *84-85*; brood parasites and hosts, AN *114-115*; camouflage, AN *50-51, 52, 58-59*; and caterpillars, IN *114, 118-119*; chickens, EV *18,*

71, 133; convergence, EV *137*; cooperative breeding, AN *116-117*; courtship and mating, AN *98-103*; Darwin's finches, EC *7*; desert, EC *89*; extinct, EC *112*, EV *144*; eyespots as defense against, AN *51, 64-65*; flight formations, AN *132-133*; in food chain, EC *124-125, 126-127, 144*; after forest fire, EC *136, 137*; of Galápagos Islands, EV *12, 13*; giant birds of prey, extinct, EV *106-107*; Mesozoic, EV *68-69, 70-71, 100-101*; navigation methods, AN *134-137*; parenting, AN *88-89, 112-113*; and poisonous prey, AN *67, 68*; as pollinators, EC *114-115*; predatory methods, AN *4-5, 36-39, 113*; savanna, EC *82*; seeds spread by, EC *123*, PL *78-79, 82*; species and subspecies, EV *10*; temperature control, EV *81*; threatened with extinction, EC *113*; tool-using, AN *47*; tropical rain forest, EC *28-29, 60-61*; wetlands, EC *138, 139, 140*; wings, EV *130-131, 135*; woodpeckers, AN *16-17*. *See also* Seabirds

Birds of paradise: EC *60*

Bison: and rattlesnakes, AN *62-63*

Bitterlings: deep-bodied, coloration of, UN *64*; egg laying by, UN *73*

Bivalve mollusks: crabs living in, UN *38-39*; in food chain, UN *126*; in ocean trenches, UN *34*; reproduction, UN *99*; scallops, UN *138*; as starfish prey, UN *138, 139*

Black ants: fighting, IN *126-127*; food gathering, IN *42*; mountain, IN *127*; symbiosis, IN *78-79*; tandem running, IN *43*

Black-headed gulls: courtship, AN *103*

Black hornets: stinging by, IN *124*

Black pines: PL *48*; cones, PL *89*; leaves (needles), PL *43, 48-49*; winged fruit, PL *73*

Black smokers: EV *32-33*, UN *34, 35*

Blackspot angelfish: sex changes in, UN *66-67*

Blackspot cardinalfish: mouthbrooding by, UN *80*

Black-winged dwarf bagworms, nest of: IN *102*

Bladder: urinary, HU *12, 13, 94*

Bladderworts: PL *47*; aquatic, EC *116*

Blakeslee, Albert: PL *138*

Blennies: egg protection by, UN *78*; saber-toothed, cleaner wrasses vs., UN *134, 135*

Blind cave dwellers: EC *40, 41, 42-43*

Blood, human: HU *64-65*; clotting, HU *65*; formation of, HU *66-67*; pumping of, HU *61, 68-69*; types, HU *70-71*; in wounds, HU *48-49*

Blood cells: HU *6, 64-65*; agglutination of, HU *70-71*; death and removal of, HU *67*; of fetus and mother, HU *21*; formation of, HU *66-67*; hemoglobin in, HU 64, 72, *73*; skin cuts and, HU *48, 49*. *See also* White blood cells

Blood pressure: HU *68-69*

Bloodsucking insects: IN *84*; mosquitoes as, IN *68-69*

Blood sugar (glucose): HU *142*, 143

Blood types: HU *70-71*; and genes, HU *chart* 71

Blood vessels of fish: and body temperature, UN *14, 15*; and gas in swim bladder, UN *13*; in gills, UN *9*

Blood vessels of humans: HU *62-63*; blood pressure in, HU *68-69*; clogged, HU *144*; of fetus and mother, HU *20-21*; and gas exchange, HU *56*; histamine, effect of, HU *135*; of kidney, HU *94, 95*; of liver, HU *86, 87*

Blood vessels of insects: dorsal, IN *8*; grasshopper's, IN *9*

Blubber: blue whale's, UN *117*

Blue butterflies: large, IN *78*

Bluefin tuna: UN *9, 73*; circulatory system, UN *14-15*

Bluefish: Japanese, UN *22-23*

Bluegirdled angelfish: UN *133*

Bluegrass, Kentucky: PL *63*

Blue-green algae: EV 34, *37*; evolution of, EV *6*; stromatolites, EV *26-27, 34-35*

Blue molds: penicillin from, PL *132-133*

Blue parrotfish: UN *104-105*

Bluering angelfish: UN *133*

Blue-spotted mudskippers: UN *29*

Blue-striped swallowtail butterflies: IN *31*

Blue whales: UN *4-5, 107, 116-117*

Blue wrasses and red wrasses: UN *63, 66*

Bluffing as defense: AN *84-85*

B lymphocytes: HU *126, 128, 129, 131*; and allergies, HU *135*; and measles, HU *132, 133*

Body language: chimpanzees, AN *143*

Body temperature of fish: circulatory system and, UN *14-15*

Bombardier beetles: IN *122-123*

Bombykol: IN *27*

Bones: HU 30, *32-33*; ear, EV *135*; finger, in bats, EV *114-115, 134*; fish with, EV *48, 49*; growth of, HU *26, 34-35*; marrow, blood-cell-producing, HU *66, 128*; and muscles, HU *6, 30-31, 38, 39*; spine, HU *40-41*. *See also* Skeletons; Skulls

Bony fishes: UN *6*. *See also individual names*

Bony (osseous) tissue: HU *7*

Planet Earth
PE

Plant Life
PL

Physical Forces
PH

Structure of Matter
ST

Space & Planets
SP

Transportation
TR

Underwater World
UN

Weather & Climate
WE

Boobies: Peruvian, EC *32*

Boomslang: AN *63*

Boryhyaena (extinct mammal): EV *120*

Bottle-nosed dolphins: conversational sounds of, UN *115*

Bottle trees: PL *117*

Bowerbirds: courtship of, AN *100-101*

Bowman's capsule: HU *95*

Bowman's gland: HU *117*

Brachiosaurus (dinosaur): EV *76*

Bracken: PL *108-109*

Brain, human: HU *96-97*; cerebral cortex, HU *104-105*; development of, HU *24-25*; and goose bumps, HU *45*; and hearing, HU *113*; hemispheres of, HU *120-121*, *124*; nerve impulses to, HU *100-101*; pituitary gland, HU *74*; salivary control center, HU *78*; and sleep, HU *122-123*, *124-125*; and smell, HU *116*; and sweating, HU *42*; and taste, HU *119*; and vision, HU *107*

Brain, insect: grasshopper's, IN *8, 9*

Brain waves: HU *120, 121, 124, 125*

Breadfruit: EC *65*

Bream, sea: UN *21*; eye, UN *45*; swim bladder type, UN *13*

Breathing by aquatic animals: crabs, UN *36-37*; by fish, out of water, UN *28-29, 30-31, 36-37*; by fish, through gills, UN *8-9, 36-37*

Breathing by humans: *See* Respiration by humans

Breathing by insects: IN *10-11*

Breathing roots: EC *25, 34, 35*

Breeding of animals: and mutations, EV *14*; between species, EV *11*; vs. evolution, EV *18-19*; within species, EV *10-11*. *See also* Mating, courtship and; Parenting; Reproduction by animals

Breeding of plants: grafting, PL *134-135*; tissue culture, PL *140-141, 143*. *See also* Crop plants

Breeds of species: EV *11, 18, 19*

Bridled dolphins: UN *114-115*

Brine shrimp: life cycle of, EC *92-93*

Bristlecone pines: PL *123*

Broad-leaved cacti: PL *112*

Broad- vs. needle-leaved trees: EC *24-25*

Bromeliad: frog in, UN *90*

Brontotherium (extinct mammal): EV *116*

Brood parasites: cuckoos, AN *114-115*

Broomrape: PL *57*

Brown algae: PL *104, 105*

Brown ant: AN *13*

Brown newt: Australian, AN *52*

Brown planthoppers: outbreaks of, IN *88*

Brown skuas: AN *113*

Bubbles: crabs blowing, UN 36, *37, 96*; spittlebugs, IN *100-101*; water spiders, IN *96-97*

Buckwheat: PL *73*

Budding: reproduction by, UN 101

Buds: formation of, PL *16*; in vegetative reproduction, PL *90, 91*; winter, PL *41*

Buffalo: Cape, EC *83*

Bulbuls in flight: AN *133*

Bulldog ants: Australian, IN *139*

Bullhead catfish: AN *21*

Bull-horn acacia plants: IN *99*

Bulls, blue: Indian, EC *11*

Bumblebee: toad avoiding, AN *54-55*

Buntings, Japanese: eggs, AN *114*

Buoyancy control: spermaceti oil for, UN 32, *33*; swim bladders for, UN *12-13*, 23

Burgess Shale fossils: EV *42-43*

Bur marigolds: EC *123*; PL *75*

Burrowing crickets: care of young, IN *74*

Burying beetles: IN *131*

Bush katydid: AN *53*

Butcher's-broom: PL *29*

Butterflies: Alpine, EC *52-53, 57*; coloration of wings, IN *30-31, 58, 83, 121*; defenses, IN *118, 119, 121, 123*; differentiation, EV *22-23*; egg laying, IN *79, 130*; eggs guarded by, IN *74*; evolutionary path, IN *7*; eyespots on caterpillar of, AN *64*; with eyespots, AN *65*; in feeding order, EC *110, 111*; flying method, IN *15*; foot structures, IN *21*; leaf butterfly, AN *53*; living fossil, EV *141*; mantis capturing, AN *30-31*; mate selection, IN *58-59*; metamorphosis, IN *56-57, 78-83, 114-115*; vs. moths, IN *32-33*; natural enemies, IN *114-115*; poisonous, mimicry of, AN *68-69*; pollination by, EC *115*, PL *8, 50, 52-53*; pupae, IN *35, 57, 78, 82-83, 115*; in spider web, IN *38*; symbiosis with ants, IN *78-79*

Butterflyfish: AN *65, 71*

Butting: bighorn sheep, AN *106-107*

Buttress roots: EC *24, 35, 64-65*, PL *23*

C

Cabbage butterflies: IN *32*; foot structure, IN *21*; mate selection, IN *58-59*; metamorphosis, IN *80-81, 114-115*; natural enemies, IN *114-115*; pupae, IN *35, 115*

Cabbages: types of, EV *19*

Cacti: EC *86, 87, 94, 95*, PL *111, 112-113*; adaptation in, EV *21*; and euphorbia, convergence of, EV *137*; Galápagos, EC *6, 119*; owl in, EC *89*

California gray whale: migration of, UN *94-95*

California newt: AN *67*

Callidulid moths: IN *33*

Calling song of crickets: AN *96*

Callus culture: PL *140*

Camarasaurus (dinosaur): EV *75*

Cambium in tree trunk: PL *25, 26, 27*

Cambrian period: life in, EV *40-45*

Camels: EC *88*; temperature, EC *chart* 88

Camouflage: AN *30-31, 50-53*, IN 113, *116-117*; color changes in, AN *32, 50-51, 56-59*; by crabs, UN *136-137*; by octopuses, UN *143*

Camphor cicadas: IN *29*

Cancer: HU *138-139*

Canine teeth: HU *26*

Cannibalism in praying mantises: IN *64, 65*

Capillaries: HU 62, *63*; alveoli surrounded by, HU *56, 57*; sinusoid, HU *63, 66-67*

Capybaras: EC *20*

Carbon dioxide: in photosynthesis, PL 10, *38*

Carbon dioxide-oxygen cycle: HU *56-57, 65*

Carboniferous period: flying insects, EV *54-55*; life in, EV *41*; plants, EV *52, 53*

Carbon monoxide: poisoning by, HU *72-73*

Carcinogens: HU *138*

Cardiac (myocardial) muscle: HU *7, 60, 144*

Cardinalfish: blackspot, mouthbrooding by, UN *80*; luminescent, and sea urchins, UN *144*

Cardiovascular system: HU *7, 52, 60-71*. *See also* Blood cells; Blood vessels of humans; Heart, human

Caribou: EC *50-51*

Carotene in storage grains: PL *7*

Carp: feeding method, UN *105*; sensory organs, UN *44-45, 46-47*; swim bladder, UN *12-13*

Carpels: PL 51, *52-53, 58, 59, 62, 66*; corn stigma and style, PL *84, 85*; impatiens (touch-me-not), PL *76, 77*; mistletoe stigma, PL *83*

Carpenter ants, black: fighting, IN *126-127*; tandem running, IN *43*

Carriers: nutrients absorbed by, HU *89*

Cartilaginous fishes: UN *6*; eyes, UN *44, 45, 54*; ratfish, UN *73*; rays, UN *107, 123*; skates, UN *104*. *See also* Sharks

Cartilaginous tissue: HU *7*

Carvalho's pipa: UN *91*

Caryophyllaceae flower: EV *103*

Castes: honeybees, AN *128-131*

Caterpillars: and ants, IN *78, 79*; aphids vs., IN *144*; bagworm, IN *102, 103*; defenses, IN *113, 118-119, 120-121, 123*; and enemies, IN *114, 125*; eyespots on, AN *64*; in metamorphosis, IN *56-57, 78-83, 114*; respiration, IN *11*; tiger moth (fall

Animal Behavior
AN

Computer Age
CO

Ecology
EC

Evolution of Life
EV

Geography
GE

Human Body
HU

Insects & Spiders
IN

Machines &
Inventions **MA**

webworms), IN *88-89*

Catfish: barbels, use of, AN 20, *21*; cuckoo, UN *84-85*; eeltail, UN *123*; electric, UN *57*; parenting behavior of, UN *86-87*; poison, UN *122, 123*

Cats: breeds of, EV *19*; golden, EC *10, 11*; marsupial, EC *17*; saber-toothed, EV *107, 121*

Cattleya orchids: PL *140-141*

Caudal fin: use of, in swimming, UN *18, 20-21*

Caudal peduncle: swordfish's use of, UN *20, 21*

Cauliflorous trees: EC *65*

Cavefish: EC *40, 41, 43*

Caves: and cave dwelling animals, EC *28, 38-43*

Cecum: HU *90*

Cedar trees: bark, PL *27*; cone, PL *89*; seed, PL *94*

Ceiba tree: PL *123*

Cell bodies of neurons: HU 100, *101, 103*

Cells: of blue-green algae, EV *34-35*; DNA and RNA in, EV 30, *36*; evolution of, EV *36-37*; first, EV *32*; insect, ordinary vs. cold-resistant, IN *35*; multiple, rise of, EV *38-39*; plant, structure of, PL *4-5, 6-7*

Cells, human: HU *6, 7*; anatomy of, HU *8-9*; and colds, HU *140*; division by meiosis, HU *14-15*; division by mitosis, HU *8-9*; ear, inner, HU *113, 114, 115*; fallopian tube, HU *16*; in healing, HU *48-49*; liver, HU *86-87*; melanocytes, HU *50-51*; metabolism, HU 52, *57*; olfactory, HU 116, *117*; pancreatic, HU *85, 142, 143*; reproductive, HU *12, 13, 15, 16-17, 22, 23, 28-29*; retinal, HU *108-109*; salivary glands, HU *79*; small intestine, HU *88-89*; stomach, HU *82-83*; taste bud, HU *119*; and tumors, HU *138-139*. *See also* Blood cells; Neurons (nerve cells) of human brain

Cenozoic era: EV 105-129. *See also* Mammals

Centipedes: EC *37*, IN *12-13*; maternal care in, IN *76*

Central nervous system: IN *8-9*

Centrioles: HU *8*

Centrosomes: PL *6*

Ceratoid anglerfish: UN *70-71*

Ceratopsians: EV *88-89*; *Protoceratops*, EV *78-79, 89*

Ceratosaurus (dinosaur): EV *75*

Cerebrum: HU 24, *25, 104-105*; auditory cortex, HU *113*; hemispheres, HU *120-121*, 124; nerve impulses to, HU *101*; olfactory areas, HU *116*; taste center, HU *119*; and vision, HU *107*

Cereus: EC *94*

Chain, Ernst: PL 132

Chameleons: AN *4-5, 32-33*

Channel catfish: AN *21*

Cheetahs: EC *10, 82, 112*; Indian, EC *11*; springbok herds and, AN *60-61*

Cheiracanthium japonicum (spider): IN *75*

Cheirolepis (extinct fish): EV *49*

Chemicals: biological accumulation of, EC 144; plants' defenses, EC *98-99, 118*

Chemical weapons of insects: IN *122-123, 126, 127*

Cherry bass: UN *62, 66*

Cherry trees: leaf, PL *29*; lenticels, PL *27*

Chesapeake Bay, Md.-Va., U.S.: life in, EC *140-141*

Chestnut trees: flowers, PL *59*; fruit, PL *67, 77*; horse chestnut, leaf scar on, PL *43*

Chickens: vs. *Archaeopteryx*, EV *71*; breeding, EV *18*; early development, EV *133*

Chief cells: HU *83*

Chimpanzees: clan, AN *141*; communication, AN *124-125, 142-143*; tool use, AN *46-47*

Chlorophyll: light absorption by, PL *11*

Chloroplasts: EV *36*, PL *6, 7, 10-11*

Choking: HU *80*

Cholesterol in arteries: HU 144

Cholla cacti: EC *95*

Chordate evolution: EV *46-47*

Chorionic villi: HU *20*

Chromatin: HU *8-9, 10-11*

Chromatophores: squid, UN *142*; tree frogs, AN *56, 57*

Chromosomes: human, HU *11, 14-15*; mitosis, in human cells, HU *8-9*; and plant breeding, PL *138*

Chrondrichthian: extinct, EV *49*

Chum salmon: UN *11*

Cicada fungus: PL *97*

Cicadas: EC *106-107*, IN *4*; evolutionary path, IN *7*; flying method, IN *14*; head, IN *4, 22*; life cycles, IN *89*; New Guinea, AN *50, 53*; sound production, IN *29*

Cichlids, reproduction by: family care of young, UN *79*; and incubation of cuckoo catfish's eggs, UN *84-85*; mouthbrooding, UN *80-81*

Cilia: olfactory cells, human, HU *117*; paramecium, AN *6, 7*; trachea, human, HU *6*

Ciliary body and muscles: HU *110-111*

Ciliated cells: HU *16, 140*

Circadian rhythm: HU *122*

Circle dance, honeybees': IN *135*

Circulatory system of fish: and body temperature, UN *14-15*. *See also* Blood vessels of fish

Circulatory system of humans: HU *7*, 52, 60-71. *See also* Blood cells; Blood vessels of

humans; Heart, human

Circulatory system of insects: IN *8*

Circumvallate papillae: HU *118*

Cirri, barnacle's: UN *41*; use of, UN *40*

Cladoselache (extinct fish): EV *49*

Clams: crabs living in, UN *38-39*; early stages of, EV *132*; in ocean trenches, UN *34*; as starfish prey, UN *138, 139*; surf clam, UN *139*

Claws: fiddler crabs, AN *108-109*; spiders, AN *29*

Cleaner shrimp: AN *22-23*

Cleaner wrasses: UN *120, 134-135*; vs. saber-toothed blennies, UN *134, 135*

Clear-winged moth: AN *55*

Climatius (extinct fish): EV *48*

Climax forest: formation of, PL *128*

Climbing perch: UN *29*

Climbing plants: parasites, PL *57*; supports for, PL *23, 29, 30-31*

Clown fish: AN *70-71*; gold-belly, UN *62, 67*; sea anemones and, UN *144*

Cobra, king: AN *62*

Cobweb mold: PL *96*

Cobwebs: IN *39*

Coccosteus (extinct fish): EV *49*

Cochlea and cochlear duct: HU *112, 113, 115*

Cochlear nerve: HU *113*

Cockleburs: EC *122*, PL *54-55*; fruit, PL *75*

Cockroaches: Australian, IN *131*; evolutionary path, IN *7*; foot structure, IN *21*

Coconut palms: EC *22-23*, PL *86-87*

Coconuts: EC *22-23*, PL *86-87*; milk, PL *87*

Cocoons: moth larvae in, IN *144*; parasitic wasps, IN *114*; spiders, IN *94-95*

Cod: Antarctic, body fluids of, UN *chart 16*; swim bladder type, UN *13*

Coelophysis (dinosaur): EV *67*

Coevolution: IN *78-79*

Colchicine: tetraploid plants from, PL *139*

Cold-adapted insects: IN *34-35*

Cold-blooded vs. warm-blooded fish: UN *14-15*

Cold-loving fish species: UN *16-17*

Colds: common, HU *140-141*

Coliform bacilli: HU *91*

Colobus monkeys: EC *71*

Colon: HU *90-91*

Colonial siphonophore: UN *42*

Colonies: *See* Social insects

Colonization of habitats: EC *120-121*

Coloration, biological: algae's auxiliary pigments, PL *105*; butterfly wings, IN *30-31, 58, 83, 121*; dinosaurs, EV *84-85*; of flowers, PL *52*; of fruits, PL *78-79*; of leaves, changing, PL *40-41*; male fish, UN *64-65*; mutation, in plants, PL *139*;

Planet Earth
PE

Plant Life
PL

Physical Forces
PH

Structure of Matter
ST

Space & Planets
SP

Transportation
TR

Underwater World
UN

Weather & Climate
WE

squid's markings, changing of, UN *142-143*. *See also* Coloration, protective

Coloration, protective: angelfish, UN *132-133*; bright, poisonous amphibians with, AN *66-67*; chameleons', changes in, AN *32*; seasonal, changes in, AN *50-51, 58-59*; tree frogs', changes in, AN *56-57*; cryptic (camouflage), IN 113, *116-117*; mimicry of plant parts, AN *31, 50-53*; and natural selection, EV *16-17, 84*; squid's markings, changes in, UN *142-143*; warning, IN *112-113, 120-121*

Colugo: AN *72*

Columnar cells: HU *88-89*

Comb jelly: UN *42*

Communication: chimpanzees, AN *124-125, 142-143*; dances, bees', IN *26, 128-129, 134-135*; with pheromones, IN *27, 42-43*

Communication cords: spiders, AN 28, *29*

Complete metamorphosis in butterflies: IN *56-57, 78-83, 114-115*

Compound eyes: IN *4-5, 22*

Compsognathus (dinosaur): EV *71, 74*

Conch with bacteria in gills: UN *35*

Condylarthra: members of, EV *112*

Cones: cycad, PL *59*; pine, PL *88-89*

Cones and rods of the eye: HU *108-109*

Cone shells: UN *118-119*

Congo tetras: UN *64*

Conifers: EC *24*; acid rain and, EC *74-75*; bark, PL *27*; biggest and oldest, PL *122-123*; and cones, PL *88-89*; fire, effects of, EC *78, 79, 136-137*; larch, PL *119*; and leaves, PL *43, 48-49*; lichens on, PL *107*; near timberline, EC *54*; root modification, PL *29*; winged fruit, PL *73*

Connective tissue: HU *6*

Continental drift: PL *118, maps* 119

Continuous capillaries: HU *63*

Contractile vacuoles: paramecium, AN *7*

Convergence of species: EV *136-137, 138-139*

Convolutions of brain: HU 104

Cooperative breeding in birds: AN *116-117*

Copeinas, red-spotted: spawning by, UN *75*

Copepods: in cave, EC *41*

Copper butterflies: Japanese, IN *78*

Coral: crabs living among, UN *39*; reproduction by, UN *100-101*; as starfish prey, UN *139*

Cork cambium: PL *25, 26, 27*

Cork cells: PL *26*

Cormorants: flightless, EC *7*; pelagic, EC *33*

Corms: PL *91*

Corn: and corn silk, PL *84-85*; hybridization, PL *136-137*; leaf growth, PL *17*; starch granules in, PL *11*; support roots, PL *23*

Cornea, fish's: for seeing through air, UN *51*

Cornea, human: HU *110-111*

Corneal lens of ocellus: IN *23*

Cornicles: aphids, AN *12*

Coronary artery, clogged: HU *144*

Corpus callosum: HU *120*; severed, HU *121*

Cortex, cerebral: *See* Cerebrum

Coscinodiscus diatom: PL *100*

Cosmos: PL *54-55*

Cottony cushion scale: IN *91*

Cotyledons (seed leaves): development of, PL *9, 12, 13, 79, 88*

Courtship: *See* Mating, courtship and

Courtship song of crickets: AN 97

Crabeater seals: EC 46, *47*

Crabs: EV *140*; on and in other animals, UN *38-39*; blue, EC *140*; breathing, UN *36-37*; camouflage, use of, UN *136-137*; claw detached by, AN *80*; early stages of, EV *132*; fiddler, courtship of, AN *108-109*; hermit, shells of, AN *76-77*; hermit, sea anemones and, AN *78-79*; in ocean trenches, UN *34*; as octopus prey, UN *60*; red-clawed, AN *123*; reproduction, UN *37, 38-39, 96-97*; as scavengers, EC *128, 129*; starfish attacked by, UN *139*

Crab spiders: mating, AN *90*

Crane flies: IN *5*

Cranes: dancing, AN *102-103*; sandhill, EC *113*; whooping, EC 113

Cranesbill: PL *77*

Crayfish: cave, EC *41, 42*; as snakes' prey, AN *15*

Crèches: penguin chicks in, AN *112-113*

Crematogaster ant: IN *99*

Crested grebes: courtship, AN *102*

Cretaceous period: ammonites, EV *94-95, 98-99*; birds, EV *100-101*; domehead dinosaurs, EV *86-87*; flowering plants, EV *102-103*; hadrosaurs, EV *76, 85*; horned dinosaurs, EV *78-79, 88-89*; life in, EV *74-75*; marine reptiles, EV *92-93, 94-95*

Cribellum: spiders, IN *95*

Crickets: burrowing, care of young by, IN *74*; courtship, AN *96-97*; sound production, IN *28*

Crocodiles: family tree, EV *chart* 66-67; heart, EV *59*; *Protosuchus*, EV *62-63*; swimming style of, UN *18-19*; temperature control, EV *81*

Crop plants: PL 130-131; genetic resources, PL 131, *142-143*; grains, kinds of, PL *67, 144*; hybrids, PL *136-137*; improvement, PL *138-139*; progenitors, origin areas of, PL *maps* 130-131. *See also individual names*

Crossbreeding: PL *136-137, 142*; artificial, PL *139*

Crossopterygians: EV *56, 57*

Crowberry: PL *78*

Crow butterfly: AN *68*

Crown of thorns (starfish): defense against, UN *139*

Crustaceans: barnacles, EC *100-101*, UN *40-41*; brine shrimp, EC *92-93*; cave, EC *40, 41, 42*; estuarine, EC *140*; luminous, UN *24*; scavengers, EC *128, 129*; shrimp, AN *22-23, 86-87*; starfish attacked by, UN *139*. *See also* Crabs

Crustaceous lichen: PL *106-107*

Cryptic coloration (camouflage): IN 113, *116-117*

Cryptomeria cone: PL *89*

Cuckoo catfish: UN *85*; incubation of, by cichlids, UN *84-85*

Cuckoos as brood parasites: AN *114-115*

Cucumber plants: PL *30*; squirting, PL *77*; tendrils, PL *30-31*

Culex mosquitoes: IN *47*; eggs, IN *69*

Cup fungi: PL *98*

Cupula: HU *114, 115*

Currant tomato: PL *142*

Cuscuses: EC *17*

Cutleria cylindrica algae: PL *103*

Cuts: healing of, HU *48-49*

Cuvieronius (mastodon): EV *121*

Cyanobacteria (blue-green algae): EV 34, *37*; evolution of, EV *6*; stromatolites, EV *26-27, 34-35*

Cycadeoidea (gymnosperm): EV *102*

Cycad flowers: PL *59*

Cynodonts: *Cynognathus*, EV *62, 64-65, 73*; *Diademodon*, EV *64*

Cynognathus (mammal-like reptile): EV *62, 64-65*; *C. crateronotus*, EV *73*

Cypress trees: bald, PL *22*; Japanese, cone of, PL *89*

Cypris larvae: barnacles, UN *40-41*

D

Dace: Japanese, UN *73*

Dahlias: PL *55*

Dairying ants: AN *12-13*

Daisies, blue: tetraploid, PL *139*

Damaster blaptoides (beetle): IN *85*

Damselflies: mating, IN *63*; nymph, IN *10*

Danaidae butterfly caterpillars: IN *121*

Dance flies: mating by, IN *67*

Dances: of bees', IN *26, 128-129, 134-135*; of cleaner wrasses, UN *134, 135*; of saber-toothed blenny, UN *135*

Dances, courtship: bowerbirds, AN *100*; cranes, AN *102-103*; flytrap spiders, AN *90*

Dandelion seeds: PL *67, 72-73*

| Animal Behavior **AN** | Computer Age **CO** | Ecology **EC** | Evolution of Life **EV** | Geography **GE** | Human Body **HU** | Insects & Spiders **IN** | Machines & Inventions **MA** |

Darkness adaptation of eyes: HU *108-109*

Dart-poison frogs: AN *66-67*

Darwin, Charles: EC 7, EV *12*, IN 61; theories, EV 12, 13

Darwin's finches: EC 7

Darwin's toads: UN *91*

Dasyures: EV *138*

Dayflowers: stomas of, PL *38-39*

Dead-leaf mantis: AN *31*

Death caps (mushrooms): PL *98-99*

Decay-producing organisms: PL *110-111*, 124, 125, *126-127*

Deciduous forests: temperate, EC *5, 25*

Deciduous vs. evergreen trees: EC *24-25*

Decomposers: PL *126*; in food chain, PL 124, 125

Decorator crabs: use of camouflage by, UN *136-137*

Deep-bodied bitterlings: UN *64*

Deep-sea creatures: anglerfish, UN *23, 70-71, 111, 112*; food-hunting adaptations, UN *112-113*; luminescence, cause of, UN *24-25, 26-27*; notothen, UN *17*; in ocean trenches, UN *34-35*; pressure, water, and, UN *22-23*; squid, luminous ink squirted by, UN *140*

Deer: after forest fire, EC *136*; moose, EC *58-59*; moose, wolves attacking, AN *44-45*; plants' defenses against, EC *118*; reindeer, EC *50-51*; white-tailed, EC *139*; white-tailed, warning signal by, AN *61*

Defenses of animals: AN 50-87, UN 120-144; angelfish, UN *132-133*; bluffing, AN *84-85*; breaking off body parts, AN *80-81*; camouflage, crab's, UN *136-137*; camouflage, insects', IN 113, *116-117*; camouflage, octopus's, UN *143*; chemical weapons of insects, IN *122-123, 126, 127*; cleaner wrasse, UN *120, 134-135*; eye-spots, AN *51, 64-65*, IN *112-113, 118, 119*; fighting ants, IN *126-127*; flounder, UN *130-131*; flying fish, UN *120-121, 128-129*; gliding, AN *72-73, 82-83*; hermit crab, AN *76-79*; hosts exploited for, UN *144*; ink, use of, UN *140-141*; insects, IN 112-127; look-alike animals, AN *54-55, 68-69*; mimicry, insects', IN *112, 113, 118-119*, 120; need for, example of, IN *114-115*; poison fish, UN *120-121, 122-123, 126-127*; porcupinefish, UN *121, 124-125*; pufferfish, UN *126-127*; schooling by fish, AN *74-75*; snake, AN *62-63*; soldier aphid, IN *114*; squid, UN *140-141, 142-143*; against starfish, UN *138-139*; stinging by insects, IN *124-125, 126, 127*, 137; symbiosis as, AN *12-13, 70-71, 78-79, 86-87*; warning coloration of insects, IN *112-113, 120-121*;

warning signals by herd animals, AN *60-61. See also* Coloration, protective

Defenses of plants: EC *98-99, 118-119*

Deinonychus (dinosaur): hunting by, EV *82*

Deinotherium (elephant ancestor): EV *110*

Dendrites: HU 100

Dendrobates frogs: AN *66-67*

Deoxyribonucleic acid: *See* DNA

Dermaptera (earwigs): IN *74, 84*

Dermis and epidermis: *See* Skin, fish's; Skin, human; Skin, prehistoric animals'

Descending colon: HU *91*

Deserts: animals, EC *28, 88-93*; plants, EC *86-87, 89, 94-95*

Desert species: EV *20-21*; convergence, EV *137*

Desmostylus (extinct mammal): EV *118-119*; skeleton, EV *104-105*; teeth, EV *119*

Devil angler: UN *23*

Devilfish: UN *25*

Devonian period, life in: EV *41*; amphibian, first, EV *57*; fish, EV *46, 47, 56, 57*; insect, oldest, EV *50-51*; plants, EV *52*, 53

Diabetes: HU *142-143*

Diademodon (mammal-like reptile): EV *64*

Diadromous fish: UN *11*

Diaphragm: movement in breathing, HU *54, 55*

Diapsids: EV *chart* 63; thecodonts, EV *62, 66-67*

Diatoms: PL *100-101*

Diatryma (extinct flightless bird): EV *106*

Dickinsonia (extinct animal): EV *39*

Dicotyledons: seed leaves of, PL *9, 12, 13*

Dictyoploca japonica (butterfly): IN *33*

Didinium: AN *7*

Didolodus (extinct mammal): EV *120*

Differentiation of species: EV *12, 22-23*

Digestion by humans: HU *92-93. See also* Digestive system of humans

Digestion by insects: of wood, methods for, IN *48-49*

Digestive system of humans: HU 6, 76-91, *92-93, 94-95*; esophagus, HU *81*; kidneys, role of, HU *94-95*; large intestine, HU *90-91*; liver, HU *86-87*; pancreas, role of, HU *84-85*; saliva and salivary glands, HU *78-79, 118*; small intestine, HU *88-89*; stomach, HU *82-83*; surfaces, kinds of, HU *76-77, 82-83, 88-89, 90*; swallowing, HU *80-81*

Digestive system of insects: of butterflies, changes in, IN *83*; of mosquitoes, IN 68

Dik-diks: EC *82*

Dimetrodon (extinct reptile): EV *59, chart* 65

Dinosaurs: EV *60-61*; bird-hipped vs. lizard-hipped, EV *chart* 66-67, *74-75*; birds' evolution from, EV *68-69, 70-71*; *Coelophysis*,

EV *67*; coloration, EV *84-85*; diet, EV *76-77*; domehead, EV *86-87*; extinction, EV 20, *24*, 61; family tree, EV *chart* 66-67; horned, EV *78-79, 88-89*; origin of, EV *66-67*; relative *(Euparkeria)*, EV *62, 66*; reproduction, EV *78-79*; skin, EV 96, *97*; as social animals, EV *78-79, 82-83*; and warm-blooded animals, similarity of, EV *80-81*

Dioecious plants: PL *59*

Diplocaulus (extinct amphibian): EV *58-59*

Diplodocus (dinosaur): EV *84-85*

Discus, mating pair of: with eggs, UN *86*; with fry, UN *87*

Disease: *See* Illness

Disks, spinal: HU *40, 41*

Ditch reeds: EC *27*, PL *129*

Diving by sperm whales: UN *32-33*

Dizziness: cause of, HU *114-115*

DNA (deoxyribonucleic acid): HU *4-5, 10-11*; damaged, and tumors, HU *138-139*; and RNA (ribonucleic acid), EV 30, 36; viral, HU *136*, 137

Dodder: PL *57*

Dodos: EV *144*

Dogfish: spiny, fetus of, UN *76*

Dogs: African hunting, EC *13*; bear dog, EV *121*; breeds of, EV *11*; Cape hunting, EC *82*

Dogtooth violet seeds: PL *79*

Dolichocebus (monkey ancestor): EV *123*

Dolomedes sulfureus (spider): wasp stinging, IN *54*

Dolphins: bottle-nosed, EV *136*; communication by, UN *114-115*; as predators, UN *58-59, 114-115*; river, UN *58-59*; swimming style of, UN *18-19*

Domehead dinosaurs: EV *86-87*

Dominance: bighorn sheep, AN *106-107*; lions, AN *138-139*; wolves, AN 45

Dominant and recessive traits: EV *13, 14*

Dorsal vessel: IN *8*; grasshopper's, IN *9*

Doryaspis (extinct fish): EV *47*

Douglas firs: PL *122*

Dragonflies: IN *5*; as butterfly enemy, IN *115*; evolutionary path, IN *7*; flying method, IN *14, 15*; mating, IN *62-63*; metamorphosis, IN *80-81*; nymphs, IN *10, 36-37, 44-45, 80-81*

Dragons (lizards): flying, AN *72-73*; Komodo, AN *15*

Dreams: sleep and, HU *124-125*

Drepanaspis (extinct fish): EV *47*

Drinking by saltwater vs. freshwater fish: UN *10-11*

Driver ants: African, IN *138, 141*

Dromedaries: EC *88*; temperature, EC *chart* 88

Planet Earth
PE

Plant Life
PL

Physical Forces
PH

Structure of Matter
ST

Space & Planets
SP

Transportation
TR

Underwater World
UN

Weather & Climate
WE

Droneflies: as pollinators, EC *115*; striped, AN *54*

Drones (bees): AN *130-131*, IN *71*; nursery, IN *70-71*

Drosophila flies: mutations in, EV *14*

Drugs from plants: PL *132-133*

Drupes: PL *66-67*; coconuts, PL *86-87*

Dryopithecus (ape ancestor): EV *123*

Dry season: adaptations to, UN *30-31*

Duckbilled platypuses: AN *18-19*

Duckweed: PL *23*

Dugong: AN *25*

Duiker: EC *21*

Dung beetles: IN *92-93, 106-107, 130, 131*

Dunkleosteus (extinct fish): EV *49*

Duodenum: lining of, HU *77*; location of, HU *82*; and pancreas, HU *84*

Dwarf gouramis: UN *64*

E

Eagles: EC *124-125, 126-127*

Ears, animal: bones, evolution of, EV *135*; cricket, IN *28*; inner, of fish, UN *52*; moth, IN *24*; shark, UN *55*; troughs, barn owl's, AN *38-39*; tympanic membrane, cricket's, AN *97*

Ears, human: bones, evolution of, EV *135*; bones of, HU *32*; and dizziness, HU *114-115*; sounds, identifying, HU *112-113*

Earth: life's beginnings on, EV *30-31*; young, EV *28-29*

Earthstars (mushrooms): PL *99*

Earthworms: EC *36*; as mole's prey, AN *105*

Earwigs: IN *84*; care of eggs by, IN *74*

Eastern mud snake: AN *63*

Eccrine sweat glands: HU *42-43*

Echinoderms as chordate ancestor: EV *46, 47*

Echolocation: bats' use of, AN *42-43*

Ecological niches: adaptation, EV *5, 20-21*; isolation, EV *23*

Ecology: EC entire volume

Edaphosaurus (extinct reptile): EV *59, chart 65*

Edelweiss: PL *121*

Eelgrass: EC *26, 27, 140*; pollination, EC *27*

Eels: UN *47*; Atlantic snipe eel, UN *112*; barbels, UN *123*; electric, UN *19, 57*; freshwater, UN *11*; Japanese, UN *73*; leopard moray, AN *22*; moray, UN *63, 67, 104*; swimming types, UN *19*

Eeltail catfishes: UN *123*

Egg and sperm, human: HU *12, 13*; fertilization, HU 12, *15, 16-17*; formation of, HU *14-15*; and twins, HU *22, 23*; in vitro fertilization, HU *28-29*

Egg cases: false trumpet, UN *99*; shark, UN *76*

Eggs and egg laying: alligators, AN *110*; amphibians, UN *88, 90, 91*; amphibian vs. reptile, EV *59*; aphids, IN *73*; aquatic animals, UN *62*; Aztec ants, IN *99*; barnacles, UN *41*; butterflies, IN *74, 79, 130*; cicadas, IN *89*; corals and sponges, UN *100*; crabs, UN *39, 96*; cuckoos and host species, AN *114, 115*; dinosaurs, EV *78, 79*; discus, UN *86*; dragonflies, IN *62, 63*; drought survival, UN *31*; dung beetles, IN *92, 106, 107, 130*; family behavior, range of, IN *130*; fertilization, AN *88-89*; flounders, UN *130*; as food for fry, UN *87*; glacier midges, IN *34*; ground bees' chambers, IN *108-109*; honeybees, IN *70, 132*; hunting wasps, IN 54, *55, 110, 111*; insects and spiders, IN *56*; in larvae, IN *114, 124*; leaf-rolling weevils, IN *104, 105*; mollusks, UN *98, 99*; mosquitoes, IN *46, 69*; mouthbrooders, UN *73, 79, 80-81, 84-85*; number of eggs, UN *72-73*; ostrich, vulture cracking, AN *47*; other species, incubation by, UN *84-85*; parental care, IN *74, 75, 76, 77, 130*; protection of eggs, UN *73, 74-75, 78, 79, 80-81, 84-85*; salmon, UN *82*; sharks, UN *76, 77*; shrikes, AN *114*; spiders' cocoons for, IN *94-95*; spring-tide laying of, AN *122-123*; tiger moths, IN *88*; tubes for, IN *124*. *See also* Mating, courtship and

Eggs of plants: fertilized, PL *9*

Egrets: EC *139*

Egyptian mouthbrooder: UN *73*

Egyptian vulture: AN *47*

Elaeagnus: thorny, PL *29*

Elands: EC *10, 83, 85*

Elasmosaurus (plesiosaur): EV *92-93*

Elbow movement: HU *39*

Elcysma westwoodii (moth): IN *33*

Elder trees: red-berry, bark of, PL *27*

Electrical receptors: platypus's, AN *19*; shark's, UN *55*

Electric eels: UN *19, 57*

Electric fish: UN *56-57*; eels, UN *19, 57*

Electricity: paramecium's reaction to, AN *6*; platypus's reaction to, AN 18, *19*

Elephant fishes (mormyrids): UN 56; relative of, UN *56-57*

Elephants: African, EC *10, 82-83, 84-85, 113*; ancestors, EV *105, 110-111, 121, 128-129*; Indian, EC *11*; temperature control, EV *81*

Elephant seals: UN *93*

Elodea nuttalli (water plant): PL *129*

Embryo culture, plant: PL *140*

Embryo, human: HU *18*; implanting, HU *29*

Embryo, plant: PL *12*; development of, PL *9*

Embryo, shark: UN 76, *77*

Emerald notothen: UN *17*

Emotional perspiration: HU *43*

Emperor, yellow (soapfish): UN *126*

Emperor penguins: EC *9, 49*

Endangered species: EC *96-97, 112-113*

End digestive enzymes: HU *89*

Endocrine glands and hormones: HU *74-75*; islets of Langerhans, HU *75, 84, 85, 142-143*

Endodermis of root: PL *15*

Endoplasmic reticulum: PL *6, 7*

Endosperm: PL *8-9, 12*, 66; coconut, PL *86-87*

Endothelium, blood vessels': HU *62, 63, 66-67*

Enzymes, digestive: HU *93*; end, HU *89*; pancreatic, HU *84, 85*; in stomach, HU *82, 83*

Eogyrinus (extinct amphibian): EV *58*

Eosinophils: HU *128*

Epidermis and dermis of fish: UN *7*

Epidermis and dermis of humans: *See* Skin, human

Epidermis of plants: PL *20*; cactus, PL *113*; pine needles, PL *49*; prickles as outgrowths of, PL *28*; of root, PL *15*; stomas in, PL *39*

Epiglottis: HU *58*; during swallowing, HU *80-81*

Epiphytes (air plants): EC *68-69*, PL *22-23*; and ants, symbiosis of, IN *98*

Episinus affinis (spider): web of, IN *39*

Epithelial cells: HU *6, 88-89, 135*

Equilibrium: loss of, HU *114-115*

Equus (horse): EV *109, 121*

Erector muscles: HU *44, 47*

Ermine: seasonal color changes in, AN *58-59*

Eryops (extinct amphibian): EV *58-59*

Esophagus, fish's: and swim bladder, UN *12, 13*

Esophagus, human: HU *55*; lining of, HU *76-77*; movement of food through, HU *81*

Estivation by lungfish: UN *31*

Estuarine species: EC *140-141*; mangrove, EC *34*

Ethiopian Region: animals of, EC *4*

Eucalyptus trees: PL *118-119*; giant, PL *122*

Eudimorphodon (early reptile): EV *63*

Eukaryotes: cell type, EV *36-37*; evolution of, EV *6, 7*; multicelled, rise of, EV *38-39*

Eulalia (grass): EC *78*

Euparkeria (early reptile): EV *62, 66*

Euphorbia: EV *137*

Animal Behavior
AN

Computer Age
CO

Ecology
EC

Evolution of Life
EV

Geography
GE

Human Body
HU

Insects & Spiders
IN

Machines &
Inventions **MA**

Euploca bagworms: nest of, IN *103*

European midwife toads: UN *90*

European starlings: sun, navigation by, AN *134*

Europlocephalus (dinosaur): EV *97*

Euryapsids: EV *chart* 63

Eurypterid fossil: EV *50*

Eusthenopteron (amphibian ancestor): EV *56*; structure, EV *57*

Evening primroses: PL *53*

Everglades, Fla., U.S.: animals of, EC *138-139*

Evergreens: vs. deciduous trees, EC *24-25*; defoliation, PL *43*; and ice ages, PL *120-121*; mistletoe, PL *23, 82-83*; oak, fruit of, PL *77. See also* Conifers

Evolution: EV entire volume; beginnings of life, EV *30-31*; vs. breeding, EV *18-19*; of camouflage in crabs, UN *137*; of cells, EV *36-37*; coevolution of insects, IN *78-79*; convergence, EV *136-137, 138-139*; fossil evidence of, EV *130*; and fossils, living, EV *130-131, 140-141*; over geologic time periods, EV *8-9, chart* 24; homologous structures, EV *130-131, 134-135*; human effect on, EV *142-143, 144*; of insects, possible path, IN *6-7*; living things, first, EV *32*; of male fish's colors, UN *64*; of multicellular organisms, EV *27, 38-39*; oxygen, atmospheric, and, EV *34*; of stingers on insects, IN *124*; theory of, EV *12-13*; of wings on insects, IN *84*; young organisms as clues to, EV *131, 132-133. See also* Mammals; Mesozoic era; Paleozoic era; Species

Exocrine glands vs. endocrine glands: HU *74*

Exocrine system of ants: IN *43*

Extensors and flexors: HU *38, 39*

External respiration vs. internal respiration: HU 52

Extinctions: EV 8, 60-61; of animals, EC *18-19, 20, 112*; of dinosaurs, EV *20, 24, 61*; modern, EV *144*

Eyeglasses: corrective, HU *110-111*

Eyes, animals': aquatic animals, UN *44-45, 48, 49*; aquatic animals, vs. human, UN *48, 61*; butterflies, and mating, IN *59*; chameleons, AN *33*; compound, IN *4-5, 22*; flounder, UN *130-131*; octopus, UN *44, 60, 61*; praying mantises, IN *5, 22, 40*; rattlesnake's, range of, AN *34*; seeing in air with, UN *45, 50-51*; sharks, UN *44, 54*

Eyes, human: HU *110-111*; darkness adaptation, HU *108-109*; vs. fish, 48; misshaping of, HU *110-111*; vs. octopus, UN *61*; in REM sleep, HU *124, 125*; stereoscopic

vision, HU *106-107*

Eyespots: AN *51, 64-65*, IN *112-113, 118, 119*; jellyfish, UN *43*

F

Facial language: chimpanzees, AN *124-125, 142*

Fallopian tubes: HU *13, 16-17*; blocked, HU *28*

Fall webworms: IN *88-89*

False acacia trees: PL *28*

False trumpet: egg laying by, UN *99*

Farsightedness: HU 110, *111*

Feces: creation and excretion of, HU *90-91*

Feeding: beaks, EC *7, 115*; deer family, EC *50-51, 58-59, 118*; insect-eating plants, EC *116-117*; insects, order of, EC *110-111*; sloths, EC *62. See also* Food chain; Predators

Feet: chameleons, AN *33*; flies', AN *8, 9*; insects, structure of, IN *21*

Female anatomy: HU *13, 16-17, 28-29, 75*

Fenestraria (window-leaf plant): PL *115*

Fenestrated capillaries: HU *63*

Fennecs: adaptation by, EV *20-21*

Ferns: PL *95, 108-109*; seed, Paleozoic, EV *53*; staghorn, EC *69*

Fertilization: in algae, PL *103*; in ferns and mosses, PL *109*; human, HU 12, *15, 16-17*; in vitro, of humans, HU *28-29*; plants, PL *8*, 66

Fescue: red, PL *63*

Fetal sharks: UN *76-77*

Fetus, human: brain development, HU *24-25*; growth of, HU *18-19*; nourishment, HU *20-21*; twins, HU *22-23*

Fibrin: HU *65*

Fibroblasts: HU *6, 49*

Ficus trees: buttress roots of, PL *23*

Fiddler crabs: AN *108-109*

Field cricket: Taiwan, AN *96*

Fighting song of crickets: AN 97

Figs and fig wasps: PL *67, 68-69*

Figworts: PL *57*

Filiform papillae: HU *118*

Filter-feeding mosquito larvae: IN *46-47*

Finches: bullfinches, subspecies of, EV *10*; Darwin's, EC *7*, EV *12, 13*; woodpecker, AN *47*

Finger bones in bats: EV *114-115, 134*

Fingerling salmon: UN *82*

Fingernails and toenails: HU *46*

Fins, use of: by flying fish, UN *128, 129*; by gurnard, UN *47*; by mudskipper, UN *28*; poisonous spines, UN *120-121, 122, 123*; in reproduction, UN *81*; by spiderfish, UN *113*; in swimming, UN *18, 19, 20-21*

Fire: forest, effects of, EC *136-137*; grassland, effects of, EC *78-79*; use of by *Homo erectus*, EV *126*

Fire ants: food gathering by, IN *42-43*

Fireflies: IN *52-53*; light, signaling with, AN *88-89, 92-93*

Firethorn: PL *78*

Firs: Douglas, PL *122*

Fish: EV *chart* 56-57; at alligator hole, EC *138, 139*; amphibian evolution from, EV *56-57*; anatomy, UN *6-7*; Antarctic, EC *47*; barbels, use of, AN *20-21*; bat's method of catching, AN *42*; breathing, UN *8-9, 28-29, 30-31*; cavefish, EC *40, 41, 43*; Chesapeake Bay, EC *140, 141*; cold-blooded vs. warm-blooded, UN *14-15*; convergence, EV *136*; definition of, UN 7; differentiation, EV *23*; dragonfly nymphs catching, IN *36-37, 44-45*; drinking by, UN *10-11*; with eyespots, AN *65*; in food chain, EC *128-129, 144*; in freezing waters, UN *16-17*; goldfish, breeds of, EV *18*; green heron's method of catching, AN *36-37*; humpback whale's method of catching, AN *40*; jawless, evolution of, EV *46-47, 48*; with jaws, evolution of, EV *48-49*; living fossils, EV *140*; luminescent, UN *22, 23, 24-25, 26-27, 70-71, 111, 112, 144*; mutations in trout, EV *14-15, 17*; navigation by, AN *120-121*; pressure, surviving, UN *22-23*; schools, swimming in, AN *74-75*; and sea anemones, AN *22-23, 48-49, 70-71*; shark development, EV *132-133*; springtide breeders, AN *122-123*; swim bladders, UN *12-13, 23, 52, 53*; swimming types, UN *18, 19, 20-21*; in symbiotic relationships, AN *22-25, 70-71, 86-87*; types of, major, UN *6. See also* Defenses of animals; Predators; Reproduction by animals

Fishing bat: AN *42*

Fishing spiders: six-starred, AN *27*

Five-lined skink: AN *80, 81*

Flagellates: EV *38*

Flatworms: acoel, EV *39*; in cave, EC *41*

Fleas: IN *84*; hosts, finding, IN *17*; jumping, IN *16-17*

Fleming, Sir Alexander: PL *132*

Flexors and extensors: HU *38, 39*

Flies: bee-mimicking, AN *54, 55*; evolutionary path, IN *7*; gift giving, IN *66*; houseflies, AN *8-9*; hover flies, aphids and, AN *118-119*; ocelli, effect of, IN *23*; walking on ceiling, IN *20-21*

Flightlessness in insects: IN *84-85*

Floating gobies: UN *73, 78*

Floral regions of Earth: PL *map 118-119*

| Planet Earth | Plant Life | Physical Forces | Structure of Matter | Space & Planets | Transportation | Underwater World | Weather & Climate |
| PE | PL | PH | ST | SP | TR | UN | WE |

Florey, Howard: PL 132

Flotation bladders: leaves with, EC 27

Flounders: UN 19, 130-131

Flower flies: IN 144; aphids vs., IN 144

Flower mantises: AN 30-31

Flowers and flowering plants: PL 50-63; alpine meadows, EC 56-57; alpine zone, PL 120, 121; animal-pollinated, EC 114-115; appearance of, EV 102-103; biggest (*Rafflesia arnoldii*), PL 51, 56-57; cactus, EC 87; day length and blooming of, PL 54-55; vs. gymnosperms, PL 8, 88; in vitro cultivation of, PL 140-141; male and female parts, PL 51, 52-53, 58-59, 62; medicines from, PL 132; opening and closing of, PL 60-61; orchids, EC 68-69; parasites, PL 23, 51, 56-57, 82-83; pollination, PL 8, 50, 52-53, 56, 58, 59, 62, 68, 69, 84, 85, 95, 136-137; sexes, separate, PL 58-59, 68, 69, 83, 84-85; structure of, PL 52-53; tetraploid, PL 139; *Tillandsia cyanea*, EC 94; vegetative reproduction, PL 62, 90-91, 134-135, 140-141, 143. See also Crop plants; Fruits; Seeds; and individual names

Flu: symptoms, HU chart 141; viruses, HU 141

Flycatchers: navigation, AN 136-137

Flying animals: EV 114-115, 130-131, 134-135; arthropods, first, EV 54-55; birds, evolution of, EV 68-69, 70-71, 101; reptiles, EV 63, 90-91, 96, 130, 134. See also Birds; Flying insects; and individual names

Flying dragon (flying lizard): AN 72-73

Flying fish: UN 120-121, 128-129; vision, UN 51

Flying frog: AN 73

Flying gecko: AN 73

Flying insects: body structures, varying, IN 4-5; methods of flight used by, IN 14-15; speeds, IN chart 14. See also individual names

Flying lemur: AN 72

Flying squid: AN 82-83

Flying squirrel: giant, AN 73

Flytrap spiders: courtship, AN 90

Flytrap, Venus's: See Venus's-flytrap

Food, digestion of: See Digestion; Digestive system

Food, finding and gathering: AN 4-49; ants, IN 42-43, 99, 138; aphids, IN 72; bagworm larvae, IN 102; barbels, use of, AN 20-21; bats, AN 42-43; bees, IN 26-27, 109, 134, 135; birds, AN 4-5, 16-17, 36-39, 47, 113; butterflies and moths, IN 33; catfish, AN 20-21; chameleons, AN 4-5, 32-33; centipedes, IN 12; dragonfly

nymphs, IN 36-37, 44-45; family behavior, range of, IN 130-131; fireflies, IN 52-53; gift giving, IN 66-67; glowworms, IN 50-51; insects, AN 8-13, 30-31, IN 36-55; loaches, AN 20-21; locusts, IN 87; millipedes, IN 12; moles, AN 105; mosquito larvae, IN 46-47; paramecia, AN 6-7; platypuses, AN 18-19; praying mantises, IN 40-41; sea anemones, AN 22, 48-49, 71; snakes, AN 14-15, 34-35; spiders, AN 26-29; in spiders' webs, IN 36-37, 38-39; spider wasps, IN 54-55; spittlebug nymphs, IN 100, 101; through symbiosis, AN 12-13, 22-25; tools used for, AN 46-47; water spiders, IN 97; whales, AN 40-41; wolves, AN 44-45; wood-eating insects, IN 48-49, 130

Food chain: EC 124-144, PL 124-125, UN 126-127; at alligator hole, EC 138-139; biological accumulation in, EC 144; in caves, EC 40-41; of eagle, EC 124-125, 126-127; estuarine, EC 140; fish in, EC 128-129, 144, UN 126-127; forest cycle, EC 104-105, 124-125, 132-133, 136-137; mushrooms in, EC 134-135; oil spills, effects of, EC 142; puffer fish, effects on, UN 126-127; savanna, EC 80-85; sea otters in, EC 130-131

Food vacuole: paramecium, AN 7

Forests: EC 4-5, 24-25; acid rain and, EC 74-75; boreal, EC 4, 24, 29; cycle of, EC 104-105, 124-125, 132-133, 136-137; fire, recovery from, EC 136-137; floor of, EC 36-37, 66-67; lichen in, EC 50; mushrooms in, EC 134; near timberline, EC 54. See also Rain forests

Formed elements of blood: See Blood cells

Formic acid: ants using, IN 123, 126, 127

Formica vessensis (ant): IN 127

Fossils: EV 130; ammonites, EV 94, 98, 99; arthropods, earliest on land, EV 50, 51; birds, first, EV 68, 70; of Burgess Shale, EV 42-43; dinosaur eggs, EV 78, 79; dinosaurs, EV 81, 82, 83, 88; dinosaur skin, EV 96, 97; gaps in record of, EV 115; living, EV 130-131, 140-141; mammal-like reptiles, EV 64, 73; Precambrian, EV 26-27, 38, 39

Four-eyed fish: UN 50-51; eyes, UN 45, 50, 51

Fovea centralis: location of, HU 108, 111

Foxes: adaptation in, EV 20-21; bag foxes, EV 139; fennec, EC 89; plovers' tricking of, AN 84-85; red, EC 136

Fraternal twins: HU 22, 23

Freezing waters, fish in: UN 16-17

Frenulum: moth's, IN 33

Freshwater eel: UN 11

Freshwater fish: drinking by, vs. saltwater fish, UN 10-11

Frigate birds: EC 7

Fringefin goby: UN 127

Frogfish: UN 111

Frogs: EC 138, 139; arrow-poison, UN 90; desert, EC 93; eyespots resembling, IN 118; flying, AN 73; gastric-brooding, Australian, UN 90-91; marsupial, pygmy, UN 90; poisonous, AN 66-67; reproduction, UN 62, 63, 88-89, 91; as snakes' prey, AN 15; tree frogs, color changes in, AN 56-57

Frog's-bits: EC 27; flotation system of, EC 27

Fruit bats: as pollinators, EC 114

Fruit flies: mutations in, EV 14

Fruits: PL 8, 64-65; baobab, PL 117; coconuts, PL 86-87; coloration of, PL 78-79; corn, PL 84-85; cucumbers, PL 30, 77; figs, PL 67, 68-69; flowers' making of, PL 66-67, 68-69; popping open of, PL 76-77; simple vs. complex, PL 66-67; squash, PL 58. See also Crop plants; Seeds

Fruit seeds: dispersal of, EC 122

Fungi: PL 96-97; in caves, EC 40; and decomposition, EC 132, 133, PL 126; in lichens, PL 106, 107; mushrooms, EC 50, 134-135, PL 92-93, 95, 98-99, 126; as penicillin source, PL 132-133

Fungiform papillae: HU 118

Fungus gnats: IN 51; larvae, IN 50-51

Fungus-growing insects: IN 49; leaf-cutter ants, IN 138-139; termites, IN 48, 142-143

Funnel weavers (spiders): IN 94

Funnel webs, spiders': IN 38

Fur seals: reproduction by, UN 92-93

G

Galápagos Islands: albatrosses, courtship of, AN 102; animals, EC 6-7, 113, 119, EV 12-13, 80; plants, EC 119

Gall aphids: AN 13

Galls and gall aphids: AN 13

Gametophytes: See Spore-bearing plants

Gamma field: PL 138-139

Ganges River dolphins: UN 58, 59

Ganglia, human: spinal, HU 101, 103

Ganglia, insect: IN 8-9

Gannets: northern, EC 32

Garden crickets: Oriental, AN 97

Gardeners: orange-crested, bower of, AN 101

Garden spiders: web use, AN 28, 29

Garter snakes: life of, EC 12-13

Gas, poisonous: beetles' use of, IN 122-123

Animal Behavior
AN

Computer Age
CO

Ecology
EC

Evolution of Life
EV

Geography
GE

Human Body
HU

Insects & Spiders
IN

Machines &
Inventions **MA**

Gas bladder: UN *12-13*; for hearing, UN *52, 53*; and pressure, UN 23

Gas exchange in lungs: HU *56-57, 65*

Gastric-brooding frogs: Australian, UN *90-91*

Gastric glands and juices: HU *82-83*

Gastrin cells and gastrin: HU *83*

Gastropods: abalone, UN *98*; conch, UN *35*; cone shells, UN *118-119*; escape from starfish, UN *139*; in food chain, UN *126, 127*; limpet, UN*138-139*; mud snail, giant, UN *98*; whelk, UN *127*

Gazelles: EC *10*; Indian, EC *11*; springboks, AN *60-61*; Thompson's, EC *82*

Geckos: flying, AN *73*

Gemmules: sponge, UN *101*

Gene bank: field, PL *143*

General Sherman (sequoia): PL 122

Genes: blood-type, HU *chart* 71; chromosomes carrying, HU *8-9, 11, 14-15*

Genetic resources and genetic diversity: PL 131, *142-143*

Genetics: and breeding of animals, EV 10, 11; and breeding of plants, PL 136, *138-139*; and differentiation, EV *22*; Mendel's laws and, EV *13*; mutations, EV *14-15*

Genji fireflies: AN *93*

Gentians: opening and closing of, PL *61*

Geotropism: PL *15*

Gerenuk: EC *84*

Germination: PL *8, 12-13, 79, 80, 81, 88, 95*; algae, PL *102*; mosses, PL *109*

Germs: *See* Infectious diseases

Giant flying squirrel: AN *73*

Giant mud snail: UN *98*

Giant purple butterfly: IN *31*

Giant silkworm moth: antennae of, IN *32*; mating, AN *94-95*

Giant squid: sperm whale attacking, AN *40-41*

Giant water bug: IN *75*

Gibbons: AN *140-141*, EC *70, 71*

Gift giving by male insects: IN *66-67*

Gill arches: UN *9*; evolution of, EV *48-49*

Gill chambers: gill bailers in, crabs', UN *36*; mudskippers', UN *28*

Gill cover (operculum): UN *8*

Gill rakers: UN *9, 106*

Gill respirators, upper: climbing perch's, UN *29*

Gills: aquatic insects with, IN *10*; breathing through, UN *8-9, 36-37*; of conch, bacteria in, UN *35*; crabs' use of, UN *36-37*; and osmosis, UN *10, 11*; "physical gill," aquatic insects', IN *11*; tadpoles', UN *88*

Ginkgoes: EV *102, 141*

Ginsburg's gobies: AN *87*

Giraffes: EC *21, 83, 85*; in Lamarck's theory, EV *13*

Glaciation: and tundra plants, PL *120-121*

Glacier midges: IN *34*; larvae, IN *35*

Glaciers: in ice ages, EV 128

Gladiolus: PL *91*

Glands, human: HU *74-75*; Bowman's, HU *117*; intestinal, HU *88, 90*; lymph nodes, HU *90, 130-131*; pancreas, HU *75, 84-85, 142-143*; salivary, HU *78, 79, 118*; sebaceous, HU *44, 47*; in stomach, HU *82-83*; sweat, HU *42-43, 44, 45*

Glands, insect: exocrine, of ant, IN *43*

Gliders (aircraft): and flying fish, similarities of, UN *129*

Gliding animals: AN *72-73*; flying fish, UN *128-129*; flying squid, AN *82-83*; pygmy glider, EC *114*; sugar glider, EC *16*

Globefish: egg laying by, AN *123*

Glowworms: IN *50-51*

Glucose in blood: HU *142*, 143

Glycoprotein and freezing point: UN 16, *chart* 16

Glyptodon (extinct mammal): EV *120*

Gnathostomes: evolution of, EV *48-49*

Gnats: fungus, IN *51*; larvae, IN *50-51*

Gnu: EC *84*

Gobies: AN *86-87*; floating, UN *73, 78*; fringefin, UN *127*; as prey of cone shell, UN *118-119*

Goblet cells: HU *88, 140*

Goblin sharks: UN *22-23*

Gold beds: woodpeckers', AN *16*

Gold-belly clownfish: UN *62, 67*

Golden bowerbird: Newton's, bower of, AN *101*

Golden cats: African, EC *10*; Indian, EC *11*

Goldenrod: EC *98*

Golden-striped grouper: UN *126*

Golden web spiders: IN *94-95*

Goldfish: wild, EV *18, 23*

Golgi apparatus: PL *6, 7*

Gomphotherium (elephant ancestor): EV *110*

Goose bumps: HU *44-45*

Goosefish: UN *102-103, 110-111*

Gorillas: mountain, EC *112*

Gossamer-winged butterfly: IN *31*

Gouramis: bubble nests made by, UN *79*; dwarf, UN *64*

Gourds: grafting onto, PL *135*; leaf growth in, PL *17*; root pressure in, PL *21*

Grafting: PL *134-135*

Grains: PL *144*; corn as, PL *84-85, 136-137*; rice, PL *67, 139*; wheat, PL *55, 67, 144*

Grana in chloroplasts: PL *10-11*

Granulocytes: HU *6, 128*; development of, HU *67*

Grapes: PL *67*; tendrils on plants, PL *29, 30*

Grasses: bamboo, PL *32-33, 91*; flowers, PL *62-63*; *Oplismenus, PL 75*; pampas,

Japanese, PL *73. See also* Grains

Grass guppies: UN *65*

Grasshoppers: AN *52, 53*; anatomy, IN *8-9*; egg laying, IN *130*; evolutionary path, IN *7*; head, IN *4*; metamorphosis, IN *56-57, 80-81*; ocelli, effect of, IN *22-23*; sound production, IN *28*; swarming, IN *86-87*

Grasslands: EC *76-77*; Alpine meadows, EC *56-57*; fires, effects of, EC *78-79*; marshes, EC *138-139, 140*; savanna (African), EC *29, 76, 80-85*

Grass snakes: AN *15*

Grayling butterfly: AN *65*

Gray whales: AN *41*; migration of, UN *94-95*

Greater horseshoe bat: AN *42-43*

Great white sharks: UN *104*

Grebes: crested, courtship of, AN *102*; food chain of, EC *144*

Green algae: PL *105*

Green bean seeds: germination of, PL *12-13*

Green heron: AN *36-37*

Grinding pads: platypus, AN *19*

Grizzled mantis: AN *31*

Gromwell: callus culture of, PL *140*

Ground bees: nests of, IN *108-109*

Ground beetles: walking method of, IN *12*

Groupers: with cleaner wrasses, UN *120, 134-135*; crab's protection from, UN *136*; golden-striped, UN *126*; tail, use of, UN *20*

Growth rings: on fish's scales, UN *7*; tree trunk's, PL *18-19, 24-25*

Grunions: egg laying by, AN *122-123*

Guard cells: stomas', PL *39*

Gulls: EC *7, 29, 33*; black-headed, courtship of, AN *103*

Gulpers: UN *22, 112-113*

Gum (eucalyptus) trees: PL *118-119, 122*

Guppies: reproduction by, UN *64-65*

Gurnard: UN *47*

Gustatory nerves: HU *118, 119*

Gymnosperms: EV *102*; vs. angiosperms, PL *8, 88*; cycads, PL *59. See also* Conifers

H

Habitats: EC *28-29*; Australian, EC *chart* 16; caves, EC *28, 38-43*; estuarine, EC *34, 140-141*; mountain, EC *52-57*; recolonization, EC *120-121*; wetlands, EC *138-139, 140, map* 141. *See also* Biomes

Hadrosaurs: *Maiasaura*, EV *83*; *Parasaurolophus*, EV *76, 85*

Hair and hair follicles, human: HU *46, 47*; standing up, HU *44-45*; sweat glands near, HU *43*; touch detection by, HU *99*

Hair cells: HU *114, 115*

Hair grass: Antarctic, EC *45*

Hairs, sensory: flies, AN 8, *9*; moths, IN *26*; praying mantises, IN *40*

Hairstreak butterflies: IN *32, 33, 78*; purple, IN *74*

Halfbeak: UN *105*

Hamlets: reproduction by, UN 68-69

Hammer jaw: UN *69*

Hammerschlag, Freddi: PL *143*

Hands, human: fingers as sensitive surfaces, HU *98, 100, 102-103*; palms, sweating of, HU *43*

Haptonasty: PL 44, *45*

Harbor seals: UN *92, 93*

Harems: blackspot angelfish, UN *66-67*; fur seals, UN *93*

Hares: jack rabbit, EC *127*; Smith's red rock, EC *21*; snowshoe, seasonal color changes in, AN *58-59*

Hatchetfish: UN *23*

Haustoria (parasitic roots): PL *23, 57, 83*

Hawk moths: as day fliers, IN *32*; ear, IN *24*; flying speed, IN *chart* 14

Hay fever: HU *134-135*

Head butting: bighorn sheep, AN *106-107*

Heads, insect: IN *4-5, 22*; mosquito larva, IN *46*; praying mantis, IN *5, 22, 40*

Hearing, sense of: barn owls, AN 38, 39; carp, UN *44*; crickets, IN *28*; fish, UN *52-53*; humans, HU *112-113*; insects, IN *24-25*; sharks, UN *55*

Heart, animal: amphibian vs. reptile, EV *59*; insects, IN *8*

Heart, human: HU *52-53, 60*; beating of, HU *60-61, 68-69*; and blood pressure, HU *68-69*; disease of, HU *144*; muscle, HU *7, 60, 144*

Heart attack: HU *144*

Heartwood: formation of, PL 24

Heat adaptation: desert animals', EC *88-89*

Heat sensors (pit organs), rattlesnakes': AN *34*; mouse as sensed by, AN 35

Heike fireflies: AN *92*

Heliconius butterflies: AN *69*

Helper T cells: HU *128, 129, 131*; and AIDS virus, HU *136-137*

Heme: HU *72, 73*

Hemichordate: EV *46*

Hemicyclaspis (extinct fish): EV *46*

Hemlock trees: decomposition of, EC *132-133*

Hemoglobin: HU 64, 72; and carbon monoxide, HU *72, 73*

Henodus (early reptile): EV *62*

Hepatic lobules: HU *86-87*

Herbivores: of Africa, EC *80-85*

Hercules beetles: IN *60, 61*

Herd animals: warning signals by, AN *60-61*

Heredity: HU *10*; of blood types, HU *chart*

71; chromosomes, HU *8-9, 11, 14-15*

Hermaphroditic plants: techniques of, PL *59*

Hermaphroditism in fish: UN *62-63, 66-67, 68-69*

Hermit crabs: new shells, finding, AN *76-77*; and sea anemones, AN *78-79*

Herniated disks: HU 40, *41*

Herons: EC *138, 139, 140*; green, AN *36-37*

Herrings: round, mouth of, UN *106*; sardines, UN *102, 106-107*; swimming type, UN *19, 21*

Hesperornis (bird): EV *100*; skeleton, EV *101*

Heterodontosaurus (dinosaur): EV *74*

Heterosis (hybrid vigor): PL 136, 137

Hibernation: bats, EC *39*; garter snakes, EC *12*

High blood pressure: effects of, HU *69*

Himalayan cedar cones: PL *89*

Hinge joint: HU *38*

Hip joint: HU *38*

Hippopotamuses: pygmy, EC *21*

Histamine: release of, HU *135*

HIV (human immunodeficiency virus): HU *136*

Hognose snakes: bluffing, AN *85*

Hominids: EV *105, 124, 125, 126-127*

Homo erectus (extinct hominid): EV *126, 127*

Homo habilis (extinct hominid): EV *125, 126*

Homologous structures: EV *130-131, 134-135*

Homology and analogy: PL *29*

Homo sapiens (human species): EV *126, 127*; skeleton, EV *105*

Honeybees: AN 125, *130*; drones' roles, AN *130-131*; and mimics, AN *54*; workers' roles, AN *128-129, 131*. See Bees

Honeycomb: cells of, IN *70-71, 132-133*

Honeycomb spider: Australian, AN *27*

Honeydew: aphids' production of, AN *12*

Honey eaters: white-cheeked, EC *114*

Honey-pot ants: IN *138*

Horizons of soil: EC *37*

Hormones, human, glands producing: HU *74-75*; islets of Langerhans, HU *75, 84, 85, 142-143*

Hormones, insect: and pupation, IN 82

Horned dinosaurs: EV *78-79, 88-89*

Horned toads: Asian, AN *51, 52*

Hornets, black: stinging by, IN *124*

Hornito: UN *34*

Horns: beetles, IN *60-61*; bighorn sheep, AN *107*; dinosaurs, EV *78-79, 88-89*

Horntails: IN *124*

Horses: ancestors of, EV *106, 108-109*; modern, EV *109, 121*; wild, EC *113*

Horseshoe bats: EC *38-39*; greater, AN *42-43*

Horsetails: PL *94, 95*

Hot-water vents (black smokers): UN 34, *35*

Houseflies: food, finding, AN *8-9*; ocelli, effect of, IN *23*; walking on ceiling, IN *20-21*

House mosquitoes: IN *46-47*

Hover flies and aphids: AN *118-119*

Howler monkeys: EC *71*

Human body: HU entire volume

Human immunodeficiency virus (HIV): HU *136*

Humans: ancestors of, EV *105, 124-125, 126*; arms, EV *130-131, 135*; ear bones, EV *135*; early development of, EV *133*; evolution affected by, EV *142-143, 144*; evolution of, EV *126-127*

Hummingbirds: EC *60-61, 114, 115*

Humpback whales: AN *40*

Hunting wasps and nests: IN *54-55, 92-93, 110-111*

Hybrid plants: PL *136-137, 142*

Hydras: AN *48*

Hydrochloric acid: stomach cells secreting, HU *83*

Hyenas: EC *82*

Hylaeosaurus (dinosaur): EV *75*

Hylonomus (early reptile): EV *58, 62*

Hyoid: woodpeckers, AN *17*

Hypermetamorphosis: IN *81*

Hyperopia (farsightedness): HU *110, 111*

Hypertension: possible effects of, HU *69*

Hyphae: EC *134, 135*

Hypocotyl: PL *12-13*

Hypothalamus: HU *74*; and goose bumps, HU *45*; and sweating, HU *42*

Hypsilophodon (dinosaur): EV *74*

Hyracotherium (horse ancestor): EV *106, 108*

H zones: HU *36*

I

Ibis: Japanese crested, EC *113*

Icaronycteris (bat ancestor): EV 114, *115*

Icarosaurus (early reptile): EV *63*

Ice: insects living in, IN *34-35*

Ice ages: EV *chart* 129; and Alpine habitats, EC 52, *53, maps* 57; animal life in, EV *128-129*; survivors of, EV *141*; and tundra plants, PL *120-121*

Ice fish: EC 46, *47*

Ice worms: IN *35*

Ichneumon: IN *124*

Ichthyornis (primitive bird): EV *101*

Ichthyosaurs: EV *136-137*; belemnites eaten by, EV *95*; *Mixosaurus*, EV *62*; vs.

plesiosaurs, EV *92*; reproduction, EV *93*; skin, EV *96*; *Stenopterygius*, EV *92*

Ichthyostega (early amphibian): EV *57*

Idea leuconoe (caterpillar): IN *121*

Identical twins: HU *22*

Iguanas: Galápagos, EC *6*, EV *12, 13, 80*; land, EC *6, 113*

Iguanodon (dinosaur): EV *74-75*

Illness: HU *126*; atherosclerosis, HU *144*; cancer, HU *138-139*; carbon monoxide poisoning, HU *72-73*; diabetes, HU *142-143*; hay fever, HU *134-135*; heart attack, HU *144*; hypertension, possible effects of, HU *69. See also* Infectious diseases

Imitation: *See* Mimicry

Immune globulin E: HU *134, 135*

Immune system: HU *126, 128-129*; cancer and, HU *139*; destruction of, by AIDS, HU *136, 137*; and hay fever, HU *134-135*

Immunity: HU *126-129*; natural, HU *132*

Immunizations: HU *133*

Inarching: PL *135*

Inbreeding of corn: PL *136-137*

Incisors: HU *26*

Incomplete vs. complete metamorphosis: IN *56-57, 80-81*

India: EC *map* 11; animals of, EC *10, 11*; river dolphins of, UN *58, 59*

Indian leaf bugs: AN *50, 53*

Indricotherium (extinct mammal): EV *117*; skeleton, EV *104*

Indus River dolphins: UN *59*

Industrial melanism: IN *116-117*

Infectious diseases: HU *126*; AIDS, HU *136-137*; colds and complications, HU *140-141*; and immune system, HU *126, 128-129*; and lymphatic system, HU *130-131*; measles, HU *132-133*; and neutrophils, HU *65, 128, 132*

Inflorescences: dandelion, PL *72*; fig vs. pineapple, PL *69*; sunflower, PL *70, 71*; thistle, PL *74*

Influenza: symptoms, HU *chart* 141; viruses, HU *141*

Initiator: tumor, HU *138*

Injuries: faking of, by plovers, AN *84-85*; healing of, human, HU *48-49*

Ink, squirting of: by octopuses, UN *141*; by squid, UN *140-141*

Inner ear of fish: UN *52*; shark's, UN *55*

Inner ear of humans: HU *112, 113*; and dizziness, HU *114-115*

Insectivorous plants: EC *116-117*, PL *34-35, 46-47*

Insects: Alpine butterflies, EC *52-53, 57*; anatomy, IN *8-9*; antennae, IN *26-27, 32*; ants, AN *12-13, 124-127*; aphids, relationships with, AN *12-13, 118-119*; bats

catching, AN *42-43*; bees, AN *26, 54-55, 125, 128-131*; biological pest control, IN *90-91*; birds evolved for catching, EV *137*; bloodsucking, IN *68-69, 84*; bluffing, AN *85*; body parts, IN *5, 6*; breathing, IN *10-11*; butterflies vs. moths, IN *32-33*; butterfly wings, coloration of, IN *30-31, 58, 83, 121*; in caves, EC *43*; chameleons catching, AN *4-5, 32-33*; cicadas, EC *106-107*; coevolution, IN *78-79*; cold-resistant, IN *34-35*; crickets, AN *96-97*; differentiation, EV *22-23*; disguises, use of, AN *30-31, 50-55, 68-69*; earliest, EV *50-51*; evolutionary path, possible, IN *6-7*; eyes, compound, IN *4-5, 22*; eyespots, AN *51, 64-65*; feeding order, EC *110-111*; fireflies, AN *88-89, 92-93*; flightlessness, IN *84-85*; flying, first, EV *54-55*; flying, types of, IN *4-5, 14-15*; in food chain, EC *125, 127*; fungi living off, PL *97*; hearing, IN *24-25, 28*; horns, use of, IN *60-61*; houseflies, AN *8-9*; jumping, IN *16-17*; living fossils, EV *141*; mosquitoes, AN *10-11*; mutations, EV *14, 16-17*; ocelli, IN *22-23*; orchid resembling, PL *53*; outbreaks, IN *88-89*; pheromones, use of, AN *94-95*; plants trapping, EC *116-117*, PL *34-35, 46-47, 53*; pollination by, EC *115*, PL *8, 50, 52-53, 56, 68, 69*; as primary consumers, PL *125*; reproduction, EC *108-109*; seeds spread by, PL *79*; soil animals, EC *36-37*, PL *127*; sounds made by, IN *28-29*; spiders catching, AN *26, 27, 28-29*; stick insects, AN *52, 80*; swarming, IN *86-87, 133, 135*; temperature ranges, IN *chart* 35; tool used for collecting, AN *47*; walking, IN *12, 18-19, 20-21. See also* Defenses of animals; Food, finding and gathering; Reproduction by animals; Social insects; *and individual names*

In situ vs. *ex situ* conservation: PL *142-143*

Instars: IN *80-81, 114*

Insulin and diabetes: HU *142-143*

Intercostal muscles: HU *54*

Intermediate neurons: HU *103*

Internal respiration vs. external respiration: HU *52*

Intertidal zone: barnacles in, UN *40*

Intervertebral (spinal) disks: HU *40, 41*

Intestines: HU *88-89, 90-91*; lining, HU *6, 76, 77, 88-89, 90*

Inulin grain: PL *7*

In vitro cultivation: PL *140-141, 143*

In vitro fertilization: HU *28-29*

Irdomyrmex ants: IN *98*

Iridophores: AN *56-57*

Irises: PL *55*; fruit of, PL *67*

Islets of Langerhans: HU *75, 84, 85, 142-143*

Isolation: and differentiation, EV *22-23*; and living fossils, EV *140*

Ivy: roots of, for support, PL *23, 29*

J

Jacamars: great, EC *61*

Jackdaws: courtship, AN *103*

Jacobson, L. I.: AN *14*

Jacobson's organ: animals with, AN *14-15, 34*

Jamoytius kerwoodie (extinct fish): EV *46*

Japanese bluefish: UN *22-23*

Japanese bunting: eggs, AN *114*

Japanese copper butterfly: IN *78*

Japanese crane: dancing, AN *102-103*

Japanese dace: UN *73*

Japanese eel: UN *73*

Japanese jay: seeds buried by, EC *123*

Japanese macaque: learning, AN *144*

Japanese pampas grass: PL *73*

Japanese pilchard: UN *73*

Jawbone: growth of, HU *26, 34, 35*

Jawless fish (agnathans): UN *6*; earliest, EV *46-47, 48*

Jaws: fish with, evolution of, EV *48-49*; reptilian, EV *135*; whales, evolution of, EV *113*

Jays: Japanese, seeds buried by, EC *123*; scrub, AN *116-117*

Jellyfish: UN *4-5, 42-43*; medusafish's relationship with, UN *144*

Jellyfish-like animals: extinct, EV *39*

Jerboas: EC *89*

Jew's ears (mushrooms): PL *98*

Johnston's organ: mosquito's, IN *27*

Joints: muscles and, HU *38*

Jumping: fleas' method of, IN *16-17*

Jurassic period: dinosaurs, EV *74-75, 84-85*; ichthyosaurs, EV *92*; pterosaurs, EV *90, 91, 96*

K

Kandelia mangrove seedlings: PL *80*

Kangaroo rats: EC *90*

Kangaroos: EC *17*

Kaniska canace (butterfly): IN *32*

Kapok trees: PL *123*

Katydids: camouflage, AN *50, 52, 53*

Kauri pines: PL *123*

Kelp: life cycle of, PL *103*; sea otters and, EC *130*

Kentrosaurus (dinosaur): EV *74*

Keyhole limpet: starfish attack repelled by, UN *138-139*

Planet Earth
PE

Plant Life
PL

Physical Forces
PH

Structure of Matter
ST

Space & Planets
SP

Transportation
TR

Underwater World
UN

Weather & Climate
WE

Keystone species: sea otters as, EC *130-131*

Kiaeraspis (agnathan): underside of, EV *46*

Kidneys, human: HU *94-95*

Killer (Africanized) bees: IN *136-137*

Killer cells: HU *128, 129*

Killer whales: AN *41*, UN *114*

Killifish: EC *139, 140*; African, UN *64*

King cobra: AN *62*

King cobra guppy: UN *65*

Kingfishers: courtship, AN *103*

King termite: IN *128, 141, 143*

Kittiwakes: EC *32-33*

Knee joint: HU *38*

Knee roots: mangroves', EC *34, 35*

Koalas: EC *16*, PL *118*

Komodo dragons: AN *15*, EC *13*

Krakatoa (volcanic island), Indonesia: recol-
    onization of, EC *120-121*

Krause end bulbs: HU *98*

Krill eaters: UN *107, 116-117*

Kudzu vine: PL *75*

Kupffer cells: HU *87*

L

Labyrinths: membranous and bony, HU *115*

Ladybird beetles: *See* Ladybugs

Ladybugs: IN *4-5*; as aphid enemies, IN *144*;
    aphids protected from, AN *13*; for biolog-
    ical pest control, IN *91*; Japanese lady-
    birds, EC *108-109*; pupa, IN *113*; walk-
    ing upside down, IN *20*; warning
    coloration, IN *113, 120*

Lamarck, Jean-Baptiste: and theory, EV *13*

Lambeosaurus (dinosaur): EV *84*

Lamellae of fish's gills: UN *8, 9*

Lamellicorn beetles: IN *61*

Lancetfish: UN *69*

Land crabs: breathing by, UN *36-37*

Land races: beans as, PL *142*

Language: aquatic mammals' production of,
    UN *114-115*; chimpanzees, AN *124-125,
    142-143*; dance, of bees, IN *26, 128-129,
    134-135*

Language areas of human brain: HU *120,
    121*

Lanternbelly: UN *24, 25*

Lanternfish: UN *22*

La Plata River dolphin: UN *59*

Larch trees: EC *56*, PL *119*; cone, PL *89*;
    Japanese, EC *55*; trunk, PL *24-25*

Large blue butterflies: IN *78*

Large intestine: HU *90-91*; lining of, HU *76,
    90*

Larvae: abalone, UN *98*; barnacles, EC *101*,
    UN *40-41*; beetles, EC *37, 43*; cicadas,
    EC *106-107*; coral planulae, UN *101*;
    crabs, UN *39, 96-97*; desert species, EC

92-93; dung beetles, IN *93, 107*, 130,
    131; eggs deposited in, IN *114, 124*; fam-
    ily behavior, range of, IN *130, 131*; floun-
    der, UN *130*; fungus gnats (glowworms),
    IN *50-51*; glacier midges, IN *35*; ground
    bees, IN *108*; honeybees, IN *71, 132-
    133*; hypermetamorphosis, IN *81*; ice
    worms, IN *35*; metamorphosis, incom-
    plete vs. complete, IN *56-57, 80-81*; mos-
    quitoes, IN *46-47*; oysters, UN *99*; simi-
    larity of, EV *132*; soldier aphids'
    enemies, IN *144*; sponges, UN *100*; tad-
    poles, UN *88-89, 90, 91*; urochordate,
    EV *47*; wasp's prey, IN *110*; wood-eating,
    IN *49, 130*. *See also* Caterpillars

Laryngitis, viral: symptoms of, HU *chart* 141

Larynx: vocal cords in, HU *58-59*

Lateral line: UN *53*; shark's system, UN *54*

Lateral roots: PL 14, *15*

Lawn grass: PL *62-63*

Leaf bugs: Indian, AN *50, 53*

Leaf butterflies: AN *53*

Leaf-cutter ants: IN *139*; fungus growing, IN
    138-139

Leaf katydids: AN *50*

Leaf-rolling weevils: IN *104-105*

Leafy sea dragon: UN *105*

Leakey, Mary: EV 124

Leaves: PL 34-49; arrangement of, PL *36-37*;
    bamboo sheaths, PL *32, 33*; blooming
    triggered by, PL *54-55*; cactus, primitive,
    PL *113*; cells, PL *4-5*; color changes, PL
    40-41; eucalyptus, PL *118*; fallen, decay
    of, PL *126-127*; falling, cause of, PL *41,
    42-43*; ferns vs. mosses, PL 108; growth
    of, PL 16, *17*; of insect-eating plants, PL
    34-35, 46-47; mimosa, curling of, PL *44-
    45*; modifications of, PL *28, 29, 30*; mu-
    tant, PL *139*; new plants grown on, PL
    90-91; palm tree, PL *86-87*; photosynthe-
    sis in, PL 6, *10-11, 38*; pine needles, PL
    43, 48-49; rosette of, PL *8*; seasonal
    changes, PL *34-35, 40-41, 42-43, 126*;
    seed leaves (cotyledons), development
    of, PL *9, 12, 13, 79, 88*; shape of, PL *37*;
    stomas, PL *20, 21, 38-39, 40, 49*; of
    stone plant, PL *110, 114-115*; transporta-
    tion of water to, PL *20-21, 40-41*

Legs, human: movement, HU *38*

Legs, insect: centipedes vs. millipedes, IN
    12, 13; dung beetles, IN *106-107*; fleas,
    IN *16-17*; praying mantises, IN *40, 41*;
    walking methods, IN *12, 13*; walking up-
    side down, IN *20, 21*; water striders, IN
    18, 19

Legs, reptile: evolution of, EV *67*

Lemmings: EC *102-103*; burrows, EC *48*

Lemurs: flying, AN *72*

Lenses, biological: of fish eye, UN *48, 49,
    50-51*; of four-eyed (bifocal) fish, UN *50-
    51*; of human eye, HU *110-111*

Lenticels on tree trunks: PL *27*

Leontopodium fauriei (alpine plant): PL *121*

Leopard guppy: UN *65*

Leopard moray eel: AN *22*

Leopards: EC *10, 11*; and leopons, EV *11*

Leopard seal: EC *46-47*

Leopons: and leopards, EV *11*

Lepidodendron (Paleozoic plant): EV *52, 53*

Leptoceratops (dinosaur): EV *88*

Lesothosaurus (dinosaur): EV *74*

Lespedeza: EC *79*

Lianas: EC *65*

Lice: sucking, IN *84*

Lichens: PL *106-107*; Antarctica, EC *44, 45*;
    reindeer's food, EC *50, 51*

Lie detectors: working of, HU *43*

Life: beginnings of, EV *30-31*; living things,
    first, EV *32*

Life cycles: IN *56-91*; abalone, UN *98*; Alpine
    butterfly, EC *53*; anglerfish, deep-sea,
    UN *70-71*; aphids, IN *72-73*; barnacles,
    EC *100-101*, UN *40-41*; butterflies, IN
    56-57, 78-83, 114-115; cicadas, EC *106-
    107*; corals, UN *100-101*; crabs, UN *38-
    39, 96-97*; desert species, rain and, EC
    92-93; dung beetles, IN *92-93, 107*;
    flounders, UN *130-131*; forest, EC *104-
    105, 124-125, 132-133, 136-137*; frogs,
    UN *88-89*; garter snakes, EC *12-13*; gla-
    cier midges, IN *34-35*; honeybees, IN *70-
    71, 132-133*; kinds of metamorphosis, IN
    56-57, 80-81; medakas, UN *31*; mosqui-
    toes, IN *46-47*; mushrooms, EC *135*; and
    outbreaks of insects, IN *88-89*; oysters,
    UN *99*; salmon, UN *82-83*; scavenger
    beetles, EC *43*; sponges, UN *100-101*;
    sunfish, ocean, UN *88-89*

Light: absence of, and germination, PL *13*;
    fireflies signaling with, AN *88-89, 92-93*;
    flowers affected by, PL *53, 54-55, 61*;
    and growth rings, PL *24*; and leaf
    arrangement, PL *36*; nastic reaction to,
    PL *44, 45*; in photosynthesis, PL *10, 11,
    104, 105, 125*; and seasonal color
    changes, AN *59*; windows for, plants
    with, PL *114-115*

Light-emitting fish: UN *24-25, 26-27*; angler-
    fish, UN *23, 70-71, 111, 112*; cardinal-
    fish, UN *144*; lanternfish, UN *22*

Light-emitting insects: fireflies, IN *52-53*;
    glowworms, IN *50-51*

Light-emitting squid ink: UN *140*

Light-sensitive organs (ocelli): IN *22-23*

Lilies: arum, fly trapped by, PL *53*; vegeta-
    tive reproduction, PL *91, 140*

Limpets: keyhole, starfish attack repelled by, UN *138-139*

Linden seeds: PL *73*

Line webs, spiders': IN *39*

Lionfish: UN *120-121, 122*

Lions: African, EC *10, 81, 82*; breeding of, EV *10-11*; cave lions, EV *129*; Indian, EC *11*; prides of, AN *138-139*

Livebearing fish: guppies, UN *64-65*; mosquitofish, UN *73*; scorpionfish, UN *72*; sharks, UN *76-77*; surffish, UN *87*

Live oaks: EC *25*

Liver: HU *86-87*

Liverworts: PL *93, 109*

Living fossils: EV *130-131, 140-141*

Living stones (stone plants): PL *110, 114-115*

Lizard-hipped dinosaurs: EV *67*; vs. bird-hipped, EV *chart 66-67, 74-75*; birds' evolution from, EV *68-69*; *Compsognathus*, EV *71, 74*; sauropods, EV *83, 84-85*; *Tyrannosaurus*, EV *74, 77, 97*

Lizards: as caterpillar enemy, IN *120-121*; chameleons, AN *4-5, 32-33*; desert, EC *88, 91*; flying, AN *72-73*; of Galápagos, EV *12, 13, 80*; iguanas, EC *6, 113*; Komodo dragon, AN *15*, EC *13*; mosasaurs, EV *94-95*; recolonization, EC *121*; tails breaking off, AN *80-81*; temperature control, EV *80*

Loaches: barbels of, AN *20-21*

Lobe-finned fish: amphibian evolution from, EV *56-57*

Locus coeruleus and norepinephrine: HU *123*

Locusts (migratory grasshoppers): egg laying, IN *130*; evolutionary path, IN *7*; ocelli, effect of, IN *22-23*; swarming, IN *86-87*

Lodgepole pines: EC *79, 136-137*

Long-horned beetles: AN *69*; flying method, IN *15*; foot structure, IN *21*; larva, IN *49*; sound production, IN *29*; tiger, AN *55*

Longleaf pines: PL *49*

Long-legged wasps: IN *114, 125*

Long-waisted ground bee: nest of, IN *108*

Lotuses: EC *27*

Louse: sucking, IN *84*

Lugworms: AN *80*; as cone shell's prey, UN *119*; in food chain, UN *126-127*

Luminescent fish: UN *24-25, 26-27*; anglerfish, UN *23, 70-71, 111, 112*; cardinalfish, UN *144*; lanternfish, UN *22*

Luminescent squid ink: UN *140*

Luna moths: eyespots, use of, AN *64*

Lungfish: UN *30-31*

Lungs, human: alveoli, HU *56-57, 72-73*; breathing movements and, HU *54, 55*; carbon monoxide in, HU *72-73*; and gas exchange, HU *56-57, 65*

Lures, fishing: green heron's use of, AN *36-37*

Lycaenid butterflies, relationship of, with ants: IN *78-79*

Lymph: HU *130*; in ear, HU *114, 115*

Lymphatic system: HU *130-131*

Lymph nodes: HU *130-131*; large intestine, HU *90*

Lymphocytes: HU *6*; B cells, HU *126, 128, 129, 131, 132, 133, 135*; development of, HU *67*; in lymphatic system, HU *130, 131*; T cells, HU *128, 129, 131, 136-137*

Lystrosaurus (early reptile): EV *63*

M

Macaques: clan, AN *141*; learning, AN *144*

Macaws: scarlet, EC *61*

MacCready, Paul: EV *91*

MacGregor's bowerbird: bower of, AN *101*

Macrauchenia (extinct mammal): EV *120*

Macroevolution (adaptive radiation): EV *24-25*, 138

Macrophages: HU *128, 129*; in lymphatic system, HU *131*; measles and, HU *132, 133*

Madder: PL *78-79*

Magnetism: navigation aid for birds, AN *137*; navigation aid for salmon, AN *121*

Magpies, azure-winged: AN *115*; eggs, AN *114, 115*

Mahasena bagworms: nest of, IN *102*

Maiasaura (dinosaur): EV *83*

Mako sharks: shortfin, UN *15*

Malawi, Lake, Africa: catfish of, UN *86-87*

Malayan butterfly: caterpillar of, AN *64*

Male anatomy: HU *12*; pelvis, HU *12, 13*

Malignant tumors: growth of, HU *138-139*

Mammal-like reptiles: EV *59, 62, 63, 64-65*; family tree, EV *charts 63-65*; skull, EV *73*

Mammals: EV *104-129*; adaptation, EV *20-21*; adaptive radiation, EV *24-25*, 138; African and Indian, EC *10-11*; African and South American, EC *20-21*; of African grasslands, EC *29, 80-85*; at alligator hole, EC *138, 139*; aquatic, EC *7, 46-47, 49, 112, 130-131, 142*, EV *112-113, 136, 144*, UN *4-5, 18-19, 32-33, 58-59, 63, 92-93, 94-95, 107, 114-115, 116-117*; Arctic, EC *48-49*; Australian, EV *138-139, 144*; bats, AN *42-43*, EC *28, 38-39, 114*, EV *114-115, 130, 134*; biggest, land, EV *104, 116-117*; breeds and breeding, EV *10-11, 19*; color changes in, seasonal, AN *58-59*; convergence, EV *136, 138-139*; deer family, EC *50-51, 58-59, 118, 136, 139*; desert, EC *28, 88-91*; *Desmostylus*, EV *104-105, 118-119*; developmental similarities among, EV *133*; dolphins, UN *18-19, 58-59, 114-115*; elephants, EV *105, 110-111, 121, 128-129*; endangered species, EC *96-97, 112-113*; extinctions, modern, EV *144*; first true, EV *65, 72-73*; after forest fire, EC *136, 137*; gliding, AN *72, 73*; in herds, warning signals, AN *60-61*; homologous structures, EV *130-131, 134-135*; horses, EV *106, 108-109, 121*; human ancestors, EV *105, 124-125, 126*; human beings, EV *126-127*; ice ages and, EV *128-129, 141*; Indian and African, EC *10-11*; in Lamarck's theory, EV *13*; lions, AN *138-139*; living fossils, EV *140, 141*; marine, EC *7, 46-47, 49, 112, 130-131, 142*, EV *112-113, 136, 144*, UN *4-5, 32-33, 63, 92-93, 94-95, 107, 114-115, 116-117*; marsupials, EC *16-17, 114*; migrations, EC *map 51, 102-103*; moles, AN *104-105*, EC *17, 37, 106-107*; opossums, AN *85*; platypuses, AN *18-19*; primates, AN *46-47, 124-125, 140-141*, EC *18-19, 28, 70-71, 112*, EV *122-123, 124*; vs. reptiles, EC *13*; seals, UN *92-93*; seed dispersers, EC *96-97, 122-123*; sloths, EC *20, 62-63*; South American, EV *107, 120-121*; South American and African, EC *20-21*; tapirs, EC *14-15*; temperature control, EV *81*; tool-using, AN *46-47*; whales, AN *40-41*, EV *112-113*, UN *4-5, 32-33, 94-95, 107, 114-115, 116-117*; wolves, AN *44-45*

Mammoths: skeletons, EV *105*; skulls, EV *110*; woolly, EV *111, 128-129*

Mandibles: ants' use of, IN *126-127*

Mangrove trees: EC *34-35*, PL *80-81*; forests, EC *25*

Man-of-war, Portuguese: UN *42*

Manta rays: AN *25*, UN *107*

Mantises: *See* Praying mantises

Maple trees: leaves, color change in, PL *40-41*; seeds, PL *67, 73*

Maras: EC *20*

Marigolds: bur, PL *75*

Marine mammals: UN *63*; dolphins, EV *136*, UN *18-19, 114-115*; otters, EC *130-131, 142*; sea lions, EC *7*; seals, EC *46-47, 49*, UN *92-93*; Steller's sea cows, EV *144*; whales, EC *112*, EV *112-113*, UN *4-5, 32-33, 94-95, 107, 114-115, 116-117*

Marine reptiles: iguanas, EV *12, 13, 80*; prehistoric, EV *62, 92-93, 94-95, 96, 136-137*

Marrow, bone: blood-cell-producing, HU *66, 128*

Planet Earth
PE

Plant Life
PL

Physical Forces
PH

Structure of Matter
ST

Space & Planets
SP

Transportation
TR

Underwater World
UN

Weather & Climate
WE

Marsh dwellers: EC *138-139, 140*

Marsupial frogs: pygmy, UN *90*

Marsupials: EC *16-17, 114*; Australian, EV *138-139, 144*; opossums, AN *85*; South American, extinct, EV *107, 120*

Mast cells: HU 134, *135*

Mastodons: EV *110, 111, 121*

Mating, courtship and: AN *88-109*; alligators, AN 110; angelfish, blackspot, UN *66, 67*; anglerfish, UN *70-71*; barnacles, UN 40, *41*; bees, AN *130-131*; beetles, IN *60, 61*; bighorn sheep, head butting by, AN *106-107*; birds, AN *98-103, 112*; cabbage white butterflies, IN *58-59*; cichlids, UN *80-81*; crabs, UN *37, 38, 96*; crickets, singing by, AN *96-97*; damselflies, IN *63*; dances, AN *90, 100, 102-103*; dinosaurs' ritual, EV *86-87*; discus, UN *86*; dragonflies, IN *62-63*; fertilization of eggs, AN *88-89*; fiddler crabs, AN *108-109*; fireflies, AN *88-89, 92-93*, IN *52, 53*; fish, UN *62*; flightless moths, IN *85*; and gift giving among insects, IN *66-67*; glacier midges, IN *34*; guppies, UN *64-65*; hamlets, UN *68-69*; moles, AN *104*; moths, AN *94-95*; mudskippers, UN *29*; and pheromones, insects, IN *27*; praying mantises, IN *64-65*; salmon, UN 82, AN *120-121*; sound production, insects, IN *28, 29*; spiders, AN *90-91*; splashing tetras, UN *74-75*; spring-tide breeders, AN *122-123*; squid's color change before, UN *142. See also* Breeding of animals

Mayfly nymphs: IN *10*

Meadows, Alpine: EC *56-57*

Measles: HU *132-133*

Medakas: as diadromous fish, UN *11*; reproduction by, UN *31*

Medicines from plants: PL *132-133*

Medulla oblongata: nerve impulses to, HU *101*; salivary control center, HU *78*

Medusafish: relationship of, with jellyfish, UN *144*

Megakaryocytes: HU *66, 67*

Megaloceros (extinct deer): EV *105, 129*

Megalops larva, crab: UN *97*

Meganeura (early flying insect): EV *54-55*

Megatheres: EC *20*

Meiosis: HU *14-15*

Meissner's corpuscles: HU *98, 99*

Melanin: in hair, HU *47*; in skin, HU *50-51*

Melanocytes: HU *50-51*

Melanophores: tree frogs, AN *56, 57*

Memory B cells: HU *129*

Mendel, Gregor: and genetics, EV *13*

Meristem: root, PL *14*; shoot, PL *16, 32*

Meristem culture: PL *140-141*

Mesohippus (horse ancestor): EV *108*

Mesonyx (extinct mammal): EV *112*

Mesophyll: PL *39, 49*

Mesopithecus (monkey ancestor): EV *123*

Mesosaurus (early reptile): EV *58*

Mesozoic era: birds, EV *68-69, 70-71, 100-101*; flowering plants, EV *102-103*; flying reptiles, EV *63, 90-91, 96, 130, 134*; life in, EV 60, *62-63*; mammal-like reptiles, EV *59, 62, 63, 64-65, 73*; mammals, first, EV *65, 72-73*; marine reptiles, EV *62, 92-93, 94-95, 96, 136-137*; mollusks, EV *94-95, 98-99*; thecodonts, EV *62, 66-67. See also* Dinosaurs

Mesquite: EC *95*

Metabolism, cell: oxidation and, HU 52, *57*

Metamorphosis: UN *88-89*; anglerfish, UN *70*; butterflies, IN *56-57, 78-83, 114-115*; hypermetamorphosis, IN *81*; incomplete vs. complete, IN *56-57, 80-81*; simple, IN *80-81. See also* Larvae

Metastasis: HU *139*

Mice: deer, EC *136*; as prey of barn owls, AN *4-5, 38, 39*; as prey of rattlesnakes, AN *34-35*; as prey of spiders, AN *27*; and rats, seed dispersal by, EC *123*; tree, Congo, EC *21*

Microvelia douglasi (water strider): IN *18-19*

Microvilli: HU *8-9*; small intestine, HU *88-89*

Middle ear: HU *112*

Midges: glacier, IN *34*; larvae, IN *35*

Midgut: grasshoppers, IN *9*; mosquitoes, IN *69*

Midwife toads: European, UN *90*

Migration: birds, navigation, AN *134-137*; birds, V-formation, AN *132-133*; fur seals, for breeding, UN *92*; gray whales, for breeding, UN *94-95*; lemmings, EC *102-103*; reindeer, EC *map 51*

Migratory grasshoppers (locusts): egg laying, IN *130*; evolutionary path, IN *7*; ocelli, effect of, IN *22-23*; swarming, IN *86-87*

Milk (baby) teeth: HU *26, 27, 35*

Milkweed butterflies: AN *68*

Miller, Stanley M.: experiment by, EV *31*

Millipedes: EC *36*, IN *12-13*; blind, EC *43*

Mimicry: IN *112, 113, 118-119, 120*; Batesian, AN *54-55, 68, 69*; of butterflies, poisonous, AN *68-69*; eyespots, AN *51, 64-65*; mantises using, AN *30-31, 51*; Müllerian, AN *69*; of plant parts, AN *30-31, 50-53*; of stinging insects, AN *54-55*

Mimosa leaves: curling of, PL *44-45*

Miscoptera (early flying insect): EV *55*

Mistletoe: PL *23, 82-83*

Mites: EC *36*

Mitochondria: PL *6, 7*

Mitosis: HU *8-9*

Mixosaurus (early reptile): EV *62*

Moeritherium (elephant ancestor): EV *110*

Molars and premolars: HU *26, 27*

Molds: PL *96-97*; as decomposers, PL *126*; as penicillin source, PL *132-133*

Molecules: organic, EV *30*

Moles: AN *104-105*; cicada larvae eaten by, EC *106-107*; greater Japanese shrews, EC *37*; marsupial, EC *17*

Mollusks: conch, UN *35*; cone shells, UN *118-119*; crabs living in, UN *38-39*; extinct, EV *42, 94-95, 98-99*; in food chain, UN *126, 127*; in ocean trenches, UN *34*; octopuses, UN *60-61, 104, 141, 143*; reproduction, UN *98-99*; squid, UN *33, 113, 140-141, 142-143*; as starfish prey, defenses used by, UN *138-139*

Molting: and color changes, AN *59*; and instars, IN *80-81*; rattlesnakes, AN *63*

Monarch butterflies: IN 31, *82-83*

Monkeys: ancestors of, EV *123*; groups, AN 140, *141*; learning in groups, AN *144*; North American ancestors, extinct, EC *18-19*; rain forest, EC *28, 70-71*

Monocotyledons: bamboo as, PL *32*; vs. dicotyledons, PL *9*

Monocytes: HU *128*

Monoecious plants: PL *59*; squash, PL *58-59*

Moorhens: cooperative breeding in, AN *117*

Moose: EC *58-59*; wolves attacking, AN *44-45*

Moray eels: UN *63, 67, 104*; leopard, AN *22*

Morganucodon (early mammal): EV *72-73*

Mormyrids: UN *56*; relative of, UN *56-57*

Morning glories: PL *54*; dodder, PL *57*; grafting of, PL *135*

Morpho butterflies: wing coloration of, IN *30*

Mosasaurs: EV *94-95*

Mosquitoes: AN *10-11*; blood sucking, IN *68-69*; flying method, IN *15*; food gathering, IN *46-47*; Johnston's organ, IN *27*

Mosquitofish: UN *73*

Mosses: EC *133*, PL *92, 95, 108-109*; Antarctica, EC *44, 45*

Moths: antennae, IN *26, 32*; as aphid enemy, IN *144*; bagworms, IN *85, 102-103*; bat catching, AN *42-43*; vs. butterflies, IN *32-33*; camouflage, use of, AN *53*; chameleons catching, AN *4-5*; defenses, IN *112-113, 116-117, 118-119*; with eyespots, AN *51, 64*; fastest flier, IN *chart 14*; in feeding order, EC *110, 111*; flightless, IN *85*; hearing, IN *24-25*; mating, AN *94-95*; mimics of other insects, AN *55, 69*; natural selection in, EV *16-17*; outbreaks, IN *88-89*; spiders catching,

| Animal Behavior **AN** | Computer Age **CO** | Ecology **EC** | Evolution of Life **EV** | Geography **GE** | Human Body **HU** | Insects & Spiders **IN** | Machines & Inventions **MA** |

AN *27, 28-29*; wing coloration, IN *31*

Motmots: blue-crowned, EC *61*

Motor and sensory cortex of brain: HU *105*

Motor cells: mimosa's, PL *45*

Motor nerves: HU *7, 102-103*

Mouthbrooders: UN *79, 80-81, 84*; Egyptian, UN *73*; other species' eggs incubated by, UN *84-85*

Mouths: adaptations for feeding, UN *104-105*; amphibians born through, UN *62, 90-91*; archerfish, UN *108*; blue whale, UN *116*; breathing, role in, UN *8, 9*; round herring, UN *106*

Mucous membrane, olfactory: HU *117*

Mucus and sense of smell: HU *116, 117*

Mucus-secreting cells: HU *6*; in fallopian tubes, HU *16*; goblet cells, HU *88, 140*; in stomach, HU *82, 83*

Mudskippers: UN *28-29*

Mud snails: UN *98*

Mud snake, eastern: AN *63*

Mulberry trees: mutation in, PL *139*

Müllerian mimicry: AN *69*

Multicellular organisms: evolution of, EV *27, 38-39*

Multiple births: HU *22-23*

Multiple fruits: PL *67, 68-69*

Mundiopsis: UN *34*

Murrelets: ancient, EC *8, 33*

Murres: EC *8, 33*; oil spills and, EC *143*

Muscles of aquatic animals: fish, UN *6-7*; red, and body heat, UN *14, 15*; retractor lentis, use of, UN *49*; squid's, and changes in coloring, UN *142*

Muscles of humans: HU *6, 30*; arm, HU *30-31, 39*; and breathing, HU *54*; contraction of, HU *36-37, 38, 39*; erector, HU *44, 47*; eye, HU *110-111*; heart, HU *7, 60, 144*; and joints, HU *38*; kinds of tissue, HU *7, 30, 60*; peristalsis, HU *81, 90, 91*; in reflex actions, HU *102*; and vocal sounds, HU *58*

Muscles of insects: dorsal vessel and, IN *8*; dragonfly nymph's lip, IN *44, 45*; wings and, IN *15*

Mushrooms: EC *134-135*, PL *92-93, 95, 98-99*; as decomposers, PL *126*; reindeer food, EC *50*

Musk dwarf antelope: EC *21*

Muskoxen: EC *48-49*

Mutations: EV *14-15*; breeding for, EV *18*, PL *138-139*; and natural selection, EV *16-17*

Mutualism: ants and butterflies, IN *78-79*; ants and plants, IN *98-99*

Mycelia: mosses', PL *109*; in mushroom reproduction, PL *99*; of mushrooms, EC *135*

Mycorrhiza: EC *134*

Myelin sheath: HU *100-101*

Myocardial infarction: HU *144*

Myocardial (cardiac) muscle: HU *7, 60, 144*

Myofibrils: HU *36-37*

Myopia (nearsightedness): HU *110*

Myosin and actin: HU *36, 37*

Myriad leaf: EC *26, 27*

Myxomycetes (slime molds): PL *96, 97*

N

Nails: HU *46*

Nares: UN *46, 47*

Nasal passages: sperm whale's use of, UN *33*

Nastic movement: PL *44-45*

Natural immunity: HU *132*

Natural killer cells: HU *128, 129*

Natural selections: EV *12, 16-17*

Nauplius larvae: barnacle, UN *41*

Nautiluses: chambered, EV *99, 140*

Navigation methods of animals: birds, AN *134-137*; river dolphins, UN *58-59*; salmon, AN *120-121*

Neanderthals: EV *126, 127*

Nearsightedness: HU *110*

Necrolemurs (extinct primates): EV *122*

Nectar guide and nectar gland: PL *52*

Needle-leaved trees: vs. broad-leaved, EC *24-25*; pines, PL *43, 48-49*. *See also* Conifers

Negative taxis: paramecium, AN *6*

Nematocysts: sea anemones, AN *48*

Nematodes: EC *36*

Neofinetia falcata (epiphyte): PL *22-23*

Neopterans: EV *54, 55*

Neotropical Region: animals of, EC *5*

Nepenthes pitcher plant: PL *47*

Nephrons: HU *95*

Nerve cells: *See* Neurons of human brain

Nerves: HU *100-101*; cochlear, HU *113*; gustatory, HU *118, 119*; motor, HU *102-103*; olfactory, HU *116, 117*; optic, HU *111*; receptors in skin, HU *98-99, 100*; in reflex actions, HU *102-103*; spinal, pinched, cause of, HU *41*. *See also* Neurons of human brain

Nervous system of humans: HU *7, 96-125*; spinal cord, HU *41, 101, 103*. *See also* Brain, human; Nerves; Sense organs, human

Nervous system of insects: IN *8-9*

Nesting holes: mudskippers', UN *29*

Nests: Africanized bees, IN *136-137*; ants, IN *78-79, 98-99, 127, 138-139*; bagworms, IN *102-103*; bees, site selection,

IN *135*; dinosaurs, EV *78*; dung beetles, IN *92-93, 106-107, 130, 131*; family life, range of, IN *130-131*; ground bees, IN *108-109*; hunting wasps, IN *55, 92-93, 110-111*; insects, IN *92-111*; leaf-rolling weevils, IN *104-105*; male fish building, UN *79*; seabirds, EC *32-33*; spiders, IN *75, 94-95, 96-97*; spittlebugs, IN *100-101*; sticklebacks, male, UN *79*; termite mounds, IN *142-143*

Net-winged beetles: AN *69*

Neurons (nerve cells) of human brain: HU *7, 96, 100-101*; in cerebral cortex, HU *24, 104-105*; in reflex actions, HU *102, 103*; and sleep, HU *123*

Neuropteris (Paleozoic seed fern): EV *53*

Neurotransmitters: HU *100, 101*; sleep-inducing, HU *123*

Neutrophils: HU *65, 128, 132*

New Guinea cicada: AN *50*

Newton's golden bowerbird: bower of, AN *101*

Newts: Australian brown, AN *52*; California, poisonous, AN *67*; early development of, EV *133*

New World monkeys: ancestors of, EV *123*

Niches, ecological: adaption to, EV *5, 20-21*; and differentiation of species, EV *23*

Night-blooming flowers: PL *53*

Nightjars: AN *52*

Niphanda fusca (butterfly): IN *78-79*

Noctuid moths: antennae, IN *32*; ear, IN *24*

Nodes of Ranvier: HU *100*

Non-insulin-dependent diabetes: HU *143*

Non-REM vs. REM (rapid eye movement) sleep: HU *122, chart 122, 123, 124-125*

Norepinephrine: and sleep, HU *123*

Northern banded water snake: favorite prey, AN *graph 15*

Northern cricket, Japan: AN *96*

Norway lemmings: range of, EC *map 103*

Nose: odor detection by, HU *116-117*

Notch grafting: PL *134-135*

Nothosaurus (early reptile): EV *62*

Notothens: UN *17*; spotted, UN *16-17*

Nucleic acids: *See* DNA; RNA

Nucleoli: of plant cell, PL *6, 7*

Nucleus: DNA in human cell, HU *4-5, 10-11*; of human cell, HU *8-9*; of plant cell, PL *6, 7*

Nucleus pulposus: HU *40, 41*

Nuts: PL *65, 77*; methods of cracking, AN *16, 46*

Nymphs: cicada, IN *89*; cricket's care of, IN *74*; dragonfly, IN *10, 36-37, 44-45, 80-81*; with gills, IN *10*; grasshopper, IN *56-57, 80-81*; spittlebug, IN *100-101*

Planet Earth
PE

Plant Life
PL

Physical Forces
PH

Structure of Matter
ST

Space & Planets
SP

Transportation
TR

Underwater World
UN

Weather & Climate
WE

O

Oak trees: bark, PL *27*; leaves, PL *43*; nuts, PL *77*

Oats: PL *144*

Oblique hatchetfish: UN *23*

Oceans: black smokers, EV *32-33*; formation of, EV *28-29*; life's beginnings in, EV *30-31*; stromatolites, EV *26-27, 34-35*

Ocean sunfish: metamorphosis in, UN *88-89*

Ocean trenches: *See* Trenches, ocean

Ocelli: IN *22-23*

Ocotillos: EC *86, 87*

Octopuses: camouflage, use of, UN *143*; hermit crab's protection against, AN *78-79*; ink squirted by, UN *141*; as prey of moray eel, UN *104*; vision, UN *44, 60-61*

Odors: detection of, by humans, HU *116-117*

Oil, spermaceti: in whale, UN *32, 33*

Oil spills: effects of, EC *142-143*

Oily secretion from sebaceous gland: HU *44*

Old-man cactus: PL *113*

Old-man's-beard lichen: PL *107*

Olfactory sense of aquatic animals: carp, UN *45, 46-47*; eels, UN *47*; fish, general, UN *46-47*; sharks, UN *55*

Olfactory sense of humans: HU *116-117*

Olfactory sense of insects: silkworm moth's, IN *26*

Oligokyphus (mammal-like reptile): EV *65*

Olive (tree): PL *78-79*

Onions: PL *29*; seeds, germination of, PL *13*

Operculum: UN *8*

Oplismenus grass: PL *75*

Opossums: bluffing by, AN *85*

Optical axis of fish eyes: UN *48, 51*

Optic nerves, human: HU *111*; vs. octopus, UN *61*

Oral groove: paramecium, AN *7*

Orange-crested gardener: bower of, AN *101*

Oranges: PL *66, 67*

Orangutans: AN *140*, EC *70*

Orb webs, spiders': IN *36-37, 38, 94*

Orcas: UN *114*

Orchids: EC *68, 69*, PL *22-23*; mantis resembling, AN *30-31*; pollinating devices, PL *52, 53*; tissue culture, PL *140-141*

Organelles: PL *5, 6-7, 10-11*

Organ of Corti: HU *112, 113*

Organs, human: and organ systems, HU *6-7*. *See also individual names*

Oriental garden crickets: AN *97*

Oriental great reed warblers: AN *98-99*; eggs, AN *114*

Oriental Region: animals of, EC *4-5*

Oriental saddleback caterpillars: IN *121*

Ornithischians vs. saurischians: EV *chart 66-67, 74-75*

Ornitholestes (dinosaur): EV *74*

Ornithosuchus (early reptile): EV *67*

Osmeterium: swallowtail's, IN *123*

Osmosis: and gas in swim bladder, UN *13*; and saline balance, UN *10, 11*

Osteichthians: EV *49*; amphibian evolution from, EV *56-57*

Osteoblasts: HU 34, *35*

Osteoclasts: HU 34, *35*

Ostracod: UN *24*

Ostriches: EC *82*

Otoliths: fish, UN *52*; jellyfish, UN *43*

Otters: river, EC *139*; sea, AN *47*, EC *130-131, 142*

Ouranosaurus (dinosaur): EV *75*

Outer ear, human: HU *112*

Ova: *See* Egg and sperm, human

Oval body in fish: function of, UN *13*

Ovaries of humans: HU *13, 16, 28, 75*

Ovaries of plants: corn kernels, PL *84-85*; fruits from, PL *66-67, 68*; squash flower's, PL *59*

Ovipositors: IN *124*

Oviraptor (dinosaur): EV *77, 79*

Ovule: development in, PL *8-9*

Owl butterflies: eyespots on, IN *118*

Owls: barn, AN *4-5, 38-39*; elf, EC *89*

Oxidation: and cell metabolism, HU 52, 57

Oxygen: atmospheric, EV 27, 34; displacement by carbon monoxide, HU 72, *73*; hemoglobin and, HU 64, 72; in photosynthesis and respiration, PL *38*; respiratory roots for, PL *22*; supplying body with, HU *56-57*, 65

Oxygen conservation by sperm whale: UN 32

Oxygen in atmosphere: EV 27, 34

Oxyntic cells: HU *83*

Oyster crabs: UN 38

Oysters: reproduction by, UN *99*

P

Pacas: EC *20*

Pacemaker, human (sinoatrial node): HU *61*

Pachycephalosaurus (dinosaur): EV *86-87*

Pacinian corpuscles: HU *98, 99*

Paddlefish: UN *107*

Pakicetus (whale ancestor): EV *112-113*

Palaelama (extinct mammal): EV *121*

Paleozoic era: amphibian evolution, EV *56-57*; backboned animals, evolution of, EV *46-47*; Cambrian period, EV *40-45*; fliers, first, EV *54-55*; jaws, evolution of, EV *48-49*; land creatures, first, EV *50-51*; land plants, evolution of, EV *52-53*; life in, EV *40-59*; reptile evolution, EV *58-59*

Palisade tissue: PL *39, 40, 41*

Palm trees: PL *86-87*; coconut, EC *22-23*; peach, PL *143*

Pampas: EC *77*

Pampas grass, Japanese: PL *73*

Pancreas, human: HU *84-85*; and diabetes, HU *142-143*; islets of Langerhans, HU *75, 84, 85, 142-143*

Pandas, giant: EC *112*

Pangaea (hypothetical supercontinent): EC 10, *map* 11, *map* 16, 20

Panther puffer: UN *127*

Panthers: Florida, EC *138*

Paper wasp: nest of, IN *92-93, 110-111*

Papilionid butterfly caterpillar: IN *119*

Papillae on tongue: HU *118*

Pappus on dandelion fruit: PL *72, 73*

Parahippus (horse ancestor): EV *109*

Paramecia (single-celled organisms): AN *6-7*, EV *39*

Parasaurolophus (dinosaur): EV *76, 85*

Parasites: cleaner shrimp removing, AN *23*; crabs, UN *38-39*; cuckoo catfish, UN *84-85*; insects, flightless, IN *16-17, 84*; mushrooms, EC *134-135*; plants, PL *23, 57, 82-83*; plants, roots of, PL *23, 57, 83*; *Rafflesia*, PL *51, 56-57*; remora removing, AN *24*; sexual (anglerfish), UN *70-71*; wasps, IN *90, 91, 114*. *See also* Fungi

Parasitic wasps: for biological pest control, IN *90, 91*; cocoons, IN *114*

Parathyroid glands: HU *75*

Parenting: AN 89, *110-123*; alligators, AN *110-111*; bats, EC *39*; cooperative breeding, AN *116-117*; cuckoos and hosts, AN *114-115*; eagles, EC *124, 126*; fish, UN *78-79, 86-87*; fish, care of other species' hatchlings, UN *84-85*; feeding of young by fish, UN *86-87*; frogs, UN *90-91*; hover fly egg laying, site selection for, AN *118-119*; insects, IN *74-75, 76-77, 130-131*; lions, AN *139*; penguins, AN *88-89, 112-113*; pill bugs, IN *76-77*; polar bears, EC *49*; sloths, EC *63*; spiders, IN *74-75*; toads, UN *90-91*; whooping cranes, EC *113*

Parnara guttata (butterfly): IN *33*

Parnassius (butterfly): EV *141*

Parnassus glacialis (butterfly): IN *31*

Parotid glands: HU *78, 79*

Parr (salmon): UN *82*

Parrotfish: blue, UN *104-105*; food chain involving, EC *129*

Passenger pigeons: EC *112*

Passive submission: wolves, AN *45*

Patagia: EV *114-115, 134*

Pathogens: *See* Infectious diseases

Pattern recognition in octopuses: UN *61*

Animal Behavior
AN

Computer Age
CO

Ecology
EC

Evolution of Life
EV

Geography
GE

Human Body
HU

Insects & Spiders
IN

Machines &
Inventions **MA**

Peach palms: PL *143*

Peach trees: fruit, PL *66-67*; shoots, tissue culture of, PL *143*

Pea crabs in clams: UN *38-39*

Pearleye: UN *69*

Pearlfish: relationship of with sea cucumbers, UN *144*

Peas: laws of genetics in, EV *13*; plants, PL *94*; tendrils of plants, PL *29, 30*

Pectoral fins: of flying fish, UN *128-129*; of gurnard, UN *47*; of mudskipper, UN *28*; of porcupinefish, UN *20*

Pedicellariae: sea urchin's, UN *139*

Pedipalps: male spider's, AN 90, *91*

Pelagic fish: hermaphrodites, UN *69*; with rete mirabile, UN *14-15*; tail type, UN 20, *21*

Pelvic fins: mudskipper's, UN *28*

Pelvis, human: male vs. female, HU *12, 13*

Pelycosaurs: evolution from, EV *chart* 65

Penguins: EC 8, *9*, 46, *47, 49*; with chicks, AN *88-89, 112-113*; Galápagos, EC *6*; swimming style of, UN *18-19*

Penicillin: source of, PL *132-133*

Pentaceratops (dinosaur): EV *89*

Peppered moths: camouflage by, IN *116-117*; natural selection in, EV *16-17*

Peppers: green, PL *136*

Pepsin: HU 82, *83*

Perch: anatomy, UN *6-7*; climbing, UN *29*; surfperch, body fluids of, UN *chart* 16; white, EC *141*

Pericarp of fruit: PL *66-67*; coconut, PL *86-87*

Pericycle of root: PL *15*

Perilymph: HU 112, *113, 115*

Peripheral nerves: *See* Nerves

Peristalsis: in esophagus, HU 80; in large intestine, HU *90, 91*

Permanent teeth: HU *26, 27, 35*

Persimmon seed, inside of: PL *12*

Pesticides: biological accumulation of, EC 144; biological control vs., IN *90-91*

Petals: opening and closing of, PL *60-61*; sunflower, PL *71*

Petrels: EC *46*; snow, EC *45*

Petunias: PL *55*

Pharyngoconjunctival fever: symptoms of, HU *chart* 141

Pharynx: HU *80*

Pheromones: ants' use of, IN *43*; moth's, AN *94-95*, IN 27

Phiomia (elephant ancestor): EV *110*

pH levels in European regions: EC *maps* 75

Phloem: in roots, PL *14*; in stems, PL *20*; in tree trunks, PL *25, 26, 27*

Phororhacos (giant extinct bird): EV *107*

Photoblepharon: UN *27*

Photophores: UN *24, 25*; blinking, UN 26, *27*

Photosynthesis: PL 6, *10-11, 38*, 124, 125; beginnings of, EV 27, 34; organs for, PL *29*; in seaweed, PL *104, 105*

Phyllotaxis: PL *36-37*

Phytoplankton: EC *46, 140*

Pigeons: navigation experiment with, AN *137*; passenger, EC *112*

Pigments in humans: in hair, HU *47*; in skin, HU *50-51*

Pigments in plants: algae's auxiliary pigments, PL *105*; of flowers, PL *52*; of fruits, PL *78*; of leaves, changing, PL *40-41*. *See also* Coloration, biological

Pigs: early development of, EV *133*

Pigweed: PL *75*

Pikaia (Paleozoic chordate): EV *47*

Pikas: EV *128, 141*

Pilchard: Japanese, UN *73*

Pill bugs: evolutionary path, IN *6*; parenting behavior, IN *76-77*; sowbugs, EC *37*; spider's capture of, AN *26*; wood lice, EC *36*

Pinched spinal nerves: cause of, HU *41*

Pineal body: location of, HU *74*

Pineapples: PL *67*; vs. figs, PL *69*

Pine cone fish: UN *26*

Pine cones: PL *88-89*

Pines: EC *54*, PL *43, 49, 89*; bark, PL *27*; bristlecone, PL *123*; cones, PL *88-89*; creeping, EC *53, 55*; fire's effect on, EC *78*, 79, *136-137*; kauri, PL *123*; leaves (needles), PL *43, 48-49*; winged fruit, PL *73*

Pipa: Carvalho's, UN *91*

Piranha: UN *105*

Pistils: PL 51, *53*, 58; of angiosperms, EV *103*. *See also* Carpels

Pitcher plant: EC *116*, PL *47, 118*

Pit organs, rattlesnakes': AN *34*; mouse as sensed by, AN *35*

Pituitary gland and hormones: HU *74*

Placenta, human: HU 18, *19, 20*; of twins, HU *22, 23*

Placental animals vs. marsupial animals: EV *138-139*

Placoderms: EV *49*

Placodus (early reptile): EV *62*

Planing by bees: AN *129*

Plankton: EC *46, 140*

Plankton eaters: UN *102, 105, 106-107*

Plant and ant symbiosis: IN *98-99*

Planthoppers: brown, outbreaks of, IN 88; eyespots, IN *112, 119*

Plants: PL entire volume; and adaptation, EV *21*; with air roots, EC *68-69*; Alpine, EC *52-53*, 54, *55, 56-57*; angiosperms, evolu-

tion of, EV *102-103*; Antarctica, EC *44-45, 46*; cabbages, breeding of, EV *19*; cells, evolution of, EV *37*; cell structure, PL *4-5, 6, 7*; classification, example of, EV *6*; convergence, EV *137*; dead, conversion of, PL *110-111*, 124, 125, *126-127*; deer family feeding on, EC *50-51, 58-59*, 118; defenses, EC *98-99, 118-119*; desert, EC *86-87, 89, 94-95*; evolution of, EV *6-7*, 105; floral regions, PL *map* 118-119; flowering, first appearance of, EV *102-103*; in food chain, EC 124, PL *124-125*; after forest fire, EC *136-137*; fungi, EC *40, 50*, 132, 133, *134-135*; Galápagos, EC *6, 119*; gymnosperms, evolution, EV *102*; hybrids, PL *136-137, 142*; insect-eating, EC *116-117*; kelp, EC 130; lakes filled in by, PL *128-129*; living fossils, EV *141*; medicines from, PL *132-133*; naturalized, PL *75*; Paleozoic, EV *52-53*; peas, genetics of, EV *13;* recolonization, EC *120, 121*; reproduction, animals aiding, EC *96-97, 114-115, 122-123*; thistles, EC *108-109*; vegetative reproduction, PL *62, 90-91, 134-135, 140-141, 143*; in water, EC *26-27. See also* Adaptation; Flowers and flowering plants; Grasslands; Leaves; Roots; Spore-bearing plants; Stems; Trees; *and individual names*

Planulae: coral, UN *101*

Plasma, human: HU *6, 64*; agglutinins, HU *70-71*; histamine, effect of, HU *135*

Plasmodia: PL 96, *97*

Platelets: HU *6, 64, 65*; development, HU *66-67*

Plateosaurus (early reptile): EV *63*

Platybelodon (mastodon): EV *110*

Platypuses: AN *18-19*

Plesiadapis (early primate): EV *122*, 123

Plesiosaurs: EV *92-93*

Pleural arch: flea's, IN *16, 17*

Pliohippus (horse ancestor): EV *109*

Plotosids: UN *123*

Plovers: injury faked by, AN *84-85*

Plumules: PL *9, 12*

Pneumatophores (breathing roots): EC *25*, 34, *35*; PL 22

Pneumonia bacteria: HU *141*

Poinsettias: PL *55*

Poisoning: carbon monoxide, HU *72-73*

Poisonous amphibians: AN *66-67*

Poisonous insects: butterflies, AN *68-69*; chemical weapons, IN *122-123, 126, 127*; stinging, IN *124-125, 126, 127*, 137; warning coloration, IN *112-113*, 120, 121

Poisonous sea creatures: UN *120-121, 122-123, 126-127*; catfish, UN *122, 123*; cone shells, UN *118-119*; fringefin goby, UN

Planet Earth
PE

Plant Life
PL

Physical Forces
PH

Structure of Matter
ST

Space & Planets
SP

Transportation
TR

Underwater World
UN

Weather & Climate
WE

127; lionfish, UN *120-121, 122*; puffer-fish, UN 126, *127*; rabbitfish, UN *123*; stingray, UN *123*; stonefish, UN *124*; trunkfish, UN *126*

Polar bears: EC *49*

Pollen: PL 52; corn, PL *85*; and hay fever; HU *134-135*; pine, PL *89*; and pollen tube, PL *8, 66*

Pollination: PL *95*; corn, PL 84, 85, *136-137*; grasses, PL 62; pines, PL *89*; self- vs. cross-pollination, PL 58, *59, 69, 136-137*; of water plants, EC *27*

Pollinators: animals, EC *97, 114-115*; insects, PL *8, 50, 52-53*, 56, 68, 69

Pollution: acid rain, EC *74-75*; biological accumulation, EC *144*; and natural selection, EV *16-17*; oil spills, EC *142-143*

Polyergus ants: IN *138*

Polygraphs: HU *43*

Polyploidic breeding: PL *138-139*

Polyps, coral: UN 100, 101; as starfish prey, UN *139*

Pomegranate fruits: PL *67*

Pondweed: EC *26, 27*

Ponerine ants: termites and, IN *140*

Poplar trees: leaves of, PL *42*

Porcupinefish: UN *20, 121, 124-125*

Porcupines: crested, EC *10*; Indian, EC *11*

Portal vein: HU *86, 87*

Portuguese man-of-war: UN *42*

Positive taxis: paramecium, AN *6*

Possum: EC *17*

Potatoes: PL *29, 91, 142*; starch granules, PL *11*; sweet potatoes, PL *29, 135*

Prairies: EC *77*

Praying mantises: butterfly enemy, IN *115*; cannibalism, IN 64, *65*; evolutionary path, IN *7*; head of, IN *5, 22, 40*; hunting, adaptations for, IN *40-41*; mating, IN *64-65*; mimicry, use of, AN *30-31, 51*

Precambrian fossils: EV 26-27, 38, 39

Precursor cells: blood cells', HU *66-67, 128*

Predators: ants, IN 42, *140, 141*; aquatic animals, UN *102-119*; archerfish, UN *108-109*; for biological pest control, IN *90-91*; cabbage butterfly's natural enemies, IN *114-115*; centipedes as, IN 12; cleaner wrasses' protection from, UN *120, 134-135*; crabs' protection from, UN *136-137*; deep-sea adaptations of, UN *112-113*; dolphins as, UN *58-59, 114-115*; dragonfly nymphs as, IN *36-37, 44-45*; electric fish, UN *57*; fireflies, IN *52-53*; flounders' defenses against, UN *130-131*; flying fish's defenses against, UN *120-121, 128-129*; glowworms, IN *50-51*; hosts for protection against, UN *144*; hunting wasps as, IN *54-55, 110-111*; ink as defense

against, UN *140-141*; lures, use of, UN *23, 25, 26, 27, 102-103, 110-111, 112*; mosquito larvae as, IN *47*; mouth adaptations of, UN *104-105*; octopuses as, UN *60-61*; plankton eaters, UN *102, 105, 106-107*; poison fish's defenses against, UN *120-121, 122-123, 126-127*; porcupinefish's defenses against, UN *121, 124-125*; praying mantises as, IN *40-41, 64, 65, 115*; pufferfish's defenses against, UN *126-127*; saber-toothed blennies, UN *134, 135*; sharks as, UN *54-55, 103, 104, 105*; shellfish as, UN *118-119*; spiders as, IN *36-37, 38-39, 94, 95, 96-97, 115*; squids' defenses against, UN *140-141, 142-143*; starfish as, UN *138-139*; tail design of predatory fish, UN *20, 21*; whales as, UN 33, 107, *114, 116-117*. *See also* Defenses of animals

Pregnancy: *See* Reproduction

Premolars and molars: HU 26, 27

Pressure: water, and deep-sea fish, UN *22-23*

Prickly pear cacti: PL *112*

Prides of lions: AN *138-139*

Primates: chimpanzees, AN *46-47, 124-125, 141, 142-143*; endangered, EC *112*; evolution of, EV *122-123, 124*; extinct, EC *18-19*; learning in monkeys, AN *144*; rain forest, EC *28, 70-71*; social groups, AN *140-141*

Primroses: evening, PL *53*

Princess fireflies: AN *93*; flashing patterns, AN *92, 93*

Probainognathus (mammal-like reptile): EV *65*

Proboscides: flies, AN *8*; mosquitoes, AN *10, 11*

Proconsul (extinct primate): EV *124*

Proganochelys (early reptile): EV *62*

Prokaryotes: cell type, EV *36, 37*; evolution from, EV 6, 7

Prominent moths: yellow-tipped, AN *53*

Promoters: cancer stimulated by, HU *139*

Pronator muscles: HU *39*

Pronghorns: AN *61*

Prop roots: EC *35, 64-65*

Prostate gland: HU *12*

Proteins: EV *30*; in cells, EV 30, *36*; laboratory creation of, EV *31*

Proterogyrinus (anthracosaur): EV *58*

Protoavis (ancestral bird): EV *68-69*, 70

Protoceratops (dinosaur): EV *78-79, 89*

Protophasma (early flying insect): EV *55*

Protosuchus (early crocodile): EV *62-63*

Protozoans: in cave, EC *40*; didinium, AN *7*; paramecium, AN *6-7*; in termites' intestines, IN *49*

Pryeria sinica caterpillars: IN *120-121*

Pseudomyrmex ant: IN *99*

Pseudoscorpions: EC *37*

Pseudosuchians: EV *67*; *Euparkeria*, EV *62, 66*

Psittacosaurus (dinosaur): EV *88*

Psyche bagworms: nests of, IN *103*

Ptarmigans: seasonal color changes in, AN *50-51, 58-59*

Pteranodon (pterosaur): EV *90, 130, 134*

Pteraspis (extinct fish): EV *47*

Pteridines: IN *58*

Pterobranch: EV *46*

Pterodactyls: EV 90, *91*

Pterodaustro (pterodactyloid): EV *91*

Pteromalus wasps: IN *115*

Pterosaurs: EV *90-91*; family tree, EV *chart 66-67*; *Pteranodon*, EV *90, 130, 134*; skin, EV *96*

Puddingwife: UN *63, 66*

Puffballs: PL *98-99*

Pufferfish: UN *105*, 126, *127*; food chain of, UN *126-127*

Puffing up of porcupinefish: UN *121, 124-125*

Puffins: horned, EC *8*; tufted, EC *33*

Pumpkin: starch granules in, PL *11*

Pupae: IN *81*; butterflies, IN *35, 57, 78, 82-83, 115*; glacier midges, IN *34*; ladybugs, IN *113*; mosquitoes, IN *47*

Purple hairstreak butterflies: IN *74*

Purse web spiders: IN *94*

Pushrods in platypus bill: AN *18*

Pygmy marsupial frog: UN *90*

Pyrotherium (extinct mammal): EV *120*

Pyrrhulinas: reproduction by, UN *75*

Pythons: African, EC *10*; Indian, EC *11*

Q

Quadruplets: HU *23*

Quagga: EV *144*

Queen insects: IN *129*; ants, AN 125, *126, 127*, IN *99*; bees, AN 125, *130, 131*, IN *70-71, 131, 132-133*; termites, IN *128, 141, 142, 143*

Queen snakes: favorite prey of, AN *graph* 15

Queen substance: honeybees', IN *132*

Quetzalcoatlus (pterodactyl): EV 90, *91*

R

Rabbitfish: UN *123*

Rabbits: Ryukyu, EV *140*

Raccoons: EC *139*

Race and skin color: HU *51*

Radiation: mutation by, PL *138-139*

Radicle: PL *9*; and germination, PL *12*

| Animal Behavior **AN** | Computer Age **CO** | Ecology **EC** | Evolution of Life **EV** | Geography **GE** | Human Body **HU** | Insects & Spiders **IN** | Machines & Inventions **MA** |

Radishes: white, root of, PL *15*

Radius and ulna: HU *33, 39*

Radula teeth: cone shell's, UN *118,* 119

Ragweed: EC *98-99;* pollen, HU *134*

Rain: acid, EC *74-75;* and beginnings of life, EV *30-31;* on desert species, effects of, EC *92-93;* on young Earth, EV *28-29*

Rain forests: EC *4, 5, 24-25, 28-29, map* 66; birds, EC *28-29, 60-61;* destruction of, EC *72-73;* epiphytes, EC *68-69;* Krakatoa, EC *121;* layers, EC *66-67,* 69; primates, EC *28, 70-71;* tree species, EC *64-65*

Rams: bighorn sheep, AN *106-107*

Raphe nuclei: HU *123;* location of, HU *123*

Rapid eye movement (REM) sleep: HU 122, *chart* 122, 123, *124-125*

Ratels: EC *10,* 11

Ratfish: UN *73*

Rattlesnakes: AN *34-35;* rattles, AN *62-63*

Rays: eye, UN *45;* manta, AN *25,* UN *107;* stingray, UN *123*

Razorbills: EC *8*

Receptacle tissue in fruits: PL *67, 68, 69*

Receptor cells: olfactory, HU 116, *117;* in skin, HU *98-99, 100*

Recessive and dominant traits: EV *13, 14*

Rectum: HU *91*

Red abalone: single-shelled, UN *98*

Red algae: PL *105*

Red ants: IN *127*

Red blood cells: HU *6, 64, 65;* agglutination, HU *70-71;* development, HU *66-67;* and gas exchange, HU *56,* 57, 65; hemoglobin in, HU 64, 72, *73;* role of, HU *65*

Red-clawed crabs: larvae released by, AN *123*

Red gland in fish: function of, UN *13*

Red muscles and body heat: UN *14, 15*

Red pines: PL *49;* bark, PL *27*

Red scale: IN *91*

Red-spotted copeinas: reproduction by, UN *75*

Red-tailed shrike eggs: AN *114*

Redwoods: PL *122*

Red wrasses and blue wrasses: UN *63, 66*

Reflex: saliva secretion as, HU *78, 79*

Reflex actions: HU *102-103*

Refraction of light: by water, archerfish's correction for, UN *109*

Regal moths: AN *53*

Regeneration of body parts: AN 80, *81*

Regeneration of skin cells: HU *48-49*

Reindeer: EC *50-51*

Remoras and hosts: AN *24-25*

REM (rapid eye movement) sleep: HU 122, *chart* 122, 123, *124-125*

Renal arteries and veins: HU *94, 95*

Reproduction by animals: amphibians, UN *62-63, 88-89, 90-91;* aquatic animals, UN 62-63; coloration of male fish and, UN *64-65;* crabs, UN *37, 38-39, 96-97;* dinosaurs, EV *78-79;* golden eagles, EC *127;* guppies, UN *64-65;* ichthyosaurs, EV 93; insects, parenting behavior, IN *74-75, 76-77, 130-131;* mollusks, UN *98-99;* population control, EC *108-109;* seals, UN *92-93;* sex changes among fish species, UN *62-63, 66-67, 68-69;* sexual parasites, UN *70-71;* sharks, UN *76-77;* sunfish, UN *72-73, 88-89;* turtles, EC *30-31;* whales, gray, migration of, UN *94-95.* *See also* Eggs and egg laying; Life cycles; Mating, courtship and; Nests; Parenting

Reproduction by humans: HU 4; brain development, HU *24-25;* DNA in, HU *4-5, 10-11;* growth, fetal, HU *18-19;* multiple births, HU *22-23;* nourishment, fetal, HU *20-21. See also* Egg and sperm, human

Reproduction by plants: animals and, EC *96-97, 114-115, 122-123;* coconut palms, EC *22-23;* diatoms, PL *101;* mangroves, EC *34;* vegetative, PL *62, 90-91, 134-135, 140-141, 143. See also* Flowers and flowering plants; Fruits; Spore-bearing plants

Reptiles: EV *58, 59, 62-63;* alligators, AN *110-111,* EC *138;* cold-climate, EC *12-13;* crocodiles, swimming style of, UN *18-19;* family tree, EV *charts* 63-67; flying, EV *63, 90-91, 96, 130, 134;* iguanas, EV *12, 13, 80;* jawbones, EV *135;* lizards, AN *4-5, 15, 32-33, 72-73, 80-81,* EC *6, 13, 88, 91, 113, 121,* EV *12, 13, 80, 94-95;* mammal-like, EV *59, 62, 63, 64-65, 73;* marine, prehistoric, EV *62, 92-93, 94-95, 96, 136-137;* snakes, AN *14-15, 34-35, 47, 62-63, 85, 117,* EC *10, 11, 12-13, 120, 125, 127,* IN *113,* 118, *119;* snapping turtle, alligator, UN *110-111;* temperature-control methods, EV *65, 80, 81, 84-85;* thecodonts, EV *62, 66-67;* tortoises, EV *12, 133, 140;* turtles, AN *25,* EC *6-7, 29, 30-31, 91, 113, 119, 139*

Requiem sharks: eye, UN *44;* with fetus, UN *76-77*

Respiration by animals: *See* Breathing

Respiration by humans: HU 52, *54-59;* breathing process, HU *54-55;* carbon monoxide's interference with, HU *72-73;* gas exchange, HU *56-57, 65;* and voice, HU *58-59*

Respiration by plants: PL *38, 39*

Respiratory diseases: HU *140-141*

Respiratory roots: EC 25, 34, *35*

Respiratory system of humans: HU 52, *54-59*

Respiratory system of insects: IN *10-11*

Rete mirabile in fish: UN *14-15*

Retina, fish's: UN *49,* 51

Retina, human: cells, HU *108-109;* and vision defects, HU *110-111*

Retractor lentis muscle: fish's use of, UN *49*

Rhamphorhynchoids: EV 90

Rhinoceros: black, EC *82-83,* 84; Javan, EC *113;* white, EC *85;* woolly, EV *129*

Rhinoceros beetle: EC *110, 111,* IN *21, 60, 61*

Rhizocarpon (lichen): PL *106-107*

Rhizoids: of lichens, PL *106;* of mosses, PL 108

Rhizomes: PL *91*

Rhododendrons: EC *52-53,* 54; leaves of, PL *43*

Rhyniaceae: EV *52*

Rhyniella (extinct insect): EV *50-51*

Ribonucleic acid: *See* RNA

Ribosomes: PL *6,* 7

Ribs, human: and breathing, HU *54*

Rice: PL *67;* short, breeding, PL *139*

Rings in tree trunk: PL *18-19, 24-25*

River dolphins: UN *58-59*

RNA (ribonucleic acid): and DNA (deoxyribonucleic acid), EV 30, *36*

Robber flies: bumblebees mimicked by, AN *54-55*

Rock ptarmigans: seasonal color changes in, AN *58-59*

Rodents: African, EC *21, 89;* desert, EC 89, *90;* after forest fire, EC *136, 137;* giant, South American, EC *20;* lemmings, EC *48, 102-103;* seed dispersal by, EC *123*

Rods and cones: HU *108-109*

Root grafting: PL *135*

Root hairs: PL *15,* 20

Root pressure: PL *21*

Roots: PL *18-19;* aboveground, kinds of, PL *22-23;* air, plants with, EC *68-69;* Alpine perennials, EC *57;* desert plants, EC *94, 95;* ferns vs. mosses, PL *108;* in germination, PL *12-13;* growth of, PL *14-15;* mangrove, EC *25, 34-35,* PL *80, 81;* mistletoe, PL *23, 83;* modifications of, PL *29;* mycorrhiza, EC *134;* rain forest trees, EC *24, 64-65;* water transportation from, PL *20, 21, 40-41*

Roses: PL *28-29*

Rotifers: EC *36,* 40

Round dance: honeybees', IN *135*

Round herring: mouth of, UN *106*

Rowan seeds: spreading of, PL *78-79*

Royal chambers: of termites, IN *141, 142, 143*

Ruffini endings: HU *98*

Planet Earth
PE

Plant Life
PL

Physical Forces
PH

Structure of Matter
ST

Space & Planets
SP

Transportation
TR

Underwater World
UN

Weather & Climate
WE

Runners: reproduction by, PL *91*
Running spiders: courtship, AN *90*
Ryegrass: Italian, PL *63*

S

Saber-toothed blennies: cleaner wrasses vs., UN *134, 135*
Saber-toothed cats: EV *107, 121*
Saddleback caterpillars: Oriental, IN *121*
Saddle joint: HU *38*
Saguaro cacti: EC *86, 87,* PL *111, 113;* owls in, EC *89*
Salamanders: as cave dwellers, EC *28, 42*
Salivary glands: HU *78-79, 118*
Salmon: AN *120;* baby, UN *12, 82;* chum, UN *11;* navigation methods, AN *120-121;* reproduction, UN *82-83;* swim bladder type, UN *12*
Salt glands: EC *34*
Saltwater fish vs. freshwater fish: drinking by, UN *10-11*
Salvia flowers: PL *53*
Sand gobies: AN *86*
Sand lizards: EC *88*
Sand shark: embryonic, UN *77*
Saprophytes: defined, PL *57, 96*
Saprophytic chain: defined, PL *126*
Sarcomeres: HU *36*
Sarcopterygians: amphibian evolution from, EV *56-57*
Sardines: UN *102, 106-107*
Sarracenia pitcher plants: PL *47*
Satin bowerbirds: AN *100-101*
Saurischians: *See* Lizard-hipped dinosaurs
Sauropods: EV *83; Diplodocus,* EV *84-85*
Savannas: EC *76;* animals of, EC *29, 80-85*
Sawflies: eggs guarded by, IN *75*
Saw-scaled vipers: AN *62*
Scale ants: food gathering by, IN *42*
Scale insects: biological control of, IN *90, 91*
Scales of fish: UN *7*
Scallops: escape from starfish by, UN *138*
Scaphonyx (early reptile): EV *63*
Scarab beetles: in feeding order, EC *110, 111;* pollination by, EC *115*
Scavenger beetles: EC *43*
Scavengers: fungi as, EC *133;* ocean, EC *128-129*
Schools of fish: AN *74-75*
Scopura langa (aquatic insect): IN *34*
Scorpionfish: UN *72;* lionfish, UN *120-121, 122;* as scavengers, EC *128, 129*
Scorpionflies: mating, IN *66-67;* snow, IN *34*
Scorpions: EC *88;* fossils, EV *51,* maternal care in, IN *75, 76;* vinegarroon, IN *123*
Scrub jays: cooperative breeding, AN *116-117*

Sea anemones: AN *22-23, 48-49,* UN *34;* and clown fish, AN *70-71,* UN *144;* crab living in, UN *39;* and hermit crabs, AN *78-79*
Sea bass: black, EC *141;* swim bladder type, UN *13*
Seabirds: EC *29, 32-33;* Arctic and Antarctic, EC *8-9, 45, 46, 47, 49;* Galápagos, EC *6, 7;* oil spills and, EC *143*
Sea bream: UN *21;* eye, UN *45;* swim bladder type, UN *13*
Sea cows: Steller's, EV *144*
Sea cucumbers: pearlfish's relationship with, UN *144*
Sea fan: PL *105*
Sea horses: leafy sea dragon, UN *105;* reproduction, father's role in, UN *78*
Sea lettuce: PL *102-103;* spores, PL *95, 102*
Sea lilies: EV *42*
Sea lions: Galápagos, EC *7*
Seals: Antarctic, EC *46-47, 49;* reproduction by, UN *92-93*
Sea otters: AN *47,* EC *130-131, 142*
Sea pens: fossils suggesting, EV *38*
Sea scorpions: EV *44-45;* fossil of, EV *50*
Sea squirts: EV *47*
Sea turtles: AN *25*
Sea urchins: EC *46;* cardinalfish among spines of, UN *144;* crab parasite on, UN *39;* in food chain, EC *130;* starfish attack repelled by, UN *139*
Seaweed: PL *95, 102-103, 104-105;* crabs' use of, for camouflage, UN *136*
Sebaceous glands: HU *44, 47*
Sedum: PL *90-91;* stomas, PL *38*
Seed-bearing plants: EV *102-103*
Seed beetles: EC *109*
Seed ferns: Paleozoic, EV *53*
Seeds: PL *64-65;* animals dispersing, EC *96-97, 122-123,* PL *65, 74, 75, 77, 78-79, 82;* climate and, EC *56;* coconuts, EC *22-23;* dandelion, PL *67, 72-73;* development of, on tree, PL *80-81;* after fires, EC *79;* germination of, PL *8, 12-13, 79, 80, 81, 88, 95;* making of, PL *8-9, 66;* mangrove, EC *34;* mistletoe, spreading of, PL *82-83;* nuts, PL *65, 77;* in pine cones, PL *88-89;* polyploidic breeding, PL *138-139;* from popping fruits, PL *76-77; Rafflesia,* PL *56;* recolonization, EC *120;* simple vs. complex fruits, PL *66, 67;* vs. spores, PL *94-95;* with sticking properties, PL *74-75;* storage of, PL *143;* sunflower, PL *70;* wind-borne, PL *72-73, 88*
Segmented worms: ancestors, possible, EV *38, 39;* early stages of, EV *132*
Self-protection: *See* Defenses of animals
Semicircle angelfish: UN *132*

Semicircular canal of fish: UN *52;* sharks, UN *55*
Semicircular canal of humans: HU *114-115*
Seminal vesicles: HU *12*
Sense organs, human: ear, HU *112-115;* eyes, HU *106-111;* nose, HU *116-117;* skin as, HU *98-99, 100;* tongue, HU *99, 118-119*
Senses of animals: *See individual senses*
Sensitization of mast cells: HU 134, *135*
Sensory and motor cortex of brain: HU *105*
Sensory nerves: HU *100-101, 102-103*
Sensory pits and hairs: flies, AN *8, 9*
Sensory speech field (Wernicke's area): HU *120,* 121
Sequoias: PL *122-123*
Serotonin: and sleep, HU 123
Sex changes in fish: UN *62-63, 66-67, 68-69*
Sexes of flowers, separate: PL *58-59;* corn, PL *84-85;* fig, PL *68, 69;* mistletoe, PL *83*
Sex pheromones: ants, IN *53;* moths, AN *94-95,* IN *27*
Sexual parasites: UN *70-71*
Seymouria (reptile ancestor): EV *58*
Shamrock spiders: AN *26*
Sharks: early development of, EV *132-133;* eyes, UN *44, 54;* goblin, UN *22-23;* mako, shortfin, UN *15;* Paleozoic, EV *49;* as predators, UN *54-55, 103, 104, 105;* and remoras, as hosts, AN *24-25;* reproduction, UN *76-77*
Sheep: bighorn, AN *106-107*
Sheet webs: spider's, IN *38*
Shellfish: early stages of, EV *132;* extinct, EV *94-95, 98-99;* living fossils, EV *140. See also* Crustaceans; Mollusks
Shepherd's-purse: PL *8, 67*
Shield lichen: PL *107*
Shiitake mushrooms: PL *95;* spores, PL *99*
Shoots: bamboo, PL *32-33, 91;* growth of, PL *16*
Shoot-tip culture: PL *140-141*
Shortfin mako shark: UN *15*
Shrikes: eggs, AN *114*
Shrimp: brine, EC *92-93;* cave, EC *41, 42;* cleaner, AN *22-23;* early stages of, EV *132;* gobies and, AN *86-87;* starfish attacked by, UN *139*
Siever blue butterfly: IN *78*
Sight: *See* Vision
Silk: for bagworm bags, IN *102;* glowworm threads, IN *50-51;* spider webs, IN *36-37, 38-39, 94-95*
Silkworm moths: AN *51,* IN *85, 119;* antennae, IN *26, 32;* larvae, eyespots on, IN *113, 118-119;* mating, AN *94-95*
Silurian period: fish from, EV *46, 47;* fossils from, EV *50, 51*

| Animal Behavior **AN** | Computer Age **CO** | Ecology **EC** | Evolution of Life **EV** | Geography **GE** | Human Body **HU** | Insects & Spiders **IN** | Machines & Inventions **MA** |

Silverfish: IN *6, 84*; metamorphosis, IN *80-81*

Simple metamorphosis: IN *80-81*

Sinoatrial node: HU *61*

Sinusoid capillaries: HU *63, 66-67*

Siphons: crabs' use of, UN *36, 37*

Sixbar angelfish: UN *132*

Six-starred fishing spiders: AN *27*

Skates: UN *104*

Skeletal types of fish: UN *6*

Skeletons: birds, EV *71, 101*; Cenozoic mammals, EV *104-105*; dinosaurs, EV *60-61, 71, 74, 88*; human, HU *30, 32*; mammal-like reptile, EV *64. See also* Bones

Skin, fish's: UN *7*

Skin, human: HU *6, 30-31*; colors of, HU *50-51*; cooling of, HU *42-43*; goose bumps on, HU *44-45*; hair, HU *44-45, 46, 47, 99*; healing of, HU *48-49*; nails, HU *46*; as sensory organ, HU *98-99, 100*

Skin, prehistoric animals': EV *96-97*

Skinks: as caterpillar enemy, IN *120-121*; five-lined, AN *80, 81*

Skipjack tuna: UN *15*

Skippers: antennae of, IN *32*

Skuas: brown, AN *113*

Skulls: *Cynognathus*, EV *73*; dinosaurs, EV *76, 77, 87, 88*; elephants, EV *110*; fish, EV *48, 49*; hominids, EV *126*; human, HU *32*; human, bone growth in, HU *35*; whales, EV *113*

Slavemakers (ants): IN *138*

Sleep: HU *122-123*; and dreams, HU *124-125*

Sleep deprivation: results of, HU *123*

Slender sweeper: UN *24*

Slickhead: UN *22*

Slime molds: PL *96, 97*

Sloths: EC *62-63*; giant, extinct, EC *20*

Small intestine: HU *88-89*; surface of, HU *77, 88-89*; villi, HU *6, 88*

Smell, sense of, animals': carp, UN *45, 46-47*; eels, UN *47*; fish, UN *46-47*; flies, AN *8, 9*; insect antennae for, IN *26-27*; salmon's use of, AN *120*; sharks, UN *55*; snakes' use of, AN *14-15*

Smell, sense of, human: HU *116-117*

Smilodon (saber-toothed cat): EV *121*

Smoky moths: IN *32*

Smolt: UN *83*

Smoothhead: bighead, UN *22-23*

Smooth muscle: HU *7, 60*; large intestine, HU *90*

Snails: EC *46, 139*; as cone shell's prey, UN *119*; mud, UN *98*; scavengers, EC *128-129*

Snakes: bird scaring, AN *117*; blind, EC *120*; caterpillars mimicking, IN *113*, 118, *119*; chimpanzee probing, AN *47*; defenses, AN *62-63, 85*; eagle's prey, EC *125, 127*; garter, EC *12-13*; hog-nose, AN *85*; pythons, EC *10-11*; rattlesnakes, AN *34-35, 62-63*; tongues, odor detection with, AN *14-15*

Snapping shrimps: AN *86-87*

Snapping turtles: alligator, UN *110-111*

Snipe eel: Atlantic, UN *112*

Snout beetles: bluffing, AN *85*

Snow scorpionflies: IN *34*

Snowshoe hares: seasonal color changes in, AN *58-59*

Soapfishes: UN *126*

Social behavior, animals': AN 124-144; ants, AN *124-127*, IN *138-139*; bees, AN 125, *128-131*, IN *130-131*; birds in flight, AN *132-137*; fish in schools, AN *74-75*; lions in prides, AN *138-139*; primates, AN *124-125, 140-144*; wolves in packs, AN *44-45*

Social insects: IN 128-129; family behavior, vs. other insects', IN *130-131*; soldier aphids, IN *144*; termites as, IN *128-129, 140-141, 142-143. See also* Wasps

Soft palate: during swallowing, HU *80-81*

Soil: animals in, EC *36-37*, PL *110-111, 127*; horizons, EC *37*

Soldier ants: AN *126, 127*

Soldier aphids: IN *144*

Soldier termites: IN *140, 141, 143*

Solidago: PL *73*

Sonar: bats' use of, AN *42-43*; dolphins' use of, UN *58-59*, 115

Songs: birds', AN 98, 99; crickets', AN 96-97

Sooty terns: EC *32*

Sordes (pterosaur): EV *96*

Sorrel, wood: PL *77*; photonasty in, PL *45*

Sound: barn owl's hunting by, AN 38, *39*; human ears' detection of, HU *112-113*

Sound organs of insects: and sound production, IN *28-29*

South America: Africanized honeybees, spread of, IN *map* 137; Aztec ants, IN *98-99*; butterflies, IN *30, 118, 121*; discus, UN *86-87*; dolphins, UN *59, 114-115*; electric eels, UN *19, 57*; extinct animals of, EV *107, 120-121*; lungfish, UN *31*; marsupial frog, pygmy, UN *90*; mud snail, giant, UN *98*; splashing tetra, UN *74-75*

Southern toads: AN *54-55*

Sow bugs (pill bugs): EC *36, 37*; evolutionary path, IN *6*; parenting behavior, IN *76-77*; spider's capture of, AN *26*

Sow thistles: PL *73*

Soybeans: PL *13, 54, 67*

Sparrow moth caterpillars: IN *119*

Spawning: salmon, UN 82, 83. *See also* Eggs and egg laying; Mating, courtship and

Species: EV 4-5; adaptation, EV 5, *20-21*; adaptive radiation, EV *24-25*, 138; branching, EV *4-5, 6-7*; breeds and breeding, EV *10-11, 14, 18-19*; classification of, EV *6*; defining characteristic of, EV *10-11*; differentiation, EV *12, 22-23*; of Galápagos, EV *12-13, 80*; mutations in, EV *14-15, 16-17, 18*; natural selection, EV 12, *16-17*; number of, EV *8-9*; subspecies of, EV *10. See also* Evolution

Spectacled spiders: AN *26*

Speech areas of brain: HU *120*, 121

Speech production, human: HU 58

Sperm, fertilization in plants by: PL *8, 66*; in algae, PL *103*; in ferns and mosses, PL *109*

Sperm, human: *See* Egg and sperm, human

Sperm ducts: HU *12*

Sperm webs: male spider's, AN *90-91*

Sperm whales: AN *40-41*; diving by, UN *32-33*

Sperry, Roger: experiment by, HU *121*

Sphincter, anal: HU *91*

Spider crabs: use of camouflage by, UN *136*

Spiderfish: UN *113*

Spider monkeys: EC *71*

Spiders: EC *37, 120*; butterfly enemy, IN *115*; courtship, AN *90-91*; evolutionary path, IN *6*; and hunting wasps, IN *54-55, 111*; methods of catching prey, AN *26-27*; parenting behavior, IN *74, 75*; sensing prey, AN *28-29*; water spiders, IN *96-97*; as web spinners, IN *36-37, 38-39, 94-95*

Spider wasps: IN *54-55*

Spiderwort stoma: PL *38*

Spikelets, grass: PL *62*; on oats, PL *144*

Spinach: PL *136*; as long-day plant, PL 54

Spinal cord: HU *41, 101, 103*

Spinal ganglia: HU *101, 103*

Spinal reflexes: HU *102-103*

Spindle tree: PL *78*

Spine, human: HU *40-41*

Spines, creatures with: poison fish, UN *120-121, 122-123*; porcupinefish, UN *121, 124-125*; sea urchins, UN *39, 139, 144. See also* Vertebrates

Spines, on plants: PL *28*; of cacti, PL *112, 113*

Spinner dolphins: UN *115*

Spinnerets: spiders', IN 94, *95*

Spiny dogfish fetus: UN *76*

Spiny hatchetfish: UN *23*

Spiracles: IN *10, 11*

Spittlebugs: IN *100-101*

Planet Earth
PE

Plant Life
PL

Physical Forces
PH

Structure of Matter
ST

Space & Planets
SP

Transportation
TR

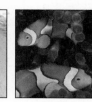
Underwater World
UN

Weather & Climate
WE

Splashing tetras: reproduction by, UN *74-75*

Spleen: role of, HU *67*

Split-brain experiment: HU *121*

Sponge gourds: leaf growth, PL *17*; root pressure, PL *21*

Sponges: ammonite in, EV *99*; evolution of, EV *6*; flagellate cells, EV *38*; repair of, UN *101*; reproduction by, UN *100-101*

Spongy tissue: PL *39, 40, 41*

Spoonbills: roseate, EC *138*

Spore-bearing plants: PL *92-109*; ascocarps (fruiting bodies), PL *97, 106*; in evolution, PL *93, 94*; ferns, PL *95, 108-109*; molds as, PL *96-97*; mosses as, PL *95, 108-109*; mushrooms as, PL *95, 99*; seaweed as, PL *95, 102-103*; vs. seed plants, PL *94-95*

Spores: mushroom, EC *135*

Sporophytes: *See* Spore-bearing plants

Spotted notothens: UN *16-17*

Spriggina (extinct wormlike animal): EV *39*

Springboks: AN *60-61*

Springtails: EC *36*

Spring-tide breeders: AN *122-123*

Spring trap: spider's, IN *39*

Spruce needles and buds: EC *24*

Spy hopping by gray whales: UN *94*

Squash: male and female flowers of, PL *58-59*

Squid: UN *113*; flying, AN *82-83*; giant, AN *40-41*; ink, use of, UN *140-141*; markings, changing of, UN *142-143*; sperm whale diving for, UN *33*

Squirrel monkeys: EC *70, 71*

Squirrels: seed dispersal by, EC *123*

Squirrels, flying: AN *73*; as owl's prey, AN *39*

Squirting cucumbers: PL *77*

Stag beetles: EC *111*

Stamens: PL *51, 52-53, 58, 59, 62*; and pistils, EV *103*

Starch grains: PL *7, 11*

Starfish: EC *47*; anatomy, UN *138*; in food chain, UN *126-127*; as predators, UN *138-139*; as scavengers, EC *128*

Starlings: sun, navigation by, AN *134*

Stars: birds' navigation by, AN *136-137*

Statocysts (static organs): UN *43*

Stegoceras (dinosaur): EV *75*

Stegodon (elephant ancestor): EV *110-111*

Stegosaurus (dinosaur): EV *81*; skeleton, EV *74*

Stele: PL *15*

Stem cells: HU *128*

Stems: PL *19*; bamboo, PL *32-33*; bark on, trees', PL *25, 26-27*; big tree trunks, PL *116, 117, 122-123*; cacti, PL *112, 113*; ferns vs. mosses, PL *108*; growth of, PL *16*, 17; growth rings, trees', PL *18-19, 24-25*; hypocotyl, PL *12-13*; layers of, PL *20*; leaf arrangement on, PL *36-37*; modifications of, PL *28, 29, 30-31*; of parasite and host, PL *57*; receptacle tissue in fruits, PL *67, 68, 69*; runners, PL *91*; underground, reproduction by, PL *62, 91*; water transportation through, PL *20-21, 40-41*

Stenodictya (early flying insect): EV *54*

Stenopterygius (ichthyosaur): EV *92*

Steppes: EC *76*

Stereoscopic vision: HU *106-107*

Stick insects: AN *52, 80*

Stickleback: nest building by, UN *79*

Stick-mimicking mantis: AN *51*

Stilt roots: EC *35, 64*

Stinging cells, sea anemones, AN *48*

Stinging insects: ants, IN *126, 127*; bees, IN *124, 125, 137*; and mimics, AN *54-55*; wasps, IN *54, 124, 125*

Stingray: UN *123*

Stink bugs: AN *69*, IN *123*; egg laying, IN *130*; mating, IN *66*; warning coloration, IN *112, 120*

Stomach, human: HU *82-83*; lining of, HU *77, 82-83*

Stomas: PL *20, 21, 38-39, 40*; cactus, PL *113*; pine needles, PL *49*

Stonecrop (sedum): PL *90-91*; stomas, PL *38*

Stonefish: UN *123*

Stone plants: PL *110, 114-115*

Storage grains: PL *7, 11*

Stotting: AN 60, *61*

Strained back: HU *40-41*

Stranglers (plants): EC *65*

Strawberries: anther culture, PL *140*; fruit, PL *67*; plants with runners, PL *91*

Streptomyces antibiotics: PL *132, 133*

Striated muscle: *See* Muscles of humans

Striped droneflies: AN *54*

Striped shrimp: AN *87*

Stromatolites: EV *26-27, 34-35*

Struthiomimus (dinosaur): EV *74*

Styrocosaurus (dinosaur): EV *89*

Sublingual glands: HU *78*

Submaxillary glands: HU *78, 79*

Submission in wolves: AN *45*

Succession of plants: PL *128-129*

Sucker: remora's, AN *25*

Sugar: blood (glucose), HU *142, 143*

Sulfur butterflies, wing coloration of: IN *30*

Sulfur-eating bacteria: UN *35*

Sun: birds' navigation by, AN *134, 135*; salmon's navigation by, AN *121*; ultraviolet light from, HU 50, *51*

Sunbirds, malachite: as pollinators, EC *114*

Sundew plants: EC *116-117*; PL *34-35, 47*

Sunfish: UN *72-73*; metamorphosis, UN *88-89*

Sunflowers: PL *70-71*; and phyllotaxis, PL *36-37*

Sunlight: *See* Light

Suppressor T cells: HU *128, 129*

Surf clam: starfish attack escaped by, UN *139*

Surffish: UN *87*

Surfperch: body fluids of, UN *chart* 16

Surinam toads: UN *91*

Swallowing: HU *80-81*

Swallows: and swifts, convergence of, EV *137*

Swallowtail butterflies: antennae, IN *32*; atypical behavior, IN *32, 33*; caterpillar with scent gland, IN *123*; egg laying, IN *130*; emergence of, from chrysalis, IN *83*; foot structure, IN *21*; metamorphosis, IN *56-57*; as pollinators, EC *114*, PL *50, 53*; wing coloration, IN *30, 31, 83*

Swans in flight: AN *133*

Swarming: honeybees, IN *133, 135*; locusts, IN *86-87*

Sweat: HU *42-43*

Sweeper: slender, UN *24*

Sweet peas: PL *55*

Sweet potatoes: PL *29*; grafting onto, PL *135*

Swell shark: emergence of, from egg case, UN *76*

Swifts: and swallows, convergence of, EV *137*

Swim bladder: UN *12-13*; for hearing, UN *52, 53*; and pressure, UN 23

Swimming styles: UN *4-5, 18-19, 20-21*; dance of cleaner wrasse, UN *134, 135*; jellyfish, UN *4-5, 42-43*; on side, by river dolphins, UN *58*

Swordfish: EV *136*; swimming style of, UN *20-21*

Sycamore trees: PL *26-27*

Symbiosis: ants and aphids, AN *12-13*; ants and butterflies, IN *78-79*; ants and plants, IN *98-99*; cleaner wrasses and hosts, UN *120, 134-135*; crabs and hosts, UN *38-39*; cuckoo catfish and cichlids, UN *84-85*; exploitation of hosts, UN *144*; remoras and sharks, AN *24-25*; sea anemones and fish, AN *22-23, 70-71*; sea anemones and hermit crabs, AN *78-79*; sexual parasites, UN *70-71*; shrimp and fish, AN *22-23, 86-87*

Symphylids: EC *37*

Synapses: HU *100-101*

Synapsids (mammal-like reptiles): EV *59, 62, 63, 64-65, 73*

T

Tadpoles: EC *93*, UN *88-89, 90, 91*

Taenophyllum root: PL *29*

Taiga (boreal forest): EC *4, 24, 29*

Tails: fish's use of, in swimming, UN *18-19, 20-21*; lizards, breaking of, AN *80-81*; rattlesnakes, rattles in, AN *62, 63*

Tamarins: lion, EC *71*

Tanagers: scarlet, EC *61*

Tanystropheus (early reptile): EV *62*

Tapirs: EC *14-15*

Tasmanian wolves: EV *138, 144*

Taste, sense of, aquatic animals': UN *46*; in gurnard, UN *47*

Taste, sense of, human: and taste buds, HU *118-119*

Taste buds, animals': in fish's barbels, AN *20*; flies, AN 8, *9*

Taste buds, human: HU *118-119*

Taxis: positive, negative, AN *6*

T cells (T lymphocytes): HU *128, 129, 131*; and AIDS virus, HU *136-137*

Teeth of animals: aquatic animals, adaptations of, for feeding, UN *104, 105*; birds with, EV *100, 101*; *Desmostylus*, EV 118, *119*; dinosaurs, EV *76, 77*; *Pterodaustro*, EV *91*; radula, cone shell's, UN *118*, 119; whales, EV *113*

Teeth of humans: development of, HU *26-27, 35*

Temperate coniferous forests: acid rain and, EC *74-75*

Temperate deciduous forests: EC *5, 25*

Temperate rain forests: EC *4, 25*

Temperature: of fish, circulatory system and, UN *14-15*; of spermaceti oil, control of, UN *33*; of water, and fish's body fluids, UN 16, *chart 16*

Tendrils: PL *29*; cucumber, coiling of, PL *30-31*

Tenontosaurus (dinosaur): EV *74-75*

Termites: ants attacking, IN *140, 141*; chimpanzee collecting, AN *47*; colonies, IN *128-129, 140-141*; evolutionary path, IN *7*; fungus-growing, mounds of, IN *142-143*; poisonous adhesive, IN *123*; wood digestion, IN *48-49*

Terns: EC *32*; Antarctic, EC *47*; Arctic, AN *135*

Territories: bowerbirds' creation of, AN *100-101*; moles', AN *104-105*; singing to defend, AN 96, 97, *98, 99*

Testicles, human (testes): HU *12, 75*

Test-tube babies: *See* In vitro fertilization

Test-tube cultivation: PL *140-141, 143*

Tetraploid plants: PL *139*

Tetras: Congo, UN *64*; splashing, reproduc-

tion by, UN *74-75*

Thalamus: nerve impulses to, HU *101*

Thallus lichens: PL *107*

Thecodonts: EV *66-67*; *Euparkeria*, EV *62, 66*

Thelodus (extinct fish): EV *47*

Theory of evolution: EV *12-13*

Theosodon (extinct mammal): EV *120*

Therapsids: EV *chart 65*

Thermal perspiration: HU *42-43*

Thick-billed murres: EC *33*

Thistles: PL *74*; beetles on, EC *108-109*

Thoatherium (extinct mammal): EV *121*

Thorns: PL *28*; parts analogous to, PL *28, 29*

Throat, human: structure of, HU *80*

Thrombi: HU *144*

Thylacosmilus (extinct mammal): EV *107, 120*

Thylakoids: PL *10-11*

Thymus gland: HU *75*

Thyroid gland: HU *75*

Tickseed: EC *122*, PL *75*

Tides, ocean: and breeding, AN *122-123*; effect of, on barnacles, UN *40*

Tides, spring: breeding during, AN *122-123*

Tiger long-horned beetles: AN *55*

Tiger moths: IN *33, 88*; larvae, IN *88-89*

Tiger swallowtail butterflies: wing coloration of, IN *30*

Tilapias: diadromous fish, UN *11*; reproduction, UN *79*

Tillandsia cyanea (plant): EC *94*

Timberline: EC *54-55*, PL *120*

Tissue culture: PL *140-141, 143*

Tissues, human: kinds of, HU *6, 7*

T lymphocytes (T cells): HU *128, 129, 131*; and AIDS virus, HU *136-137*

Toads: Asian horned, AN *51, 52*; bee avoidance by, AN *54-55*; Carvalho's pipa, UN *91*; Darwin's, UN *91*; in food chain, EC *125*; midwife, European, UN *90*; spadefoot, life cycle of, EC *92-93*; Surinam, UN *91*; with young, UN *62-63, 90-91*

Toadstools: PL *92-93, 98-99*

Toenails and fingernails: HU *46*

Tomatoes: crossbred, PL *136, 142*

Tongues of animals: chameleons, AN *4-5, 32, 33*; snakes, AN *14, graph 15*; woodpeckers, AN *17*

Tongues of humans: and taste, HU *118-119*; and touch, HU *99*

Tool-using animals: AN *46-47*

Toothfish: Antarctic, UN *17*

Topi: EC *85*

Torosaurus (dinosaur): EV *89*

Tortoise ladybugs: IN *120*

Tortoises: EC *91*; early development of, EV

133; Galápagos, EC *6-7, 113, 119*; giant, EV *12, 140*

Tortoise shell wasps: IN *111*

Toucans: EC *28-29, 61*

Touch: mimosa's response to, PL 44, *45*

Touch, sense of, fish's: UN *45*

Touch, sense of, human: HU *98-99*

Touch-me-not: PL *76, 77*

Toxodon (extinct mammal): EV *120*

Toxorhynchites mosquito and larva: IN *47*

Trachea, human: HU 6, *7*, 54, *55*, 58; cutaway view, HU *59*; during swallowing, HU *80-81*

Trachea, insect's: IN 10, *11*

Tracheal gills: IN *10*

Tracheoles, insect's: IN 10, *11*

Trail pheromones: ants' use of, IN *42-43*

Transfusions: blood types and, HU *70-71*

Transpiration: PL *20, 21*

Transverse colon: HU *90-91*

Trapdoor spiders: AN *26*

Tree frogs: color changes in, AN *56-57*

Tree kangaroos: black, EC *17*

Tree mice: Congo, EC *21*

Tree rats: spiny, EC *20*

Trees: acacia, false, PL *28*; baobab, PL *116-117*; bark, PL *25, 26-27*; bottle tree, PL *117*; chestnut, PL *43, 59, 67, 77*; coconut palms, EC *22-23*; with colorful fruits, PL *78-79*; eucalyptus, PL *118-119, 122*; and fire, EC *78, 79, 136-137*; grafting, PL *134-135*; growth rings, PL *18-19, 24-25*; ice ages and, PL *120-121*; larches, PL *119*; largest, PL *122-123*; lichens on, PL *107*; mangroves, EC *25, 34-35*, PL *80-81*; needles, PL *43, 48-49*; oldest, PL *123*; palm, PL *86-87, 143*; parasites on, PL *23, 82-83*; roots, PL *18-19, 22, 23, 29*; seasonal changes, PL *34-35, 40-41, 42-43, 126*; seeds, PL *67, 73, 77, 79, 88-89, 94*; sequoias, PL *122-123*; succession of, PL *128*; water transportation through, PL *20-21, 40-41*. *See also* Forests

Trenches, ocean: life in, UN *34-35*

Triangle spiders: web of, IN *39*

Triassic period: birds, EV *68-69*; mammals, first, EV *65, 72-73*; reptiles, EV *62-63, 64-65, 66-67*

Triceratops (dinosaur): EV *89*; skeleton, EV *88*

Trichogramma wasps: IN *114*

Triconodonts: EV *72-73*

Trigodon (extinct mammal): EV *120*

Trilobites: EV *40-41, 42, 44-45*

Tritylodont reptiles: EV *65*

Trochophore larvae: oyster, UN *99*

Trogons: collared, EC *61*

Troödon (dinosaur): EV *80-81*

Planet Earth
PE

Plant Life
PL

Physical Forces
PH

Structure of Matter
ST

Space & Planets
SP

Transportation
TR

Underwater World
UN

Weather & Climate
WE

Trophoblast: HU *21*

Tropical rain forests: *See* Rain forests

Trout: mutations in, EV *14-15, 17*; swim bladder, type of, UN *12*

Trumpet trees: Aztec ants and, IN *98-99*

Trunkfish: UN *19, 126*

Tube feet, starfish's: UN *138*; attack on, UN *139*

Tubers: PL *91*

Tubeworms: UN *35*

Tulips: bulbs, PL *60-61, 91*

Tumors: HU *138-139*

Tuna: bluefin, UN *9, 14-15, 73*; body temperature, UN *chart 14*; circulatory system, UN *14-15*; skipjack, UN *15*; squid's defense against, UN *140-141*; swimming style, UN *18*

Tundra plants: ice ages and, PL *120-121*

Tundras: Alpine, EC *54, 55, 57*; Arctic, EC *28, 48*

Turtles: EC *29, 139*; gender, determinant of, EC *30-31*; sea, AN *25*; snapping, alligator, UN *110-111*; tortoises, EC *6-7, 91, 113, 119*

Tussock moths: IN *85*

Tuxedo guppy: UN *65*

Twins: HU *22-23*

Two-point discrimination test: HU *99*

Tympanic and vestibular canals, human: HU *113*

Tympanic membrane: crickets, AN *97*

Tympanic organ: moth's, IN *24*

Types A, B, AB, and O blood: HU *70-71*

Tyrannosaurus (dinosaur): EV *74, 77, 97*

U

Uintatherium (extinct mammal): EV *116-117*; skeleton, EV *104*

Ulna and radius: HU *33, 39*

Ultrasaurus (dinosaur): EV *75*

Ultraviolet radiation: solar, HU *50, 51*

Umbilical cord: blood vessels, HU *21*

Univalves: *See* Gastropods

Upper gill respirators: climbing perch's, UN *29*

Ureters and urethra: HU *12, 13, 94*

Urinary bladder: HU *12, 13, 94*

Urine and urine production: HU *94, 95*

Urochordates: EV *46-47*

Urocteid spider: web of, AN *29*

Uterus: HU *13, 17*; fetuses in, HU *18-23*; and in vitro fertilization, HU *28, 29*

V

Vacuoles: PL *6, 7*; paramecia, AN *7*

Valves, biological: in human veins, HU *63*

Vascular bundles: PL *20, 49, 113*

Vascular plants: first, EV *52, 53*

Vavilov, Nikolai: PL *142*

Vegetative reproduction: PL *90-91*; grafting, PL *134-135*; tissue culture, PL *140-141, 143*; underground stems, PL *62, 91*

Veins, human: HU *6, 62-63*; of fetus and mother, HU *20-21*; of liver, HU *86, 87*; renal, HU *94, 95*

Veliger larvae: oyster, UN *99*

Venom glands: ants', IN *126*

Venom sac and duct: stinger with, IN *125*

Ventricles: *See* Heart, human

Venus's-flytrap: EC *116*, PL *46*

Venus's girdle: UN *42*

Vertebrae, human: HU *33, 40-41*

Vertebrates: early development of, EV *132-133*; evolution of, EV *46-47*. *See also* Amphibians; Birds; Fish; Mammals; Reptiles

Vestibular and tympanic canals: HU *113*

V-formation: birds flying in, AN *132-133*

Vibration range of rattlesnakes: AN *34*

Villi: chorionic, HU *20*; small intestine, HU *6, 88*

Vinegarroon scorpion: IN *123*

Vines: ivy, roots of, PL *23, 29*; kudzu, PL *75*; *Nepenthes, PL 47*; tendrils, PL *29, 30-31*

Violets: fruit and seeds, PL *67, 77, 79*; self-pollinating, PL *69*

Vipers: saw-scaled, AN *62*

Viral diseases: AIDS, HU *136-137*; colds and flu, HU *140-141*; measles, HU *132-133*

Vision, aquatic animals': UN *44-45, 48-49*; in air, UN *45, 50-51*; octopuses', UN *44, 60-61*; sharks', UN *44, 54*

Vision, human: HU *110-111*; darkness adaptation, HU *108-109*; stereoscopic, HU *106-107*

Vision, insects': IN *22-23*; as butterfly mating stimulus, IN *58, 59*

Visual vs. optical axes in fish vs. humans: UN *48*

Vocal cords: and voice production, HU *58-59*

Voice: production of, HU *58-59*

Vultures: Egyptian, AN *47*

W

Waggle dance, honeybees': IN *134-135*

Wahoo: UN *15*

Waksman, Selman: PL *132*

Walcott, Charles Doolittle: EV *42*

Walking by insects: IN *12*; on ceiling, IN *20-21*; centipedes, IN *13*; ocelli's effect on, IN *22-23*; on water, IN *18-19*

Wallabies: EC *16, 17*

Warblers: cooperative breeding, AN *116*; eggs, AN *114*; mating, AN *98-99*

Warm-blooded animals: EV *81*; fish, vs. cold-blooded fish, UN *14-15*. *See also* Birds; Mammals

Warning coloration: IN *112-113, 120-121*

Warthogs: EC *84*

Washington grass: EC *26*

Wasps: EC *109*; for biological pest control, IN *90, 91*; as butterfly enemies, IN *114, 115*; in feeding order, EC *110, 111*; fig, pollination by, PL *68, 69*; hunting, and nests, IN *54-55, 92-93, 110-111*; stinging, IN *54, 124, 125*; warning coloration, IN *112, 120*; yellow jackets and mimics, AN *54, 55*

Water: drinking of, by fish, UN *10-11*; fish breathing out of, UN *28-29, 30-31, 36-37*; fish breathing under, UN *8-9, 36*; freezing, fish in, UN *16-17*; pressure of, surviving, UN *22-23*

Water beetles: IN *11*

Waterbucks: EC *85*

Water bugs: care of eggs by, IN *75*

Water chestnuts: EC *26, 27*

Water dwelling insects: breathing methods, IN *10, 11*; cold-adapted, IN *34*; dragonfly nymphs as, IN *10, 36-37, 44-45*; eggs, care of, IN *75*; mosquito larvae, IN *46-47*; nest building, IN *96-97*; walking methods, IN *18-19*

Water ferns: EC *26*

Water hyacinths: EC *26*

Water lilies: EC *27*, PL *119, 129*

Water measurer: IN *19*

Watermelons: grafting, PL *135*; seedless, PL *139*

Water plants: EC *26-27*, PL *129*; diatoms, PL *100-101*; roots of, PL *23*; seaweed, PL *95, 102-103, 104-105*; water lilies, PL *119, 129*

Water potential: PL *20, 21*

Water spiders: nest building by, IN *96-97*

Water striders: IN *18-19*

Water supply: desert species', EC *86, 87, 90-95*

Waxwings, Bohemian: fruit eaten by, PL *78-79*

Weberian ossicles: UN *52*

Webs, spider: IN *36-37, 38-39, 94-95*; and mating, AN *90-91*; methods of using, AN *26, 27*; sensing prey in, AN *28-29*

Webworms: IN *88-89*

Weddell seals: EC *49*

Weedfish: vision in, UN *51*

Weevils, leaf-rolling: nest building by, IN *104-105*

Wegener, Alfred: PL *119*

Weigela shrubs: EC *79*

Wernicke's area of brain: HU *120, 121*

Animal Behavior
AN

Computer Age
CO

Ecology
EC

Evolution of Life
EV

Geography
GE

Human Body
HU

Insects & Spiders
IN

Machines &
Inventions **MA**

Wetlands: EC *138-139, 140, map* 141

Whalefish: UN *22*

Whales: AN *40-41*; blue, EC *112*, UN *4-5, 107, 116-117*; communication by, UN *114-115*; evolution of, EV *112-113*; gray, migration of, UN *94-95*; as hunters, UN *33, 114*; sperm, UN *32-33*

Whale shark: UN *105*

Wheat: PL *55, 67, 144*

Whelks: UN *127*

White blood cells: HU *64, 65*; and AIDS virus, HU *136-137*; and allergies, HU *135*; development, HU *66-67*; immune system, HU *126, 128-129*; and lymphatic system, HU 130, *131*; measles and, HU *132, 133*; skin cuts and, HU *48, 49*

White-eyes: as pollinators, EC *114*

White pine: PL *49*

White-tailed deer: AN *61*

Willow ptarmigans: AN *50-51*

Window-leaf plant: PL *115*

Windpipe (trachea): HU *6, 7, 55, 58*; cutaway view, HU *59*; during swallowing, HU *80-81*

Wings, insect: IN *4-5*; absence of, IN *84-85*; bees', analyzing, IN *137*; coloration of, in butterflies, IN *30-31, 58, 83, 121*; defenses, IN *112-113, 116-117, 118, 119, 121*;

flying methods, IN *14-15*; in sound production, IN *28*

Wolf spiders: AN *27*; care of young by, IN *74*

Wolves: AN *44-45*, EV *138*; Tasmanian, EV *138, 144*

Wombats: common, EC *17*

Wood-eating insects: IN *48-49, 130*

Wood lice (pill bugs): EC *36*

Woodpecker finches: AN *47*

Woodpeckers: AN *16-17*

Wood sorrel: PL *77*; photonasty in, PL *45*

Woolly mammoths: EV *111, 128-129*; skeleton, EV *105*; skull, EV *110*

Woolly monkeys: EC *70*

Worker insects: ants, AN *126, 127*, IN *42-43, 85, 123, 126-127, 138-139, 140, 141*; bees, AN *128-129, 130, 131*, IN *26, 70-71, 128-129, 132, 133, 134-135*; termites, IN *140, 141, 142, 143*; wasps, nests made by, IN *92-93, 110-111*

Worms: EC *36*; ancestors, possible, EV *38, 39*; early stages of, EV *132*; flatworms, EC *41*, EV *39*; lugworms, AN *80*, UN *119, 126-127*; marine, EC *129*; as mole's prey, AN *105*; tubeworms, UN *35*

Wrasses: blue, UN *63, 66*; cleaner, UN *120, 134-135*; eye, UN *44*; red, UN *63, 66*

X

X and Y chromosomes: HU *15*

Xylem: in roots, PL *14, 15*; in stems and trunks, PL 19, *20, 24-25, 26, 27*

Y

Yangtze River dolphins: UN *59*

Yellow emperor: UN *126*

Yellowface angelfish: changes in markings on, UN *133*

Yellow jackets: IN *112;* and mimics, AN *55*; nests, IN *110*

Yellow pigment cells: tree frogs, AN *56, 57*

Yellowtail: UN *21*

Yellowtail ants: IN *127*

Yellow-tipped prominent moths: AN *53*

Z

Zebras: EC *80-81, 84-85*; extinct (quagga), EV *144*

Zelkova: bark of, PL *27*

Z lines: HU *36*

Zoea larvae: crab, UN *39, 96, 97*

Zosterophyllum (early plant): EV *52, 74*

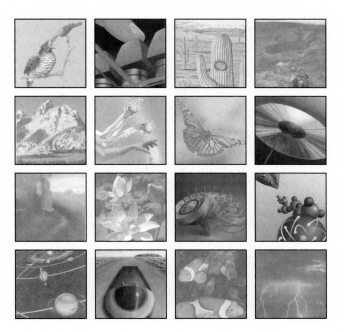

Physical Science

The five volumes of the physical science group—*Computer Age, Machines & Inventions, Physical Forces, Structure of Matter,* and *Transportation*—offer a fresh look at physical science. Unlike most textbooks, these books put science into a familiar context, from the physics of baseball to the chemical and mechanical processes that power a car. Detailed process diagrams and compelling cutaways, teamed with brief, easy-to-understand text, keep students engaged in and excited about science.

Physical Forces and *Structure of Matter* directly supplement any physical science curriculum. Between them, they cover a range of standard topics from the structure of an atom to the complicated mechanics of sound. Students will have an easier time following illustrated explanations of difficult concepts such as inertia or phase change than traditional textbook treatments. These two books also investigate everyday mysteries—such as why bubbles form in boiling water or why a sliced apple turns brown.

The remaining volumes in this group describe the more complex applications of physical science concepts. Each volume traces the history of a certain branch of technology, investigates current applications, and explores possible future advances. These books uncover the inner workings of common devices. *Machines & Inventions,* for example, describes several historically important inventions, including the telephone and the camera. It also examines the machines students see every day, such as television and the automatic dishwasher. *Computer Age* surveys the history of computers, discusses their theory and structure, and explains how each component functions. *Transportation* explains the mechanics of land, air, and water vehicles.

Physical Forces

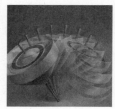

Physical Forces explores the basic principles taught in any physics classroom, taking aim at such hard-to-explain topics as how scientists measure the speed of light. Diagrams, magnified cutaways, and molecular models help students understand the invisible forces at work in the world around them.

Chapter 1: Force and Pressure. A number of basic forces affect the behavior of objects. This chapter introduces them and explains how they interact to produce visible effects. It shows how gravity and buoyancy keep ships afloat and how the low pressure of gas allows a balloon to fly. Sections on rocket engines, barometers, and whirlpools show how forces can be measured, created, and controlled.

Chapter 2: Gravity and Motion. Motion is governed by a few fundamental laws. Using familiar examples, this chapter investigates Newton's laws of motion. A skier's run demonstrates the effects of friction on speed, while a subway ride illustrates the principle of inertia. Diagrams show how the forces of circular motion that keep riders safe in loop-the-loop roller coasters are similar to those that keep satellites in orbit.

Chapter 3: Simple Machines. Even the most complex modern machines consist of only a few basic parts. Each part descends from what physicists call simple machines—the lever, the wheel and axle, the pulley, the inclined plane, and the screw. This section examines everyday devices—from bottle openers and brooms to multispeed bicycles—to show how humans use simple machines to manipulate force and make their tasks easier.

Chapter 4: Temperature, Heat, and Molecules. In scientific terms, temperature represents the energy of an object's molecules. This chapter explains the difference between thermal energy and heat energy. It also introduces the concept of phase change and, with molecular models, shows students how the invisible structure of matter determines its visible properties.

Chapter 5: Electricity and Magnetism. Electricity and magnetism are particularly hard for students to understand because they can't be seen. This chapter exposes the charged particles that interact to create electricity, magnetism, and radioactivity. Colorful diagrams define the flow of electrons in a light bulb and the arc of field lines from an electromagnet.

Chapter 6: Generating Electricity. All generators—from portable gasoline-powered models to huge hydroelectric plants—operate on the same principle: Energy moves a magnet past a coil of wire to generate a current. Chapter 6 explores how scientists harness energy from water, sunlight, atoms, fossil fuels, the heat of the Earth, and wind.

Chapter 7: The Mysteries of Light. Light has five properties: propagation, reflection, refraction, diffraction, and interference. These properties are exploited in devices from magnifying glasses to lasers and holograms. In this chapter, students learn about wave and corpuscular theories of light. They also learn about light-based phenomena, such as the prismatic effect of soap bubbles and the curious three-dimensional image of a hologram.

Chapter 8: The Physics of Sound. Sound exists because of waves produced by subtle vibrations of air. This chapter explores that wave motion. Singing violin strings show how wavelength affects pitch, while a study of echoes demonstrates the effect of climate on sound. A force diagram reveals how supersonic aircraft compress sound waves to create a sonic boom. The chapter also discusses Doppler phenomena and electronic manipulation of sound.

Structure of Matter

Like *Physical Forces, Structure of Matter* helps students see the invisible forces behind everyday phenomena—this time with a focus on chemistry. Large models reveal the tiny molecules and atoms that make up all matter and show how those particles interact. *Structure of Matter* also explores the relationship between energy and physical or chemical change using commonplace examples.

Chapter 1: The World of Matter. *Structure of Matter* begins with an examination of the unseen particles that constitute matter. This chapter focuses on the atom and its constituents: protons, neutrons, and electrons. The chapter also explores atomic processes such as nuclear fission and fusion. Molecular diagrams of sodium chloride show how electrons change when atoms form compounds. A discussion of the nitrogen cycle explains how atoms are recycled in the environment. Finally, a review of the structure of metal and rubber illustrates the effect of atomic arrangement on a substance's physical properties.

Chapter 2: Changes in Matter. Many familiar events involve unseen changes in the interaction of atoms. The second chapter of *Structure of Matter* deals with these changes. Drawings and molecular models explain how water freezes and turns to steam. Phase diagrams of dry ice illustrate sublimation—the process in which a substance changes directly from solid to gas. The immiscibility of oil and water demonstrates the relationship of polar and nonpolar molecules, while a study of blimps illustrates the properties of gases.

Chapter 3: Chemical Energy. Countless chemical reactions occur throughout nature, each one causing a change in the composition of matter. When iron rusts, for example, oxygen reacts with iron to form red iron oxide. Chapter 3 focuses on these reactions and their relationship to energy—from the production of electricity in a battery to the combustion of coal. Students will be intrigued by the discussions of rocket engines and fire extinguishers, and will also be interested in learning about topical issues such as acid rain and the depletion of the ozone layer.

Chapter 4: The Chemistry of Food. In few areas are chemical reactions more apparent than in the production and preparation of food. A boiled egg undergoes a phase change from liquid to solid. Water and heat change the molecular structure of flour to make it digestible. This chapter examines the chemical changes associated with these and other foods. Molecular drawings of ice cream show how chemical structure affects the properties of foods. The chapter also investigates the desalination of seawater and the purification of drinking water, drawing attention to the worldwide shortage of clean drinking water.

Chapter 5: Engineering a Way of Life. From paper and textiles to railroads and skyscrapers, the products of industrial chemistry have changed the 20th century. This chapter investigates the impact new materials have had on modern life.

Chapter 6: Exploring the New Materials. Long before the first alchemists sought a formula to turn base metals into gold, people have looked for ways to transform natural materials into new substances. From wear-resistant ceramic bone implants to lightweight plastics that make cars more fuel efficient, today's custom-engineered synthetics are transforming life. The last chapter in *Structure of Matter* is dedicated to the latest developments in chemistry, including industrial ceramics, artificial diamonds, carbon fiber polymers, and shape-memory metal alloys. It also explains new materials vital to the electronics industry, such as liquid crystals and silicon chips.

Machines & Inventions

Students have a natural curiosity about how things work. *Machines & Inventions* satisfies that curiosity. Using this book, students actually see and understand how an electron beam forms the picture on a TV screen, or why quartz watches are so accurate. They learn about devices too dangerous to get close to and about machines they would never be allowed to take apart. Cutaway drawings focus attention on a machine's components and on the principles that make them work.

Chapter 1: Inventions That Changed History. Science and technology have often altered the course of history. This chapter surveys some of history's most important inventions—from Gutenberg's printing press to the first V-2 rocket. Inventions such as the telegraph, dynamite, and the electric generator are also described in a historical context.

Chapter 2: The Machines of Industry and Science. Industrial machines and the tools of scientific research are the focus of this chapter. From the electron microscope to the latest printing presses, these inventions have extended humanity's senses and communications.

Chapter 3: An Explosion in Office Equipment. As recently as the 1970s, most offices relied on no more than an electric typewriter and a telephone to help get their work done. The development of the integrated circuit, however, has caused a revolution in office technology. Chapter 3 shows how innovations have changed the way we do business. Because of their importance to modern life, personal computers are not discussed here but are the subject of their own volume, *Computer Age.*

Chapter 4: Machines for Leisure Time. Many of the things people do for fun—munching popcorn at a movie, dancing to music recorded on a compact disk, or even sitting at home in front of the television—would not be possible without modern innovations in electronics and chemistry. Chapter 4 dissects the inventions that help us play. VCRs, music synthesizers, and high-definition TV are all explained in detail, as are a few "old-fashioned" devices such as the quartz watch, Polaroid cameras, and binoculars.

Chapter 5: Machines for the Home. Technology for the home ranges from the very old to the very new. The water faucet is an adaptation of one of the earliest machines, the screw, while the microwave oven uses modern discoveries about radiation to heat food. This chapter investigates these and other domestic machines. The text explains the refrigerator, air conditioner, and sewing machine as well as an iron's thermostat and an electric meter.

Chapter 6: Medical Marvels. In the last 100 years, scientists and engineers have developed a wondrous array of instruments that prevent, diagnose, or treat illness and trauma. The final chapter of *Machines & Inventions* presents modern medical tools, including the fiberscope, CAT scanners, and ultrasound. The chapter also discusses more familiar medical equipment, such as the stethoscope and the digital thermometer.

Computer Age

Computer Age eliminates the mystery of the digital box, explaining how computers work and how they affect our daily lives. Because many adults would like to have a better understanding of computers, this volume is as valuable a resource for teachers as it is for students.

Chapter 1: History of the Computer. Computers began with numbers. As ancient societies searched for ways to make counting easier, they created the first mechanical computing devices. These led to the invention of adding machines, steam-powered calculators, and finally to the first electronic computer. From the abacus to ENIAC, this chapter explores the history of computers and shows how the first counting stones eventually led to the advanced personal computers people use today.

Chapter 2: Modern Computers. Since the first electronic computer was built in 1946, computers have become smaller, faster, and more powerful. Today, they coordinate traffic lights, run factory assembly lines, and process bank deposits. These adaptable devices share an amazing ability to perform simple tasks—such as addition or comparison—at lightning speed. This chapter examines modern computers to see how they accomplish these tasks. It uncovers the structure and the operation of integrated circuits and also shows how data is entered and stored. In addition, illustrated charts and diagrams explain the basics of binary code mathematics.

Chapter 3: Software. Until a program has been loaded into the computer's memory, the computer is like a body without a brain, unable to function. Chapter 3 explores software, the languages it is written in, and the processes that make it function. The chapter also investigates memory and storage.

Chapter 4: Computer Graphics. The first computers generated simple, unrealistic images. But today's computers can produce pictures that are virtually indistinguishable from photographs. Many of the most stunning special effects in movies were generated by computer; computers have even been used to create feature-length animated films. From automobile design and map making to video games and flight simulators, this chapter shows how computer graphics have changed both science and entertainment.

Chapter 5: Digitizing Daily Life. As the computer has become smaller, faster, and more affordable, it has found its way into all aspects of life. This chapter explains the many interesting ways in which computers can—or will—affect our daily routine, examining the use of computers in bar code scanners and bank machines, cars and crime.

Chapter 6: Computer Networks. A computer's ability to store and process data is remarkable. Even more remarkable is its ability to share data when linked to other computers in a network. Chapter 6 looks into the many possibilities of networking, from electronic mail to videophones. It explains how networks work and how data can be transmitted by phone lines, fiberoptic cables, or radio waves.

Chapter 7: Science and Computers. Science has found many uses for computers. Tiny devices implanted in the body can control the heart's rhythm; computer models help meteorologists predict the weather. Computers can help an athlete analyze performance, or guide a cruise missile on its deadly path. This chapter explores the many ways in which scientists use computers, from creating detailed models to devising practical applications that make our lives easier.

Transportation

Many of the most dramatic advances in technology have come in the field of transportation. The development of the first ships opened the world to discovery. The steam engine gave settlers the incentive to go west; the invention of the automobile made it even easier to visit neighbors across the country. Developments in each area of transport—from fuel-efficient solar cars to supersonic aircraft—are still changing our lives. These are the subject of *Transportation*. In this volume, students will learn about the history and future of land, air, and sea travel and will examine the scientific principles that make each mode of transportation work.

Chapter 1: Riding the Changing Rails. The train is one of the great engineering triumphs of modern times. Rail travel played an important role in the success of the Industrial Revolution in England, and was vital to the increased westward expansion of the United States in the 1800s. Today, trains still haul freight and passengers all over the world. This chapter surveys train travel, from the first steam locomotive to the magnetic-levitation trains of the future. Detailed illustrations examine a train's features—flanged wheels, coupling systems, brakes, traffic control systems, and signals.

Chapter 2: The Machine That Moves Humanity. The first automobile, invented by Nicolas-Joseph Cugnot in 1769, was a steam-powered three-wheeler that raced along at 3 mph. With the help of new discoveries, new designs, and new materials, today's models are faster, safer, and more efficient. This chapter explores the insides of these useful machines, including the brakes, transmission, steering, drive system, engine, and tires. The chapter also features racing cars, electric cars, motorcycles, and experimental solar-powered and self-driving cars.

Chapter 3: A Vehicle for Every Need. Using the automobile as a basic model, engineers have developed an array of specialized vehicles to fill every need. Vehicles equipped with skis or tracks can reach treacherous terrain once accessible only on foot. A cumbersome crane, now mounted on a chassis, can be driven to a construction site for heavy lifting jobs. Specialty vehicles—snowmobiles, fire trucks, cranes, power shovels, and construction rollers—and their unusual features are the subject of Chapter 3.

Chapter 4: From Sail to Sub. The next chapter deals with vehicles that travel on, under, or over the water. From clipper ships to hovercraft, from steam boats to submarines, chapter 4 explores the past and present of ocean travel, including the navigational techniques that aid each kind of vehicle.

Chapter 5: Dreaming of the Heavens. The ability to fly has long been the subject of human fascination. Is it possible for people to sail through the skies? How can flight be controlled? Can it be safe? The last chapter of *Transportation* answers these questions. It describes the history of air travel from the Wright *Flyer* to the Stealth bomber. Diagrams and cutaways explain the physics of the airfoil, the forces of lift and drag, and the principles of jet propulsion. A section on navigation reviews modern air-traffic control and examines the on-board instruments that allow pilots to fly at night or in bad weather.

Classroom Applications

Perhaps the best reason to use the physical science books in the classroom is that they motivate students to learn by tying science to a student's daily life. A quick look through *Machines & Inventions* will teach students about compact disks and vending machines. A discussion of surfing in *Physical Forces* springboards into an exploration of wave-forms, gravity, and buoyancy. Their friendly approach makes these books exciting tools for introducing students to physical science. Thumbing through the pages will lead students to inventions or processes that demonstrate the science they have just learned and their discoveries will make the foundation for a great report.

The information found in this group relates naturally to most physical science curricula, including basic physical science, physics, or chemistry. The following topic list shows some of the possible connections.

Acids, Bases, Salts	*Structure of Matter* (p. 64-65, 80-83)
Alternative Energy Sources	*Physical Forces* (p. 98-111) *Transportation* (p. 62-63)
Atomic Structure	*Structure of Matter* (p. 6-11, 14-17, 22-23)
Carbon and Organic Chemistry	*Structure of Matter* (p. 94-95, 106-109, 116-119, 126-127, 132-133, 138-139)
Chemical Properties of Matter	*Structure of Matter* (p. 42-43, 48-49, 52-77, 80-85)
Chemical Reactions	*Structure of Matter* (p. 60-61, 66-71, 74-75, 84-85) *Machines & Inventions* (p. 24-25)
Electricity	*Physical Forces* (p. 96-97) *Structure of Matter* (p. 18-19, 58-59 *Machines & Inventions* (p. 28-29)
Electricity and Magnetism	*Physical Forces* (p. 68-91) *Machines & Inventions* (p. 10-11, 56-57, 82-83, 118-121)
Energy	*Physical Forces* (p. 52-67)
Forces and Motion	*Physical Forces* (p. 4-39) *Transportation* (p. 130-131)
Light	*Physical Forces* (p. 118-127) *Machines & Inventions* (p. 16-19, 76-77)
Measurement	*Physical Forces* (p. 56 - 57) *Machines & Inventions* (p. 34-39, 46-49, 118-119, 126-144) *Transportation* (p. 132-133)
Metals	*Structure of Matter* (p. 28-29, 56-57, 62-63, 70-71, 110-115, 140-143)
Mirrors and Lenses	*Physical Forces* (p. 114-117)
Nonmetallic Elements	*Structure of Matter* (p. 26-27, 36-37, 46-47, 74-77, 134-135)
Radioactivity and Nuclear Reactions	*Structure of Matter* (p. 14-17, 24-25)
Simple Machines	*Physical Forces* (p. 40-51) *Machines & Inventions* (p. 108-109) *Transportation* (p. 72-73)
Solutions and Colloids	*Structure of Matter* (p. 18-21, 40-43, 48-49) *Machines and Inventions* (p. 112-113)
States of Matter	*Structure of Matter* (p. 34-35, 38-39, 46-47, 86-87, 92-93) *Physical Forces* (p. 10-11, 22-23, 62-63, 66-67) *Machines & Inventions* (p. 100-101, 106-107, 122-125) *Transportation* (p. 16-17)
Waves and Sound	*Physical Forces* (p. 128-144) *Machines & Inventions* (p. 84-87, 90-91)

Activity: Boiling Bubbles

Background. Everyone is familiar with the bubbles that appear in boiling water and other liquids, but few people pay attention to the interesting sequence of changes that occur as a liquid is heated from room temperature to boiling. In this activity, students heat a sample of cold water to the boiling point, making and recording observations of the various stages of bubbling that occur along the way.

Group Size. Students may perform this activity individually or in pairs.

Duration. One class period (about 45 minutes).

Materials. Each student or pair of students will need:

> 1 600-milliliter beaker, about 2/3 full of cold tap water
> 1 ring stand
> 2 iron rings
> some wire gauze
> 1 gas burner
> some boiling stones (if beakers are new)
> 1 thermometer (optional)
> safety goggles

Procedure.

1. Set up the ring stand: Use one ring and the wire gauze to support the beaker of water; use the second ring as a safety ring about three-fourths of the way up the sides of the beaker.
2. Put on safety goggles. Adjust the gas burner to make a clear blue flame.
3. Place the beaker on the ring stand, with the burner centered under it. Add the boiling stones if the beaker is new.
4. Observe the changes and record them as the water heats to boiling.
5. *Optional:* Record the temperature of the water in the middle of the beaker every two minutes. Make a temperature chart showing the times when bubbles appeared or disappeared.

To the Teacher. The first bubbles, made of dissolved air, appear almost immediately. These are small and may form all over the inside surface of the beaker. As the water heats up, these bubbles grow in size; eventually they break loose from the glass and rise to the surface of the water. You might point out that this dissolved air is what fish survive on in water. Gasses become less soluble in a liquid as the liquid's temperature rises. This is why hot water vented from a power plant (thermal pollution) can pose such a hazard to aquatic animals even if it contains no chemical pollutants.

After this initial formation of dissolved-air bubbles, a relatively long, bubble-free period follows as the water, now rid of air, is heated to boiling.

The first true "boiling bubbles" appear at the bottom of the beaker near the heat source. These break free of the bottom, but as they rise through the cooler water, they shrink and eventually collapse. The collapse of these bubbles creates a crackling sound, familiar to cooks as a sign that water is about to boil. As the water temperature increases, the bubbles rise higher in the liquid before collapsing; however, they still form only on the bottom of the beaker.

True boiling is achieved when bubbles form at various places throughout the liquid and grow larger as they rise to the surface, where they burst. If the water is allowed to cool without being agitated and is then reheated to boiling, the boiling bubbles will go through the same changes in size. No dissolved-air bubbles will appear, however; the air dissolved in the water was driven off in the first heating.

Reference Guide. On pages 62-63, *Physical Forces* describes the changes that students will observe and explains why they happen.

Activity: Making Yogurt

Background. In 1854, while helping a local distiller ferment beet sugar to make alcohol, Louis Pasteur discovered that fermentation was not a simple chemical process. He learned that fermentation could take place only in the presence of the living organisms we now know as bacteria. Today, manufacturers

use many types of bacteria to make the foods we eat. The *Lactobacillus* bacterium—used in this activity—is especially important. It plays a vital role in the production of yogurt and other dairy products such as cheese, sour cream, and buttermilk. In this activity, students will create conditions favorable to bacteria growth and then transfer active cultures of *Lactobacillus* into milk to make yogurt.

Group size. Two or three students per group.

Duration. The class will need one day to prepare the *Lactobacillus* cultures. The cultures will have to sit overnight to allow the bacteria to grow. Students will need the next class period to examine the results of their experiment.

Materials. Each group of students will need:

2 200 ml beakers	beaker tongs
1 20 ml graduated cylinder	1 plastic spoon
1 hot plate	parafilm to cover beakers
stirring rod	20 ml unflavored or vanilla yogurt containing active scissors
300 ml milk	yogurt cultures
safety goggles	

Procedure.
A. Sterilization and Control

1. Label the beakers *A* and *B*.
2. Measure 150 ml milk into each beaker.
3. Cover beaker *A* with parafilm. Label the beaker "control" and set it aside.
4. Put on safetly goggles. Heat beaker *B* until the milk just reaches boiling. Use beaker tongs to remove *B* from the hot plate.
5. Allow the milk to cool to room temperature.

B. Inoculation

1. Add 20 ml (about 1 tbs) yogurt to the cooled milk in beaker *B*.
2. Stir the mixture until it is smooth.
3. Cover beaker *B* with parafilm and label the beaker "experiment."

C. Incubation
Leave both beakers overnight in a protected place at room temperature. Keep them away from windows and other sources of heat or cold.

D. Observation

After 24 hours, compare and describe the odor and appearance of the milk in each beaker.

Post-lab analysis. Discuss how each step in the lab procedure creates the necessary environment for bacterial growth. First, the milk was sterilized to make sure that no unwanted bacteria were still alive. Next, the milk was cooled so the *Lactobacillus* bacteria could survive after inoculation. Finally, the inoculated milk was left at room temperature to permit the *Lactobacillus* to grow.

Questions for discussion. Have your students write down their answers to the following questions, or use the questions to foster class discussion after the lab.

1. What conditions are ideal for bacterial growth?
2. What conditions would be likely to slow or stop bacterial growth?
3. Why do packaged dairy products have an expiration date?
4. What causes milk to turn sour?
5. Is sour milk harmful to drink?

Notes. It is not a good idea for your students eat the yogurt they have made in class; if they wish to taste their results, have them repeat the experiment at home. Make sure to use yogurt that contains active yogurt cultures as a starter. If the label of the yogurt does not specifically mention active cultures, or if the label says that the yogurt has been pasteurized, then it is unlikely to have sufficient *Lactobacillus* bacteria for this experiment.

As most students have not had much experience using beaker tongs to handle hot liquids, demonstrate the technique for them and have them practice before they begin the lab.

Reference Guide. Students will find the background information they need for this activity in *Structure of Matter*, pages 84-85.

Animal Behavior
AN

Computer Age
CO

Ecology
EC

Evolution of Life
EV

Geography
GE

Human Body
HU

Insects & Spiders
IN

Machines &
Inventions **MA**

Physical Science Index

Numerals in italics indicate an illustration of the subject mentioned.

A

Abacuses and counting stones: CO *4-5, 6-7*
AC (alternating current): and DC (direct current), PH *85, 86*; generators, working of, PH *96-97*
Acceleration: and inertia, PH *28*; in Newton's second law of motion, PH 24
Accelerator: automobile's, TR *41, 47*
Accelerometer: in aircraft's INS, TR *124*; integral, V-2 rocket's, MA *27*
Acidity in yogurt formation: ST *84-85*
Acid rain: ST *64-65*
Acids and alkalines: foods, ST *82-83*; neutralizing, ST 52, *53*, 64, 65
Acoustic analysis: CO *62-63*
Acrylic: molecular structure of, ST *109*
Activated carbon: air purification with, MA *50-51*; removing odors with, ST *52-53*
Adder circuits: CO 28, *29*
Adding machines: CO *4-5, 8-9*
Addition by computers: CO 24, *25*; logic gates and, CO 28, *29*; programs for, CO 51
Addresses in computer memory: CO *30-31*; disk, CO 56, 57
Advanced materials: *See* Materials technology
Aerodynamics: of automobiles, CO 75; of hang gliders, PH *14-15*
Aerosols: ST *20*
Aging phenomenon of starch: ST 100, *101*
Agitator: washing machine's, MA *113*
Agriculture: combines used in, MA *14-15*
Aiken, Howard: CO 14
Ailerons: TR *111*
Air: around baseball during pitch, PH *34, 35*; blimp's displacement of, ST *46-47*; bubbles in liquid, PH *63*; convection in, PH *59*; down's interference with convection in, PH 60, *61*; hang glider in, PH *14-15*; hot, balloons filled with, PH *4-5, 10-11*; in ice cream, ST *92, 93*; pressure, temperature, and volume of, PH *11*; in

sauna, PH *64-65*; sound waves through, PH *130-131, 133. See also* Wind
Air bags: automobile's, TR *50-51*
Air brakes: automatic, trains', TR *10-11*
Air circulation: in airplanes, TR *128-129*
Air conditioners: MA *122-123*; basement system, MA *51*; ideal placement of, PH *59*
Aircraft: TR 108-144; airships, TR *108, 116-117*; altitude, measuring, TR 132, *133*; first, TR *108, 134-135*; flying, basic method of, TR *110-111*; with forward-swept wings, TR *142-143*; gliders, TR *118-119*; helicopters, TR *109, 114-115*; INS (inertial navigation system), TR *124-125*; jet engines, working of, TR *130-131, 139*; landing system for (ILS), TR *126-127*; navigational aids for, TR *122-123, 124-125*; Omega System for, TR *map* 125; propellers, use of, TR *112-113, 134, 139*; sideways-flying, TR *140-141*; simulation of flight, CO *82-83*; sonic booms from, PH *140-141*; speed, measuring, TR *132-133*; Stealth bomber, TR *109, 144*; supersonic, TR *108-109, 136-137*; traffic control, TR *120-121*; ventilation system for, TR *128-129*; and VOR stations, TR *122-123*; VTOL (vertical takeoff and landing), TR *138-139*
Air currents: glider's use of, TR *119*
Air-cushion vehicle (hovercraft): TR *78, 96-97*
Air drying: dehumidifier for, MA *124-125*
Airfoil: type of (hang glider), PH *14-15*
Airline computers: CO *96-97*
Air molecules: heated, PH *10-11*; and heat loss, PH 60; pressure, temperature, and volume of, PH *11*
Airplanes: *See* Aircraft
Air pollution: from automobiles, computerized control of, CO 102
Airport security gates: MA *42-43*
Air purifier systems: MA *50-51*
Airships: TR *108, 116-117*
Airspeed indicators: TR *132-133*
Air supply: for airplanes, TR *128-129*; for submarines, TR *99*; for subways, TR *26-27*
Air traffic: control of, TR *120-121*
Alarm systems: burglar, MA *114-115*; fire, MA *64-65*
Alcohol: ethanol, water and, ST *43*; and lowering of freezing point, ST *40*; in perfume, ST *127*
Algae: blue-green, and oxygen, ST 36
Algorithms: CO *52-53*
Alkalines and acids: foods, ST *82-83*; neutralizing, ST 52, *53*, 64, 65

Alloys: ST *112-113*; shape-memory, ST *128-129, 140-141*
Alpha decay: PH *91*
Alpha-starch vs. beta-starch: ST *100-101*
Alternating current (AC): and direct current (DC), PH *85, 86*; generators, working of, PH *96-97*
Altimeters: TR 132, *133*
Altitude: and boiling point, PH *22-23*
Alumina: refining, ST 114, *115*
Aluminosilicate glass: ST *125*
Aluminum: burning, conditions for, ST 70, *71*; extruded beams, ST *28-29*; glass enhanced with, ST *125*; number of atoms in, ST *8*; refining, ST 114, *115*; space shuttle powered by, ST *71, 74-75*
Alvin (bathyscaphe): TR *107*
Ammeters: PH *76-77*
Amorphous metals: ST *142-143*
Amplifier: radio's, MA *84-85*; sound spectrograph's, MA 35
Amplitude modulation: MA *85*
Amplitude of sound, variations in: MA *90*; and recording of compact disks, MA 86
AM radio transmissions: MA *84-85*
Analog and digital conversion: CO *40-41, 67, 110-111, 119*
Analog and digital signals: compact disks, recording of, MA *86*; fax machine's use of, MA *68-69*; synthesizer's use of, MA *91*
Analytical Engine: CO 4, *10-11*
AND gate: CO *28*; in half-adder, CO 29
Aneroid barograph: PH *17*
Aneroid barometers: PH *16-17*; airplane instruments with, TR *132-133*
Angle of attack: airplane's, TR *110*
Angular momentum: PH *32*
Anode: sacrificial, ST *57*
Anodes and cathodes: in automobile batteries, ST *58-59*; in electrolytic conduction, ST *18-19*; in electroplating, ST *62-63*; and iron reactions, ST *56-57*
Antarctica: ozone hole over, ST *map* 77
Antennas, electromechanical: ground, CO *128, 129*; orbiting, CO *129*; radar, ship's, TR *83*; in space, ST *139, 141*; space probe's, CO *143*; transmitting, PH *88-89*
Antimatter vs. matter: ST *22-23*
Antinodes and nodes: PH *137*
Apollo spacecraft: PH *19*
Apples: browning of, ST *80-81*
Appliances: computer-controlled, CO *104-105*
Arago, François: MA 119
Archimedes' principle: PH *9*
Architectural models: CO *133*
Architecture of computers: CO *18-19*

Arithmetic logic units (ALUs): CO *24-25*; location, CO *18*

Arm, mechanical: artificial (prosthetic), CO *138*; robotic, automakers' use of, CO *100-101*

Arteries: blood pressure in, MA *130, 131*

Artificial heart: MA *132-133*

Artificial Intelligence (AI): CO *69*

Artificial limbs and organs: CO *138-139*

ASCII code table: CO *chart 27*

Assembly lines: robot use on, CO *100-101*

Astrolabe: TR *86*

Astronauts: weight of, on Earth vs. Moon, PH *6-7*

Asuka STOL aircraft: TR *139*

Athletes: computer use by, CO *136-137*

ATM (automated teller machine): CO *88-89*

Atmosphere of Earth: history of, ST *36-37*; nitrogen in, ST *25, 26-27*; ozone layer, hole in, ST *76-77*

Atmospheric pressure: measuring, PH *16-17*; states of matter and, ST *38, charts 38-39*; vapor pressure and, PH *22*

Atmospheric pressure altimeter vs. radio altimeter: TR *132, 133*

Atomic nuclei: fission of, TR *102, 103*

Atomic reactors: PH *108-109*; core, PH *94-95, 108*

Atoms: ST *4*; of antimatter, vs. matter, ST *22-23*; fission of, ST *14-15*; fusion of nuclei, ST *16-17*; light emission by, ST *50-51*; makeup of, ST *6-7*; of metals, ST *13, 19, 28-29, 31, 121, 140-141, 142-143*; radioactive, PH *90-91, 108*; of silicon, in quartz crystal, MA *96*; of silicon, microscope's magnification of, MA *32*; size of, ST *8-9*. *See also* Electrons; Ions; Molecules

Audio equipment: compact disks (CDs) and CD players vs. phonograph records, MA *86-87*; microphones and speakers, MA *80-81*; radios, MA *84-85*

Audio recording head in VCR: MA *83*

Autofocus (AF): cameras with, MA *74-75*

Automated-teller machines (ATMs): CO *88-89*

Automatic air brakes: trains', TR *10-11*

Automatic cars: TR *60-61*

Automatic trains: TR *24-25*

Automatic transmission: automobile's, TR *47*

Automatons: *See* Robots

Automobiles: TR *36-65*; air bags, TR *52-53*; automated, TR *60-61*; batteries, ST *58-59*; brakes, TR *44-45, 58*; computers in, CO *102-103*; design of, CO *74-75*; electric, TR *64-65*; engine, ST *60-61*; first, TR *36, 38-39*; four-wheel drive (4WD), TR *48-49*; four-wheel steering (4WS), TR *50-*

51; motorcycles vs., TR *42-43*; phones in, CO *120-121*; power for, TR *40-41, 47, 54-55, 58, 59*; racing cars, Formula One, TR *58-59*; robot use in manufacture of, CO *100-101*; solar-powered, TR *62-63*; traffic patterns, computer modeling of, CO *132-133*; transmission, TR *40, 46-47*; tread on tires, TR *56-57*; turbocharged, TR *54-55*; wheel types, TR *36-37*

Aviation, flight simulators used in: CO *82-83*

B

Babbage, Charles: CO *4, 10*; inventions, CO *4, 10-11*

Babies, unborn: ultrasound monitoring of, MA *142-143*

Bacteria: in fermentation, ST *85, 90-91*; food protected from, ST *88, 89*; in nitrogen cycle, ST *26, 27*; removal from water, ST *98-99*

Baird, John L.: mechanical scanning televisor built by, MA *22-23*

Ballast tanks, use of: by icebreakers, TR *101*; by submarines, TR *98*

Ballonet: blimp's use of, TR *116*

Balloons: hot-air, PH *4-5, 10-11*; rubber, ST *30-31*

Balls: baseball pitches, PH *24-25, 34-35*; in inertia experiment, PH *29*

Bank machines (automated-teller machines; ATMs): CO *88-89*

Barbules of feathers: PH *60, 61*

Bar codes: CO *86-87*

Barium: fission producing, ST *14-15*

Barograph: aneroid, PH *17*

Barometers: aneroid, PH *16-17*; aneroid, airplane instruments with, TR *132-133*; mercury, PH *16, 17*

Baseball pitches: PH *24-25, 34-35*; speed guns for clocking, MA *38-39*

Base stations for cellular phone calls: CO *120*; zones covered by, CO *120, 121*

Base stations for paging devices: CO *122-123*

BASIC (programming language): CO *50-51*; program in, CO *51*

Bathroom scales: MA *108-109*

Bathyscaphes: TR *107*

Batteries: automobile, working of, ST *58-59*; electric, automobiles powered by, TR *64-65*; solar, PH *110-111*; solar, automobiles powered by, TR *62-63*

Battle, transportation in: *See* Military transportation

Bauxite: ST *115*

Beam-interference alarms: MA *114*

Beams: extruded aluminum, ST *28-29*

Beat (pulsating tone): PH *142-143*

Beepers (pagers): electronic, CO *122-123*

Bell, Alexander Graham: MA *11*; telephone invented by, MA *10-11, 56*

Bernoulli, Daniel: MA *47*

Beryllium: lithium's decay into, PH *91*

Beta decay: PH *91*

Beta-starch vs. alpha-starch: ST *100-101*

Bias tires: TR *57*

Bicycle: working of, PH *46-47*

Big Bang: antimatter created in, ST *22-23*

Bimetal thermal sensors: MA *121*; in fire alarm, MA *65*; in iron, MA *120-121*

Binary code: CO *26, chart 27*; bar codes, CO *86-87*; and logic gates, CO *28-29*

Binary conversion: CO *chart 27*

Binary notation: CO *26-27*

Binary search: CO *57*

Binoculars: MA *94-95*

Biomedical engineering: computer use in, CO *138-139*

Bits and bytes: CO *26*; magnetic storage, CO *36, 37*; memory addresses, CO *30-31*; telephone transmissions, CO *110-111*

Blackboard: electronic, MA *70-71*

Blast furnaces: pig iron in, ST *102-103, 110-111, 112*

Blasting cap: dynamite, MA *24*

Bleaches: ink removal with, ST *72-73*

Blimps: TR *116-117*; buoyancy of, ST *46-47*

Block and tackle: PH *49*

Blood: cleaning of, CO *139*

Blood pressure: lie detector's measurement of, MA *37*; measurement of, MA *130-131*

Blown glass: ST *123*

Boats: hydrofoils, TR *79, 94-95*; motorboats, TR *79*; sailing of, into wind, PH *12-13*; steamboats, TR *90-91*

Boiled eggs: ST *94-95*

Boilers: steam car with, TR *38-39*; on steam locomotives, TR *14, 17*; in thermoelectric plants, PH *100, 101*

Boiling of liquids: PH *62*; temperature of, variation in, PH *22-23*; water, MA *100*, PH *62-63*, ST *32-33, 35*

Boiling stone: PH *63*

Bombers: Stealth, TR *109, 144*

Bones: microscope's magnification of, MA *32*; x-raying, MA *140, 141*

Booms: crane's, TR *66-67, 72-73*; power shovel's, TR *67, 76-77*

Borosilicate glass: ST *125*

Bottle opener as lever: PH *43*

Box camera, Kodak: MA *18, 19*

Brain, human: CAT scan of, MA *135*; computers resembling, CO *44-45*

Brakes: automobile, TR *44-45, 58*; automobile, computerized control of, CO *103*;

Animal Behavior
AN

Computer Age
CO

Ecology
EC

Evolution of Life
EV

Geography
GE

Human Body
HU

Insects & Spiders
IN

Machines &
Inventions **MA**

cable car, TR *30*; racing car, TR *58*; snowmobile, TR *69*; train, TR *10-11*; and train stop system, automatic, TR *21*

Brake shoes: in car's drum brakes, TR *45*; train's, TR *11*

Braun, Karl: MA 23

Braun, Wernher von: MA *26*

Bread: starch in, ST *101*

Breathing: lie detector's measurement of, MA *36*

Bronze: electroplating, ST *62-63*

B-2 Stealth bomber: TR *109, 144*

Bubbles: formation of, in liquid, PH *62-63*; soap, colors of, PH *120-121*

Bubble sort: CO 54, *55*

Buffer: printer's, data in, CO *39*

Building construction: self-raising crane used in, MA *52-53*

Buildings: computer models of, CO *133*

Bulldozers: TR *66-67, 77*; on excavator, TR *76*

Bulletin boards: electronic, CO 116, *117*

Bullet trains: TR *4-5, 33*

Buoyancy of blimps: ST *46-47*

Buoyancy vs. gravity: in air, PH *4-5, 10-11*; in water, PH *8-9*

Burglar alarms: MA *114-115*

Burning: *See* Combustion

Buses: CO *20-21, 30-31*

Bus tires: TR *57*

Business computers: CO *92-93*

Bytes and bits: CO *26*; magnetic storage, CO *36, 37*; memory addresses, CO *30-31*; in telephone transmissions, CO *110-111*

C

Cable cars: TR *30-31*

Cables: optical-fiber, ST *124-125*; telegraph, MA 8, *9*

CAD/CAM (computer-aided design/manufacturing) and automobiles: CO *74-75*

Calculators: CO *4*; abacuses and counting stones, CO *4-5, 6-7*; Babbage's, CO *4, 10-11*; seventeenth-century, CO *4-5, 8-9*

Calendars: electronic, CO *91*

Calipers: micrometer, MA *48-49*; vernier (slide), MA 48, *49*

Camera lenses: leaded glass for, ST *125*

Camera obscura: MA 16

Cameras: with autofocus (AF), MA *74-75*; automated cars' use of, TR 60, *61*; first, MA *16-17*; instant, color, working of, MA *92-93*; kinetograph, MA *20*; Kodak, MA *18, 19*; submersible with, TR *106*; TV, iconoscope, MA 22, *23*

Canals: locks, Panama Canal's, TR *92-93*

Canards: automated car's, TR *61*; CCV's, TR *140-141*; Wright *Flyer's*, TR *135*; X-29A's, TR *142*

Canned food: ST *89*

Cans: dispensing of, by vending machine, MA *58*

Carbon: ST *4*; activated, odor removal with, ST *52-53*; aluminum refined with, ST *115*; carbon fibers from, ST *138-139*; in cellulose, ST *12-13*; combustion products, ST *67*; graphite, diamonds synthesized from, ST *132, chart* 133; iron refined with, ST *102-103, 110-111*; in polymers, ST *30-31, 106-107*; in steel, content of, ST *112, chart* 113

Carbon cycle: ST *25*

Carbon dioxide: from aluminum refining, ST *115*; from combustion, ST *67*; frozen (dry ice), ST 38, *39, 40*; in oxygen cycle, ST *37*; phase changes in, ST 32, *38, 39*; in photosynthesis, ST *66*

Carbon fiber: ST *138-139*

Carbon filter: air purification with, MA *50-51*

Carbon-14 dating: ST *24-25*

Carbon granules: telephone's use of, MA *56*

Carboniferous period: forests during, and atmospheric oxygen, ST *36-37*

Carbon monoxide: as combustion product, ST *67*; and pig iron, ST *110, 112-113*

Carburetor: role of, TR *41*; throttle plate, TR *45*

Card counters: CO *12*

Card feeders: CO *13*

Card punches: CO *12*

Card readers: CO *12, 13, 18*

Card sorters: CO *13*

Car phones: CO *120-121*

Carracks: Columbus's *(Santa Maria)*, TR *88-89*

Carrier waves for radio transmissions: MA *84-85*

Cars: *See* Automobiles

Cartography: *See* Maps and mapping

Casting of pig iron: ST *112*

Catalytic reformers: ST *117*

Cathodes: *See* Anodes and cathodes

CAT (computerized axial tomographic) scanners: MA *134-135*

CCDs: *See* Charge-coupled devices

CCV (control-configured vehicle; fighter jet): TR *140-141*

CDI (course deviation indicator) dial: aircraft's, TR *123*

CD-ROM (compact disk read-only memory): CO *95*

CDs (compact disks): MA *86-87*

Cellular phones: CO *120-121*

Cellulose fibers: ST *104*

Cellulose molecules: cotton, ST *12-13, 107*; papermaking, ST 104, *105*; wood, ST *67*

Cement: hydration of, ST *120*; in lattice structure, ST *121*

Census, U.S.: tabulating machine used in, CO *12-13*

Center of gravity: ship's shifting, PH *9*; top's, PH *32, 33*

Central processing units (CPUs): CO *18, 24-25*; and memory, CO *30*; microprocessors as, CO 22

Centrifugal pump: fire engine's, TR *71*

Centripetal force: on roller coaster, PH 30, *31*; on satellite, PH *37*

Ceramics: ST 130, *131*; advanced, ST *130-131*

Cerium: neodymium's decay into, PH *91*

Chain reactions: in nuclear fission, ST *14-15*; of uranium 235, PH *108*

Chainwheel gear: bicycle's, PH 46, *47*

Change bit coding vs. constant bit coding: CO *36*

Character maps in computer games: CO *78*

Character recognition: CO *64-65*

Charge-coupled devices (CCDs): in cameras, MA *75*; in color copiers, MA *62-63*; in fax machines, CO *114*, MA 68, *69*

Charges, electrical: *See* Electrons

Charles V, King (France): clock commissioned by, MA *12-13*

Charlotte Dundas (steam vessel): TR *91*

Charts: navigational, TR *80*

Checkout counters: scanner type used in, CO *86-87*

Chemistry and matter: ST entire volume

Chest monitor: stethoscope's, MA *144*

Chest x-ray: MA *141*

Chevalier, C. L.: lens type made by, MA *16*

Chinese abacuses: CO *7*

Chip log: TR *87*

Chips: *See* Integrated circuits

Chloride, and sodium ions: ST *43*; and electron conduction, ST *18-19*; and freezing point of water, ST 40, *41*; and reclamation of salt from seawater, ST *96*

Chlorine: disinfecting water with, ST 98, *99*; ozone broken down by, ST *76*

Chlorofluorocarbons (CFCs): ST *76*

Cholesteric liquid crystals: ST *137*

Chroma key process: CO *80-81*

Circuits, electrical: PH *74-75*; measuring current, PH *76-77*

Cladding: fiberoptic cable's, CO 124, *125*

Clarinet: working of, PH *136-137*

Cleaning of air: MA *50-51*

Clermont (Fulton's paddle steamer): TR *90-91*

Climbing crane: MA *52-53*

Planet Earth
PE

Plant Life
PL

Physical Forces
PH

Structure of Matter
ST

Space & Planets
SP

Transportation
TR

Underwater World
UN

Weather & Climate
WE

Clipper ship: TR *78-79*

Clocks: mechanical, MA *12-13*; use of quartz in, MA *96-97*

Clothes iron with thermostat: MA *120-121*

Clothes washers: MA *112-113*

Coal: ST *67*; burning of, ST *66*

COBOL (programming language): CO *50-51*; program in, CO *51*

Cockpit in flight simulator: CO *82-83*

Code, Morse: MA *9*

Codec (coder/decoder), picture phone's use of: CO *126, 127*

Code tables: binary, CO chart *27*

Coffee, instant: making of, ST *86-87*

Coil springs: PH *51*

Coin-operated machines: MA *58-59*; movie viewer, MA *20-21*

Coke in iron refining: ST *110*

Collisions: simulated, CO *74-75*

Colloids: ST *20-21*

Colon polyp: fiberscope's view of, MA *139*

Colors: electronic publishing of, CO *94-95*; of fireworks, elements and, ST *50, 51*; of light, primary, MA *77, 92*; pens, electronic blackboard's, MA *71*; photocopying, MA *62-63*; photography, instant, MA *92-93*; printing, MA *40-41*; television, MA *76-77*

Columbus, Christopher, expedition of: route, TR map *89*; ship, TR *88-89*

Combat, transportation for: *See* Military transportation

Combines (grain harvesting machines): MA *14-15*

Combustion: ST *66-67, 68*; in car engine, ST *60*; extinguishing, ST *68-69*; of food in body, ST *82-83*; of metals, conditions for, ST *70-71*; photosynthesis and, ST *66-67*; of rocket fuel, craft powered by, ST *54-55, 71, 74-75*; of wood, ST *67, 68*

Communications: *See* Networks, computer

Communications cables: optical, ST *124-125*

Commutator: Pixii generator with, MA *28*

Commuter trains: TR *4-5*; cable car, TR *30*; computer-controlled, TR *24-25*; contact couplings, TR *9*; doors, TR *12-13, 25*; electromagnetic brakes, TR *10, 11*; subways' air supply, TR *26-27*

Compact disk read-only memory (CD-ROM): CO *95*

Compact disks (CDs): MA *86-87*

Compasses: gyrocompass, TR *80*; medieval, TR *87*

Composing stick: MA *6*

Composition of music: CO *66-67*

Compression molding of resins: ST *119*

Compression of gases: principle of, MA *123*

Compressors: hydrofoil's, TR *95*; jet engines', TR *130, 131*; turbocharger's, TR *54, 55*

Computer-aided design (CAD): of automobiles, CO *74-75*

Computer-aided manufacturing (CAM): of automobiles, CO *74-75*

Computer applications: CO 16, *84-107, 130-144*; airlines, CO *96-97*; automobiles, CO *102-103*; automotive industry, CO *74-75, 100-101*; banking, CO *88-89*; building design, CO *133*; business, CO *92-93*; crime, CO *106-107*; house, running of, CO *104-105*; Landsat mapping, CO *140-141*; medicine, CO *138-139*; missiles, cruise, CO *144*; publishing, CO *94-95*; robots, CO *98-99, 100-101*; space probes, CO *142-143*; sports, CO *136-137*; store products, bar codes on, CO *86-87*; traffic patterns, CO *132-133*; weather prediction, CO *134-135*. *See also* Graphics, computer; Networks, computer; Software and programs

Computer crime: CO *106-107*

Computer games: CO *78-79*

Computerized axial tomographic (CAT) scanners: MA *134-135*

Computerized reservation system (CRS): CO *96-97*

Computerized sewing machine: MA *105*

Computer models and simulations: *See* Simulations and models, computer

Computer networks: *See* Networks, computer

Computers: CO entire volume; addition by, CO 24, *25, 28, 29, 51*; aircraft, TR *124, 125*; analog and digital conversion, CO *40-41, 67, 110-111, 119*; architecture of, CO *18-19*; automated cars, TR *60, 61*; binary notation, use of, CO *26-27*; cranes, TR *73*; hydrofoils, TR *94, 95*; integrated circuits, CO *20-21, 22-23*; keyboards, CO *32-33, 90-91*; logic gates, CO *21, 28-29*; magnetic data storage, CO *19, 36-37, 56-57*; memory addresses, CO *30-31*; mouse, CO *34-35*; neurocomputers, CO *44-45*; pocket, CO *90-91*; printers, CO *38-39, 90-91, 95*; supercomputers, CO *15, 42-43, 134*; trains controlled by, TR *24-25*; vs. humans, CO *68-69*. *See also* Computer applications; History of computers; Software and programs

Computer simulations and models: *See* Simulations and models, computer

Concave surfaces: lenses, PH *117*; mirrors, PH *114-115*

Concorde (supersonic aircraft): TR *108-109, 136-137*

Concrete: ST *120-121*

Condensation of liquids: in distillation, ST 116, *117, 127*; of water vapor, ST *39*; of water vapor, and heat transfer, PH *64*; of water vapor on skin, in sauna, PH *64-65*

Condensers: in air conditioners, MA *122-123*; in dehumidifiers, MA *124-125*; in refrigerators, MA *106-107*

Conduction of electricity: by metals, ST *19*; by salt, ST *18-19*

Conductivity: thermal, PH chart *61*

Conferencing: audio, CO *112-113*

Conning room of nuclear submarine: TR *103*

Conning tower, submarine's: TR *99*

Constant bit coding vs. change bit coding: CO *36*

Construction equipment: cranes, TR *66-67, 72-73*; power shovels, TR *66-67, 76-77*; rollers, TR *66, 74-75*

Contact couplers for train cars: TR *9*

Control-configured vehicle (CCV; fighter jet): TR *140-141*

Controller chips: kinds of, CO 22

Control unit of central processing unit (CPU): CO *24-25*; location, CO *18*

Convection: PH *58-59, 66*; insulation against, PH *60-61*

Conversion I and II in nitrogen cycle: ST 27

Converters: in copper refining, ST *111*; pig iron in, ST *111, 112-113*

Convex surfaces: lenses, PH *116-117*; mirrors, PH 114, *115*

Cooking: microwave ovens, MA *102-103*; pressure cookers, MA *100-101*

Cooling mechanisms: air conditioners, MA *122-123*; in dehumidifiers, MA *124-125*; refrigerators, MA *106-107*

Copiers: MA *62*; color, MA *62-63*

Copolymers vs. homopolymers: ST 106

Copper: ST *114*; refining of, ST *111, 114*; structure of, ST *19*

Corpuscular vs. wave theory of light: PH 122

Cosmic rays: in carbon-14 formation, ST 25

Cotton: structure of, ST *12-13, 107*

Counting stones and abacuses: CO *4-5, 6-7*

Couplings: train cars', TR *8-9*

Course deviation indicator (CDI) dial: aircraft's, TR *123*

CPUs (central processing units): CO *18, 24-25*; and memory, CO *30*; microprocessor as, CO *22*

Cranes (mechanical): TR *66-67, 72-73*; block and tackle used with, PH *49*; jib, MA *52*; self-raising, MA *52-53*

Cray-1 supercomputer: CO *15*

Cray Y-MP supercomputer: CO *43*

Crime: computer, CO *106-107*

Animal Behavior
AN

Computer Age
CO

Ecology
EC

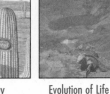
Evolution of Life
EV

Geography
GE

Human Body
HU

Insects & Spiders
IN

Machines &
Inventions **MA**

Cross-linked molecules: proteins, ST *84, 95.*
See also Polymers

Cross-staff: TR *87*

CRS (computer reservation system): CO *96-97*

Crude oil: refining of, ST *116-117*

Cruise missiles: CO *144*

Cruiser (ship): military, TR *78-79*

Cryogens: ST *40-41*

Crystal glassware: ST *125*

Crystalline lattices: metals, ST *13, 19, 28, 29, 31, 121, 140-141, 142, 143*; quartz, ST *122*

Crystals: ceramic, ST 130, *131*; ice, ST *39, 41, 93*; liquid, ST *136-137*; and piezoelectricity, MA *96*; quartz, ST *122*; quartz watches using, MA *96-97*; salt, ST *41*; silicon, ST *134-135*; silicon, microscopic view of, MA *32*

Cugnot, Nicolas Joseph: automobile invented by, TR 36, *38-39*

Current, electric: *See* Electricity

Cursor: mouse movement and, CO *34*

Curve ball: PH *24-25, 34-35*

Cyclone separator: PH *102*

Cylinders, automobiles': TR *40, 41*; steam car, TR *38-39*; turbocharger and, TR 54, 55

Cylinders, steam locomotive's: TR *14, 15*

D

Daguerre, Louis: MA 16, *17*

Daguerreotypes: MA *16*; camera for, MA *16-17*

Dams: and hydroelectric plants, PH *98-99*

Darrieus windmill: PH *104*

Databases: computerized reservation systems, CO *96, 97*; map information, CO *77*

Data networks: smart houses, CO *104*

Data retrieval: smart cards, MA *60-61*

Data storage: CO *30-31*; CD-ROM, CO *95*; magnetic, CO *19, 36-37, 56-57*; smart cards, MA *60-61*; after sorting, CO *55*

Data transfer between computers: CO *118-119*; pocket computer, CO *91*

Dating: of fossils, ST *24-25*

DC (direct current) and AC (alternating current): PH *85, 86*

Deadbeat escapement: pendulum clock's, MA *13*

Dead reckoning: TR *81*; with chip log, TR *87*

Dead zone: sailboat's, PH *13*

Debugging of programs: CO *49*

Decibels of sound: PH 128, 135

Decimal vs. binary notation: CO 26, *chart* 27

Deep Space Network: CO *142*

Deflection coils in TV picture tube: MA *77*

De Galley, Blasco: steamboat built by, TR *91*

Dehumidifiers: MA *124-125*

Demodulator, radio's: working of, MA *85*

Density: of gases, ST *46*; of water, PH *chart* 67, ST *chart* 35

Deoxyribonucleic acid (DNA): *See* DNA

Depth finders: TR *82*

Derailleur: bicycle's, PH *46*

Desktop computers: vs. mainframe computers, CO *18-19*

Desktop publishing: defined, CO *94*

Destiny 2000 electric car: TR *65*

Detergent: action of, MA *112*

Detonation wave: MA 25

Deuterium nuclei: fusion of, ST *17*

Developer in instant color photography: MA *92-93*

DeVries, William: MA 132

Dew point: MA 125

Diamonds: ST 132, *133*; synthetic, ST *132-133*

Diastole in artificial heart: MA *133*

Diastolic pressure: measuring, MA *131*

Dickson, W. K. L.: MA 20

Diesel-powered locomotives: TR *4-5*

Difference Engine: CO *10*

Differential: automobile's, TR *41, 49*

Differential flow device: MA *46-47*

Differential pressure sensor: MA *46*

Diffraction: defined, PH *112*; holograms and, PH *125*

Diffusion vacuum pumps: MA *44, 45*

Digestion, human: waste products of, ST *82-83*

Digital and analog conversion: CO *40-41, 67, 110-111, 119*

Digital and analog signals: compact disks, recording of, MA *86*; fax machine's use of, MA *68-69*; synthesizer's use of, MA *91*

Digitized illustrations in electronic publishing: CO *95*

Digitized strings: faxing, CO *114-115*

Dikes: in tidal power generating station, PH *106-107*

Diode: PH *85*

DIP (dual in-line package): CO *23*

Dirac, Paul: ST 22

Direct current (DC) and alternating current (AC): PH *85, 86*

Direct search: CO *57*

Dirt: removal of, by soap, ST *48-49*

Disappearing-filament optical pyrometers: PH 56, *57*

Disc brakes: automobile, TR *44, 58*; snowmobile, TR *69*; train, high-speed, TR *33*

Dishwashers: MA *116-117*

Disinfection of water: ST *98-99*

Disks, computer: and disk drives, CO *19, 36-37, 56-57*; CD-ROM, CO *95*

Distillation: fractional, of oil, ST *116-117*; steam, in perfume making, ST *126-127*

Distributor, automobile: role of, TR *41*

Divider circuit in quartz watch: MA *97*

DNA (deoxyribonucleic acid): ST *4-5*

Doctor blade in intaglio printing: MA *41*

Domains: magnetic, PH *78, 79*

Doors: commuter trains', TR *12-13, 25*

Doppler effect (Doppler shift): MA *39*, PH *138-139*; speed gun's use of, MA *38*; ultrasound's use of, MA *142*

Dot-matrix printers: CO *38-39*

Down jackets: insulation by, PH *60-61*

Downlink and uplink antennas: CO *128*

Drag: on baseball, PH *34*; in hang gliding, PH *14, 15*; vs. lift on airplane, TR *110*

Drains: whirlpools in, PH *20-21*

Drilling rigs: synthetic diamonds in, ST *133*

Drinking water: purifying, ST *98-99*

Drive shaft: automobile's, and differential gear, TR *41*

Drum brakes: automobile's, TR 44, *45*

Dry ice: ST 38, *39*; and alcohol, ST *40*

Dual in-line package (DIP): CO *23*

Dump trucks: tires for, TR *57*

Dyes in ink: ST 72, *73*; removal of, ST *72-73*

Dynamic microphones: MA *80*

Dynamic speakers: MA 80, *81*

Dynamite: working of, MA *24-25*

Dynamo: invention of, PH *94*

E

Ears, human: CO *63*

Earthmover: TR *77*

Eastman, George: MA 18, *19*; camera invented by, MA *18, 19*

Echo (U.S. satellite): CO *128*

Echoes: PH *132-133*

Echo sounder: TR *82*

Eckert, J. P.: CO *14*

Edison, Thomas: generator built by, MA *29*; movie by, MA *20*; movie equipment built by, MA *20-21*

Editors: electronic publishing by, CO *94-95*; word processors for, CO *58-59*

Eggs, boiled: ST *94-95*

Einstein, Albert: PH *126-127*

EKGs (electrocardiograms): MA *136-137*

Elastic limit of springs: PH 50, 51

E layer and F layer: CO *128*

Electrical generators: MA *28-29*

Electrical imbalance in polar molecules: ST *42, 43*

Planet Earth
PE

Plant Life
PL

Physical Forces
PH

Structure of Matter
ST

Space & Planets
SP

Transportation
TR

Underwater World
UN

Weather & Climate
WE

Animal Behavior
AN

Computer Age
CO

Ecology
EC

Evolution of Life
EV

Geography
GE

Human Body
HU

Insects & Spiders
IN

Machines &
Inventions **MA**

Ferrous and ferric tannate in ink: ST *72-73*

Fetal monitoring with ultrasound: MA *142-143*

Fiberoptic communications: CO *124-125*

Fibers: ST *12-13, 104*; carbon, ST *138-139*; glass, ST *124-125*; natural vs. synthetic, ST *109*; silk, ST *108*; synthetic, ST *108-109*

Fiberscopes: MA *138-139*

Field, Cyrus W.: MA 9

Field lines: *See* Magnetic field lines

Fighter jets: CCV (control-configured vehicle), TR *140-141*; Harrier, TR *138-139*

Filament of incandescent bulb: PH *72-73*

Files and records: CO 55, 56

Film: movie, projectors for, MA *20-21, 88-89*; Polaroid, working of, MA *92-93*; roll, Kodak camera's use of, MA 18, *19*

Films: *See* Movies

Filters: color, MA *62-63, 92*; VC (voltage control), sound quality affected by, MA *90*

Financial uses of computers: CO 92; banking, CO *88-89*

Fire: in combustion reactions, ST 66, 67, *68*; extinguishing, ST *68-69*

Fire alarm systems: MA *64-65*

Fire pumpers (fire engines): TR *66-67, 70-71*

Fireworks: ST *50-51*

First-class levers: PH *43*

First law of motion, Newton's: PH 24, 28

Fission, nuclear: ST *14-15*, TR 102, *103*; power production by, PH *108-109*; reactor core, PH *94-95, 108*

Fixing of nitrogen: ST *26*

Fizeau, Armand: experiment by, PH *118-119*

Flagpole: fixed pulley atop, PH *48*

Flaps, airplane's: function of, TR *110*

Flashbulb: magnesium, ST *71*

Flat package (FLP): CO *23*

Flavor enhancers: food, ST *90-91*

F layer and E layer: CO *128*

Flight corridors for aircraft: TR *120-121*; following, TR *122-123*

Flight director (FD), aircraft's: TR *127*

Flight reservations: computerized, CO *96-97*

Flight simulator: CO *82-83*

Floating: PH *8-9*

Florida, southern, U.S.: Landsat image of, CO *141*

Flour: starch in, ST *100-101*

Flow chart: CO *53*

Flowers and flowering plants: extracting oils from, ST *126-127*

FLP (flat package): CO *23*

Fluids: *See* Gases; Liquids

Fluorescent lamps: PH 72, *73*

Flyer (Wright airplane): TR *108, 134-135*

FM vs. AM radio transmissions: MA *85*

Foams: ST *20*; from fire extinguisher, ST *69*; fire pumper's use of, TR *71*

Focal point: reflection from curved surface, PH *114-115*; through lenses, PH *116, 122*

Focusing of cameras: automatic, MA *74-75*; Polaroid, MA *93*

Fog: navigation in, TR *82-83*

Food chain: nitrogen in, ST *27*

Food science: ST *78-101*; acidic vs. alkaline foods, ST *82-83*; apple, browning of, ST *80-81*; coffee, instant, ST *86-87*; eggs, boiled, ST *94-95*; flavor enhancers, ST *90-91*; flour, starch in, ST *100-101*; freezing rates, ST *93*; ice cream, ST *92-93*; preservation, ST *88-89*; salt reclamation from sea, ST *96-97*; water purification, ST *98-99*; yogurt, ST *84-85*

Forces, kinds of: PH *4*; buoyancy vs. gravity, PH *4-5, 8-9, 10-11*; lift and drag in hang gliding, PH *14, 15*; Magnus effect, PH *34, 35*; on roller coasters, PH *30-31*; on sailboats, PH *12-13*; on skiers, PH *26-27*; on surfboards, PH *38*; torque, PH *32*; on train passengers, PH *28-29*. *See also* Electricity; Friction; Gravity; Machines, simple; Magnetism; Pressure

Forger VTOL aircraft: TR *139*

Formula One racing cars: TR *58-59*

FORTRAN (programming language): CO *50-51*; program in, CO 51

Forward-swept wings: aircraft with, TR *142-143*

Fossil fuels: energy from, and thermoelectric power, PH *100-101*

Fossils: dating, ST *24-25*

Foucault, Jean-Bernard-Léon: speed of light measured by, PH 118, *119*

Four-color processes: photocopying, MA *62-63*; printing, MA *40*

Four-wheel drive (4WD) vehicles: TR *48-49*; tires for, TR *57*

Four-wheel steering (4WS): TR *50-51*

Fractals: CO *70*

Fractional distillation: ST *116-117*

France: high-speed train in, TR *33*

Frank, Barney: MA *132*

Free electrons: in conductors, PH 82, *84*; radioactive decay and, PH *90*; in semiconductors, PH *84*

Freewheel gear: bicycle's, PH *46-47*

Freeze-drying: of coffee, ST *86-87*

Freezing: ST *34, 35*; foods, ST *89, 92, 93*; temperature of, lowering, ST *40-41*; of water, PH *66-67*

Freight trains: automatic air brakes, TR *10-11*; diesel-powered locomotives, TR *4-5*

Frequency modulation: CO *66*, MA *85*

Frequency of sound: PH 128, 131, *135*; and Doppler effect, PH *138*; and pitch, MA *90*; of tuning forks, PH *142*

Friction: and skiers, PH *26-27*; and static electricity, PH 70, *71*; and water flow, PH *20, 21*

Front-loading washing machine: MA *113*

Fulcrum: lever's, PH *42, 43*

Full adder: half-adder vs., CO 28, *29*

Fulton, Robert: paddle steamer built by *(Clermont)*, TR *90-91*

Fundamental tone: PH *134, 137*

Funicular cable car system: TR *31*

Fusion, nuclear: ST *16-17*

G

Galileo Galilei: PH 28; experiment by, PH *29*

Galley, Blasco de: steamboat built by, TR *91*

Gallows phone: Bell's, MA *10-11*

Galvanizing of metal: ST *63*

Galvanometers: PH 76, *96*; Thomson's, MA *9*

Games: computer, CO *78-79*

Gamma decay: PH *91*

Gases: atmospheric, ST *25, 26-27, 36-37, 76-77*; and buoyancy, ST *46-47*; in colloids, ST *20*; exhaust, ST 60, *61*, 74, *chart* 75; in fluorescent lamps, PH 72, *73*; lighter-than-air, PH *10*; phase changes, ST *38, 39*; pressure, temperature, and volume of, PH *11*; vs. liquids and solids, determinants of, ST *44-45*; water as, ST *32-33*, 34, *35*. *See also* Air; Water vapor

Gasoline: combustion in car engine, ST *60-61*; production, ST *117*

Gasoline tractor combine: MA *14-15*

Gas-pressure sensors: MA *120*

Gastroscope: MA *138-139*

Gates, logic: CO *21, 28*; in adder circuits, CO 28, *29*

Gatun Locks, Panama Canal: ship passing through, TR *92-93*

Gearbox: hydrofoil's, TR *95*

Gear ratios: bicycle's, PH *46*, *charts* 46

Gears, automobile: differential, TR *41, 49*; planetary, TR *47*; shifting, TR *46*; transfer, in optional 4WD, TR *49*; viscous coupling, TR *49*

Gears, bicycle: PH *46-47*

Geese: feathers of, PH *60*

Geiger counters: PH *91*; working of, PH *90, 91*

Generators, electrical: MA *28-29*. *See also* Electricity, generating

Geostationary orbit: CO *128-129*

Planet Earth
PE

Plant Life
PL

Physical Forces
PH

Structure of Matter
ST

Space & Planets
SP

Transportation
TR

Underwater World
UN

Weather & Climate
WE

Geostationary satellites: CO *128-129*; PH 37

Geothermal power: generation of, PH *102-103*

Germany, trains in: Intercity Express (ICE), TR *33*; maglevs, TR *34, 35*; monorail, TR *29*

Geysers: PH 102

Glass: making of, ST *122-123*; uses for, ST *124-125*

Glassblowing: ST *123*

Glass-break sensors: MA *114*

Glide-path indicator in airport's ILS (instrument landing system): TR 126, 127

Gliders (aircraft): TR *118-119*

Gliders, hang: PH *14-15*

Global Positioning System (GPS) satellites: TR 84

Glucose molecules: from photosynthesis, ST *66*; in starch, ST *100-101*

Glutamic acid: production of, ST *90-91*

Goddard, Robert H.: MA 26

Gold leaf: ST 29

Golf: computer analysis of, CO *137*

Gondola: blimp's, TR *117*

Goodyear, Charles: ST 30

Goose: feathers of, PH *60*

GPS (Global Positioning System) satellites: TR 84

Graded-index optical fibers: CO *125*

Grain harvesting: combines for, MA *14-15*

Gramme, Zénobe-Théophile: generator built by, MA *29*

Graphics, computer: CO *70-83*; automobile design, CO *74-75*; face, image of, CO *72-73*; flight simulator, CO *82-83*; games, CO *78-79*; maps, CO *76-77*; special effects, CO *80-81*; from word-processing programs, CO *59*

Graphite: diamonds synthesized from, ST *132, chart* 133

Gravity: PH 4, 6; center of, ship's, PH *9*; center of, top's, PH *32, 33*; escape of, by three-stage rocket, PH *18-19*; and inclined plane, PH *44*; lift vs., in hang gliding, PH *14, 15*; and skiers, PH *26-27*; viscosity vs., and whirlpool formation, PH *20*; vs. buoyancy, in air, PH *4-5, 10-11*; vs. buoyancy, in water, PH *8-9*; vs. inertia, PH *28, 29*, 30, 31, *37*; and weight, PH *6-7*

Gravity wells: PH *7*

Gravure (intaglio) printing: MA 40, *41*

Greek abacus: CO *7*

Guidance system, automatic: V-2 rocket's, MA 27

Gutenberg, Johannes: MA *7*; printing method of, MA *6-7*

Gutenberg Bible: MA *7*

Gyroaccelerometer: V-2 rocket's, MA 27

Gyrocompass: TR *80*

Gyroscope: PH 32; in aircraft's INS (inertial navigation system), TR 124

H

Hackers: computer crime by, CO *106-107*

Half-adder circuit: CO 28, *29*

Hands, robotic: CO *98*

Hang gliders: PH *14-15*

Hard disks and disk drives: CO *36-37, 57*

Harrier jet: TR *138-139*

Harvesting of grain: combines for, MA *14-15*

Hearing aid: computerized, CO *139*

Heart, human: MA *132*; and blood pressure, MA 130; computerized assistance for, CO *138-139*; current fluctuations, EKGs of, MA *136-137*; fetus's, ultrasound monitoring of, MA 142; listening to, stethoscope for, MA 144; mechanical, MA *132-133*; pacemaker for, MA *133*; rate, lie detector's measurement of, MA 36

Heart-lung machine: CO *139*

Heat: combustion and, ST 66, 67, 68; conductivity, PH *chart* 61; and electrons in fireworks, ST *50-51*; extreme, measuring, PH *56-57*; geothermal energy, PH *102-103*; and kinetic energy, ST *34, 35*; loss of, insulation against, PH *60-61*; in nuclear reactor, PH *109*; and phase changes, PH *22-23, 52-53, 54-55, 62-63*; reducing, in extinguishing fire, ST 68; of rocket fuel's combustion, ST *chart* 74; in sauna, effects of, PH *64-65*; shape-memory alloys and, ST *128-129, 140*; solar, as power source, PH 110, *111*; spreading of, in fluids, PH *58-59*; in thermoelectric plant, PH *100-101*; water vapor's transfer of, PH *64*

Heat energy vs. thermal energy: PH 52

Heating: of air, PH *10-11*; convection by, PH *58-59*; in steamer, PH 65

Heat-pump-type air conditioner: MA *122*

Heat-sensitive devices: MA *120-121*; in fire alarms, MA 64, 65; in thermometer, MA *128*

Heat transfer: by water vapor, PH *64*

Heavy oil: ST *117*

Heeling operation: icebreaker's, TR *100*

Helical springs: PH *51*

Helicopters: TR *109, 114-115*

Helium: in blimps, use of, ST *46-47*; formation of, in fusion reactions, ST *16-17*

Hemodialysis machine: CO *139*

High-definition television: MA *78-79*

High-level vacuum: pump producing, MA *44-45*

High-speed printing press: MA *40-41*

High-speed trains: TR *32-33*; bullet trains, TR *4-5, 33*

Hill, James J.: quoted, TR 18

Hiller, Lejaren: *Illiac Suite for String Quartet*, CO 66, 67

History of computers: CO *4-15*; abacuses and counting stones, CO *4-5, 6-7*; calculators, seventeenth-century, CO *4-5, 8-9*; first computer, Babbage's, CO 4, *10-11*; first electronic computer, CO 4, *14-15*, 84; first supercomputer, CO *15*; Hollerith's contribution, CO *12-13*

Hoists: PH *49*

Holes in semiconductors: PH *84, 85*

Hollerith, Herman: CO *13*; invention, CO *12-13*

Holograms: PH *124-125*

Homopolymers vs. copolymers: ST *106-107*

Hooke, Robert: Hooke's law, PH 50

Horizontal canard: CCV's, TR *141*

Horse-drawn combine: MA *14*; area harvested by, MA *14-15*

Hot-air balloons: PH *4-5, 10-11*

Hot dip galvanizing, continuous: ST *63*

Household network in smart house: CO *105*

Houses: computer-run, CO *104-105*

Hovercraft: TR *78, 96-97*

Hulls, Jonathan: steam-driven tugboat patented by, TR *91*

Hull tanks for ships: use of, PH *9*

Humanoid robot: hypothetical, CO *98-99*

Humans vs. computers: CO *68-69*; brain, CO *44-45*; organs, CO *138-139*; speech production, CO *60-61*; speech recognition, CO *62-63*

Humidity control: dehumidifier for, MA *124-125*

Humidity in sauna: effect of, PH *64-65*

Huygens, Christiaan: MA 13

Hydrated cement: ST *120*

Hydraulic cylinder: on climbing crane, MA *52-53*

Hydraulic systems: TR *66*; climbing crane's, MA *52-53*; standard crane's, TR *73*; power shovel's, TR 76, *77*

Hydrochloric acid: formation of, ST *99*

Hydroelectric power plant: PH *98-99*

Hydrofoils: TR *79, 94-95*

Hydrogen: ST *6, 7*; buoyancy of, ST *46*; fusion of, ST *17*; as rocket fuel, PH 18, ST *74, 75*; size of atoms, relative, ST *8, 9*; vs. antihydrogen, ST *22-23*; in water molecules, PH *54-55*

Hydrogenation refining device: ST *117*

Hydrophilic and hydrophobic components of soap molecules: ST 48, 49

Hydroplaning: treadless vs. treaded tires

Animal Behavior
AN

Computer Age
CO

Ecology
EC

Evolution of Life
EV

Geography
GE

Human Body
HU

Insects & Spiders
IN

Machines &
Inventions **MA**

and, TR 56

Hydro-rods: hovercraft's use of, TR 97

Hydroxide ions: ST 56

Hydroxyl groups in cellulose molecules: ST 104, 105

Hyperfusion filter: CO 139

Hypochlorite ion: ST 76

I

IC chips: *See* Integrated circuits

Ice: crystals, ST 39, 41, 93; dry ice, ST 38, 39, 40; formation of, PH 66-67; freezing point, lowering of, ST 40-41; molecular structure of, ST 34, 35; phase change in, heat and, PH 52-53, 54-55; skating on, PH 26, 27

Icebreakers: TR 100-101

Ice cream: making of, ST 92-93

IC logic cards: MA 60-61

Iconoscope: MA 22, 23

Ignition coil, automobile's: role of, TR 41

Illiac Suite for String Quartet (Hiller and Isaacson): CO 66, 67

Illustrations: electronic publishing of, CO 94-95; faxing, CO 114-115. *See also* Graphics, computer

ILS (instrument landing system) for aircraft: TR 126-127

Impact printers: CO 38-39

Impulse turbine: PH 99

Incandescent bulb: working of, PH 72-73

Inclined planes: PH 44-45

Indirect reduction of ore: ST 110-111

Induction: electromagnetic, PH 94

Industrial chemistry: ST 102-127; alloys in, ST 112-113; concrete, ST 120-121; glass, ST 122-123, 124-125; metal refining, ST 102-103, 110-111, 114-115; oil refining, ST 116-117; papermaking, ST 104-105; perfume making, ST 126-127; plastics, ST 118-119; polymerization, ST 106-107; synthetic fibers, ST 108-109. *See also* Materials technology

Inertia: PH 28-29; Galileo's experiment, PH 29; law of, PH 24, 28; and train passengers, PH 28-29; vs. gravity, PH 28, 29, 30, 31, 37

Inertial guidance system: V-2 rocket's, MA 27

Inertial navigation system (INS): TR 124-125

Information searches: CO 56-57

Infrared, use of: burglar alarms, MA 114, 115; camera's autofocus system, MA 75

Infrared radiation: measuring, PH 56-57

Injection molding of resins: ST 118-119, 138

Ink and ink removers: ST 72-73

Inking of type: MA 6

Input devices: CO 18, 19; game controller, CO 79; keyboards, CO 32-33, 90-91; mouse, CO 34-35

INS (inertial navigation system): TR 124-125

Instant coffee: making of, ST 86-87

Instant photography: color, MA 92-93

Instrument flights, aircraft on: inertial navigation system (INS), TR 124-125; landing system for (ILS), TR 126-127; Omega System for, TR map 125; traffic corridors for, TR 120-121; VHF omni-range stations and, TR 122-123

Instrument landing system (ILS): TR 126-127

Instruments: *See* Musical instruments

Insulation: electrical, PH 82, 83, 84; thermal, PH 60-61

Intaglio printing: MA 40, 41

Integrated circuits: CO 20-21, 22-23, MA 54; in cameras, MA 75; packages for, CO 23; quartz watch, circuitry in, MA 97; silicon for, ST 134-135; in smart cards, MA 60-61; in telephones, MA 56

Integrated Services Digital Network: CO 108

INTELSAT satellites: CO 128-129

Intercity Express (ICE; German high-speed train): TR 33

Intercom: working of, PH 84, 85

Interference of waves: light waves, PH 112, 120-121; light waves, and holograms, PH 124, 125; microwaves, speed gun's use of, MA 38-39

Intermolecular forces, breaking of: by ions, ST 40, 41; by kinetic energy, ST 34, 35

Ion exchange film: glutamic acid and, ST 91; in salt reclamation, ST 96, 97

Ions: from acid and alkaline substances, ST 64, 65, 82, 83; in automobile batteries, ST 58-59; copper, ST 114; hypochlorite, ST 76; in iron reactions, ST 56; silver, in electroplating, ST 62-63; sodium and chloride, ST 18-19, 40, 41, 43, 96

Iron: burning, conditions for, ST 70-71; casting, ST 112; galvanizing, ST 63; molten, measuring temperature of, PH 56-57; pig iron, refining into pig iron, ST 102-103, 110-111; rusting, ST 56-57; steel from, ST 111, 112-113. *See also* Ferromagnetic materials

Iron, electric: with thermostat, MA 120-121

Iron hydroxide: ST 56, 57, 110

Iron oxide: ST 56, 57, 110

Isaacson, Leonard: *Illiac Suite for String Quartet*, CO 66, 67

J

Jackets, down: insulation by, PH 60-61

Jackscrew: PH 45

Jacquard, Joseph-Marie: loom invented by, CO 10, 11

Japan: Atomic Energy Research Institute, nuclear power plant at, PH 109; bullet trains, TR 4-5, 33; icebreaker (*Shirase*), TR 101; luxury train (*Twilight Express*), TR 18-19; solar-powered automobile (*Southern Cross*), TR 62-63; superconducting train design, PH 93

Japanese abacus: CO 7

Jarvik-7 artificial heart: MA 132-133

Jet action in dishwasher: MA 117

Jet aircraft: TR 108-109; CCV (control-configured vehicle), TR 140-141; Concorde, TR 108-109, 136-137; engines, working of, TR 130-131, 139; sonic booms from, PH 140-141; Stealth bomber, TR 109, 144; VTOL (vertical takeoff and landing), TR 138-139; X-29A, TR 142-143

Jib crane: MA 52

Joint implants: ceramic, ST 130

Jordan snowplow: TR 23

Joystick: CO 35

Jumbo jets: TR 108-109; engines, TR 131

Jump jet fighters: Harrier, TR 138-139

K

Kamerlingh Onnes, Heike: PH 92

Kawaguchi, Yoichiro: image by, CO 70-71

Kelvin, William Thomson, 1st Baron: MA 9

Kerosene: as fraction of crude oil, ST 117; as rocket fuel, ST 74

Keyboards: computer's, CO 32-33, 58, 90-91; synthesizer's, MA 91

Keys for records: CO 56, 57

Kidneys: artificial, CO 139

Kinetic energy: of molecules, PH 23, 52; of rolled ball, PH 29; of roller coaster, PH 31; vs. intermolecular forces, ST 34, 35

Kinetograph: MA 20

Kinetoscope: MA 20-21

"Kiss, The" (Edison movie): MA 20

Kitchen items: dishwasher, MA 116-117; microwave oven, MA 102-103; pressure cooker, MA 100-101; refrigerator, MA 106-107

Knives: ceramic, ST 130

Knuckle-type couplers for train cars: TR 8-9

Kodak cameras: MA 18; ad for, MA 18; working of, MA 18, 19

Korotkoff sounds: MA 131

Krypton: fission producing, ST 14-15

Planet Earth
PE

Plant Life
PL

Physical Forces
PH

Structure of Matter
ST

Space & Planets
SP

Transportation
TR

Underwater World
UN

Weather & Climate
WE

L

Laënnec, René: stethoscope invented by, MA *144*

Lamps: electricity illuminating, PH *72-73*

Landing of aircraft: glider, TR *118*; instrument landing system (ILS) for, TR *126-127*

Landsat satellites: CO *140-141*

Languages, computer: CO *50-51*; programs in, CO 51

LANs (local area networks): CO 108

Laser beams: bar codes scanned by, CO *86-87*; color copiers using, MA *62-63*; compact disks read by, MA *87*; fiberoptic cables guiding, CO *124-125*

Lasers: PH *112-113, 122-123*; and holograms, PH *124, 125*; speed of light measured with, PH *119*

Latent heat of fusion: defined, PH 54

Lattices: crystalline, of metal, ST *13, 19, 28, 29, 31, 121, 140-141, 142, 143*

Lawn mowers: tires for, TR *57*

Laws of motion, Newton's: PH 18, 24, 28

LCC (leadless chip carrier): CO 23

LCDs (liquid-crystal displays): ST *136-137*

Leaded glass: ST *125*

Leadless chip carrier (LCC): CO 23

Lead storage battery: automobile, ST *58-59*

Leaf springs: PH *51*

LEDs: *See* Light-emitting diodes (LEDs)

Left-hand rule: TR *105*

Legs, robotic: CO *99*

Leibniz, Baron Gottfried Wilhelm von: CO 8; calculator invented by, CO *9*

Lenses, mechanical: PH *116-117*; autofocus camera, MA *74-75*; binoculars, MA *95*; camera, leaded glass for, ST *125*; daguerrotype camera, MA *16*; natural light vs. lasers through, PH *122*; Polaroid camera, MA *93*

Letters: electronic mail (E-mail), CO *116-117*

Level converters: use of, CO *91*

Lever action and screws: PH *44-45*

Levers: PH *42-43*; bathroom scales' use of, MA *108-109*

Lie detectors: MA *36-37*

Lift: airplane's wings and, TR *110-111*; and drag, in hang gliding, PH *14, 15*; eagle's use of, TR *118*; glider's use of, TR 118; helicopter's rotor and, TR *114*

Lifting: TR *66*; cranes for, TR *66-67, 72-73*; excavators for, TR *67, 76-77*

Light: PH *112-127*; in binoculars, path of, MA *94*; in camera, single-lens reflex, MA *75*; in color copier, MA *62-63*; colors of, primary, MA *77, 92*; compact disks read

by, MA *87*; corpuscular vs. wave theory of, PH 112; curved surfaces, reflection from, PH *114-115*; electricity and, PH *72-73*; and holograms, PH *124-125*; in instant color photography, MA 92, *93*; through lenses, PH *116-117, 122*; and liquid crystals, ST *136-137*; movie projector's use of, MA 88, *89*; through optical fiber, CO *124-125*, ST *125*; and photosensitive resin, ST *144*; properties of, PH 112; release of, in fireworks, ST *50-51*; scattering of, ST *20*; sensor, photoelectric, in smoke detector, MA *65*; and soap bubbles, PH *120-121*; spectrum of, PH *120*; speed of, measuring, PH *118-119*; speed of, nearing, PH *126-127*; in temperature measurement, PH 56, *57*; wavelengths, and color, ST *51*; wave vs. corpuscular theory of, PH 112

Light, laser: PH *112-113, 119, 122-123, 124, 125*; bar codes scanned by, CO *86-87*; fiberoptic cables guiding, CO *124-125*

Light bulbs: working of, PH *72-73*

Light-emitting diodes (LEDs): automated cars' use of, TR *60;* in mouse, CO *34, 35*; in pen-type scanners, CO *87*

Lightning: in nitrogen cycle, ST *26*

Lightning fixing: of nitrogen, ST *26*

Light-sensitive emulsions in Polaroid film: MA *92-93*

Liquid crystal displays (LCDs): ST *136-137*

Liquid crystals: ST *136-137*

Liquid-fuel rockets: ST *75*

Liquid rocket fuel: PH *18*

Liquids: in colloids, ST *20*; contraction of, PH 66; flow of, measuring, MA *46-47*; freezing of, PH *66-67*; phase changes, ST *38, 39*; vs. gases and solids, determinants of, ST *44-45. See also* Water

Lithium 8: beta decay of, PH *91*

Lithography as printing method: MA *40-41*

Litmus paper: use of, ST *82*

Liver: computerized assistance for, CO *139*

Loader: TR 77

Local area networks (LANs): CO 108

Localizer in airport's ILS: TR 126, 127

Locks, canal: Panama Canal's, TR *92-93*

Locomotion (early locomotive): TR *15*

Locomotives: diesel-powered, TR *4-5*; with snowplows, TR *22-23*; steam-powered, TR *4-5, 14-15, 16-17*; traction for, TR *6*

Logarithms: inventor of, CO 8

Logic cards, IC: MA *60-61*

Logic chips: CO 22, *23*

Logic elements (gates): CO *21, 28*; in adder circuits, CO 28, *29*

Looms: Jacquard, CO 10, *11*

Loran (long-range navigation): determining

ship's position with, TR *81, 82-83*

Loudness of sound: wave height and, MA *90*

Loudspeakers: dynamic, MA 80, *81*

Low-level vacuums: water-seal pump producing, MA *45*

Luxury trains: TR *18-19*

M

Mach cone: TR *136-137*

Mach indicator: airplane's, TR *132-133*

Machine language: CO 50; translation into, CO *51*

Machines: MA entire volume

Machines, simple: PH 40-51; inclined planes, PH *44-45*; levers, PH *42-43*; pulleys, PH *48-49*; screws, PH *44-45*; springs, PH *50-51*; wheel and axle, bicycle's use of, PH *46-47*

Macromolecules: *See* Polymers

Magdeburg hemispheres: PH *16-17*

Magellan, Ferdinand, expedition of: route, TR *map* 86-87; ship, TR *87*

Maglev (magnetic levitation) trains: TR *4-5, 34-35*

Magnesium: forms of, ST 70, *71*

Magnetic brakes: trains', TR *10, 11*

Magnetic data storage: CO *19, 36-37, 56-57*

Magnetic domains: PH *78, 79*

Magnetic field lines: PH *78-79*; in AC generator, PH *96-97*; of electromagnet, PH *80-81*; shapes of, PH *68-69, 81*; and superconductor vs. normal conductor, PH *92-93*

Magnetic fields: metal detectors', MA *42, 43*; TV deflection coils', MA *77. See also* Magnets

Magnetic levitation (maglev) trains: TR *4-5, 34-35*

Magnetic recording by VCR: MA 82, *83*

Magnetism: in AC generators, PH *96-97*; attraction of metals by, PH *78-79*; and electricity, PH *68-69, 80-81*, 94; in electromagnetic waves, PH *88-89*; electromagnets, PH *80-81, 99*, 100, *101*; in measurement of electricity, PH 76, *77*; and superconductors, PH *92-93*; and transformers, PH *86*

Magnetrons: MA *102, 103*; working of, MA *103*

Magnets: in burglar alarms, MA *114*; direction of motion, rule for, TR *105*; in electrocardiograph, MA *137*; in generators, electrical, MA 28, *29*; in maglevs, TR *34*; in microphones, MA *80*; in power meters, MA *118-119*; in speakers, MA *81*; superconducting, TR *104-105*; in telephones, MA *57*; in VCRs, MA *83*

| Animal Behavior **AN** | Computer Age **CO** | Ecology **EC** | Evolution of Life **EV** | Geography **GE** | Human Body **HU** | Insects & Spiders **IN** | Machines & Inventions **MA** |

Magnification: by binoculars, MA *94-95*; by electron microscope, MA *32-33*; by magnifying glass, PH *116-117*

Magnifying glasses: PH *116-117*

Magnus effect: on baseball, PH *34-35*

Mail, electronic (E-mail): CO *116-117*

Mainframe computer: architecture of, CO *18-19*

MALTRON layout of keys: CO *33*

Management functions of computers: CO 93

Manipulator (robotic hand): CO *98*

Manual transmission: automobile's, TR *46*

Maps and mapping: sixteenth-century, TR *86-87*; computer, CO *76-77, 135, 140-141*; Landsat satellites for, CO *140-141*; weather, CO *135*

Marketing functions of computers: CO 93

Mark I calculator: CO *14*

Mass vs. weight: PH 6

Matter and chemistry: ST entire volume

Materials technology: ST 128-144; amorphous metals, ST *142-143*; carbon fiber, ST *138-139*; ceramics, advanced, ST *130-131*; diamonds, synthetic, ST *132-133*; liquid crystals, ST *136-137*; photosensitive resin, ST *144*; shape-memory alloys, ST *128-129, 140-141*; single-crystal silicon, ST *134-135*

Mauchly, John: CO *14*

Measurements: precision, MA *48-49*

Mechanical devices: See Machines, simple

Mechanical heart: MA *132-133*; auxiliary, MA *133*

Mechanical mouse vs. optical mouse: CO *34-35*

Mechanical scanning television: MA *22-23*

Medical instruments and machines: MA 126-144; for blood pressure measurement, MA *130-131*; CAT scanner, MA *134-135*; electrocardiograph, MA *136-137*; fiberscope, MA *138-139*; heart, mechanical, MA *132-133*; pacemaker, MA *133*; stethoscope, MA *144*; thermometer, electronic, MA *128-129*; for ultrasound, MA *142-143*; x-ray machine, MA *140-141*

Medical uses of computers: CO *138-139*

Meissner effect: PH *93*

Melting of ice: PH *52-53, 54-55*, ST *34*; ions and, ST *41*

Memory, digital: CO 18, *30-31*; CD-ROM, CO *95*; smart card's, MA 61

Memory cards for pocket computers: CO *91*

Memory chips: CO 22

Mendeleev, Dmitri: ST 10

Mercury barometers: PH 16, *17*

Message-display vs. tone-only pagers: CO 122, *123*

Message handling system (MHS): CO 116, 117

Metal detectors: MA *42-43*

Metals: and advance of civilization, ST 102; alloys, ST *112-113*; alloys, shape-memory, ST *128-129, 140-141*; amorphous, ST *142-143*; atoms of, ST *13, 19, 28-29, 31, 121, 140-141, 142-143*; burning, conditions for, ST *70-71*; electric conduction by, ST *19*; flexibility, ST *28-29*; glass enhanced with, ST *125*; in periodic table, ST *chart* 10-11; plating methods, ST *62-63*; refining, ST *102-103, 110-111, 114-115*; rusting, ST *56-57*; vs. ceramics, advanced, ST *charts* 131

Metal spraying: ST *63*

Metal testers in vending machines: MA 58, 59

Metal thermal sensors: MA *121*; in fire alarm, MA *65*; in iron, MA *120-121*

Meteorology: computer use in, CO *134-135*

Meters: electric power, MA *118-119*; water, MA *46, 47*

Metrorail commuter trains, Washington, D.C.: control room for, TR *24*

Micelles: formation of, ST *48-49*

Michelson, Albert: experiment by, PH 126

Microchips: See Integrated circuits

Microfibrils in cotton fibers: ST *13*

Micrometers: MA *48-49*

Microphones: dynamic, MA *80*

Microprocessors: camera's, MA *75*; chips, CO *16-17*, 22, *23*; and keyboard, CO *32, 33*; multiple, CO *42-43*; robotic eye with, CO *99*; sewing machine with, MA *105*; thermometer's, MA 128, *129*

Microscopes: electron, MA *32-33*

Microwave landing system (MLS) for aircraft: TR 126

Microwave ovens: MA *102-103*

Microwaves: speed gun's use of, MA *38-39*

Military transportation: TR *109*; bombers, Stealth, TR *109, 144*; cruisers, TR *78-79*; fighter jets, CCV, TR *140-141*; fighter jets, Harrier, TR *138-139*; submarines, TR *98-99, 102-103*

Milk: as colloid, ST *20, 21*; yogurt from, ST *84-85*

Mirrors: curved, reflection by, PH *114-115*; galvanometer, Thomson's, MA *9*; Polaroid camera's use of, MA *93*

Missiles: cruise, CO *144*

Mitsubishi Model MSRII (automated car): TR *60-61*

MLS (microwave landing system): TR 126

Mobile phone calls: CO *120-121*

Mobile robots: problem of, CO *99*

Models and simulations, computer: See Simulations and models, computer

Modems (modulator/demodulators), use of: CO 118, *119*; by pocket computers, CO *91*

Modulation: of carrier waves, MA *85*; in faxing, CO *115*; of frequency, CO *66*

Molasses: sugarcane, MSG from, ST *90-91*

Molding of plastics: compression, ST *119*; injection, ST *118-119*, 138

Molecules: ST *13*; air, PH *10-11*, 60; alumina, ST *115*; in apples, and browning, ST *80, 81*; aromatic, ST *126-127*; cellulose, ST *12-13, 67*, 104, *105*; in colloids, ST *20*; DNA, ST *4-5*; in glass, ST *122, 123*; glucose, ST *66, 100-101*; glutamic acid, ST 90, *91*; of liquid crystals, ST *137*; makeup of, ST *6-7*; nitrogen, ST *26-27*; odor, removal of, ST *52-53*; ozone, ST *76-77*; in photosynthesis, ST *66*; polar and nonpolar, ST 42, *43*, 48; soap, ST *48-49*; sodium chloride, ST *18*; water, PH *20-23, 52-53, 54-55*, 62. See also Polymers

Momentum: PH 30; angular, PH 32

Money sorters: in vending machines, MA 58, *59*

Monomers: polymerization of, ST *106-107*

Monorails: TR *28-29*

Monosodium glutamate (MSG): manufacture of, ST *90-91*

Moon, Earth's: Apollo spacecraft shot toward, PH *19*; vs. Earth, weight on, PH *6-7*

Morley, Edward, experiment by: PH 126

Morse, Samuel F. B.: MA *8*

Morse code: MA *9*

Motherboards: CO *22-23*

Motion: changes in, and inertia, PH *28-29*; energy of (kinetic energy), PH *23, 29, 31*, 52; Newton's laws of, PH 18, 24, 28

Motion analysis programs for athletes: CO *136-137*

Motorboats: TR *79*

Motorcycles: TR *42-43*

Mountainside cable car systems: brakes, TR *30*; funicular, TR *31*

Mountain updrafts: and gliders, TR *119*

Mouse: CO *34-35*

Movie camera: first (kinetograph), MA *20*

Movie projectors: MA *88-89*; kinetoscope, MA *20-21*

Movies: special effects for, CO *80-81*

Music: compact disks (CDs) and phonograph records for playing, MA *86-87*; making, with computers, CO *66-67*; synthesizers for producing, MA *90-91*

Musical instruments: PH *128-129*; tones, production of, PH *134-135, 136-137*;

Planet Earth
PE

Plant Life
PL

Physical Forces
PH

Structure of Matter
ST

Space & Planets
SP

Transportation
TR

Underwater World
UN

Weather & Climate
WE

tuning, PH *142-143*; wind instruments, PH *135, 136-137*

N

Napier, John: CO 8

Napier's rods: CO *5, 8*

Naval Navigation Satellite System (NNSS), U.S.: TR *84-85*

Navigation: TR 78, *80-81*; aircraft, aids for, TR *122-123, 124-125*; automatic car's system, TR *60*; in fog, TR *82-83*; on-board navigation computers, in automobiles, CO *103*; in past, TR *86-87*; rules of the road for, TR *83*; satellite, TR *84-85*; submarine, aids for, TR *103*

Negative-channel metal-oxide semiconductor (n-MOS): CO *22*

Nematic liquid crystals: ST *137*

Neodymium 144: alpha decay of, PH *91*

Nerve cells: *See* Neurons (nerve cells) of human brain

Networks, computer: CO *108-129*; business computers, CO *92-93*; car phones, CO *120-121*; data transfer between computers, CO *91, 118-119*; electronic mail, CO *116-117*; fax machines, CO *114-115*; fiberoptic communications, CO *124-125*; pagers, electronic, CO *122-123*; picture phones, CO *126-127*; satellites, communications, CO *128-129*; teleconferencing, CO *112-113*; telephone lines, voice transmission through, CO *110-111*

Neurocomputers: CO *44-45*

Neurons (nerve cells) of human brain: CO *45*

Neutral gear: automobile's, TR *46*

Neutrons: ST *7*; in carbon-14 formation, ST *25*; in nuclear fission, PH *108*; in nuclear fusion, ST *16-17*

New materials: *See* Materials technology

Newton, Sir Isaac: PH 24, 112; laws of motion, PH 18, 24, 28

Niepce, Joseph-Nicéphore: MA 16

Nipkow, Paul: MA 22

Nipkow scanning disks: use of, MA *22-23*

Nitrates: ST *27*; production of, ST *26*

Nitrogen: carbon 14 and, ST *24, 25*; reactions involving, ST *26-27*

Nitrogen cycle: ST *26-27*

Nitrogen dioxide and acid rain: ST 64

Nitroglycerin explosion: chain reaction in, MA *24-25*

n-MOS (negative-channel metal-oxide semiconductor): CO *22*

NNSS (U.S. Naval Navigation Satellite System): TR *84-85*

Nobel, Alfred: MA 24

Nodes and antinodes: PH *137*

Nonpolar and polar molecules: separation of, ST *42, 43*; soap, working of, ST 48

NPN transistor: PH 84, *85*

N-type and P-type semiconductors: PH *84, 85*; silicon, PH 84, *85, 110-111*

Nuclear fission: PH *108*, ST *14-15*, TR 102, *103*

Nuclear fusion: ST *16-17*

Nuclear reactors: PH *108-109*, ST *15*; control rods, ST *14*; core, PH *94-95, 108*; fusion, experimental, ST *17*

Nuclear submarines: TR *102-103*

Nuclei, atomic: ST 6, *7*; fission of, ST *14-15*; fusion of, ST *16-17*; radioactive, PH *91, 108*

Nylon: ST *108*; spinning of, ST *108-109*

O

Objective and ocular lenses: PH *116*

Oceans: floating on, PH *8-9*; as power source, PH *106-107*; sonar use in, PH *130*; surfers riding waves of, PH *38-39*; whirlpools, PH *20*

Ocean travel: *See* Water travel

Ocular and objective lenses: PH *116*

Odors: removal of, ST *52-53*

Office equipment: copiers, MA *62-63*; electronic blackboards, MA *70-71*; fax machines, MA *68-69*

Offices: computer use in, CO *92-93*

Offset printing: MA *40-41*

Oil: crude, refining of, ST *116-117*; drilling rigs, synthetic diamonds used in, ST *133*; fragrant, extracting, ST *126-127*; removal of, by soap, ST *48-49*; and water, separation of, ST *42-43, 127*

Oil film: colors on, PH *120*

Oil-seal vacuum pump: MA 45

Omega System: TR *map* 125

Onnes, Heike Kamerlingh: PH 92

Optical fibers: communication by, CO *124-125*; glass, ST *124-125*

Optical mouse: CO *34*

Optical pyrometers: PH 56, *57*

Optics: binoculars, MA *94-95*; in fax machine, MA *69*; fiberscope, MA *138-139*; microscope, electron, MA *32-33*; movie projector, MA *88-89*. *See also* Cameras

Optional four-wheel drive: TR *49*

Orbit: satellites, PH *36-37*

Ores: refining, ST *102-103, 110-111, 114-115*; and rust, ST 56, *57*

Organs, human: artificial, CO *138-139*

OR gate: CO *28*

Orient Express (luxury train): TR *19*

Orifice plate: MA *46-47*

Ørsted, Hans Christian: PH 94

Oscillators: in quartz watch, MA *97*; VC (voltage control), and sound frequency, MA *90*

Oscilloscope: PH *135*

Output devices: CO 18, *19*; for pocket computers, CO *90-91*; printers, CO *38-39*

Ovens: microwave, MA *102-103*

Overripening of foods: ST *88-89*

Overtones: PH 134, *135, 137*

Oxalic acid: ink removal with, ST *72-73*

Oxidation-reduction (redox) reactions: ST 56, *73*; in automobile batteries, ST *58-59*; ink and ink removal, ST *72-73*; iron in, ST *56*; ores, creation and refining of, ST 110, *111*

Oxygen: ST *6-7*; atmospheric, ST *36-37*; and browning of apples, ST *80, 81*; and burning of metals, ST *70*; carbon combustion and, ST *67*; for disinfection of water, ST *98, 99*; fire extinguishers and, ST *69*; food protected from, ST *88, 89*; ink, reactions with, ST *72, 73*; iron, reaction with, ST *56, 57*; liquid, as rocket fuel, PH *18*; ozone layer, hole in, ST *76-77*; pig iron converted with, ST 111, *112-113*; rocket fuel, ST *74, 75*; vs. antioxygen, ST *22-23*; in water molecules, PH *54-55*

Oxygen in atmosphere: source of, ST *36-37*

Oxygen cycle: ST *37*

Ozone for disinfection: ST *98*

Ozone layer: hole in, ST *76-77*

P

Pacemaker, artificial: CO *138*, MA *133*

Packet switching: CO *118-119*

Pack ice: cracking of, by icebreakers, TR 100, *101*

Paddle steamers: TR *90-91*

Pagers, electronic: CO *122-123*

Painting of automobiles: robot use in, CO *101*

Panama Canal, Panama: TR *92-93*

Pancreas, human: artificial system for, CO *138*

Pantograph: high-speed train's, TR *33*

Papermaking: ST *104-105*

Paper punch as lever: PH *42*

Parallel circuits: PH *75*

Parallel (pipeline) processing: CO *42-43*

Parking system: automated car's, TR *61*

Particle (corpuscular) vs. wave theory of light: PH *112*

Pascal, Blaise: CO 8, *9*; quoted, CO 9

Pascaline (adding machine): CO *4-5, 8-9*

Animal Behavior
AN

Computer Age
CO

Ecology
EC

Evolution of Life
EV

Geography
GE

Human Body
HU

Insects & Spiders
IN

Machines &
Inventions **MA**

Passenger trains: cable cars, TR *30-31*; electromagnetic air brakes, TR *10, 11*; high-speed, TR *4-5, 32-33*; luxury, TR *18-19*; monorails, TR *28-29*. *See also* Commuter trains

Passwords: CO 106; possible, number of, CO *chart* 107

PCBs (printed circuit boards): CO *20-21*; motherboard, CO *22-23*

PCs: *See* Personal computers

Pedal and sprocket on bicycle: PH 46, *47*

Pendulums: clock's, working of, MA *13*; sympathetic vibrations in, PH *143*

Pens: electronic blackboard's, MA *71*

Perfume: making of, ST *126-127*

Periodic table: ST 4, *chart* 10-11

Peripherals: CO 19

Periscope: use of, on submarines, TR *103*

Personal computers: CO *19*; E-mail, use of, CO 116, *117*; graphics, CO 70; motherboard, CO *22-23*; pocket computer's communication with, CO *91*; as word processors, CO *58-59*

Personal identification numbers (PINs): CO 88, 89

Personnel functions of computers: CO 93

Phase changes: ST *32-33, 34-35, 38-39*; boiling, MA 100, PH *22-23, 62-63*; in coolants, systems using, MA *106-107, 122-125*; freezing, PH *66-67*; freezing point, lowering of, ST *40-41*; heat and, PH *22-23, 52-53, 54-55, 62-63*; melting, PH *52-53, 54-55*; vaporization/evaporation, PH *22-23, 53, 62-63, 64-65*; water vapor and, PH *64*

Phase-detection autofocus: MA *75*

Phenols in apple: ST *80*

Phones: *See* Telephones and telephone lines

Phonograph records: MA *86*

Phosphors in TV picture tube: MA 76

Photocopiers: MA 62; color, MA *62-63*

Photodetectors: bar codes scanned by, CO *86*; in mouse, CO *34*

Photodiodes: in fiberoptic communication, CO *125*; in mouse, CO *35*; in scanners, CO *87*

Photoelectric sensors in smoke detectors: MA *65*

Photography: autofocus (AF), cameras with, MA *74-75*; first cameras, MA *16-17*; holographic, PH *124-125*; instant, color, MA *92-93*; movie camera, first, MA *20*; movie projectors, MA *20-21, 88-89*; popularization of, MA *18-19*

Photosensitive resin: ST *144*

Photosynthesis: and atmospheric oxygen, ST 36, *37*; and stored energy, ST *66*

pH scale: ST *83*

Physical forces: PH entire volume

Piano: tuning of, PH *142-143*

Picture elements: *See* Pixels

Picture phones: CO *126-127*

Pictures: electronic publishing of, CO *94-95*; faxing, CO *114-115*. *See also* Graphics, computer

Picture tube, TV: MA *76*; working of, MA 77

Piezoelectric crystals: MA *96*; watches using, MA *96-97*

Pig iron: casting, ST *112*; converting, ST *111, 112-113*; producing, ST *102-103, 110-111*

Pilot training: flight simulator for, CO *82-83*

Pins: external, smart card's, MA 61

PINs (personal identification numbers): CO 88, 89

Pipeline (parallel) processing: CO *42-43*

Pistons: in automatic air brake system, train's, TR *11*; automobile, TR *38, 40, 41*; in hydraulic systems, TR 66, 77; motorcycle, TR *42*; steam car, TR *38*; steam train, TR *15, 17*

Pitch, baseball: PH *24-25, 34-35*

Pitch, of sound: Doppler effect, PH *138-139*; frequency and, MA *90*, PH 128, *135*, 138, 142; tones, production of, PH *134-135, 136-137*

Pitching machine: baseball, PH 35

Pitching of ships: reducing, PH *9*

Pitot tubes: TR *132-133*

Pixels: CO 70; in electronic publishing, CO *95*; in fax transmission, CO 114, *115*, MA *68*; in television, MA 76, *77*; in TV vs. videophone images, CO *127*

Pixii, Hippolyte: generator built by, MA *28*

Planetary gear: transmission's, TR *47*

Plants: acid rain and, ST *64-65*; and atmospheric oxygen, ST *36-37*; energy stored by, ST *66*; fragrant oils from, ST *126-127*

Plastics: ST *118-119*; carbon fibers bonded with, ST *138-139*; electroless plating, ST *63*

Plate glass: making of, ST *122-123*

Plating methods for metal: ST *62-63*

Pliers as lever: PH *43*

Pneumatic tube detector in fire alarm system: MA *65*

PNP transistor: PH *85*

Pocket calendars: CO *91*

Pocket computers: CO *90-91*

Polarizing filters in LCDs: ST *136-137*

Polar molecules: and nonpolar molecules, separation of, ST 42, *43*; soap, working of, ST *48*

Polaroid film: working of, MA *92-93*

Pollutants, air: removal of, MA *50-51*; size of, MA *chart* 50

Pollution: from automobiles, computerized control of, CO 102

Polycrystalline grains: ST 130, *131*; silicon, ST 134, *135*

Polyester: molecular structure of, ST *109*

Polyethylene: production of, ST *106-107*

Polygraphs: MA *36-37*

Polymers: ST 106; carbon fibers from, ST *138-139*; in cotton, ST *12-13, 107*; making of, ST *106-107*; natural, kinds of, ST 106, *107*; from photosensitive resins, ST *144*; plastics molded from, ST *118-119*; rubber, ST *30-31, 107*; silk, ST *108*; as synthetic fibers, ST *108-109*; wool, ST 107, *109*

Polyphenols: and browning of apple, ST *80*

Port and starboard tacks: PH *13*

Positrons: ST 22, 23

Potential energy: of roller coaster, PH *31*

Power cord: structure of, PH *82-83*

Power grid: PH *99*

Power meters: MA *118-119*

Power plants (power stations): nuclear reactors, PH *94-95, 108-109*; windmills, PH *104-105*. *See also* Electricity, generating

Power shovels: TR *67, 76-77*; bulldozers, TR *66-67, 77*

Precession: PH *32*

Precision measurements: MA *48-49*

Prenatal monitoring with ultrasound: MA *142-143*

Preservation of food: ST *88-89*

Pressure: PH 4; on baseball, PH 34; and hang gliding, PH 14; on liquid, and boiling temperature, PH 22; and phase changes, MA 100, 107; rocket thrust, PH 18; and sailing into wind, PH 12; of skis and skates, PH 26, 27; supersonic shock waves and, PH 140; and temperature and volume of gas, PH 11; water, depth and, TR 107

Pressure, atmospheric: *See* Atmospheric pressure

Pressure cookers: MA *100-101*, PH 23

Pressure differences: airplane instruments measuring, TR *132-133*; measuring flow rate with, MA *46, 47*

Pressurization of aircraft: TR *128-129*

Primary memory: CO *30-31*

Printed circuit boards (PCBs): CO *20-21*; motherboards, CO *22-23*

Printers: CO 19, *38-39*; pocket computers and, CO *90-91*

Printing and printing presses: MA *6-7, 40-41*

Printing plates: photosensitive resins for, ST 144

Prisms: in binoculars, MA *94*; white light through, PH *120*

Production area of business: computer use in, CO 93

Production lines: robot use on, CO *100-101*

Program counter: CO 24

Programming languages: CO *50-51*; programs in, CO 51

Programs and software: *See* Software and programs

Program signal: radio's, MA *84, 85*

Projectors, movie: MA *88-89*; kinetoscope, MA *20-21*

Propagation of light: defined, PH 112

Propellers: TR *112-113*; blimp, TR *116*; icebreaker's screw, TR *101*; turboprop engine, TR *131*; Wright *Flyer*, TR *134*; XV-15 VTOL aircraft, TR *139*

Propeller turbine: PH *99*

Prosthetic (artificial) limbs: CO *138*

Proteins: egg, ST *94, 95*; milk, ST *84, 85*

Protons: PH 68, ST *7*; and antimatter counterpart, ST *22-23*; in nuclear fusion, ST *16-17*; and static electricity, PH *70*

Pry bar as lever: PH *43*

P-type and N-type semiconductors: PH *84, 85*; silicon, PH 84, 85, *110-111*

Publishing: electronic, CO 94-95

Pulleys: PH *48-49*; crane's use of, TR *73*

Pulp: in papermaking, ST *105*; producing, ST *104*

Pulse: lie detector's measurement of, MA *36*

Pumps: fire engine's, TR *70-71*; waterjet, hydrofoil's, TR *95*

Punch cards: CO *4-5*, 10, *11*; census tabulating machines's system, CO *12-13*

P waves in electrocardiogram: MA *136*

Pyrometers: optical, PH 56, *57*

Q

QFP (integrated circuit package): CO *23*

QRS complex in electrocardiogram: MA *136*

Quadrant (navigation instrument): TR *86*

Quarks: ST 6, *7*

Quartz: MA *96*; structure of, ST *122*; watches using, MA *96-97*

Quinones in browning apple: ST *80*

QWERTY layout of keys: CO *33*

R

Racing cars: Formula One, TR *58-59*

Radar: ship's navigation with, TR *82-83*; Stealth bomber's evasion of, TR *144*

Radial tires: high-performance, TR *57*

Radiant thermal energy: measuring, PH *56-57*

Radiation: *See* Electromagnetic radiation

Radiator: racing car's, working of, TR *59*

Radioactive elements: carbon 14, ST *24-25*; fission of, ST *14-15*

Radioactive fuel: submarines using, TR *102-103*

Radioactivity: PH *90-91*; core of nuclear reactor, PH *94-95, 108*

Radio altimeter vs. atmospheric pressure altimeter: TR 132, *133*

Radiocarbon dating: ST *24-25*

Radio direction finders: use of, TR *81*

Radiography: MA *140-141*

Radio magnetic indicator (RMI) dial: aircraft's, TR *123*

Radios: AM/FM, working of, MA *84-85*; two-way, PH *88*

Radio signals, communications with: cellular phones, CO *120-121*; pagers, electronic, CO *122-123*; satellites, CO *128-129*; space probes, Voyager, CO *142-143*

Radio waves: PH *88-89*; landing system (ILS) using, TR *126-127*; Omega System using, TR *map* 125; ships' use of, in navigation, TR *81-85*; VOR stations emitting, TR *122-123*

Railroads: *See* Trains

Rails, trains': TR *6-7*; high-speed trains, TR *33*

Rain: acid, ST *64-65*

Rally tires: TR *57*

RAM (random-access memory) chips: CO 22

Ramps as inclined planes: PH *44, 45*

Random-access memory (RAM) chips: CO 22

Rate-of-rise sensors in fire alarm systems: MA *64*

RCA Victor television set: MA *22*

Reach: sailing on, PH *12*

Reaction: turbine, PH *98-99*

Reactors, nuclear: *See* Nuclear reactors

Reading of text: CO *64-65*

Read-only memory (ROM): CD-ROM, CO *95*; chips, CO 22

Reaping and threshing: combines for, MA *14-15*

Rearview mirror, convex: PH *115*

Recharger: electric car's, TR *64*

Recorder (musical instrument): PH *135*

Recording: of compact disks, MA *86-87*; of phonograph records, MA *86*; of television signals, by VCR, MA *82-83*

Records, phonograph: MA *86*

Records and files, computer: CO 55, 56

Redox reactions: *See* Oxidation-reduction (redox) reactions

Reduction-oxidation (redox) reactions: *See* Oxidation-reduction (redox) reactions

Refining processes: ST 102, *110-111*; elec-

trolytic, ST *114-115*; iron, ST *102-103, 110-111*; oil, crude, ST *116-117*

Reflection of electromagnetic waves: PH 89

Reflection of light: from curved surfaces, PH *114-115*; defined, PH 112; off soap bubble, PH *120-121*

Reflection of sound waves: and echoes, PH *132-133*; in sonar, PH 130

Reforming: catalytic device for, ST 117

Refraction of electromagnetic waves: PH 89

Refraction of light: defined, PH 112; by lenses, PH *116-117, 122*; by prism, PH *120*

Refraction of sound waves: PH *133*

Refrigerated vending machines: MA 58-59

Refrigerators: MA *106-107*; gas-pressure sensor used in, MA *120*

Relativity, special theory of: PH *126-127*

Relief printing: MA 40, *41*

Reservation system: computerized (CRS), CO *96-97*

Resins: epoxy, carbon fibers bonded with, ST *138-139*; molded, ST *118-119*, 138; photosensitive, ST *144*

Resistors, thermal (thermistors): MA *120*; in electronic thermometer, MA *128*

Resistors in circuits: PH *74-75*; and voltmeter, PH *77*

Respiration: lie detector's measurement of, MA *36*

Reverse gear: automobile's, TR *46*

Rice starch: ST *100*

Right-hand rule of electromagnetism: PH *76, 81*

Ripening of foods: excessive, ST *88-89*

RMI (radio magnetic indicator) dial: aircraft's, TR *123*

Road construction: rollers for, TR *66, 74-75*

Road roller: TR *75*

Robots: CO *98-101*; arms, CO *100-101*; in automotive industry, CO *100-101*; eyes, CO *99*; hands (manipulators), CO *98*; humanoid, hypothetical, CO *98-99*; mobile, CO *99*

Rocket, the (train): TR *4, 14-15*

Rockets: launching of, PH *18-19*; matter-antimatter as fuel, ST *23*; near speed of light, PH *126-127*; and rocket fuel, ST *54-55, 71, 74-75*; V-2, MA *26-27*

Roentgen, Wilhelm: MA *140*

Rogallo, Francis: PH 14

Roller coasters: PH *30-31*

Rollers, construction: TR *66, 74-75*

Roll film: Kodak camera's use of, MA 18, *19*

Rolling of ships: reducing, PH *9*

ROM (read-only memory): CD-ROM, CO *95*; chips, CO 22

Roman counting tablet: CO *6-7*

Rømer, Ole: PH 118

Animal Behavior
AN

Computer Age
CO

Ecology
EC

Evolution of Life
EV

Geography
GE

Human Body
HU

Insects & Spiders
IN

Machines &
Inventions MA

Ropeway cable car system: TR *31*

Rotary oil-seal vacuum pump: MA *45*

Rotary snowplow: train's, TR *22-23*

Rotating objects: baseball, PH *24-25, 34-35*; top, spinning, PH *25, 32-33*

Rotors, helicopter's: TR *114*; auxiliary, function of, TR *114, 115*; hub, TR *115*; pilot's use of, TR *115*

Rubber: molecular structure of, ST *30-31, 107*; vulcanization of, ST 30

Rudders: airplane's, TR *111*; blimp's use of, TR *117*; hovercraft's use of, TR *97*; hydroplanes, submarine with, TR *98-99*

Rules of the road at sea: TR *83*

Russell snowplow: TR *23*

Russian abacus: CO *7*

Rusting of iron: ST *56-57*; prevention, ST *57*

S

Saccharin: glutamic acid from, ST *91*

Sacrificial anodes: ST *57*

Safety glass: laminated, ST *125*

Sailing into wind: PH *12-13*

Sailing ships: TR *78-79*; Columbus's, TR *88-89*; Magellan's, TR *87*

Sailors: *See* Water travel

Salt: ST *43*; electric conduction by, ST *18-19*; freezing point lowered by, ST *40-41*; natural formations of, ST *96*; preserving food with, ST *89*; reclaiming, from sea, ST *96-97*

Sand: in concrete, ST *120, 121*

Sandglass: estimating longitude with, TR *87*

San Francisco, Calif., U.S.: cable cars in, TR *30*

Santa Maria (Columbus's ship): TR *88-89*

Satellite navigation: TR *84-85*

Satellites: carbon fibers in, ST *139*; communications, CO *128-129*; Landsat, CO *140-141*; navigation using, TR *84-85*; orbit of, PH *36-37*; ozone hole detected by, ST *map 77*; solar cells for, PH *111*; weather, CO *134*

Saturn V rocket: launching of, PH *18-19*

Sauna: air in, and skin, PH *64-65*

Scales: bathroom, MA *108-109*; springs used in, PH *50*

Scanners: bar codes and, CO *86-87*; digitization of pictures by, in electronic publishing, CO *95*; text read by, CO *64, 65*

Scanning electron microscopes: MA *32, 33*

Scanning of images by television: MA *22, 23, 77*; scan lines, MA *78*

Schickard, Wilhelm: CO *8*

Scientific uses of computers: CO *130*; biomedical engineering, CO *138-139*; Landsat satellites, CO *140-141*; meteorology,

CO *134-135*; missiles, cruise, CO *144*; space probes, CO *142-143*. *See also* Simulations and models, computer

Scissors: ceramic, ST *130*; as levers, PH *43*

Screwball (pitch): PH *35*

Screw propellers: icebreaker's, TR *101*

Screws: PH *44-45*

SDPS (stereo digital photogrammetric station): CO *76*

Sea lanes: opening of, icebreakers' strategies for, TR *100, 101*; rules of, TR *83*

Searches: information, CO *56-57*

Sea travel: *See* Water travel

Seawater: salt recovered from, ST *96-97*

Second-class levers: PH *42-43*

Second law of motion, Newton's: PH *24*

Security gates: airport, MA *42-43*

Self-raising crane: MA *52-53*

Semiconductors: CO 20, PH *84-85*; electrical resistance of, MA *chart 128*; silicon, PH 84, *85, 110-111*

Separated photoelectrics in smoke detector: MA *65*

Separator lenses in camera: MA *75*

Sequential processing: CO *42-43*

Sequential search: CO *57*

Sewing machines: MA *104-105*

Shanks, William: CO 68

Shape-memory alloys: ST *128-129, 140-141*

Sheet metal: production of, ST *28-29*

Shifting of gears: automobile's, TR *46*

Shinkansen line (bullet trains): TR *4-5, 33*

Ships: TR 78; clipper, TR *78-79*; Columbus's, TR *88-89*; cruiser, military, TR *78-79*; floating, PH *8-9*; in fog, TR *82-83*; future, TR *104-105*; historical navigational instruments, TR *86-87*; icebreakers, TR *100-101*; Magellan's, TR *87*; navigation, TR 78, *80-87*; navigation, satellite use in, TR *84-85*; rules of the road for, TR *83*; steam-powered, TR *79, 90-91*; submarines, TR *79, 98-99, 102-103, 106-107*; through Panama Canal, TR *92-93*; wave power generators on, PH *107*

Shirase (icebreaker): TR *101*

Shock absorbers: computerized control of, CO *103*; motorcycle's, TR *43*

Shock waves: and sonic booms, PH *140-141*

Short takeoff and landing (STOL) aircraft: Asuka, TR *139*

Shovels, power: TR *67, 76-77*; bulldozers, TR *66-67, 77*

Shutter: rotating, movie projector's, MA *89*

Shutter sensors: MA *115*

Siemens, Werner von: generator built by, MA *29*

Signals: trains controlled by, TR *20-21*

Silica (silicon dioxide): MA *96*; glass made

from, ST *122-123*; quartz, structure of, ST *122*; rock, ST *134*

Silicon: ST *134-135*; microscope's magnification of, MA *32*; in quartz crystal, MA *96*; as semiconductor, PH 84, 85; solar cells, PH *110-111*

Silicon dioxide: *See* Silica

Silk: ST *108*

Silver: electroplating with, ST *62-63*

Silver iodide: on daguerreotype plates, MA *16*

Simple machines: *See* Machines, simple

Simulations and models, computer: CO 130, *132-133*; automotive design, CO *74-75*; buildings, CO *133*; flight simulator, CO *82-83*; sports analysis programs, CO *136-137*; traffic patterns, CO *132-133*; train station, crowds in, CO *133*; weather conditions, CO *134*

Single-crystal silicon: ST *134-135*

Single in-line package (SIP): CO *23*

Single-lens reflex camera: MA *74*; autofocus (AF) for, MA *74-75*

Single-mode optical fibers: CO *125*

Sink: whirlpool formation in, PH *20-21*

SIP (single in-line package): CO *23*

Skaters and skating: PH *26, 27*

Skid control in automobiles: CO *102, 103*

Skiers and skiing: PH *26-27*

Ski jumping: computer analysis of, CO *136-137*

Skin: electrical properties of, lie detector's measurement of, MA *36*; sauna air and, PH *64-65*

Skylab (space station): PH *37*

Skyscraper: computer model of, CO *133*

Slide (vernier) calipers: MA *48, 49*

Smart cards: MA *60-61*

Smart houses: CO *104-105*

Smectic liquid crystals: ST *137*

Smelting of copper: ST *111*

Smoke detectors: MA *64, 65*

Snorkels: submarine's, TR *99*

Snow: lowering freezing point of, ST *40, 41*

Snowmobiles: TR *67, 68-69*

Snowplows: trains, TR *22-23*

Snow tires: TR *57*

Soap: removal of dirt by, ST *48-49*

Soap bubbles: colors of, PH *120-121*

Soaring: eagles, TR *118*; gliders, TR *118*

Society for Space Travel, German: MA *26*

Sodium: electron shells, ST *7, 50-51*; ions, ST *18-19, 40, 41, 43, 96*; light emission by, ST *50-51*

Sodium hypochlorite: ink removal with, ST *72*

Sodium 24: gamma decay of, PH *91*

Software and programs: CO *46-69*; algo-

rithms, CO *52-53*; in computer crime, CO *106*; games, CO *78-79*; languages, CO *50-51*; motion analysis, in sports, CO *136-137*; music making, CO *66-67*; reading of text, CO *64-65*; robots controlled by, CO *99*; role of, CO *48*; searches for information, CO *56-57*; sorting, CO *54-55*; voice recognition, CO *62-63*; voice synthesis, CO *60-61*; vs. human thinking, CO *68-69*; word processors, CO *58-59*; writing of, CO *48-49*

Soil: acid rain and, ST *64*, 65; nitrogen compounds in, ST *26*, 27

Solar energy: PH *110-111*; automobiles powered by, TR *62-63*; stored, ST *66*

Solar Flair (solar-powered automobile): TR *63*

Solar power: *See* Solar energy

Solar-powered automobiles: TR *62-63*

Solar satellites: CO *128-129*

Solenoids: PH *69, 81*; in electromagnet, PH *80-81*

Solid-fuel rockets: ST *74*

Solids: ST *44-45*; in colloids, ST *20*; freezing point, lowering, ST *40-41*; phase changes in, PH *52-53, 54-55*, ST *34, 35, 38, 39*

Solvent extraction in perfume making: ST *126*

Sonar: PH *130*

Sonar depth finder: TR *82*

Sonic booms: PH *140-141*; Mach cones created by, TR *136-137*

Sonograms: production of, MA *142-143*

Sound: PH *128-144*; air temperature and, PH *133*; on compact disks, MA *86-87*; Doppler effect, PH *138-139*; echoes, PH *132-133*; microphones' and speakers' conversion of, MA *80-81*; movie projectors' playing back of, MA *88*; on phonograph records, MA *86*; qualities of, MA *90*; and radio transmissions, MA *84-85*; sonic booms, PH *140-141*, TR *136-137*; spectrographs' use of, MA *34-35*; speed of, TR *136*; stethoscopes' transmission of, MA *144*; surround sound, PH *144*; synthesizers' use of, MA *90-91*; telephones' transmission of, MA *56-57*; tones, production of, PH *134-135, 136-137*; transmission of, PH *130-131*; tuning of musical instruments, PH *142-143*; ultrasonic, use of, MA *75, 142-143*; VCRs' recording of, MA *83*; wind, traveling with, PH *133*; wind instruments, PH *135, 136-137*

Sound barrier: breaking, PH *140-141*, TR *136-137*

Sound production by computers: music, CO *66-67*; speech, CO *60-61*

Sound recognition by computers: CO *62-63*

Sound waves: PH *131*; forms, and timbre, MA *90*; wave fronts, PH *131, 138-139*

Southern Cross (solar-powered automobile): TR *62-63*

South Pole: ozone hole over, ST *map* 77

Spacecraft: ceramic tiles on, ST *131*; launching, PH *18-19*; near speed of light, PH *126-127*; orbit, PH *36-37*; rockets and rocket fuel, ST *23, 54-55, 71, 74-75*; and shape-memory antenna, ST *141*; solar cells for, PH *111*. *See also* Satellites

Space probes: CO *142-143*

Space shuttle: ST *71, 74-75, 131*

Spark plugs: computerized control of, CO *102*; role of, TR *40, 41*

Speakers: dynamic, MA *80, 81*; radio's, MA *85*

Special effects: CO *80-81*

Special-purpose vehicles: TR *66-77*; construction rollers, TR *66, 74-75*; cranes, TR *66-67, 72-73*; fire engines, TR *66-67, 70-71*; power shovels, TR *66-67, 76-77*; snowmobiles, TR *67, 68-69*

Special theory of relativity: PH *126-127*

Spectrographs: sound, MA *34-35*; sound, and spectrum analysis, CO *62-63*

Spectrum: of white light, PH *120*

Speech production by computers: CO *60-61*

Speech recognition by computers: CO *62-63*

Speech transmission by telephones: CO *110-111*; car phones, CO *120-121*; teleconferencing, CO *112-113*

Speed guns: MA *38-39*

Speed indicators: airplanes', TR *132-133*

Speed of light: approaching, PH *126-127*; measuring, PH *118-119*

Speed of sound: exceeding, PH *140-141*, TR *136-137*; medium and, PH *chart* 130; temperature and, PH *133*

Sphygmomanometer: medical use of, MA *130-131*

Spinning machines for fibers: glass, ST *124*; synthetic, ST *109*

Spinning tops: PH *25, 32-33*

Spoilage of food: controlling, ST *88-89*

Spoilers: automated car's, TR *61*; glider's, use of, TR *118, 119*; racing car's, TR *58*

Sporting goods: carbon fibers in, ST *138-139*

Sports analysis programs: CO *136-137*

Spot welding: robot use in, CO *101*

Spray arm: dishwasher's, MA *117*

Spray-dried coffee: ST *86, 87*

Spray plating: ST *63*

Springs: PH *50-51*; bathroom scales' use of, MA 108, *109*

Sprocket and pedal on bicycle: PH 46, *47*

Staircases: moving (escalators), MA *66-67*

Standing waves: PH 134, *137*

Stapler as lever: PH *42*

Starboard and port tacks: PH *13*

Starch in flour: ST *100-101*

Stars: nuclear fusion in, ST *16-17*

Star wheel in vending machine: MA *58*

Static electricity: PH *70-71*

Stealth bomber: TR *109, 144*

Steam: in extinguishing of fire, ST *68*; water's phase change into, ST *32-33*

Steam car: Cugnot's, TR 36, *38-39*

Steam distillation in perfume making: ST *126-127*

Steam engine: TR *90*

Steamer: heating food in, PH *65*

Steam generator: nuclear engine with, TR *102*

Steam-powered tractor combine: MA *15*

Steam trains: TR *4, 16-17*; earliest, TR *4-5, 14-15*

Steam turbines, power for: geothermal, PH *102-103*; nuclear, PH *109*; ocean, PH *107*; solar, PH 110, *111*; thermoelectric, PH *100-101*

Steam vessels: TR *79, 90-91*

Steel: ST *111, 112*; burning, conditions for, ST *70-71*; galvanizing, ST *63*; pig iron for, producing, ST *102-103, 110-111*; types of, ST *chart* 113; uses for, ST *chart* 113

Steel wool: burning of, ST *70*

Steering: automobile's, four-wheel vs. two-wheel, TR *50-51*; snowmobile's, TR *69*

Stephenson, George: train built by (Rocket), TR *4, 14-15*

Step-type optical fibers: CO *125*

Step-up transformers: PH *86, 99*

Stereo digital photogrammetric station (SDPS): CO *76*

Stethoscopes: MA *144*; in blood pressure measurement, MA *130, 131*

Stitches: forming of, by sewing machines, MA *104-105*

STOL (short takeoff and landing) aircraft: Asuka, TR *139*

Stomach: fiberscope's viewing of, MA *139*

Storage of data: CO *30-31*; CD-ROM, CO *95*; magnetic, CO *19, 36-37, 56-57*; after sorting, CO 55

Stores: bar codes and scanners used in, CO *86-87*

Storms: computer models of, CO *134*

Straddle-type monorail: TR *28-29*

Stratosphere: ozone layer, hole in, ST *76-77*

Stringed instruments: PH *134-135*

Studded tires: TR *57*

Subatomic particles: ST *4, 5, 6-7*; antiparticles, ST *22-23*; in fusion reactions, ST

Animal Behavior
AN

Computer Age
CO

Ecology
EC

Evolution of Life
EV

Geography
GE

Human Body
HU

Insects & Spiders
IN

Machines &
Inventions **MA**

16-17; neutrons, ST *7, 14, 15, 16-17, 25.* *See also* Electrons

Sublimation of carbon dioxide: ST 38, *39*

Submarines: TR *79, 98-99;* diving and surfacing, TR *98;* nuclear, TR *102-103;* submersibles, TR *79, 106-107*

Submersibles, deep-diving: TR *79, 106-107*

Subways: air supply, TR *26-27;* contact couplings, TR *9;* doors, TR *13*

Sugarcane: MSG from, ST *90-91*

Sugar: in fermentation, ST *85*

Sulfur dioxide: and acid rain, ST *64*

Sulfuric acid: batteries with, ST *58-59*

Sun: energy from, stored, ST *66;* energy generated by, PH *110-111;* nuclear fusion in, ST *16-17*

Supercomputers: CO *42-43;* first, CO *15;* weather conditions modeled by, CO *134*

Superconducting ships: future, TR *104-105*

Superconductivity: PH *92-93*

Supermarkets: scanner type used in, CO *86-87*

Supersonic aircraft: TR *108-109, 136-137;* sonic booms from, PH *140-141*

Supertrains: TR *32-33;* bullet trains, TR *4-5, 33*

Surfers and surfing: PH *38-39*

Surgery: heart-lung machine used in, CO *139*

Surround sound: PH *144*

Suspension: motorcycle's, TR *43;* racing, TR *59*

Suspension monorails: TR *29*

Swash plate on helicopter's rotor shaft: use of, TR *115*

Sweat: evaporating, in sauna, PH *64-65;* gland activity, lie detector's measurement of, MA *36*

Switching circuitry: synthesizer's, MA *91;* telephone signal passing through, MA *57*

Switch rails: TR *7*

Symington, William: steam vessel engineered by *(Charlotte Dundas)*, TR *91*

Sympathetic vibrations: PH *143*

Synthesized images: CO *81*

Synthesized sound: music, CO *66;* voice, CO *60-61*

Synthesizers: MA *90-91*

Synthetic materials: ST *108-109, 118-119.* *See also* Materials technology

Systole in artificial heart: MA *133*

Systolic pressure: measuring, MA *130-131*

T

Tabulating machine, Hollerith's: CO *12-13*

Tacking by sailboat: PH *13*

Tanker in Panama Canal: TR *92*

Tape: magnetic, and tape drives, CO *19, 36, 37;* recording on, by VCR, MA *82-83*

Teleconferencing: CO *112-113*

Telegraph: MA *8-9*

Telephones and telephone lines: CO *108-109,* MA *56-57;* car phones, CO *120-121;* earliest, MA *10-11;* fax transmissions over, CO *114-115,* MA *68-69;* modems, use of, CO *91,* 118, *119;* pagers, calls to, CO *122;* picture phones, CO *126-127;* teleconferencing, CO *112-113;* voice transmission through, CO *110-111*

Telescopes: convex lenses in, PH *116*

Television: color images on, MA *76-77;* early, MA *22-23;* high-definition, MA *78-79;* images, vs. videophone images, CO *127;* liquid-crystal, ST *137;* VCR's recording of signals from, MA *82-83;* and video games, CO *78-79*

Temperature: PH *52;* of boiling point, MA 100, *chart* 100; and density of water, PH *chart* 67; of dew point, MA *125;* extreme, measuring, PH *56-57;* and phase changes, PH *22-23, 52-53, 54-55, 62-63;* and pressure and volume of gas, PH *11;* sensors, fire alarm systems', MA *64, 65;* and speed of sound, PH *133;* thermometer, electronic, for measuring, MA *128-129;* thermostats controlling, MA *120-121;* and vapor pressure, PH *chart* 22

Tender: steam train's, TR *14-15*

Tennis ball: path of, in computer model, CO *136*

Tennis racket: carbon-fiber, ST *138-139*

Text: electronic publishing of, CO *94-95;* faxing, CO *114-115;* reading, by computer, CO *64-65;* saving, CO *59*

TGV (Train à Grande Vitesse): TR *33*

Thematic mappers (TMs): CO *140*

Theory of relativity, special: PH *126-127*

Thermal conductivity: PH *chart* 61

Thermal energy: from ocean, PH 106, *107;* radiant, measuring, PH *56-57;* vs. heat energy, PH *52. See also* Heat

Thermal insulation: PH *60-61*

Thermal resistors: *See* Thermistors

Thermals (rising air currents): PH *15;* and gliders, TR *119*

Thermistors (thermal resistors): MA *120;* in electronic thermometer, MA *128*

Thermoelectric power plants: PH *100-101*

Thermogram: working of, PH *56-57*

Thermometers: electronic, MA *128-129;* high-temperature, PH *56-57;* liquid-crystal, ST *137*

Thermoplastic vs. thermosetting resins: ST *118-119*

Thermostats: MA *120-121*

Thinking: computer vs. human, CO *68-69*

Third-class levers: PH *43*

Third law of motion, Newton's: PH *18,* 24

Thomson, Sir William: MA 9

Threshing of grain: combines for, MA *14-15*

Throttle plate: carburetor's, TR *47*

Thunderstorms: computer models, CO *134*

Tidal power generating station: PH *106-107*

Timbre of sound: wave-forms and, MA *90*

Time: in special theory of relativity, PH *126-127*

Timepieces: mechanical clocks, MA *12-13;* quartz watches, MA *96-97*

Tire roller: TR *75*

Tires, automobile: racing vs. passenger, TR *58-59;* tread on, TR *56-57*

TMs (thematic mappers): CO *140*

Tomograms: CAT scanner for producing, MA *134-135*

Tone-only vs. message-display pagers: CO 122, *123*

Toner: application of, in photocopiers, MA *62-63*

Tones of sound: production of, PH *134-135, 136-137*

Tools: *See* Machines, simple

Tops: spinning, PH *25, 32-33*

Torque: PH *32;* car's transmission and, TR *46*

Torque converter: automatic transmission's, TR *47*

Torricelli, Evangelista: barometer invented by, PH 16, *17*

Torrs: vacuums measured in, MA 44

Torsion springs: PH *51*

Tracking stations: satellite, TR *map* 84, 85

Tracks, trains': TR *6-7;* automatic train, TR *25;* cable cars, TR *30-31;* monorail, TR *28*

Tractors: combines drawn by, MA *14-15;* tires for, TR *57*

Traffic patterns: computer modeling of, CO *132-133*

Train à Grande Vitesse (TGV): TR *33*

Trains: TR 4-35; automatic, TR *24-25;* brakes, TR *10-11;* cable cars, TR *30-31;* couplings, TR *8-9;* diesel-powered, TR *4-5;* doors, commuter trains', TR *12-13,* 25; earliest, TR *4-5, 14-15;* flange and rail system, TR *6-7;* luxury, TR *18-19;* maglev, TR *4-5, 34-35;* monorails, TR *28-29;* passengers, inertia's effect on, PH *28-29;* superconducting, *93;* signals controlling, TR *20-21;* snowplows, TR *22-23;* steam-powered, TR *4-5, 14-15, 16-17;* subways' air supply, TR *26-27;* supertrains, TR *4-5, 32-33;* tracks, TR *6-7,* 25,

      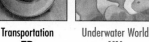

| Planet Earth | Plant Life | Physical Forces | Structure of Matter | Space & Planets | Transportation | Underwater World | Weather & Climate |
| PE | PL | PH | ST | SP | TR | UN | WE |

28, 30-31; whistle and Doppler effect, PH 138-139

Train station: crowds in, computer simulation of, CO 133

Transatlantic telegraph cable: MA map 9

Transducer: use of, in ultrasound technique, MA 142-143

Transformers: PH 86, 111; step-up, PH 86, 99; on utility pole, PH 87

Transistors: CO 20, 21, 22, PH 84, 85

Transition probability: CO chart 67

Transmission: TR 40; electric car without, TR 64-65; motorcycle, TR 42; working of, TR 46-47

Transmission electron microscope: MA 32-33

Transportation: TR entire volume. See also Aircraft; Automobiles; Motorcycles; Special-purpose vehicles; Trains; Water travel

Transrapid system (German maglev trains): TR 34

Travel agents: computer use by, CO 96-97

Tread on automobile tires: TR 56-57

Trevithick, Richard: steam locomotive built by, TR 15

Triangulation with infrared light: autofocus system using, MA 75

Triple point (of phase change): ST charts 38-39

Tritium in fusion reactions: ST 17

Trombone: PH 136

Truck tires: TR 57

Tsiolkovsky, Konstantin: MA 26

Tugboats: steam-driven, TR 91

Tuner: radio's, MA 84

Tuning forks: PH 142

Tuning of musical instruments: PH 142-143

Tunnels, train: signal for, TR 20; subway, ventilation for, TR 26, 27

Turbine (jet) engines: TR 130-131, 139

Turbine flow meter: MA 47

Turbines: hydroelectric, PH 98-99; hydrofoil's, TR 95; jet engines', TR 131; nuclear engine's, TR 102; ocean-powered, PH 106, 107; steam, PH 100-101, 103, 107, 109, 110, 111; turbocharger's, TR 54, 55

Turbocharged engines: automobile, TR 54-55

Turbofan engines: TR 130-131; VTOL aircraft's, TR 139

Turbojet engines: TR 131

Turbomolecular vacuum pumps: MA 44-45

Turboprop engines: TR 131

TV: color images on, MA 76-77; early, MA 22-23; high-definition, MA 78-79; images, vs. videophone images, CO 127; VCR's

recording of signals from, MA 82-83; and video games, CO 78-79

T waves in electrocardiogram: MA 137

Tweezers as levers: PH 43

Twilight Express (Japanese train): TR 18-19

Two-color offset printing: MA 40-41

Two-stroke engine: motorcycle's, TR 43

Two-wheel drive (2WD): automobile's, TR 48, 49

Two-wheel steering (2WS): automobile's, TR 50, 51

Tyndall effect: ST 20

Type, movable: casting, MA 77; use of, MA 6-7

U

Ultrasonic sound waves, use of: MA 142-143; by camera's autofocus system, MA 75

Ultraviolet radiation: and ozone layer, ST 76-77; and photosensitive resin, ST 144

Underwater exploration: submersibles for, TR 106-107

Union Pacific railroad: Big Boy locomotives built by, TR 4

Universal Product Codes (UPC bar codes): CO 86-87

Updrafts: and gliders, TR 119

Upholder (submarine): TR 98-99

Uplink and downlink antennas: CO 128

Upside-down top: PH 33

Uranium: fission of, ST 14-15

Uranium fuel: submarines using, TR 102-103

Uranium 235: fissioning, PH 108

Utilities: electricity supplied by, PH 86-87

V

Vaccine programs: computer viruses vs., CO 106

Vacuum-packed foods: ST 89

Vacuum pumps: MA 44-45; in fire engines, TR 71

Vacuum tubes: CO 5, 14-15; in electron microscope, MA 32-33; in x-ray machine, MA 140

Valves, mechanical: deadweight and safety, for pressure cooker, MA 101

Vapor diffusion vacuum pumps: MA 44, 45

Vaporization: PH 22-23, 53, 62-63; in distillation, ST 116, 126-127; evaporation, PH 62, 64-65; of water, ST 32-33, 34, 35. See also Steam turbines, power for

Vapor pressure: PH 22; temperature and, PH chart 22

Variable-pitch propellers: TR 113

VCA (voltage control amplifier), synthesizer's: sound qualities produced by, MA 90

VCF (voltage control filter), synthesizer's: sound qualities produced by, MA 90

VCO (voltage control oscillator), synthesizer's: sound qualities produced by, MA 90

VCRs (videocassette recorders): MA 82-83

Vector processing: CO 43

Velocity of baseball: use of speed gun for calculating, MA 38-39

Vending machines: MA 58-59

Ventilation systems: for airplanes, TR 128-129; for subway stations, TR 26-27

Ventricles: artificial, MA 132, 133. See also Heart, human

Venturi flap: automated car's, TR 61

Venturi tube: MA 47

Verge escapement mechanism: mechanical clock's, MA 12, 13

Vernier (slide) calipers: MA 48, 49

Vertical canard: CCV's, TR 140

Vertical takeoff and landing (VTOL) aircraft: TR 138-139

VHF Omni-range (VOR) stations: TR 122-123

Vibration roller: TR 74-75

Vic, Henri de: clock by, MA 12-13

Victoria (Magellan's ship): TR 87

Videocassette recorders (VCRs): MA 82-83

Video editing room: CO 80

Video games: CO 78-79

Videophones: CO 126-127

Vidie, Lucien: barometer type invented by, PH 16-17

Vinylon: molecular structure of, ST 109

Violin: working of, PH 134-135

Virtual image: PH 116

Virus programs: computer, CO 106

Viscosity vs. gravity: and whirlpool formation, PH 20

Viscous coupling: TR 49

Vise: PH 44-45

Vitamin C: cut apple coated with, ST 80, 81

Voice: recognition, CO 62-63; recording, by sound spectrographs, MA 34-35; synthesizers, CO 60-61; transmission, by car phone, CO 120-121; transmission, by teleconferencing, CO 112-113; transmission, by telephone, CO 110-111, MA 10, 11, 56-57

Voiceprints: MA 35

Voltage control (VC): kinds of, synthesizer's, MA 90

Voltage drop: PH 74-75

Voltmeters: PH 77

VOR (VHF Omni-range) stations: TR 122-123

Vortexes: formation of, PH 20-21

Animal Behavior
AN

Computer Age
CO

Ecology
EC

Evolution of Life
EV

Geography
GE

Human Body
HU

Insects & Spiders
IN

Machines &
Inventions **MA**

Voyager space probes: communication with Earth, CO *142-143*

VTOL (vertical takeoff and landing) aircraft: TR *138-139*

V-2 rocket: MA *26-27*

Vulcanized rubber: ST 30

W

War, transportation for: *See* Military transportation

Washers, faucet: MA *110*; working of, MA *110, 111*

Washing machines: MA *112-113*

Washing of dishes: MA *116-117*

Watches: quartz, MA *96-97*

Water: boiling, MA *100*, PH *22-23, 62*; bubbles in, PH *62-63*; in concrete, ST *120*; convection in, PH *58-59, 66*; density and expansion of, PH *chart 67*; fire extinguished with, ST 68, *69*; floating on, PH *8-9*; freezing, PH *66-67*; heat and phase changes in, PH *22-23, 52-53, 54-55, 62-63*; heat transfer, PH *58-59, 64*; hydroelectric power from, PH *98-99*; iron exposed to, ST *56-57*; lowering freezing point of, ST *40-41*; molecules, makeup of, ST *6-7*; molecules, microwaves and, MA *102*; as neutral substance, ST *65*; ocean, as power source, PH *106-107*; and oil, separation of, ST *42-43, 127*; phase changes, ST *32-33, 34-35, 39, 40-41*; in photosynthesis, ST *66*; purifying, ST *98-99*; removal from coffee, ST *86-87*; removal in papermaking, ST *104, 105*; sea, salt recovered from, ST *96-97*; skiing and skating on film of, PH 26, 27; and soap, dirt removal by, ST *48-49*; sound waves through, PH *130*; starch and, ST 100, *101*; steam from, generating power with, PH *100-101, 102-103, 109*, 110, *111*; substances in, ST *43*; vapor, ST 34, *35, 39*, PH *22-23, 53, 62-63, 64-65*; whirlpools, formation of, PH *20-21*

Water faucets: MA *110-111*

Waterjet pump: hydrofoil's, TR *95*

Water meters: MA *46, 47*

Water molecules: boiling and, MA *100*; escape into air, PH *62*; heat and, PH *52-53, 54-55*; kinetic energy, PH *23, 52*; makeup of, ST *6-7*; microwaves and, MA *102*; in whirlpool formation, PH *20*

Water pipe: measuring flow in, MA *46-47*

Water-seal vacuum pump: MA *45*

Water system: MA *111*

Water travel: TR 78-107; Columbus's expedition, ships of, TR *88-89*; in fog, TR *82-83*; future, superconducting ships for, TR *104-105*; historical navigational instruments for, TR *86-87*; hovercraft, TR *78, 96-97*; hydrofoils, TR *79, 94-95*; icebreakers, TR *100-101*; navigation, TR 78, *80-87, 103*; nuclear vessels, TR *102-103*; through Panama Canal, TR *92-93*; rules of the road for, TR *83*; satellites, use of, TR *84-85*; steam vessels, TR *79, 90-91*; submarines, TR *79, 98-99, 102-103, 106-107*; submersibles, deep-diving, TR *79, 106-107*

Water vapor: ST 34, *35*; bubbles, PH *62-63*; condensation of, PH *64-65*, ST *39*; phase change into, PH *22-23, 53, 62-63, 64-65*

Watt, James: steam engine perfected by, TR 90

Wave-forms: CO *40, 41, 66, 110, 111*; sound, PH *131*; and timbre of sound, MA 90

Wave fronts, sound: PH *131*; and Doppler effect, PH *138-139*

Wavelengths: and color of light, ST *51*

Wave mechanics: PH *88-89*

Waves, light: *See* Light

Waves, ocean: as power source, PH 106, *107*; surfers riding, PH *38-39*

Waves, sound: *See* Sound waves

Wave vs. corpuscular theory of light: PH 112

Wax: solidification of, PH *67*

Weather: computer studies of, CO *134-135*

Weather satellites: CO *134*

Wedge: PH *45*

Weighing mechanism: PH *50*; bathroom scales', MA *108-109*

Weight: gravity and, PH *6-7*

Welding of automobile parts, robot use in: CO *101*

Wet plate photography: difficulty of, MA 18, 19

Wheat: harvesting, combines for, MA *14-15*; starch, ST *100-101*

Wheel and axle: bicycle's use of, PH *46-47*; faucet as, MA 110

Wheelbarrow as lever: PH *42*

Wheels: TR *36-37*; brakes and, TR *11, 44-45*; drive systems, TR *48-49*; flanged, trains', TR *6-7, 31*; paddle, steamers', TR *90, 91*; steam car's, TR *38*; steam locomotives', TR *14, 15, 17*; steering, TR *50-51*

Wheel trucks: trains', TR *7, 33*

Whirlpools, formation of: PH *20-21*

Wiener, Norbert: MA 4

Winch: crane's, TR *72*

Wind: and hang gliding, PH *14-15*; as power source, PH *104-105*; and sailing, PH *12-13*; sound traveling with, PH *133*

Wind instruments: PH *135, 136-137*

Windmills: PH *104-105*

Window air conditioner: MA *122-123*

Wings, aircraft: delta, *Concorde*'s, TR *136*; forward-swept, TR *142-143*; and lift, TR *110-111*; in soaring, TR *118*; Wright *Flyer*'s, twisting tips of, TR *135*

Wire: shape-memory, ST *128-129, 140-141*

Wood: burning, extinguishing, ST *69*; combustion, ST *67, 68*; paper made from, ST *104-105*

Woodwinds: clarinet, PH *136-137*; recorder, PH *135*

Wool: molecular structure of, ST *107, 109*

Word processors: CO *58-59*

Work stations: computers for, CO *92*

World solar challenge race (1990): car competing in, TR *63*

Worms (self-replicating programs): CO *106*

Wright, Orville and Wilbur: aircraft built by, TR *108, 134-135*

Writers: word processors for, CO *58-59*

X

Xenon gas: CAT scanner using, MA *134*

XOR gate: CO 28; in half-adder, CO *29*

X-rays: MA *140-141*; CAT scanner's use of, MA *134-135*

X-29A (forward-swept-wing aircraft): TR *142-143*

XV-15 VTOL aircraft: TR *139*

Y

Yeager, Chuck: TR 136

Yogurt: making of, ST *84-85*

Z

Zigzag in-line package (ZIP): CO *23*

Zinc: galvanizing metal with, ST *63*; sacrificial anodes from, ST *57*

ZIP (zigzag in-line package): CO *23*

Zworykin, Vladimir K.: iconoscope invented by, MA 22, *23*

Planet Earth
PE

Plant Life
PL

Physical Forces
PH

Structure of Matter
ST

Space & Planets
SP

Transportation
TR

Underwater World
UN

Weather & Climate
WE

Master Index

Numerals in italics indicate an illustration of the subject mentioned.

A

Abacuses and counting stones: CO *4-5, 6-7*

Abalone, single-shelled red: reproduction by, UN *98*

Aberration of starlight: SP *55*

Abscission layer, leaf stalk's: PL *41, 43*

Absolute vs. apparent magnitude: SP *80-81*

Absorption lines: SP *29, 78*; redshift of, SP *115*

Abyssal currents: PE *116-117*

Abyssal plains: PE *map 112-113, 115*

AC (alternating current): and DC (direct current), PH *85, 86*; generators, working of, PH *96-97*

Acacia plants: bull-horn, IN *99*

Acanthodians: EV *48*

Acarina (extinct arachnid): EV *50*

Acceleration: and inertia, PH *28*; in Newton's second law of motion, PH *24*

Accelerator: automobile's, TR *41, 47*

Accelerometer: in aircraft's INS, TR *124*; integral, V-2 rocket's, MA *27*

Accretion disks around black holes: SP *94, 95*

Acellular organisms: EV *39*

Acidity in yogurt formation: ST *84-85*

Acid rain: ST *64-65*, WE *28-29*; effects of, EC *74-75*

Acids and alkalines: foods, ST *82-83*; neutralizing, ST *52, 53, 64, 65*

Acinar cells: HU *85*

Acoustic analysis: CO *62-63*

Acquired immune deficiency syndrome (AIDS): HU *136-137*

Acrylic: molecular structure of, ST *109*

Actin and myosin: HU *36, 37*

Activated carbon: air purification with, MA *50-51*; removing odors with, ST *52-53*

Active submission: wolves, AN *45*

Adam's apple: HU *58*; development of, HU *59*

Adapis (extinct primate): EV *122*

Adaptation: EV *5, 20-21*, PL *110*; alpine plants, PL *120-121*; baobab tree, PL *116-117*; cacti, PL *111, 112-113*; stone plant, PL *110, 114-115*

Adaptive radiation: EV *24-25*, 138

Addax: EC *91*

Adder circuits: CO 28, *29*

Adding machines: CO *4-5, 8-9*

Addition by computers: CO 24, *25*; logic gates and, CO 28, *29*; programs for, CO 51

Addresses in computer memory: CO *30-31*; disk, CO 56, 57

Adélie penguins: AN *88-89, 112-113*, EC *9, 46, 47*

Adenosine triphosphate (ATP): HU 36, *37, 57*

Adiabatic cooling: WE *24*

Adrenal glands: HU *75*

Adriatic Sea and bora winds: WE *48-49*

Advanced materials: *See* Materials technology

Advection fog: WE *71*

Aedes albopictus mosquito: AN *11*

Aerial roots: PL *22*

Aerial surveys: GE *6-7, 19*; of ore deposits, PE *99*; of volcanoes, PE *79*

Aerodynamics: of automobiles, CO *75*; of hang gliders, PH *14-15*

Aerosol plasma theory of ball lightning: WE *107*

Aerosols: ST *20*

Africa: beetles, IN *60, 61, 107*; catfish, UN 57, *84-85, 86-87*; cattle, GE *131*; cichlids, UN *79, 84-85*; climate zones, GE *112-113*; desert animals, EC *89, 91*; diamond formation, PE *91*; driver ants, IN 138, *141*; electric fish, UN *56-57*; elephants, EC *10, 82-83, 84-85, 113*; Great Rift Valley, PE *22-23, 40-41*; hunting dogs, EC *13, 82*; and India, animals of, EC *10-11*; killifish, UN *64*; locust swarming, IN *map 87*; lungfish, UN *30-31*; Nile River, GE *4-5, 33*; Sahara dunes, GE *100-101, 105, 109*; savannas, EC *29, 76, 80-85*, GE *113*; vs. South America, animals of, EC *20-21*

Africanized honeybees: IN *136-137*

Aftershocks following earthquakes: PE *54*

Agave: EC *95*

Agglutinins: HU *70-71*

Agglutinogens: HU *70-71*

Aggregate fruits: PL *67*

Aggressive mimicry: AN *30-31*

Aging phenomenon of starch: ST 100, *101*

Agitator: washing machine's, MA *113*

Agnathans: EV *46-47, 48*

Agouti: EC *20*

Agriculture: climate and, GE *130-131, 136-137*; combines used in, MA *14-15*; dryland farming, GE 138; grain production, GE *122-123*; irrigation, GE *35, 63, 138-139*; Mediterranean, GE *131, 136-137*; slash-and-burn, GE *107*; South America,

GE *141*; transhumance, GE *142-143*; Whittlesey's zones, GE *map 130-131*

AIDS (acquired immune deficiency syndrome): HU *136-137*

Aiken, Howard: CO 14

Ailerons: TR *111*

Air: around baseball during pitch, PH *34, 35*; blimp's displacement of, ST *46-47*; bubbles in liquid, PH *63*; convection in, PH *59*; down's interference with convection in, PH 60, *61*; hang glider in, PH *14-15*; hot, balloons filled with, PH *4-5, 10-11*; in ice cream, ST *92, 93*; pressure, temperature, and volume of, PH *11*; in sauna, PH *64-65*; sound waves through, PH *130-131, 133. See also* Atmosphere of Earth; Wind

Air bags: automobile's, TR *50-51*

Air (swim) bladder: UN *12-13*; for hearing, UN *52, 53*; and pressure, UN 23

Air brakes: automatic, trains', TR *10-11*

Air-breathing fish: UN *28-29, 30-31*

Air circulation: in airplanes, TR *128-129*; in Earth's atmosphere, SP *48*

Air conditioners: MA *122-123*; basement system, MA *51*; placement of, PH *59*

Aircraft: TR *108-144*; airships, TR *108, 116-117*; air turbulence and, WE *52-53*; altitude, measuring, TR 132, *133*; cloud seeding from, WE *78-79*; contrails, WE *64-65*; first, TR *108, 134-135*; flying, basic method of, TR *110-111*; with forward-swept wings, TR *142-143*; gliders, TR *118-119*; helicopters, TR *109, 114-115*; hurricane hunters, WE *94-95*; INS (inertial navigation system), TR *124-125*; jet engines, working of, TR *130-131, 139*; landing system for (ILS), TR *126-127*; navigational aids for, TR *122-123, 124-125*; Omega System for, TR *map 125*; propellers, use of, TR *112-113, 134, 139*; sideways-flying, TR *140-141*; simulation of flight, CO *82-83*; sonic booms from, PH *140-141*, TR *136-137*; speed, measuring, TR *132-133*; Stealth bomber, TR *109, 144*; supersonic, TR *108-109, 136-137*; traffic control, TR *120-121*; ventilation system for, TR *128-129*; and VOR stations, TR *122-123*; VTOL (vertical takeoff and landing), TR *138-139*; in weather observation, WE *94-95, 111, 116, 123*

Air currents: glider's use of, TR *119*

Air-cushion vehicle (hovercraft): TR *78, 96-97*

Air drying: dehumidifier for, MA *124-125*

Air eddies: and contrails, WE *64*; mountains and, WE *69*

Animal Behavior **AN** · Computer Age **CO** · Ecology **EC** · Evolution of Life **EV** · Geography **GE** · Human Body **HU** · Insects & Spiders **IN** · Machines & Inventions **MA**

Airfoil: type of (hang glider), PH *14-15*

Airline computers: CO *96-97*

Air molecules: heated, PH *10-11*; and heat loss, PH 60; pressure, temperature, and volume of, PH *11*

Airplanes: *See* Aircraft

Air plants: *See* Epiphytes

Air pollution: WE *26-27*; and acid rain, WE *28-29*; from automobiles, computerized control of, CO 102; and ozone holes, WE *30-31*

Airport security gates: MA *42-43*

Air pressure: *See* Atmospheric pressure

Air purifier systems: MA *50-51*

Air roots: plants with, EC *68-69*

Air sacs in lungs: HU *56-57*

Airships: TR *108, 116-117*

Airspeed indicators: TR *132-133*

Air supply: for airplanes, TR *128-129*; for submarines, TR *99*; for subways, TR *26-27*

Air traffic: control of, TR *120-121*

Air turbulence: WE *52-53*

Akagi stink bugs: IN *120*

Akebia flowers: PL *59*

Akiyoshi Cave, Japan: GE *54-55*

Alarm systems: burglar, MA *114-115*; fire, MA *64-65*

Alaska, U.S.: aurora, WE *16*; rainbow, WE *99*

Albatrosses: Galápagos, courtship of, AN *102*; short-tailed, EC *33*

Albedo: WE *map 123*

Albino long fin guppy: UN *65*

Alcaid (star): movement, SP *90-91*

Alcohol: ethanol, water and, ST *43*; and lowering of freezing point, ST *40*; in perfume, ST *127*

Alevins: UN *82*

Alexander's horned aphid: IN *144*

Alfonsino: UN *23*

Algae: PL *95, 102-103, 104-105*; blue-green, and oxygen, ST 36; chlorophyll in, EV *37*; diatoms, PL *100-101*; evolution of, EV *6-7*, 53; and formation of atmosphere, WE *7*; fossils (stromatolites), EV *26-27, 34-35*, WE *6*; in lichens, PL *106, 107*

Algol (binary star system): SP *82-83*

Algorithms: CO *52-53*

Alioth (star): movement, SP *90-91*

Alkalines and acids: foods, ST *82-83*; neutralizing, ST 52, *53*, 64, 65

Allergies: HU 135; hay fever, HU *134-135*

Alligators: and alligator holes, EC *138-139*; planthopper resembling, IN *112, 119*; and young, AN *110-111*

Alligator snapping turtle: UN *110-111*

Allosaurus (dinosaur): EV *74-75*

Alloys: ST *112-113*; shape-memory, ST *128-129, 140-141*

Alluvial fans: GE *27, 30-31*

Alluvium: terraces from, GE *88-89*

Alpha decay: PH *91*

Alpha-starch vs. beta-starch: ST *100-101*

Alpha waves, brain's: HU *120, 124, 125*

Alpine butterflies: EC *52-53, 57*

Alpine glaciers: GE *42*; landforms created by, GE *44-45*

Alpine meadows: EC *56-57*

Alpine plants: PL *120-121*

Alpine tundra: EC 54, *55, 57*

Alpine zone of Alps: GE *142, chart* 142

Alps (mountains), Europe: GE *45, 142-143*; Dinaric (Yugoslavia), bora winds over, WE *48-49*

Alternating current (AC): and direct current (DC), PH *85, 86*; generators, PH *96-97*

Alternation of generations: *See* Spore-bearing plants

Altimeters: TR 132, *133*

Altiplano (plateau): Bolivian, GE *140-141*

Altitude: and boiling point, PH *22-23*; and gravity, PE *18*

Altocumulus clouds: WE *61, 63*

Altostratus clouds: WE *61, chart 74*

Alumina: refining, ST 114, *115*

Aluminosilicate glass: ST *125*

Aluminum: burning, conditions for, ST 70, *71*; extruded beams, ST *28-29*; glass enhanced with, ST *125*; number of atoms in, ST *8*; refining, ST 114, *115*; space shuttle powered by, ST *71, 74-75*

Alveoli and alveolar sacs: HU *56-57*; carbon monoxide in, HU *72-73*

Alvin (bathyscaphe): TR *107*

Amaranth: PL *75*

Amazon River, Brazil-Peru: GE *36-37*; dolphins, UN *59*

Amino acids: formation, SP *23*

Ammeters: PH *76-77*

Ammonia: Jupiter's, absorption pattern, SP *29*

Ammonites: EV *98-99*; mosasaurs eating, EV *94-95*

Amniotic sac: HU *19*; of twins, HU *22, 23*

Amoebas: evolution of, EV *6*

Amorphous metals: ST *142-143*

Amphibians: evolution of, EV *56-57*; frogs, AN 15, *56-57, 66-67*, 73, EC 93, *127, 138, 139*; newts, AN *52, 67*, EV *133*; reproduction in, UN *62-63, 88-89, 90-91*; and reptile evolution, EV *58-59*; salamanders, EC *28, 42*; toads, AN 51, *52, 54-55*, EC *92-93, 125*

Amplifier: radio's, MA *84-85*; sound spectrograph's, MA *35*

Amplitude modulation: MA *85*

Amplitude of sound, variations in: MA *90*; and recording of compact disks, MA *86*

Ampullae and ampullar crests: HU *114, 115*

Ampullae of Lorenzini: shark's, UN *55*

AM radio transmissions: MA *84-85*

Anaerobic bacteria: EV 32, *33*, 37

Anak Krakatoa (volcanic island), Indonesia: PE *72*

Anal fin: mouthbrooder's, spots on, UN *81*

Analog and digital conversion: CO *40-41, 67, 110-111, 119*

Analog and digital signals: compact disks, recording of, MA *86*; fax machine's use of, MA *68-69*; synthesizer's use of, MA *91*

Analogous parts: PL 28, *29, 30*

Anal pore: paramecium, AN *7*

Anal sphincter: HU *91*

Analytical Engine: CO 4, *10-11*

Anancus (elephant ancestor): EV *110*

Anapsids: EV *chart 63*; *Hylonomus*, EV 58, 62

Anchiceratops (dinosaur): EV *75*

Andesite: PE *89*

Andes (mountains), South America: PE *map* 39; Altiplano, GE *140-141*; and fog, WE *72-73, 135*; formation of, PE *38-39*; source of Amazon, GE *36*

AND gate: CO *28*; in half-adder, CO *29*

Andrews, Roy Chapman: EV *78*

Andrewsarchus (extinct mammal): EV *112*

Andromeda (galaxy): SP *103*

Anemones, sea: AN *22-23, 48-49*, UN *34*; and clown fish, AN *70-71*, UN *144*; crabs living in, UN *39*; and hermit crabs, AN *78-79*

Aneroid barograph: PH *17*

Aneroid barometers: PH *16-17*; airplane instruments with, TR *132-133*

Angelfish: blackspot, sex changes in, UN *66-67*; coloration, UN *132-133*

Angiosperms: *See* Flowers and flowering plants

Angle of attack: airplane's, TR *110*

Anglerfish: UN 110, *111, 112*; devil angler, UN *23*; goosefish, UN *102-103, 110-111*; reproduction, UN *70-71*

Angular momentum: PH *32*

Animal behavior: AN entire volume

Animals: Antarctic and Arctic, EC *8-9*, 28, *46-49*; cells of, PL *6-7*; as consumers, PL 124, *125*; crowding of, EC *100-101*; endangered, EC *96-97, 112-113*; extinct, EC *18-19, 20, 112*, EV 8, 20, 24, *60-61, 144*; after forest fire, EC *136-137*; of Galápagos, EC *6-7, 113, 119*; plant reproduction aided by, EC *96-97, 114-115,*

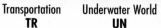

Planet Earth **PE** — Plant Life **PL** — Physical Forces **PH** — Structure of Matter **ST** — Space & Planets **SP** — Transportation **TR** — Underwater World **UN** — Weather & Climate **WE**

122-123; plants' defenses against, EC 118-119; by region, EC 4-5; seeds spread by, PL 65, 74-75, 77, 78-79, 82; soil, PL 110-111, 127. See also Africa; Amphibians; Biomes; Birds; Food chain; Gastropods; Habitats; Insects; Mammals; Reptiles; and individual names

Ankle joint: HU 38

Annular eclipse of Sun: SP 63

Annularia (Paleozoic plant): EV 52

Anode: sacrificial, ST 57

Anodes and cathodes: in automobile batteries, ST 58-59; in electrolytic conduction, ST 18-19; in electroplating, ST 62-63; and iron reactions, ST 56-57

Anomalops: UN 26; photophore, UN 27

Antarctica: GE 52-53; albedo, WE map 123; animals, EC 9, 46-47, 48, 49; icecap, possible melting of, effects of, GE 72-73; ice fog and solar displays, WE 103; moraines, GE 46; ozone hole over, ST map 77, WE 30-31; plants, EC 44-45, 46; atmospheric pressure over, WE 122; weather observation of, WE 122-123

Antarctic cod: body fluids of, UN chart 16

Antarctic Ocean: fish in, UN 16-17

Antarctic toothfish: UN 17

Antarctic Transverse Range: GE 53

Anteater: banded, EC 17

Antelope: AN 60-61; African, EC 10, 21, 82-85, 91; pronghorn, AN 61

Antennae, insect: IN 26-27; ants' use of, AN 12; butterflies' vs. moths', IN 32; flies', AN 8, 9; mosquitoes', AN 10; moths', AN 94

Antennas, electromechanical: ground, CO 128, 129; orbiting, CO 129; radar, ship's, TR 83; in space, ST 139, 141; space probe's, CO 143; transmitting, PH 88-89

Anther culture: PL 140

Anthers: mistletoe, PL 83; pine cone, PL 89

Anthracite and bituminous coal: deposits, PE map 104; formation of, PE 105

Anthracosaur: EV 58

Antibiotics: PL 132-133

Antibodies: HU 133; B cells producing, HU 126, 128, 129, 132, 135; immune globulin E, HU 134, 135

Antimatter vs. matter: ST 22-23

Antinodes and nodes: PH 137

Ant plants: IN 98

Ants: aphids' use of, AN 12-13; army, AN 124-127; defenses, IN 123, 126-127; food gathering, IN 42-43, 99, 138; societies, IN 138-139; symbiosis, IN 78-79, 98-99; termites attacked by, IN 140, 141; as wingless insects, IN 85

Anus: HU 91

Anvil clouds: WE 62, 63; stratocumulus, WE 60

Apanteles wasps: IN 114

Apes: arboreal, EC 70, 71; chimpanzees, AN 46-47, 124-125, 141, 142-143; evolutionary ancestry, EV 123, 124; gorillas, EC 112; social groups, AN 140-141

Aphids: ants' use of, AN 12-13; and butterfly-ant coevolution, IN 79; hover flies and, AN 118-119; reproduction, IN 72-73; soldier, IN 144; as wingless insects, IN 72-73, 85

Aphytis (parasitic wasp): IN 91

Apocrine sweat glands: HU 43

Apollo asteroids: SP 34-35

Apollo 11 mission: view of Moon from, SP 69

Apollo 17 astronauts: Moon buggy used by, SP 74

Apollo spacecraft: PH 19

Appalachian Mountains, U.S.: formation of: GE 87, 96-97

Apparent vs. absolute magnitude: SP 80-81

Appendix: HU 90; lining of, HU 77

Apples: PL 67; browning of, ST 80-81

Appliances: computer-controlled, CO 104-105

Aquatic insects: See Water dwelling insects

Aquatic mammals: UN 63; dolphins, EV 136, UN 18-19, 58-59, 114-115; otters, EC 130, 131, 142; sea lions, EC 7; seals, EC 46-47, 49, UN 92-93; Steller's sea cows, EV 144; whales, EC 112, EV 112-113, UN 4-5, 32-33, 94-95, 107, 114-115, 116-117

Aquatic plants: EC 26-27; moose feeding on, EC 58-59

Aquifers: GE 56; and artesian water, GE 56; formation of, GE 57; and oases, GE 62, 63; and subsidence, GE 64-65

Arable zone of Alps: GE 142, chart 142

Arachnids: earliest, on land, EV 50-51. See also Spiders

Arago, François: MA 119

Araucaria (gymnosperm): EV 102

Arborescent lichens: PL 107

Archaeopteryx (ancestral bird): EV 68, 69, 70-71

Archerfish: UN 108-109

Arches: sea cliffs and, GE 68-69, 76-77

Archimedes' principle: PH 9

Architectural models: CO 133

Architecture of computers: CO 18-19

Arctic animals: EC 8, 28, 48-49; gray whales, UN 94; seals' birthplace, UN 92; seasonal color changes in, AN 50-51, 58-59; terns, AN 135

Arctic Circle: summer, SP 58-59

Arctic temperature vs. Antarctica's: EC chart 45

Ardis tyrannus amurensis (moth): IN 32

Areole: cactus's, PL 113

Argiope amoena (spider): attack on, IN 54-55

Argiope bruennichi (spider): insect trapping by, IN 38-39

Argyros (water spider): IN 96-97

Arithmetic logic units (ALUs): CO 24-25; location, CO 18

Arizona, U.S.: Grand Canyon, GE 84-85, 94-95; Monument Valley, GE 110-111; Sun City, planned community in, GE 118-119

Arm, human: movement, HU 30-31, 39; nerves, HU 103; wing, relationship to, EV 131, 135

Arm, mechanical: artificial (prosthetic), CO 138; robotic, automakers' use of, CO 100-101

Army ants: AN 124-127

Arrow-poison frogs: UN 90

Arsinoitherium (extinct mammal): EV 117

Arteries: HU 62-63; blood pressure in, HU 68-69, MA 130, 131; clogged, HU 144; of fetus and mother, HU 20-21; renal, HU 94, 95

Artesian springs: GE 56; and oases, GE 62, 63

Artesian wells: GE 56; at oases, GE 62

Arthropods: EV 42; flying, first, EV 54-55; land, earliest, EV 50-51; larvae, similarity of, EV 132; trilobites, EV 40-41, 42, 44-45

Artificial heart: MA 132-133

Artificial Intelligence (AI): CO 69

Artificial limbs and organs: CO 138-139

Artiodactyls: EC 20

Ascending colon: HU 90

ASCII code table: CO chart 27

Ascocarps: lichen's, PL 106; perithecia, PL 97

Ascomycetes fungi: PL 98

Asian horned toad: AN 51, 52

Asian warbler: AN 98

Assassin bug: IN 114; mantis resembling, AN 31

Assembly lines: robot use on, CO 100-101

Asteroids: SP 30-31; Apollo, SP 34-35; belt, SP 4-5, 30, 31, 35; orbits, SP 31, 35

Asthenosphere: PE 9, 28, 29

Astrapotherium (extinct mammal): EV 120

Astrolabe: TR 86

Astronauts: weight of, on Earth vs. Moon, PH 6-7. See also Space travel

Asuka STOL aircraft: TR 139

Atherosclerosis: HU 144

Athletes: computer use by, CO 136-137

Animal Behavior
AN

Computer Age
CO

Ecology
EC

Evolution of Life
EV

Geography
GE

Human Body
HU

Insects & Spiders
IN

Machines & Inventions **MA**

Atlantic Ocean: continental margin, PE *114-115*; fishing grounds, GE *126*; Sargasso Sea, PE *132-133*; seacoast, formation of, GE *28-29*; temperatures, PE *117*

Atlantic salmon: reproduction by, UN *82-83*

Atlantic snipe eel: UN *112*

Atlas moth: IN *112-113*

ATM (automated-teller machine): CO *88-89*

Atmosphere of Earth: WE 4-31; acid rain, WE *28-29*; aurora, WE *8, 11, 16-17*; composition of, WE 6, 8, 10, *14-15*; Earth's protection by, WE *20-21*; end of, WE *10-11*; formation of, WE 4, *6-7*; greenhouse effect, WE *136-137, 139*; history of, PE 6, 110, *111*, ST *36-37*; inversion layer, WE *60, 138-139*; ionosphere, WE 4, 8, 9, 10, *14-15*, 16; layers of, WE 4, *8-9, 10-11, 112-113*; nitrogen in, ST *25, 26-27*; optical phenomena, WE *96-105*; ozone layer, ST *76-77*, WE 4, 7, *8-9, 12-13*, 25, *30-31*; pollution, WE *26-27*; pollution effects, WE *28-29, 30-31*; sky color, WE *22-23*; from space, WE *10*; spacecraft above, SP *124, 130-131*; Sun's radiation and, SP *48-49*; Sun through, WE *4-5*; temperature of, altitude and, WE 24, 25, *113*; Van Allen belts, WE *10-11, 18-19. See also* Atmospheric pressure; Wind

Atmospheres: Jupiter, SP *14-15, 16, 17, 28*; Sun's chromosphere, SP *40, 41, 42-43*; Sun's corona, SP *40, 41, 50-51, 63, 123*; Titan (moon of Saturn), SP 22, *23*; Venus, SP 10, *11*

Atmospheric circulation: WE *34-35, 36-37, 112-113*, 124, *134*; and jet streams, WE *38, 53*

Atmospheric pressure: WE 82; altitude and, WE *24*; at center of hurricane, WE *charts* 92-93; isobars, WE *40, 41, 44, 84, 85, 93, 118-119, 122*; measuring, PH *16-17*; states of matter and ST, 38, ST *charts* 38-39; vapor pressure and, PH 22. *See also* High pressure; Low pressure

Atmospheric pressure altimeter vs. radio altimeter: TR 132, *133*

Atolls: GE *81*; coral, PE *114-115*

Atomic nuclei: fission of, TR 102, *103*

Atomic reactors: PH *108-109*; core, PH *94-95, 108*

Atoms: ST 4; of antimatter, vs. matter, ST *22-23*; birth of, SP *108*; fission of, ST *14-15*; fusion of nuclei, ST *16-17*; light emission by, ST *50-51*; makeup of, ST *6-7*; of metals, ST *13, 19, 28-29, 31, 121, 140-141, 142-143*; radioactive, PH *90-91, 108*; of silicon, MA *96*; of silicon, microscope's magnification of, MA *32*; size of, ST *8-9. See also* Electrons; Ions; Molecules

ATP (adenosine triphosphate): HU 36, *37, 57*

Audio equipment: compact disks (CDs) and CD players vs. phonograph records, MA *86-87*; microphones and speakers, MA *80-81*; radios, MA *84-85*

Audio recording head in VCR: MA *83*

Auditory system of fish: UN *52-53*; carp, UN *44*; sharks, UN *55*

Auditory system of humans: receptors and cortex, HU *113*

Auks: EC *8*; great, EC 8, EV *144*

Aurelia jellyfish: UN *43*

Aurora: WE *16-17*; in atmospheric layers, WE *8, 11*; australis, WE 16; borealis, WE 16; in Norway, SP *49*

Auroral oval: WE *17*

Australia: animals, EV *138-139, 144*; bulldog ants, IN *139*; capital (Canberra), GE *128-129*; cockroaches, IN *131*; desert, EC *87*; gastric-brooding frogs, UN *90-91*; Great Barrier Reef, GE *80-81*; ladybug from, IN *91*; lungfish, UN *31*; in map projections, GE *17*; marsupials, EC *16-17, 114*; pollinators, EC *114*; sheep, GE *131*; stromatolites, EV *35*

Australian brown newt: AN *52*

Australian honeycomb spider: AN *27*

Australian Region: animals of, EC *4-5*

Australopithecus (extinct hominid): EV *124-126*; skeleton, EV *105*

Austria: Alps in, GE *45*

Autofocus (AF): cameras with, MA *74-75*

Automated-teller machines (ATMs): CO *88-89*

Automatic air brakes: trains', TR *10-11*

Automatic cars: TR *60-61*

Automatic trains: TR *24-25*

Automatic transmission: automobile's, TR *47*

Automatons: *See* Robots

Automobiles: TR 36-65; air bags, TR *52-53*; automated, TR *60-61*; batteries, ST *58-59*; brakes, TR *44-45, 58*; computers in, CO *102-103*; design of, CO *74-75*; electric, TR *64-65*; engine, ST *60-61*; first, TR 36, *38-39*; four-wheel drive (4WD), TR *48-49*; four-wheel steering (4WS), TR *50-51*; motorcycles vs., TR *42-43*; phones in, CO *120-121*; power for, TR *40-41, 47, 54-55*, 58, 59; racing cars, Formula One, TR *58-59*; robot use in manufacture of, CO *100-101*; solar-powered, TR *62-63*; traffic patterns, computer modeling of, CO *132-133*; transmission, TR *40, 46-47*; tread on tires, TR *56-57*; turbocharged, TR *54-55*; wheel types, TR *36-37*

Autumnal equinox: SP *56, 57*

Aviation, flight simulators used in: CO *82-83*

Axis cylinder: HU *100-101*

Axons: HU 100; terminal, HU *100-101*

Azaleas: PL *50, 52*; Japanese, EC *118*

Aztec ants and trumpet trees: IN *98-99*

Azure-winged magpies: AN *115*; eggs, AN *114, 115*

B

Babbage, Charles: CO 4, *10*; inventions, CO 4, *10-11*

Babies, unborn: ultrasound monitoring of, MA *142-143*

Baboons: AN 140

Babylonian world map: GE *14*

Baby (milk) teeth: HU 26, 27, 35

Bacilli: coliform, HU *91*

Back: strained, HU *40-41*

Backboned animals: early development of, EV *132-133*; evolution of, EV *46-47. See also* Amphibians; Birds; Fish; Mammals; Reptiles

Background radiation: cosmic, SP *113*

Bacteria: EV *32, 33, 37*, HU *141*; and antibiotics, PL 132, *133*; in conch's gills, UN *35*; as decomposers, PL *126*; decomposition by, EC 128, 129; evolution of, EV 6; in fermentation, ST *85, 90-91*; in food chain, UN *126*; food protected from, ST *88, 89*; intestinal, HU *89, 91*; luminous, sea creatures with, UN *24, 25, 26, 27, 111, 140, 144*; in nitrogen cycle, ST 26, 27; in ocean trenches, UN 35; plasmodium and, PL *97*; removal from water, ST *98-99*; white blood cell engulfing, HU *65*

Bagworm moths: IN *85*; nests, IN *102-103*

Baird, John L.: mechanical scanning televisor built by, MA *22-23*

Bait: green heron's use of, AN *36-37*

Baker, Mount, Wash., U.S.: study of, PE *79*

Balance: organs of, UN *52*

Bald cypress: PL *22*

Bald nototen: UN *17*

Baleen plate, blue whale's: UN *116, 117*

Baleen whales: AN *40*; blue, UN *116-117*; gray, AN *41*; humpback, AN *40*

Bali (island), Indonesia: tropical squall on, WE *76*

Ball-and-socket joint: HU *38*

Ballast tanks, use of: by icebreakers, TR *101*; by submarines, TR *98*

Ball lightning: WE *106-107*

Ballonet: blimp's use of, TR *116*

Balloons: atmospheric, WE *116*; hot-air, PH *4-5, 10-11*; radiosondes, WE 11, *112, 116, 118, 123*; rubber, ST *30-31*

Balls: baseball pitches, PH *24-25, 34-35*; in inertia experiment, PH *29*

Planet Earth
PE

Plant Life
PL

Physical Forces
PH

Structure of Matter
ST

Space & Planets
SP

Transportation
TR

Underwater World
UN

Weather & Climate
WE

Balsam seeds: PL *67*; germination of, PL *13*

Baltic Sea: predecessors of, GE *maps 66-67*

Bamboo: PL *32-33, 91*

Bandicoots: long-nosed, EC *16*

Bank machines (automated-teller machines; ATMs): CO *88-89*

Banks' pine cone: PL *89*

Baobab tree: PL *116-117*

Barbel eel: UN *123*

Barbels: of catfish and loaches, AN *20-21*

Barberry: PL *29*

Barbets: crimson-breasted, EC *61*

Barbules of feathers: PH *60, 61*

Barchan dunes: GE *108*; movement of, GE *109*

Barchanoid dunes: GE *108*

Bar codes: CO *86-87*

Barges: on Rhine River, GE *40*

Barium: fission producing, ST *14-15*

Bark beetles: IN *49, 131*

Bark of tree: PL *25, 26-27*

Barley: PL *144*

Barnacles: EC *100-101*, UN *40-41*; early stages of, EV *132*

Barn owls: AN *4-5, 38-39*

Barograph: aneroid, PH *17*

Barometers: aneroid, PH *16-17*; aneroid, airplane instruments with, TR *132-133*; mercury, PH 16, *17*

Barometric (pressure) gradient force: WE *40, 41*

Barracudas as predators: UN *103, 104-105*

Barred spiral galaxies: SP *103*

Barrel cacti: EC *94*, PL *113*

Barrier reefs: GE *80-81*

Barringer Crater, Ariz., U.S.: SP *35*

Baryonyx (dinosaur): EV *77*

Basalt: PE *89*; columnar, PE *84-85*; in layers of Earth's crust, PE *10*; lunar maria, SP *69*

Baseball pitches: PH *24-25, 34-35*; speed guns for clocking, MA *38-39*

Base stations for cellular phone calls: CO *120*; zones covered by, CO 120, *121*

Base stations for paging devices: CO *122-123*

BASIC (programming language): CO *50-51*; program in, CO 51

Basidia: EC *135*

Basidiomycetes vs. Ascomycetes: PL 98

Basilosaurus (whale ancestor): EV *113*

Basophils: HU 128

Bass: cherry, UN *62, 66*; largemouth, EC *138, 141*; sea, EC *141*; sea, swim bladder type in, UN *13*

Bates, Henry: AN 68

Batesian mimicry vs. Müllerian: AN *68*; of poisonous butterflies, AN *68*; of stinging

insects, AN *54-55*

Bathroom scales: MA *108-109*

Bathymetric map: GE *19*

Bathyscaphes: TR *107*

Bats: AN *42-43*; cave dwellers, EC *28, 38-39*; droppings (guano), EC *40*; evolution of, EV *114-115*; as insect predators, IN *24-25*; as pollinators, EC *114*; wing of, EV *130, 134*

Batteries: automobile, working of, ST *58-59*; electric, automobiles powered by, TR *64-65*; solar, PH *110-111*; solar, automobiles powered by, TR *62-63*

Battle, transportation in: *See* Military transportation

Bauxite: ST *115*

Bays: Carmel Bay, Calif., U.S., GE *19*; estuaries, GE *38-39*; Osaka Bay, Japan, GE *144*; and sand bar formation, GE *74, 75*; in sea cliffs, GE *76-77*; Suruga Bay, Japan, GE *23*

B cells: HU *126, 128, 129, 131*; and allergies, HU *135*; and measles, HU *132, 133*

Beach drift: GE *74*

Beaches: sand ridge with, GE *75*; sea cliffs and, GE *68-69, 76-77*

Beam-interference alarms: MA *114*

Beams: extruded aluminum, ST *28-29*

Beans: PL *142*; germination, PL *12-13*; soybeans, PL *13, 54, 67*; starch granules, PL *11*

Bears: EC *142*; anthill attacked by, IN *127*; black, EC *137*; polar, EC *49*; stinging of, IN *124, 125*

Beat (pulsating tone): PH *142-143*

Beautyberries: PL *78*

Beavertail cacti: EC *86, 87*

Beech trees: EC *25, 75*; Japanese, fruit of, PL *77*

Beepers (pagers): electronic, CO *122-123*

Bees: AN 125, *130*; Africanized, IN *136-137*; antennae, use of, IN *26-27*; dancing, IN *26, 128-129, 134-135*; drones' roles, AN *130-131*; evolutionary path, IN *7*; flying method, IN *15*; foot structure, IN *21*; ground, nests of, IN *108-109*; head, IN *5, 22*; and mimics, AN *54-55*; ocelli, effect of, IN *23*; as pollinators, EC *115*; reproduction, IN *70-71, 131, 132-133*; respiration, IN *10-11*; spider's capture of, AN *26*; stinging, IN 124, *125, 137*; workers' roles, AN *128-129, 131*

Beetles: bark, IN *49, 131*; bombardier, IN *122-123*; in caves, EC *43*; *Damaster blaptoides*, IN *85*; dung, IN *92-93, 106-107, 130, 131*; egg laying, EC *108-109*; evolutionary path, IN *7*; family life, range of, IN *130-131*; feeding order, EC *110-111*;

fireflies, AN *88-89, 92-93*; foot structures, IN *21*; ground, IN *12*; horns, use of, IN *60-61*; hypermetamorphosis, IN *81*; ladybugs, AN *13*, EC *108-109*, IN *4-5, 20, 91, 113, 120, 144*; leaf-rolling weevils, IN *104-105*; long-horned, AN *55, 69*, IN *15, 21, 29, 49*; net-winged, AN *69*; as pollinators, EC *115*; snout beetle, bluffing by, AN *85*; in soil, EC *36, 37*; spiracles, IN *10*; tiger, larva of, as wasp's prey, IN *110*; water, IN *11*

Beggar-ticks (bur marigold seeds): EC *123*, PL *75*

Behaim, Martin: globe by, GE *14*

Belemnites as food for ichthyosaurs: EV *95*

Bell, Alexander Graham: MA *11*; telephone invented by, MA *10-11*, 56

Bellflowers: PL *59*

Benches: coastal, wave-cut, GE *77*

Bench marks: GE *6*

Bent grass and Bermuda grass: PL *63*

Bernoulli, Daniel: MA 47

Berries: PL *66, 67*; eaten by birds, PL *78-79*; mistletoe, PL *82*

Beryl: PE *100*

Beryllium: lithium's decay into, PH *91*

Bess beetles: IN *130*

Bessel, Friedrich: SP 54

Beta decay: PH *91*

Beta Lyrae (binary star system): SP *83*

Beta-starch vs. alpha-starch: ST *100-101*

Betelgeuse (star): magnitude, SP *80*; spectrographic analysis of, SP *78-79*

Bias tires: TR *57*

Bicycle: working of, PH *46-47*

Big Bang: aftermath of, SP *108-109, 112-113*; antimatter created in, ST *22-23*

Big Crunch in closed universe: SP *115*

Big Dipper (Ursa Major constellation): SP *60, 90*; changes in, SP *90-91*

Bighead smoothhead: UN *22-23*

Bighorn sheep: AN *106-107*

Bile canaliculi and bile ducts: HU *86, 87*

Bimetal thermal sensors: MA *121*; in fire alarm, MA *65*; in iron, MA *120-121*

Binary code: CO 26, *chart* 27; bar codes, CO *86-87*; and logic gates, CO *28-29*

Binary conversion: CO *chart* 27

Binary notation: CO *26-27*

Binary search: CO *57*

Binary star systems: with black hole, possible, SP *94-95*; eclipsing variables, SP *82-83*; with neutron star, SP *96-97*; and Type I supernova, SP *85*

Bingham mine, Utah, U.S.: PE *96-97*

Binoculars: MA *94-95*

Bioelectric sensing system of shark: UN *55*

Biological accumulation: EC *144*

Animal Behavior
AN

Computer Age
CO

Ecology
EC

Evolution of Life
EV

Geography
GE

Human Body
HU

Insects & Spiders
IN

Machines &
Inventions **MA**

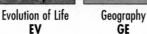

Planet Earth
PE

Plant Life
PL

Physical Forces
PH

Structure of Matter
ST

Space & Planets
SP

Transportation
TR

Underwater World
UN

Weather & Climate
WE

Animal Behavior
AN

Computer Age
CO

Ecology
EC

Evolution of Life
EV

Geography
GE

Human Body
HU

Insects & Spiders
IN

Machines &
Inventions **MA**

Cacti: EC *86, 87, 94, 95*, PL *111, 112-113*; adaptation in, EV *21*; and euphorbia, convergence of, EV *137*; Galápagos, EC *6, 119*; owl in, EC *89*

CAD/CAM (computer-aided design/manufacturing) and automobiles: CO *74-75*

Calcite in formation of cave features: GE 61

Calculators: CO *4*; abacuses and counting stones, CO *4-5, 6-7*; Babbage's, CO *4, 10-11*; seventeenth-century, CO *4-5, 8-9*

Calderas: PE *67, 68*; formation of, PE *68-69*; hot-spot volcanic island, PE *77*; Krakatoa, PE *72*; Yellowstone, PE *80*

Calendars: electronic, CO *91*

California, U.S.: Carmel Bay, GE *19*; Death Valley, GE *115*; Loma Prieta earthquake (1989), effects of, PE *55, 61*; San Andreas fault, PE *42-43*, 49

California Current: WE 126

California gray whale: migration of, UN *94-95*

California newt: AN *67*

Calipers: micrometer, MA *48-49*; vernier (slide), MA 48, *49*

Callidulid moths: IN *33*

Calling song of crickets: AN 96

Callus culture: PL *140*

Calms: morning and evening, WE *42, 43*

Camarasaurus (dinosaur): EV *75*

Cambium in tree trunk: PL *25, 26, 27*

Cambrian period: life in, EV *40-45;* species, WE *142*; temperatures, WE *chart* 142

Camels: EC *88*; temperature, EC *chart* 88

Camera lenses: leaded glass for, ST *125*

Camera obscura: MA 16

Cameras: with autofocus (AF), MA *74-75*; automated cars' use of, TR 60, *61*; first, MA *16-17*; instant, color, working of, MA *92-93*; kinetograph, MA *20*; Kodak, MA *18, 19*; submersible with, TR *106*; TV, iconoscope, MA 22, *23*

Camouflage: AN *30-31, 50-53*, IN 113, *116-117*; color changes in, AN *32, 50-51, 56-59*; by crabs, UN *136-137*; by octopuses, UN *143*

Camphor cicadas: IN *29*

Canada: forests, GE *125*; Laurentian Plateau, GE *29*; Rockies, GE *24-25*

Canals: European, GE *map* 41; locks, GE *40*, TR *92-93*; Panama Canal, TR *92-93*

Canards: automated car's, TR *61*; CCV's, TR *140-141*; Wright *Flyer*'s, TR *135*; X-29A's, TR *142*

Canberra, Australia: GE *128-129*

Cancer: HU *138-139*

Canine teeth: HU *26*

Canned food: ST *89*

Cannibalism in praying mantises: IN 64, *65*

Cans: dispensing of, by vending machine, MA *58*

Cap clouds: WE *68-69*

Capes, sea cliffs': GE *76-77*

Capillaries: HU 62, *63*; alveoli surrounded by, HU *56, 57*; sinusoid, HU *63, 66-67*

Capture theory of Moon's origin: SP *67*

Capybaras: EC *20*

Carbon: ST *4*; activated, odor removal with, ST *52-53*; aluminum refined with, ST *115*; carbon fibers from, ST *138-139*; in cellulose, ST *12-13*; combustion products, ST *67*; content of coal, PE 104; diamonds, PE *90-91*; graphite, diamonds synthesized from, ST *132, chart* 133; iron refined with, ST *102-103, 110-111*; in polymers, ST *30-31, 106-107*; in steel, content of, ST *112, chart* 113

Carbon cycle: ST *25*

Carbon dioxide: from aluminum refining, ST *115*; in cities, and greenhouse effect, WE *139*; from combustion, ST *67*; frozen (dry ice), ST 38, *39, 40*; and global warming, GE 72, *73*, WE *136-137*; and greenhouse effect, GE *73*, WE *136-137, 139*; in oxygen cycle, ST *37*; phase changes in, ST 32, *38, 39*; in photosynthesis, PL 10, *38*, ST *66*; rain and, rock dissolved by, GE 58, *110*

Carbon dioxide-oxygen cycle: HU *56-57*, 65

Carbon fiber: ST *138-139*

Carbon filter: air purification with, MA *50-51*

Carbon-14 dating: PE 95, ST *24-25*

Carbon granules: telephone's use of, MA *56*

Carboniferous period: coal formation in, PE *104*; flying insects, EV *54-55*; forests during, and atmospheric oxygen, ST *36-37*; life in, EV 41; plants, EV *52, 53*; species, WE *142*; temperatures, WE *chart* 142

Carbon monoxide: as combustion product, ST *67*; and pig iron, ST *110, 112-113*; poisoning by, HU *72-73*

Carburetor: role of, TR *41*; throttle plate, TR *45*

Carcinogens: HU *138*

Card counters: CO *12*

Card feeders: CO *13*

Cardiac (myocardial) muscle: HU *7, 60, 144*

Cardinalfish: blackspot, mouthbrooding by, UN *80*; luminescent, UN *144*

Cardiovascular system: HU *7*, 52, 60-71. *See also* Blood cells; Blood vessels of humans; Heart, human

Card punches: CO *12*

Card readers: CO *12, 13, 18*

Card sorters: CO *13*

Cargo transport, Europe's: GE *40, map* 40-41

Caribou: EC *50-51*

Carmel Bay, Calif., U.S.: GE *19*

Carotene in storage grains: PL *7*

Carp: feeding method, UN *105*; sensory organs, UN *44-45, 46-47*; swim bladder, UN *12-13*

Carpels: PL 51, *52-53*, 58, *59, 62*, 66; corn stigma and style, PL 84, *85*; impatiens (touch-me-not), PL *76, 77*; mistletoe stigma, PL *83*

Carpenter ants, black: fighting, IN *126-127*; tandem running, IN *43*

Car phones: CO *120-121*

Carracks: Columbus's *(Santa Maria)*, TR *88-89*

Carriers: nutrients absorbed by, HU *89*

Carrier waves for radio transmissions: MA *84-85*

Cars: *See* Automobiles

Cartilaginous fishes: UN *6*; eyes, UN *44, 45, 54*; ratfish, UN *73*; rays, UN *107, 123*; skates, UN *104. See also* Sharks

Cartilaginous tissue: HU *7*

Cartography: *See* Maps and mapping

Carvalho's pipa: UN *91*

Caryophyllaceae flower: EV *103*

Cassiopeia (constellation): SP *60*

Cassiopeia A (supernova remnant): SP *85*

Castes: honeybees, AN *128-131*

Casting of pig iron: ST *112*

Catalytic reformers: ST *117*

Caterpillars: and ants, IN *78, 79*; aphids vs., IN *144*; bagworm, IN *102, 103*; defenses, IN *113, 118-119, 120-121, 123*; and enemies, IN *114, 125*; eyespots on, AN *64*; in metamorphosis, IN *56-57, 78-83, 114*; respiration, IN *11*; tiger moth (fall webworms), IN *88-89*

Catfish: barbels, use of, AN 20, *21*; cuckoo, UN *84-85*; eeltail, UN *123*; electric, UN 57; parenting behavior of, UN *86-87*; poison, UN *122, 123*

Cathodes: *See* Anodes and cathodes

Cats: breeds of, EV *19*; golden, EC *10, 11*; marsupial, EC *17*; saber-toothed, EV *107, 121*

CAT (computerized axial tomographic) scanners: MA *134-135*

Cattle raising: GE *130, 131*; Alpine, GE *143*; overgrazing and desertification, GE *107*

Cattleya orchids: PL *140-141*

Caudal fin: use of, in swimming, UN *18, 20-21*

Caudal peduncle: swordfish's use of, UN 20, *21*

Cauliflorous trees: EC *65*

Cavefish: EC *40, 41, 43*

Caves: GE *54-55*; and cave dwelling animals,

Planet Earth
PE

Plant Life
PL

Physical Forces
PH

Structure of Matter
ST

Space & Planets
SP

Transportation
TR

Underwater World
UN

Weather & Climate
WE

EC *28, 38-43*; formation of, GE *59, 60-61*; in sea cliffs, GE *76, 77*

Cavity geyser: PE *81*

CCDs: *See* Charge-coupled devices

CCV (control-configured vehicle; fighter jet): TR *140-141*

CDI (course deviation indicator) dial: aircraft's, TR *123*

CD-ROM (compact disk read-only memory): CO *95*

CDs (compact disks): MA *86-87*

Cecum: HU *90*

Cedar trees: bark, PL *27*; cone, PL *89*; seed, PL *94*

Ceiba tree: PL *123*

Celestial sphere: GE *10, 11, 21*, SP *50, 60-61, 100*; ecliptic on, SP *54-55, 60-61, 70*

Cell bodies of neurons: HU *100, 101, 103*

Cells: of blue-green algae, EV *34-35*; DNA and RNA in, EV *30, 36*; evolution of, EV *36-37*; first, EV *32*; multiple, rise of, EV *38-39*; insect, ordinary vs. cold-resistant, IN *35*; plant, structure of, PL *4-5, 6-7*

Cells, human: HU *6, 7*; anatomy of, HU *8-9*; and colds, HU *140*; division by meiosis, HU *14-15*; division by mitosis, HU *8-9*; ear, inner, HU *113, 114, 115*; fallopian tube, HU *16*; in healing of wound, HU *48-49*; liver, HU *86-87*; melanocytes, HU *50-51*; metabolism, oxidation and, HU *52, 57*; olfactory, HU *116, 117*; pancreatic, HU *85, 142, 143*; reproductive, HU *12, 13, 15, 16-17, 22, 23, 28-29*; retinal, HU *108-109*; salivary glands, HU *79*; small intestine, HU *88-89*; stomach, HU *82-83*; taste bud, HU *119*; and tumors, HU *138-139*. *See also* Blood cells; Neurons (nerve cells) of human brain

Cellular phones: CO *120-121*

Cellulose fibers: ST *104*

Cellulose molecules: cotton, ST *12-13, 107*; papermaking, ST *104, 105*; wood, ST *67*

Cement: hydration of, ST *120*; in lattice structure, ST *121*

Cenozoic era: EV *105-129*; configuration of continents during, PE *102*; species during, WE *143*. *See also* Mammals

Census, U.S.: tabulating machine used in, CO *12-13*

Center of gravity: ship's shifting, PH *9*; top's, PH *32, 33*

Centipedes: EC *37*, IN *12-13*; maternal care in, IN *76*

Central nervous system: IN *8-9*

Central processing units (CPUs): CO *18, 24-25*; and memory, CO *30*; microprocessors as, CO *22*

Centrifugal force: in Earth-Moon system, SP

73; and Earth's rotation, PE *18*; and hurricanes, WE *91*; and tides, PE *128*; and wind, WE *41*

Centrifugal pump: fire engine's, TR *71*

Centrioles: HU *8*

Centripetal force: on roller coaster, PH *30, 31*; on satellite, PH *37*

Centrosomes: PL *6*

Cepheid variables (stars): SP *83*

Cepheus (constellation): SP *60, 61*

Ceramics: ST *130, 131*; advanced, ST *130-131*

Ceratoid anglerfish: UN *70-71*

Ceratopsians: EV *88-89*; *Protoceratops*, EV *78-79, 89*

Ceratosaurus (dinosaur): EV *75*

Cerebrum: HU *24, 25, 104-105*; auditory cortex, HU *113*; hemispheres, HU *120-121, 124*; nerve impulses to, HU *101*; olfactory areas, HU *116*; taste center, HU *119*; and vision, HU *107*

Cereus: EC *94*

Cerium: neodymium's decay into, PH *91*

Chain, Ernst: PL *132*

Chain reactions: in nuclear fission, ST *14-15*; of uranium 235, PH *108*

Chainwheel gear: bicycle's, PH *46, 47*

Chameleons: AN *4-5, 32-33*

Change bit coding vs. constant bit coding: CO *36*

Channel catfish: AN *21*

Character maps in computer games: CO *78*

Character recognition: CO *64-65*

Charge-coupled devices (CCDs): in cameras, MA *75*; in color copiers, MA *62-63*; in fax machines, CO *114*, MA *68, 69*

Charges, electrical: *See* Electrons

Charles V, King (France): clock commissioned by, MA *12-13*

Charlotte Dundas (steam vessel): TR *91*

Charts: navigational, TR *80*

Checkout counters: scanner type used in, CO *86-87*

Cheetahs: EC *10, 82, 112*; Indian, EC *11*; springbok herds and, AN *60-61*

Cheiracanthium japonicum (spider): IN *75*

Cheirolepis (extinct fish): EV *49*

Chemicals: biological accumulation of, EC *144*; plants' defenses, EC *98-99, 118*

Chemical surveys of mineral deposits: PE *99*

Chemical weapons of insects: IN *122-123, 126, 127*

Chemistry and matter: ST entire volume

Cherry bass: UN *62, 66*

Cherry trees: leaf, PL *29*; lenticels, PL *27*

Chert (rock): PE *87*

Chesapeake Bay, Md.-Va., U.S.: GE *38*; life

in, EC *140-141*

Chest monitor: stethoscope's, MA *144*

Chestnut trees: flowers, PL *59*; fruit, PL *67, 77*; horse chestnut, leaf scar on, PL *43*

Chest x-ray: MA *141*

Chevalier, C. L.: lens type made by, MA *16*

Chiba Peninsula, Japan: earthquake effects on, PE *54, 55*

Chickens: vs. *Archaeopteryx*, EV *71*; breeding of, EV *18*; early development of, EV *133*

Chief cells: HU *83*

Chimpanzees: clan, AN *141*; communication, AN *124-125, 142-143*; tool use, AN *46-47*

China: oasis, GE *63*; tower karst, GE *59*; Yellow River, course changes in, GE *34-35*

Chinese abacuses: CO *7*

Chinooks: WE *44-45*

Chip log: TR *87*

Chips: *See* Integrated circuits

Chloride, and sodium ions: ST *43*; and electron conduction, ST *18-19*; and freezing point of water, ST *40, 41*; and reclamation of salt from seawater, ST *96*

Chlorine: disinfecting water with, ST *98, 99*; ozone broken down by, ST *76*

Chlorofluorocarbons (CFCs): ST *76*; destruction of ozone layer by, WE *30-31*

Chlorophyll: light absorption by, PL *11*

Chloroplasts: EV *36*, PL *6, 7, 10-11*

Choking: HU *80*

Cholesteric liquid crystals: ST *137*

Cholesterol in arteries: HU *144*

Cholla cacti: EC *95*

Chordate evolution: EV *46-47*

Chorionic villi: HU *20*

Chroma key process: CO *80-81*

Chromatin: HU *8-9, 10-11*

Chromatophores: squid, UN *142*; tree frogs, AN *56, 57*

Chromosomes: human, HU *11, 14-15*; mitosis, in human cells, HU *8-9*; and plant breeding, PL *138*

Chromosphere: SP *40, 41, 42-43*

Chrondrichthian: extinct, EV *49*

Chum salmon: UN *11*

Cicada fungus: PL *97*

Cicadas: EC *106-107*, IN *4*; evolutionary path, IN *7*; flying method, IN *14*; head, IN *4, 22*; life cycles, IN *89*; New Guinea, AN *50, 53*; sound production, IN *29*

Cichlids, reproduction by: family care of young, UN *79*; and incubation of cuckoo catfish's eggs, UN *84-85*; mouthbrooding, UN *80-81*

Cilia: olfactory cells, human, HU *117*; paramecium, AN *6, 7*; trachea, human, HU *6*

Ciliary body and muscles: HU *110-111*

Animal Behavior	Computer Age	Ecology	Evolution of Life	Geography	Human Body	Insects & Spiders	Machines &
AN	**CO**	**EC**	**EV**	**GE**	**HU**	**IN**	Inventions **MA**

Ciliated cells: HU *16, 140*

Cinder cones: PE *67*

Circadian rhythm: HU 122

Circle dance, honeybees': IN *135*

Circuits, electrical: PH *74-75*; measuring current, PH *76-77*

Circulation, atmospheric: WE *34-35, 36-37, 112-113,* 124, *134*; and jet streams, WE *38,* 53

Circulatory system of fish: and body temperature, UN *14-15*

Circulatory system of humans: HU *7,* 52, *60-71. See also* Blood cells; Blood vessels of humans; Heart, human

Circulatory system of insects: IN 8. *See also* Heart, animal

Circumpolar Currents: Antarctic, PE *map* 120-121; bottom, PE *116-117*

Circumvallate papillae: HU *118*

Cirques: GE *45;* horns formed from, GE *44*

Cirrostratus clouds: WE *61, chart* 74

Cirrus clouds: WE 60, *61;* in atmospheric layers, WE *8,* 11; from cumulonimbus top, WE *63;* and subtropical jet stream, WE *38*

Cladding: fiberoptic cable's, CO 124, *125*

Cladoselache (extinct fish): EV *49*

Clams: crabs living in, UN *38-39;* early stages of, EV *132;* in ocean trenches, UN *34;* as starfish prey, UN *138, 139;* surf clam, UN *139*

Clarinet: working of, PH *136-137*

Claws: fiddler crabs, AN *108-109;* spiders, AN *29*

Cleaner shrimp: AN *22-23*

Cleaner wrasses: UN *120, 134-135;* vs. saber-toothed blennies, UN *134, 135*

Cleaning of air: MA *50-51*

Clear-cutting of rain forest: GE *125*

Clear-weather turbulence: WE *53*

Clear-winged moth: AN *55*

Clermont (Fulton's paddle steamer): TR *90-91*

Cliffs: sea, GE *68-69, 76-77, 88-89*

Climate: GE 100-117, WE 124-144; and agriculture, GE *130-131, 136-137;* of Alps, GE *142-143;* of Andes, GE 140, GE *charts* 140; changes over time, WE *142-143;* cities vs. suburbs, WE *138-139;* deserts, GE *51, 100-101, 104-109,* WE *72, 124-125, 134-135;* El Niño phenomenon, WE *140-141;* factors determining, WE *128-129;* geography's effect on, GE 100, *114-115, 116-117;* greenhouse effect, WE *136-137,* 139; ice ages, WE 142, *chart* 143, *144;* land elevation and, GE *maps* 114, *142-143;* and landslides, GE

102-103; monsoon seasons, WE *130-131,* 132; and Monument Valley's formation, GE *110-111;* ocean currents and, GE 70, *71, 116-117,* WE *72-73, 126-127, 140-141;* Pleistocene glaciations, GE *charts* 50, *maps* 51; rainy season, WE *88-89, 132-133;* and soil types, GE 112, *map* 113; and vegetation zones, GE *maps* 51, 112, *map* 113, 142, *chart* 142; in water cycle, global, GE 82, 83; western U.S. zones, GE *map* 114; world zones, GE *charts* 112, WE *128-129, map* 128-129. *See also* Wind

Climatius (extinct fish): EV *48*

Climax forest: formation of, PL *128*

Climbing crane: MA *52-53*

Climbing perch: UN *29*

Climbing plants: parasites, PL *57;* supports for, PL *23, 29, 30-31*

Clinch River, Tenn.-Va., U.S.: dam, GE *134*

Clipper ship: TR *78-79*

Clocks: mechanical, MA *12-13;* use of quartz in, MA *96-97*

Closed vs. open universe: SP *115*

Clothes iron with thermostat: MA *120-121*

Clothes washers: MA *112-113*

Clouds: WE 56; and adiabatic cooling, WE *24;* over Antarctica, WE *122;* around low pressure, WE *86, 87, 111, 122;* atmospheric layers and, WE *8-9, 10,* 11; bora winds and, WE *49;* cap, WE *68-69;* cirrus, WE *8, 11, 38,* 60, *61, 63;* contrails, WE *64-65;* cumulonimbus, WE *9, 10, 50, 51,* 60, *62-63,* 66, 67, *74-75,* 76, 78, 89, *90-91;* electricity in, WE 66, *67;* equatorial waves, WE *132;* and foehns, WE *45;* fog, WE *70-71, 72-73;* formation and growth of, WE *58-59, 60-61, 62-63,* 89; on Jupiter, SP *14-15;* and mountain halos, formation of, WE *104-105;* in primitive atmosphere, WE *6;* and radar, WE *115;* satellite images, WE *111, 121;* seeding of, WE *78-79;* shapes, WE *60-61;* sirocco and, WE 46, *47;* solar energy reflected and absorbed by, WE *20-21;* squalls, tropical, and, WE 76, *77;* test-tube, WE *58;* thermal air turbulence and, WE *52;* on Venus, SP *10-11*

Cloud seeding: WE *78-79*

Clown fish: AN *70-71;* gold-belly, UN *62,* 67; sea anemones and, UN *144*

Clusters and superclusters of galaxies: SP *110-111;* Local Group, SP *102, 110-111;* recession of, SP *graph* 115

Coal: ST *67;* burning of, ST 66; formation of, PE *104-105;* locations of, PE *100, 101;* reserves of, PE *map* 104; strip mining of, PE *105*

Coastal areas: aerial surveying of, GE *19;* deltas, GE *4-5,* 26, *32-33,* 39; estuaries, GE *38-39;* inundation of, GE *90-91;* plains, formation of, GE *28-29;* rain, sea winds and, GE *114-115;* saltwater intrusion in, GE 64; sand bars, formation of, GE *74-75;* sea's shaping of, GE *68-69, 76-77, 88-89*

Coastal plain estuaries: GE *38*

Coastal terraces: GE *88-89*

COBOL (programming language): CO *50-51;* program in, CO 51

Cobra, king: AN *62*

Cobweb mold: PL *96*

Cobwebs: IN *39*

Coccosteus (extinct fish): EV *49*

Cochlea and cochlear duct: HU *112, 113, 115*

Cochlear nerve: HU *113*

Cockleburs: EC *122,* PL *54-55;* fruit, PL *75*

Cockpit in flight simulator: CO *82-83*

Cockroaches: Australian, IN *131;* evolutionary path, IN *7;* foot structure, IN *21*

Coconut palms: EC *22-23,* PL *86-87*

Coconuts: EC *22-23,* PL *86-87;* milk, PL *87*

Cocoons: moth larvae in, IN *144;* parasitic wasps, IN *114;* spiders, IN *94-95*

Cod: Antarctic, body fluids of, UN *chart* 16; swim bladder type, UN *13*

Code, Morse: MA *9*

Codec (coder/decoder), picture phone's use of: CO 126, 127

Code tables: binary, CO *chart* 27

Coelophysis (dinosaur): EV *67*

Coevolution: IN *78-79*

Coffee, instant: making of, ST *86-87*

Coil springs: PH *51*

Coin-operated machines: MA *58-59;* movie viewer, MA *20-21*

Coke in iron refining: ST *110*

Colchicine: tetraploid plants from, PL *139*

Cold-adapted insects: IN *34-35*

Cold-blooded vs. warm-blooded fish: UN *14-15*

Cold-loving fish species: UN *16-17*

Colds: common, HU *140-141*

Coliform bacilli: HU *91*

Collisions: simulated, CO *74-75*

Collision theory of Moon's origin: SP *66-67*

Colloids: ST *20-21*

Colobus monkeys: EC *71*

Colon: HU *90-91*

Colonial siphonophore: UN *42*

Colonies: *See* Social insects

Colonization of habitats: EC *120-121*

Colonization of space, possible: SP 128, *140-141;* and Moon base, SP *74-75;* and transport, SP *143*

Planet Earth
PE

Plant Life
PL

Physical Forces
PH

Structure of Matter
ST

Space & Planets
SP

Transportation
TR

Underwater World
UN

Weather & Climate
WE

| Animal Behavior | Computer Age | Ecology | Evolution of Life | Geography | Human Body | Insects & Spiders | Machines & |
| AN | CO | EC | EV | GE | HU | IN | Inventions MA |

Constellations: changes in, SP *90-91*; precession and, SP *60-61*; zodiac, SP *54-55*. *See also individual names*

Construction equipment: cranes, TR *66-67, 72-73*; power shovels, TR *66-67, 76-77*; rollers, TR *66, 74-75*

Contact couplers for train cars: TR *9*

Contact vs. regional metamorphic rock: PE *87*

Continental crust: collisions, PE *11, 34, 36-37, 48-49, 64-65*; vs. oceanic crust, PE *8, 9, 10*; splitting of, PE *29, 33, 40, 41*

Continental drift: PL 118, *maps* 119, WE *142-143*; and mountain building, GE 86, 87, 96-99; and seafloor spreading, GE *78-79*. *See also* Plate tectonics

Continental margin (continental shelf and continental slope): PE *114-115*

Continuous capillaries: HU *63*

Contractile vacuoles: paramecium, AN *7*

Contrails: WE *64-65*

Control-configured vehicle (CCV; fighter jet): TR *140-141*

Controller chips: kinds of, CO 22

Control unit of central processing unit (CPU): CO *24-25*; location, CO *18*

Convection: PH *58-59, 66*; atmosphere, PE *120*; insulation against, PH *60-61*; in plate tectonics, PE *28, 29*

Convection currents: WE *59*; and atmospheric circulation, WE *34*; formation of, WE *40-41*

Convection zone of ocean: PE 134, *135*

Convection zone of Sun: SP *17, 40, 41, 42*

Convergence of species: EV *136-137, 138-139*

Convergence of trade winds: WE *90, 132-133*

Convergent boundaries: and mountain building, PE *11, 34, 36-37, 38-39, 49. See also* Subduction

Conversion I and II in nitrogen cycle: ST *27*

Converters: in copper refining, ST *111*; pig iron in, ST *111, 112-113*

Convex surfaces: lenses, PH *116-117*; mirrors, PH 114, *115*

Convolutions of brain: HU 104

Cooking: microwave ovens, MA *102-103*; pressure cookers, MA *100-101*

Cooling, kinds of: adiabatic, WE *24*; insulation, WE *58, 64*; radiation, WE *76, 85*

Cooling mechanisms: air conditioners, MA *122-123*; in dehumidifiers, MA *124-125*; refrigerators, MA *106-107*

Cooperative breeding in birds: AN *116-117*

Copeinas, red-spotted: spawning by, UN *75*

Copepods: in cave, EC *41*

Copernicus, Nicolaus: SP 52

Copiers: MA 62; color, MA *62-63*

Copolymers vs. homopolymers: ST 106

Copper: ST *114*; refining of, ST *111, 114*; structure of, ST *19*

Copper butterflies: Japanese, IN *78*

Copper mine: PE *96-97*

Coral: atolls, PE *114-115*; crabs living among, UN *39*; reefs, formation of, GE *80-81*; reproduction by, UN *100-101*; as starfish prey, UN *139*

Core of Earth: PE *8*; formation of, PE *7*; and magnetic field, PE *20, 21*; and seismic waves, PE *15*

Cores: Mars, SP *12*; Milky Way, SP *104-105*; Moon, SP *68*; Neptune, SP *29*; Saturn, SP *29*; Sun, SP *17, 40, 41*; Uranus, SP *29*; Venus, SP *11*

Coriolis force and effect: SP *53*; on climate, WE *124*; and ocean currents, GE 70, *71*, PE 118, *119*; on prevailing winds, WE 36

Cork cambium: PL *25, 26, 27*

Cork cells: PL *26*

Cormorants: flightless, EC *7*; pelagic, EC *33*

Corms: PL *91*

Corn: and corn silk, PL *84-85*; hybridization, PL *136-137*; leaf growth, PL *17*; production of, GE 122, *123*; starch granules in, PL *11*; support roots, PL *23*

Cornea, human: HU *110-111*

Cornea, fish's: for seeing through air, UN *51*

Corneal lens of ocellus: IN *23*

Cornicles: aphids, AN *12*

Corona: atmospheric, WE *105*; of comet, SP *32-33*; lunar, WE *105*; solar, SP *40, 41, 123*, WE 105; solar, telescopes for studying, SP *122, 123*; solar, during total eclipse, SP *41, 50-51, 63*

Coronagraph: SP *123*; photograph by, SP *123*

Coronary artery, clogged: HU *144*

Corpus callosum: HU *120*; severed, HU *121*

Corpuscular vs. wave theory of light: PH 122

Cortex, cerebral: *See* Cerebrum

Coscinodiscus diatom: PL *100*

Cosmic background radiation: SP *113*

Cosmic rays: WE *9*; in carbon-14 formation, ST *25*; and electricity in clouds, WE *67*; and Van Allen belts, WE *18*

Cosmos: PL *54-55*

Cotton: growing, GE *map* 130, *131*; structure of, ST *12-13, 107*

Cottony cushion scale: IN *91*

Cotyledons (seed leaves): development of, PL *9, 12, 13, 79, 88*

Counting stones and abacuses: CO *4-5, 6-7*

Couplings: train cars', TR *8-9*

Course deviation indicator (CDI) dial: aircraft's, TR *123*

Courtship: *See* Mating, courtship and

Courtship song of crickets: AN 97

CPUs (central processing units): CO 18, *24-25*; and memory, CO *30*; microprocessor as, CO 22

Crabeater seals: EC 46, *47*

Crab nebula: SP *85, 96*

Crabs: EV *140*; on and in other animals, UN *38-39*; blue, EC *140*; breathing, UN *36-37*; and camouflage, UN *136-137*; claw detached by, AN *80*; early stages of, EV *132*; fiddler, courtship of, AN *108-109*; hermit, new shells of, AN *76-77*; hermit, sea anemones and, AN *78-79*; in ocean trenches, UN *34*; as octopus prey, UN *60*; red-clawed, AN *123*; reproduction, UN *37, 38-39, 96-97*; as scavengers, EC *128, 129*; starfish attacked by, UN *139*

Crab spiders: mating, AN *90*

Crane flies: IN *5*

Cranes: dancing, AN *102-103*; sandhill, EC *113*; whooping, EC *113*

Cranes (mechanical): TR *66-67, 72-73*; block and tackle used with, PH *49*; jib, MA *52*; self-raising, MA *52-53*

Cranesbill: PL *77*

Crater Lake, Oreg., U.S.: PE *68*

Craters: asteroids, SP *30*; Earth, SP *35*; Mercury, SP *8-9*; Moon, SP *64-65, 68-69*; Triton (moon of Neptune), SP *27. See also* Calderas; Meteor craters

Crayfish: cave, EC *41, 42*; as snakes' prey, AN *15*

Cray-1 supercomputer: CO *15*

Cray Y-MP supercomputer: CO *43*

Crèches: penguin chicks in, AN *112-113*

Creep meter: PE *57*

Crematogaster ant: IN *99*

Crested grebes: courtship, AN *102*

Cretaceous period: ammonites, EV *94-95, 98-99*; birds, EV *100-101*; climate, WE *chart* 143; domehead dinosaurs, EV *86-87*; flowering plants, EV *102-103*; hadrosaurs, EV *76, 85*; horned dinosaurs, EV *78-79, 88-89*; life in, EV *74-75*, WE *143*; marine reptiles, EV *92-93, 94-95*

Cribellum: spiders', IN *95*

Crickets: burrowing, care of young by, IN *74*; courtship, AN *96-97*; sound production, IN *28*

Crimes: computer, CO *106-107*

Critical density of universe: SP 115

Crocodiles: family tree, EV *chart* 66-67; heart, EV *59*; *Protosuchus*, EV *62-63*; swimming style of, UN *18-19*; temperature control, EV *81*

Planet Earth
PE

Plant Life
PL

Physical Forces
PH

Structure of Matter
ST

Space & Planets
SP

Transportation
TR

Underwater World
UN

Weather & Climate
WE

Crop plants: PL 130-131; and climate, GE 130-131; genetic resources, PL 131, *142-143*; grains, kinds of, PL *67, 144*; hybrids, PL *136-137*; improvement, PL *138-139*; progenitors, origin areas of, PL *maps 130-131*. *See also individual names*

Crossbreeding: PL *136-137, 142*; artificial, PL *139*

Cross-linked molecules: proteins, ST *84, 95*. *See also* Polymers

Crossopterygians: EV *56, 57*

Cross-staff: TR *87*

Cross winds in tornado formation: WE 50

Crowberry: PL *78*

Crow butterfly: AN *68*

Crown of thorns (starfish): defense against, UN *139*

CRS (computer reservation system): CO *96-97*

Crude oil: refining of, ST *116-117*

Cruise missiles: CO *144*

Cruiser (ship): military, TR *78-79*

Crustaceans: barnacles, EC *100-101*, UN *40-41*; brine shrimp, EC *92-93*; cave, EC *40, 41, 42*; estuarine, EC *140*; luminous, UN *24*; scavengers, EC *128, 129*; shrimp, AN *22-23, 86-87*; starfish attacked by, UN *139*. *See also* Crabs

Crustaceous lichen: PL *106-107*

Crusts: Earth, PE *8, 9, 10-11*; Earth, formation of, PE *7, 111*; Earth, igneous rocks in, PE *88, 89*; Io (moon of Jupiter), SP *18-19*; Mars, SP *12*; Moon of Earth, SP *68*; Venus, SP *11*. *See also* Plate tectonics

Cryogens: ST *40-41*

Cryptic coloration (camouflage): IN *113, 116-117*

Cryptomeria cone: PL *89*

Crystal glassware: ST *125*

Crystalline lattices: metals, ST *13, 19, 28, 29, 31, 121, 140-141, 142, 143*; quartz, ST *122*

Crystals: ceramic, ST *130, 131*; ice, ST *39, 41, 93*; ice, images formed by, WE *102-103*; liquid, ST *136-137*; and piezoelectricity, MA *96*; quartz, ST *122*; quartz watches using, MA *96-97*; salt, ST *41*; silicon, ST *134-135*; silicon, microscopic view of, MA *32*

Cuckoo catfish: UN *85*; incubation of, by cichlids, UN *84-85*

Cuckoos as brood parasites: AN *114-115*

Cucumber plants: PL *30*; squirting, PL *77*; tendrils, PL *30-31*

Cuesta ridges: GE *92-93*

Cugnot, Nicolas Joseph: automobile invented by, TR 36, *38-39*

Culex mosquitoes: IN *47*; eggs, IN *69*

Cumulonimbus clouds: atmospheric layers and, WE *9, 10*; and cloud seeding, WE 78; formation of, WE *60, 62-63, 89*; and hurricanes, WE *90-91*; and lightning, WE *66, 67*; and precipitation, WE *63, 74-75, 76*; and tornadoes, WE *50, 51*

Cumulus clouds: WE *60*; cumulonimbus clouds from, WE *50, 62*

Cup fungi: PL *98*

Cupula: HU *114, 115*

Currant tomato: PL *142*

Current, electric: *See* Electricity

Currents, auroral: WE *16-17*

Currents, ocean: GE 68, *70-71*, WE *126-127*; bottom, PE *116-117*; cause of, SP *49*; effect of, on climate, GE 100, *116-117*; and fishing areas, GE *126-127*; and garúa, WE *72-73*; and sand bars, GE *74-75*; and Sargasso Sea, PE *132-133*; southern oscillation and, WE *140-141*; surface, PE *118-119, map 120-121*; warm and cool, PE *120-121*; and whirlpool formation, PE *122-123*

Cursor: mouse movement and, CO *34*

Curve ball: PH *24-25, 34-35*

Cuscuses: EC 17

Cutleria cylindrica algae: PL *103*

Cuts: healing of, HU *48-49*

Cuvieronius (mastodon): EV *121*

Cyanobacteria (blue-green algae): EV 34, 37; evolution of, EV 6; stromatolites, EV *26-27, 34-35*

Cycadeoidea (gymnosperm): EV *102*

Cycad flowers: PL *59*

Cyclones: Coriolis force affecting, SP *53*; formation of, WE 86

Cyclone separator: PH *102*

Cygnus (constellation): and precession, SP *60*; x-ray sources in, SP *94, 97*

Cygnus X-1 (x-ray source): SP *94*

Cylinders, automobiles': TR *40, 41*; steam car, TR *38-39*; turbocharger, TR 54, 55

Cylinders, steam locomotive's: TR *14, 15*

Cylindrical map projections: GE *13*

Cynodonts: *Cynognathus*, EV 62, *64-65, 73*; *Diademodon*, EV *64*

Cynognathus (mammal-like reptile): EV *62, 64-65*; *C. crateronotus*, EV *73*

Cypress trees: bald, PL *22*; Japanese, cone of, PL *89*

Cypris larvae: barnacles, UN *40-41*

D

Dace: Japanese, UN *73*

Daguerre, Louis: MA *16, 17*

Daguerreotypes: MA *16*; camera for, MA *16-17*

Dahlias: PL *55*

Dairying ants: AN *12-13*

Daisies, blue: tetraploid, PL *139*

Damaster blaptoides (beetle): IN *85*

Dams: and hydroelectric plants, PH *98-99*; for irrigation, GE *138*; in the Netherlands, GE *133*; Ogouchi Dam, Tokyo, Japan, WE *79*; Tennessee Valley Authority (TVA) projects, GE *134, map 134-135*; tidal, PE *139*

Damselflies: mating, IN *63*; nymph, IN *10*

Danaidae butterfly caterpillars: IN *121*

Dance flies: mating by, IN *67*

Dances: bees', IN *26, 128-129, 134-135*; of cleaner wrasses, UN *134, 135*; of saber-toothed blenny, UN *135*

Dances, courtship: bowerbirds, AN *100*; cranes, AN *102-103*; flytrap spiders, AN *90*

Dandelion seeds: PL *67, 72-73*

Dark nebulas: SP *87*

Darkness adaptation of eyes: HU *108-109*

Darrieus windmill: PH *104*

Dart-poison frogs: AN *66-67*

Darwin, Charles: EC 7, EV *12*, GE 81, IN 61; theories, EV 12, 13

Darwin's finches: EC 7

Darwin's toads: UN *91*

Dasyures: EV *138*

Databases: computerized reservation systems, CO *96, 97*; map information, CO *77*

Data networks: in smart houses, CO *104*

Data retrieval: smart cards, MA *60-61*

Data storage: CO *30-31*; CD-ROM, CO *95*; magnetic, CO *19, 36-37, 56-57*; smart cards, MA *60-61*; after sorting, CO 55

Data transfer between computers: CO *118-119*; pocket computer, CO *91*

Dating: of fossils, ST *24-25*; geological, PE *94, 95*

Dayflowers: stomas of, PL *38-39*

DC (direct current) and AC (alternating current): PH *85, 86*

Deadbeat escapement: pendulum clock's, MA *13*

Dead-leaf mantis: AN *31*

Dead reckoning: TR *81*; with chip log, TR *87*

Dead zone: sailboat's, PH *13*

Death caps (mushrooms): PL *98-99*

Death Valley, Calif., U.S.: GE *115*

Debugging of programs: CO *49*

Decay-producing organisms: PL *110-111, 124, 125, 126-127*

Decibels of sound: PH 128, 135

Deciduous forests: temperate, EC *5, 25*

Deciduous vs. evergreen trees: EC *24-25*

Decimal vs. binary notation: CO 26, *chart* 27

Decomposers: PL *126*; in food chain, PL 124, 125

Decorator crabs: use of camouflage by, UN *136-137*

Deep-bodied bitterlings: UN *64*

Deep-sea creatures: anglerfish, UN *23, 70-71, 111, 112*; food-hunting adaptations, UN *112-113*; luminescence, cause of, UN *24-25, 26-27*; notothen, UN *17*; in ocean trenches, UN *34-35*; pressure, water, and, UN *22-23*; squid, luminous ink squirted by, UN *140*

Deep-sea drilling: PE *31*

Deep Space Network: CO *142*

Deer: after forest fire, EC *136*; moose, EC *58-59*; moose, wolves attacking, AN *44-45*; plants' defenses against, EC *118*; reindeer, EC *50-51*; white-tailed, EC *139*; white-tailed, warning signal by, AN *61*

Defenses of animals: AN 50-87, UN 120-144; angelfish, UN *132-133*; bluffing, AN *84-85*; breaking off body parts, AN *80-81*; camouflage, crab's, UN *136-137*; camouflage, insects', IN 113, *116-117*; camouflage, octopus's, UN *143*; chemical weapons of insects, IN *122-123, 126, 127*; cleaner wrasse, UN *120, 134-135*; eye-spots, AN *51, 64-65*, IN *112-113, 118, 119*; fighting ants, IN *126-127*; flounder, UN *130-131*; flying fish, UN *120-121, 128-129*; gliding, AN *72-73, 82-83*; hermit crab, AN *76-79*; hosts exploited for, UN *144*; ink, use of, UN *140-141*; insects, IN 112-127; look-alike animals, AN *54-55, 68-69*; mimicry, insects', IN *112, 113, 118-119*, 120; need for, example of, IN *114-115*; poison fish, UN *120-121, 122-123, 126-127*; porcupinefish, UN *121, 124-125*; pufferfish, UN *126-127*; schooling by fish, AN *74-75*; snakes, AN *62-63*; soldier aphids, IN *114*; squid, UN *140-141, 142-143*; against starfish, UN *138-139*; stinging by insects, IN *124-125, 126, 127*, 137; symbiosis as, AN *12-13, 70-71, 78-79, 86-87*; warning coloration of insects, IN *112-113, 120-121*; warning signals by herd animals, AN *60-61. See also* Coloration, protective

Defenses of plants: EC *98-99, 118-119*

Deflection coils in TV picture tube: MA *77*

De Galley, Blasco: steamboat built by, TR *91*

Dehumidifiers: MA *124-125*

Deinonychus (dinosaur): hunting by, EV *82*

Deinotherium (elephant ancestor): EV *110*

Deltas: GE *26, 32-33*; estuaries from, GE *39*; Nile River, GE *4-5, 33*

Demodulator, radio's: working of, MA *85*

Dendrites: HU 100

Dendrobates frogs: AN *66-67*

Deneb (star): distance and magnitude, SP *81*

Density: of gases, ST *46*; of planets, SP *28-29*; of water, PH *chart 67*, ST *chart 35*

Deoxyribonucleic acid: *See* DNA

Deposition: terraces formed by, GE *88-89*

Depositional plains: GE 28, *29*; alluvial fans, GE *27, 30-31*; deltas, GE *4-5, 26, 32-33, 39*; flood plains, GE *27, 29*

Depressions: tropical, WE 82, *90-91*

Depth charts: GE *18*; soundings for, GE *18*

Depth finders: TR *82*

Derailleur: bicycle's, PH *46*

Dermaptera (earwigs): IN *74, 84*

Dermis and epidermis: *See* Skin, fish's; Skin, human; Skin, prehistoric animals'

Desalinization plants: PE *139*

Descending colon: HU *91*

Desertification: and overgrazing, GE *107*

Deserts: GE 100, WE *124-125, 134-135*; animals, EC *28, 88-93*; creation of, by wind, GE *104-105*; distribution of, WE *map* 135; dunes, GE *100-101, 105, 108-109*; expansion and contraction of, GE *106-107*; human activities as cause of, GE 106, *107*; ice ages' effect on, GE *51*; mirages, type of, WE *100, 101*; Monument Valley's floor, GE *110-111*; oases in, GE *62-63*; plants, EC *86-87, 89, 94-95*; rain-shadow, formation of, WE *134-135*; sirocco from, WE *46-47*; South American coastal, WE *72, 135*

Desert species: EV *20-21*; convergence, EV *137*

Desktop computers vs. mainframe computers: CO *18-19*

Desktop publishing: defined, CO 94

Desmostylus (extinct mammal): EV *118-119*; skeleton, EV *104-105*; teeth, EV *119*

Destiny 2000 electric car: TR *65*

Detergent: action of, MA *112*

Detonation wave: MA *25*

Deuterium nuclei: fusion of, ST *17*

Deuteron formation: SP *44*

Developer in instant color photography: MA *92-93*

Devil angler: UN *23*

Devilfish: UN *25*

Devonian period, life in: EV *41*; amphibian, first, EV *57*; fish, EV *46, 47, 56, 57*; insect, oldest, EV *50-51*; plants, EV *52, 53*

DeVries, William: MA *132*

Dew point: MA *125*, WE *58, 62*

Diabetes: HU *142-143*

Diademodon (mammal-like reptile): EV *64*

Diadromous fish: UN *11*

Diamonds: PE *90*, ST 132, *133*; formation of, PE *90-91*; synthetic, ST *132-133*

Diaphragm: movement in breathing, HU *54, 55*

Diapsids: EV *chart* 63; thecodonts, EV 62, *66-67*

Diastole in artificial heart: MA *133*

Diastolic pressure: measuring, MA *131*

Diatoms: PL *100-101*

Diatryma (extinct flightless bird): EV *106*

Dickinsonia (extinct animal): EV *39*

Dickson, W. K. L.: MA 20

Dicotyledons: seed leaves of, PL *9, 12, 13*

Dictyoploca japonica (butterfly): IN *33*

Didinium: AN *7*

Didolodus (extinct mammal): EV *120*

Diesel-powered locomotives: TR *4-5*

Difference Engine: CO *10*

Differential: automobile's, TR *41, 49*

Differential flow device: MA *46-47*

Differential pressure sensor: MA *46*

Differentiation of species: EV *12, 22-23*

Diffraction: WE *104*; defined, PH *112*; effects, WE *104-105*; holograms and, PH *125*

Diffusion vacuum pumps: MA 44, *45*

Digestion by humans: HU *92-93*; waste products of, ST *82-83. See also* Digestive system of humans

Digestion by insects: of wood, methods for, IN *48-49. See also* Digestive system of insects

Digestive system of humans: HU 6, 76-91, *92-93*, 94-95; esophagus, HU *81*; kidneys, role of, HU *94-95*; large intestine, HU *90-91*; liver, HU *86-87*; pancreas, role of, HU *84-85*; saliva and salivary glands, HU *78-79, 118*; small intestine, HU *88-89*; stomach, HU *82-83*; surfaces, kinds of, HU *76-77, 82-83, 88-89, 90*; swallowing, HU *80-81*

Digestive system of insects: of butterflies, changes in, IN *83*; of mosquitoes, IN *68*

Digital and analog conversion: CO *40-41, 67, 110-111, 119*

Digital and analog signals: compact disks, recording of, MA *86*; fax machine's use of, MA *68-69*; synthesizer's use of, MA *91*

Digitized illustrations in electronic publishing: CO *95*

Digitized strings: faxing, CO *114-115*

Dik-diks: EC *82*

Dikes: in the Netherlands, GE *132*; in tidal power generating station, PH *106-107*; Yellow River's, GE 34, *35*

Dimetrodon (extinct reptile): EV *59, chart* 65

Planet Earth
PE

Plant Life
PL

Physical Forces
PH

Structure of Matter
ST

Space & Planets
SP

Transportation
TR

Underwater World
UN

Weather & Climate
WE

Dinaric Alps (mountains), Yugoslavia: bora winds over, WE *48-49*

Dinosaurs: EV *60-61*, WE *143*; bird-hipped vs. lizard-hipped, EV *chart 66-67, 74-75*; birds' evolution from, EV *68-69, 70-71*; *Coelophysis*, EV *67*; coloration, EV *84-85*; diet, EV *76-77*; domehead, EV *86-87*; extinction, EV 20, *24*, 61; family tree, EV *chart 66-67*; horned, EV *78-79, 88-89*; origin of, EV *66-67*; relative (*Euparkeria*), EV *62, 66*; reproduction, EV *78-79*; skin, EV 96, *97*; as social animals, EV *78-79, 82-83*; and warm-blooded animals, similarity of, EV *80-81*

Diode: PH *85*

Dioecious plants: PL *59*

DIP (dual in-line package): CO *23*

Diplocaulus (extinct amphibian): EV *58-59*

Diplodocus (dinosaur): EV *84-85*

Dirac, Paul: ST 22

Direct current (DC) and alternating current (AC): PH *85, 86*

Direct search: CO 57

Dirt, removal of: by detergent, MA *112*; by soap, ST *48-49*

Disappearing-filament optical pyrometers: PH 56, *57*

Disc brakes: automobile, TR *44*, 58; snowmobile, TR *69*; train, high-speed, TR *33*

Discontinuities between layers of Earth: PE *14*

Discus, mating pair of: with eggs, UN *86*; with fry, UN *87*

Disease: *See* Illness

Dishwashers: MA *116-117*

Disinfection of water: ST *98-99*

Disks, computer, and disk drives: CO *19, 36-37, 56-57*; CD-ROM, CO *95*

Disks, spinal: HU 40, *41*

Distillation: fractional, of oil, ST *116-117*; steam, in perfume making, ST *126-127*

Distributor, automobile: role of, TR *41*

Ditch reeds: EC *27*, PL *129*

Divergent boundaries: PE *34*; and normal faults, PE *48*. *See also* Mid-ocean ridges; Rift valleys

Divider circuit in quartz watch: MA *97*

Diving by sperm whales: UN *32-33*

Dizziness: cause of, HU *114-115*

D layer of ionosphere: WE *9, 14-15*

DNA (deoxyribonucleic acid): HU *4-5, 10-11*, ST *4-5*; damaged, and tumors, HU *138-139*; and RNA (ribonucleic acid), EV 30, *36*; viral, HU *136*, 137

Doctor blade in intaglio printing: MA *41*

Dodder: PL *57*

Dodos: EV *144*

Dogfish: spiny, fetus of, UN *76*

Dogs: African hunting, EC *13*; bear dog, EV *121*; breeds of, EV *11*; Cape hunting, EC *82*

Dogtooth violet seeds: PL *79*

Dolichocebus (monkey ancestor): EV *123*

Dolomedes sulfureus (spider): wasp stinging, IN *54*

Dolphins: bottle-nosed, EV *136*; communication by, UN *114-115*; as predators, UN *58-59, 114-115*; river, UN *58-59*; swimming style of, UN *18-19*

Domains: magnetic, PH 78, *79*

Domehead dinosaurs: EV *86-87*

Dominance, establishing: bighorn sheep, AN *106-107*; lions, AN *138-139*; wolves, AN *45*

Dominant and recessive traits: EV *13, 14*

Doors: commuter trains', TR *12-13, 25*

Doppler effect (Doppler shift): MA *39*, PH *138-139*, SP *91*; redshift, SP *91, 115*; speed gun's use of, MA 38; ultrasound's use of, MA 142

Dorsal vessel: IN *8*; grasshopper's, IN *9*

Doryaspis (extinct fish): EV *47*

Dot-matrix printers: CO *38-39*

Douglas firs: PL *122*

Downdrafts: and air turbulence, WE *52-53*; mountain and valley breezes, WE *43*; in tornado formation, WE *50, 51*; in wind formation, WE *41*

Down jackets: insulation by, PH *60-61*

Downlink and uplink antennas: CO *128*

Draco (constellation): SP *60, 61*

Drag: on baseball, PH 34; lift and, in hang gliding, PH *14, 15*; vs. lift on airplane, TR *110*

Dragonflies: IN *5*; as butterfly enemy, IN *115*; evolutionary path, IN *7*; flying method, IN *14, 15*; mating, IN *62-63*; metamorphosis, IN *80-81*; nymphs, IN *10, 36-37, 44-45, 80-81*

Dragons (lizards): flying, AN *72-73*; Komodo, AN *15*

Drains: whirlpools in, PH *20-21*

Dreams: sleep and, HU *124-125*

Drepanaspis (extinct fish): EV *47*

Drift motion in Van Allen belts: WE *18-19*

Drilling rigs: synthetic diamonds in, ST *133*

Drinking by saltwater vs. freshwater fish: UN *10-11*

Drinking water: purifying, ST *98-99*

Driver ants: African, IN 138, *141*

Drive shaft: automobile's, and differential gear, TR *41*

Dromedaries: EC *88*; temperature, EC *chart* 88

Droneflies: as pollinators, EC *115*; striped, AN *54*

Drones (bees): AN *130-131*, IN *71*; nursery, IN *70-71*

Dropsondes: use of, WE 95

Drosophila flies: mutations in, EV *14*

Drowned valleys: GE *90-91*

Drugs from plants: PL *132-133*

Drum brakes: automobile's, TR 44, *45*

Drumlins: glaciers' formation of, GE *44-45*

Drupes: PL *66-67*; coconuts, PL *86-87*

Dry ice: ST 38, *39*; and alcohol, ST *40*

Dryland farming: GE 138

Dryopithecus (ape ancestor): EV *123*

Dry season: adaptations to, UN *30-31*

Dual in-line package (DIP): CO 23

Dubhe (star): movement, SP *90-91*

Duckbilled platypuses: AN *18-19*

Duckweed: PL *23*

Dugong: AN *25*

Duiker: EC *21*

Dump trucks: tires for, TR *57*

Dunes: formation of, GE *108-109*; Sahara's, GE *100-101, 105, 109*

Dung beetles: IN *92-93, 106-107, 130, 131*

Dunkleosteus (extinct fish): EV *49*

Duodenum: lining of, HU *77*; location of, HU *82*; and pancreas, HU *84*

Dust tail of comet: SP *33*

Dwarf gouramis: UN *64*

Dwarf stars: SP *93*; Sun as, SP *47*; and supernova, SP *85*

Dyes in ink: ST 72, *73*; removal of, ST *72-73*

Dynamic microphones: MA *80*

Dynamic speakers: MA 80, *81*

Dynamite: working of, MA *24-25*

Dynamo: invention of, PH *94*

Dynamo theory of Earth: PE *20*

E

Eagles: EC *124-125, 126-127*

Ears, animal: bones, evolution of, EV *135*; cricket's, IN *28*; inner, fish's, UN *52*; moth's, IN *24*; shark's, UN *55*; troughs, barn owl's, AN *38-39*; tympanic membrane, cricket's, AN *97*

Ears, human: CO *63*; bones, evolution of, EV *135*; bones of, HU *32*; and dizziness, HU *114-115*; sounds, identifying, HU *112-113*

Earth: PE entire volume; density, SP *29*; eclipses seen from, SP 41, *50-51, 62-63*; formation of, PE *6-7, 110-111*; gravitational variation, PE 17, *18-19*; heat, internal, PE *12-13, 28, 29*; life's beginnings on, EV *30-31*; magnetic field, PE *20-21*; Mercury's view of, SP *8*; meteorite crater, SP *35*; midnight Sun, land of, SP *58-59*; Milky Way seen from, SP *100-*

| Animal Behavior **AN** | Computer Age **CO** | Ecology **EC** | Evolution of Life **EV** | Geography **GE** | Human Body **HU** | Insects & Spiders **IN** | Machines & Inventions **MA** |

101; Moon's distance from, increasing, SP *72-73*; Moon's eclipses caused by, SP *62-63*; and Moon's formation, theories of, SP *66-67*; Moon's orbit around, SP *70-71*; Moon's view of, SP *67*; motion of, SP *50, 52-61*; nebulas seen from, SP *86-87*; nuclear fusion, experimental, SP *45*; orbit, SP *54-55*; precession, SP *60-61*; rotation, effects of, SP *52-53*; rotation, slowing of, SP *73*; satellites above, SP *124*; seasons, cause of, SP *56-57*; seismic study of, PE *14-15, 98, 99*; shape, PE *4-5, 16, 17*; size, PE *16-17*; solar radiation on, SP *45, 48-49*; star motions relative to, SP *90-91*; stars' distances from, and magnitude, SP *80-81*; tides, cause of, SP *73*; universe's evolution seen from, SP *112-113*; young, EV *28-29*. *See also* Earthquakes; Layers of Earth; Minerals; Oceans; Plate tectonics; Rocks; Volcanoes

Earth-approaching asteroids: orbits, SP *31, 35*

Earthmover: TR *77*

Earthquakes: PE *46-61*; around volcanoes, detecting, PE *79*; cause of, PE *42, 46, 48-49*; effects of, PE *46-47, 48, 54-55, 58-59, 60-61*; focus, locating, PE *52-53*; and liquefaction of ground, PE *55, 60-61*; predicting, PE *56-57*; S-P time of seismic waves from, PE *51, 52, 53, chart 53*; studying seismic waves from, PE *14-15*; traveling of seismic waves from, PE *50-51*; and tsunamis, PE *54, 58-59*

Earth's Moon: *See* Moon, Earth's

Earthstars (mushrooms): PL *99*

Earthworms: EC *36*; as mole's prey, AN *105*

Earwigs: IN *84*; care of eggs by, IN *74*

Easterlies (winds): WE *34-35, 36, 37*; convergence of trade winds, WE *90, 132-133*; southern oscillation and, WE *140-141*

Eastern mud snake: AN *63*

Eastman, George: MA *18, 19*; camera invented by, MA *18, 19*

East Pacific Rise: PE *35*

Eating in space: SP *132, 133*

Eccrine sweat glands: HU *42-43*

Echinoderms as chordate ancestor: EV *46, 47*

Echo (U.S. satellite): CO *128*

Echoes: PH *132-133*

Echolocation: bats' use of, AN *42-43*

Echo sounder: TR *82*; survey ship using, GE *18*

Eckert, J. P.: CO *14*

Eclipses: of Moon, SP *62-63*; of Sun, SP *41, 50-51, 62-63*

Eclipsing variables (stars): SP *82-83*

Ecliptic: SP *54-55, 60-61, 70*

Ecological niches: adaptation, EV *5, 20-21*; isolation, EV *23*

Ecology: EC entire volume

Edaphosaurus (extinct reptile): EV *59, chart* 65

Eddies, air: and contrails, WE *64*; mountains and, WE *69*

Edelweiss: PL *121*

Edison, Thomas: generator built by, MA *29*; movie by, MA *20*; movie equipment built by, MA *20-21*

Editors: electronic publishing by, CO *94-95*; word processors for, CO *58-59*

Eelgrass: EC *26, 27, 140*; pollination, EC *27*

Eels: UN *47*; Atlantic snipe eel, UN *112*; barbels, UN *123*; electric, UN *19, 57*; freshwater, UN *11*; Japanese, UN *73*; leopard moray, AN *22*; moray, UN *63, 67, 104*; swimming types, UN *19*

Eeltail catfishes: UN *123*

Egg and sperm, human: HU *12, 13*; fertilization, HU 12, *15, 16-17*; fertilization, in vitro, HU *28-29*; formation of, HU *14-15*; and twins, HU *22, 23*

Egg cases: false trumpet, UN *99*; shark, UN *76*

Eggs, boiled: ST *94-95*

Eggs and egg laying: alligators, AN *110*; amphibians, UN *88, 90, 91*; amphibian vs. reptile, EV *59*; aphids, IN *73*; aquatic animals, UN *62*; Aztec ants, IN *99*; barnacles, UN *41*; butterflies, IN *74, 79, 130*; cicadas, IN *89*; corals and sponges, UN *100*; crabs, UN *39, 96*; cuckoos and host species, AN *114, 115*; dinosaurs, EV *78, 79*; discus, UN *86*; dragonflies, IN *62, 63*; drought survival, UN *31*; dung beetles, IN *92, 106, 107, 130*; family behavior, range of, IN *130*; fertilization, AN *88-89*; flounders, UN *130*; as food for fry, UN *87*; glacier midges, IN *34*; ground bees' chambers, IN *108-109*; honeybees, IN *70, 132*; hunting wasps, IN 54, *55*, 110, 111; insects and spiders, IN *56*; in larvae, IN *114, 124*; leaf-rolling weevils, IN *104, 105*; mollusks, UN *98, 99*; mosquitoes, IN *46, 69*; mouthbrooders, UN *73, 79, 80-81, 84-85*; number of eggs, UN *72-73*; ostrich, vulture cracking, AN *47*; other species, incubation by, UN *84-85*; parental care, IN *74, 75, 76, 77, 130*; protection of eggs, UN *73, 74-75, 78, 79, 80-81, 84-85*; salmon, UN *82*; sharks, UN *76, 77*; shrikes, AN *114*; spiders' cocoons for, IN *94-95*; spring-tide laying, AN *122-123*; tiger moths, IN *88*; tubes for, IN

124. See also Mating, courtship and

Eggs of plants: fertilized, PL *9*

Egrets: EC *139*

Egypt: Nile, GE *4-5, 33*; Sahara, GE *100-101*

Egyptian mouthbrooder: UN *73*

Egyptian vulture: AN *47*

Einstein, Albert: SP 44, 95; relativity theory of, PH *126-127*

EKGs (electrocardiograms): MA *136-137*

Ekman spiral (current): PE *119*

Elaeagnus: thorny, PL *29*

Elands: EC *10, 83, 85*

Elasmosaurus (plesiosaur): EV *92-93*

Elastic limit of springs: PH 50, 51

E layer and F layer: CO *128*

E layer of ionosphere: WE *9, 14-15*

Elbow movement: HU *39*

Elcysma westwoodii (moth): IN *33*

Elder trees: red-berry, bark of, PL *27*

Electrical and gravitational studies: of ore deposits, PE *98*; of volcanoes, PE *79*

Electrical generators: MA *28-29*

Electrical imbalance in polar molecules: ST 42, 43

Electrical receptors: platypus's, AN *19*; shark's, UN *55*

Electric eels: UN *19, 57*

Electric fish: UN *56-57*; eels, UN *19, 57*

Electricity: automobiles powered by, TR *64-65*; batteries, automobile, ST *58-59*; circuits, PH *74-75*; in clouds, WE *66, 67*; conduction, ST *18-19*; conductors of, vs. insulators, PH *82-83, 84*; and electromagnetic waves, PH *88-89*; electromagnets created by, PH *80-81*; for homes, PH *86-87*; lamps illuminated by, PH *72-73*; and liquid crystals, ST *136-137*; and magnetism, PH *68-69, 80-81, 94*; measuring, PH *76-77*; paramecium's reaction to, AN *6*; in plating of metals, ST *62-63*; platypus's reaction to, AN 18, *19*; in reclamation of salt, ST 96; in refining of metals, ST *114-115*; rust prevention with, ST *57*; and semiconductors, PH *84-85*; solar automobiles powered by, TR *62-63*; static, PH *70-71*; superconductivity, PH *92-93*

Electricity, generating: PH 94-111; AC generators, PH *96-97*; dynamo, invention of, PH 94; geothermal energy, PH *102-103*; hydroelectric power, PH *98-99*; nuclear reactors, PH *94-95, 108-109*, ST *15*; ocean power, PH *106-107*; solar power, PH *110-111*; thermoelectric power, PH *100-101*; windmills, PH *104-105. See also* Power plants

Electricity theory of ball lightning: WE *107*

Electric power meters: MA *118-119*

Planet Earth
PE

Plant Life
PL

Physical Forces
PH

Structure of Matter
ST

Space & Planets
SP

Transportation
TR

Underwater World
UN

Weather & Climate
WE

Electric trains: high-speed, TR *4-5, 32-33*; monorails, TR *28-29. See also* Commuter trains

Electrocardiograms (EKGs): MA *136-137*

Electrocardiograph: MA *136-137*

Electrodermal response: lie detector's measurement of, MA *36*

Electroless plating: ST *63*

Electrolysis: conduction, ST *18-19*; plating, ST *62-63*; reclamation of salt, ST *96-97*; refining of metals, ST *114-115*

Electromagnetic brakes: trains', TR *10, 11*

Electromagnetic force in measurement of electricity: PH *76, 77*

Electromagnetic induction: MA *28*, PH *94*

Electromagnetic radiation: PH *88*; high-temperature thermometers measuring, PH *56-57*; radio waves, PH *88-89*; types of, MA *chart* 141; wavelengths of, PH *chart* 72, 88

Electromagnetic wave theory of ball lightning: WE *107*

Electromagnets: direction of motion in, rule for, TR *105*; Edison generator with, MA *29*; in maglevs, TR *34*; microphone with, MA *80*; in power meter, MA *118, 119*; superconducting, TR *104-105*; in telephone, MA *57*; in videocassette recorder (VCR), MA *83*

Electron guns: electron microscope's use of, MA *32-33*; in TV picture tubes, MA *76, 77*

Electronic blackboard: MA *70-71*

Electronic blood-pressure gauge: MA *131*

Electronic bulletin boards: CO 116, *117*

Electronic mail (E-mail): CO *116-117*

Electronic Numerical Integrator and Computer (ENIAC): CO 4, 14, *15*; vacuum tubes, CO *5, 14-15*

Electronic pagers: CO *122-123*

Electronic publishing: CO *94-95*

Electronic thermometer: MA *128-129*

Electron microscopes: MA *32-33*

Electrons: PH 68, ST *7*; in AC generators, PH *96-97*; and antimatter counterpart, ST *22, 23*; and auroras, WE 16, *17*; in automobile batteries, ST *58-59*; combustion and, ST *67*; in conductors vs. insulators, PH *82-83, 84*; in current electricity, PH *72-73, 74-75*; and electricity, ST *18-19*; energy levels, ST *7*; and fireworks, ST *50-51*; and Geiger counters, PH *90, 91*; in ionosphere, WE *14*; in iron reactions, ST *56-57*; and laser formation, PH 122, *123*; of magnets, PH *78*; in oxidation-reduction reactions, ST *56, 58, 59, 72, 73,* 110; in semiconductors, PH *84, 85*; in silver-plating, ST *62, 63*; and static elec-

tricity, PH *70, 71*; in Van Allen belts, WE *18-19*

Electron scanning: development of, MA 22

Electroplating: ST *62-63*

Electrostatic filter: air purification with, MA *50-51*

Elements: ST *10-11*; in fireworks, colors produced by, ST 50, *51*; periodic table of, ST 4, *chart* 10-11; radioactive, ST *14-15, 24-25*; as solids, ST *44-45. See also* Metals; *and individual names*

Elephant fishes (mormyrids): UN 56; relative of, UN *56-57*

Elephants: African, EC 10, 82-83, *84-85, 113*; ancestors, EV *105, 110-111, 121, 128-129*; Indian, EC *11*; temperature control, EV *81*

Elephant seals: UN *93*

Elevators: MA *66*

Elevators, airplane's: TR *111*; Wright *Flyer's*, working of, TR *135*

Elliptical galaxies: SP *103*

El Niño phenomenon: PE *124-125*, WE *140-141*

Elodea nuttalli (water plant): PL *129*

Eltanin Fracture Zone: PE *map* 112-113

E-mail (electronic mail): CO *116-117*

Embryo culture, plant: PL *140*

Embryo, human: HU *18*; implanting, HU *29*

Embryo, plant: PL *12*; development of, PL *9*

Embryo, shark: UN *76, 77*

Emerald notothen: UN *17*

Emission lines in spectra of stars: SP *78*

Emission nebulas: SP *86*

Emissions control: computer use in, CO 102

Emotional perspiration: HU *43*

Emperor, yellow (soapfish): UN *126*

Emperor penguins: EC *9, 49*

Emperor seamounts: PE *44*

Emulsions: ST *20*

Encke comet, orbit: SP *32*

Endangered species: EC *96-97, 112-113*

End digestive enzymes: HU *89*

Endocrine glands and hormones: HU *74-75*; islets of Langerhans, HU *75, 84, 85, 142-143*

Endodermis of root: PL *15*

Endoplasmic reticulum: PL *6, 7*

Endoscope: MA *138*

Endosperm: PL *8-9, 12,* 66; coconut, PL *86-87*

Endothelium, blood vessels': HU *62, 63, 66-67*

Energy: ST *54*; in car batteries, ST *58-59*; kinetic, vs. intermolecular forces, ST *34, 35. See also* Combustion; Electricity; Heat; Kinetic energy; Magnetism

Engine control on automobiles: CO *102*

Engines: aircraft, TR 108, *130-131, 134, 139*; automobile, TR *40, 41, 47, 54-55,* 58, 59, ST *60-61*; icebreaker, TR *101*; jet, TR *130-131, 139*; motorcycle, TR *42-43*; nuclear, TR *102*; racing car, Formula One, TR 58, *59*; rocket, ST 74, *75*; snowmobile, TR *68*; steam, TR *90*; steam vs. gasoline, for tractors pulling combines, MA *14-15*; turbocharged, TR *54-55*; Wright *Flyer*, TR *134*

England: Greenwich meridian, GE *21*; London, GE *116,* 128; Thames River, GE *38*

ENIAC (Electronic Numerical Integrator and Computer): CO 4, 14, *15*; vacuum tubes, CO *5, 14-15*

Envelope of sound: envelope generator (EG) and, MA *90*

Enzymes: in apples, ST *80, 81*

Enzymes, digestive: HU *93*; end, HU *89*; pancreatic, HU *84, 85*; in stomach, HU *82, 83*

Eogyrinus (extinct amphibian): EV *58*

Eosinophils: HU *128*

Epicenter of earthquake: PE *50*; locating, PE *52-53*

Epidermis and dermis of fish: UN *7*

Epidermis and dermis of humans: *See* Skin, human

Epidermis of plants: PL *20*; cactus, PL *113*; pine needles, PL *49*; prickles as outgrowths of, PL *28*; of root, PL *15*; stomas in, PL *39*

Epiglottis: HU *58*; during swallowing, HU *80-81*

Epiphytes (air plants): EC *68-69*, PL *22-23*; and ants, symbiosis of, IN *98*

Episinus affinis (spider): web of, IN *39*

Epithelial cells: HU *6, 88-89,* 135

Epoxy resin: carbon fibers bonded with, ST *138-139*

Equal-area map projections: GE *17*

Equator, Earth's: Foucault pendulum at, SP *52-53*; stars' apparent motion at, SP *53*; Sun's angle to, and seasons, SP *56-57*

Equatorial convergence zone: WE *90, 132-133*

Equatorial waves (clouds): WE *132*

Equilibrium: floating ship in, PH *8*; loss of, HU *114-115*

Equinox: autumnal, SP *56, 57*; vernal, SP *56*

Equus (horse): EV *109, 121*

Eratosthenes (Greek scientist): PE 16, 17

Erector muscles: HU *44, 47*

Ermine: seasonal color changes in, AN *58-59*

Erosion: in Appalachian Mountains' formation, GE *96-97*; aquifers exposed by, GE *62, 63*; cuestas formed by, GE *92-93*; by

Animal Behavior **AN** | Computer Age **CO** | Ecology **EC** | Evolution of Life **EV** | Geography **GE** | Human Body **HU** | Insects & Spiders **IN** | Machines & Inventions **MA**

Himalayan rivers, GE *98-99*; of limestone, GE *58-59*; marine, effects of, GE *68-69, 76-77, 88-89*; Monument Valley's formation by, GE *110-111*; plains formed by, GE *28, 29*; and terraces, GE *88-89*

Erosional plains: GE *28, 29*

Eryops (extinct amphibian): EV *58-59*

Escalators: MA *66-67*

Escapements, mechanical clocks': deadbeat, MA *13*; verge, MA *12, 13*

Eskers: GE *66*; formation of, GE *44, 67*

Esophagus, fish's: and swim bladder, UN *12, 13*

Esophagus, human: HU *55*; lining of, HU *76-77*; movement of food through, HU *81*

Estivation by lungfish: UN *31*

Estuaries: GE *38-39*

Estuarine species: EC *140-141*; mangrove, EC *34*

Ethanol and water: mixing of, ST *43*

Ethiopian region: animals of, EC *4*

Ethylene: ST *107*; polymerization, ST *106-107*

Eucalyptus trees: PL *118-119*; giant, PL *122*

Eudimorphodon (early reptile): EV *63*

Eukaryotes: cell type, EV *36-37*; evolution of, EV *6, 7*; multicelled, rise of, EV *38-39*

Eulalia (grass): EC *78*

Eumycetes vs. Myxomycetes: PL *96*

Euparkeria (early reptile): EV *62, 66*

Euphorbia: EV *137*

Euploca bagworms: nest of, IN *103*

European midwife toads: UN *90*

European Space Agency: satellites launched by U.S. and, SP *124, 125*

European starlings: sun, navigation by, AN *134*

Europlocephalus (dinosaur): EV *97*

Euryapsids: EV *chart 63*

Eurypterid fossil: EV *50*

Eusthenopteron (amphibian ancestor): EV *56*; structure, EV *57*

Evaporation: PH *22-23, 53, 62-63*; in global water cycle, GE *68, 82*; and heat transfer, PH *64*; vs. precipitation, GE *83*; of sweat in sauna, PH *64-65*

Evaporators: in air conditioners, MA *122-123*; in dehumidifiers, MA *124-125*; in refrigerators, MA *106-107*

Evening primroses: PL *53*

Everglades, Fla., U.S.: animals, EC *138-139*

Evergreens: vs. deciduous trees, EC *24-25*; defoliation, PL *43*; and ice ages, PL *120-121*; mistletoe, PL *23, 82-83*; oak, fruit of, PL *77*. *See also* Conifers

Evolution: EV entire volume; beginnings of life, EV *30-31*; vs. breeding, EV *18-19*; of

camouflage in crabs, UN *137*; of cells, EV *36-37*; coevolution of insects, IN *78-79*; convergence, EV *136-137, 138-139*; fossil evidence of, EV *130*; and fossils, living, EV *130-131, 140-141*; over geologic time periods, EV *8-9, chart 24*; homologous structures, EV *130-131, 134-135*; human effect on, EV *142-143, 144*; of insects, possible path, IN *6-7*; living things, first, EV *32*; of male fish's colors, UN *64*; of multicellular organisms, EV *27, 38-39*; oxygen, atmospheric, and, EV *34*; of stingers on insects, IN *124*; theory of, EV *12-13*; of wings on insects, IN *84*; young organisms as clues to, EV *131, 132-133*. *See also* Mammals; Mesozoic era; Paleozoic era; Species

Excavators: TR *67, 76-77*

Exchange offices, telephone: for cellular calls, CO *120, 121*; use of, MA *57*

Exciter lamp in movie projector: MA *88*

Exercising in space: SP *132, 133*

Exhaust: automobile, ST *60, 61*, TR *40*; automobile, turbochargers' use of, TR *54, 55*; jet, for creation of thrust, TR *130-131*; rocket, ST *74, chart 75*; VTOL aircraft's use of, TR *138, 139*

Exhaust velocity: rocket's, ST *74, chart 75*

Exocrine glands vs. endocrine glands: HU *74*

Exocrine system of ants: IN *43*

Exosphere: WE *8-9*

Expanding universe: SP *98, 114-115*

Explorer 1 (satellite): WE *18*

Explosives: MA *24-25*

Extensometer: PE *57*

Extensors and flexors: HU *38, 39*

External pins: smart card's, MA *61*

External respiration: vs. internal respiration, HU *52*

Extinctions: EV *8, 60-61*; of animals, EC *18-19, 20, 112*; of dinosaurs, EV *20, 24, 61*; modern, EV *144*

Extruded aluminum beams: ST *28-29*

Extrusive vs. intrusive igneous rocks: PE *87, 89*

Eyeglasses: corrective, HU *110-111*

Eye of hurricane or typhoon: WE *91, 92, chart 93, 95, 115*

Eyes, animals': aquatic animals, UN *44-45, 48, 49*; aquatic animals, vs. human, UN *48, 61*; butterflies, and mating, IN *59*; chameleon, AN *33*; compound, IN *4-5, 22*; flounder, UN *130-131*; octopus, UN *44, 60, 61*; praying mantises, IN *5, 22, 40*; rattlesnakes, range of, AN *34*; seeing in air with, UN *45, 50-51*; sharks, UN *44, 54*

Eyes, human: HU *110-111*; darkness adaptation, HU *108-109*; vs. fish's, UN *48*; misshaping of, HU *110-111*; vs. octopus's, UN *61*; in REM sleep, HU *124, 125*; stereoscopic vision, HU *106-107*

Eyes, robotic: CO *99*

Eyespots: AN *51, 64-65*, IN *112-113, 118, 119*; jellyfish's, UN *43*

F

Fabrics: synthetic, ST *108*

Fabricus, David: SP *82*

Face, human: images of, CO *72-73*

Facial language: chimpanzees, AN *124-125, 142*

Facsimile (fax) machines: CO *114-115*, MA *68-69*; in E-mail systems, CO *116*

Faculae: SP *41*

Fall equinox: SP *56, 57*

Fallopian tubes: HU *13, 16-17*; blocked, HU *28*

Fall webworms: IN *88-89*

False acacia trees: PL *28*

False trumpet: egg laying by, UN *99*

Fans for ventilating subway stations: TR *26-27*

Faraday, Michael: MA *28*, PH *94*

Farallon plate: subduction of, PE *42, 43*

Farming: combines used in, MA *14-15*. *See also* Agriculture

Farnsworth, Philo: MA *22*

Farsightedness: HU *110, 111*

Fastball: PH *35*

Fat in ice cream: ST *92, 93*

Faucets: water, MA *110-111*

Fault-block mountains: GE *86*

Faults: PE *48, 49*; measuring movement of, PE *56, 57*; from shallow-focus earthquakes, PE *54*; transform, PE *34, 35, 42-43, 49*

Fax machines: *See* Facsimile (fax) machines

Feathers, down: insulation by, PH *60-61*

Feces: creation and excretion of, HU *90-91*

Feed dog: sewing machine's, working of, MA *104*

Feeding: beaks, EC *7, 115*; deer family, EC *50-51, 58-59, 118*; insect-eating plants, EC *116-117*; insects, order of, EC *110-111*; sloths, EC *62*. *See also* Food chain; Predators

Feet: chameleons, AN *33*; flies', AN *8, 9*; insects, structure of, IN *21*

Felsic rocks: PE *88, 89*

Female anatomy: HU *13, 16-17, 28-29, 75*

Fenestraria (window-leaf plant): PL *115*

Fenestrated capillaries: HU *63*

Fennecs: adaptation by, EV *20-21*

Planet Earth
PE

Plant Life
PL

Physical Forces
PH

Structure of Matter
ST

Space & Planets
SP

Transportation
TR

Underwater World
UN

Weather & Climate
WE

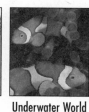

Fermentation: of milk, yogurt from, ST *84-85*; of molasses, MSG from, ST *90-91*

Ferns: PL *95, 108-109*; seed, Paleozoic, EV *53*; staghorn, EC *69*

Ferrel cells: WE *34-35, 38, 53, 112*

Ferric tannate in ink: ST *72-73*

Ferromagnetic materials: in electromagnets, PH *80-81*; magnetic domains of, PH *78, 79*; vs. superconductors, PH *93*

Ferromagnetic metals: detection of, MA *42, 43*

Ferrous and ferric tannate in ink: ST *72-73*

Fertilization: human, HU *12, 15, 16-17*; in vitro, of humans, HU *28-29*; plants, PL *8, 66*; in algae, PL *103*; in ferns and mosses, PL *109*

Fescue: red, PL *63*

Fetal monitoring, ultrasound: MA *142-143*

Fetal sharks: UN *76-77*

Fetus, human: brain development, HU *24-25*; growth of, HU *18-19*; nourishment, HU *20-21*; twins, HU *22-23*

Fiberoptic communications: CO *124-125*

Fibers: ST *12-13, 104*; carbon, ST *138-139*; glass, ST *124-125*; natural vs. synthetic, ST *109*; silk, ST *108*; synthetic, ST *108-109*

Fiberscopes: MA *138-139*

Fibrin: HU *65*

Fibroblasts: HU *6, 49*

Ficus trees: buttress roots of, PL *23*

Fiddler crabs: AN *108-109*

Field, Cyrus W.: MA *9*

Field-aligned current, auroral: WE *16-17*

Field cricket: Taiwan, AN *96*

Field lines: *See* Magnetic field lines

Fighter jets: CCV (control-configured vehicle), TR *140-141*; Harrier, TR *138-139*

Fighting song of crickets: AN *97*

Figs and fig wasps: PL *67, 68-69*

Figworts: PL *57*

Fiji Islands: GE *21*

Filament of incandescent bulb: PH *72-73*

Files and records: CO *55*, 56

Filiform papillae: HU *118*

Film: movie, projectors for, MA *20-21, 88-89*; Polaroid, working of, MA *92-93*; roll, Kodak camera's use of, MA *18, 19*

Films: *See* Movies

Filter-feeding mosquito larvae: IN *46-47*

Filters: color, MA *62-63, 92*; VC (voltage control), and sound quality, MA *90*

Financial uses of computers: CO *92*; banking, CO *88-89*

Finches: bullfinches, subspecies of, EV *10*; Darwin's, EC *7*, EV *12, 13*; woodpecker, AN *47*

Finger bones in bats: EV *114-115, 134*

Fingerling salmon: UN *82*

Fingernails and toenails: HU *46*

Finland: landscape formation in, GE *66-67*

Fins, use of: by flying fish, UN *128, 129*; by gurnard, UN *47*; by mudskipper, UN *28*; poisonous spines, UN *120-121, 122, 123*; in reproduction, UN *81*; by spiderfish, UN *113*; in swimming, UN *18, 19, 20-21*

Fire: in combustion reactions, ST 66, 67, 68; extinguishing, ST *68-69*; forest, effects of, EC *136-137*; grassland, effects of, EC *78-79*; use of by *Homo erectus*, EV *126*

Fire alarm systems: MA *64-65*

Fire ants: food gathering by, IN *42-43*

Fireballs: WE *106-107*

Fireflies: IN *52-53*; light, signaling with, AN *88-89, 92-93*

Fire pumpers (fire engines): TR *66-67, 70-71*

Firethorn: PL *78*

Fireworks: ST *50-51*

Firn zone of Alps: GE *142, chart* 142

Firs: Douglas, PL *122*

First-class levers: PH *43*

First law of motion, Newton's: PH 24, 28

Fish: EV *chart* 56-57; at alligator hole, EC *138, 139*; amphibian evolution from, EV *56-57*; anatomy, UN *6-7*; Antarctic, EC *47*; barbels, use of, AN *20-21*; bat's method of catching, AN *42*; breathing, UN *8-9, 28-29, 30-31*; cavefish, EC *40, 41, 43*; Chesapeake Bay, EC *140, 141*; cold-blooded vs. warm-blooded, UN *14-15*; convergence, EV *136*; definition of, UN 7; differentiation, EV *23*; dragonfly nymphs catching, IN *36-37, 44-45*; drinking by, UN *10-11*; with eyespots, AN *65*; in food chain, EC *128-129, 144*; in freezing waters, UN *16-17*; goldfish, breeds of, EV *18*; green heron's method of catching, AN *36-37*; humpback whale's method of catching, AN *40*; jawless, evolution of, EV *46-47, 48*; with jaws, evolution of, EV *48-49*; living fossils, EV *140*; luminescent, UN *22, 23, 24-25, 26-27, 70-71, 111, 112, 144*; mutations in trout, EV *14-15, 17*; navigation by, AN *120-121*; pressure, surviving, UN *22-23*; schools, swimming in, AN *74-75*; and sea anemones, AN *22-23, 48-49, 70-71*; shark development, EV *132-133*; spring-tide breeders, AN *122-123*; swim bladders, UN *12-13, 23, 52, 53*; swimming types, UN *18, 19, 20-21*; in symbiotic relationships, AN *22-25, 70-71, 86-87*; types of, major, UN *6*. *See also* Defenses of animals; Predators; Reproduction by animals

Fish farming: PE *142-143*

Fishing areas: GE *126-127*

Fishing bat: AN *42*

Fishing spiders: six-starred, AN *27*

Fission, nuclear: ST *14-15*, TR 102, *103*; power production by, PH *108-109*; reactor core, PH *94-95, 108*

Fission theory of Moon's origin: SP *67*

Five-lined skink: AN *80, 81*

Fixing of nitrogen: ST *26*

Fizeau, Armand: experiment by, PH *118-119*

Fjords: GE *91*

Flagellates: EV *38*

Flagpole: fixed pulley atop, PH *48*

Flaps, airplane's: function of, TR *110*

Flares, solar: SP *36-37, 40, 41*

Flashbulb: magnesium, ST *71*

Flat package (FLP): CO *23*

Flatworms: acoel, EV *39*; in cave, EC *41*

Flavor enhancers: food, ST *90-91*

F layer and E layer: CO *128*

F layer of ionosphere: WE *9, 14-15*

Fleas: IN *84*; hosts, finding, IN *17*; jumping, IN *16-17*

Fleming, Sir Alexander: PL *132*

Flexors and extensors: HU *38, 39*

Flies: houseflies, AN *8-9*; bee-mimicking, AN *54, 55*; evolutionary path, IN *7*; gift giving, IN *66*; hover flies, aphids and, AN *118-119*; ocelli, effect of, IN *23*; walking on ceiling, IN *20-21*

Flight corridors for aircraft: TR *120-121*; following, TR *122-123*

Flight director (FD), aircraft's: TR *127*

Flightlessness in insects: IN *84-85*

Flight reservations: computerized, CO *96-97*

Flight simulator: CO *82-83*

Floating: PH *8-9*

Floating gobies: UN *73, 78*

Flooding of rivers: and alluvial fans, GE *30-31*; and estuaries, GE *39*; Yellow River, GE *34*

Flood plains: GE *27*; of Mississippi, GE *29*

Flood tides: and estuaries, GE *38*; South American, GE *36, 37*

Floral regions of Earth: PL *map* 118-119

Florey, Howard: PL 132

Florida, southern, U.S.: Landsat image of, CO *141*

Flotation bladders: leaves with, EC *27*

Flounders: UN *19, 130-131*

Flour: starch in, ST *100-101*

Flow (landslide): GE *103*

Flow chart: CO *53*

Flower flies: IN *144*; aphids vs., IN *144*

Flower mantises: AN *30-31*

Flowers and flowering plants: PL *50-63*; alpine meadows, EC *56-57*; alpine zone,

| Animal Behavior **AN** | Computer Age **CO** | Ecology **EC** | Evolution of Life **EV** | Geography **GE** | Human Body **HU** | Insects & Spiders **IN** | Machines & Inventions **MA** |

PL *120, 121;* animal-pollinated, EC *114-115;* appearance of, EV *102-103;* biggest (*Rafflesia arnoldii*), PL *51, 56-57;* cactus, EC *87;* day length and blooming of, PL *54-55;* extracting oils from, ST *126-127;* vs. gymnosperms, PL 8, 88; in vitro cultivation of, PL *140-141;* male and female parts, PL *51, 52-53, 58-59, 62;* medicines from, PL *132;* opening and closing of, PL *60-61;* orchids, EC *68-69;* parasites, PL *23, 51, 56-57, 82-83;* pollination, PL *8, 50, 52-53,* 56, 58, *59,* 62, 68, *69,* 84, 85, *95, 136-137;* sexes, separate, PL *58-59,* 68, 69, *83, 84-85;* structure of, PL *52-53;* sundew, EC *117;* tetraploid, PL *139; Tillandsia cyanea,* EC *94;* vegetative reproduction, PL *62, 90-91, 134-135, 140-141, 143. See also* Crop plants; Fruits; Seeds; *and individual names*

FLP (flat package): CO *23*

Flu: symptoms, HU *chart* 141; viruses, HU *141*

Fluids: *See* Gases; Liquids

Fluorescent lamps: PH 72, *73*

Flux tubes: Sun, SP *42*

Flycatchers: navigation, AN *136-137*

Flyer (Wright airplane): TR *108, 134-135*

Flying animals: EV *114-115, 130-131, 134-135;* arthropods, first, EV *54-55;* birds, evolution of, EV *68-69, 70-71, 101;* reptiles, EV 63, *90-91,* 96, 130, 134. *See also* Birds; Flying insects; *and individual names*

Flying dragon (flying lizard): AN *72-73*

Flying fish: UN *120-121, 128-129;* vision, UN *51*

Flying frog: AN *73*

Flying gecko: AN *73*

Flying insects: body structures, varying, IN *4-5;* methods used by, IN *14-15;* speeds, IN *chart* 14. *See also individual names*

Flying lemur: AN *72*

Flying squid: AN *82-83*

Flying squirrel: giant, AN *73*

Flytrap spiders: courtship, AN *90*

Flytrap, venus's: *See* Venus's-flytrap

FM vs. AM radio transmissions: MA *85*

Foams: ST *20;* from fire extinguisher, ST *69;* fire pumper's use of, TR *71*

Focal point: reflection from curved surface, PH *114-115;* in telescopes, SP 118, *119;* through lenses, PH *116, 122*

Focusing of cameras: automatic, MA *74-75;* Polaroid, MA *93*

Focus of earthquake: locating, PE *52-53;* seismic waves traveling from, PE *50-51*

Foehns: WE *44-45;* in Sicily, WE *47*

Fog: WE *70-71;* advection, WE *71;* garúa,

WE *72-73;* ice, WE *103;* and mountain halos, formation of, WE *104-105;* navigation in, TR *82-83;* radiant, WE *70;* sliding, WE *71;* South America, WE *72-73, 135;* steam, WE *71*

Fog forests: WE *72*

Fontana Dam, N.C., U.S.: power station, GE *134*

Food chain: EC 124-144, PL *124-125,* UN *126-127;* at alligator hole, EC *138-139;* biological accumulation in, EC *144;* in caves, EC *40-41;* of eagle, EC *124-125, 126-127;* estuarine, EC *140;* fish in, EC *128-129,* 144, UN *126-127;* forest cycle, EC *104-105, 124-125, 132-133, 136-137;* mushrooms in, EC *134-135;* nitrogen in, ST *27;* oil spills, effects of, EC *142;* puffer fish, effects on, UN *126-127;* savanna, EC *80-85;* sea otters in, EC *130-131*

Food, digestion of: *See* Digestion; Digestive system

Food, finding and gathering: AN *4-49;* ants, IN *42-43, 99, 138;* aphids, IN *72;* bagworm larvae, IN *102;* barbels, use of, AN *20-21;* bats, AN *42-43;* bees, IN *26-27,* 109, 134, 135; birds, AN *4-5, 16-17, 36-39, 47, 113;* butterflies and moths, IN *33;* centipedes, IN *12;* catfish, AN *20-21;* chameleons, AN *4-5, 32-33;* dragonfly nymphs, IN *36-37, 44-45;* family behavior, range of, IN *130-131;* fireflies, IN *52-53;* gift giving, IN *66-67;* glowworms, IN *50-51;* insects, AN *8-13, 30-31,* IN 36-55; loaches, AN *20-21;* locusts, IN *87;* millipedes, IN *12;* moles, AN *105;* mosquito larvae, IN *46-47;* paramecia, AN *6-7;* platypuses, AN *18-19;* praying mantises, IN *40-41;* sea anemones, AN *22, 48-49,* 71; snakes, AN *14-15, 34-35;* spiders, AN *26-29,* IN *36-37, 38-39;* spider wasps, IN *54-55;* spittlebug nymphs, IN 100, *101;* through symbiosis, AN *12-13, 22-25;* tools used for, AN *46-47;* water spiders, IN *97;* whales, AN *40-41;* wolves, AN *44-45;* wood-eating insects, IN *48-49, 130*

Food science: ST *78-101;* acidic vs. alkaline foods, ST *82-83;* apple, browning of, ST *80-81;* coffee, instant, ST *86-87;* eggs, boiled, ST *94-95;* flavor enhancers, ST *90-91;* flour, starch in, ST *100-101;* freezing rates, ST *93;* ice cream, ST *92-93;* preservation, ST *88-89;* salt reclamation from sea, ST *96-97;* water purification, ST *98-99;* yogurt, ST *84-85*

Food vacuole: paramecium, AN *7*

Forces, kinds of: PH 4; buoyancy vs. gravity, PH *4-5, 8-9, 10-11;* lift and drag in hang

gliding, PH *14, 15;* Magnus effect, PH *34, 35;* on roller coasters, PH *30-31;* on sailboats, PH *12-13;* on skiers, PH *26-27;* on surfboards, PH 38; torque, PH *32;* on train passengers, PH *28-29. See also* Electricity; Friction; Gravity; Machines, simple; Magnetism; Pressure

Forecasts, weather: WE 108, *120-121*

Forests: EC *4-5, 24-25;* acid rain and, EC *74-75;* boreal, EC *4,* 24, 29; cycle of, EC *104-105, 124-125, 132-133, 136-137;* fire, recovery from, EC *136-137;* floor of, EC *36-37, 66-67;* lichen in, EC *50;* lumber exports from, GE 124, *maps* 124-125, *125;* mushrooms in, EC *134;* near timberline, EC *54. See also* Rain forests

Forger VTOL aircraft: TR *139*

Formed elements of blood: *See* Blood cells

Formic acid: ants using, IN *123, 126, 127*

Formica vessensis (ant): IN *127*

Formula One racing cars: TR *58-59*

FORTRAN (programming language): CO *50-51;* program in, CO 51

Forward-swept wings: aircraft with, TR *142-143*

Fossil algae (stromatolites): WE *6*

Fossil fuels: coal, formation of, PE *104-105;* energy from, and thermoelectric power, PH *100-101;* and greenhouse effect, WE 136; locating deposits of, PE 98, *99;* locations of, PE 100, *101;* oil and natural gas, formation of, PE *102-103;* pollution by, WE *26, 27, 28-29*

Fossils: EV 130; ammonites, EV *94,* 98, *99;* arthropods, EV *50, 51;* birds, first, EV *68, 70;* of Burgess Shale, EV *42-43;* and continental drift, PE *26;* dating, ST *24-25;* dinosaur eggs, EV 78, *79;* dinosaurs, EV 81, 82, 83, 88; dinosaur skin, EV *96, 97;* and Earth's history, PE *94;* gaps in record, EV *115;* index fossils, PE *chart* 95; living, EV *130-131, 140-141;* mammal-like reptiles, EV *64, 73;* Precambrian, EV 26-27, 38, 39; trilobites, PE *95*

Foucault, Jean-Bernard-Léon: rotation of the earth proven by, SP *52;* speed of light, measured by PH 118, *119*

Foucault's pendulum: SP *52-53*

Four-color processes: photocopying, MA *62-63;* printing, MA *40*

Four-eyed fish: UN *50-51;* eyes, UN *45, 50, 51*

Four-wheel drive (4WD) vehicles: TR *48-49;* tires for, TR *57*

Four-wheel steering (4WS): TR *50-51*

Fovea centralis: location of, HU 108, 111

Foxes: adaptation in, EV *20-21;* bag foxes,

Planet Earth **PE** — Plant Life **PL** — Physical Forces **PH** — Structure of Matter **ST** — Space & Planets **SP** — Transportation **TR** — Underwater World **UN** — Weather & Climate **WE**

EV *139*; fennec, EC *89*; plovers' tricking of, AN *84-85*; red, EC *136*

Fractals: CO 70

Fractional distillation: ST *116-117*

France: beach, Normandy, GE *68-69*; cuestas, GE *93*; high-speed train in, TR *33*; temperature, Paris's, GE *chart* 116

Frank, Barney: MA 132

Free electrons: in conductors, PH *82, 84*; radioactive decay and, PH *90*; in semiconductors, PH *84*

Freewheel gear: bicycle's, PH *46-47*

Freeze-drying: of coffee, ST *86-87*

Freezing: ST *34, 35*; foods, ST *89, 92, 93*; temperature of, lowering, ST *40-41*; of water, PH *66-67*

Freezing waters, fish in: UN *16-17*

Freight trains: automatic air brakes, TR *10-11*; diesel-powered locomotives, TR *4-5*

Frenulum: moth's, IN *33*

Frequency modulation: CO *66*, MA *85*

Frequency of sound: PH 128, 131, *135*; and Doppler effect, PH *138*; and pitch, MA *90*; of tuning forks, PH 142

Freshwater eel: UN *11*

Freshwater fish: drinking by, vs. saltwater fish, UN *10-11*

Friction: and skiers, PH *26-27*; and static electricity, PH *70, 71*; and water flow, PH *20, 21*

Frigate birds: EC *7*

Fringefin goby: UN *127*

Fringing reefs: GE *81*

Frogfish: UN *111*

Frogs: EC *138, 139*; arrow-poison, UN *90*; desert, EC *93*; eyespots resembling, IN *118*; flying, AN *73*; gastric-brooding, Australian, UN *90-91*; marsupial, pygmy, UN *90*; poisonous, AN *66-67*; reproduction, UN *62, 63, 88-89, 91*; as snakes' prey, AN *15*; tree frogs, color changes in, AN *56-57*

Frog's-bits: EC *27*; flotation system, EC *27*

Front-loading washing machine: MA *113*

Fronts: WE *84, 86, 87*; Antarctica, WE *122*; and cloud formation, WE *59, 60, 61*; and downpours, WE *88, 89, 133*; occluded, WE *87*; stationary, WE *120-121*; on weather maps, WE *118-119, 120-121*

Fruit bats: as pollinators, EC *114*

Fruit flies: mutations in, EV *14*

Fruits: PL *8, 64-65*; baobab, PL *117*; coconuts, PL *86-87*; coloration of, PL *78-79*; corn, PL *84-85*; cucumbers, PL *30, 77*; figs, PL *67, 68-69*; flowers' making of, PL *66-67, 68-69*; popping open of, PL *76-77*; simple vs. complex, PL *66-67*; squash, PL *58*. *See also* Crop plants; Seeds

Fruit seeds: dispersal of, EC 122

Fuji, Mount, Japan: GE *22-23*, WE *24, 25*; cap cloud, WE *68*; radar antenna, WE *115*

Fulcrum: lever's, PH *42, 43*

Full adder: half-adder vs., CO *28, 29*

Fulton, Robert: paddle steamer built by (*Clermont*), TR *90-91*

Fundamental tone: PH *134, 137*

Fungi: PL *96-97*; in cave, EC *40*; and decomposition, EC *132, 133*, PL *126*; in lichens, PL *106, 107*; mushrooms, EC *50, 134-135*, PL *92-93, 95, 98-99, 126*; as penicillin source, PL *132-133*

Fungiform papillae: HU *118*

Fungus gnats: IN *51*; larvae, IN *50-51*

Fungus-growing insects: IN 49; leaf-cutter ants, IN *138-139*; termites, IN *48, 142-143*

Funicular cable car system: TR *31*

Funnel cloud in tornado formation: WE 50, *51*

Funnel weavers (spider): IN *94*

Funnel webs, spiders': IN *38*

Fur seals: reproduction by, UN *92-93*

Fusion, nuclear: ST *16-17*; on Earth, SP *45*; stars, SP *76, 92*; Sun, SP 40, *44-45*

G

Gabbro as layer of crust: PE *32, 89*

Galápagos Islands: albatrosses, courtship of, AN *102*; animals, EC *6-7, 113, 119*, EV *12-13, 80*; plants, EC *119*

Galaxies: SP *98*; evolution of, SP *108-109, 112-113*; groups of, SP *102, 110-111, graph* 115; infant, quasars as, SP 112, *113*; recession of, SP *98, 114-115*; shapes of, SP *103*; spiral, SP *89, 98-99, 103, 106-107*. *See also* Milky Way

Galaxy clusters: SP *110-111*; Local Group, SP *102, 110-111*; recession of, SP *graph* 115

Galileo Galilei: PH 28, SP 116; experiment by, PH *29*

Galley, Blasco de: steamboat built by, TR *91*

Gallows phone: Bell's, MA *10-11*

Gall aphids: AN *13*

Galls and gall aphids: AN *13*

Galvanizing of metal: ST *63*

Galvanometers: PH *76, 96*; Thomson's, MA *9*

Games: computer, CO *78-79*

Gametophytes: *See* Spore-bearing plants

Gamma decay: PH *91*

Gamma field: PL *138-139*

Gamma rays: Sun's production of, SP *40, 44*

Ganges River dolphins: UN *58, 59*

Ganglia, human: spinal, HU *101, 103*

Ganglia, insect: IN *8-9*

Gannets: northern, EC *32*

Garden crickets: Oriental, AN *97*

Gardeners: orange-crested, bower of, AN *101*

Garden spiders: web use, AN *28, 29*

Garter snakes: life of, EC *12-13*

Garúa (fog): WE *72-73*

Gas, natural, and oil: formation of, PE *102-103*; in reservoir rocks, PE *103*

Gas, poisonous: beetles' use of, IN *122-123*

Gas bladder: UN *12-13*; for hearing, UN *52, 53*; and pressure, UN 23

Gases: atmospheric, ST *25, 26-27, 36-37, 76-77*; and buoyancy, ST *46-47*; in colloids, ST *20*; exhaust, ST 60, 61, 74, *chart* 75; in fluorescent lamps, PH *72, 73*; lighter-than-air, PH *10*; vs. liquids and solids, determinants of, ST *44-45*; phase changes, ST *38, 39*; pressure, temperature, and volume of, PH *11*; water as, ST *32-33, 34, 35. See also* Air; Water vapor

Gas exchange in lungs: HU *56-57, 65*

Gas jets: at galactic center, SP *104*; from quasar, SP *113*

Gasoline: combustion in car engine, ST *60-61*; production, ST *117*

Gasoline tractor combine: MA *14-15*

Gas-pressure sensors: MA *120*

Gastric-brooding frogs: Australian, UN *90-91*

Gastric glands and juices: HU *82-83*

Gastrin cells and gastrin: HU *83*

Gastropods: abalone, UN *98*; conch, UN *35*; cone shells, UN *118-119*; escape from starfish, UN *139*; in food chain, UN *126, 127*; limpet, UN *138-139*; mud snail, giant, UN *98*; whelk, UN *127*

Gastroscope: MA *138-139*

Gas-type planets vs. rock-type planets: SP *7, 28-29*

Gates, logic: CO *21, 28*; in adder circuits, CO *28, 29*

Gatun Locks, Panama Canal: ship passing through, TR *92-93*

Gazelles: EC *10*; Indian, EC *11*; springboks, AN *60-61*; Thompson's, EC *82*

Gearbox: hydrofoil's, TR *95*

Gear ratios: bicycle's, PH *46, charts* 46

Gears, automobile: differential, TR *41, 49*; planetary, TR *47*; shifting, TR *46*; transfer, in optional 4WD, TR *49*; viscous coupling, TR *49*

Gears, bicycle: PH *46-47*

Geckos: flying, AN *73*

Geese: feathers of, PH *60*

Geiger counters: PH *91*; use of, PE *57*; working of, PH *90, 91*

Animal Behavior
AN

Computer Age
CO

Ecology
EC

Evolution of Life
EV

Geography
GE

Human Body
HU

Insects & Spiders
IN

Machines &
Inventions **MA**

Gemmules: sponge, UN *101*

Gene bank: field, PL *143*

General circulation of atmosphere: WE *34-35, 36-37, 112-113*, 124, *134*; and jet streams, WE *38, 53*

General Sherman (sequoia): PL 122

Generators, electrical: MA *28-29. See also* Electricity, generating

Genes: blood-type, HU *chart* 71; chromosomes carrying, HU *8-9, 11, 14-15*

Genetic resources and genetic diversity: PL 131, *142-143*

Genetics: and breeding of animals, EV 10, 11; and breeding of plants, PL 136, *138-139*; and differentiation, EV 22; laws of, Mendel and, EV *13*; and mutations, EV *14-15*

Genji fireflies: AN *93*

Gentians: opening and closing of, PL *61*

Geochemical surveys: PE *99*

Geography: GE entire volume

Geoid: Earth as, PE *17*

Geologic surveys: PE 98; improved, PE *98-99*

Geology: PE entire volume

Geomagnetism: *See* Magnetism

Geostationary orbit: CO *128-129*

Geostationary satellites: CO *128-129*, PH 37, WE *11, 94, 110-111*, 117

Geothermal power: generation of, PH *102-103*

Geothermal (hot) springs: PE *12, 82-83*; distribution, PE *map* 83

Geotropism: PL *15*

Gerenuk: EC *84*

Germany, trains in: Intercity Express (ICE), TR *33*; maglevs, TR *34, 35*; monorail, TR *29*

Germination: PL *8, 12-13, 79*, 80, *81, 88, 95*; algae, PL *102*; mosses, PL *109*

Germs: *See* Infectious diseases

Geysers: PE *80-81*, PH 102

Ghawar oil field, Saudi Arabia: PE *102*

Giant flying squirrel: AN *73*

Giant mud snail: UN *98*

Giant purple butterfly: IN *31*

Giant silkworm moth: antennae of, IN *32*; mating, AN *94-95*

Giant squid: sperm whale attacking, AN *40-41*

Giant stars, red: *See* Red giants

Giant water bug: IN *75*

Gibbons: AN *140-141*, EC *70, 71*

Gift giving by male insects: IN *66-67*

Gill arches: UN *9*; evolution of, EV *48-49*

Gill chambers: gill bailers in, crabs', UN *36*; mudskippers', UN *28*

Gill cover (operculum): UN *8*

Gill rakers: UN *9, 106*

Gill respirators, upper: climbing perch's, UN *29*

Gills: aquatic insects with, IN *10*; breathing through, UN *8-9, 36-37*; of conch, bacteria in, UN *35*; crabs' use of, UN *36-37*; and osmosis, UN *10, 11*; "physical gill," IN *11*; tadpoles', UN *88*

Ginkgoes: EV *102, 141*

Ginsburg's gobies: AN *87*

Giraffes: EC *21, 83, 85*; in Lamarck's theory, EV *13*

Glaciation: WE *map* 144; and tundra plants, PL *120-121*

Glacier midges: IN *34*; larvae, IN *35*

Glaciers: GE 24, *52-53*; Columbia Icefield, GE *24-25*; continental drift and, PE *26*; Finland, effect on, GE *66-67*; and fjord formation, GE *91*; formation of, GE *42-43*; Great Lakes formed by, GE *48-49*; in ice ages, EV *128*; landforms created by, GE *44-45, 46-47*; melting, possible, effects of, GE *72-73*; Pleistocene glaciations, GE *charts* 50, *maps* 51

Gladiolus: PL *91*

Glands, human: HU *74-75*; Bowman's, HU *117*; intestinal, HU *88, 90*; lymph nodes, HU *90, 130-131*; pancreas, HU *75, 84-85, 142-143*; salivary, HU *78, 79, 118*; sebaceous, HU *44, 47*; in stomach, HU *82-83*; sweat, HU *42-43, 44, 45*

Glands, insect: exocrine, of ant, IN *43*

Glass: making of, ST *122-123*; uses for, ST *124-125*

Glassblowing: ST *123*

Glass-break sensors: MA *114*

Glide-path indicator in airport's ILS (instrument landing system): TR 126, 127

Gliders (aircraft): TR *118-119*; and flying fish, similarities of, UN *129*

Gliders, hang: PH *14-15*

Gliding animals: AN *72-73*; flying fish, UN *128-129*; flying squid, AN *82-83*; pygmy glider, EC *114*; sugar glider, EC *16*

Global Positioning System (GPS) satellites: TR 84

Global warming: GE 72, 73, WE *136, 137*, 138

Globefish: egg laying by, AN *123*

Globes: Martin Behaim's, GE *14*

Glowworms: IN *50-51*

Glucose in blood: HU *142*, 143

Glucose molecules: from photosynthesis, ST *66*; in starch, ST *100-101*

Glutamic acid: production of, ST *90-91*

Glycoprotein and freezing point: UN 16, *chart* 16

Glyptodon (extinct mammal): EV *120*

Gnathostomes: evolution of, EV *48-49*

Gnats: fungus, IN *51*; larvae, IN *50-51*

Gneiss (rock): PE *7, 87*

Gnu: EC *84*

Gobi Desert, China-Mongolia: effect of ice ages on, GE *51*; oasis in, GE *63*

Gobies: AN *86-87*; floating, UN *73, 78*; fringefin, UN *127*; as prey of cone shell, UN *118-119*

Goblet cells: HU *88, 140*

Goblin sharks: UN *22-23*

Goddard, Robert H.: MA *26*

Gold: PE *101*

Gold beds: woodpeckers', AN *16*

Gold-belly clownfish: UN *62, 67*

Golden bowerbird: Newton's, bower of, AN *101*

Golden cats: African, EC *10*; Indian, EC *11*

Goldenrod: EC *98*

Golden-striped grouper: UN *126*

Golden web spiders: IN *94-95*

Goldfish: wild, EV *18, 23*

Gold leaf: ST *29*

Golf: computer analysis of, CO *137*

Golgi apparatus: PL *6, 7*

Gomphotherium (elephant ancestor): EV *110*

Gondola: blimp's, TR *117*

Goodyear, Charles: ST 30

Goose: feathers of, PH *60*

Goose bumps: HU *44-45*

Goosefish: UN *102-103, 110-111*

Gorillas: mountain, EC *112*

Gossamer-winged butterfly: IN *31*

Gouramis: bubble nests made by, UN *79*; dwarf, UN *64*

Gourds: grafting onto, PL *135*; leaf growth in, PL *17*; root pressure in, PL *21*

GPS (Global Positioning System) satellites: TR 84

Graded-index optical fibers: CO *125*

Grafting: PL *134-135*

Grain harvesting: combines for, MA *14-15*

Grain production: GE *122-123*

Grains: PL *144*; corn as, PL *84-85, 136-137*; rice, PL *67, 139*; wheat, PL *55, 67, 144*

Gramme, Zénobe-Théophile: generator built by, MA *29*

Grana in chloroplasts: PL *10-11*

Grand Canyon, Ariz., U.S.: GE *84-85, 94-95*, PE *94*

Granite in Earth's crust: PE *10, 88*; erosion of, PE *92*

Granodiorite (rock): PE *88*

Granules: photosphere, SP *41*

Granulocytes: HU *6, 128*; development of, HU *67*

Grapes: PL *67*; growing, GE *136-137*; roots, GE *137*; tendrils on plants, PL *29*, 30

Planet Earth
PE

Plant Life
PL

Physical Forces
PH

Structure of Matter
ST

Space & Planets
SP

Transportation
TR

Underwater World
UN

Weather & Climate
WE

Graphics, computer: CO *70-83*; automobile design, CO *74-75*; face, image of, CO *72-73*; flight simulator, CO *82-83*; games, CO *78-79*; maps, CO *76-77*; special effects, CO *80-81*; from word-processing programs, CO *59*

Graphite vs. diamonds: PE *chart* 90; diamonds synthesized from, ST *132, chart* 133

Grasses: bamboo, PL *32-33, 91*; flowers, PL *62-63*; *Oplismenus, PL 75*; pampas, Japanese, PL *73. See also* Grains

Grass guppies: UN *65*

Grasshoppers: AN *52, 53*; anatomy, IN *8-9*; egg laying, IN *130*; evolutionary path, IN *7*; head, IN *4*; metamorphosis, IN *56-57, 80-81*; ocelli, effect of, IN *22-23*; sound production, IN *28*; swarming, IN *86-87*

Grasslands: EC *76-77*; Alpine meadows, EC *56-57*; fires, effects of, EC *78-79*; marshes, EC *138-139, 140*; savannas (African), EC *29, 76, 80-85*, GE *113*

Grass snakes: AN *15*

Gravitational interactions with Earth: and precession, SP *60-61*; and tides, PE *128,* SP *73*

Gravitational lens: SP *95*

Gravity: PH *4, 6*; vs. buoyancy, in air, PH *4-5, 10-11*; vs. buoyancy, in water, PH *8-9*; center of, ship's, PH *9*; center of, top's, PH *32, 33*; detecting ore deposits with, PE *98*; Earth's, variations in, PE *17, 18-19*; escape of, by three-stage rocket, PH *18-19*; and inclined plane, PH *44*; vs. inertia, PH *28, 29,* 30, 31, *37*; lift vs., in hang gliding, PH *14, 15*; lunar, and tides, PE *128*; and skiers, PH *26-27*; viscosity vs., and whirlpool formation, PH *20*; volcano's, measuring, PE *79*; and weight, PH *6-7*

Gravity waves: SP *95*

Gravity wells: PH *7*

Gravure (intaglio) printing: MA 40, *41*

Grayling butterfly: AN *65*

Gray whales: AN *41*; migration of, UN *94-95*

Great Barrier Reef, Australia: GE *80-81*

Great circles: GE *17, 21*

Great Dark Spot, Neptune: SP *27*

Greater horseshoe bat: AN *42-43*

Great Lakes, Canada-U.S.: formation of, GE *48-49*

Great Mazarin (galaxy): SP *103*

Great Plains, Canada-U.S.: GE *29*; wheat crop, GE *123*

Great Red Spot, Jupiter: SP *14-15, 16*

Great Rift Valley, Africa: PE *22-23*; formation of, PE *40-41*

Great white sharks: UN *104*

Grebes: crested, courtship of, AN *102*; food chain of, EC *144*

Greek abacus: CO *7*

Green algae: PL *105*

Green bean seeds: germination of, PL *12-13*

Green heron: AN *36-37*

Greenhouse effect: GE *73*, WE *136-137*; in cities, WE *139*; Venus, SP *11*

Greenhouse gases: buildup of, GE *73*; in primitive atmosphere, WE *6*

Greenland: gneiss formations in, PE *7*

Greenstone: PE *87*

Greenwich, England: prime meridian at, GE *21*

Grinding pads: platypus, AN *19*

Grizzled mantis: AN *31*

Gromwell: callus culture of, PL *140*

Ground bees: nests of, IN *108-109*

Ground beetles: walking method of, IN *12*

Ground moraine: GE *46*

Ground subsidence: GE *64-65*

Ground water: GE *54*; and caverns, GE *54-55, 59, 60-61*; landscape shaped by, GE *58-59*; movement of, gravity and, GE *56-57*; and oases, GE *62-63*; overpumping of, and subsidence, GE *64-65*

Groupers: with cleaner wrasses, UN *120, 134-135*; crab's protection from, UN *136*; golden-striped, UN *126*; tail of, UN *20*

Growth rings: on fish's scales, UN *7*; tree trunk's, PL *18-19, 24-25*

Grunions: egg laying by, AN *122-123*

Guard cells: stomas', PL *39*

Guidance system, automatic: V-2 rocket's, MA *27*

Guilin, China: tower karst of, GE *59*

Gulf Stream: WE *126, 127*; whirlpool formation in, PE *122-123*

Gulls: EC *7, 29, 33*; black-headed, courtship of, AN *103*

Gulpers: UN *22, 112-113*

Gum (eucalyptus) trees: PL *118-119, 122*

Guppies: reproduction by, UN *64-65*

Gurnard: UN *47*

Gustatory nerves: HU *118, 119*

Gutenberg, Johannes: MA *7*; printing method of, MA *6-7*

Gutenberg Bible: MA *7*

Guyots: PE *115*

Gymnosperms: EV *102*; vs. angiosperms, PL 8, *88*; cycads, PL *59. See also* Conifers

Gyoki Bosatsu: map by, GE *15*

Gyres (circular currents): GE *70, 71*, PE *118, 119, map* 120-121, *132*

Gyroaccelerometer: V-2 rocket's, MA *27*

Gyrocompass: TR *80*

Gyroscope: PH *32*; in aircraft's INS (inertial navigation system), TR *124*

H

Habitats: EC *28-29*; Australian, EC *chart* 16; caves, EC *28, 38-43*; estuarine, EC *34, 140-141*; mountain, EC *52-57*; recolonization, EC *120-121*; wetlands, EC *138-139, 140, map* 141. *See also* Biomes

Hackers: computer crime by, CO *106-107*

Hadley cells: WE *34-35, 36-37, 38, 112*

Hadrosaurs: *Maiasaura*, EV *83; Parasaurolophus*, EV *76, 85*

Hail: cause of, WE *74, 75*; electricity produced in clouds by, WE *66, 67*

Hair and hair follicles, human: HU *46, 47*; standing up, HU *44-45*; sweat glands near, HU *43*; touch detection by, HU *99*

Hair cells: HU *114, 115*

Hair grass: Antarctic, EC *45*

Hairs, sensory: flies, AN 8, *9*; moths, IN *26*; praying mantises, IN *40*

Hairstreak butterflies: IN *32, 33, 78*; purple, IN *74*

Haleakala (extinct volcano), Hawaii, U.S.: PE *45*

Hale telescope, Mount Palomar, Calif., U.S.: SP *118-119*

Half-adder circuit: CO 28, *29*

Halfbeak: UN *105*

Halley, Edmond: SP *90*

Halley's comet: SP *32-33*

Halos: mountain, WE *104-105*; solar and lunar, WE *102-103*

Hamlets: reproduction by, UN *68-69*

Hammer jaw: UN *69*

Hammerschlag, Freddi: PL *143*

Hands, human: fingers as sensitive surfaces, HU *98, 100, 102-103*; palms, sweating of, HU *43*

Hands, robotic: CO *98*

Hang gliders: PH *14-15*

Haptonasty: PL *44, 45*

Harbor seals: UN *92, 93*

Hard disks and disk drives: CO *36-37, 57*

Harems: blackspot angelfish, UN *66-67*; fur seals, UN *93*

Hares: jack rabbit, EC *127*; Smith's red rock, EC *21*; snowshoe, seasonal color changes in, AN *58-59*

Harrier jet: TR *138-139*

Harvesting of grain: combines for, MA *14-15*

Hatchetfish: UN *23*

Haustoria (parasitic roots): PL *23, 57, 83*

Hawaii, U.S.: formation of, PE *44-45*; ocean wave, PE *108-109*; tsunami damage to, PE *59*; volcanically extinct islands, PE *77*; volcanic lava, makeup of, PE *chart* 65; volcanoes, PE *45, 62, 64, 68, 78, 79*

Hawaiian type of volcanic eruptions: PE *66*

Animal Behavior
AN

Computer Age
CO

Ecology
EC

Evolution of Life
EV

Geography
GE

Human Body
HU

Insects & Spiders
IN

Machines &
Inventions **MA**

Hawk moths: as day fliers, IN *32*; ear, IN *24*; flying speed, IN *chart* 14

Hay fever: HU *134-135*

HDE226868 (star): SP *94-95*

Head butting: bighorn sheep, AN *106-107*

Head (coma) of comet: SP *32-33*

Heads, insect: IN *4-5, 22*; mosquito larva, IN *46*; praying mantis, IN *5, 22, 40*

Hearing, sense of: barn owls, AN 38, 39; carp, UN *44*; crickets, IN *28*; fish, UN *52-53*; humans, HU *112-113*; insects, IN *24-25*; sharks, UN 55

Hearing aids: computerized, CO *139*

Heart, animal: amphibian vs. reptile, EV *59*; insects, IN *8*

Heart, human: HU *52-53, 60*, MA *132*; beating of, HU *60-61, 68-69*; and blood pressure, HU *68-69*, MA 130; computerized assistance for, CO *138-139*; current fluctuations, EKGs of, MA *136-137*; disease of, HU *144*; fetus's, ultrasound monitoring of, MA 142; listening to, stethoscope for, MA 144; mechanical, MA *132-133*; muscle, HU *7, 60, 144*; pacemaker for, MA 133; rate, lie detector's measurement of, MA *36*

Heart attack: HU *144*

Heart-lung machine: CO *139*

Heartwood: formation of, PL 24

Heat: combustion and, ST 66, 67, 68; conductivity, PH *chart* 61; and electrons in fireworks, ST *50-51*; extreme, measuring, PH *56-57*; geothermal energy, PH *102-103*; and kinetic energy, ST *34, 35*; loss of, insulation against, PH *60-61*; in nuclear reactor, PH *109*; and phase changes, PH *22-23, 52-53, 54-55, 62-63*; reducing, in extinguishing fire, ST 68; of rocket fuel's combustion, ST *chart* 74; in sauna, effects of, PH *64-65*; shape-memory alloys and, ST *128-129, 140*; solar, as power source, PH 110, *111*; spreading of, in fluids, PH *58-59*; in thermoelectric plant, PH *100-101*; water vapor's transfer of, PH 64

Heat, internal, of Earth: PE *12-13*; and plate tectonics, PE *28, 29*

Heat adaptation: desert animals', EC *88-89*

Heat balance map: WE *34*

Heat energy vs. thermal energy: PH 52

Heating: of air, PH *10-11*; convection by, PH *58-59*; in steamer, PH *65*

Heat island: WE *138-139*

Heat-pump-type air conditioner: MA *122*

Heat-sensitive devices: MA *120-121*; in fire alarms, MA 64, *65*; in thermometer, MA *128*

Heat sensors (pit organs), rattlesnakes': AN *34*; mouse as sensed by, AN 35

Heat transfer: WE *20, 21*; in atmospheric circulation, WE *34-35*, 124; by ocean currents, WE 126, 127; by water vapor, PH *64*

Heavy oil: ST *117*

Heeling operation: icebreaker's, TR *100*

Heike fireflies: AN *92*

Heliconius butterflies: AN *69*

Helicopters: TR *109, 114-115*

Helium: in blimps, use of, ST *46-47*; formation of, in fusion reactions, ST *16-17*; in history of universe, SP *108, 109, 113*; hydrogen conversion to, in Sun, SP 40, *44-45, 46-47*

Helper T cells: HU *128, 129, 131*; and AIDS virus, HU *136-137*

Heme: HU 72, *73*

Hemichordate: EV *46*

Hemicyclaspis (extinct fish): EV *46*

Hemlock trees: decomposition of, EC *132-133*

Hemodialysis machine: CO *139*

Hemoglobin: HU 64, 72; and carbon monoxide, HU 72, *73*

Henodus (early reptile): EV *62*

Hepatic lobules: HU *86-87*

Herbivores: of Africa, EC *80-85*

Herculaneum and Pompeii (ancient cities), Italy: destruction of, PE *74-75*

Hercules (constellation): SP *61*

Hercules beetles: IN *60, 61*

Herd animals: warning signals by, AN *60-61*

Heredity: HU 10; of blood types, HU *chart* 71; chromosomes, HU *8-9, 11, 14-15*

Hermaphroditic plants: techniques of, PL *59*

Hermaphroditism in fish: UN *62-63, 66-67, 68-69*

Hermit crabs: new shells, finding, AN *76-77*; and sea anemones, AN *78-79*

Herniated disks: HU 40, *41*

Herons: EC *138, 139, 140*; green, AN *36-37*

Herrings: round, mouth of, UN *106*; sardines, UN *102, 106-107*; swimming type, UN *19, 21*

Hertzsprung-Russell diagram: SP *chart* 79

Hesperornis (bird): EV *100*; skeleton, EV *101*

Heterodontosaurus (dinosaur): EV *74*

Heterosis (hybrid vigor): PL 136, 137

Hibernation: bats, EC *39*; garter snakes, EC *12*

High blood pressure: effects of, HU *69*

High-definition television: MA *78-79*

High-level vacuum: pump producing, MA *44-45*

High pressure: WE *40, 41, 82, 84-85*; belts, WE *34-35, 37, 134*; cold systems, WE 85; and deserts, WE 134; forecast map, WE *120, 121*; jet streams and, WE *39, 88*; migratory vs. stationary systems, WE *85*; Pacific, WE *85, 88, 93, 133*; Sea of Okhotsk, WE *133*; warm systems, WE 85; Yugoslavia, WE 48

High-speed printing press: MA *40-41*

High-speed trains: TR *32-33*; bullet trains, TR *4-5, 33*

Hill, James J.: quoted, TR 18

Hiller, Lejaren: *Illiac Suite for String Quartet*, CO 66, 67

Hilo harbor, Hawaii, U.S.: tsunami damage to, PE *59*

Himalayan cedar cones: PL *89*

Himalayas (mountains), Asia: PE *36*; formation of, PE *11, 36, 49*, 101; and gravity, PE *19*; and limestone deposit, PE *101*; rivers crossing, GE *98-99*

Hinge joint: HU *38*

Hip joint: HU *38*

Hippopotamuses: pygmy, EC *21*

Histamine: release of, HU *135*

History of computers: CO *4-15*; abacuses and counting stones, CO *4-5, 6-7*; calculators, seventeenth-century, CO *4-5, 8-9*; first computer, Babbage's, CO 4, *10-11*; first electronic computer, CO 4, *14-15*, 84; first supercomputer, CO *15*; Hollerith's contribution, CO *12-13*

HIV (human immunodeficiency virus): HU *136*

Hognose snakes: bluffing, AN *85*

Hoists: PH *49*

Hokkaido (island), Japan: sand spit on, GE *75*

Holes in semiconductors: PH *84, 85*

Hollerith, Herman: CO *13*; invention, CO *12-13*

Holograms: PH *124-125*

Hominids: EV *105, 124, 125, 126-127*

Homo erectus (extinct hominid): EV *126, 127*

Homo habilis (extinct hominid): EV *125, 126*

Homologous structures: EV *130-131, 134-135*

Homology and analogy: PL *29*

Homopolymers vs. copolymers: ST *106-107*

Homo sapiens (human species): EV *126, 127*; skeleton, EV *105*

Honeybees: AN 125, *130*; drones' roles, AN *130-131*; and mimics, AN *54*; workers' roles, AN *128-129, 131*. *See also* Bees

Honeycomb: cells of, IN *70-71, 132-133*

Honeycomb spider: Australian, AN *27*

Honeydew: aphids' production of, AN *12*

Planet Earth
PE

Plant Life
PL

Physical Forces
PH

Structure of Matter
ST

Space & Planets
SP

Transportation
TR

Underwater World
UN

Weather & Climate
WE

Honey eaters: white-cheeked, EC *114*

Honey-pot ants: IN *138*

Honshu (island), Japan: mountain on, GE *22-23*; tsunami hitting, PE *map* 59

Hooke, Robert: Hooke's law, PH *50*

Horizons of soil: EC *37*

Horizontal canard: CCV's, TR *141*

Hormones, human, glands producing: HU *74-75*; islets of Langerhans, HU *75, 84, 85, 142-143*

Hormones, insect: and pupation, IN 82

Horned dinosaurs: EV *78-79, 88-89*

Horned toads: Asian, AN *51, 52*

Hornets, black: stinging by, IN *124*

Hornfels: PE *87, 92*

Hornito: UN *34*

Horns: beetles' use of, IN *60-61*; bighorn sheep, AN *107*; dinosaurs, EV *78-79, 88-89*; glacial, GE *44*

Horntails: IN *124*

Horse-drawn combine: MA *14*; area harvested by, MA *14-15*

Horsehead nebula: SP *87*

Horses: ancestors of, EV *106, 108-109*; modern, EV *109, 121*; wild, EC *113*

Horseshoe bats: EC *38-39*; greater, AN *42-43*

Horsetails: PL *94, 95*

Hot-air balloons: PH *4-5, 10-11*

Hot dip galvanizing, continuous: ST *63*

Hot spots: mantle, volcanoes formed by, PE *44-45, 76, 77*

Hot springs: PE *12, 82-83*; distribution of, PE *map* 83; geysers, PE *80-81*

Hot-water vents (black smokers): UN 34, *35*

Houseflies: food, finding, AN *8-9*; ocelli, effect of, IN *23*; walking on ceiling, IN *20-21*

Household network in smart house: CO *105*

House mosquitoes: IN *46-47*

Houses: computer-run, CO *104-105*

Hovercraft: TR *78, 96-97*

Hover flies and aphids: AN *118-119*

Howler monkeys: EC *71*

Hubble, Edwin P.: SP *114*

Hubble's law: SP 114, *graph* 115

Hubble Space Telescope: SP *124*

Hulls, Jonathan: steam-driven tugboat patented by, TR *91*

Hull tanks for ships: use of, PH *9*

Human body: HU entire volume

Human immunodeficiency virus (HIV): HU *136*

Humanoid robot: hypothetical, CO *98-99*

Humans: ancestors of, EV *105, 124-125, 126*; arms, EV *130-131, 135*; ear bones, EV *135*; early development of, EV *133*; evolution affected by, EV *142-143, 144*;

evolution of, EV *126-127*

Humans vs. computers: CO *68-69*; brain, CO *44-45*; organs, CO *138-139*; speech production, CO *60-61*; speech recognition, CO *62-63*

Humboldt (Peru) Current: WE *127*; and garúa, WE *72-73*

Humidity control: dehumidifier for, MA *124-125*

Humidity in sauna: effect of, PH *64-65*

Hummingbirds: EC *60-61, 114, 115*

Humpback whales: AN *40*

Hundred Dishes (terraced pools), Akiyoshi Cave, Japan: GE *54-55*

Hunting wasps and nests: IN *54-55, 92-93, 110-111*

Hurricanes and typhoons: WE *82-83, 90*; cause of, WE *90-91*; development of, WE *92-93*; eye of, WE *91, 92, chart* 93, *95, 115*; observing, WE *94-95, 115*; storm tides and waves caused by, PE *130-131*; zones, WE *map* 91

Huygens, Christiaan: MA 13

Hybrid plants: PL *136-137, 142*

Hydras: AN *48*

Hydrated cement: ST *120*

Hydraulic cylinder: on climbing crane, MA *52-53*

Hydraulic systems: TR 66; climbing crane's, MA *52-53*; standard crane's, TR *73*; power shovel's, TR *76, 77*

Hydrochloric acid: formation of, ST *99*; stomach cells secreting, HU *83*

Hydroelectric power plant: PH *98-99*

Hydrofoils: TR *79, 94-95*

Hydrogen: ST *6, 7*; vs. antihydrogen, ST *22-23*; buoyancy of, ST *46*; fusion of, ST *17*; in history of universe, SP *108, 109, 113*; Jupiter's, SP *15, 17, 28*; Jupiter's absorption pattern, SP *29*; as rocket fuel, PH *18*, ST *74, 75*; size of atoms, relative, ST *8, 9*; Sun's conversion to helium, SP 40, *44-45, 46-47*; in water molecules, PH *54-55*

Hydrogenation refining device: ST *117*

Hydrophilic and hydrophobic components of soap molecules: ST 48, 49

Hydroplaning: treadless vs. treaded tires and, TR *56*

Hydro-rods: hovercraft's use of, TR *97*

Hydrothermal deposits: PE *100, 101, 106-107*

Hydroxide ions: ST *56*

Hydroxyl groups in cellulose molecules: ST *104, 105*

Hyenas: EC *82*

Hylaeosaurus (dinosaur): EV *75*

Hylonomus (early reptile): EV *58, 62*

Hyoid: woodpeckers, AN *17*

Hyperfusion filter: CO *139*

Hypermetamorphosis: IN *81*

Hyperopia (farsightedness): HU 110, *111*

Hypertension: possible effects of, HU *69*

Hyphae: EC *134, 135*

Hypochlorite ion: ST *76*

Hypocotyl: PL *12-13*

Hypothalamus: HU *74*; and goose bumps, HU *45*; and sweating, HU *42*

Hypsilophodon (dinosaur): EV *74*

Hyracotherium (horse ancestor): EV *106, 108*

H zones: HU *36*

I

Ibis: Japanese crested, EC *113*

Icaronycteris (bat ancestor): EV 114, *115*

Icarosaurus (early reptile): EV *63*

IC chips: *See* Integrated circuits

Ice: crystals, ST *39, 41, 93*, WE 102, *103*; dry ice, ST 38, *39, 40*; formation of, PH *66-67*; freezing point, lowering of, ST *40-41*; insects living in, IN *34-35*; molecular structure of, ST *34, 35*; and optical phenomena, WE *102-103*; phase change in, heat and, PH *52-53, 54-55*; skating on, PH 26, *27*

Ice ages: EV *chart* 129, GE 50, *charts* 50, *maps* 51, WE 142, *chart* 143; and Alpine habitats, EC 52, *53, maps* 57; animal life in, EV *128-129*; cause of, WE *144*; vs. interglacial periods, effect of, on deserts, GE *51, 106-107*; melting after, and estuaries, GE *38*; survivors of, EV *141*; and tundra plants, PL *120-121*

Icebreakers: TR *100-101*

Icecaps, polar: GE *52-53*; changes in, effect of, on deserts, GE *106-107*; Mars, SP *12*; melting, possibility of, GE *72-73*

Ice cream: making of, ST *92-93*

Ice fish: EC 46, *47*

Ice fog: WE *103*

Ice sheets: *See* Glaciers

Ice worms: IN *35*

Ichneumon: IN *124*

Ichthyornis (primitive bird): EV *101*

Ichthyosaurs: EV *136-137*; belemnites eaten by, EV *95*; *Mixosaurus*, EV *62*; vs. plesiosaurs, EV *92*; reproduction, EV *93*; skin, EV *96*; *Stenopterygius*, EV *92*

Ichthyostega (early amphibian): EV *57*

Icing: WE *80-81*

IC logic cards: MA *60-61*

Iconoscope: MA 22, *23*

Idea leuconoe (caterpillar): IN *121*

Identical twins: HU *22*

Animal Behavior
AN

Computer Age
CO

Ecology
EC

Evolution of Life
EV

Geography
GE

Human Body
HU

Insects & Spiders
IN

Machines &
Inventions **MA**

Igneous rocks: classification of, PE *88-89*; columnar basalt, PE *84-85*; cycle of, PE 93; extrusive vs. intrusive, PE *87, 89*; formation of, PE 86

Ignition coil, automobile's: role of, TR *41*

Iguanas: Galápagos, EC *6*, EV *12, 13, 80*; land, EC *6, 113*

Iguanodon (dinosaur): EV *74-75*

Ijssel, Lake, the Netherlands: GE *133*

Illiac Suite for String Quartet (Hiller and Isaacson): CO 66, 67

Illness: HU 126; atherosclerosis, HU *144*; cancer, HU *138-139*; carbon monoxide poisoning, HU *72-73*; diabetes, HU *142-143*; hay fever, HU *134-135*; heart attack, HU *144*; hypertension, possible effects of, HU *69*. See also Infectious diseases

Illustrations: electronic publishing of, CO *94-95*; faxing, CO *114-115*. See also Graphics, computer

ILS (instrument landing system) for aircraft: TR *126-127*

Imitation: *See* Mimicry

Immune globulin E: HU 134, *135*

Immune system: HU *126, 128-129*; cancer and, HU *139*; destruction of, by AIDS, HU 136, *137*; and hay fever, HU *134-135*

Immunity: HU *126-129*; natural, HU 132

Immunizations: HU *133*

Impact craters: *See* Craters

Impact printers: CO 38; dot-matrix, CO *38-39*

Impulse turbine: PH *99*

Inarching: PL *135*

Inbreeding of corn: PL *136-137*

Incandescent bulb: working of, PH *72-73*

Incisors: HU *26*

Inclined planes: PH *44-45*

Incomplete vs. complete metamorphosis: IN *56-57, 80-81*

Index fossils: PE *chart* 95

India: EC *map* 11; animals of, EC 10, *11*; collision of, with Asia, GE *98-99*; equatorial convergence zone and, WE *132-133*; monsoon, WE *130*; river dolphins of, UN *58, 59*; satellite, WE *111*

Indian leaf bugs: AN *50, 53*

Indirect reduction of ore: ST *110-111*

Indricotherium (extinct mammal): EV *117*; skeleton, EV *104*

Induction: electromagnetic, PH 94

Indus River dolphins: UN *59*

Industrial chemistry: ST 102-127; alloys in, ST *112-113*; concrete, ST *120-121*; glass, ST *122-123, 124-125*; metal refining, ST *102-103, 110-111, 114-115*; oil refining, ST *116-117*; papermaking, ST *104-105*; perfume making, ST *126-127*; plastics,

ST *118-119*; polymerization, ST *106-107*; synthetic fibers, ST *108-109. See also* Materials technology

Industrial melanism: IN *116-117*

Inertia: PH *28-29*; Galileo's experiment, PH *29*; vs. gravity, PH *28, 29*, 30, 31, *37*; law of, PH 24, 28; and train passengers, PH *28-29*

Inertial guidance system: V-2 rocket's, MA 27

Inertial navigation system (INS): TR *124-125*

Infectious diseases: HU 126; AIDS, HU *136-137*; colds and complications, HU *140-141*; and immune system, HU 126, *128-129*; and lymphatic system, HU *130-131*; measles, HU *132-133*; and neutrophils, HU *65, 128, 132*

Infinium planetarium: Tsukuba Expo Center, Japan, SP *126*

Inflorescences: dandelion, PL *72*; fig vs. pineapple, PL *69*; sunflower, PL *70, 71*; thistle, PL *74*

Influent streams: formation of, GE *30-31*

Influenza: symptoms, HU *chart* 141; viruses, HU *141*

Information searches: CO *56-57*

Infrared, use of: by burglar alarms, MA *114, 115*; by autofocus system, MA *75*

Infrared Astronomical Satellite: SP *124*

Infrared detector: satellite with, WE *110-111*

Infrared images: satellite, WE *121*

Infrared light and observatory: SP *124*

Infrared radiation: WE *9, 11, 24*; and greenhouse effect, WE *136, 137*; measuring, PH *56-57*

Infrared sensors: Landsat's use of, PE *79, 136*

Infrared spectroscopy: SP *29*; telescope, SP 28

Initiator: tumor, HU *138*

Injection molding of resins: ST *118-119*, 138

Injuries: faking of, by plovers, AN *84-85*; healing of, human, HU *48-49*

Ink, squirting of: by octopuses, UN *141*; by squid, UN *140-141*

Ink and ink removers: ST *72-73*

Inking of type: MA 6

Inlets: drowned valleys with, GE *90*; and sand bar formation, GE *74-75*

Inner ear of fish: UN *52*; shark's, UN *55*

Inner ear of humans: HU *112, 113*; and dizziness, HU *114-115*

Input devices: CO 18, *19*; game controller, CO *79*; keyboards, CO *32-33, 90-91*; mouse, CO *34-35*

INS (inertial navigation system): TR *124-125*

Insectivorous plants: EC *116-117*, PL *34-35, 46-47*

Insects: Alpine butterflies, EC *52-53, 57*; anatomy, IN *8-9*; antennae, IN *26-27, 32*; ants, AN *12-13, 124-127*; aphids, relationships with, AN *12-13, 118-119*; bats catching, AN *42-43*; bees, AN *26, 54-55*, 125, *128-131*; biological pest control, IN *90-91*; birds evolved for catching, EV *137*; bloodsucking, IN *68-69, 84*; bluffing, AN *85*; body parts, IN 5, 6; breathing, IN *10-11*; butterflies vs. moths, IN *32-33*; butterfly wings, coloration of, IN *30-31, 58, 83, 121*; in caves, EC *43*; chameleons catching, AN *4-5, 32-33*; cicadas, EC *106-107*; coevolution, IN *78-79*; cold-resistant, IN *34-35*; crickets, AN *96-97*; differentiation, EV *22-23*; disguises, use of, AN *30-31, 50-55, 68-69*; earliest, EV *50-51*; evolutionary path, possible, IN *6-7*; eyes, compound, IN *4-5, 22*; eyespots, AN *51, 64-65*; feeding order, EC *110-111*; fireflies, AN *88-89, 92-93*; flightlessness, IN *84-85*; flying, first, EV *54-55*; flying, types of, IN *4-5, 14-15*; in food chain, EC *125, 127*; fungi living off, PL *97*; hearing, IN *24-25, 28*; horns, use of, IN *60-61*; houseflies, AN *8-9*; jumping, IN *16-17*; living fossils, EV *141*; mosquitoes, AN *10-11*; mutations, EV *14, 16-17*; ocelli, IN *22-23*; orchid resembling, PL *53*; outbreaks, IN *88-89*; pheromones, use of, AN *94-95*; plants trapping, EC *116-117*, PL *34-35, 46-47*, *53*; pollination by, EC *115*, PL *8, 50, 52-53*, 56, 68, *69*; as primary consumers, PL *125*; reproduction, EC *108-109*; seeds spread by, PL *79*; soil animals, EC *36-37*, PL *127*; sounds made by, IN *28-29*; spiders catching, AN *26, 27, 28-29*; stick insects, AN *52, 80*; swarming, IN *86-87, 133, 135*; temperature ranges, IN *chart* 35; tool used for collecting, AN *47*; walking, IN *12, 18-19, 20-21. See also* Defenses of animals; Food, finding and gathering; Reproduction by animals; Social insects; *and individual names*

In situ vs. *ex situ* conservation: PL *142-143*

Insolation: varying, and ice ages, WE *144*

Instant coffee: making of, ST *86-87*

Instant photography: color, MA *92-93*

Instars: IN *80-81, 114*

Instrument flights, aircraft on: inertial navigation system (INS), TR *124-125*; landing system for (ILS), TR *126-127*; Omega System for, TR *map* 125; traffic corridors for, TR *120-121*; VHF omnirange (VOR) stations and, TR *122-123*

Planet Earth
PE

Plant Life
PL

Physical Forces
PH

Structure of Matter
ST

Space & Planets
SP

Transportation
TR

Underwater World
UN

Weather & Climate
WE

nstrument landing system (ILS): TR *126-127*

nstruments: *See* Musical instruments

nsulation: electrical, PH *82, 83,* 84; thermal, PH *60-61*

nsulation cooling (insulation expansion): and contrails, WE *64;* demonstration of, WE *58*

nsulin and diabetes: HU *142-143*

ntaglio printing: MA 40, *41*

ntegrated circuits: CO *20-21, 22-23,* MA 54; in cameras, MA *75;* packages for, CO *23;* quartz watch, circuitry in, MA *97;* silicon for, ST *134-135;* in smart cards, MA *60-61;* in telephones, MA 56

ntegrated Services Digital Network: CO 108

NTELSAT satellites: CO *128-129*

Intercity Express (ICE; German high-speed train): TR *33*

Intercom: working of, PH *84, 85*

Intercostal muscles: HU 54

Interference of waves: lightwaves, PH 112, *120-121;* lightwaves, and holograms, PH *124, 125;* microwaves, speed gun's use of, MA *38-39*

Interferometry: radio, SP *121;* very long baseline (VLBI), uses of, PE *31, 56-57*

Intermediate neurons: HU *103*

Intermolecular forces, breaking of: by ions, ST 40, 41; by kinetic energy, ST *34, 35*

Internal respiration vs. external respiration: HU 52

International Date Line: GE *20, 21*

International Ultraviolet Explorer (IUE satellite): SP *125*

Intertidal zone: barnacles in, UN *40*

Intervertebral (spinal) disks: HU *40, 41*

Intestines: HU *88-89, 90-91;* lining, HU *6, 76, 77, 88-89, 90*

Intrusive igneous rocks: PE *88;* vs. extrusive, PE *87, 89*

Inulin grain: PL *7*

Inversion layer: WE *60;* heat island, WE *138-139*

In vitro cultivation: PL *140-141, 143*

In vitro fertilization: HU *28-29*

Io (moon of Jupiter): orbit, SP *19;* volcanoes, SP *18-19*

Ion engine: SP *143;* craft using, SP *142-143*

Ion exchange film: glutamic acid and, ST *91;* in salt reclamation, ST *96, 97*

Ionosphere: WE 4, 8, *9,* 10, *14-15;* and aurora, WE 16

Ions: from acid and alkaline substances, ST *64, 65, 82, 83;* in automobile batteries, ST *58-59;* copper, ST *114;* hypochlorite, ST *76;* in iron reactions, ST *56;* silver, in

electroplating, ST *62-63;* sodium and chloride, ST *18-19,* 40, *41, 43,* 96

Ion tail of comet: SP *33*

Irdomyrmex ants: IN *98*

Iridophores: AN *56-57*

Irises: PL *55;* fruit of, PL *67*

Irkutsk, Russia: climate of, GE *117*

Iron: burning, conditions for, ST *70-71;* casting, ST *112;* galvanizing, ST *63;* molten, measuring temperature of, PH *56-57;* refining into pig iron, ST *102-103, 110-111;* rusting, ST *56-57;* steel from, ST *111, 112-113. See also* Ferromagnetic materials

Iron, electric: with thermostat, MA *120-121*

Iron hydroxide: ST 56, *57, 110*

Iron meteorite: SP *34*

Iron oxide: ST 56, *57, 110*

Irregular galaxies: SP *103*

Irrigation: GE *138-139;* kanats for, GE *63, 139;* with Yellow River water, GE *35*

Isaacson, Leonard: *Illiac Suite for String Quartet,* CO 66, 67

Island-arc volcanoes: formation of, PE *76;* Pacific Rim, PE *115*

Islands: Antarctic, GE *52-53;* coastal terraces around, GE *89;* coral reefs around, GE *80-81;* drowned valleys with, GE *90;* hot-spot, formation of, PE *44-45, 76, 77*

Islets of Langerhans: HU *75, 84, 85, 142-143*

Isobars: WE *40, 41, 84, 85, 118-119;* Antarctica, WE *122;* chinook, WE *44;* typhoon, WE *93*

Isochrones: seismic waves', PE *53*

Isolation: and differentiation, EV *22-23;* and living fossils, EV *140*

Isostasy: theory of, PE *10*

Isotherms: WE *126, 139*

Italy: agriculture, GE *131, map* 137; climate, GE *chart* 137; Tiber River delta, GE *33*

Ivy: roots of, for support, PL *23, 29*

Iwaki, Japan: GE *77*

Izu Peninsula, Japan: earthquake's effect on, PE *55*

J

Jacamars: great, EC *61*

Jackdaws: courtship, AN *103*

Jackets, down: insulation by, PH *60-61*

Jackscrew: PH *45*

Jacobson, L. I.: AN 14

Jacobson's organ: animals with, AN *14-15, 34*

Jacquard, Joseph-Marie: loom invented by, CO 10, *11*

Jamoytius kerwoodie (extinct fish): EV *46*

Japan: air pollutants, WE *chart* 27; airport construction, GE *144;* Akiyoshi Cave, GE *54-55;* alluvial fan, GE *31;* Atomic Energy Research Institute, nuclear power plant at, PH *109;* ball lightning, WE *106;* bullet trains, TR *4-5, 33;* coal formation, PE *105;* computer mapping, GE *22-23;* delta, GE *26;* earthquake effects, PE *54, 55,* 60; Fuji, Mount, GE *22-23,* WE *24, 25, 68, 115;* Gyoki map of, GE *15;* heat island, Tokyo's, WE *map* 139; icebreaker *(Shirase),* TR *101;* Iwaki, GE *77;* landslide, GE *103;* luxury train *(Twilight Express),* TR *18-19;* Notsukezaki, Cape, GE *75;* Ogouchi Dam, Tokyo, WE *79;* planetarium, SP *126;* radio astronomy, SP *105, 120-121;* satellite, WE *111;* solar-powered automobile *(Southern Cross),* TR *62-63;* subsidence, GE *65;* superconducting train design, PH *93;* terraces, GE *89;* tsunami, PE *map* 59; volcanoes, PE *62-63, 67, 78;* V-shaped canyon, GE *26;* whirlpools, PE *122, 123;* x-ray observatory, SP *125;* Zao, Mount, ice formations on, WE *80*

Japan Current: PE *123*

Japanese abacus: CO *7*

Japanese bluefish: UN *22-23*

Japanese bunting: eggs, AN *114*

Japanese copper butterfly: IN *78*

Japanese crane: dancing, AN *102-103*

Japanese dace: UN *73*

Japanese eel: UN *73*

Japanese jay: seeds buried by, EC *123*

Japanese macaque: learning, AN *144*

Japanese pampas grass: PL *73*

Japanese pilchard: UN *73*

Jarvik-7 artificial heart: MA *132-133*

Jasper National Park, Canada: GE *24-25*

Jawbone: growth of, HU *26, 34, 35*

Jawless fish (agnathans): UN *6;* earliest, EV *46-47,* 48

Jaws: fish with, evolution of, EV *48-49;* reptilian, EV *135;* whales, evolution of, EV *113*

Jays: Japanese, seeds buried by, EC *123;* scrub, AN *116-117*

Jellyfish: UN *4-5, 42-43;* medusafish's relationship with, UN *144*

Jellyfish-like animals: extinct, EV *39*

Jerboas: EC *89*

Jet action in dishwasher: MA *117*

Jet aircraft: TR *108-109;* air turbulence and, WE *52-53;* CCV (control-configured vehicle), TR *140-141; Concorde,* TR *108-109, 136-137;* contrails, WE *64-65;* engines, working of, TR *130-131, 139;* sonic booms from, PH *140-141;* Stealth

Animal Behavior
AN

Computer Age
CO

Ecology
EC

Evolution of Life
EV

Geography
GE

Human Body
HU

Insects & Spiders
IN

Machines &
Inventions **MA**

bomber, TR *109, 144*; VTOL (vertical takeoff and landing), TR *138-139*; X-29A, TR *142-143*

Jets, gas: galactic center, SP *104*; from quasar, SP *113*

Jet streams: WE *37, 38-39, 112*; and clear-weather turbulence, WE *53*; and downpours, WE *88-89*; and monsoons, WE *130-131*

Jew's ears (mushrooms): PL *98*

Jib crane: MA *52*

Jizuki, Mount, Japan: landslide on, GE *103*

Johnston's organ: mosquito's, IN *27*

Joint implants: ceramic, ST *130*

Joints: muscles and, HU *38*

Jordan snowplow: TR *23*

Joystick: CO *35*

Jumbo jets: TR *108-109*; engines, TR *131*

Jumping: fleas' method of, IN *16-17*

Jump jet fighters: Harrier, TR *138-139*

Jupiter (planet): SP *14-17, 28*; Great Red Spot, SP *14-15, 16*; moon of (Io), SP *18-19*; rings, SP *16, 20*; spectrum, SP *29*; Sun compared to, SP *17*; Voyager missions to, SP *139*

Jurassic period: dinosaurs, EV *74-75, 84-85*; ichthyosaurs, EV *92*; pterosaurs, EV *90, 91, 96*; species, WE *143*; temperatures, WE *chart* 143

K

Kahoolawe (island), Hawaii, U.S.: PE *77*

Kaibab Plateau, Ariz., U.S.: GE *95*

Kamerlingh Onnes, Heike: PH 92

Kanats: GE *63, 139*

Kandelia mangrove seedlings: PL *80*

Kangaroo rats: EC *90*

Kangaroos: EC *17*

Kaniska canace (butterfly): IN *32*

Kapok trees: PL *123*

Karrens: formation of, GE *58-59*

Karst topography: GE *58*; development, GE *58-59*

Katashina River, Japan: terraces, GE *89*

Katydids: camouflage, AN *50, 52, 53*

Kauai (island), Hawaii, U.S.: rainfall on, GE *115*

Kauri pines: PL *123*

Kawaguchi, Yoichiro: image by, CO *70-71*

Kekaha, Hawaii, U.S.: rainfall on, GE *115*

Kelp: giant, beds of, PE *142*; life cycle of, PL *103*; sea otters and, EC 130

Kelvin, William Thomson, 1st Baron: MA *9*

Kentrosaurus (dinosaur): EV *74*

Kerosene: as fraction of crude oil, ST *117*; as rocket fuel, ST 74

Keyboards: computer's CO *32-33, 58*; pock-et computer's, CO *90-91*; synthesizer's, MA *91*

Keyhole limpet: starfish attack repelled by, UN *138-139*

Keys for records: CO 56, 57

Keystone species: sea otters as, EC *130-131*

Kiaeraspis (agnathan): underside of, EV *46*

Kidneys, human: HU *94-95*; artificial, CO *139*

Kilauea, Mount, Hawaii, U.S.: PE *45, 62, 64, 68, 78, 79*; lava, makeup of, PE *chart* 65

Killer (Africanized) bees: IN *136-137*

Killer cells: HU *128, 129*

Killer whales: AN *41*, UN *114*

Killifish: EC *139, 140*; African, UN *64*

Kimberlite pipes: formation of, PE *90-91*

Kinetic energy: vs. intermolecular forces, ST *34, 35*; of molecules, PH *23, 52*; of rolled ball, PH *29*; of roller coaster, PH *31*

Kinetograph: MA *20*

Kinetoscope: MA *20-21*

King cobra: AN *62*

King cobra guppy: UN *65*

Kingfishers: courtship, AN *103*

King termite: IN *128, 141, 143*

"Kiss, The" (Edison movie): MA *20*

Kitchen items: dishwasher, MA *116-117*; microwave oven, MA *102-103*; pressure cooker, MA *100-101*; refrigerator, MA *106-107*

Kittiwakes: EC *32-33*

Knee joint: HU *38*

Knee roots: mangroves', EC *34, 35*

Knives: ceramic, ST *130*

Knuckle-type couplers for train cars: TR *8-9*

Koalas: EC *16*; PL *118*

Kodak cameras: MA *18*; ad for, MA *18*; working of, MA 18, *19*

Komodo dragons: AN *15*, EC *13*

Köppen, Wladimir: WE 128-129

Köppen system: WE 128-129, *map* 128-129

Korotkoff sounds: MA 131

Krakatoa (volcanic island), Indonesia: eruption of, PE 62, *72-73*; recolonization of, EC *120-121*

Krause end bulbs: HU *98*

Krill eaters: UN 107, *116-117*

Krypton: fission producing, ST *14-15*

Kudzu vine: PL *75*

Kupffer cells: HU *87*

Kurobe Canyon, Japan: GE *26*

Kwanto earthquake, Japan (1923): effects of, PE *54, 55*

L

Labyrinths: membranous and bony, HU *115*

Ladybird beetles: *See* Ladybugs

Ladybugs: IN *4-5*; as aphid enemies, IN *144*; aphids protected from, AN *13*; for biological pest control, IN *91*; Japanese ladybirds, EC *108-109*; pupa, IN *113*; walking upside down, IN *20*; warning coloration, IN *113, 120*

Laënnec, René: stethoscope invented by, MA *144*

Lagoons, formation of: by coral reefs, GE *80-81*; by sand ridges, GE *74*

Lakes: artificial, for irrigation, GE *138*; Burley Griffin, Canberra, Australia, GE *128*, *map* 129; Finland's, formation of, GE *66-67*; Great Lakes, formation of, GE *48-49*; Ijssel, the Netherlands, GE 133; oxbow, formation of, GE *26-27*; Titicaca, Bolivia-Peru, GE *140, 141*

Lamarck, Jean-Baptiste: and theory, EV *13*

Lambeosaurus (dinosaur): EV *84*

Lamellae of fish's gills: UN 8, *9*

Lamellicorn beetles: IN *61*

Laminar air currents: WE *69*

Lamps: electricity illuminating, PH *72-73*

Lancetfish: UN *69*

Land and sea breezes: WE *42, 43, 76*

Land crabs: breathing by, UN *36-37*

Landfill: airport constructed on, GE *144*

Landing of aircraft: glider, TR *118*; instrument landing system (ILS) for, TR *126-127*

Land of midnight Sun: SP *58-59*

Land races: beans as, PL *142*

Land reclamation: GE *132-133*

Landsat satellites: CO *140-141*, PE *136*; volcanoes studied with, PE *79*

Landslides: GE *102-103*

Language: aquatic mammals' production of, UN *114-115*; chimpanzees, AN *124-125, 142-143*; dance, of bees, IN *26, 128-129, 134-135*

Language areas of human brain: HU *120, 121*

Languages, computer: CO *50-51*; programs in, CO 51

La Niña phenomenon: WE *141*

LANs (local area networks): CO 108

Lanternbelly: UN *24, 25*

Lanternfish: UN *22*

La Paz, Bolivia: GE *141*; climate, GE *chart* 140

La Plata River dolphin: UN *59*

Larch trees: EC *54*, PL *119*; cone, PL *89*; Japanese, EC *55*; trunk, PL *24-25*

Large blue butterflies: IN *78*

Large intestine: HU *90-91*; lining of, HU *76, 90*

Larvae: abalone, UN *98*; barnacles, EC *101*, UN *40-41*; beetles, EC *37, 43*; cicadas,

Animal Behavior	Computer Age	Ecology	Evolution of Life	Geography	Human Body	Insects & Spiders	Machines &
AN	**CO**	**EC**	**EV**	**GE**	**HU**	**IN**	Inventions **MA**

color copier, MA *62-63*; colors of, primary, MA *77, 92*; compact disks read by, MA *87*; corpuscular vs. wave theory of, PH 112; curved surfaces, reflection from, PH *114-115*; electricity and, PH *72-73*; fireflies signaling with, AN *88-89, 92-93*; flowers affected by, PL *53, 54-55, 61*; and growth rings, PL *24*; and holograms, PH *124-125*; in instant color photography, MA 92, *93*; and leaf arrangement, PL 36; through lenses, PH *116-117, 122*; and liquid crystals, ST *136-137*; movie projector's use of, MA *88, 89*; nastic reaction to, PL 44, *45*; ocean's absorption of sunlight, PE *chart* 135; through optical fiber, CO *124-125*, ST *125*; and photosensitive resin, ST *144*; in photosynthesis, PL *10, 11, 104*, 105, *125*; properties of, PH 112; release of, in fireworks, ST *50-51*; scattering of, ST *20*; and seasonal color changes, AN *59*; sensor, photoelectric, in smoke detector, MA *65*; and soap bubbles, PH *120-121*; spectrum of, PH *120*; speed of, measuring, PH *118-119*; speed of, nearing, PH *126-127*; in temperature measurement, PH 56, *57*; wavelengths, and color, ST *51*; wave vs. corpuscular theory of, PH 112; windows for, plants with, PL *114-115*

Light, laser: PH *112-113, 119, 122-123, 124, 125*; bar codes scanned by, CO *86-87*; fiberoptic cables guiding, CO *124-125*

Light bulbs: working of, PH *72-73*

Light-emitting diodes (LEDs): automated cars' use of, TR *60*; in mouse, CO *34, 35*; in pen-type scanners, CO *87*

Light-emitting fish: UN *24-25, 26-27*; anglerfish, UN *23, 70-71, 111, 112*; cardinalfish, UN *144*; lanternfish, UN *22*

Light-emitting insects: fireflies, IN *52-53*; glowworms, IN *50-51*

Light-emitting squid ink: UN *140*

Lightning: WE *56-57, 67*; artificial, WE *66*; ball, WE *106-107*; cause of, WE *66-67*; fireballs related to, WE *107*; from ground up, WE *67*; in nitrogen cycle, ST *26*; and thunder, WE 67

Lightning fixing: of nitrogen, ST *26*

Light-sensitive emulsions in Polaroid film: MA *92-93*

Light-sensitive organs (ocelli): IN *22-23*

Lignite: deposits, PE *map* 104; formation, PE *105*

Lilies: arum, fly trapped by, PL *53*; vegetative reproduction, PL *91, 140*

Limestone: PE *101*; caverns, GE *54-55, 59, 60-61*; karst topography, formation of,

GE *58-59*; shoreline, cliffs along, GE *68-69*

Limpets: keyhole, starfish attack repelled by, UN *138-139*

Linden seeds: PL *73*

Line webs, spiders': IN *39*

Lionfish: UN *120-121, 122*

Lions: African, EC *10, 81, 82*; breeding of, EV *10-11*; cave lions, EV *129*; Indian, EC *11*; prides of, AN *138-139*

Liquefaction of ground: earthquakes and, PE 55, *60-61*

Liquid crystal displays (LCDs): ST *136-137*

Liquid crystals: ST *136-137*

Liquid-fuel rockets: ST *75*

Liquid rocket fuel: PH *18*

Liquids: in colloids, ST *20*; contraction of, PH *66*; freezing of, PH *66-67*; vs. gases and solids, determinants of, ST *44-45*; phase changes, ST *38, 39. See also* Water

Lithium 8: beta decay of, PH *91*

Lithography as printing method: MA *40-41*

Lithosphere: PE *9, 28, 29*; regeneration, PE *32*

Litmus paper: use of, ST *82*

Little Dipper (Ursa Minor constellation): SP *60, 61*

Little Tennessee River, U.S.: power station on, GE *134*

Livebearing fish: guppies, UN *64-65*; mosquitofish, UN *73*; scorpionfish, UN *72*; sharks, UN *76-77*; surffish, UN *87*

Live oaks: EC *25*

Liver: HU *86-87*; computerized assistance for, CO *139*

Liverworts: PL *93, 109*

Livestock raising: GE *130, 131*; llamas, GE 140, *141*; overgrazing and desertification, GE *107*; transhumance, GE *142-143*

Living fossils: EV *130-131, 140-141*

Living stones (stone plants): PL *110, 114-115*

Lizard-hipped dinosaurs: EV *67*; vs. birdhipped, EV *chart* 66-67, *74-75*; birds' evolution from, EV *68-69*; *Compsognathus*, EV *71, 74*; sauropods, EV *83, 84-85*; *Tyrannosaurus*, EV *74, 77, 97*

Lizards: as caterpillar enemy, IN *120-121*; chameleons, AN *4-5, 32-33*; desert, EC *88, 91*; flying, AN *72-73*; of Galápagos, EV *12, 13, 80*; iguanas, EC *6, 113*; Komodo dragon, AN *15*, EC *13*; mosasaurs, EV *94-95*; recolonization, EC *121*; tails breaking off, AN *80-81*; temperature control, EV *80*

Llamas: GE 140, *141*

Loaches: barbels of, AN *20-21*

Loader: TR *77*

Lobe-finned fish: amphibian evolution from, EV *56-57*

Local area networks (LANs): CO 108

Local Group of galaxies: SP *102, 110-111*

Localizer in airport's ILS: TR 126, 127

Local Supercluster of galaxies: SP *110*

Locks, canal: Panama Canal's, TR *92-93*; Rhine River's, GE *40*

Locomotion (early locomotive): TR *15*

Locomotives: diesel-powered, TR *4-5*; with snowplows, TR *22-23*; steam-powered, TR *4-5, 14-15, 16-17*; traction for, TR *6*

Locus coeruleus: HU 123

Locusts (migratory grasshoppers): egg laying, IN *130*; evolutionary path, IN *7*; ocelli, effect of, IN *22-23*; swarming, IN *86-87*

Lodgepole pines: EC 79, *136-137*

Loess Plateau, China: GE 34, *map* 34

Logarithms: inventor of, CO *8*

Logic cards, IC: MA *60-61*

Logic chips: CO 22, *23*

Logic elements (gates): CO *21, 28*; in adder circuits, CO 28, *29*

Loma Prieta earthquake, Calif., U.S. (1989): effects of, PE *55, 61*

Long-horned beetles: AN *69*; and flight , IN *15*; foot structure, IN *21*; larva, IN *49*; sound production, IN *29*; tiger, AN *55*

Longitude: GE 10, *11*; on Mercator projections, GE *16*; and time zones, GE *20-21*

Longitudinal dunes: GE *109*

Longleaf pines: PL *49*

Long-legged wasps: IN *114, 125*

Long-waisted ground bee: nest of, IN *108*

Looms: Jacquard, CO 10, *11*

Loran (long-range navigation): determining ship's position with, TR *81, 82-83*

Lotuses: EC *27*

Loudness of sound: wave height and, MA *90*

Loudspeakers: dynamic, MA 80, *81*

Louse: sucking, IN *84*

Love waves: PE *51*

Low-level vacuums: water-seal pump producing, MA *45*

Low pressure: WE *41, 82, 86-87*; above cold high-pressure systems, WE *85*; over Antarctica, WE *122*; belts, WE *34-35, 37*; and bora winds, WE *48-49*; and chinooks, WE *44-45*; forecast map, WE *120, 121*; jet streams and, WE *38-39*, 88, 89; and monsoon, WE *130*; monsoon lows, formation of, WE *132-133*; in satellite image, WE *111*; and seasonal downpours, WE 88, 89, 133; and sirocco, WE *46-47*; tropical depressions, WE 82, *90-91*; troughs, WE *84*, 86, 87; warm system, WE *87*

Planet Earth
PE

Plant Life
PL

Physical Forces
PH

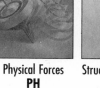
Structure of Matter
ST

Space & Planets
SP

Transportation
TR

Underwater World
UN

Weather & Climate
WE

Low-velocity zone (asthenosphere): PE 9, 28, 29

Lugworms: AN 80; as cone shell's prey, UN 119; in food chain, UN 126-127

Luminescent fish: UN 24-25, 26-27; anglerfish, UN 23, 70-71, 111, 112; cardinalfish, UN 144; lanternfish, UN 22

Luminescent squid ink: UN 140

Luna moths: eyespots, use of, AN 64

Lunar coronas: WE 105

Lunar eclipses: SP 62-63

Lunar halos: WE 102-103

Lungfish: UN 30-31

Lungs, human: alveoli, HU 56-57, 72-73; breathing movements and, HU 54, 55; carbon monoxide in, HU 72-73; and gas exchange, HU 56-57, 65

Lures, fishing: green heron's use of, AN 36-37

Luxury trains: TR 18-19

Lycaenid butterflies, relationship of, with ants: IN 78-79

Lymph: HU 130; in ear, HU 114, 115

Lymphatic system: HU 130-131

Lymph nodes: HU 130-131; large intestine, HU 90

Lymphocytes: HU 6; B cells, HU 126, 128, 129, 131, 132, 133, 135; development of, HU 67; in lymphatic system, HU 130, 131; T cells, HU 128, 129, 131, 136-137

Lyot, Bernard-Ferdinand: invention, SP 123

Lyra (constellation): and precession, SP 60, 61; Ring nebula in, SP 87

Lystrosaurus (early reptile): EV 63

M

Maar volcano: PE 67

Macaques: clan, AN 141; learning, AN 144

Macaws: scarlet, EC 61

MacCready, Paul: EV 91

MacGregor's bowerbird: bower of, AN 101

Mach cone: TR 136-137

Mach indicator: airplane's, TR 132-133

Machine language: CO 50; translation into, CO 51

Machines: MA entire volume

Machines, simple: PH 40-51; inclined planes, PH 44-45; levers, PH 42-43; pulleys, PH 48-49; screws, PH 44-45; springs, PH 50-51; wheel and axle, bicycle's use of, PH 46-47

McMath solar telescope, Ariz., U.S.: SP 122-123

Macrauchenia (extinct mammal): EV 120

Macroevolution (adaptive radiation): EV 24-25, 138

Macromolecules: *See* Polymers

Macrophages: HU 128, 129; in lymphatic system, HU 131; measles and, HU 132, 133

Madder: PL 78-79

Mafic and ultramafic rocks: PE 88, 89

Magdeburg hemispheres: PH 16-17

Magellan, Ferdinand, expedition of: route, TR *map* 86-87; ship, TR 87

Maglev (magnetic levitation) trains: TR 4-5, 34-35

Magma: in formation of Andes, PE 38; in formation of hot springs, PE 82, 83; in formation of igneous rocks, PE 86, 88, 89, 93; in formation of minerals, PE 100, 106; in formation of ocean floor, PE 32; in formation of rift valley, PE 41; in formation of volcanoes, PE 44-45, 64, 65, 66, 67, 69, 76, 77, 79, 83; Moon, SP 68, 69

Magma reservoirs: PE 64, 65; and caldera formation, PE 68, 69; and Mount St.. Helens eruption, PE 70; Yellowstone, PE 80

Magnesium: forms of, ST 70, 71

Magnesium gas: spectrum of, SP 78

Magnetic brakes: trains', TR 10, 11

Magnetic data storage: CO 19, 36-37, 56-57

Magnetic domains: PH 78, 79

Magnetic field lines: PH 78-79; in AC generator, PH 96-97; of Earth, PE 21; of electromagnet, PH 80-81; shapes of, PH 68-69, 81; and superconductor vs. normal conductor, PH 92-93

Magnetic fields: of Earth, PE 20-21, WE 10-11, 16, 17, 19; of Galaxy, and gas jet, SP 104; metal detectors', MA 42, 43; of neutron star, SP 97; of Sun, SP 42-43, 46, WE 16; TV deflection coils', MA 77. *See also* Magnets

Magnetic levitation (maglev) trains: TR 4-5, 34-35

Magnetic recording by VCR: MA 82, 83

Magnetism: in AC generators, PH 96-97; attraction of metals by, PH 78-79; as dating method, PE 94; in detection of ore deposits, PE 99; and electricity, PH 68-69, 80-81, 94; in electromagnetic waves, PH 88-89; electromagnets, PH 80-81, 99, 100, 101; in measurement of electricity, PH 76, 77; as navigation aid for birds, AN 137; as navigation aid for salmon, AN 121; as proof of continental drift, PE 27; as proof of seafloor spreading, PE 30, 94; and superconductors, PH 92-93; and transformers, PH 86

Magnetogram of Sun: SP 43

Magnetopause: WE 16, 19

Magnetosheath: WE 16

Magnetosphere: WE 10-11, 16

Magnetotail: WE 16, 19

Magnetrons: MA 102, 103

Magnets: in burglar alarms, MA 114; direction of motion, rule for, TR 105; in electrocardiograph, MA 137; in generators, electrical, MA 28, 29; in maglevs, TR 34; in microphones, MA 80; in power meters, MA 118-119; in speakers, MA 81; superconducting, TR 104-105; in telephones, MA 57; in VCRs, MA 83

Magnification: by binoculars, MA 94-95; by electron microscope, MA 32-33; by magnifying glass, PH 116-117

Magnifying glasses: PH 116-117

Magnitude of stars: SP 80-81; variable, SP 82-83

Magnus effect: on baseball, PH 34-35

Magpies, azure-winged: AN 115; eggs, AN 114, 115

Mahasena bagworms: nest of, IN 102

Maiasaura (dinosaur): EV 83

Mail, electronic (E-mail): CO 116-117

Mainframe computer: architecture of, CO 18-19

Main sequence of stars: SP *chart* 79

Mako sharks: shortfin, UN 15

Malawi, Lake, Africa: catfish of, UN 86-87

Malayan butterfly: caterpillar of, AN 64

Malaysia: rain forests of, GE 124

Male anatomy: HU 12; pelvis, HU 12, 13

Malignant tumors: growth of, HU 138-139

MALTRON layout of keys: CO 33

Mammal-like reptiles: EV 59, 62, 63, 64-65; family tree, EV *charts* 63-65; skull, EV 73

Mammals: EV 104-129; adaptation, EV 20-21; adaptive radiation, EV 24-25, 138; African and Indian, EC 10-11; African and South American, EC 20-21; of African grasslands, EC 29, 80-85; at alligator hole, EC 138, 139; aquatic, EC 7, 46-47, 49, 112, 130-131, 142, EV 112-113, 136, 144, UN 4-5, 18-19, 32-33, 58-59, 63, 92-93, 94-95, 107, 114-115, 116-117; Arctic, EC 48-49; Australian, EV 138-139, 144; bats, AN 42-43, EC 28, 38-39, 114, EV 114-115, 130, 134; biggest, land, EV 104, 116-117; breeds and breeding, EV 10-11, 19; color changes in, seasonal, AN 58-59; convergence, EV 136, 138-139; deer family, EC 50-51, 58-59, 118, 136, 139; desert, EC 28, 88-91; *Desmostylus*, EV 104-105, 118-119; developmental similarities among, EV 133; dolphins, UN 18-19, 58-59, 114-115; elephants, EV 105, 110-111, 121, 128-129; endangered species, EC 96-97, 112-113; extinctions, modern, EV 144; first true,

| Animal Behavior **AN** | Computer Age **CO** | Ecology **EC** | Evolution of Life **EV** | Geography **GE** | Human Body **HU** | Insects & Spiders **IN** | Machines & Inventions **MA** |

EV *65, 72-73*; after forest fire, EC *136, 137*; gliding, AN *72, 73*; in herds, warning signals, AN *60-61*; homologous structures, EV *130-131, 134-135*; horses, EV *106, 108-109, 121*; human ancestors, EV *105, 124-125, 126*; human beings, EV *126-127*; ice ages and, EV *128-129, 141*; Indian and African, EC *10-11*; in Lamarck's theory, EV *13*; lions, AN *138-139*; living fossils, EV *140, 141*; marine, aquatic, EC *7, 46-47, 49, 112, 130-131, 142*, EV *112-113, 136, 144*, UN *4-5, 32-33, 63, 92-93, 94-95, 107, 114-115, 116-117*; marsupials, EC *16-17, 114*; migrations, EC *map 51, 102-103*; moles, AN *104-105*, EC *17, 37, 106-107*; opossums, AN *85*; platypuses, AN *18-19*; primates, AN *46-47, 124-125, 140-141*, EC *18-19, 28, 70-71, 112*, EV *122-123, 124*; vs. reptiles, EC *13*; seals, UN *92-93*; seed dispersers, EC *96-97, 122-123*; sloths, EC *20, 62-63*; South American, EV *107, 120-121*; South American and African, EC *20-21*; tapirs, EC *14-15*; temperature control, EV *81*; tool-using, AN *46-47*; whales, AN *40-41*, EV *112-113*, UN *4-5, 32-33, 94-95, 107, 114-115, 116-117*; wolves, AN *44-45*

Mammoths: skeletons, EV *105*; skulls, EV *110*; woolly, EV *111, 128-129*

Management functions of computers: CO *93*

Mandibles: ants' use of, IN *126-127*

Manganese deposits: PE *100*; nodules on ocean floor, PE *140-141*

Mangrove trees: EC *34-35*, PL *80-81*; forests, EC *25*

Manipulator (robotic hand): CO *98*

Manned Maneuvering Unit (MMU): SP *135*

Man-of-war, Portuguese: UN *42*

Manta rays: AN *25*, UN *107*

Mantises: *See* Praying mantises

Mantle, Earth's: PE *8, 9*; convection in, PE *28, 29*; diamond formation in, PE *90-91*; formation of, PE *7*; heat from, PE *12-13, 28, 29*; hot spots, volcanoes formed by, PE *44-45, 76, 77*; in magma formation, PE *64*; peridotite rock in, PE *88, 89*

Mantles: Io (moon of Jupiter), SP *18-19*; Mars, SP *12*; Moon, Earth's, SP *68, 69*; Venus, SP *11*

Manual transmission: automobile's, TR *46*

Maple trees: leaves, color change in, PL *40-41*; seeds, PL *67, 73*

Maps and mapping: GE *4-23*; sixteenth-century, TR *86-87*; computer, CO *76-77, 135, 140-141*, GE *19, 22-23*; first, GE *14-15*; forecast map, WE *120-121*; Landsat satellites, CO *140-141*; latitude and longitude, GE *10-11, 16*; nautical charts, GE *18-19*; printing of, GE *7*; projection types, GE *13, 16-17*; scale, GE *12*; surveying for, GE *6-7, 8-9, 18, 19*; time zones on, GE *20-21*; topographic vs. thematic, GE *12*; weather, CO *135*, WE *118-119*

Maras: EC *20*

Maria: Moon, SP *69*

Marigolds: bur, PL *75*

Marine erosion: effects of, GE *68-69, 76-77, 88-89*

Marine mammals: UN *63*; dolphins, EV *136*, UN *114-115*; otters, EC *130-131, 142*; sea lions, EC *7*; seals, EC *46-47, 49*, UN *92-93*; Steller's sea cows, EV *144*; whales, EC *112*, EV *112-113*, UN *4-5, 32-33, 94-95, 107, 114-115, 116-117*

Marine reptiles: iguanas, EV *12, 13, 80*; prehistoric, EV *62, 92-93, 94-95, 96, 136-137*

Mariner spacecraft: SP *125*; *Mariner 9*, Martian features studied by, SP *12-13*; *Mariner 10*, Mercury photographed by, SP *8*

Marketing functions of computers: CO *93*

Mark I calculator: CO *14*

Marrow, bone: blood-cell-producing, HU *66, 128*

Mars (planet): SP *12-13, 29, 31*; moon of (Phobos), SP *30*; travel to, possible, SP *144*; Viking missions to, SP *125*

Marsh dwellers: EC *138-139, 140*

Marsupial frogs: pygmy, UN *90*

Marsupials: EC *16-17, 114*; Australian, EV *138-139, 144*; opossums, bluffing by, AN *85*; South American, extinct, EV *107, 120*

Mass: of planets, SP *28-29*; of stars, and lifetimes, SP *46, 76, 92, 93*; of Sun and Jupiter, SP *17*; Sun's conversion of, into energy, SP *44*; vs. weight, PH *6*

Mast cells: HU *134, 135*

Mastodons: EV *110, 111, 121*

Materials technology: ST *128-144*; amorphous metals, ST *142-143*; carbon fiber, ST *138-139*; ceramics, advanced, ST *130-131*; diamonds, synthetic, ST *132-133*; liquid crystals, ST *136-137*; photosensitive resin, ST *144*; shape-memory alloys, ST *128-129, 140-141*; single-crystal silicon, ST *134-135*

Mating, courtship and: AN *88-109*; alligators, AN *110*; angelfish, blackspot, UN *66, 67*; anglerfish, UN *70-71*; barnacles, UN *40, 41*; bees, AN *130-131*; beetles, IN *60, 61*; bighorn sheep, head butting by, AN *106-107*; birds, AN *98-103, 112*;

cabbage white butterflies, IN *58-59*; cichlids, UN *80-81*; crabs, UN *37, 38, 96*; crickets, singing by, AN *96-97*; damselflies, IN *63*; dances, AN *90, 100, 102-103*; dinosaurs' ritual, EV *86-87*; discus, UN *86*; dragonflies, IN *62-63*; fertilization of eggs, AN *88-89*; fiddler crabs, AN *108-109*; fireflies, AN *88-89, 92-93*, IN *52, 53*; fish, UN *62*; flightless moths, IN *85*; and gift giving among insects, IN *66-67*; glacier midges, IN *34*; guppies, UN *64-65*; hamlets, UN *68-69*; moles, AN *104*; moths, AN *94-95*; mudskippers, UN *29*; and pheromones, insects, IN *27*; praying mantises, IN *64-65*; salmon, AN *120-121*, UN *82*; sound production, insects, IN *28, 29*; spiders, AN *90-91*; splashing tetras, UN *74-75*; spring-tide breeders, AN *122-123*; squid's color change before, UN *142*. *See also* Breeding

Matter and chemistry: ST entire volume

Matterhorn (mountain), Switzerland: GE *142*

Mauchly, John: CO *14*

Maui (island), Hawaii, U.S.: PE *77*; Haleakala, PE *45*

Mauna Kea (volcano), Hawaii, U.S.: observatory, SP *28*

Mayfly nymphs: IN *10*

Meadows, Alpine: EC *56-57*

Meanders: development of, GE *26-27*

Measles: HU *132-133*

Measurements: precision, MA *48-49*

Mechanical devices: *See* Machines, simple

Mechanical heart: MA *132-133*; auxiliary, MA *133*

Mechanical mouse vs. optical mouse: CO *34-35*

Mechanical scanning television: MA *22-23*

Mechanical weathering: desert sand created by, GE *104-105*

Medakas: as diadromous fish, UN *11*; reproduction by, UN *31*

Medial and lateral moraines: GE *46-47*

Medical instruments and machines: MA *126-144*; for blood pressure measurement, MA *130-131*; CAT scanner, MA *134-135*; electrocardiograph, MA *136-137*; fiberscope, MA *138-139*; heart, mechanical, MA *132-133*; pacemaker, MA *133*; stethoscope, MA *144*; thermometer, electronic, MA *128-129*; for ultrasound, MA *142-143*; x-ray machine, MA *140-141*

Medical uses of computers: CO *138-139*

Medicines from plants: PL *132-133*

Mediterranean Sea: agriculture around, GE

Planet Earth
PE

Plant Life
PL

Physical Forces
PH

Structure of Matter
ST

Space & Planets
SP

Transportation
TR

Underwater World
UN

Weather & Climate
WE

131, 136-137; Nile meeting, GE 4-5, 33; and the sirocco, WE 46-47

Medulla oblongata: nerve impulses to, HU 101; salivary control center, HU 78

Medusafish: relationship of, with jellyfish, UN 144

Megakaryocytes: HU 66, 67

Megaloceros (extinct deer): EV 105, 129

Megalops larva, crab: UN 97

Meganeura (early flying insect): EV 54-55

Megatheres: EC 20

Megrez (star): movement, SP 90-91

Meiosis: HU 14-15

Meissner effect: PH 93

Meissner's corpuscles: HU 98, 99

Melanin: in hair, HU 47; in skin, HU 50-51

Melanocytes: HU 50-51

Melanophores: tree frogs, AN 56, 57

Melting of ice: PH 52-53, 54-55, ST 34; ions and, ST 41

Memory, digital: CO 18, 30-31; CD-ROM, CO 95; smart card's, MA 61

Memory B cells: HU 129

Memory cards for pocket computers: CO 91

Memory chips: CO 22

Mendel, Gregor: and genetics, EV 13

Mendeleev, Dmitri: ST 10

Merak (star): movement, SP 90-91

Mercator projections: GE 16-17

Mercury (planet): SP 8-9, 29

Mercury barometers: PH 16, 17

Meridians: GE 10, 11; on Mercator map, GE 16; and time zones, GE 20-21

Meristem: root, PL 14; shoot, PL 16, 32

Meristem culture: PL 140-141

Mesohippus (horse ancestor): EV 108

Mesonyx (extinct mammal): EV 112

Mesophyll: PL 39, 49

Mesopithecus (monkey ancestor): EV 123

Mesosaurus (early reptile): EV 58

Mesosphere: WE 8-9, 10-11

Mesozoic era: birds, EV 68-69, 70-71, 100-101; flowering plants, EV 102-103; flying reptiles, EV 63, 90-91, 96, 130, 134; life in, EV 60, 62-63, WE 143; mammal-like reptiles, EV 59, 62, 63, 64-65, 73; mammals, first, EV 65, 72-73; marine reptiles, EV 62, 92-93, 94-95, 96, 136-137; mollusks, EV 94-95, 98-99; thecodonts, EV 62, 66-67. See also Dinosaurs

Mesquite: EC 95

Message-display vs. tone-only pagers: CO 122, 123

Message handling system (MHS): CO 116, 117

Metabolism, cell: oxidation and, HU 52, 57

Metal detectors: MA 42-43

Metallic hydrogen in planets: SP 17, 28-29

Metals: and advance of civilization, ST 102; alloys, ST 112-113; alloys, shape-memory, ST 128-129, 140-141; amorphous, ST 142-143; atoms of, ST 13, 19, 28-29, 31, 121, 140-141, 142-143; burning, conditions for, ST 70-71; vs. ceramics, advanced, ST *charts* 131; electric conduction by, ST 19; flexibility, ST 28-29; glass enhanced with, ST 125; in periodic table, ST *chart* 10-11; plating methods, ST 62-63; refining, ST 102-103, 110-111, 114-115; rusting, ST 56-57

Metal spraying: ST 63

Metal testers in vending machines: MA 58, 59

Metal thermal sensors: MA 121; in fire alarm, MA 65; in iron, MA 120-121

Metamorphic rocks: PE 86, 87, 92

Metamorphosis: UN 88-89; anglerfish, UN 70; butterflies, IN 56-57, 78-83, 114-115; hypermetamorphosis, IN 81; incomplete vs. complete, IN 56-57, 80-81; simple, IN 80-81. See also Larvae

Metastasis: HU 139

Meteor craters: Barringer Crater, Ariz., U.S., SP 35; Mercury, SP 8-9

Meteorites: SP 34

Meteoroids and meteors: SP 34

Meteorology: computer use in, CO 134-135

Meteor showers: SP 34, 35

Meters: electric power, MA 118-119; water, MA 46, 47

Methane: on Titan (moon of Saturn), SP 22-23

Metrorail commuter trains, Washington, D.C., U.S.: control room for, TR 24

Mexico City, Mexico: earthquake destruction in, PE 46-47

M51 (galaxy): SP 106

Mice: deer, EC 136; as prey of barn owls, AN 4-5, 38, 39; as prey of rattlesnakes, AN 34-35; as prey of spiders, AN 27; and rats, seed dispersal by, EC 123; tree, Congo, EC 21

Micelles: formation of, ST 48-49

Michelson, Albert: experiment by, PH 126

Microchips: See Integrated circuits

Microfibrils in cotton fibers: ST 13

Micrometers: MA 48-49

Microphones: dynamic, MA 80

Microprocessors: camera's, MA 75; chips, CO 16-17, 22, 23; and keyboard, CO 32, 33; multiple, CO 42-43; robotic eye with, CO 99; sewing machine with, MA 105; thermometer's, MA 128, 129

Microscopes: electron, MA 32-33

Microvelia douglasi (water strider): IN 18-19

Microvilli: HU 8-9; small intestine, HU 88-89

Microwave landing system (MLS) for aircraft: TR 126

Microwave ovens: MA 102-103

Microwaves: radar, WE 115; speed gun's use of, MA 38-39

Mid-Atlantic Ridge: exposed portion of, PE 34; and seafloor spreading, PE 30

Middle ear: HU 112

Midges: glacier, IN 34; larvae, IN 35

Midgut: grasshoppers, IN 9; mosquitoes, IN 69

Mid-ocean ridges: GE 78, 79, PE 10, 34, 35, 112, *map* 113; formation of, PE 29; hydrothermal deposits at, PE 106; as location of normal faults, PE 49; and ocean-ridge volcanoes, PE 77; and San Andreas fault, PE 42, 43; and seafloor building, PE 32; and seafloor spreading, PE 30, 94

Midwife toads: European, UN 90

Migration: birds, navigation, AN 134-137; birds, V-formation, AN 132-133; fur seals, for breeding, UN 92; gray whales, for breeding, UN 94-95; lemmings, EC 102-103; reindeer, EC *map* 51

Migratory grasshoppers (locusts): egg laying, IN 130; evolutionary path, IN 7; ocelli, effect of, IN 22-23; swarming, IN 86-87

Migratory high pressure: WE 85

Mihara, Mount, Japan: PE 62-63, 78

Milankovitch, Milutin: WE 144

Military transportation: TR 109; bombers, Stealth, TR 109, 144; cruisers, TR 78-79; fighter jets, CCV, TR 140-141; fighter jets, Harrier, TR 138-139; submarines, TR 98-99, 102-103

Milk: as colloid, ST 20, 21; yogurt from, ST 84-85

Milk (baby) teeth: HU 26, 27, 35

Milkweed butterflies: AN 68

Milky Way (galaxy): SP 98, 100-107; and celestial sphere, SP 100; center, SP 100, 102, 104-105; Earth's view of, SP 100-101; shape, maintenance of, SP 106-107; stars in, locations of, SP 101; structure of, SP 102-103

Miller, Stanley M.: experiment by, EV 31

Millipedes: EC 36, IN 12-13; blind, EC 43

Mimicry: IN 112, 113, 118-119, 120; Batesian, AN 54-55, 68, 69; of butterflies, poisonous, AN 68-69; eyespots, AN 51, 64-65; mantises using, AN 30-31, 51; Müllerian, AN 69; of plant parts, AN 30-31, 50-53; of stinging insects, AN 54-55

Mimosa leaves: curling of, PL 44-45

Minerals: PE 96-107; coal, formation of, PE 104-105; copper mine, PE 96-97; diamonds, PE 90-91; locating, PE 98-99;

| Animal Behavior **AN** | Computer Age **CO** | Ecology **EC** | Evolution of Life **EV** | Geography **GE** | Human Body **HU** | Insects & Spiders **IN** | Machines & Inventions **MA** |

locations of, PE *100-101*; in oceans, PE *100, 101, 106-107, 138-139, 140-141*; oil and natural gas, formation of, PE *102-103*. *See also* Rocks

Mines: copper, PE *96-97*; strip, PE *105*

Minolta optical projector: SP *127*

Mir (space station): SP *144*

Mira (star): SP *82*

Mirages: WE *100-101*

Mirrors: curved, reflection by, PH *114-115*; galvanometer, Thomson's, MA *9*; Polaroid camera's use of, MA *93*; radio telescope, SP *121*; telescope, SP *118, 119, 122, 123*

Miscoptera (early flying insect): EV *55*

Missiles: cruise, CO *144*

Mission specialists: space shuttle, SP *136, 137*

Mississippi River, U.S.: delta, GE *33*; flood plains, GE *29*

Missouri, U.S.: cotton growing, GE *131*; St. Louis, topographic maps of, GE *12*

Mistletoe: PL *23, 82-83*

Mites: EC *36*

Mitochondria: PL *6, 7*

Mitosis: HU *8-9*

Mitsubishi Model MSRII (automated car): TR *60-61*

Miura Peninsula, Japan: earthquake's effects on, PE *maps 55*

Mixosaurus (early reptile): EV *62*

Mizar (star): movement, SP *90-91*

MLS (microwave landing system): TR *126*

Mobile phone calls: CO *120-121*

Mobile robots: problem of, CO *99*

Mock suns: WE *102, 103*

Models and simulations, computer: *See* Simulations and models, computer

Modems (modulator/demodulators), use of: CO *118, 119*; by pocket computers, CO *91*

Modulation: of carrier waves, MA *85*; in faxing, CO *115*; of frequency, CO *66*

Moeritherium (elephant ancestor): EV *110*

Mohorovičić discontinuity (Moho): PE *14*

Molars and premolars: HU *26, 27*

Molasses: sugarcane, MSG from, ST *90-91*

Molding of plastics: compression, ST *119*; injection, ST *118-119, 138*

Molds: PL *96-97*; as decomposers, PL *126*; as penicillin source, PL *132-133*

Molecules: ST *13*; air, PH *10-11, 60*; alumina, ST *115*; in apples, and browning, ST *80, 81*; aromatic, ST *126-127*; cellulose, ST *12-13, 67, 104, 105*; in colloids, ST *20*; DNA, ST *4-5*; in glass, ST *122, 123*; glucose, ST *66, 100-101*; glutamic acid, ST *90, 91*; of liquid crystals, ST *137*;

makeup of, ST *6-7*; nitrogen, ST *26-27*; odor, removal of, ST *52-53*; organic, EV *30*; ozone, ST *76-77*; in photosynthesis, ST *66*; polar and nonpolar, ST *42, 43, 48*; soap, ST *48-49*; sodium chloride, ST *18*; water, PH *20, 23, 52-53, 54-55, 62*. *See also* Polymers

Moles: AN *104-105*; cicada larvae eaten by, EC *106-107*; greater Japanese shrews, EC *37*; marsupial, EC *17*

Mollusks: conch, UN *35*; cone shells, UN *118-119*; crabs living in, UN *38-39*; extinct, EV *42, 94-95, 98-99*; in food chain, UN *126, 127*; in ocean trenches, UN *34*; octopuses, UN *60-61, 104, 141, 143*; reproduction, UN *98-99*; squid, UN *33, 113, 140-141, 142-143*; as starfish prey, defenses used by, UN *138-139*

Molting: and color changes, AN *59*; and instars, IN *80-81*; rattlesnakes, AN *63*

Momentum: PH *30*; angular, PH *32*

Monarch butterflies: IN *31, 82-83*

Money sorters in vending machines: MA *58, 59*

Monkeys: ancestors of, EV *123*; groups, AN *140, 141*; learning in groups, AN *144*; North American ancestors, extinct, EC *18-19*; rain forest, EC *28, 70-71*

Monocotyledons: bamboo as, PL *32*; vs. dicotyledons, PL *9*

Monocytes: HU *128*

Monoecious plants: PL *59*; squash, PL *58-59*

Monomers: polymerization of, ST *106-107*

Monorails: TR *28-29*

Monosodium glutamate (MSG): manufacture of, ST *90-91*

Monsoon lows: formation of, WE *132-133*

Monsoons: PE *118*, WE *130-131*; flooding, WE *132*

Monument Valley, Ariz., U.S.: GE *110-111*

Moon, Earth's: SP *64-75*; Apollo spacecraft, PH *19*; coronas around, WE *105*; crater formation, SP *64-65, 68*; Earth rising over, SP *67*; vs. Earth, weight on, PH *6-7*; eclipses of, SP *62-63*; far side, visible portion of, SP *71*; halos around, WE *102-103*; human bases on, possible, SP *74-75*; inside, SP *68-69*; motion of, SP *63, 70-73*; origin, SP *64, 66-67*; and precession of Earth, SP *60-61*; recession from Earth, SP *72-73*; role of, in tides, PE *128-129*; and solar eclipses, SP *41, 50-51, 62-63*; surface features, SP *64, 69*

Moons: formation of, SP *7*; of Jupiter (Io), SP *18-19*; of Mars (Phobos), SP *30*; of Neptune (Triton), SP *26-27*; of Saturn (Titan), SP *22-23*; of Uranus, SP *25*

Moorhens: cooperative breeding in, AN *117*

Moose: EC *58-59*; wolves attacking, AN *44-45*

Moraines: formation of, GE *44-45, 46-47*

Moray eels: UN *63, 67, 104*; leopard, AN *22*

Morganucodon (early mammal): EV *72-73*

Morley, Edward, experiment by: PH *126*

Mormyrids: UN *56*; relative of, UN *56-57*

Morning glories: PL *54*; dodder, PL *57*; grafting of, PL *135*

Morpho butterflies: wing coloration of, IN *30*

Morse, Samuel F. B.: MA *8*

Morse code: MA *9*

Mosasaurs: EV *94-95*

Moscow, Russia, climate of: GE *116-117*

Mosquitoes: AN *10-11*; blood sucking, IN *68-69*; flying method, IN *15*; food gathering, IN *46-47*; Johnston's organ, IN *27*

Mosquitofish: UN *73*

Mosses: EC *133*, PL *92, 95, 108-109*; Antarctica, EC *44, 45*

Motherboards: CO *22-23*

Mother-of-pearl clouds: WE *8, 11*

Moths: antennae, IN *26, 32*; as aphid enemy, IN *144*; bagworms, IN *85, 102-103*; bat catching, AN *42-43*; vs. butterflies, IN *32-33*; camouflage, use of, AN *53*; chameleons catching, AN *4-5*; defenses, IN *112-113, 116-117, 118-119*; with eyespots, AN *51, 64*; fastest flier, IN *chart 14*; in feeding order, EC *110, 111*; flightless, IN *85*; hearing, IN *24-25*; mating, AN *94-95*; mimics of other insects, AN *55, 69*; natural selection in, EV *16-17*; outbreaks, IN *88-89*; spiders catching, AN *27, 28-29*; wing coloration, IN *31*

Motion: changes in, and inertia, PH *28-29*; energy of (kinetic energy), PH *23, 29, 31, 52*; Newton's laws of, PH *18, 24, 28*

Motion analysis programs for athletes: CO *136-137*

Motmots: blue-crowned, EC *61*

Motor and sensory cortex of brain: HU *105*

Motorboats: TR *79*

Motor cells: mimosa's, PL *45*

Motorcycles: TR *42-43*

Motor nerve cells and nerves: HU *7, 102-103*

Mountain and valley breezes: WE *42, 43*

Mountain halos: WE *104-105*

Mountains: GE *86-87*; air currents over, WE *59, 68-69*; Alps, GE *45, 142-143*; Andes, GE *36, 140-141*, PE *38-39, map 39*, WE *72-73, 135*; Antarctica, GE *52, 53*; Appalachians, GE *87, 96-97*; cap clouds over, WE *68-69*; climate, effect on, GE *114-115*; and deserts, rain-shadow, WE *134-135*; Dinaric Alps, Yugoslavia, bora

Planet Earth
PE

Plant Life
PL

Physical Forces
PH

Structure of Matter
ST

Space & Planets
SP

Transportation
TR

Underwater World
UN

Weather & Climate
WE

winds over, WE *48-49*; fault-block, GE *86*; and foehns, WE *44-45*; and fog, WE *71, 72, 135*; formation of, GE *86, 87, 96-99*, PE *11, 34, 36-37, 38-39, 49*; glaciers in, GE *24-25, 42-47*; and gravity, PE *19*; Himalayas, GE *98-99*, PE *11, 19, 36, 49, 101*; icing on, WE *80-81*; in isostasy theory, PE *10*; landslides on, GE *102-103*; mineral deposits in, PE *100*; pressure and temperature on, WE *24, 25*; Rocky Mountains, Canada-U.S., GE *24-25, 115*, WE *44-45, 53*; subduction and, GE *87*; Teton Range, Wyo., GE *86*; turbulence over, WE *52, 53*; weather observation on, WE *108-109, 115*; young Earth's volcanoes, WE *7*. See also Mid-ocean ridges; Volcanoes; *and individual names*

Mountainside cable car systems: brakes, TR *30*; funicular, TR *31*

Mountain updrafts and gliders: TR *119*

Mountain-wave turbulence: WE *53*

Mouse: CO *34-35*

Mouthbrooders: UN *79, 80-81, 84*; Egyptian, UN *73*; other species' eggs incubated by, UN *84-85*

Mouths: adaptations for feeding, UN *104-105*; amphibians born through, UN *62, 90-91*; archerfish, UN *108*; blue whale, UN *116*; breathing, role in, UN *8, 9*; round herring, UN *106*

Movie camera: first (kinetograph), MA *20*

Movie projectors: MA *88-89*; kinetoscope, MA *20-21*

Movies: special effects for, CO *80-81*

M33 (galaxy): location of, SP *110*

Mucous membrane, olfactory: HU *117*

Mucus and sense of smell: HU *116, 117*

Mucus-secreting cells: HU *6*; in fallopian tubes, HU *16*; goblet cells, HU *88, 140*; in stomach, HU *82, 83*

Mudflows from Mount St. Helens: PE *70, 71*

Mudskippers: UN *28-29*

Mud snails: UN *98*

Mud snake, eastern: AN *63*

Mudstone: PE *87*; and fossil fuels, PE *102, 103*; hornfels from, PE *87, 92*; layers of, PE *86*

Mulberry trees: mutation in, PL *139*

Müllerian mimicry: AN *69*

Multicellular organisms: evolution of, EV *27, 38-39*

Multiple births: HU *22-23*

Multiple fruits: PL *67, 68-69*

Mundiopsis: UN *34*

Murrelets: ancient, EC *8, 33*

Murres: EC *8, 33*; oil spills and, EC *143*

Muscles of aquatic animals: fish, UN *6-7*; red, and body heat, UN *14, 15*; retractor

lentis, use of, UN *49*; squid's, and changes in coloring, UN *142*

Muscles of humans: HU *6, 30*; arm, HU *30-31, 39*; and breathing, HU *54*; contraction of, HU *36-37, 38, 39*; erector, HU *44, 47*; eye, HU *110-111*; heart, HU *7, 60, 144*; and joints, HU *38*; kinds of tissue, HU *7, 30, 60*; peristalsis, HU *81, 90, 91*; in reflex actions, HU *102*; and vocal sounds, HU *58*

Muscles of insects: dorsal vessel and, IN *8*; dragonfly nymph's lip, IN *44, 45*; wings and, IN *15*

Mushrooms: EC *134-135*, PL *92-93, 95, 98-99*; as decomposers, PL *126*; reindeer food, EC *50*

Music: compact disks (CDs) and phonograph records for playing, MA *86-87*; making, with computers, CO *66-67*; synthesizers for producing, CO *67*, MA *90-91*

Musical instruments: PH *128-129*; tones, production of, PH *134-135, 136-137*; tuning, PH *142-143*; wind instruments, PH *135, 136-137*

Musk dwarf antelope: EC *21*

Muskoxen: EC *48-49*

Mutations: EV *14-15*; breeding for, EV *18*, PL *138-139*; natural selection, EV *16-17*

Mutualism: ants and butterflies, IN *78-79*; ants and plants, IN *98-99*

Mycelia: mosses', PL *109*; in mushroom reproduction, PL *99*; of mushrooms, EC *135*

Mycorrhiza: EC *134*

Myelin sheath: HU *100-101*

Myocardial infarction: HU *144*

Myocardial (cardiac) muscle: HU *7, 60, 144*

Myofibrils: HU *36-37*

Myopia (nearsightedness): HU *110*

Myosin and actin: HU *36, 37*

Myriad leaf: EC *26, 27*

Myxomycetes (slime molds): PL *96, 97*

N

Nails: HU *46*

Napier, John: CO *8*

Napier's rods: CO *5, 8*

Nares: UN *46, 47*

Nasal passages: sperm whale's use of, UN *33*

Nastic movement: PL *44-45*

National Weather Service forecasts: WE *121*

Natural gas and oil: formation of, PE *102-103*; in reservoir rocks, PE *103*

Natural immunity: HU *132*

Natural killer cells: HU *128, 129*

Natural resources: See Minerals

Natural selections: EV *12, 16-17*

Nauplius larvae: barnacle, UN *41*

Nautical charts: making of, GE *18-19*

Nautiluses: chambered, EV *99, 140*

Naval Navigation Satellite System (NNSS), U.S.: TR *84-85*

Navigation: TR *78, 80-81*; aircraft, aids for, TR *122-123, 124-125*; automatic car's system, TR *60*; in fog, TR *82-83*; maps used for, GE *18-19*; Mercator projections used for, GE *16-17*; on-board navigation computers, in automobiles, CO *103*; in past, TR *86-87*; portolans used for, GE *15*; rules of the road for, TR *83*; satellite, TR *84-85*, PE *16, 137*; submarine, aids for, TR *103*

Navigation methods of animals: birds, AN *134-137*; river dolphins, UN *58-59*; salmon, AN *120-121*

Nazca plate: boundary of, PE *35*; and formation of Andes mountains, PE *38-39*

Neanderthals: EV *126, 127*

Neap tides: cause of, PE *129*

Nearsightedness: HU *110*

Nebulas: SP *86-87*; Crab, SP *85, 96*; in Orion, SP *6, 86, 87, 121*; Pleiades, SP *86, 88*; and star formation, SP *76-77, 87, 88-89*; Sun's formation from, SP *6, 38*; x-ray sources, location of, SP *97*

Necrolemurs (extinct primates): EV *122*

Nectar guide and nectar gland: PL *52*

Needle-leaved trees: vs. broad-leaved, EC *24-25*; pines, PL *43, 48-49*. See also Conifers

Negative-channel metal-oxide semiconductor (n-MOS): CO *22*

Negative taxis: paramecium, AN *6*

Nematic liquid crystals: ST *137*

Nematocysts: sea anemones, AN *48*

Nematodes: EC *36*

Neodymium 144: alpha decay of, PH *91*

Neofinetia falcata (epiphyte): PL *22-23*

Neopterans: EV *54, 55*

Neotropical Region: animals of, EC *5*

Nepenthes pitcher plant: PL *47*

Nephrons: HU *95*

Neptune (planet): SP *5, 26, 27, 29*; moon of (Triton), SP *26-27*; rings, SP *20, 26-27*; Voyager mission to, SP *138*

Nerve cells: See Neurons (nerve cells) of human brain

Nerves: HU *100-101*; cochlear, HU *113*; gustatory, HU *118, 119*; motor, HU *102-103*; olfactory, HU *116, 117*; optic, HU *111*; receptors in skin, HU *98-99, 100*; in reflex actions, HU *102-103*; pinched, cause of, HU *41*. See also Neurons

| Animal Behavior **AN** | Computer Age **CO** | Ecology **EC** | Evolution of Life **EV** | Geography **GE** | Human Body **HU** | Insects & Spiders **IN** | Machines & Inventions **MA** |

Nervous system of humans: HU *7*, 96-125; spinal cord, HU *41, 101, 103. See also* Brain, human; Nerves; Sense organs, human

Nervous system of insects: IN *8-9*

Nesting holes: mudskippers', UN *29*

Nests: Africanized bees, IN *136-137*; ants, IN *78-79, 98-99, 127, 138-139*; bagworms, IN *102-103*; bees, site selection, IN *135*; dinosaurs, EV *78*; dung beetles, IN *92-93, 106-107, 130, 131*; family life, range of, IN *130-131*; ground bees, IN *108-109*; hunting wasps, IN *55, 92-93, 110-111*; insects, IN *92-111*; leaf-rolling weevils, IN *104-105*; male fish building, UN *79*; seabirds, EC *32-33*; spiders, IN *75, 94-95, 96-97*; spittlebugs, IN *100-101*; sticklebacks, male, UN *79*; termite mounds, IN *142-143*

Netherlands, the: land reclamation in, GE *132-133*

Net-winged beetles: AN *69*

Networks, computer: CO *108-129*; business computers, CO *92-93*; car phones, CO *120-121*; data transfer between computers, CO *91, 118-119*; electronic mail, CO *116-117*; fax machines, CO *114-115*; fiberoptic communications, CO *124-125*; pagers, electronic, CO *122-123*; picture phones, CO *126-127*; satellites, communications, CO *128-129*; teleconferencing, CO *112-113*; telephone lines, voice transmission through, CO *110-111*

Neurocomputers: CO *44-45*

Neurons (nerve cells) of human brain: CO *45*, HU *7*, 96, *100-101*; in cerebral cortex, HU *24, 104-105*; in reflex actions, HU 102, *103*; and sleep, HU 123

Neuropteris (Paleozoic seed fern): EV *53*

Neurotransmitters: HU 100, *101*; sleep-inducing, HU 123

Neutral gear: automobile's, TR *46*

Neutrinos: Sun's production of, SP *40, 44*

Neutron core of supernova: SP *84*

Neutrons: ST *7*; in carbon-14 formation, ST *25*; in nuclear fission, PH *108*; in nuclear fusion, SP *44-45*, ST *16-17*

Neutron stars: SP *93*, 96, *97*; Crab nebula and, SP *85, 96*

Neutrophils: HU *65, 128, 132*

New Guinea cicada: AN *50*

New materials: *See* Materials technology

Newton, Sir Isaac: PH 24, 112; laws of motion, PH 18, 24, 28

Newton's golden bowerbird: AN *101*

Newts: Australian brown, AN *52*; California, poisonous, AN *67*; early development of, EV *133*

New World monkeys: ancestors of, EV *123*

NGC1073 (galaxy): SP *103*

NGC1300 (galaxy): SP *103*

NGC3031 (galaxy): SP *103*

NGC5128 (galaxy): SP *103*

Niagara Falls, N.Y., U.S.: rainbow over, WE *96-97*

Niches, ecological: adapation to, EV 5, *20-21*; and differentiation of species, EV 23

Niepce, Joseph-Nicéphore: MA 16

Night-blooming flowers: PL *53*

Nightjars: AN *52*

Nile River, Africa: GE *4-5*; delta, GE *4-5, 33*

Nimbostratus clouds: WE *61, chart* 74

Ninetyeast Ridge: PE *map* 112-113

Niphanda fusca (butterfly): IN *78-79*

Nipkow, Paul: MA 22

Nipkow scanning disks: use of, MA *22-23*

Nitrates: ST *27*; production of, ST *26*

Nitrogen: carbon 14 and, ST *24, 25*; reactions involving, ST *26-27*

Nitrogen cycle: ST *26-27*

Nitrogen dioxide and acid rain: ST 64

Nitrogen in atmosphere: WE *8*; and aurora, WE *17*; ionosphere, WE *14*

Nitrogen oxides: in ionosphere, WE *14, 15*; and sulfur oxides, pollution by, WE 26, *27, 28-29*

Nitrogen volcanoes: Triton (moon of Neptune), SP *27*

Nitroglycerin explosion: chain reaction in, MA *24-25*

n-MOS (negative-channel metal-oxide semiconductor): CO 22

NNSS (U.S. Naval Navigation Satellite System): TR *84-85*

Nobel, Alfred: MA 24

Nobeyama Radio Observatory, Japan: radio map from, SP *105*; telescope, SP *120-121*

Noctuid moths: antennae, IN *32*; ear, IN *24*

Nodes and antinodes: PH *137*

Nodes of Ranvier: HU *100*

Non-insulin-dependent diabetes: HU 143

Nonpolar and polar molecules: separation of, ST *42, 43*; soap, working of, ST 48

Non-REM vs. REM (rapid eye movement) sleep: HU 122, *chart* 122, 123, *124-125*

Norepinephrine: and sleep, HU 123

Normal vs. reverse faults: PE *48*

Normandy (region), France: cuestas, GE *93*; shoreline of, GE *68-69*

Norris Dam, Tenn., U.S.: GE *134*

North: true vs. magnetic, PE *21*

North America nebula: SP *86*

North American plate and San Andreas fault: PE *42, 43*

North Atlantic Drift (ocean current): effect of, GE 116

North Carolina, U.S.: Appalachian Mountains, GE *96*; dam's power station, GE *134*

Northern banded water snake: favorite prey, AN *graph* 15

Northern cricket, Japan: AN *96*

North Pole: Foucault pendulum at, SP *52, 53*; precession, SP *60-61*; seasons at, SP *59*; solar wind, effects of, SP *49*; stars' apparent motion at, SP *53*

North Sea, rivers emptying into: Rhine, GE *map* 41; Thames, GE *38*

North Star: changing of, SP *60-61. See also* Polaris

Norway: fjords in, GE *91*

Norway lemmings: range of, EC *map* 103

Nose: odor detection by, HU *116-117*

Notch grafting: PL *134-135*

Nothosaurus (early reptile): EV *62*

Notothens: UN *17*; spotted, UN *16-17*

Notsukezaki, Cape, Japan: GE *75*

NPN transistor: PH 84, *85*

N-type and P-type semiconductors: PH *84, 85*; silicon, PH 84, *85, 110-111*

Nuclear fission: PH 108, ST *14-15*, TR 102, *103*

Nuclear fusion: ST *16-17*; Earth, SP *45*; stars, SP 76, *92*; Sun, SP 40, *44-45*

Nuclear reactors: PH *108-109*, ST *15*; control rods, ST *14*; core, PH *94-95, 108*; fusion, experimental, ST *17*

Nuclear submarines: TR *102-103*

Nuclei, atomic: ST 6, *7*; fission of, ST *14-15*; fusion of, ST *16-17*; radioactive, PH *91, 108*

Nucleic acids: *See* DNA; RNA

Nucleoli: of plant cell, PL *6, 7*

Nucleus: DNA in human cell, HU *4-5, 10-11*; of human cell, HU *8-9*; of plant cell, PL *6, 7*

Nucleus of comet: SP *32, 33*

Nucleus pulposus: HU 40, *41*

Nuts: PL 65, *77*; methods of cracking, AN *16, 46*

Nylon: ST *108*; spinning of, ST *108-109*

Nymphs: cicada, IN *89*; cricket's care of, IN *74*; dragonfly, IN *10, 36-37, 44-45, 80-81*; with gills, IN *10*; grasshopper, IN *56-57, 80-81*; spittlebug, IN *100-101*

O

Oak trees: bark, PL *27*; leaves, PL *43*; nuts, PL *77*

Oases: GE *62-63*

Oats: PL *144*

Objective and ocular lenses: PH *116*

Oblique hatchetfish: UN *23*

Planet Earth
PE

Plant Life
PL

Physical Forces
PH

Structure of Matter
ST

Space & Planets
SP

Transportation
TR

Underwater World
UN

Weather & Climate
WE

Observatories: *See* Telescopes

Occluded front: WE *87*

Ocean currents: *See* Currents, ocean

Oceanic crust: vs. continental crust, PE *8, 9, 10;* formation of, PE *32, 41;* and seamounts, PE *44, 76-77, 114-115. See also* Subduction

Oceanic plate interactions: GE *86, 87*

Oceanic ridges: *See* Mid-ocean ridges

Oceanographic satellites: PE *136-137*

Oceanographic vessels: PE *31, 137*

Ocean-ridge volcanoes: formation of, PE *77*

Oceans: GE *68-83,* PE *108-144;* advection fog, WE *71;* black smokers, EV *32-33;* bottom currents, PE *116-117;* breakers, PE *108-109, 126, 127;* changes in, with depth, PE *117, 134-135;* continental margins, PE *114-115;* coral reefs, formation of, GE *80-81;* desalinization of, PE *139;* and deserts, WE *134, 135;* El Niño phenomenon, PE *124-125;* as energy source, PE *139;* farming of, PE *142-143;* fishing areas, GE *126-127;* floating on, PH *8-9;* floor, GE *78-79;* formation of, EV *28-29,* PE *7, 33, 110-111,* WE *6-7;* fossil fuels formed in, PE *102;* future uses of, possible, PE *144;* in global water cycle, GE *68, 82-83;* heat flow, PE *map 13;* hurricanes, WE *82-83, 90-95, 115;* importance of, PE *108;* invasion of land by, GE *90-91;* vs. land, PE *chart 113;* life's beginnings in, EV *30-31;* manganese nodules in, PE *140-141;* maps for navigating, GE *15, 16-17, 18-19;* melted icecaps' effect on, possible, GE *72-73;* as mineral location, PE *98, 100, 101, 106-107, 138-139, 140-141;* mirages over, WE *100;* and monsoons, WE *130;* as power source, PH *106-107;* saltwater intrusion from, GE *64;* Sargasso Sea in, PE *132-133;* satellite scanning of, PE *136-137, 143;* sea and land breezes, WE *42, 43, 76;* seafloor building, PE *32-33, 41;* seafloor spreading, PE *30-31, 32, 94;* seamounts, PE *44, 76-77, 114-115;* sonar use in, PH *130;* storm waves, PE *130-131;* stromatolites, EV *26-27, 34-35;* surfers riding waves of, PH *38-39;* terrain under, PE *112-113;* tsunamis, PE *54, 58-59;* wave motions, PE *126-127;* weather ships and buoys, WE *110-111, 117;* whirlpools, PE *122-123,* PH *20. See also* Coastal areas; Currents, ocean; Tides, ocean; Trenches, ocean; *and individual names*

Ocean sunfish: metamorphosis in, UN *88-89*

Ocean tides: *See* Tides, ocean

Ocean travel: *See* Water travel

Ocean trenches: *See* Trenches, ocean

Ocelli: IN *22-23*

Ocotillos: EC *86, 87*

Octopuses: camouflage, use of, UN *143;* hermit crab's protection against, AN *78-79;* ink squirted by, UN *141;* as prey of moray eel, UN *104;* vision, UN *44, 60-61*

Ocular and objective lenses: PH *116*

Odors: detection of, by humans, HU *116-117;* removal of, ST *52-53*

Office equipment: copiers, MA *62-63;* electronic blackboards, MA *70-71;* fax machines, MA *68-69*

Offices: computer use in, CO *92-93*

Offset printing: MA *40-41*

Ogouchi Dam, Tokyo, Japan: WE *79*

Oil: crude, refining of, ST *116-117;* distribution of, in rock layers, PE *103;* drilling rigs, synthetic diamonds used in, ST *133;* formation of, PE *102-103;* fragrant, extracting, ST *126-127;* locating deposits of, PE *98, 99;* removal of, by soap, ST *48-49;* and water, separation of, ST *42-43, 127*

Oil, spermaceti: in whale, UN *32, 33*

Oil fields: Saudi Arabian, PE *102*

Oil film: colors on, PH *120*

Oil-seal vacuum pump: MA *45*

Oil spills: effects of, EC *142-143*

Oily secretion from sebaceous gland: HU *44*

Okhotsk, Sea of: high (weather system), WE *133*

Old Faithful (geyser), Yellowstone National Park, U.S.: PE *80*

Old-man cactus: PL *113*

Old-man's-beard lichen: PL *107*

Olfactory nerves: human, HU *116-117;* silkworm moth's, IN *26*

Olfactory sense of aquatic animals: carp, UN *45, 46-47;* eels, UN *47;* fish, general, UN *46-47;* sharks, UN *55*

Olfactory sense of humans: HU *116-117*

Olfactory sense of insects: silkworm moth's, IN *26*

Oligokyphus (mammal-like reptile): EV *65*

Olive (tree): PL *78-79;* growing, GE *131, 136-137*

Olympus, Mount, Mars: SP *12-13*

Omega System: TR *map 125*

Omori formula for earthquake focus: PE *53*

O'Neill, Gerard: space colony designed by, SP *140-141*

Onions: PL *29;* seeds, germination of, PL *13*

Onnes, Heike Kamerlingh: PH *92*

Open vs. closed universe: SP *115*

Operculum: UN *8*

Oplismenus grass: PL *75*

Opossums: bluffing by, AN *85*

Optical axis of fish eyes: UN *48, 51*

Optical fibers: communication by, CO *124-125;* glass, ST *124-125*

Optical mouse: CO *34*

Optical pyrometers: PH *56, 57*

Optical telescopes: SP *118-119;* Galileo's, SP *116;* Hubble Space Telescope, SP *124;* for solar astronomy, SP *122-123*

Optic nerves, human: HU *111;* vs. octopus, UN *61*

Optics: binoculars, MA *94-95;* in fax machine, MA *69;* fiberscope, MA *138-139;* microscope, electron, MA *32-33;* movie projector, MA *88-89. See also* Cameras; Optical telescopes

Optional four-wheel drive: TR *49*

Oral groove: paramecium, AN *7*

Orange-crested gardener: bower of, AN *101*

Oranges: PL *66, 67*

Orange trees: GE *131*

Orangutans: AN *140,* EC *70*

Orbits: asteroids, SP *31, 35;* comets, SP *4-5, 32-33;* Earth, SP *54-55;* Earth, and ice ages, WE *144;* Io (moon of Jupiter), SP *19;* Moon, Earth's, SP *63, 70-73;* planets, SP *4-5, 25, 31, 35;* satellites, PH *36-37*

Orb webs, spiders': IN *36-37, 38, 94*

Orcas: UN *114*

Orchids: EC *68, 69,* PL *22-23;* mantis resembling, AN *30-31;* pollinating devices, PL *52, 53;* tissue culture, PL *140-141*

Ordovician period: species, WE *142;* temperatures, WE *chart 142*

Ores: refining, ST *102-103, 110-111, 114-115;* and rust, ST *56, 57*

Organelles: PL *5, 6-7, 10-11*

Organ of Corti: HU *112, 113*

Organs, human: artificial, CO *138-139;* and organ systems, HU *6-7. See also individual names*

OR gate: CO *28*

Oriental garden crickets: AN *97*

Oriental great reed warblers: AN *98-99;* eggs, AN *114*

Oriental Region: animals of, EC *4-5*

Oriental saddleback caterpillars: IN *121*

Orient Express (luxury train): TR *19*

Orifice plate: MA *46-47*

Orion (constellation): movement, apparent, SP *54;* nebulas in, SP *6, 86, 87, 121;* stars in, SP *78, 80*

Orion nebula: SP *6, 86;* gas analysis, SP *121*

Ornithischians vs. saurischians: EV *chart 66-67, 74-75*

Ornitholestes (dinosaur): EV *74*

Ornithosuchus (early reptile): EV *67*

Orogeny (mountain building): PE *11, 34, 36-37, 38-39, 49;* belts of, PE *map 11*

| Animal Behavior **AN** | Computer Age **CO** | Ecology **EC** | Evolution of Life **EV** | Geography **GE** | Human Body **HU** | Insects & Spiders **IN** | Machines & Inventions **MA** |

Ørsted, Hans Christian: PH 94

Osaka Bay, Japan: as airport site, GE 144

Oscillators: in quartz watch, MA 97; VC (voltage control), and sound frequency, MA 90

Oscilloscope: PH 135

Oshima Island, Japan: volcanoes on, PE 62-63, 78

Osmeterium: swallowtail's, IN 123

Osmosis: and gas in swim bladder, UN 13; and saline balance, UN 10, 11

Osseous (bony) tissue: HU 7

Osteichthians: EV 49; amphibian evolution from, EV 56-57

Osteoblasts: HU 34, 35

Osteoclasts: HU 34, 35

Ostracod: UN 24

Ostriches: EC 82

Ota River delta, Japan: GE 26

Otoliths: fish, UN 52; jellyfish, UN 43

Otters: river, EC 139; sea, AN 47, EC 130-131, 142

Ouranosaurus (dinosaur): EV 75

Outer ear, human: HU 112

Output devices: CO 18, 19; for pocket computers, CO 90-91; printers, working of, CO 38-39

Ova: *See* Egg and sperm, human

Oval body in fish: function of, UN 13

Ovaries of humans: HU 13, 16, 28, 75

Ovaries of plants: corn kernels, PL 84-85; fruits from, PL 66-67, 68; squash flower's, PL 59

Ovens: microwave, MA 102-103

Overgrazing and desertification: GE 107

Overripening of foods: ST 88-89

Overtones: PH 134, 135, 137

Ovipositors: IN 124

Oviraptor (dinosaur): EV 77, 79

Ovule: development in, PL 8-9

Owl butterflies: eyespots on, IN 118

Owls: barn, AN 4-5, 38-39; elf, EC 89

Oxalic acid: ink removal with, ST 72-73

Oxbow lakes, formation of: GE 26-27

Oxidation: and cell metabolism, HU 52, 57

Oxidation-reduction (redox) reactions: ST 56, 73; in automobile batteries, ST 58-59; ink and ink removal, ST 72-73; iron in, ST 56; ores, creation and refining of, ST 110, 111

Oxygen: ST 6-7; vs. antioxygen, ST 22-23; atmospheric, EV 27, 34, ST 36-37, WE 7, 8, 13, 14, 17, 29, 30, 31; and browning of apples, ST 80, 81; and burning of metals, ST 70; carbon combustion and, ST 67; for disinfection of water, ST 98, 99; displacement by carbon monoxide, HU 72, 73; fire extinguishers and, ST 69;

food protected from, ST 88, 89; hemoglobin and, HU 64, 72; ink, reactions with, ST 72, 73; iron, reaction with, ST 56, 57; liquid, as rocket fuel, PH 18; ozone layer, hole in, ST 76-77; in photosynthesis and respiration, PL 38; pig iron converted with, ST 111, 112-113; respiratory roots for, PL 22; rocket fuel, ST 74, 75; supplying body with, HU 56-57, 65; in water molecules, PH 54-55

Oxygen conservation by sperm whale: UN 32

Oxygen cycle: ST 37

Oxygen in atmosphere: EV 27, 34, WE 8; and acid rain, WE 29; and aurora, WE 17; formation of, WE 7; ionosphere, WE 14; ozone from, WE 13; and ozone holes, WE 30, 31; source of, ST 36-37

Oxyntic cells: HU 83

Oyashio Current: PE 123

Oyster crabs: UN 38

Oysters: reproduction by, UN 99

Ozone for disinfection: ST 98

Ozone layer: WE 4, 8-9, 12-13, 25; formation of, WE 7; holes in, ST 76-77, WE 30-31

P

Pacas: EC 20

Pacemaker, artificial: CO 138, MA 133

Pacemaker, human (sinoatrial node): HU 61

Pachycephalosaurus (dinosaur): EV 86-87

Pacific Ocean: Andes along, GE 36, 140-141; coral reefs, GE 81; currents, WE 72-73, 127; El Niño phenomenon, PE 124-125, WE 140-141; fishing areas, GE 126-127; and garúa, WE 72-73; high pressure, WE 85, 88, 93, 133; International Date Line, GE 21; low pressure, WE 86, 111; saltiness, variation in, PE *chart* 134; satellite information on, WE 84, 111; tides, PE *map* 129; typhoon birthplace, WE *maps* 90, 91, 93; vertical layers of, PE 135; winds, rain from, GE 114-115

Pacific plate: boundary of, PE 35; and San Andreas fault, PE 42, 43

Pacific Rim: PE 114-115

Pacinian corpuscles: HU 98, 99

Packet switching: CO 118-119

Pack ice: cracking of, by icebreakers, TR 100, 101

Paddlefish: UN 107

Paddle steamers: TR 90-91

Pagers, electronic: CO 122-123

Pahoehoe lava: PE 65

Painting of automobiles: robot use in, CO 101

Pakicetus (whale ancestor): EV 112-113

Pakistan: kanat access holes in, GE 139

Palaelama (extinct mammal): EV 121

Paleozoic era: amphibian evolution, EV 56-57; backboned animals, evolution of, EV 46-47; Cambrian period, EV 40-45; fliers, first, EV 54-55; jaws, evolution of, EV 48-49; land creatures, first, EV 50-51; land plants, evolution of, EV 52-53; life in, EV 40-59, WE 142; reptile evolution, EV 58-59

Palisade tissue: PL 39, 40, 41

Palm trees: PL 86-87; coconut, EC 22-23; peach, PL 143

Palomar, Mount, Calif., U.S.: Hale telescope, SP 118-119

Pampas: EC 77

Pampas grass, Japanese: PL 73

Panama Canal, Panama: TR 92-93

Pancreas, human: HU 84-85; artificial system for, CO 138; and diabetes, HU 142-143; islets of Langerhans, HU 75, 84, 85, 142-143

Pandas, giant: EC 112

Pangaea (hypothetical supercontinent): EC 10, *map* 11, *map* 16, 20; breakup of, PE 24-25, 38-39

Panther puffer: UN 127

Panthers: Florida, EC 138

Pantograph: high-speed train's, TR 33

Papermaking: ST 104-105

Paper punch as lever: PH 42

Paper wasp: nest of, IN 92-93, 110-111

Papilionid butterfly caterpillar: IN 119

Papillae on tongue: HU 118

Pappus on dandelion fruit: PL 72, 73

Parahippus (horse ancestor): EV 109

Parallax: stellar, SP 55

Parallel circuits: PH 75

Parallel (pipeline) processing: CO 42-43

Paramecia (single-celled organisms): AN 6-7, EV 39

Parasaurolophus (dinosaur): EV 76, 85

Parasites: cleaner shrimp removing, AN 23; crabs, UN 38-39; cuckoo catfish, UN 84-85; insects, flightless, IN 16-17, 84; mushrooms, EC 134-135; plants, PL 23, 57, 82-83; plants, roots of, PL 23, 57, 83; *Rafflesia*, PL 51, 56-57; remora removing, AN 24; sexual (anglerfish), UN 70-71; wasps, IN 90, 91, 114. *See also* Fungi

Parasitic wasps: for biological pest control, IN 90, 91; cocoons, IN 114

Parathyroid glands: HU 75

Parenting: AN 89, 110-123; alligators, AN 110-111; bats, EC 39; cooperative breeding, AN 116-117; cuckoos and hosts, AN 114-115; eagles, EC 124, 126; feeding of young by aquatic animals, UN 86-87;

Planet Earth
PE

Plant Life
PL

Physical Forces
PH

Structure of Matter
ST

Space & Planets
SP

Transportation
TR

Underwater World
UN

Weather & Climate
WE

fish, UN *78-79, 86-87*; fish, care of other species' hatchlings, UN *84-85*; frogs, UN *90-91*; hover fly egg laying, site selection for, AN *118-119*; insects, IN *74-75, 76-77, 130-131*; lions, AN *139*; penguins, AN *88-89, 112-113*; pill bugs, IN *76-77*; polar bears, EC *49*; sloths, EC *63*; spiders, IN *74-75*; toads, UN *90-91*; whooping cranes, EC *113*

Parhelia (mock suns): WE *102, 103*

Paris Basin, France: cuesta ridges in, GE *93*

Parking system: automated car's, TR *61*

Parnara guttata (butterfly): IN *33*

Parnassius (butterfly): EV *141*

Parnassus glacialis (butterfly): IN *31*

Parotid glands: HU *78, 79*

Parr (salmon): UN *82*

Parrotfish: blue, UN *104-105*; food chain involving, EC *129*

Parry arcs: WE *102*

Particle (corpuscular) vs. wave theory of light: PH *112*

Pascal, Blaise: CO *8, 9*; quoted, CO *9*

Pascaline (adding machine): CO *4-5, 8-9*

Passenger pigeons: EC *112*

Passenger trains: cable cars, TR *30-31*; electromagnetic air brakes, TR *10, 11*; high-speed, TR *4-5, 32-33*; luxury, TR *18-19*; monorails, TR *28-29*. *See also* Commuter trains

Passive submission: wolves, AN *45*

Passwords: CO *106*; possible, number of, CO *chart 107*

Patagia: EV *114-115, 134*

Pathogens: *See* Infectious diseases

Pattern recognition in octopuses: UN *61*

Payload specialists on space shuttle: SP *133, 136, 137*

PCBs (printed circuit boards): CO *20-21*; motherboard, CO *22-23*

PCs: *See* Personal computers

Peach palms: PL *143*

Peach trees: fruit, PL *66-67*; shoots, tissue culture of, PL *143*

Pea crabs in clams: UN *38-39*

Pearleye: UN *69*

Pearlfish: relationship of with sea cucumbers, UN *144*

Peas: laws of genetics in, EV *13*; plants, PL *94*; tendrils of plants, PL *29, 30*

Peat: formation of, PE *104*

Pectoral fins: of flying fish, UN *128-129*; of gurnard, UN *47*; of mudskipper, UN *28*; of porcupinefish, UN *20*

Pedal and sprocket on bicycle: PH *46, 47*

Pedicellariae: sea urchin's, UN *139*

Pedipalps: male spider's, AN *90, 91*

Pelagic fish: hermaphrodites, UN *69*; with rete mirabile, UN *14-15*; tail type, UN *20, 21*

Pelvic fins: mudskipper's, UN *28*

Pelvis, human: male vs. female, HU *12, 13*

Pelycosaurs: evolution from, EV *chart 65*

Pendulums: clock's, working of, MA *13*; Foucault's, SP *52-53*; sympathetic vibrations in, PH *143*

Peneplains vs. structural plains: GE *28*

Penguins: EC *8, 9, 46, 47, 49*; with chicks, AN *88-89, 112-113*; Galápagos, EC *6*; swimming style of, UN *18-19*

Penicillin: source of, PL *132-133*

Peninsulas: drowned valleys with, GE *90*; sand spits, GE *75*; Sinai, GE *5*

Pens: electronic blackboard's, MA *71*

Pentaceratops (dinosaur): EV *89*

Penumbra and umbra: SP *62, 63*

Peppered moths: camouflage by, IN *116-117*; natural selection in, EV *16-17*

Peppers: green, PL *136*

Pepsin: HU *82, 83*

Pepsinogen: HU *82, 83*

Perch: anatomy, UN *6-7*; climbing, UN *29*; surfperch, body fluids of, UN *chart 16*; white, EC *141*

Perched ground water: GE *56*

Perfume: making of, ST *126-127*

Pericarp of fruit: PL *66-67*; coconut, PL *86-87*

Pericycle of root: PL *15*

Peridotite (rock): PE *88, 89*

Perilymph: HU *112, 113, 115*

Periodic table: ST *4, chart 10-11*

Peripheral nerves: *See* Nerves

Peripherals: CO *19*

Periscope: use of, on submarines, TR *103*

Peristalsis: in esophagus, HU *80*; in large intestine, HU *90, 91*

Permanent teeth: HU *26, 27, 35*

Permian period: species, WE *143*; temperatures, WE *chart 143*

Persimmon seed, inside of: PL *12*

Personal computers: CO *19*; E-mail, use of, CO *116, 117*; graphics, CO *70*; motherboard, CO *22-23*; pocket computer's communication with, CO *91*; as word processors, CO *58-59*

Personal identification numbers (PINs): CO *88, 89*

Personnel functions of computers: CO *93*

Peru: coast of, garúa along, WE *72-73*; Lima, weather conditions in, WE *chart 73*

Peru-Chile Trench: PE *map 112-113*

Peru (Humboldt) Current: WE *127*; and garúa, WE *72-73*

Pesticides: biological accumulation of, EC *144*; biological control vs., IN *90-91*

Petals: opening and closing of, PL *60-61*; sunflower, PL *71*

Petrels: EC *46*; snow, EC *45*

Petunias: PL *55*

Pharyngoconjunctival fever: HU *chart 141*

Pharynx: HU *80*

Phase changes: ST *32-33, 34-35, 38-39*; boiling, MA *100*, PH *22-23, 62-63*; in coolants, systems using, MA *106-107, 122-125*; freezing, PH *66-67*; freezing point, lowering of, ST *40-41*; heat and, PH *22-23, 52-53, 54-55, 62-63*; melting, PH *52-53, 54-55*; vaporization/evaporation, PH *22-23, 53, 62-63, 64-65*; water vapor and, PH *64*

Phase-detection autofocus: MA *75*

Phecda (star): movement, SP *90-91*

Phenols in apple: ST *80*

Pheromones: ants' use of, IN *43*; moth's, AN *94-95*, IN *27*

Phiomia (elephant ancestor): EV *110*

pH levels in European regions: EC *maps 75*

Phloem: in roots, PL *14*; in stems, PL *20*; in tree trunks, PL *25, 26, 27*

Phobos (moon of Mars): SP *30*

Phones: *See* Telephones and telephone lines

Phonograph records: MA *86*

Phororhacos (giant extinct bird): EV *107*

Phosphors in TV picture tube: MA *76*

Photoblepharon: UN *27*

Photocopiers: MA *62*; color, MA *62-63*

Photodetectors: bar codes scanned by, CO *86*; in mouse, CO *34*

Photodiodes: in fiberoptic communication, CO *125*; in mouse, CO *35*; in scanners, CO *87*

Photoelectric sensors in smoke detectors: MA *65*

Photography: autofocus (AF), cameras with, MA *74-75*; first cameras, MA *16-17*; holographic, PH *124-125*; instant, color, MA *92-93*; movie camera, first, MA *20*; movie projectors, MA *20-21, 88-89*; popularization of, MA *18-19*

Photophores: UN *24, 25*; blinking, UN *26, 27*

Photosensitive resin: ST *144*

Photosphere: SP *40, 41, 42-43*

Photosynthesis: PL *6, 10-11, 38, 124, 125*; and atmospheric oxygen, ST *36, 37*; beginnings of, EV *27, 34*; organs for, PL *29*; in seaweed, PL *104, 105*; and stored energy, ST *66*

Photosynthetic organisms: SP *48, 49*

pH scale: ST *83*

Phyllotaxis: PL *36-37*

Physical forces: PH entire volume

Phytoplankton: EC *46, 140*

Animal Behavior
AN

Computer Age
CO

Ecology
EC

Evolution of Life
EV

Geography
GE

Human Body
HU

Insects & Spiders
IN

Machines &
Inventions **MA**

Piano: tuning of, PH *142-143*

Picture elements: *See* Pixels

Picture phones: CO *126-127*

Pictures: electronic publishing of, CO *94-95*; faxing, CO *114-115. See also* Graphics, computer

Picture tube, TV: MA *76*; working of, MA *77*

Piezoelectric crystals: MA *96*; watches using, MA *96-97*

Pigeons: navigation experiment with, AN *137*; passenger, EC *112*

Pig iron: casting, ST *112*; converting, ST *111, 112-113*; producing, ST *102-103, 110-111*

Pigments in humans: in hair, HU *47*; in skin, HU *50-51*

Pigments in plants: algae's auxiliary pigments, PL *105*; of flowers, PL *52*; of fruits, PL *78*; of leaves, changing, PL *40-41. See also* Coloration, biological

Pigs: early development of, EV *133*

Pigweed: PL *75*

Pikaia (Paleozoic chordate): EV *47*

Pikas: EV *128, 141*

Pilchard: Japanese, UN *73*

Pill bugs: evolutionary path, IN *6*; parenting behavior, IN *76-77*; sow bugs, EC *37*; spider's capture of, AN *26*; wood lice, EC *36*

Pillow lava: PE *32*; around hydrothermal deposit, PE *106-107*; and hot-spot volcanic islands, PE *77*

Pilot training: flight simulator for, CO *82-83*

Pinched spinal nerves: cause of, HU *41*

Pineal body: location of, HU *74*

Pineapples: PL *67*; vs. figs, PL *69*

Pine cone fish: UN *26*

Pine cones: PL *88-89*

Pines: EC *54*, PL *43, 49, 89*; bark, PL *27*; bristlecone, PL *123*; cones, PL *88-89*; creeping, EC *53, 55*; fire's effect on, EC *78, 79, 136-137*; kauri, PL *123*; leaves (needles), PL *43, 48-49*; winged fruit, PL *73*

Pins: external, smart card's, MA *61*

PINs (personal identification numbers): CO *88, 89*

Pioneer Venus-Orbiter spacecraft: Venus photographed by, SP *10, 11*

Pipa: Carvalho's, UN *91*

Pipeline (parallel) processing: CO *42-43*

Piranha: UN *105*

Pistils: PL *51, 53, 58*; of angiosperms, EV *103. See also* Carpels

Pistons: in automatic air brake system, train's, TR *11*; automobile, TR *38, 40, 41*; in hydraulic systems, TR *66, 77*; motorcycle, TR *42*; steam car, TR *38*; steam

train, TR *15, 17*

Pitch, baseball: PH *24-25, 34-35*

Pitch, sound: Doppler effect, PH *138-139*; frequency and, MA *90*, PH *128, 135, 138, 142*; tones, production of, PH *134-135, 136-137*

Pitcher plant: EC *116*, PL *47, 118*

Pitching machine: baseball, PH *35*

Pitching of ships: reducing, PH *9*

Pit organs, rattlesnakes': AN *34*; mouse as sensed by, AN *35*

Pitot tubes: TR *132-133*

Pituitary gland and hormones: HU *74*

Pixels: CO *70*; in electronic publishing, CO *95*; in fax transmissions, CO *114, 115*, MA *68*; in television, MA *76, 77*; in TV vs. videophone images, CO *127*

Pixii, Hippolyte: generator built by, MA *28*

Placenta, human: HU *18, 19, 20*; of twins, HU *22, 23*

Placental animals vs. marsupial animals: EV *138-139*

Placoderms: EV *49*

Placodus (early reptile): EV *62*

Plages: SP *41*

Plains and plateaus: GE *28-29*; Altiplano and puna region, GE *140-141*; Antarctic, GE *53*; coastal plain estuaries, GE *38*; Colorado Plateau, history of, GE *94-95, 110-111*; Gobi Desert as, GE *51*; karst, GE *58-59*; Loess Plateau, China, GE *34*; undersea, GE *78. See also* Depositional plains

Planetariums: SP *126-127*

Planetary gear: transmission's, TR *47*

Planetary nebulas: SP *87*

Planetesimals: PE *110*; collisions, SP *7, 66*; formation of, PE *6*, SP *6*; in history of Earth, WE *6*

Planets: density, SP *28-29*; formation of, SP *7, 17, 20*; gas- vs. rock-type, SP *7, 28-29*; Jupiter, SP *14-17, 18, 19, 20, 28, 29, 139*; Mars, SP *12-13, 29, 30, 31, 125, 144*; Mercury, SP *8-9, 29*; Neptune, SP *5, 20, 26-27, 29, 138*; orbits, SP *4-5, 25, 31, 35*; Pluto, SP *29*; Saturn, SP *20-21, 22, 28-29, 138, 139*; travel between, SP *142-143, 144*; Uranus, SP *20, 24-25, 29, 138*; Venus, SP *8, 10-11, 29. See also* Earth

Planing by bees: AN *129*

Plankton: EC *46, 140*

Plankton eaters: UN *102, 105, 106-107*

Plankton theory of manganese nodules: PE *141*

Planned cities: GE *118-119, 128-129*

Plant and ant symbiosis: IN *98-99*

Planthoppers: brown, outbreaks of, IN *88*; eyespots, IN *112, 119*

Plants: PL entire volume; and adaptation, EV *21*; acid rain and, ST *64-65*; with air roots, EC *68-69*; Alpine, EC *52-53, 54, 55, 56-57*; angiosperms, evolution of, EV *102-103*; Antarctica, EC *44-45, 46*; and atmospheric oxygen, ST *36-37*; cabbages, breeding of, EV *19*; cells, evolution of, EV *37*; cell structure, PL *4-5, 6, 7*; classification, example of, EV *6*; and climate zones, GE *112, map 113*; convergence, EV *137*; dead, conversion of, PL *110-111, 124, 125, 126-127*; deer family feeding on, EC *50-51, 58-59, 118*; defenses, EC *98-99, 118-119*; desert, EC *86-87, 89, 94-95*; energy stored by, ST *66*; evolution of, EV *6-7, 105*; floral regions, PL map *118-119*; flowering, first appearance of, EV *102-103*; in food chain, EC *124*, PL *124-125*; after forest fire, EC *136-137*; fragrant oils from, ST *126-127*; fungi, EC *40, 50, 132, 133, 134-135*; Galápagos, EC *6, 119*; gymnosperms, evolution of, EV *102*; hybrids, PL *136-137, 142*; insect-eating, EC *116-117*; kelp, EC *130*; lakes filled in by, PL *128-129*; living fossils, EV *141*; medicines from, PL *132-133*; naturalized, PL *75*; Paleozoic, EV *52-53*; peas, genetics of, EV *13;* recolonization, EC *120, 121*; reproduction, animals aiding, EC *96-97, 114-115, 122-123*; thistles, EC *108-109*; vegetative reproduction, PL *62, 90-91, 134-135, 140-141, 143*; in water, EC *26-27. See also* Adaptation; Flowers and flowering plants; Grasslands; Leaves; Roots; Spore-bearing plants; Stems; Trees; *and individual names*

Planulae: coral, UN *101*

Plasma, atmospheric: WE *10-11, 14*; in solar wind, WE *19*

Plasma, human: HU *6, 64*; agglutinins, HU *70-71*; histamine, effect of, HU *135*

Plasmodia: PL *96, 97*

Plastics: ST *118-119*; carbon fibers bonded with, ST *138-139*; electroless plating, ST *63*

Plateaus: *See* Plains and plateaus

Plate glass: making of, ST *122-123*

Platelets: HU *6, 64, 65*; development, HU *66-67*

Plateosaurus (early reptile): EV *63*

Plate tectonics: PE *11, 22-45*; Andes mountains, formation of, PE *38-39*; boundaries of plates, kinds of, PE *34-35, 42, 48-49*; collision of continents, PE *11, 34, 36-37, 49*; and continental margins, PE *115*; and earthquakes, PE *46, 48-49*; force behind, PE *28-29*; and Great Rift Valley, PE *22-*

Planet Earth
PE

Plant Life
PL

Physical Forces
PH

Structure of Matter
ST

Space & Planets
SP

Transportation
TR

Underwater World
UN

Weather & Climate
WE

23, 40-41; Hawaii, formation of, PE 44-45; history of continental drift, PE 24-25, 38-39; and hot springs, PE map 83; igneous rocks, formation of, PE 86; and lava formation, PE 64-65; major plates, PE map 35; and mineral deposits, PE 100, 101, 106; and mountain building, GE 86-87, 96-97, 98-99; and ocean formation, PE 33; and ocean terrain, PE 112; proof of continental drift, PE 26-27; San Andreas fault, PE 42-43, 49; and seafloor building, PE 32-33, 41; and seafloor spreading, GE 78-79, PE 30-31, 32, 94; and seamounts, PE 44, 76-77, 114-115

Plating methods for metal: ST 62-63

Platybelodon (mastodon): EV 110

Platypuses: AN 18-19

Pleiades star cluster: SP 86, 88

Pleistocene glaciations: GE charts 50, maps 51

Plesiadapis (early primate): EV 122, 123

Plesiosaurs: EV 92-93

Pleural arch: flea's, IN 16, 17

Pliers as lever: PH 43

Pliohippus (horse ancestor): EV 109

Plotosids: UN 123

Plovers: injury faked by, AN 84-85

Plumules: PL 9, 12

Pluto (planet): SP 29

Pneumatic tube detector in fire alarm system: MA 65

Pneumatophores (breathing roots): EC 25, 34, 35, PL 22

Pneumonia bacteria: HU 141

PNP transistor: PH 85

Pocket computers: CO 90-91

Poinsettias: PL 55

Pointed deltas: GE 33

Poisoning: carbon monoxide, HU 72-73

Poisonous amphibians: AN 66-67

Poisonous insects: butterflies, AN 68-69; chemical weapons, IN 122-123, 126, 127; stinging, IN 124-125, 126, 127, 137; warning coloration, IN 112-113, 120, 121

Poisonous sea creatures: UN 120-121, 122-123, 126-127; catfish, UN 122,123; cone shells, UN 118-119; fringefin goby, UN 127; lionfish, UN 120-121, 122; pufferfish, UN 126, 127; rabbitfish, UN 123; stingray, UN 123; stonefish, UN 124; trunkfish, UN 126

Polar bears: EC 49

Polar circulation cells: WE 34, 35, 37, 38, 53, 112

Polar easterlies: WE 35, 36, 37

Polaris (star): SP 90; distance and magnitude, SP 81; and precession, SP 60, 61;

stars circling, SP 52

Polarizing filters in LCDs: ST 136-137

Polar jet stream: WE 37, 38-39, 112; and clear-weather turbulence, WE 53

Polar molecules, and nonpolar molecules: separation of, ST 42, 43; soap, working of, ST 48

Polaroid film: working of, MA 92-93

Polar orbit satellites: WE 10, 94, 110, 111, 117

Polders: in the Netherlands, GE 133

Pollen: PL 52; corn, PL 85; and hay fever, HU 134-135; pine, PL 89; and pollen tube, PL 8, 66

Pollination: PL 95; corn, PL 84, 85, 136-137; grasses, PL 62; by insects, PL 8, 50, 52-53, 56, 68, 69; pines, PL 89; self- vs. cross-pollination, PL 58, 59, 69, 136-137; of water plants, EC 27

Pollinators: animals, EC 97, 114-115; insects, PL 8, 50, 52-53, 56, 68, 69

Pollutants, air: removal of, MA 50-51; size of, MA chart 50

Pollution: acid rain, EC 74-75, WE 28-29; of atmosphere, WE 26-27; from automobiles, computerized control of, CO 102; biological accumulation, EC 144; and natural selection, EV 16-17; oil spills, EC 142-143; and ozone holes, WE 30-31

Polycrystalline grains: ST 130, 131; silicon, ST 134, 135

Polyergus ants: IN 138

Polyester: molecular structure of, ST 109

Polyethylene: production of, ST 106-107

Polygraphs: HU 43, MA 36-37

Polymers: ST 106; carbon fibers from, ST 138-139; in cotton, ST 12-13, 107; making of, ST 106-107; natural, kinds of, ST 106, 107; from photosensitive resins, ST 144; plastics molded from, ST 118-119; rubber, ST 30-31, 107; silk, ST 108; as synthetic fibers, ST 108-109; wool, ST 107, 109

Polyphenols: and browning of apple, ST 80

Polyploidic breeding: PL 138-139

Polyps, coral: UN 100, 101; as starfish prey, UN 139

Pomegranate fruits: PL 67

Pompeii (ancient city), Italy: destruction of, PE 74-75

Pondweed: EC 26, 27

Ponerine ants: termites and, IN 140

Pools, terraced: in limestone caves, GE 54-55, 60-61

Poplar trees: leaves of, PL 42

Population explosion: GE 120-121

Porcupinefish: UN 20, 121, 124-125

Porcupines: crested, EC 10; Indian, EC 11

Pororoca (flood tide): GE 36, 37

Portable Life-Support Subsystem (PLSS): SP 134

Portal vein: HU 86, 87

Port and starboard tacks: PH 13

Portolan chart: GE 15

Portuguese man-of-war: UN 42

Positive taxis: paramecium, AN 6

Positrons: ST 22, 23

Possum: EC 17

Potassium-argon dating: PE 95

Potatoes: PL 29, 91, 142; starch granules, PL 11; sweet potatoes, PL 29, 135

Potential energy: of roller coaster, PH 31

Power cord: structure of, PH 82-83

Power grid: PH 99

Power meters: MA 118-119

Power plants (power stations): nuclear reactors, PH 94-95, 108-109; oceans' energy used by, PE 139; windmills, PH 104-105. See also Electricity, generating

Power shovels: TR 67, 76-77; bulldozers, TR 66-67, 77

Prairies: EC 77

Praying mantises: butterfly enemy, IN 115; cannibalism, IN 64, 65; evolutionary path, IN 7; head of, IN 5, 22, 40; hunting, adaptations for, IN 40-41; mating, IN 64-65; mimicry, use of, AN 30-31, 51

Precambrian fossils: EV 26-27, 38, 39

Precambrian shields: PE 10, 11

Precession: PH 32, SP 60-61

Precipitation: Andes region, GE charts 140; climate zones, GE charts 112; vs. evaporation, GE 83; glaciation and, GE chart 50; in Mediterranean countries, GE charts 136-137. See also Climate; Rain; Snow

Precision measurements: MA 48-49

Precursor cells: blood cells', HU 66-67, 128

Predators: ants as, IN 42, 140, 141; aquatic animals, UN 102-119; archerfish, UN 108-109; for biological pest control, IN 90-91; cabbage butterfly's natural enemies, IN 114-115; centipedes as, IN 12; cleaner wrasses' protection from, UN 120, 134-135; crabs' protection from, UN 136-137; deep-sea adaptations of, UN 112-113; dolphins as, UN 58-59, 114-115; dragonfly nymphs as, IN 36-37, 44-45; electric, UN 57; fireflies, IN 52-53; flounders' defenses against, UN 130-131; flying fish's defenses against, UN 120-121, 128-129; glowworms, IN 50-51; hosts for protection against, UN 144; hunting wasps as, IN 54-55, 110-111; ink as defense against, UN 140-141; lures, use of, UN 23, 25, 26, 27, 102-103, 110-

Animal Behavior
AN

Computer Age
CO

Ecology
EC

Evolution of Life
EV

Geography
GE

Human Body
HU

Insects & Spiders
IN

Machines &
Inventions **MA**

111, 112; mosquito larvae as, IN *47*; mouth adaptations of, UN *104-105*; octopuses as, UN *60-61*; plankton eaters, UN *102, 105, 106-107*; poison fish's defenses against, UN *120-121, 122-123, 126-127*; porcupinefish's defenses against, UN *121, 124-125*; praying mantises as, IN *40-41*, 64, 65, *115*; pufferfish's defenses against, UN *126-127*; saber-toothed blennies, UN *134, 135*; sharks as, UN *54-55, 103, 104, 105*; shellfish as, UN *118-119*; spiders as, IN *36-37, 38-39, 94, 95, 96-97, 115*; squids' defenses against, UN *140-141, 142-143*; starfish as, UN *138-139*; tail design of, UN *20, 21*; whales as, UN *33*, 107, *114*, 116-117. *See also* Defenses of animals

Pregnancy: *See* Reproduction

Premolars and molars: HU 26, 27

Prenatal monitoring with ultrasound: MA *142-143*

Preservation of food: ST *88-89*

Pressure: PH 4; on baseball, PH *34*; and hang gliding, PH *14*; on liquid, and boiling temperature, PH 22; and phase changes, MA *100, 107*; rocket thrust, PH *18*; and sailing into wind, PH *12*; of skis and skates, PH *26, 27*; supersonic shock waves and, PH *140*; and temperature and volume of gas, PH *11*; water, and deep-sea fish, UN *22-23*; water, depth and, TR *107*

Pressure, atmospheric: *See* Atmospheric pressure

Pressure cookers: MA *100-101*, PH 23

Pressure differences: airplane instruments measuring, TR *132-133*; measuring flow rate with, MA *46, 47*

Pressure gradient force: WE *40, 41*

Pressurization of aircraft: TR *128-129*

Prevailing winds: WE *34-35, 36-37*; convergence of trade winds, WE *90, 132-133*; and El Niño phenomenon, PE *124-125*; and ocean currents, PE *118, 119, 120, 132, 133*; southern oscillation and, WE *140-141*

Prickly pear cacti: PL *112*

Prides of lions: AN *138-139*

Primary memory: CO *30-31*

Primary (P; compressional) waves, seismic: and secondary (S; shear) waves, PE *15, 50, 51*; S-P time, PE 51, 52, 53, *chart* 53

Primates: chimpanzees, AN *46-47, 124-125, 141, 142-143*; endangered, EC *112*; evolution of, EV *122-123*, 124; extinct, EC *18-19*; learning in monkeys, AN *144*; rain forest, EC 28, *70-71*; social groups, AN *140-141*

Prime focus of Hale telescope: SP *119*

Primroses: evening, PL *53*

Princess fireflies: AN *93*; flashing patterns, AN *92, 93*

Printed circuit boards (PCBs): CO *20-21*; motherboards, CO *22-23*

Printers: CO *19, 38-39*; pocket computers and, CO *90-91*

Printing and printing presses: MA *6-7, 40-41*

Printing plates: photosensitive resins for, ST *144*

Prisms: SP *78*; in binoculars, MA *94*; Hale telescope, SP *118*; light split by, WE *23, 98*; white light through, PH *120*

Probainognathus (mammal-like reptile): EV 65

Probes: *See* Space probes

Proboscises: flies, AN *8*; mosquitoes, AN *10*, 11

Proconsul (extinct primate): EV *124*

Procyon (star): spectrographic analysis of, SP *78*

Production area of business: computer use in, CO *93*

Production lines: robot use on, CO *100-101*

Proganochelys (early reptile): EV *62*

Program counter: CO 24

Programming languages: CO *50-51*; programs in, CO 51

Programs and software: *See* Software and programs

Program signal: radio's, MA *84, 85*

Projection types: maps', GE 13, *16-17*

Projectors, movie: MA *88-89*; kinetoscope, MA *20-21*

Prokaryotes: cell type, EV 36, 37; evolution from, EV 6, 7

Prominences: solar, SP *41, 43, 46*

Prominent moths: yellow-tipped, AN *53*

Promoters: cancer stimulated by, HU *139*

Pronator muscles: HU *39*

Pronghorns: AN *61*

Propagation of light: defined, PH 112

Propellers: TR *112-113*; blimp, TR *116*; icebreaker's screw, TR *101*; turboprop engine, TR *131*; Wright *Flyer*, TR *134*; XV-15 VTOL aircraft, TR *139*

Propeller turbine: PH *99*

Prop roots: EC 35, *64-65*

Prostate gland: HU *12*

Prosthetic (artificial) limbs: CO *138*

Protective coloration: *See* Coloration, protective

Proteins: EV *30*; in cells, EV 30, 36; egg, ST *94, 95*; laboratory creation of, EV *31*; milk, ST *84, 85*

Proterogyrinus (anthracosaur): EV *58*

Protoavis (ancestral bird): EV *68-69*, 70

Protoceratops (dinosaur): EV *78-79*, 89

Protogalaxies: evolution of, SP *108-109, 112-113*

Protons: PH 68, ST *7*; and antimatter counterpart, ST *22-23*; in nuclear fusion, SP *44-45*, ST *16-17*; and solar wind, WE 16-17; and static electricity, PH *70*; in Van Allen belts, WE *18-19*

Protophasma (early flying insect): EV *55*

Protostar: SP *92*

Protosuchus (early crocodile): EV *62-63*

Protozoans: in cave, EC *40*; didinium, AN *7*; paramecium, AN *6-7*; in termites' intestines, IN *49*

Pry bar as lever: PH *43*

Pryeria sinica caterpillars: IN *120-121*

Pseudomyrmex ant: IN *99*

Pseudoscorpions: EC *37*

Pseudosuchians: EV *67*; *Euparkeria*, EV *62, 66*

Psittacosaurus (dinosaur): EV *88*

Psyche bagworms: nests of, IN *103*

Ptarmigans: seasonal color changes in, AN *50-51, 58-59*

Pteranodon (pterosaur): EV *90, 130, 134*

Pteraspis (extinct fish): EV *47*

Pteridines: IN *58*

Pterobranch: EV *46*

Pterodactyls: EV 90, *91*

Pterodaustro (pterodactyloid): EV *91*

Pteromalus wasps: IN *115*

Pterosaurs: EV *90-91*; family tree, EV *chart* 66-67; *Pteranodon*, EV *90, 130, 134*; skin, EV *96*

Ptolemy, Claudius: GE 14, *map* 15

P-type and N-type semiconductors: PH *84, 85*; silicon, PH 84, 85, *110-111*

Publishing: electronic, CO *94-95*

Puddingwife: UN 63, 66

Puffballs: PL *98-99*

Pufferfish: UN *105*, 126, *127*; food chain of, UN *126-127*

Puffing up of porcupinefish: UN *121, 124-125*

Puffins: horned, EC *8*; tufted, EC *33*

Pulleys: PH *48-49*; crane's use of, TR *73*

Pulp: in papermaking, ST *105*; producing, ST *104*

Pulsars: SP *96*, 97

Pulsating variables (stars): SP 82, *83*

Pulse: lie detector's measurement of, MA *36*

Pumpkin: starch granules in, PL *11*

Pumps: fire engine's, TR *70-71*; waterjet, hydrofoil's, TR *95*

Puna region, South America: GE *140*

Punch cards: CO *4-5*, 10, *11*; census tabulating machines's system, CO *12-13*

Pupae: IN *81*; butterflies, IN 35, *57*, 78, *82-*

Planet Earth
PE

Plant Life
PL

Physical Forces
PH

Structure of Matter
ST

Space & Planets
SP

Transportation
TR

Underwater World
UN

Weather & Climate
WE

83, 115; glacier midges, IN 34; ladybugs, IN 113; mosquitoes, IN 47

Purple hairstreak butterflies: IN 74

Purse web spiders: IN 94

Pushrods in platypus bill: AN 18

P (compressional) waves, seismic: S-P time, PE 51, 52, 53, chart 53; and S (shear) waves, PE 15, 50, 51

P waves in electrocardiogram: MA 136

Pygmy marsupial frog: UN 90

Pyrometers: optical, PH 56, 57

Pyrotherium (extinct mammal): EV 120

Pyrrhulinas: reproduction by, UN 75

Pythons: African, EC 10; Indian, EC 11

Q

QFP (integrated circuit package): CO 23

QRS complex in electrocardiogram: MA 136

Quadrant (navigation instrument): TR 86

Quadruplets: HU 23

Quagga: EV 144

Quarks: ST 6, 7

Quartz: MA 96; structure of, ST 122; watches using, MA 96-97

Quasars: SP 112-113; spectra of, redshift in, SP 115; very long baseline interferometry using, PE 31, 56-57

Quaternary period: species, WE 143; temperatures, WE chart 143

Queen insects: IN 129; ants, AN 125, 126, 127, IN 99; bees, AN 125, 130, 131, IN 70-71, 131, 132-133; termites, IN 128, 141, 142, 143

Queen snakes: favorite prey of, AN graph 15

Queen substance: honeybees', IN 132

Quetzalcoatlus (pterodactyl): EV 90, 91

Quinones in browning apple: ST 80

QWERTY layout of keys: CO 33

R

Rabbitfish: UN 123

Rabbits: Ryukyu, EV 140

Raccoons: EC 139

Race and skin color: HU 51

Racing cars: Formula One, TR 58-59

Radar: Antarctica mapped with, GE 52; ship's navigation with, TR 82-83; Stealth bomber's evasion of, TR 144; weather, WE 63, 94, 108, 114-115, 118, 123

Radar map of Venus: SP 11

Radial tires: high-performance, TR 57

Radiant fog: WE 70

Radiant thermal energy: measuring, PH 56-57

Radiation: mutation by, PL 138-139. See also Electromagnetic radiation

Radiation belts: Van Allen, WE 10-11, 18-19

Radiation cooling: WE 76, 85

Radiation zone of Sun: SP 17, 40, 41

Radiator: racing car's, working of, TR 59

Radicle: PL 9; and germination, PL 12

Radioactive decay: and dating, PE 94, 95; and Earth's internal heat, PE 12; ore deposits detected with, PE 99

Radioactive elements: carbon 14, ST 24-25; fission of, ST 14-15

Radioactive fuel: submarines using, TR 102-103

Radioactivity: PH 90-91; core of nuclear reactor, PH 94-95, 108

Radio altimeter vs. atmospheric pressure altimeter: TR 132, 133

Radio astronomy: galactic center, map of, SP 105; telescopes, SP 120-121, 122, 124

Radiocarbon dating: ST 24-25

Radio direction finders: use of, TR 81

Radiography: MA 140-141

Radio interference from solar wind: SP 48

Radio magnetic indicator (RMI) dial: aircraft's, TR 123

Radios: AM/FM, working of, MA 84-85; two-way, PH 88

Radio signals, communications with: cellular phones, CO 120-121; pagers, electronic, CO 122-123; satellites, CO 128-129; space probes, Voyager, CO 142-143

Radiosondes: WE 11, 112, 116, 118, 123

Radio waves: PH 88-89, WE 9; ionosphere and, WE 15; landing system (ILS) using, TR 126-127; Omega System using, TR map 125; ships' use of, in navigation, TR 81-85; use of, in weather radar, WE 114, 115; VOR stations emitting, TR 122-123

Radishes: white, root of, PL 15

Radius and ulna: HU 33, 39

Radon: Geiger counter for measuring, PE 57

Radula teeth: cone shell's, UN 118, 119

Rafflesia flower: PL 51, 56-57

Ragweed: EC 98-99; pollen, HU 134

Railroads: See Trains

Rails, trains': TR 6-7; high-speed trains, TR 33

Rain: GE 100; acid, EC 74-75, ST 64-65, WE 28-29; artificial, WE 78-79; and beginnings of life, EV 30-31; with carbon dioxide, rock dissolved by, GE 58, 110; cause of, WE 74, 75; clouds producing, WE 58-59, 63; coastal, sea winds and, GE 114-115; days of, annual, WE chart 77; and deserts, rain-shadow, WE 134-135; on desert species, effects of, EC 92-93; downpours, seasonal, WE 88-89, 132-133; equatorial convergence zone and, WE 132-133; ground water from, GE 57;

and icing, WE 80-81; landslides caused by, GE 102-103; monsoon and, WE 130, 131, map 131; radar and, WE 115; South America, WE map 73; southern oscillation and, WE 140, 141; squalls, tropical, WE 76-77; and stratus clouds, WE 61; and tornado formation, WE 50; western U.S., variations in, GE map 114; on young Earth, EV 28-29, WE 6

Rainbows: WE 96-97, 98-99

Rain forests: EC 4, 5, 24-25, 28-29, map 66; birds, EC 28-29, 60-61; destruction of, EC 72-73; epiphytes, EC 68-69; Krakatoa, EC 121; layers, EC 66-67, 69; logging of, GE 124, 125; primates, EC 28, 70-71; tree species, EC 64-65

Rain shadow: Death Valley in, GE 115; deserts, formation of, WE 134-135

Rainy season: WE 88-89, 132-133

Rally tires: TR 57

RAM (random-access memory) chips: CO 22

Ramps as inclined planes: PH 44, 45

Rams: bighorn sheep, AN 106-107

Random-access memory (RAM) chips: CO 22

Raphe nuclei: HU 123; location of, HU 123

Rapid eye movement (REM) sleep: 122, chart 122, 123, 124-125

Ratels: EC 10, 11

Rate-of-rise sensors in fire alarm systems: MA 64

Ratfish: UN 73

Rattlesnakes: AN 34-35; rattles, AN 62-63

Rayleigh scattering: WE 23

Rayleigh waves: PE 51

Rays: eye, UN 45; manta, AN 25, UN 107; stingray, UN 123

Razorbills: EC 8

RCA Victor television set: MA 22

Reach: sailing on, PH 12

Reaction: turbine, PH 98-99

Reactors, nuclear: See Nuclear reactors

Reading of text: CO 64-65

Read-only memory (ROM): CD-ROM, CO 95; chips, CO 22

Reaping and threshing: combines for, MA 14-15

Rearview mirror, convex: PH 115

Reber, Grote: SP 120

Receptacle tissue in fruits: PL 67, 68, 69

Receptor cells: in skin, HU 98-99, 100; olfactory, HU 116, 117

Recessional moraines: GE 44, 46-47

Recessive and dominant traits: EV 13, 14

Recharger: electric car's, TR 64

Recorder (musical instrument): PH 135

Recording: of compact disks, MA 86-87; of

| Animal Behavior
AN | Computer Age
CO | Ecology
EC | Evolution of Life
EV | Geography
GE | Human Body
HU | Insects & Spiders
IN | Machines &
Inventions **MA** |

Planet Earth
PE

Plant Life
PL

Physical Forces
PH

Structure of Matter
ST

Space & Planets
SP

Transportation
TR

Underwater World
UN

Weather & Climate
WE

Rhumb lines: GE 16, *17*

Rhyniaceae: EV *52*

Rhyniella (extinct insect): EV *50-51*

Rhyolite: PE *89*

Ria coastline: GE *90-91*

Ribonucleic acid: *See* RNA

Ribosomes: PL *6, 7*

Ribs, human: and breathing, HU *54*

Rice: PL *67*; production of, GE *122*; short, breeding, PL *139*

Rice starch: ST *100*

Ride, Sally: SP *133*

Ridges, air-pressure: WE *84*

Ridges, mid-ocean: *See* Mid-ocean ridges

Rift valleys: PE *34*; formation of, PE *29, 32, 33, 40-41*; Great Rift Valley, PE *22-23, 40-41*; seafloor, PE *30, 32*

Rigel (star): distance and magnitude, SP *80-81*

Right-hand rule of electromagnetism: PH *76, 81*

Riming: WE *80-81*

Ringed seals: UN *92*

Ring nebula: SP *87*

Rings, planetary: SP *20*; Jupiter, SP *16, 20*; Neptune, SP *20, 26-27*; Saturn, SP *20-21*; Uranus, SP *20, 25*

Rings in tree trunk: PL *18-19, 24-25*

Ripening of foods: excessive, ST *88-89*

River dolphins: UN *58-59*

Rivers: GE *24*; Amazon, GE *36-37*; Colorado, Grand Canyon formed by, GE *84-85, 94-95*; deltas, GE *4-5, 26, 32-33, 39*; development projects, GE *134-135*; estuaries, GE *38-39*; and ground water, GE *57*; Himalayas crossed by, GE *98-99*; landforms created by, GE *26-33*; oasis water provided by, GE *62*; Rhine, GE *40, map 40-41*; terraces, GE *27, 88-89*; Yellow, GE *34-35*

RMI (radio magnetic indicator) dial: TR *123*

RNA (ribonucleic acid): and DNA (deoxyribonucleic acid), EV *30, 36*

Road construction: rollers for, TR *66, 74-75*

Road roller: TR *75*

Robber flies: bumblebees mimicked by, AN *54-55*

Robots: CO *98-101*; arms, CO *100-101*; in automotive industry, CO *100-101*; eyes, CO *99*; hands (manipulators), CO *98*; humanoid, hypothetical, CO *98-99*; mobile, CO *99*

Rocket, the (train): TR *4, 14-15*

Rockets: launching of, PH *18-19*; matter-antimatter as fuel, ST *23*; near speed of light, PH *126-127*; and rocket fuel, ST *54-55, 71, 74-75*; V-2, MA *26-27*; weather, WE *11, 112, 116, 123*

Rock ptarmigans: seasonal color changes in, AN *58-59*

Rocks: PE *84-95*; ages of, PE *84, 94, 95*; classifications of, PE *86, 87, 88-89*; coastal, sea's shaping of, GE *68-69, 76-77*; cuestas from, GE *92-93*; cycle of, PE *92-93*; desert sand from, GE *104-105*; diamonds in, PE *90-91*; dissolved by rain with carbon dioxide, GE *58, 110*; erosional plains, formation of, GE *28, 29*; formation of, PE *7, 84, 86-87, 92, 93*; glacial deposits, GE *44-45, 46-47*; Grand Canyon's, GE *94-95*; ground water's shaping of, GE *58-59*; history of Earth in, PE *94-95*; igneous, PE *84-85, 86, 87, 88-89, 93*; landslides, GE *102-103*; magnetic orientation of, PE *27, 30, 94, 99*; metamorphic, PE *86, 87, 92*; Monument Valley's formation, GE *110-111*; mountain formation, GE *86, 87, 96-97*; reservoir, fossil fuels in, PE *103*; sedimentary, PE *84, 86, 87, 92, 94, 95, 101, 103*. *See also* Aquifers; Minerals

Rock salt: deposit of, PE *101*

Rock-type vs. gas-type planets: SP *7, 28-29*

Rocky Mountains, Canada-U.S.: GE *24-25, 115*; chinooks, WE *44-45*; turbulence over, type of, WE *53*

Rodents: African, EC *21, 89*; desert, EC *89, 90*; after forest fire, EC *136, 137*; giant, South American, EC *20*; lemmings, EC *48, 102-103*; seed dispersal by, EC *123*

Rods and cones: HU *108-109*

Roentgen, Wilhelm: MA *140*

Rogallo, Francis: PH *14*

Roller coasters: PH *30-31*

Rollers, construction: TR *66, 74-75*

Roll film: Kodak camera's use of, MA *18, 19*

Rolling of ships: reducing, PH *9*

ROM (read-only memory): CD-ROM, CO *95*; chips, CO *22*

Roman counting tablet: CO *6-7*

Rømer, Ole: PH *118*

Root grafting: PL *135*

Root hairs: PL *15, 20*

Root pressure: PL *21*

Roots: PL *18-19*; aboveground, kinds of, PL *22-23*; air, plants with, EC *68-69*; Alpine perennials, EC *57*; desert plants, EC *94, 95*; ferns vs. mosses, PL *108*; in germination, PL *12-13*; growth of, PL *14-15*; mangrove, EC *25, 34-35*, PL *80, 81*; mistletoe, PL *23, 83*; modifications of, PL *29*; mycorrhiza, EC *134*; rain forest trees, EC *24, 64-65*; water transportation from, PL *20, 21, 40-41*

Ropeway cable car system: TR *31*

Roses: PL *28-29*

Rotary oil-seal vacuum pump: MA *45*

Rotary snowplow: train's, TR *22-23*

Rotating objects: baseball, PH *24-25, 34-35*; top, spinning, PH *25, 32-33*

Rotation: Earth's, effects of, SP *52-53*; Earth's, slowing of, SP *73*; Moon's, SP *70-71*

Rotifers: EC *36, 40*

Rotors, helicopter's: TR *114*; auxiliary, function of, TR *114, 115*; hub, TR *115*; pilot's use of, TR *115*

Round dance: honeybees', IN *135*

Round herring: mouth of, UN *106*

Rowan seeds: spreading of, PL *78-79*

Royal chambers: termites', IN *141, 142, 143*

Royal Observatory, Greenwich, England: GE *21*

Rubber: molecular structure of, ST *30-31, 107*; vulcanization of, ST *30*

Rudders: airplane's, TR *111*; blimp's use of, TR *117*; hovercraft's use of, TR *97*; hydroplanes, submarine with, TR *98-99*

Ruffini endings: HU *98*

Rules of the road at sea: TR *83*

Runners: reproduction by, PL *91*

Running spiders: courtship, AN *90*

Russell snowplow: TR *23*

Russia: climate of, GE *116-117*

Russian abacus: CO *7*

Rusting of iron: ST *56-57*; prevention, ST *57*

Ryegrass: Italian, PL *63*

S

Saber-toothed blennies: cleaner wrasses vs., UN *134, 135*

Saber-toothed cats: EV *107, 121*

Saccharin: glutamic acid from, ST *91*

Sacrificial anodes: ST *57*

Saddleback caterpillars: Oriental, IN *121*

Saddle joint: HU *38*

Sado Island, Japan: coastline of, GE *89*

Safety glass: laminated, ST *125*

Sagami trough, Japan: PE *55*

Saguaro cacti: EC *86, 87*; owls in, EC *89*; PL *111, 113*

Sahara (desert), Africa: GE *100-101, 105, 109*, SP *45*, WE *124-125, 135*; sirocco from, WE *46-47*

Sailing into wind: PH *12-13*

Sailing ships: TR *78-79*; Columbus's, TR *88-89*; Magellan's, TR *87*

Sailors: *See* Water travel

St. Helens, Mount, Wash., U.S.: PE *70-71, 78*

St. Louis, Mo., U.S.: topographic maps of, GE *12*

Salamanders: as cave dwellers, EC *28, 42*

Salinity levels: in Chesapeake Bay, EC *141*; and bottom currents, PE *116*; of ocean

| Animal Behavior **AN** | Computer Age **CO** | Ecology **EC** | Evolution of Life **EV** | Geography **GE** | Human Body **HU** | Insects & Spiders **IN** | Machines & Inventions **MA** |

waters, GE *charts* 70-71, PE *chart* 134

Saliva: HU *78-79, 118*

Salivary glands: HU *78-79, 118*

Salmon: AN *120*; baby, UN *12, 82*; chum, UN *11*; navigation methods, AN *120-121*; reproduction, UN *82-83*; swim bladder type, UN *12*

Salt: ST *43*; electric conduction by, ST *18-19*; freezing point lowered by, ST *40-41*; natural formations of, ST *96*; preserving food with, ST *89*; reclaiming, from sea, ST *96-97*; rock, deposit of, PE *101*

Salt content of bodies of water: *See* Salinity levels

Salt glands: EC *34*

Saltwater fish vs. freshwater fish: drinking by, UN *10-11*

Saltwater intrusion: GE *64*

Salvia flowers: PL *53*

San Andreas fault, Calif., U.S.: PE *42-43, 49*

Sand: in concrete, ST *120, 121*; desert, creation of, GE *104-105*; windblown, rock cut by, GE *111*

Sand bars: formation of, GE *74-75*

Sand dunes: GE *108-109*; Sahara's, GE *100-101, 105, 109*

Sandglass: estimating longitude with, TR *87*

Sand gobies: AN *86*

Sand lizards: EC *88*

Sand ridges: GE *74, 75*

Sand seas: formation of, GE *108*

Sand shark: embryonic, UN *77*

Sand spits: GE *75*

Sandstone: PE *87*; formations, Monument Valley's, GE *110-111*; and fossil fuels, PE *102*, 103; layers of, PE *86, 92*

San Francisco, Calif., U.S.: cable cars in, TR *30*

Santa Maria (Columbus's ship): TR *88-89*

Saprophytes: defined, PL *57, 96*

Saprophytic chain: defined, PL *126*

Sarcomeres: HU *36*

Sarcopterygians: amphibian evolution from, EV *56-57*

Sardines: UN *102, 106-107*

Sargasso Sea: PE *132-133*

Sarracenia pitcher plants: PL *47*

Satellite navigation: TR *84-85*

Satellite photos: Chesapeake Bay, GE *38*; Earth, PE *4-5, 133*; Grand Canyon area, GE *95*; Middle East, GE *4-5*; Osaka Bay, GE *144*

Satellites: SP *123, 124-125*; over Antarctica, WE *123*; carbon fibers in, ST *139*; communications, CO *128-129*; *Explorer 1*, WE *18*; geostationary vs. polar orbit, WE *10-11, 94*, 110, *111, 117*; global network, WE *111*; ground station monitors, WE

110; hurricanes observed by, WE *82-83, 84, 111, 121*; Landsat, CO *140-141*; navigation using, PE *16, 137*, TR *84-85*; orbit of, PH *36-37*; ozone hole detected by, ST *map* 77; repair of, in space, SP *136*; solar cells for, PH *111*; surveyors' use of, GE *9*; use of, PE *16, 99, 136-137, 143*; volcanoes studied by, PE *79*; weather, CO *134*, PE *4-5, 136*, WE *10-11, 110-111, 113, 117, 118*

Satin bowerbirds: AN *100-101*

Saturation: and cloud formation, WE 58, *62*; and fog, WE 70

Saturn (planet): SP *20-21, 28-29*; moon of (Titan), SP *22-23*; ring formation, SP *20-21*; Voyager missions to, SP 138, *139*

Saturn V rocket: launching of, PH *18-19*

Sauna: air in, and skin, PH *64-65*

Saurischians: *See* Lizard-hipped dinosaurs

Sauropods: EV *83*; *Diplodocus*, EV *84-85*

Savanna, African: EC *76*, GE *113*; animals of, EC *29, 80-85*

Sawflies: eggs guarded by, IN *75*

Saw-scaled vipers: AN *62*

Scale ants: food gathering by, IN 42

Scale insects: biological control of, IN *90, 91*

Scale of maps: GE *12*

Scales: bathroom, MA *108-109*; springs used in, PH *50*

Scales of fish: UN *7*

Scallops: escape from starfish by, UN *138*

Scanners: bar codes and, CO *86-87*; digitization of pictures by, in electronic publishing, CO *95*; text read by, CO *64, 65*

Scanning electron microscopes: MA 32, *33*

Scanning of images by television: MA *22, 23, 77*; scan lines, MA *78*

Scaphonyx (early reptile): EV *63*

Scarab beetles: in feeding order, EC *110, 111*; pollination by, EC *115*

Scarps: creation of, by slumps, GE *103*

Scavenger beetles: EC *43*

Scavengers: fungi as, EC *133*; ocean, EC *128-129*

Schickard, Wilhelm: CO *8*

Schools of fish: AN *74-75*

Scientific uses of computers: CO *130*; biomedical engineering, CO *138-139*; Landsat satellites, CO *140-141*; meteorology, CO *134-135*; missiles, cruise, CO *144*; space probes, CO *142-143*. *See also* Simulations and models, computer

Scissors: ceramic, ST *130*; as levers, PH *43*

Scopura langa (aquatic insect): IN *34*

Scorpionfish: UN *72*; lionfish, UN *120-121, 122*; as scavengers, EC *128, 129*

Scorpionflies: mating, IN *66-67*; snow, IN *34*

Scorpion fossils: EV *51*

Scorpions: EC *88*; maternal care in, IN *75, 76*; vinegarroon, IN *123*

Screwball (pitch): PH *35*

Screw propellers: icebreaker's, TR *101*

Screws: PH *44-45*

Scrub jays: cooperative breeding, AN *116-117*

SDPS (stereo digital photogrammetric station): CO *76*

Sea anemones: AN *22-23, 48-49*, UN *34*; and clown fish, AN *70-71*, UN *144*; crab living in, UN *39*; and hermit crabs, AN *78-79*

Sea bass: black, EC *141*; swim bladder type, UN *13*

Seabirds: EC *29, 32-33*; Arctic and Antarctic, EC *8-9, 45, 46, 47, 49*; Galápagos, EC *6, 7*; oil spills and, EC *143*

Sea bream: UN *21*; eye, UN *45*; swim bladder type, UN *13*

Sea breezes: and land breezes, WE *42, 43, 76*

Sea cliffs: GE *68-69, 76-77, 88-89*

Sea cows: Steller's, EV *144*

Sea cucumbers: pearlfish's relationship with, UN *144*

Sea fan: PL *105*

Seafloor building: PE *32-33, 41*

Seafloor spreading: GE *78-79*, PE *30-31, 32, 94*

Seafloor terrain: PE *112-113*

Sea horses: leafy sea dragon, UN *105*; reproduction, father's role in, UN *78*

Sea lanes: opening of, icebreakers' strategies for, TR *100, 101*; rules of, TR *83*

Sea lettuce: PL *102-103*; spores, PL *95, 102*

Sea level: Antarctica above, GE *52-53*; changes in, and formation of plains, GE *28-29*; drop in, and terraces, GE *88-89*; increase in, effects of, GE *23, 38, 39, 72-73, 90-91*

Sea lilies: EV *42*

Sea lions: Galápagos, EC *7*

Seals: Antarctic, EC *46-47, 49*; reproduction by, UN *92-93*

Seamounts: PE *76-77*; Emperor, PE *44*; Pacific Rim, PE *114-115*

Sea of Okhotsk high: WE *133*

Sea otters: AN *47*, EC *130-131, 142*

Sea pens: fossils suggesting, EV *38*

Searches: information, CO *56-57*

Seas: ancient, Finland's, GE *maps* 66-67; land reclaimed from, GE *132-133*; lunar, SP *69*. *See also* Oceans; *and individual names*

Sea scorpions: EV *44-45*; fossil of, EV *50*

Seasons, cause of: SP *56-57*; in land of midnight Sun, SP *58-59*

Planet Earth
PE

Plant Life
PL

Physical Forces
PH

Structure of Matter
ST

Space & Planets
SP

Transportation
TR

Underwater World
UN

Weather & Climate
WE

Sea squirts: EV 47

Sea stacks: GE 76, 77

Sea travel: *See* Water travel

Sea turtles: AN 25

Sea urchins: EC 46; cardinalfish among spines of, UN 144; crab parasite on, UN 39; in food chain, EC 130; starfish attack repelled by, UN 139

Seawater: salt recovered from, ST 96-97

Sea waves (tsunamis): PE 54, 58-59, map 73

Seaweed: PL 95, 102-103, 104-105; crabs' use of, for camouflage, UN 136

Sebaceous glands: HU 44, 47

Secondary (S; shear) waves, seismic: and primary (P; compressional) waves, PE 15, 50, 51; S-P time, PE 51, 52, 53, *chart* 53

Second-class levers: PH 42-43

Second law of motion, Newton's: PH 24

Security gates: airport, MA 42-43

Sediment: seafloor, PE 10, 102

Sedimentary rock: Appalachian Mountains, formation of, GE 96-97; composition of, PE 87; cuestas from, GE 92-93; formation of, PE 86, 87, 92; fossil fuels in, PE 103; in Grand Canyon, GE 94-95; history of Earth in, PE 94, 95; layers of, PE 84, 86, 92, 94, 95; limestone, PE 101; in Monument Valley's formation, GE 110-111; in Teton Range, GE 86

Sedimentation: *See* Depositional plains

Sedum: PL 90-91; stomas, PL 38

Seed-bearing plants: EV 102-103

Seed beetles: EC 109

Seed ferns: Paleozoic, EV 53

Seeds: PL 64-65; animals dispersing, EC 96-97, 122-123, PL 65, 74, 75, 77, 78-79, 82; climate and, EC 56; coconuts, EC 22-23; dandelion, PL 67, 72-73; development of, on tree, PL 80-81; after fires, EC 79; germination of, PL 8, 12-13, 79, 80, 81, 88, 95; making of, PL 8-9, 66; mangrove, EC 34; mistletoe, spreading of, PL 82-83; nuts, PL 65, 77; in pine cones, PL 88-89; polyploidic breeding, PL 138-139; from popping fruits, PL 76-77; *Rafflesia*, PL 56; recolonization, EC 120; simple vs. complex fruits, PL 66, 67; vs. spores, PL 94-95; with sticking properties, PL 74-75; storage of, PL 143; sunflower, PL 70; wind-borne, PL 72-73, 88

Segmented worms: ancestors, possible, EV 38, 39; early stages of, EV 132

Seismic tomography: PE 15

Seismic waves: PE 14-15; isochrones, PE 53; ore deposits detected with, PE 98, 99; S-P time, PE 51, 52, 53, *chart* 53; traveling of, PE 50-51

Seismograms: PE 51

Seismographs: PE 56; waves reaching, PE 50-51; working of, PE 51

Seismometers: volcanoes studied with, PE 79

Self-protection: *See* Defenses of animals

Self-raising crane: MA 52-53

Semicircle angelfish: UN 132

Semicircular canal of fish: UN 52; sharks, UN 55

Semicircular canal of humans: HU 114-115

Semiconductors: CO 20, PH 84-85; electrical resistance of, MA *chart* 128; silicon, PH 84, 85, 110-111

Seminal vesicles: HU 12

Senegal: cattle in, GE 131

Sense organs, human: HU 96-118; ears, HU 112-115; eyes, HU 106-111; nose, HU 116-117; skin, HU 98-99, 100; tongue, HU 99, 118-119

Senses of animals: *See individual senses*

Sensitization of mast cells: HU 134, 135

Sensory and motor cortex of brain: HU 105

Sensory nerves, human: HU 100-101, 102-103

Sensory pits and hairs: flies, AN 8, 9

Sensory speech field (Wernicke's area): HU 120, 121

Separated photoelectrics in smoke detector: MA 65

Separator lenses in camera: MA 75

Sequential processing: CO 42-43

Sequential search: CO 57

Sequoias: PL 122-123

Serotonin: and sleep, HU 123

Sewing machines: MA 104-105

Sex changes in fish: UN 62-63, 66-67, 68-69

Sexes of flowers, separate: PL 58-59; corn, PL 84-85; fig, PL 68, 69; mistletoe, PL 83

Sex pheromones: ants', IN 53; moths', AN 94-95, IN 27

Sexual parasites: UN 70-71

Seymouria (reptile ancestor): EV 58

Shadow zone: seismic, PE 15

Shallow-focus earthquakes: PE 53; fissuring by, PE 54

Shamrock spiders: AN 26

Shanks, William: CO 68

Shape-memory alloys: ST 128-129, 140-141

Sharks: early development of, EV 132-133; eyes, UN 44, 54; goblin, UN 22-23; mako, shortfin, UN 15; Paleozoic, EV 49; as predators, UN 54-55, 103, 104, 105; and remoras, as hosts, AN 24-25; reproduction, UN 76-77

Shear (cross wind): WE 50

Shear (transform) boundaries: PE 34, 35, 42-43, 49

Shear (S) waves, seismic: and compressional (P) waves, PE 15, 50, 51; S-P time, PE 51, 52, 53, *chart* 53

Sheep: bighorn, AN 106-107; raising of, GE *map* 130, 131

Sheet metal: production of, ST 28-29

Sheet webs: spider's, IN 38

Shellfish: early stages of, EV 132; extinct, EV 94-95, 98-99; living fossils, EV 140. *See also* Crustaceans; Mollusks

Shepherd's-purse: PL 8, 67

Shield lichen: PL 107

Shield volcanoes: formation of, PE 67, 77

Shifting of gears: automobile's, TR 46

Shiitake mushrooms: PL 95; spores, PL 99

Shinkansen line (bullet trains): TR 4-5, 33

Shipping: European, GE 40, map 40-41

Ships: TR 78; clipper, TR 78-79; Columbus's, TR 88-89; cruiser, military, TR 78-79; floating, PH 8-9; in fog, aids for, TR 82-83; future, TR 104-105; historical navigational instruments, TR 86-87; icebreakers, TR 100-101; Magellan's, TR 87; navigation, TR 78, 80-87; navigation, satellite use in, PE 16, 137, TR 84-85; oceanographic, PE 31, 137; rules of the road for, TR 83; steam-powered, TR 79, 90-91; submarines, TR 79, 98-99, 102-103, 106-107; survey, GE 18; through Panama Canal, TR 92-93; wave power generators on, PH 107; in weather observation, WE 111, 117

Shirase (icebreaker): TR 101

Shoals: sand bars formed from, GE 74-75

Shock absorbers: computerized control of, CO 103; motorcycle's, TR 43

Shock waves: and sonic booms, PH 140-141

Shooting stars: SP 34-35

Shoots: bamboo, PL 32-33, 91; growth of, PL 16

Shoot-tip culture: PL 140-141

Shortfin mako shark: UN 15

Short takeoff and landing (STOL) aircraft: Asuka, TR 139

Shortwaves: radio, WE 15

Shovels, power: TR 67, 76-77; bulldozers, TR 66-67, 77

Showa New Mountain, Japan: PE 67

Shrikes: eggs, AN 114

Shrimp: brine, EC 92-93; cave, EC 41, 42; cleaner, AN 22-23; early stages of, EV 132; gobies and, AN 86-87; starfish attacked by, UN 139

Shutter: rotating, movie projector's, MA 89

Shutter sensors: MA 115

Shuttle: *See* Space shuttle

Sicily (island), Italy: foehn in, WE 47; olive trees on, GE 131

Siemens, Werner von: generator built by, MA *29*

Siever blue butterfly: IN *78*

Sight: *See* Vision

Signals: trains controlled by, TR *20-21*

Silica (silicon dioxide): MA *96*; glass made from, ST *122-123*; lava, silica content of, PE *chart* 65; quartz, structure of, ST *122*; rock, ST *134*

Silicon: ST *134-135*; microscope's magnification of, MA *32*; in quartz crystal, MA *96*; as semiconductor, PH 84, *85*; solar cells, PH *110-111*

Silicon dioxide: *See* Silica

Silk: ST *108*; for bagworm bags, IN *102*; glowworm threads, IN *50-51*; spider webs, IN *36-37, 38-39, 94-95*

Silkworm moths: AN *51*, IN *85, 119*; antennae, IN *26, 32*; larvae, eyespots on, IN *113, 118-119*; mating, AN *94-95*

Silurian period: fish from, EV *46, 47*; fossils from, EV *50, 51*; species, WE *142*; temperatures, WE *chart* 142

Silver: electroplating with, ST *62-63*

Silverfish: IN *6, 84*; metamorphosis, IN *80-81*

Silver iodide: cloud seeding with, WE *78-79*; on daguerreotype plates, MA *16*

Simple machines: *See* Machines, simple

Simple metamorphosis: IN *80-81*

Simulations and models, computer: CO 130, *132-133*; automotive design, CO *74-75*; buildings, CO *133*; flight simulator, CO *82-83*; sports analysis programs, CO *136-137*; traffic patterns, CO *132-133*; train station, crowds in, CO *133*; weather conditions, CO *134*, WE 108

Sinai Peninsula, Egypt: GE *5*

Single-crystal silicon: ST *134-135*

Single in-line package (SIP): CO *23*

Single-lens reflex camera: MA *74*; autofocus (AF) for, MA *74-75*

Single-mode optical fibers: CO *125*

Sink: whirlpool formation in, PH *20-21*

Sinkholes: formation of, GE *58-59*

Sinoatrial node: HU *61*

Sinusoid capillaries: HU *63, 66-67*

SIP (single in-line package): CO *23*

Siphons: crabs' use of, UN *36, 37*

Sirius (star): magnitude, SP *81*; spectrographic analysis of, SP *78*

Sirocco: WE *46-47*

Sister theory of Moon's origin: SP *67*

Sixbar angelfish: UN *132*

Six-starred fishing spiders: AN *27*

Skarn: PE *100*

Skaters and skating: PH 26, *27*

Skates: UN *104*

Skeletal types of fish: UN *6*

Skeletons: birds, EV *71, 101*; Cenozoic mammals, EV *104-105*; dinosaurs, EV *60-61, 71, 74, 88*; human, HU 30, *32*; mammal-like reptile, EV *64. See also* Bones

Skid control in automobiles: CO 102, *103*

Skiers and skiing: PH *26-27*

Ski jumping: computer analysis of, CO *136-137*

Skin, fish's: UN *7*

Skin, human: HU *6, 30-31*; colors of, HU *50-51*; cooling of, HU *42-43*; electrical properties of, lie detector's measurement of, MA *36*; goose bumps on, HU *44-45*; hair, HU *44-45*, 46, *47, 99*; healing of, HU *48-49*; nails, HU *46*; sauna air and, PH *64-65*; as sensory organ, HU *98-99, 100*

Skin, prehistoric animals': EV *96-97*

Skinks: as caterpillar enemy, IN *120-121*; five-lined, AN *80, 81*

Skipjack tuna: UN *15*

Skippers: antennae of, IN *32*

Skuas: brown, AN *113*

Skulls: *Cynognathus,* EV *73*; dinosaurs, EV *76, 77, 87, 88*; elephants, EV *110*; fish, EV *48, 49*; hominids, EV *126*; human, HU *32*; human, bone growth in, HU *35*; whales, EV *113*

Sky color: cause of, WE *22-23*

Skylab (space station): PH 37; coronagraph, photograph by, SP *123*

Skyscraper: computer model of, CO *133*

Sky Water Project: WE *79*

Slash-and-burn agriculture: GE *107*

Slavemakers (ants): IN *138*

Slayton, Deke: SP *133*

Sleep: HU *122-123*; and dreams, HU *124-125*; in space, SP *132, 133*

Sleep deprivation, results of: HU *123*

Slender sweeper: UN *24*

Slickhead: UN *22*

Slide (vernier) calipers: MA *48, 49*

Sliding fog: WE *71*

Slime molds: PL 96, *97*

Slip surfaces: creation of, GE *103*

Sloths: EC *62-63*; giant, extinct, EC *20*

Slumps (landslides): GE *102-103*

Small intestine: HU *88-89*; surface of, HU *77, 88-89*; villi, HU *6, 88*

Smart cards: MA *60-61*

Smart houses: CO *104-105*

Smectic liquid crystals: ST *137*

Smell, sense of, animals': carp, UN *45, 46-47*; eels, UN *47*; fish, UN *46-47*; flies, AN 8, 9; insect antennae for, IN *26-27*; salmon's use of, AN *120*; sharks, UN *55*; snakes' use of, AN *14-15*

Smell, sense of, human: HU *116-117*

Smelting of copper: ST *111*

Smilodon (saber-toothed cat): EV *121*

Smoke: pollution by, WE *26, 27*

Smoke detectors: MA 64, *65*

Smoke machines: cloud seeding with, WE *79*

Smoky moths: IN *32*

Smolt: UN *83*

Smoothhead: bighead, UN *22-23*

Smooth muscle: HU *7, 60*; large intestine, HU *90*

Snails: EC *46, 139*; as cone shell's prey, UN *119*; mud, UN *98*; scavengers, EC *128-129*

Snakes: bird scaring, AN *117*; blind, EC *120*; caterpillars mimicking, IN *113*, 118, *119*; chimpanzee probing, AN *47*; defenses, AN *62-63, 85*; eagle's prey, EC *125, 127*; garter, EC *12-13*; hog-nose, AN *85*; pythons, EC *10-11*; rattlesnakes, AN *34-35, 62-63*; tongues, odor detection with, AN *14-15*

Snapping shrimps: AN *86-87*

Snapping turtles: alligator, UN *110-111*

Snipe eel: Atlantic, UN *112*

Snorkels: submarine's, TR *99*

Snout beetles: bluffing, AN *85*

Snow: cause of, WE *74, 75*; lowering freezing point of, ST *40, 41*; melted by chinooks, WE 44

Snowmobiles: TR *67, 68-69*

Snowplows: trains, TR *22-23*

Snow scorpionflies: IN *34*

Snowshoe hares: seasonal color changes in, AN *58-59*

Snow tires: TR *57*

Soap: removal of dirt by, ST *48-49*

Soap bubbles: colors of, PH *120-121*

Soapfishes: UN *126*

Soaring: eagles, TR *118*; gliders, TR *118*

Social behavior, animals': AN 124-144; ants, AN *124-127*, IN *138-139*; bees, AN 125, *128-131*; birds in flight, AN *132-137*; fish in schools, AN *74-75*; insects, IN *130-131*; lions in prides, AN *138-139*; primates, AN *124-125, 140-144*; wolves in packs, AN *44-45*

Social insects: IN 128-129; family behavior, vs. other insects', IN *130-131*; soldier aphids, IN *144*; termites as, IN *128-129, 140-141, 142-143. See also* Ants; Bees; Wasps

Society for Space Travel, German: MA 26

Sodium: electron shells, ST *7, 50-51*; ions, ST *18-19*, 40, *41, 43, 96*; light emission by, ST *50-51*

Sodium gas: spectrum of, SP *78*

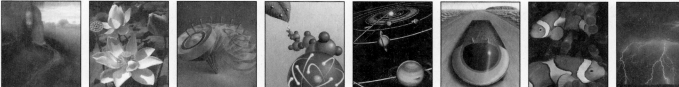

| Planet Earth PE | Plant Life PL | Physical Forces PH | Structure of Matter ST | Space & Planets SP | Transportation TR | Underwater World UN | Weather & Climate WE |

Sodium hypochlorite: ink removal with, ST *72*

Sodium 24: gamma decay of, PH *91*

Soft palate: during swallowing, HU *80-81*

Software and programs: CO *46-69*; algorithms, CO *52-53*; in computer crime, CO *106*; games, CO *78-79*; vs. human thinking, CO *68-69*; languages, CO *50-51*; motion analysis, in sports, CO *136-137*; music making, CO *66-67*; reading of text, CO *64-65*; robots controlled by, CO *99*; role of, CO *48*; searches for information, CO *56-57*; sorting, CO *54-55*; voice recognition, CO *62-63*; voice synthesis, CO *60-61*; word processors, CO *58-59*; writing of, CO *48-49*

Soil: acid rain and, ST *64, 65*; animals in, EC *36-37*, PL *110-111, 127*; horizons, EC *37*; nitrogen compounds in, ST *26, 27*; types, climate and, GE 112, GE *map* 113

Solar coronas: WE *105*

Solar eclipses: SP *41, 50-51, 62-63*

Solar energy: PH *110-111*; automobiles powered by, TR *62-63*; Earth, effects on, SP *48-49*; for Moon, possible, SP *75*; stored, ST *66*

Solar Flair (solar-powered automobile): TR *63*

Solar flares: SP *36-37, 40, 41*

Solar halos: WE *102-103*

Solar Max satellite: repair of, SP *136*

Solar panels: spacecraft with, SP *142-143*

Solar pillars: WE *102, 103*

Solar power: *See* Solar energy

Solar-powered automobiles: TR *62-63*

Solar prominences: SP *41, 43, 46*

Solar satellites: CO *128-129*

Solar System: SP 4-35; asteroids, comets, and meteors, SP *4-5, 30-35*; in Milky Way, SP *100-101, 102, 103, 111*; origins, SP *6-7, 17*; Voyager routes in, SP *138-139*. *See also* Planets; Sun

Solar telescopes: SP *122-123*

Solar wind: WE *19*; and aurora, WE *16, 17*; effects of, SP *48, 49*

Soldier ants: AN *126, 127*

Soldier aphids: IN *144*

Soldier termites: IN *140, 141, 143*

Solenoids: PH *69, 81*; in electromagnet, PH *80-81*

Solidago: PL *73*

Solid-fuel rockets: ST *74*

Solids: ST *44-45*; in colloids, ST *20*; freezing point, lowering, ST *40-41*; phase changes in, PH *52-53, 54-55*, ST *34, 35, 38, 39*

Sols: ST *20*

Solstices: summer, SP *56, 58-59*; winter, SP *57, 58*

Solvent extraction in perfume making: ST *126*

Sonar: PH *130*; bats' use of, AN *42-43*; dolphins' use of, UN *58-59, 115*

Sonar depth finder: TR *82*

Songs: birds', AN 98, *99*; crickets', AN *96-97*

Sonic booms: PH *140-141*; Mach cones created by, TR *136-137*

Sonograms: production of, MA *142-143*

Sooty terns: EC *32*

Sordes (pterosaur): EV *96*

Sorrel, wood: PL *77*; photonasty in, PL *45*

Sorting: CO *54-55*

Sound: PH 128-144; air temperature and, PH *133*; barn owl's hunting by, AN 38, *39*; on compact disks, MA *86-87*; Doppler effect, PH *138-139*; echoes, PH *132-133*; human ears' detection of, HU *112-113*; microphones' and speakers' conversion of, MA *80-81*; movie projectors' playing back of, MA *88*; on phonograph records, MA *86*; qualities of, MA *90*; and radio transmissions, MA *84-85*; sonic booms, PH *140-141*, TR *136-137*; spectrographs' use of, MA *34-35*; speed of, TR 136; stethoscopes' transmission of, MA *144*; surround sound, PH *144*; synthesizers' use of, MA *90-91*; telephones' transmission of, MA *56-57*; tones, production of, PH *134-135, 136-137*; transmission of, PH *130-131*; tuning of musical instruments, PH *142-143*; ultrasonic, use of, MA *75, 142-143*; VCRs' recording of, MA *83*; wind, traveling with, PH *133*; wind instruments, PH *135, 136-137*

Sound barrier: breaking, PH *140-141*, TR *136-137*

Sound organs of insects: and sound production, IN *28-29*

Sound production by computers: music, CO *66-67*; speech, CO *60-61*

Sound recognition by computers: CO *62-63*

Sound waves: PH *131*; forms, and timbre, MA *90*; speed of, in ocean, 134, PE *chart* 135; wave fronts, PH *131, 138-139*

South Africa: diamond formation in, PE *91*

South America: Africanized honeybees, spread of, IN *map* 137; Altiplano, GE *140-141*; Amazon River, GE *36-37*; Andes mountains, formation of, PE *38-39*; Aztec ants, IN *98-99*; butterflies, IN *30, 118, 121*; deserts, WE *72, 135*; discus, UN *86-87*; dolphins, UN *59, 114-115*; electric eels, UN *19, 57*; El Niño phenomenon, PE *124-125*; extinct animals of, EV *107, 120-121*; garúa, WE *72-73*; lungfish, UN *31*; marsupial frog, pygmy, UN *90*; mud snail, giant, UN *98*; rainfall, WE *map* 73;

southern oscillation, effect of, WE *140-141*; splashing tetra, UN *74-75*

Southern Cross (solar-powered automobile): TR *62-63*

Southern oscillation and trade winds: WE *140-141*

Southern toads: AN *54-55*

South Pole: and atmospheric circulation, WE 34; ozone hole over, ST *map* 77. *See also* Antarctica

Sow bugs (pill bugs): EC *36, 37*; evolutionary path, IN *6*; parenting behavior, IN *76-77*; spider's capture of, AN *26*

Sow thistles: PL *73*

Soybeans: PL *13, 54, 67*

Space: SP entire volume

Space colonization, possible: SP 128, *140-141*; Moon base, SP *74-75*; transport, SP *143*

Spacecraft: ceramic tiles on, ST *131*; launching, PH *18-19*; near speed of light, PH *126-127*; orbit, PH *36-37*; rockets and rocket fuel, ST *23, 54-55, 71, 74-75*; and shape-memory antenna, ST *141*; solar cells for, PH *111*. *See also* Satellites

Spacelab: SP *132*, 136; simulator, SP *137*

Space probes: CO *142-143*, SP 124, *125*; ion-powered, SP *143*; Mars studied by, SP *12-13*; Mercury studied by, SP *8*; Venus studied by, SP *10, 11*. *See also* Voyager space probes

Space shuttle: SP *128-129*, ST *71, 74-75, 131*; living in, SP *132-133*; propulsion of, SP *130-131*; replicas, training in, SP *137*; specialists, SP *136-137*

Space stations: possible, SP 128, *142, 144*

Spacesuits: SP *134-135*

Space travel: SP *128-144*; colony designs, SP *140-141*; interplanetary, craft for, SP *142-143, 144*; ion-powered craft, SP *142-143*; shuttle, SP *128-133, 136-137*; space stations, SP 128, *142, 144*; suits for, SP *134-135*; training for, SP *136-137*

Spain, agriculture in: GE *131, map* 136; climate for, GE *chart* 136

Spark plugs: computerized control of, CO *102*; role of, TR *40, 41*

Sparrow moth caterpillars: IN *119*

Spawning: salmon, UN 82, *83*. *See also* Eggs and egg laying; Mating, courtship and

Speakers: dynamic, MA 80, *81*; radio's, MA *85*

Special effects: CO *80-81*

Special-purpose vehicles: TR *66-77*; construction rollers, TR *66, 74-75*; cranes, TR *66-67, 72-73*; fire engines, TR *66-67, 70-71*; power shovels, TR *66-67, 76-77*; snowmobiles, TR *67, 68-69*

Animal Behavior
AN

Computer Age
CO

Ecology
EC

Evolution of Life
EV

Geography
GE

Human Body
HU

Insects & Spiders
IN

Machines &
Inventions **MA**

Special theory of relativity: PH *126-127*

Species: EV *4-5*; adaptation, EV *5, 20-21*; adaptive radiation, EV *24-25*, 138; branching, EV *4-5, 6-7*; breeds and breeding, EV *10-11, 14, 18-19*; classification of, EV *6*; defining characteristic of, EV *10-11*; differentiation, EV *12, 22-23*; of Galápagos, EV *12-13, 80*; mutations in, EV *14-15, 16-17, 18*; natural selection, EV *12, 16-17*; number of, EV *8-9*; subspecies of, EV *10. See also* Evolution

Spectacled spiders: AN *26*

Spectra: Doppler shifts in, SP *91, 115*; infrared, SP *29*; prisms and, SP *78, 118*

Spectral types of stars: SP *78, chart* 79

Spectrographs: sound, MA *34-35*; sound, and spectrum analysis, CO *62-63*

Spectrometers: Voyager, SP *139*

Spectroscopy: SP *29*; radio, SP *121*; telescope for, SP *28*

Spectrum: solar, WE *23*; of white light, PH *120*

Speech areas of brain: HU *120*, 121

Speech production: by computers, CO *60-61*; human, HU *58*

Speech recognition by computers: CO *62-63*

Speech transmission by telephones: CO *110-111*; car phones, CO *120-121*; teleconferencing, CO *112-113*

Speed guns: MA *38-39*

Speed indicators: airplanes', TR *132-133*

Speed of light: approaching, PH *126-127*; measuring, PH *118-119*

Speed of sound: exceeding, PH *140-141*, TR *136-137*; medium and, PH *chart* 130; temperature and, PH *133*

Sperm, fertilization in plants by: PL *8, 66*; in algae, PL *103*; in ferns and mosses, PL *109*

Sperm, human: *See* Egg and sperm, human

Sperm ducts: HU *12*

Sperm webs: male spider's, AN *90-91*

Sperm whales: AN *40-41*; diving by, UN *32-33*

Sperry, Roger: experiment by, HU *121*

Sphincter, anal: HU *91*

Sphygmomanometer: medical use of, MA *130-131*

Spicules: Sun's atmosphere, SP *41*

Spider crabs: use of camouflage by, UN *136*

Spiderfish: UN *113*

Spider monkeys: EC *71*

Spiders: EC *37, 120*; butterfly enemy, IN *115*; courtship, AN *90-91*; evolutionary path, IN *6*; and hunting wasps, IN *54-55, 111*; methods of catching prey, AN *26-27*; parenting behavior, IN *74, 75*; sensing prey, AN *28-29*; water spiders, IN *96-*

97; as web spinners, IN *36-37, 38-39, 94-95*

Spider wasps: IN *54-55*

Spiderwort stoma: PL *38*

Spikelets, grass: PL *62*; on oats, PL *144*

Spinach: PL *136*; as long-day plant, PL *54*

Spinal cord: HU *41, 101, 103*

Spinal ganglia: HU *101, 103*

Spinal reflexes: HU *102-103*

Spindle tree: PL *78*

Spine, human: HU *40-41*

Spines, creatures with: poison fish, UN *120-121, 122-123*; porcupinefish, UN *121, 124-125*; sea urchins, UN *39, 139, 144. See also* Vertebrates

Spines, on plants: PL *28*; of cacti, PL *112, 113*

Spinner dolphins: UN *115*

Spinnerets: spiders', IN *94, 95*

Spinning machines for fibers: glass, ST *124*; synthetic, ST *109*

Spinning tops: PH *25, 32-33*

Spiny dogfish fetus: UN *76*

Spiny hatchetfish: UN *23*

Spiracles: IN *10, 11*

Spiral galaxies: SP *98-99, 103*; shape, maintenance of, SP *106-107*; and star formation, SP *89. See also* Milky Way

Spits: sand, GE *75*

Spitting spiders: AN *27*

Spittlebugs: IN *100-101*

Splashing tetras: reproduction by, UN *74-75*

Spleen: role of, HU *67*

Split-brain experiment: HU *121*

Spoilage of food: controlling, ST *88-89*

Spoilers: automated car's, TR *61*; glider's, use of, TR *118, 119*; racing car's, TR *58*

Sponge gourds: leaf growth, PL *17*; root pressure, PL *21*

Sponges: ammonite in, EV *99*; evolution of, EV *6*; flagellate cells, EV *38*; repair of, UN *101*; reproduction by, UN *100-101*

Spongy tissue: PL *39, 40, 41*

Spoonbills: roseate, EC *138*

Spore-bearing plants: PL *92-109*; ascocarps (fruiting bodies), PL *97, 106*; in evolution, PL *93, 94*; ferns, PL *95, 108-109*; molds as, PL *96-97*; mosses as, PL *95, 108-109*; mushrooms as, PL *95, 99*; seaweed as, PL *95, 102-103*; vs. seed plants, PL *94-95*

Spores: mushroom, EC *135*

Sporophytes: *See* Spore-bearing plants

Sporting goods: carbon fibers in, ST *138-139*

Sports analysis programs: CO *136-137*

Spotted notothens: UN *16-17*

Spot welding: robot use in, CO *101*

Spray arm: dishwasher's, MA *117*

Spray-dried coffee: ST 86, *87*

Spray plating: ST *63*

Spriggina (extinct wormlike animal): EV *39*

Springboks: AN *60-61*

Spring (vernal) equinox: SP *56*

Springs (water): alluvial fans and formation of, GE *30-31*; artesian, GE *56, 62, 63*

Springs, mechanical: PH *50-51*; bathroom scales' use of, MA *108, 109*

Springtails: EC *36*

Spring-tide breeders: AN *122-123*

Spring tides: cause of, PE *128-129*

Spring trap: spider's, IN *39*

Sprocket and pedal on bicycle: PH *46, 47*

Spruce needles and buds: EC *24*

S-P time: PE 51, 52, 53, *chart* 53

Spy hopping: by gray whales, UN *94*

Squall line: WE *51*

Squalls: tropical, WE *76-77*

Squash: male and female flowers of, PL *58-59*

Squid: UN *113*; flying, AN *82-83*; giant, AN *40-41*; ink, use of, UN *140-141*; markings, changing of, UN *142-143*; sperm whale diving for, UN *33*

Squirrel monkeys: EC *70, 71*

Squirrels: seed dispersal by, EC *123*

Squirrels, flying: AN *73*; as owl's prey, AN *39*

Squirting cucumbers: PL *77*

Stag beetles: EC *111*

Staircases: moving (escalators), MA *66-67*

Stalactites: GE *60-61*

Stalagmites: GE *60-61*

Stamens: PL *51, 52-53, 58, 59, 62*; and pistils, EV *103*

Standing waves: PH 134, *137*

Stapler as lever: PH *42*

Starboard and port tacks: PH *13*

Starch grains: PL *7, 11*

Starch in flour: ST *100-101*

Star dunes: GE *109*

Starfish: EC *47*; anatomy, UN *138*; in food chain, UN *126-127*; as predators, UN *138-139*; as scavengers, EC *128*

Starlight: aberration of, SP *55*

Starlings: sun, navigation by, AN *134*

Stars: SP *76-97*; birds' navigation by, AN *136-137*; birth of, SP *6, 7, 38-39, 76-77, 87, 88-89, 92*; black hole in binary system, SP *94-95*; brightness, SP *chart* 79, *80-81*; colors, SP *78-79*; evolution, SP *46-47, 92, 93*; Hertzsprung-Russell diagram, SP *chart* 79; in Milky Way, SP *101*; motion, apparent, SP *52, 53, 54, 55*; motion, proper, SP *90-91*; and nebula types, SP *86-87*; North Star, changing of, SP *60-61*;

|  |  |  |  | |  | | |

| Planet Earth PE | Plant Life PL | Physical Forces PH | Structure of Matter ST | Space & Planets SP | Transportation TR | Underwater World UN | Weather & Climate WE |

nuclear fusion in, ST *16-17*; nuclear reactions in, SP 40, *44-45*, 76, 92; planetariums projecting, SP *126-127*; Pleiades, cluster of, SP *86, 88*; pulsars, SP 96, *97*; sizes, comparative, SP *78-79*; spectral types, SP *78, chart* 79; supernova explosions and remnants, SP 76, *84-85, 89, 93-97*; variable, SP *82-83. See also* Galaxies; Sun

Star wheel in vending machine: MA *58*

Static electricity: PH *70-71*

Stationary front: WE *120-121*

Stationary vs. migratory high pressure: WE *85*

Station models: WE *118-119*

Statocysts (static organs): UN *43*

Stealth bomber: TR *109, 144*

Steam: in extinguishing of fire, ST 68; water's phase change into, ST *32-33*

Steam car: Cugnot's, TR 36, *38-39*

Steam distillation in perfume making: ST *126-127*

Steam engine: TR *90*

Steamer: heating food in, PH *65*

Steam fog: WE *71*

Steam generator: nuclear engine with, TR *102*

Steam-powered tractor combine: MA *15*

Steam trains: TR 4, *16-17*; earliest, TR *4-5, 14-15*

Steam turbines, power for: geothermal, PH *102-103*; nuclear, PH *109*; ocean, PH *107*; solar, PH 110, *111*; thermoelectric, PH *100-101*

Steam vessels: TR *79, 90-91*

Steel: ST *111, 112*; burning, conditions for, ST *70-71*; galvanizing, ST *63*; pig iron for, producing, ST *102-103, 110-111*; types of, ST *chart* 113; uses for, ST *chart* 113

Steel wool: burning of, ST *70*

Steering: automobile's, four-wheel vs. two-wheel, TR *50-51*; snowmobile's, TR *69*

Stegoceras (dinosaur): EV *75*

Stegodon (elephant ancestor): EV *110-111*

Stegosaurus (dinosaur): EV *81*; skeleton, EV *74*

Stele: PL *15*

Stem cells: HU *128*

Stems: PL 19; bamboo, PL *32-33*; bark on, trees', PL *25, 26-27*; big tree trunks, PL *116, 117, 122-123*; cacti, PL 112, *113*; ferns vs. mosses, PL 108; growth of, PL *16, 17*; growth rings, trees', PL *18-19, 24-25*; hypocotyl, PL *12-13*; layers of, PL *20*; leaf arrangement on, PL *36-37*; modifications of, PL *28, 29, 30-31*; of parasite and host, PL *57*; receptacle tissue in

fruits, PL *67, 68, 69*; runners, PL *91*; underground, reproduction by, PL 62, *91*; water transportation through, PL *20-21, 40-41*

Stenodictya (early flying insect): EV *54*

Stenopterygius (ichthyosaur): EV *92*

Stephenson, George: train built by (Rocket), TR *4, 14-15*

Steppes: EC *76*

Step-type optical fibers: CO *125*

Step-up transformers: PH *86, 99*

Stereo digital photogrammetric station (SDPS): CO *76*

Stereoscopic vision: HU *106-107*

Stethoscopes: MA *144*; in blood pressure measurement, MA *130, 131*

Stick insects: AN *52, 80*

Stickleback: nest building by, UN *79*

Stick-mimicking mantis: AN *51*

Stilt roots: EC *35, 64*

Stinging cells: sea anemones, AN *48*

Stinging insects: ants, IN *126, 127*; bees, IN 124, *125*, 137; and mimics, AN *54-55*; wasps, IN *54, 124, 125*

Stingray: UN *123*

Stink bugs: AN *69*, IN *123*; egg laying, IN *130*; mating, IN *66*; warning coloration, IN *112, 120*

Stitches: forming of, by sewing machines, MA *104-105*

STOL (short takeoff and landing) aircraft: Asuka, TR *139*

Stomach, human: HU *82-83*; fiberscope's viewing of, MA *139*; lining of, HU *77, 82-83*

Stomas: PL *20, 21, 38-39, 40*; cactus, PL *113*; pine needles, PL *49*

Stonecrop (sedum): PL *90-91*; stomas, PL *38*

Stonefish: UN *123*

Stone plants: PL *110, 114-115*

Storage grains: PL *7, 11*

Storage of data: CO *30-31*; CD-ROM, CO *95*; magnetic, CO *19, 36-37, 56-57*; after sorting, CO *55*

Stores: bar codes and scanners used in, CO *86-87*

Storms: computer models of, CO *134*; Great Red Spot, Jupiter, SP *14-15, 16*; Neptune, SP *27*; thunderstorms, WE 51, *56-57, 66-67, 89. See also* Hurricanes and typhoons

Storm tides and storm waves: PE *130-131*

Stotting: AN 60, *61*

Straddle-type monorail: TR *28-29*

Strained back: HU *40-41*

Stranglers (plants): EC *65*

Stratovolcanoes: PE *67*; caldera formation in, PE *68*

Stratified zone of oceans: PE 134, *135*

Stratocumulus cloud: WE *60*

Stratosphere: WE 4, *8-9, 10-11, charts* 25; ozone layer, WE 4, *8-9, 12-13, 25, 30-31*; ozone layer, hole in, ST *76-77*; weather observation in, WE *112-113*; winds in, WE *36, 112-113*

Stratus clouds: WE *60, 61, chart* 74

Strawberries: anther culture, PL *140*; fruit, PL *67*; plants with runners, PL *91*

Street winds: WE *55*

Streptomyces antibiotics: PL *132, 133*

Striated muscle: *See* Muscles of humans

Strike-slip faults: PE *42-43, 48, 49*

Stringed instruments: PH *134-135*

Striped droneflies: AN *54*

Striped shrimp: AN *87*

Strip mine: PE *105*

Stromatolites: EV *26-27, 34-35*, WE *6*

Strombolian type of volcanic eruption: PE *66*

Structural plains vs. peneplains: GE *28*

Struthiomimus (dinosaur): EV *74*

Studded tires: TR *57*

Styrocosaurus (dinosaur): EV *89*

Subalpine zone of Alps: GE *142, chart* 142

Subatomic particles: ST 4, *5, 6-7*; antiparticles, ST *22-23*; in fusion reactions, ST *16-17*; neutrons, ST 7, 14, 15, *16-17, 25. See also* Electrons

Subduction: PE *11, 28, 33, 34, 48-49*; active theory of, PE *29*; of Farallon plate, PE *42, 43*; island arcs as result of, PE *76, 115*; and magma formation, PE *64-65*; mountains formed by, GE *87*; and rock formation, PE *86*

Sublimation of carbon dioxide: ST *38, 39*

Sublingual glands: HU *78*

Submarines: TR *79, 98-99*; diving and surfacing, TR *98*; nuclear, TR *102-103*; submersibles, TR *79, 106-107*

Submaxillary glands: HU *78, 79*

Submersibles, deep-diving: TR *79, 106-107*

Submission in wolves: AN *45*

Subreflector of radio telescope: SP *120*

Subsidence: ground, GE *64-65*

Subtropical deserts: WE *134*

Subtropical jet stream: WE *37, 38-39, 112*

Subways: air supply, TR *26-27*; contact couplings, TR *9*; doors, TR *13*

Succession of plants: PL *128-129*

Sucker: remora's, AN *25*

Sugar: blood (glucose), HU *142, 143*; in fermentation: ST *85*

Sugarcane: MSG from, ST *90-91*

Sulfur: on Io (moon of Jupiter), SP *18-19*

Sulfur butterflies, wing coloration of: IN *30*

Sulfur deposits: PE *100*

Sulfur dioxide: and acid rain, ST *64*

| Animal Behavior **AN** | Computer Age **CO** | Ecology **EC** | Evolution of Life **EV** | Geography **GE** | Human Body **HU** | Insects & Spiders **IN** | Machines & Inventions **MA** |

Sulfur-eating bacteria: UN *35*

Sulfuric acid: batteries with, ST *58-59*; Venus, SP 10, *11*

Sulfur oxides: and nitrogen oxides, WE 26, *27, 28-29*

Summer monsoon: WE *130*; flooding, WE *132*

Summer solstice: SP *56*; in Arctic, SP *58-59*

Sun: SP *4-5, 17, 36-49*; and aurora, WE 16; birds' navigation by, AN *134*, 135; chromosphere and photosphere, SP *40, 41, 42-43*; corona, SP *40, 41, 50-51, 63, 123*; corona, atmospheric, WE *105*; Earth, radiation received by, SP *45, 48-49*; Earth's angle to, and seasons, SP *56-57*; Earth's protection from, WE *20-21*; eclipse of, SP *41, 50-51, 62-63*; in eclipse of Moon, SP *62-63*; energy from, stored, ST *66*; energy generated by, PH *110-111*; flares, SP *36-37, 40, 41*; formation of, SP *6, 7, 38-39*; future of, SP 36, *46-47*; and greenhouse effect, WE *136, 137*; halos and other images around, WE *102-103*; on Hertzsprung-Russell diagram, SP *chart* 79; inside, SP *17, 40, 41*, 44; insolation from, varying, and ice ages, WE *144*; Jupiter compared to, SP *17*; life history of, SP *39, 46-47*; magnetic field, WE *16*; magnetic field lines, SP *42-43, 46*; midnight, land of, SP *58-59*; mock, WE *102, 103*; and mountain halos, WE *104-105*; nuclear fusion in, SP 40, *44-45*, ST *16-17*; path on celestial sphere (ecliptic), SP *54-55, 60-61, 70*; and precession of Earth, SP *60-61*; and rainbows, WE *96-97, 98-99*; reflection of (albedo), WE *map* 123; salmon's navigation by, AN *121*; size, comparative, SP *79*; and sky color, WE *22-23*; spectrum, WE *23*; stars around, SP *101*; sunspots on, SP *41, 42-43*; telescopes for studying, SP *122-123*; temperatures, SP *17*, 39, 41, 47; through atmosphere, WE *4-5*; and tides, PE 128, *129*; and tropical squalls, WE *76*; ultraviolet light from, HU 50, *51*, WE *7, 9, 11, 12-13, 14, 15, 30*; uneven heating by, and air movement, WE 32, 34, 40, 42, 124; and wind and ocean currents, PE *118, 119, 120*

Sunbirds, malachite: as pollinators, EC *114*

Sun City, Ariz., U.S.: GE *118-119*

Sundew plants: EC *116-117*, PL *34-35, 47*

Sunfish: UN *72-73*; metamorphosis, UN *88-89*

Sunflowers: PL *70-71*; phyllotaxis, PL *36-37*

Sunlight: *See* Light

Sunrise and sunset: sky color at, WE *22*

Sunspots: SP *41, 42, 43*; cycle of, SP *graph*

43; formation of, SP *42-43*

Superclusters of galaxies: SP *110*

Supercomputers: CO *42-43*; first, CO *15*; weather conditions modeled by, CO *134*, WE 108

Superconducting ships: future, TR *104-105*

Superconductivity: PH *92-93*

Supergiants (stars): and black holes, SP *94-95*; and supernovas, SP *84, 93*

Supergranules and granules: SP *41*

Supermarkets: scanner type used in, CO *86-87*

Supernova explosions: SP 76, *84-85, 89, 93*

Supernova remnants: black holes and neutron stars as, SP 76, *85, 93-97*

Superposition of strata: law of, PE 94, *95*

Supersonic aircraft: TR *108-109, 136-137*; sonic booms from, PH *140-141*

Supertrains: TR *32-33*; bullet trains, TR *4-5, 33*

Suppressor T cells: HU *128, 129*

Surface currents, ocean: PE *118-119, map* 120-121

Surface waves, seismic: PE 50; Love vs. Rayleigh, PE *51*

Surf clam: starfish attack escaped by, UN *139*

Surfers and surfing: PH *38-39*

Surffish: UN *87*

Surfperch: body fluids of, UN *chart* 16

Surgery: heart-lung machine used in, CO *139*

Surinam toads: UN *91*

Surround sound: PH *144*

Suruga Bay, Japan: GE *23*

Surveying: GE *6, 8-9*; aerial, GE *6-7, 19*; for nautical charts, GE *18, 19*

Suspension: motorcycle's, TR *43*; racing, TR *59*

Suspension monorails: TR *29*

Swallowing: HU *80-81*

Swallows: and swifts, convergence of, EV *137*

Swallowtail butterflies: antennae, IN *32*; atypical behavior, IN *32, 33*; caterpillar with scent gland, IN *123*; egg laying, IN *130*; emergence of, from chrysalis, IN *83*; foot structure, IN *21*; metamorphosis, IN *56-57*; as pollinators, EC *114*, PL *50, 53*; wing coloration, IN *30, 31, 83*

Swans in flight: AN *133*

Swarming: honeybees, IN *133, 135*; locusts, IN *86-87*

Swash plate on helicopter's rotor shaft: use of, TR *115*

S (shear) waves, seismic: and P (compressional) waves, PE *15*, 50, *51*; S-P time, PE 51, 52, 53, *chart* 53

Sweat: HU *42-43*; evaporating, in sauna, PH *64-65*; gland activity, lie detector's measurement of, MA *36*

Sweeper: slender, UN *24*

Sweet peas: PL *55*

Sweet potatoes: PL *29*; grafting onto, PL *135*

Swell shark: emergence of, from egg case, UN *76*

Swifts: and swallows, convergence of, EV *137*

Swim bladder: UN *12-13*; for hearing, UN *52, 53*; and pressure, UN 23

Swimming styles: UN *4-5, 18-19, 20-21*; dance of cleaner wrasse, UN *134, 135*; jellyfish, UN *4-5, 42-43*; on side, by river dolphins, UN *58*

Switching circuitry: synthesizer's, MA *91*; telephone signal passing through, MA *57*

Switch rails: TR *7*

Switzerland: Alps in, GE *142-143*

Swordfish: EV *136*; swimming style of, UN *20-21*

Sycamore trees: PL *26-27*

Syenite (rock): PE *88*

Symbiosis: ants and aphids, AN *12-13*; ants and butterflies, IN *78-79*; ants and plants, IN *98-99*; cleaner wrasses and hosts, UN *120, 134-135*; crabs and hosts, UN *38-39*; cuckoo catfish and cichlids, UN *84-85*; exploitation of hosts, UN *144*; remoras and sharks, AN *24-25*; sea anemones and fish, AN *22-23, 70-71*; sea anemones and hermit crabs, AN *78-79*; sexual parasites, UN *70-71*; shrimp and fish, AN *22-23, 86-87*

Symington, William: steam vessel engineered by *(Charlotte Dundas)*, TR *91*

Sympathetic vibrations: PH *143*

Symphylids: EC *37*

Synapses: HU *100-101*

Synapsids (mammal-like reptiles): EV 59, *62, 63, 64-65, 73*

Synchronous rotation of Moon: SP *70-71*

Synthesized images: CO *81*

Synthesized sound: music, CO *66*; voice, CO *60-61*

Synthesizers: MA *90-91*

Synthetic materials: ST *108-109, 118-119*. *See also* Materials technology

Systole in artificial heart: MA *133*

Systolic pressure: measuring, MA *130-131*

T

Tabulating machine, Hollerith's: CO *12-13*

Tacking by sailboat: PH *13*

Tadpoles: EC *93*, UN *88-89, 90, 91*

Taenophyllum root: PL *29*

| Planet Earth **PE** | Plant Life **PL** | Physical Forces **PH** | Structure of Matter **ST** | Space & Planets **SP** | Transportation **TR** | Underwater World **UN** | Weather & Climate **WE** |

Taiga (boreal forest): EC *4, 24, 29*

Tails: fish's use of, in swimming, UN *18-19, 20-21*; lizards, breaking of, AN *80-81*; rattlesnakes, rattles in, AN *62, 63*

Tails of comets: SP *33*

Tamarins: lion, EC *71*

Tanagers: scarlet, EC *61*

Tanker in Panama Canal: TR *92*

Tanystropheus (early reptile): EV *62*

Tape: magnetic, and tape drives, CO *19, 36, 37*; recording on, by VCR, MA *82-83*

Tapirs: EC *14-15*

Tasmanian wolves: EV *138, 144*

Taste, sense of, aquatic animals': UN *46*; in gurnard, UN *47*

Taste, sense of, human: and taste buds, HU *118-119*

Taste buds, animals': in fish's barbels, AN *20*; flies, AN *8, 9*

Taste buds, human: HU *118-119*

Taxis: positive, negative, AN *6*

T cells (T lymphocytes): HU *128, 129, 131*; and AIDS virus, HU *136-137*

Tectonic plate interactions: and mountain building, GE *86-87, 96-97, 98-99*; and seafloor spreading, GE *78-79*

Tectonic plates: *See* Plate tectonics

Teeth of animals: aquatic animals, adaptations of, for feeding, UN *104, 105*; birds with, EV *100, 101*; *Desmostylus*, EV *118, 119*; dinosaurs, EV *76, 77*; *Pterodaustro*, EV *91*; radula, cone shell's, UN *118, 119*; whales, EV *113*

Teeth of humans: development of, HU *26-27, 35*

Teleconferencing: CO *112-113*

Telegraph: MA *8-9*

Telemeters: laser, GE *8-9*

Telephones and telephone lines: CO *108-109*, MA *56-57*; car phones, CO *120-121*; earliest, MA *10-11*; fax transmissions over, CO *114-115*, MA *68-69*; modems, use of, CO *91, 118, 119*; pagers, calls to, CO *122*; picture phones, CO *126-127*; teleconferencing, CO *112-113*; voice transmission through, CO *110-111*

Telescopes: SP *116-125*; convex lenses in, PH *116*; earliest, SP *116*; Mauna Kea, SP *28*; optical, SP *116, 118-119, 122-123, 124*; radio, SP *120-121, 122, 124*; satellites and probes, SP *123, 124-125*; solar, SP *122-123*

Television: color images on, MA *76-77*; early, MA *22-23*; high-definition, MA *78-79*; images, vs. videophone images, CO *127*; liquid-crystal, ST *137*; VCR's recording of signals from, MA *82-83*; and video games, CO *78-79*

Temperate coniferous forests: acid rain and, EC *74-75*

Temperate deciduous forests: EC *5, 25*

Temperate rain forests: EC *4, 25*

Temperature: PH *52*; altitude and, WE *24, 25, 113*; Andes region, GE *charts* 140; of boiling point, MA *100*, *chart* 100; and chinooks, WE *44*, *chart* 45; climate zones, GE *charts* 112, WE *128-129*; and density of water, PH *chart* 67; of dew point, MA *125*; of earth, changes over time, WE *142*, *chart* 142-143; and electricity in clouds, WE *67*; extreme, measuring, PH *56-57*; of fish, circulatory system and, UN *14-15*; glaciation and, GE *chart* 50; global warming, WE *136, 137*; isotherms, WE *126, 139*; land and sea, WE *chart* 43; in Mediterranean countries, GE *charts* 136-137; and mirages, WE *100, 101*; ocean currents and, GE *charts* 116-117; of oceans, depth and, GE *70-71*, PE *117, 134*, *chart* 135; and phase changes, PH *22-23, 52-53, 54-55, 62-63*; and pressure and volume of gas, PH *11*; and saturation, WE *58, 70*; sensors, fire alarm systems', MA *64, 65*; and speed of sound, PH *133*; of spermaceti oil, control of, UN *33*; thermometer, electronic, for measuring, MA *128-129*; thermostats controlling, MA *120-121*; and vapor pressure, PH *chart* 22; of water, and fish's body fluids, UN *16*, *chart* 16; and wind, WE *40-41*; worldwide, GE *map* 117

Temperature inversion layer: WE *60*; heat island, WE *138-139*

Tender: steam train's, TR *14-15*

Tendrils: PL *29*; cucumber, PL *30-31*

Tenma (x-ray observatory): SP *125*

Tennessee River, U.S.: Tennessee Valley Authority (TVA) projects on, GE *134-135*

Tennis ball: path of, in computer model, CO *136*

Tennis racket: carbon-fiber, ST *138-139*

Tenontosaurus (dinosaur): EV *74-75*

Terminal moraine: GE *44-45, 46-47*

Termites: ants attacking, IN *140, 141*; chimpanzee collecting, AN *47*; colonies, IN *128-129, 140-141*; evolutionary path, IN *7*; fungus-growing, mounds of, IN *142-143*; poisonous adhesive, IN *123*; wood digestion, IN *48-49*

Terns: EC *32*; Antarctic, EC *47*; Arctic, AN *135*

Terpen in the Netherlands: GE *132*

Terraced farms: GE *141*

Terraced pools in caves: GE *54-55, 60-61*

Terraces: GE *27, 88-89*; slump's creation of, GE *103*

Territories: bowerbirds' creation of, AN *100-101*; moles', AN *104-105*; singing to defend, AN *96, 97, 98, 99*

Tertiary period: WE *143*; coal formation beginning in, PE *105*

Testes: *See* Testicles, human

Testicles, human (testes): HU *12, 75*

Test-tube babies: *See* In vitro fertilization

Test-tube cultivation: PL *140-141, 143*

Teton Range, Wyo., U.S.: GE *86*

Tetraploid plants: PL *139*

Tetras: Congo, UN *64*; splashing, reproduction by, UN *74-75*

Text: electronic publishing of, CO *94-95*; faxing, CO *114-115*; reading, by computer, CO *64-65*; saving, CO *59*

TGV (Train à Grande Vitesse): TR *33*

Thailand: rice harvest in, GE *122*; summer monsoon in, WE *132*

Thalamus: nerve impulses to, HU *101*

Thallus lichens: PL *107*

Thames River, England: estuary of, GE *38*

Thecodonts: EV *66-67*; *Euparkeria*, EV *62, 66*

Thelodus (extinct fish): EV *47*

Thematic mappers (TMs): CO *140*

Thematic maps: GE *12*

Theory of evolution: EV *12-13*

Theory of relativity, special: PH *126-127*

Theosodon (extinct mammal): EV *120*

Therapsids: EV *chart* 65

Thermal air turbulence: WE *52-53*

Thermal conductivity: PH *chart* 61

Thermal energy: vs. heat energy, PH *52*; from ocean, PH *106, 107*; radiant, measuring, PH *56-57*. *See also* Heat

Thermal insulation: PH *60-61*

Thermal perspiration: HU *42-43*

Thermal power stations: PE *139*

Thermal resistors: *See* Thermistors

Thermals (rising air currents): PH *15*; and gliders, TR *119*

Thermistors (thermal resistors): MA *120*; in electronic thermometer, MA *128*

Thermocline: oceans', PE *134, 135*

Thermoelectric power plants: PH *100-101*

Thermogram: working of, PH *56-57*

Thermometers: electronic, MA *128-129*; high-temperature, PH *56-57*; liquid-crystal, ST *137*

Thermoplastic vs. thermosetting resins: ST *118-119*

Thermosphere: WE *8-9, 10-11*; and winds, WE *36, 38*

Thermostats: MA *120-121*

Thick-billed murres: EC *33*

Thinking: computer vs. human, CO *68-69*

Third-class levers: PH *43*

| Animal Behavior **AN** | Computer Age **CO** | Ecology **EC** | Evolution of Life **EV** | Geography **GE** | Human Body **HU** | Insects & Spiders **IN** | Machines & Inventions **MA** |

Third law of motion, Newton's: PH 18, 24

Thistles: PL *74*; beetles on, EC *108-109*

Thoatherium (extinct mammal): EV *121*

Thomson, Sir William: MA 9

Thorns: PL *28;* parts analogous to, PL *28, 29*

3C273 (quasar): SP *113*

Threshing of grain: combines for, MA *14-15*

Throat, human: structure of, HU *80*

Thrombi: HU *144*

Throttle plate: carburetor's, TR *47*

Thuban (star): SP *60*

Thunder: production of, WE *67*

Thunderclouds: *See* Cumulonimbus clouds

Thunderstorms: computer models, CO *134*; development of, WE 66, 89; lightning, WE *56-57, 66-67*; squall line, WE *51*

Thylacosmilus (extinct mammal): EV *107, 120*

Thylakoids: PL *10-11*

Thymus gland: HU *75*

Thyroid gland: HU *75*

Tiber River, Italy: delta of, GE *33*

Tickseed: EC *122*, PL *75*

Tidal dams: PE *139*

Tidal forces in Earth-Moon system: SP *73*

Tidal pools: PE *128*

Tidal power generating station: PH *106-107*

Tidal range: PE *128, map 129*

Tide gauge as earthquake indicator: PE *56*

Tides, ocean: GE *36, 37*, PE *128-129*; and breeding, AN *122-123*; cause of, SP *73*; effect of, on barnacles, UN *40*; and estuaries, GE *38*; storm tides, PE *130-131*

Tides, spring: breeding during, AN *122-123*

Tiger long-horned beetles: AN *55*

Tiger moths: IN *33, 88*; larvae, IN *88-89*

Tiger swallowtail butterflies: wing coloration of, IN *30*

Tilapias: diadromous fish, UN *11*; reproduction, UN *79*

Tillandsia cyanea (plant): EC *94*

Tilting: vs. centrifugal force in hurricane, WE *91*

Tiltmeters: water-tube, PE *56, 79*

Timber exports: GE *124, maps 124-125, 125*

Timberline: EC *54-55*, PL *120*

Timbre of sound: wave-forms and, MA *90*

Time: and gravity, PE *18*; in special theory of relativity, PH *126-127*

Timepieces: mechanical clocks, MA *12-13*; quartz watches, MA *96-97*

Time zones: GE *20-21*

Tire roller: TR *75*

Tires, automobile: racing vs. passenger, TR *58-59*; tread on, TR *56-57*

Tissue culture: PL *140-141, 143*

Tissues, human: kinds of, HU *6, 7*

Titan (moon of Saturn): SP *22-23*

Titicaca, Lake, Bolivia-Peru: GE *140, 141*

T lymphocytes (T cells): HU *128, 129, 131*; and AIDS virus, HU *136-137*

TMs (thematic mappers): CO *140*

Toads: Asian horned, AN *51, 52*; bee avoidance, learning, AN *54-55*; Carvalho's pipa, UN *91*; Darwin's, UN *91*; in food chain, EC *125*; midwife, European, UN *90*; spadefoot, life cycle of, EC *92-93*; Surinam, UN *91*; with young, UN *62-63, 90-91*

Toadstools: PL *92-93, 98-99*

Toenails and fingernails: HU *46*

Tokyo, Japan: heat island, WE *map 139*; Ogouchi Dam, WE *79*; subsidence in, GE *65*

Tomatoes: crossbred, PL *136, 142*

Tomograms: CAT scanner for producing, MA *134-135*

Tone-only vs. message-display pagers: CO *122, 123*

Toner: application of, in photocopiers, MA *62-63*

Tones of sound: production of, PH *134-135, 136-137*

Tongues of animals: chameleons, AN *4-5, 32, 33*; snakes, AN *14, graph 15*; woodpeckers, AN *17*

Tongues of humans: and taste, HU *118-119*; and touch, HU *99*

Tools: *See* Machines, simple

Tool-using animals: AN *46-47*

Toothfish: Antarctic, UN *17*

Topi: EC *85*

Topographic maps: GE *12*; of seabed, GE *19*

Tops: spinning, PH *25, 32-33*

Tornadoes: WE *32-33, 50*; formation of, WE *50-51*

Torosaurus (dinosaur): EV *89*

Torque: PH *32*; car's transmission and, TR *46*

Torque converter: automatic transmission's, TR *47*

Torricelli, Evangelista: barometer invented by, PH *16, 17*

Torrs: vacuums measured in, MA *44*

Torsion springs: PH *51*

Tortoise ladybugs: IN *120*

Tortoises: EC *91*; early development of, EV *133*; Galápagos, EC *6-7, 113, 119*; giant, EV *12, 140*

Tortoise shell wasps: IN *111*

Toucans: EC *28-29, 61*

Touch: mimosa's response to, PL *44, 45*

Touch-me-not: PL *76, 77*

Touch, sense of, fish's: UN *45*

Touch, sense of, human: HU *98-99*

Tower karst: Guilin, China, GE *59*

Toxodon (extinct mammal): EV *120*

Toxorhynchites mosquito and larva: IN *47*

Trachea, human: HU *6, 7, 54, 55, 58*; cutaway view, HU *59*; during swallowing, HU *80-81*

Trachea, insect's: IN *10, 11*

Tracheal gills: IN *10*

Tracheoles, insects': IN *10, 11*

Tracking stations: satellite, TR *map 84, 85*

Tracks, trains': TR *6-7*; automatic train, TR *25*; cable cars, TR *30-31*; monorail, TR *28*

Tractors: combines drawn by, MA *14-15*; tires for, TR *57*

Trade winds: PE *118, 119, 132, 133*, WE *34-35, 36, 37*; convergence of, WE *90, 132-133*; deserts created by, GE *104-105*; and deserts' expansion and contraction, GE *106-107*; and El Niño phenomenon, PE *124-125*; and ocean surface currents, GE *70, 71*; and rainfall, GE *115*; southern oscillation and, WE *140-141*

Traffic patterns: computer modeling of, CO *132-133*

Trail pheromones: ants' use of, IN *42-43*

Train à Grande Vitesse (TGV): TR *33*

Trains: TR 4-35; automatic, TR *24-25*; brakes, TR *10-11*; cable cars, TR *30-31*; couplings, TR *8-9*; diesel-powered, TR *4-5*; doors, commuter trains', TR *12-13, 25*; earliest, TR *4-5, 14-15*; flange and rail system, TR *6-7*; luxury, TR *18-19*; maglev, TR *4-5, 34-35*; monorails, TR *28-29*; passengers, inertia's effect on, PH *28-29*; superconducting, *93*; signals controlling, TR *20-21*; snowplows, TR *22-23*; steam-powered, TR *4-5, 14-15, 16-17*; subways' air supply, TR *26-27*; supertrains, TR *4-5, 32-33*; tracks, TR *6-7, 25, 28, 30-31*; whistle and Doppler effect, PH *138-139*

Train station: crowds in, computer simulation of, CO *133*

Transatlantic telegraph cable: MA *map 9*

Transducer: use of, in ultrasound technique, MA *142-143*

Transform boundaries and transform faults: PE *34, 35, 49*; San Andreas fault, PE *42-43, 49*

Transformers: PH *86, 111*; step-up, PH *86, 99*; on utility pole, PH *87*

Transfusions: blood types and, HU *70-71*

Transhumance: GE *142-143*

Transistors: CO *20, 21, 22*, PH *84, 85*

Transition probability: CO *chart 67*

Transmission: TR *40*; electric car without, TR *64-65*; motorcycle, TR *42*; working

Planet Earth
PE

Plant Life
PL

Physical Forces
PH

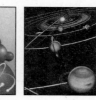
Structure of Matter
ST

Space & Planets
SP

Transportation
TR

Underwater World
UN

Weather & Climate
WE

of, TR 46-47

Transmission electron microscope: MA 32-33

Transpiration: PL 20, 21

Transportation: TR entire volume. *See also* Aircraft; Automobiles; Motorcycles; Special-purpose vehicles; Trains; Water travel

Transrapid system (German maglev trains): TR 34

Transverse colon: HU 90-91

Transverse dunes: GE 108

Trapdoor spiders: AN 26

Travel agents: computer use by, CO 96-97

Tread on automobile tires: TR 56-57

Tree frogs: color changes in, AN 56-57

Tree icing: WE 80-81

Tree kangaroos: black, EC 17

Tree mice: Congo, EC 21

Tree rats: spiny, EC 20

Trees: acacia, false, PL 28; in Appalachian Mountains, GE 96; baobab, PL 116-117; bark, PL 25, 26-27; bottle tree, PL 117; chestnut, parts of, PL 43, 59, 67, 77; coconut palms, EC 22-23; with colorful fruits, PL 78-79; crop-bearing, GE 131; eucalyptus, PL 118-119, 122; fire, effects of, EC 78, 79, 136-137; Gobi Desert formerly covered by, GE 51; grafting, PL 134-135; growth rings, PL 18-19, 24-25; ice ages and, PL 120-121; larches, PL 119; largest, PL 122-123; lichens on, PL 107; lumber exports, GE 124, maps 124-125, 125; mangroves, EC 25, 34-35, PL 80-81; needles, PL 43, 48-49; oldest, PL 123; palm, PL 86-87, 143; parasites on, PL 23, 82-83; roots, PL 18-19, 22, 23, 29; seasonal changes, PL 34-35, 40-41, 42-43, 126; seeds, PL 67, 73, 77, 79, 88-89, 94; sequoias, PL 122-123; succession of, PL 128; water transportation through, PL 20-21, 40-41. *See also* Forests

Trenches, ocean: GE 78, 79, PE 33, 34, map 35, 42, 43, 48-49, 65, 76, 112, map 112, map 115; life in, UN 34-35; Pacific Rim, PE 115

Trevithick, Richard: steam locomotive built by, TR 15

Triangle spiders: web of, IN 39

Triangulation with infrared light: autofocus system using, MA 75

Triassic period: birds, EV 68-69; mammals, first, EV 65, 72-73; reptiles, EV 62-63, 64-65, 66-67

Triceratops (dinosaur): EV 89; skeleton, EV 88

Trichogramma wasps: IN 114

Triconodonts: EV 72-73

Trigodon (extinct mammal): EV 120

Trilobites: EV 40-41, 42, 44-45, PE 95

Triple point (of phase change): ST charts 38-39

Tritium in fusion reactions: ST 17

Triton (moon of Neptune): SP 26-27

Tritylodont reptiles: EV 65

Trochophore larvae: oyster, UN 99

Trogons: collared, EC 61

Trombone: PH 136

Troödon (dinosaur): EV 80-81

Trophoblast: HU 21

Tropical convergence belt: WE 90, 132-133

Tropical depressions: WE 82, 90-91

Tropical rain forests: *See* Rain forests

Tropic of Cancer: SP 56-57

Tropic of Capricorn: SP 56-57

Trout: mutations in, EV 14-15, 17; swim bladder type of, UN 12

Truck tires: TR 57

Trumpet trees: Aztec ants and, IN 98-99

Trunkfish: UN 19, 126

Tsiolkovsky, Konstantin: MA 26

Tsunamis: earthquakes and, PE 54, 58-59; volcanoes and, PE 58, map 73

Tube feet, starfish's: UN 138; attack on, UN 139

Tube geyser: PE 81

Tubers: PL 91

Tubeworms: UN 35

Tugboats: steam-driven, TR 91

Tulips: bulbs, PL 60-61, 91

Tumors: HU 138-139

Tuna: bluefin, UN 9, 14-15, 73; body temperature, UN chart 14; circulatory system, UN 14-15; skipjack, UN 15; squid's defense against, UN 140-141; swimming style, UN 18

Tundra plants: ice ages and, PL 120-121

Tundras: Alpine, EC 54, 55, 57; Arctic, EC 28, 48

Tuner: radio's, MA 84

Tuning forks: PH 142

Tuning of musical instruments: PH 142-143

Tunnels, train: signal for, TR 20; subway, ventilation for, TR 26, 27

Turbine (jet) engines: TR 130-131, 139

Turbine flow meter: MA 47

Turbines: hydroelectric, PH 98-99; hydrofoil's, TR 95; jet engines', TR 131; nuclear engine's, TR 102; ocean-powered, PH 106, 107; steam, PH 100-101, 103, 107, 109, 110, 111; turbocharger's, TR 54, 55

Turbocharged engines: automobile, TR 54-55

Turbofan engines: TR 130-131; VTOL aircraft's, TR 139

Turbojet engines: TR 131

Turbomolecular vacuum pumps: MA 44-45

Turboprop engines: TR 131

Turtles: EC 29, 139; gender, determinant of, EC 30-31; sea, AN 25; snapping, alligator, UN 110-111; tortoises, EC 6-7, 91, 113, 119

Tussock moths: IN 85

Tuxedo guppy: UN 65

TV: color images on, MA 76-77; early, MA 22-23; high-definition, MA 78-79; images, vs. videophone images, CO 127; VCR's recording of signals from, MA 82-83; and video games, CO 78-79

T waves in electrocardiogram: MA 137

Tweezers as levers: PH 43

Twilight Express (Japanese train): TR 18-19

Twins: HU 22-23

Two-color offset printing: MA 40-41

Two-point discrimination test: HU 99

Two-stroke engine: motorcycle's, TR 43

Two-wheel drive (2WD): automobile's, TR 48, 49

Two-wheel steering (2WS): automobile's, TR 50, 51

Tympanic and vestibular canals, human: HU 113

Tympanic membrane: cricket's, AN 97

Tympanic organ: moth's, IN 24

Tyndall effect: ST 20

Type, movable: casting, MA 77; use of, MA 6-7

Type I supernova: SP 85

Types A, B, AB, and O blood: HU 70-71

Type II supernova: SP 84

Typhoons: *See* Hurricanes and typhoons

Tyrannosaurus (dinosaur): EV 74, 77, 97

U

Uintatherium (extinct mammal): EV 116-117; skeleton, EV 104

Ulm ice period: glaciation during, WE map 144

Ulna and radius: HU 33, 39

Ultrasaurus (dinosaur): EV 75

Ultrasonic sound waves, use of: MA 142-143; by camera's autofocus system, MA 75

Ultraviolet astronomy: satellite, SP 125

Ultraviolet photograph of Sun: SP 41

Ultraviolet radiation: and ozone layer, ST 76-77, WE 30; and photosensitive resin, ST 144; and primitive atmosphere, WE 7; solar, HU 50, 51, WE 9, 11, 12-13, 14, 15

Umbilical cord: artery, HU 21; vein, HU 21

Animal Behavior
AN

Computer Age
CO

Ecology
EC

Evolution of Life
EV

Geography
GE

Human Body
HU

Insects & Spiders
IN

Machines &
Inventions **MA**

Umbra and penumbra: SP 62, *63*

Underwater exploration: submersibles for, TR *106-107*

Underwater life: UN entire volume

Union Pacific railroad: Big Boy locomotives built by, TR 4

Univalves: *See* Gastropods

Universal Product Codes (bar codes): CO *86-87*

Universe: SP 98; birth, SP *108*; evolution, SP *108-109, 112-113*; expansion, SP 98, *114-115*; fate, SP *115*; structure, SP *110-111*

UPC (Universal Product Code): CO *86-87*

Updrafts: and air turbulence, WE *52-53*; and gliders, TR *119*; in tornado formation, WE *50, 51*; valley and mountain breezes, WE *43*; in wind formation, WE *41*

Upholder (submarine): TR *98-99*

Uplink and downlink antennas: CO *128*

Upper gill respirators: climbing perch's, UN *29*

Upside-down top: PH *33*

Upwelling of cold water: PE *121*

Uranium: fission of, ST *14-15*

Uranium dating: PE *95*

Uranium fuel: submarines using, TR *102-103*

Uranium recovery from seawater: PE *138*

Uranium 235: fissioning, PH *108*

Uranus (planet): SP *24-25, 29*; rings, SP *20, 25*; Voyager mission to, SP *138*

Ureters and urethra: HU *12, 13, 94*

Urinary bladder: HU *12, 13, 94*

Urine and urine production: HU *94, 95*

Urochordates: EV *46-47*

Urocteid spider: web of, AN *29*

Ursa Major (Big Dipper constellation): SP *90*; changes in, SP *90-91*; and precession, SP *60*

Ursa Minor (Little Dipper constellation): SP *60, 61*

Utah: irrigation in, GE *138*

Uterus: HU *13, 17*; fetuses in, HU *18-23*; and in vitro fertilization, HU *28, 29*

Utilities: electricity supplied by, PH *86-87*

V

Vaccine programs: computer viruses vs., CO *106*

Vacuoles: PL *6, 7*; paramecia, AN *7*

Vacuum-packed foods: ST *89*

Vacuum pumps: MA *44-45*; in fire engines, TR *71*

Vacuum tubes: CO *5, 14-15*; in electron microscope, MA *32-33*; in x-ray machine, MA *140*

Valles Marineris (canyon), Mars: SP *13*

Valley and mountain breezes: WE 42, *43*

Valleys: drowned, GE *90-91*; flooding of, and estuaries, GE *39*; glaciers in, GE *24-25, 42-47*; limestone, formation of, GE *58-59*; rivers' creation of, GE *26, 27, 99. See also* Rift valleys

Valley winds: buildings and, WE *55*

Valves, biological: in human veins, HU *63*

Valves, mechanical: deadweight and safety, for pressure cooker, MA *101*

Van Allen, James: WE *18*

Van Allen belts: WE *10-11, 18-19*

Vapor diffusion vacuum pumps: MA 44, *45*

Vaporization: PH *22-23, 53, 62-63*; in distillation, ST *116, 126-127*; evaporation, PH 62, *64-65*; of water, ST *32-33, 34, 35. See also* Steam turbines, power for

Vapor pressure: PH 22; temperature and, PH *chart 22*

Vapor trails (contrails): WE *64-65*

Variable-pitch propellers: TR *113*

Variable stars: SP *82-83*

Vascular bundles: PL *20, 49, 113*

Vascular plants: first, EV *52*, 53

Vavilov, Nikolai: PL *142*

VCA (voltage control amplifier), synthesizer's: sound qualities produced by, MA *90*

VCF (voltage control filter), synthesizer's: sound qualities produced by, MA *90*

VCO (voltage control oscillator), synthesizer's: sound qualities produced by, MA *90*

VCRs (videocassette recorders): MA *82-83*

Vector processing: CO *43*

Vega (star): SP *61*; distance and magnitude, SP *81*

Vegetation zones: climate and, GE *maps* 51, 112, *map* 113, 142, *chart* 142

Vegetative reproduction: PL *90-91*; grafting, PL *134-135*; tissue culture, PL *140-141, 143*; underground stems, PL *62, 91*

Veins, human: HU *6, 62-63*; of fetus and mother, HU *20-21*; of liver, HU *86, 87*; renal, HU *94, 95*

Veliger larvae: oyster, UN *99*

Velocity of baseball: use of speed gun for calculating, MA *38-39*

Vending machines: MA *58-59*

Venom glands: ants', IN *126*

Venom sac and duct: stinger with, IN *125*

Ventilation systems: for airplanes, TR *128-129*; for subway stations, TR *26-27*

Ventricles: artificial, MA *132, 133. See also* Heart, human

Venturi flap: automated car's, TR *61*

Venturi tube: MA *47*

Venus (planet): SP *10-11, 29*; as seen from Mercury, SP *8*

Venus's-flytrap: EC *116*, PL *46*

Venus's girdle: UN *42*

Verge escapement mechanism: mechanical clock's, MA *12, 13*

Vernal equinox: SP *56*

Vernier (slide) calipers: MA 48, *49*

Vertebrae, human: HU *33, 40-41*

Vertebrates: early development of, EV *132-133*; evolution of, EV *46-47. See also* Amphibians; Birds; Fish; Mammals; Reptiles

Vertical canard: CCV's, TR *140*

Vertical takeoff and landing (VTOL) aircraft: TR *138-139*

Very long baseline interferometry (VLBI): in earthquake prediction, PE *56-57*; seafloor spreading measured with, PE *31*

Vestibular and tympanic canals: HU *113*

Vesuvius, Mount, Italy: eruption of, PE *74-75*

V-formation: birds flying in, AN *132-133*

VHF Omni-range (VOR) stations: TR *122-123*

Vibration range of rattlesnakes: AN *34*

Vibration roller: TR *74-75*

Vic, Henri de: clock by, MA *12-13*

Victoria (Magellan's ship): TR *87*

Videocassette recorders (VCRs): MA *82-83*

Video editing room: CO *80*

Video games: CO *78-79*

Videophones: CO *126-127*

Vidie, Lucien: barometer type invented by, PH *16-17*

Viking 1 (spacecraft): SP *125*; Mars photographed by, SP *13*

Villi: chorionic, HU *20*; small intestine, HU *6, 88*

Vinegarroon scorpion: IN *123*

Vines: ivy, roots of, PL *23, 29*; kudzu, PL *75*; *Nepenthes*, PL *47*; tendrils, PL *29, 30-31*

Vinylon: molecular structure of, ST *109*

Violets: fruit and seeds, PL *67, 77, 79*; self-pollinating, PL *69*

Violin: working of, PH *134-135*

Vipers: saw-scaled, AN *62*

Viral diseases: AIDS, HU *136-137*; colds and flu, HU *140-141*; measles, HU *132-133*

Virgo (galaxy cluster): location, SP *110*

Virtual image: PH *116*

Virus programs: computer, CO *106*

Viscosity vs. gravity: and whirlpool formation, PH *20*

Viscous coupling: TR *49*

Vise: PH *44-45*

Vision, aquatic animals': UN *44-45, 48-49*; in air, UN *45, 50-51*; octopuses', UN *44, 60-61*; sharks', UN *44, 54*

Vision, human: HU *110-111*; darkness adaptation, HU *108-109*; stereoscopic, HU *106-107*

**Planet Earth
PE**

**Plant Life
PL**

**Physical Forces
PH**

**Structure of Matter
ST**

**Space & Planets
SP**

**Transportation
TR**

**Underwater World
UN**

**Weather & Climate
WE**

Vision, insects': IN *22-23*; as butterfly mating stimulus, IN 58, 59

Visual vs. optical axes in fish vs. humans: UN *48*

Vitamin C: cut apple coated with, ST 80, *81*

VLBI (very long baseline interferometry): in earthquake prediction, PE *56-57*; seafloor spreading measured with, PE *31*

Vocal cords: and voice production, HU *58-59*

Voice: production of, and vocal cords, HU *58-59*; recognition, CO *62-63*; recording, by sound spectrographs, MA *34-35*; synthesizers, CO *60-61*; transmission, by car phone, CO *120-121*; transmission, by teleconferencing, CO *112-113*; transmission, by telephone, CO *110-111*, MA 10, 11, *56-57*

Voiceprints: MA *35*

Volcanic hot springs: PE *82*

Volcanic (extrusive) igneous rocks: PE *87, 89*

Volcanic pipes: kimberlite, PE *90-91*

Volcanism and seafloor building: PE *32*

Volcanoes: PE *62-79*; along rift valleys, PE *41*; Andes formed by, PE 38, 39; calderas, PE *67, 68-69, 72, 77, 80*; differences among, PE *66-67*; Fuji, Mount, Japan, WE *24, 25, 68, 115*; from hot spots, PE *44-45, 76, 77*; and hot springs, distribution of, PE *map 83*; Io (moon of Jupiter), SP *18-19*; Krakatoa, Indonesia, PE 62, *72-73*; lava formation, PE *64-65*; Mars, SP *12-13*; Pompeii's destruction by, PE *74-75*; predicting eruption of, PE *78-79*; seamounts, PE *44, 76-77, 114-115*; St. Helens, Mount, Wash., U.S., PE *70-71, 78*; thermal air turbulence over, WE *52*; Triton (moon of Neptune), SP *27*; and tsunamis, PE *58, map 73*; wind around, WE *68*; on young Earth, PE *111*, WE *7*

Voltage control (VC): kinds of, synthesizer's, MA *90*

Voltage drop: PH *74-75*

Voltmeters: PH *77*

Volumetric strain gauge: PE *56*

VOR (VHF Omni-range) stations: TR *122-123*

Vortexes: formation of, PH *20-21*

Voyager space probes: communication with Earth, CO *142-143*; Jupiter, mission to, SP *14, 16, 18*; missions, SP *138-139*; Neptune, mission to, SP *26*; Saturn, mission to, SP *20, 22*; Uranus, mission to, SP *24, 25*; *Voyager 1*, SP *138-139*; *Voyager 1* studies, SP *16, 22*; *Voyager 2*, SP *26, 125, 138-139*; *Voyager 2* studies, SP *16, 20, 24, 25, 26*

VTOL (vertical takeoff and landing) aircraft: TR *138-139*

V-2 rocket: MA *26-27*

Vulcanian type of volcanic eruption: PE *66*

Vulcanized rubber: ST 30

Vultures: Egyptian, AN *47*

W

Waggle dance, honeybees': IN *134-135*

Wahoo: UN *15*

Waialeale, Mount, Hawaii, U.S.: rainfall on, GE *115*

Waksman, Selman: PL 132

Walcott, Charles Doolittle: EV 42

Walking, by insects: IN *12*; on ceiling, IN *20-21*; centipedes, IN *13*; millipedes, IN *13*; ocelli's effect on, IN *22-23*; on water, IN *18-19*

Wallabies: EC *16, 17*

War, transportation for: *See* Military transportation

Warblers: cooperative breeding, AN *116*; eggs, AN *114*; mating, AN *98-99*

Warm-blooded animals: EV *81*; fish, vs. cold-blooded fish, UN *14-15*. *See also* Birds; Mammals

Warning coloration: IN *112-113, 120-121*

Warthogs: EC *84*

Washers, faucet: MA *110*; working of, MA *110, 111*

Washing machines: MA *112-113*

Washing of dishes: MA *116-117*

Washington grass: EC 26

Wasps: EC *109*; for biological pest control, IN *90, 91*; as butterfly enemies, IN *114, 115*; in feeding order, EC *110, 111*; fig, pollination by, PL 68, 69; hunting, and nests, IN *54-55, 92-93, 110-111*; stinging, IN *54, 124, 125*; warning coloration, IN *112, 120*; yellow jackets and mimics, AN *54, 55*

Watches: quartz, MA *96-97*

Water: boiling, MA *100*, PH *22-23, 62*; bubbles in, PH *62-63*; in concrete, ST *120*; convection in, PH *58-59, 66*; density and expansion of, PH *chart 67*; drinking of, by fish, UN *10-11*; fire extinguished with, ST 68, 69; fish breathing out of, UN *28-29, 30-31, 36-37*; fish breathing under, UN *8-9*, 36; floating on, PH *8-9*; freezing, PH *66-67*; freezing, fish in, UN *16-17*; heat and phase changes in, PH *22-23, 52-53, 54-55, 62-63*; heat transfer, PH *58-59, 64*; hydroelectric power from, PH *98-99*; iron exposed to, ST *56-57*; irrigation with, GE *35, 63, 138-139*; land reclamation from, GE *132-133*; lowering freezing point of, ST *40-41*; molecules, makeup of, ST *6-7*; molecules, microwaves and, MA *102*; as neutral substance, ST *65*; ocean, as power source, PH *106-107*; and oil, separation of, ST *42-43, 127*; phase changes, ST *32-33, 34-35, 39, 40-41*; in photosynthesis, ST *66*; pressure of, surviving, UN *22-23*; purifying, ST *98-99*; removal from coffee, ST *86-87*; removal in papermaking, ST *104, 105*; sea, salt recovered from, ST *96-97*; skiing and skating on film of, PH 26, 27; and soap, dirt removal by, ST *48-49*; sound waves through, PH *130*; starch and, ST 100, *101*; steam from, generating power with, PH *100-101, 102-103, 109, 110, 111*; substances in, ST *43*; vapor, ST *34, 35, 39*, PH *22-23, 53, 62-63, 64-65*, WE *70*; whirlpools, formation of, PH *20-21*. *See also* Glaciers; Ground water; Lakes; Oceans; Rain; Rivers

Water beetles: IN *11*

Waterbucks: EC *85*

Water bugs: care of eggs by, IN *75*

Water chestnuts: EC *26, 27*

Water circulation: Earth, SP *49*

Water cycle: global, GE 24, 68, *82-83*

Water dwelling insects: breathing methods, IN *10, 11*; cold-adapted, IN *34*; dragonfly nymphs as, IN *10, 36-37, 44-45*; eggs, care of, IN *75*; mosquito larvae, IN *46-47*; nest building, IN *96-97*; walking methods, IN *18-19*

Waterfalls: migration of, GE *27*

Water faucets: MA *110-111*

Water ferns: EC 26

Water hyacinths: EC 26

Waterjet pump: hydrofoil's, TR *95*

Water-layer geyser: PE *81*

Water lilies: EC 27, PL *119, 129*

Water measurer: IN *19*

Watermelons: grafting, PL *135*; seedless, PL *139*

Water meters: MA *46, 47*

Water molecules: boiling and, MA *100*; escape into air, PH *62*; heat and, PH *52-53, 54-55*; kinetic energy, PH *23, 52*; makeup of, ST *6-7*; microwaves and, MA *102*; in whirlpool formation, PH *20*

Water pipe: measuring flow in, MA *46-47*

Water plants: EC *26-27*; PL *129*; diatoms, PL *100-101*; roots of, PL *23*; seaweed, PL *95, 102-103, 104-105*; water lilies, PL *119, 129*

Water potential: PL 20, 21

Water-seal vacuum pump: MA *45*

Water spiders: nest building by, IN *96-97*

Water striders: IN *18-19*

| Animal Behavior **AN** | Computer Age **CO** | Ecology **EC** | Evolution of Life **EV** | Geography **GE** | Human Body **HU** | Insects & Spiders **IN** | Machines & Inventions **MA** |

Water supply: desert species', EC 86, 87, *90-95*

Water system: MA *111*

Water table: GE 56, 57; sinking of, subsidence from, GE *64-65*

Water travel: TR 78-107; Columbus's expedition, ships of, TR *88-89*; in fog, TR *82-83*; future, superconducting ships for, TR *104-105*; historical navigational instruments for, TR *86-87*; hovercraft, TR *78, 96-97*; hydrofoils, TR *79, 94-95*; icebreakers, TR *100-101*; navigation, TR 78, *80-87, 103*; nuclear vessels, TR *102-103*; through Panama Canal, TR *92-93*; rules of the road for, TR *83*; satellites, use of, TR *84-85*; steam vessels, TR *79, 90-91*; submarines, TR *79, 98-99, 102-103, 106-107*; submersibles, deep-diving, TR *79, 106-107*

Water vapor: ST 34, *35*; bubbles, PH *62-63*; condensation of, PH *64-65*, ST *39*, WE *70*; phase change into, PH *22-23, 53, 62-63, 64-65*

Watt, James: steam engine perfected by, TR *90*

Wave-form clouds: WE *61*

Wave-form currents over mountains: WE *69*

Wave-forms: CO *40, 41, 66, 110, 111*; sound, PH *131*; and timbre of sound, MA *90*

Wave fronts, sound: PH *131*; and Doppler effect, PH *138-139*

Wavelengths: and color of light, ST *51*

Wave mechanics: PH *88-89*

Waves, light: *See* Light

Waves, ocean: PE *108-109*; marine erosion from, GE *68-69, 76-77, 88-89*; motion of, PE *126-127*; as power source, PE *139*, PH 106, *107*; and sand bar formation, GE *74*; storm waves, PE *130-131*; surfers riding, PH *38-39*

Waves, seismic: PE *14-15*; isochrones, PE *53*; ore deposits detected with, PE *98, 99*; S-P time, PE 51, 52, 53, *chart 53*; traveling of, PE *50-51*

Waves, sound: *See* Sound waves

Wave vs. corpuscular theory of light: PH 112

Wax: solidification of, PH *67*

Waxwings, Bohemian: fruit eaten by, PL *78-79*

Weather: WE entire volume; computer studies of, CO *134-135*; hail and snow, formation of, WE 74, *75*; hurricanes and typhoons, WE *82-83, 90-95, 115*; lightning, WE *56-57, 66-67, 106-107*. *See also* Atmosphere of Earth; Climate; Clouds; Rain; Weather observation

Weather forecasts: WE 108, *120-121*

Weathering: in desert sand's formation, GE *104-105*; in Monument Valley's formation, GE *110-111*

Weather maps, making: WE *118-119*; forecast map, WE *120-121*

Weather observation: WE *108-109*; of Antarctica, WE *122-123*; forecasts from, WE 108, *120-121*; history of, WE 108; of hurricanes and typhoons, WE *94-95, 115*; maps, making, WE *118-119, 120-121*; models from, supercomputer, WE 108; sources, kinds of, WE *10-11, 116-117, 123*; of upper atmosphere, WE *112-113, 119*

Weather radar: WE 94, *114-115*; Antarctica, observation of, WE *123*; antennas on, WE *108, 114, 115, 118*; cloud development, observation of, WE *63*; range of, WE 114, *115*

Weather satellites: CO *134*, PE *136*, WE *10-11, 18, 82-83, 84, 94, 110-111, 113, 117, 118, 121, 123*; image of Earth from, PE *4-5*

Weather stations: WE 116, *117*; maps, making, role in, WE *118*; on mountains, WE *108-109, 115*; network, international, WE *map* 117; satellites and, WE 110

Weberian ossicles: UN *52*

Webs, spider: IN *36-37, 38-39, 94-95*; and mating, AN *90-91*; methods of using, AN *26, 27*; sensing prey in, AN *28-29*

Webworms: IN *88-89*

Weddell seals: EC *49*

Wedge: PH *45*

Weedfish: vision in, UN *51*

Weevils, leaf-rolling: nest building by, IN *104-105*

Wegener, Alfred: PE 24, PL 119

Weigela shrubs: EC *79*

Weighing mechanism: PH *50*; bathroom scales', MA *108-109*

Weight: gravity and, PH *6-7*

Weightlessness in space: SP 132; simulating, SP *136-137*

Welding of automobile parts, robot use in: CO *101*

Wells, water: GE *139*; artesian, GE *56, 62, 139*; earthquake effects on, PE *55*; overpumping of, and subsidence, GE *64-65*

Well-to-well surveys: PE *99*

Wernicke's area of brain: HU 120, 121

Westerly winds: PE *119, 132, 133*, WE 35, *36, 37*; and El Niño phenomenon, PE *124-125*; and low-pressure troughs, WE *84, 86*; and ocean currents, GE *71*

Wetlands: EC *138-139, 140, map* 141

Wet plate photography: difficulty of, MA 18, *19*

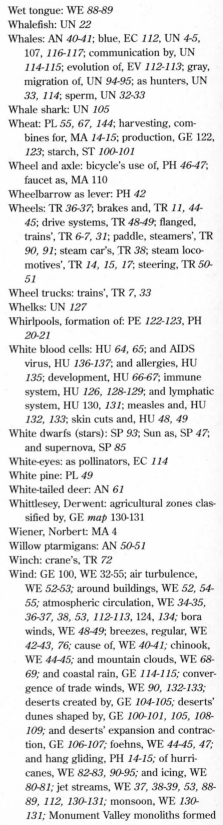

Wet tongue: WE *88-89*

Whalefish: UN *22*

Whales: AN *40-41*; blue, EC *112*, UN *4-5, 107, 116-117*; communication by, UN *114-115*; evolution of, EV *112-113*; gray, migration of, UN *94-95*; as hunters, UN *33, 114*; sperm, UN *32-33*

Whale shark: UN *105*

Wheat: PL *55, 67, 144*; harvesting, combines for, MA *14-15*; production, GE 122, *123*; starch, ST *100-101*

Wheel and axle: bicycle's use of, PH *46-47*; faucet as, MA 110

Wheelbarrow as lever: PH *42*

Wheels: TR *36-37*; brakes and, TR 11, *44-45*; drive systems, TR *48-49*; flanged, trains', TR *6-7, 31*; paddle, steamers', TR *90, 91*; steam car's, TR *38*; steam locomotives', TR *14, 15, 17*; steering, TR *50-51*

Wheel trucks: trains', TR *7, 33*

Whelks: UN *127*

Whirlpools, formation of: PE *122-123*, PH *20-21*

White blood cells: HU *64, 65*; and AIDS virus, HU *136-137*; and allergies, HU *135*; development, HU *66-67*; immune system, HU *126, 128-129*; and lymphatic system, HU 130, *131*; measles and, HU *132, 133*; skin cuts and, HU *48, 49*

White dwarfs (stars): SP *93*; Sun as, SP *47*; and supernova, SP *85*

White-eyes: as pollinators, EC *114*

White pine: PL *49*

White-tailed deer: AN *61*

Whittlesey, Derwent: agricultural zones classified by, GE *map* 130-131

Wiener, Norbert: MA 4

Willow ptarmigans: AN *50-51*

Winch: crane's, TR *72*

Wind: GE 100, WE 32-55; air turbulence, WE *52-53;* around buildings, WE 52, *54-55;* atmospheric circulation, WE *34-35, 36-37, 38, 53, 112-113*, 124, *134;* bora winds, WE *48-49;* breezes, regular, WE *42-43, 76;* cause of, WE *40-41;* chinook, WE *44-45;* and mountain clouds, WE *68-69;* and coastal rain, GE *114-115;* convergence of trade winds, WE *90, 132-133;* deserts created by, GE *104-105;* deserts' dunes shaped by, GE *100-101, 105, 108-109;* and deserts' expansion and contraction, GE *106-107;* foehns, WE *44-45, 47;* and hang gliding, PH *14-15;* of hurricanes, WE *82-83, 90-95;* and icing, WE *80-81;* jet streams, WE *37, 38-39, 53, 88-89, 112, 130-131;* monsoon, WE *130-131;* Monument Valley monoliths formed

| Planet Earth PE | Plant Life PL | Physical Forces PH | Structure of Matter ST | Space & Planets SP | Transportation TR | Underwater World UN | Weather & Climate WE |

by, GE *110-111;* and ocean surface currents, GE 70, *71;* and ocean waves, PE *126, 127;* as power source, PH *104-105;* pressure and, WE 82, 84; prevailing, and El Niño phenomenon, PE *124-125;* prevailing, and ocean currents, PE *118, 119, 120, 132, 133;* prevailing, kinds of, WE *35, 36-37;* and sailing, PH *12-13;* sirocco, WE *46-47;* sound traveling with, PH *133;* southern oscillation and, WE *140-141;* storm tides and storm waves caused by, PE *130-131;* in strato-sphere, WE *36, 112-113;* tornadoes, WE *32-33, 50-51*

Wind instruments: PH *135, 136-137*

Windmills: PH *104-105*

Window air conditioner: MA *122-123*

Window-leaf plant: PL *115*

Wind patterns: Jupiter, SP *14*

Windpipe (trachea): HU *6, 7,* 55, 58; cutaway view, HU *59;* during swallowing, HU *80-81*

Wind shadows and dune formation: GE 108

Wings, aircraft: delta, *Concorde's,* TR *136;* forward-swept, TR *142-143;* and lift, TR *110-111;* in soaring, TR *118;* Wright *Flyer's,* twisting tips of, TR *135*

Wings of insects: IN *4-5;* absence of, IN *84-85;* bees', analyzing, IN *137;* coloration of, in butterflies, IN *30-31, 58, 83, 121;* defenses, IN *112-113, 116-117, 118, 119, 121;* flying methods, IN *14-15;* in sound production, IN *28*

Winter monsoon: WE 130, *131*

Winter solstice: SP *57, 58*

Winter winds: warm, WE *44-45*

Wire: shape-memory, ST *128-129, 140-141*

Wisconsinan glaciation: Gobi Desert during, GE *51*

Wolf spiders: AN *27;* care of young by, IN *74*

Wolves: AN *44-45,* EV *138;* Tasmanian, EV *138, 144*

Wombats: common, EC *17*

Wood: burning, extinguishing, ST *69;* combustion, ST *67, 68;* exports, GE 124, *maps* 124-125, *125;* paper made from, ST

104-105

Wood-eating insects: IN *48-49, 130*

Wood lice (pill bugs): EC 36

Woodpecker finches: AN *47*

Woodpeckers: AN *16-17*

Wood sorrel: PL *77;* photonasty in, PL *45*

Woodwinds: clarinet, PH *136-137;* recorder, PH *135*

Wool: molecular structure of, ST *107, 109*

Woolly mammoths: EV *111, 128-129;* skeleton, EV *105;* skull, EV *110*

Woolly monkeys: EC *70*

Word processors: CO *58-59*

Worker insects: ants, AN *126, 127,* IN *42-43, 85, 123, 126-127, 138-139, 140, 141;* bees, AN *128-129, 130, 131,* IN *26, 70-71, 128-129, 132, 133, 134-135;* termites, IN *140, 141, 142, 143;* wasps, nests made by, IN *92-93, 110-111*

Work stations: computers for, CO *92*

World solar challenge race (1990): car competing in, TR *63*

Worms: EC *36;* ancestors, possible, EV *38, 39;* early stages of, EV *132;* flatworms, EC *41;* lugworms, AN *80,* UN *119, 126-127;* marine, EC *129;* as mole's prey, AN *105;* tubeworms, UN *35*

Worms (self-replicating programs): CO *106*

Wrasses: blue, UN *63, 66;* cleaner, UN *120, 134-135;* eye, UN *44;* red, UN *63, 66*

Wright, Orville and Wilbur: aircraft built by, TR *108, 134-135*

Writers: word processors for, CO *58-59*

Wyoming, U.S.: Teton Range in, GE *86*

X

X and Y chromosomes: HU *15*

Xenon gas: CAT scanner using, MA *134*

XOR gate: CO *28;* in half-adder, CO *29*

X-ray observatory: SP *125*

X-ray photograph of Sun: SP *41*

X-rays: MA *140-141;* black hole as possible source of, SP *94, 95;* CAT scanner's use of, MA *134-135;* sources of, SP *97*

X-29A (forward-swept-wing aircraft): TR *142-143*

XV-15 VTOL aircraft: TR *139*

Xylem: in roots, PL *14, 15;* in stems and trunks, PL *19, 20, 24-25, 26, 27*

Y

Yangtze River dolphins: UN *59*

Yardangs: formation of, GE *111*

Yeager, Chuck: TR 136

Yellow emperor: UN *126*

Yellowface angelfish: changes in markings on, UN *133*

Yellow jackets: IN *112;* and mimics, AN *55;* nests, IN *110*

Yellow pigment cells: tree frogs, AN *56, 57*

Yellow River, China: course changes in, GE *34-35*

Yellowstone National Park, Wyo., U.S.: columnar basalts, PE *84-85;* geysers, PE *80-81*

Yellowtail: UN *21*

Yellowtail ants: IN *127*

Yellow-tipped prominent moths: AN *53*

Yogurt: making of, ST *84-85*

Yoldia Sea, ancient Finland: GE *map* 67

Yugoslavia: bora winds, WE *48-49;* Dubrovnik, WE *49*

Z

Zao, Mount, Japan: ice formations on, WE *80*

Zebras: EC *80-81, 84-85;* extinct (quagga), EV *144*

Zeiss, Carl: planetariums, SP *126*

Zelkova: bark of, PL *27*

Zigzag in-line package (ZIP): CO *23*

Zinc: galvanizing metal with, ST *63;* sacrificial anodes from, ST *57*

ZIP (zigzag in-line package): CO *23*

Z lines: HU *36*

Zodiac: constellations of, SP *54-55*

Zoea larvae: crab, UN *39, 96, 97*

Zosterophyllum (early plant): EV *52, 74*

Zworykin, Vladimir K.: iconoscope invented by, MA 22, *23*

Staff for
UNDERSTANDING SCIENCE & NATURE

Managing Editor: Patricia Daniels
Editorial Directors: Allan Fallow, Karin Kinney
Publishing Associate: Marike van der Veen
Production Manager: Marlene Zack
Copyeditors: Barbara Fairchild Quarmby (Chief),
   Donna Carey, Heidi A. Fritschel, Anthony Pordes
Picture Coordinator: David A . Herod
Production: Celia A. Beattie
Library: Louise D. Forstall
Computer Composition: Deborah G. Tait (Manager),
   Monika D. Thayer, Janet Barnes Syring, Lillian Daniels
Design/Illustration: Antonio Alcalá, Nicholas Fasciano,
   David Neal Wiseman
Index: Barbara L. Klein

Staff for
RESOURCE GUIDE AND MASTER INDEX

Editor: Marike van der Veen
Designer: Angela Miner
Editorial Assistant: Mary Saxton
Quality Assurance Manager: James King
Production Manager: Marlene Zack
Copyeditor: Juli Duncan
Proofreader: April Syring
Special Contributor, Text: Andrew Pogan

Consultant:
Andrew Pogan teaches physics and chairs the science
   department at Quince Orchard High School in
   Montgomery County, Maryland. An author of the textbook *Chemistry in the Community,* Mr. Pogan has led
   teacher training workshops on laboratory management
   and demonstration techniques.

Library of Congress Cataloging-in-Publication Data
Resource guide and master index.
   P. Cm. – (Understanding science and nature)
        Includes index.
   Summary: A resources guide and index to the series
"Understanding Science and Nature," suggesting activities
and providing access to the information found in the
sixteen volumes of that set.
   ISBN 0-8094-9716-6 (hard cover)
   1. Reference books– Science–Bibliography–Juvenile
liferature. 2. Reference books–Science–Bibliography–
Indexes–Juvenile literature. 3. Science–Study and teach-
ing–Miscellanea–Juvenile literture. 4. Children's reference books.
   [1. Science –Indexes.]
I. Series: Understanding science & nature.
Z7401.R37 1995
[Q163]
016.5–dc20   95-18955
                                                   CIP
                                                    AC

TIME-LIFE EDUCATION

President: Robert H. Smith
Vice President, Marketing: Rosalyn McPherson Andrews
Vice President, Operations: James C. Armstrong
Sales Director: Cheryl L. Crowell
Promotions Director: Terrance Afer-Anderson
Operations Manager: Lisa H. Peterson
Sales Manager: Nancy H. Leppert
Executive Assistants: Barbara A. Jones, Theresa Mixon

First printing.
Printed in U.S. A.
Published simultaneously in Canada.
Time Life Inc. is a wholly owned subsidiary of
THE TIME INC. BOOK COMPANY.
TIME-LIFE is a trademark of Time Warner Inc. U.S.A.
For subscription information, call 1-800-449-2010